People-Centered Digital Technology for Ethical and Sustainable Business Practices

Sandra Castro-González
Universidade de Santiago de Compostela, Spain

Lucía Rey-Ares
ECOBAS, Universidade de Santiago de Compostela, Spain

IGI Global
Scientific Publishing
Publishing Tomorrow's Research Today

Vice President of Editorial	Melissa Wagner
Director of Acquisitions	Mikaela Felty
Director of Book Development	Jocelynn Hessler
Production Manager	Mike Brehm
Cover Design	Jose Rosado

Published in the United States of America by
IGI Global Scientific Publishing
701 East Chocolate Avenue
Hershey, PA, 17033, USA
Tel: 717-533-8845 | Fax: 717-533-7115
Website: https://www.igi-global.com E-mail: cust@igi-global.com

Library of Congress Cataloging-in-Publication Data

Names: Castro-González, Sandra, 1991- editor http://id.loc.gov/rwo/agents/n2025018512 | Rey-Ares, Lucía, 1990- editor http://id.loc.gov/rwo/agents/n2025018514

Title: People-centered digital technology for ethical and sustainable business practices / edited by Sandra Castro-González and Lucía Rey-Ares.

Description: Hershey, PA : IGI Global Scientific Publishing, [2026] | Includes bibliographical references and index. | Summary: "This book aims to synthesize research that investigates the potential of digitalization as a catalyst for promoting sustainability across various dimensions, including organizational, socioeconomic, and environmental aspects"-- Provided by publisher.

Identifiers: LCCN 2025005824 (print) | LCCN 2025005825 (ebook) | ISBN 9798337303857 hardcover | ISBN 9798337303864 paperback | ISBN 9798337303871 ebook

Subjects: LCSH: Sustainable development--Technological innovations | Technological innovations--Management http://id.loc.gov/authorities/subjects/sh2008112644 | Business ethics http://id.loc.gov/authorities/subjects/sh85018297

Classification: LCC HC79.E5 P3675 2026 (print) | LCC HC79.E5 (ebook) | DDC 338.9/27--dc23/eng/20250425

LC record available at https://lccn.loc.gov/2025005824

LC ebook record available at https://lccn.loc.gov/2025005825

British Cataloguing in Publication Data
A Cataloguing in Publication record for this book is available from the British Library.

Table of Contents

Detailed Table of Contents

In the setting up of new digital platforms such as FinTech and e-commerce in the world, the most important task that has brought businesses to open up their markets to customers is interaction between the function before and after sale. This chapter thus reflects on the factors that have created regulatory hurdles for the digital economy, along with the effects it has had on the business-consumer relationship. It tries to analyze how the rapid adoption of digital technologies will change the old patterns of market architecture by adding to the already apparent gap between regulation and industries under new design. It also tries to look at how these regulatory issues would be about consumer trust and loyalty, about consumer behavior, and how businesses can adopt a more pragmatic approach to such problems without compromising ethical principles and developing strong consumer relationships. This chapter will show provisions of regulations that would enable innovation to ensure consumer safety, thus giving an appropriate digital marketplace in which a balance is created.

This article analyses the role of hybrid public policy instruments based on the case study of the Spanish Corporate Social Responsibility Strategy (EERSE) 2014-2020. Using a mixed methodology with a predominantly qualitative focus, including questionnaires and focus groups with experts, we assess the design, implementation and degree of execution of the Spanish CSR Strategy, as well as its main advances and limitations. The results reveal that, although the EERSE represented a significant effort to institutionalise CSR and was positively valued for its technical and conceptual approach, its impact on the transformation of the business fabric was limited. The main weaknesses detected are related to the lack of follow-up, the scarcity of resources and the low visibility among the actors involved. Likewise, the need for greater inter-institutional coordination, the strengthening of participatory governance structures and the closing of the gap between large companies and SMEs in the effective incorporation of responsible practices are identified as critical challenges.

The growth of tourism has piqued the interest of political leaders, prompting them to market their countries as popular tourist destinations. Recognizing tourism's potential as a significant economic engine, authorities in certain nations have begun to focus on international relations tactics to improve their country's image and earn a portion of global tourist income. The present study is a bibliometric approach to examine the future trends in digital tourism through a review approach using R tool. The study examines the contribution of top authors, institutions, journals and countries and also examined the top cited articles and authors. Scopus database is used to extract the dataset as it is the largest repository of published articles. The thematic map technique is used to examine the trends in digital tourism to pave the way for future research directions for academicians and researchers.

This chapter explores the integration of ethics and sustainability into AInitiatives amidst rapid digital transformation. Emphasizing the centrality of ethical governance and sustainable practices, it examines how organizations can address critical ethical, social, and environmental challenges associated with AI technologies. Through a detailed analysis of the Ai.ethics program developed by the APEE and the UNA PT, the chapter demonstrates how structured frameworks such as Good Governance, Explainability, and Trust can enhance stakeholder confidence and organizational accountability. It underscores the significance of a people-centered approach,

This chapter examines the impact of digital nativeness and generational identity on ethical values and responsible consumption behaviours in Spain. Through a data-driven analysis of six generational cohorts, the findings reveal significant intergenerational differences in both the strength of ethical values and the consistency of ethical behaviour. Notably, digital immigrants demonstrate higher ethical commitment and more responsible consumption than digital natives. Accordingly, the former presents a stronger coherence between intention and behaviour, although there is no cognitive dissonance on any of the groups. The study validates key ethical consumption theories and introduces the DAS BIE scale as a novel tool for assessing generational differences. Practical implications highlight the need for targeted educational initiatives, ethical marketing strategies, and digital tools that align values with actions. This research underscores the need of a people-centred digital transformation to bridge generational disparities and foster a more sustainable, ethically engaged society..

The field of human resource management (HRM) has seen a growing body of research emphasizing the conceptualization of intellectual capital and its various dimensions. In response to increasing calls from the scientific community to deepen research in this area, the aim of this project is to analyze the role of emotional capital in fostering a socially responsible orientation in HRM decision-making. This process, in turn, could be key to building more committed and productive human capital within organizations. As emphasized in the literature, these practices are vital to the success of SMEs. This chapter sets out to explore two specific sub-objectives: to examine the effect of emotional capital on socially responsible HRM decisions and analyze whether socially responsible HRM decisions influence employee commitment and productivity levels. Main theories and articles which combine emotional capital and HRM are examined, providing implications for SDGs, conclusions and future research lines.

Digital transformation has become imperative for business survival and competitiveness in today's rapidly evolving economic landscape. While digitalization offers unprecedented opportunities through technologies it presents unique challenges for family businesses that must balance innovation with tradition. This chapter examines the multifaceted nature of digital transformation. It specifically addresses the distinctive challenges faced by family businesses, where the integration of digital technologies must be reconciled with preserved heritage and stakeholder relationships. The discussion outlines frameworks for implementing digital transformation while maintaining organizational values and emphasizes a human-centered approach. The chapter demonstrates how these organizations can leverage technological advancement for sustainable growth while preserving their distinctive identity and core values by providing practical strategies for family businesses to navigate this digital transition.

This study investigates the factors influencing the integration of mobile technology and services of Social Enterprise, to communities in South Africa. The Case study approach was employed using a South African community. We conducted a qualitative study involving semi-structured interviews with Social Enterprise (SE) employees and members of a community in South Africa. The technology acceptance model (TAM) was applied in the analysis of the data. Our analysis revealed seven key factors: connectivity, network infrastructure, capabilities, affordability, accessibility, contextualisation, language translation, and knowledgeability. The study reveals how various factors interact in complex ways to shape the integration of mobile technology with SE services in the community. The study contributes to literature by providing a nuanced understanding of how mobile technology can be integrated with SE services, highlighting the potential implications and consequences. The study has significant impact on SEs, community members, and IT specialists including those involved in policymaking.

Preface

INTRODUCTION

Understanding the scope of digital technology and its impact on key issues such as people, ethics, and sustainability is becoming one of the most important challenges today due to the speed at which innovations are emerging and being implemented. There is no doubt about the advantages of digital technology; however, it entails risks that must be carefully considered.

People-Centered Digital Technology for Ethical and Sustainable Business Practices arises from the conviction that digital transformation must not lose sight of its ultimate purpose: enhancing human well-being while preserving the planet. As editors, we have observed how the indiscriminate adoption of technology can exacerbate social inequalities, threaten privacy, and undermine environmental goals. Conversely, when applied thoughtfully, digital solutions can foster transparency, efficiency, inclusivity, and long-term sustainability.

This book contains a total of twelve chapters from various sources and authors, which together aim to provide a critical view of the convergence of digital technology, ethics, and sustainability. In the current context of digitization, there is a clear and pressing need for collective responses that involve assessing issues from multiple perspectives and integrating those perspectives into coherent solutions. The use of a single approach cannot provide clear and convincing answers. The diversity of chapters in this book—discussed in greater detail later in this preface—illustrates the broad field of study of technological digitization and its direct and indirect influence on people. To illustrate this point, consider the chapter on digital tourism, which examines the transformative impact of technologies on one of the most influential industries on a global scale. In a more general sense, some of the works contained in the book explore how trust, explainability, and governance mechanisms are vital to ensuring a sustainable digital transformation. The contributions on human resources are more people-centered in nature, emphasizing the significance of emotional capital and responsible decision-making. The book also contains other, more specific case studies focusing on family businesses, social enterprises in Africa, and the role of governments in corporate social responsibility, emphasizing that the ethical and sustainable use of technology is a global and cross-cutting challenge.

We are strongly committed to a people-centered approach—one that places human values, rights, and dignity at the heart of digital development. Technology should adapt to human needs, rather than the other way around. It is only through this orientation that digitalization can genuinely contribute to a just and sustainable future.

Our aim with this book is to stimulate meaningful dialogue and foster interdisciplinary reflection. Whether examining the ethical implications of AI deployment, exploring digital strategies for circular economies, or assessing governance models for data justice, the contributions herein collected invite readers to think critically about the paths that lie ahead.

This book is intended for a wide and varied audience, including but not limited to:

- Academics and researchers seeking to deepen their understanding of the ethical and sustainability dimensions of digital innovation.
- Students and educators engaged with these topics across business, technology, or social science disciplines.
- Business leaders and practitioners aiming to align digital strategies with responsible and sustainable values.
- Policymakers and regulators charged with navigating the complex terrain of digital governance.
- Governments and non-profit organizations advocating for inclusive and ethical technological ecosystems.

As editors, we extend our sincere gratitude to the contributors who have shared their insights, and to the readers who are joining us in reimagining the role of technology in shaping a fairer and more sustainable world.

Let us move forward with purpose—placing people, ethics, and sustainability at the heart of digital transformation.

ORGANIZATION OF THE BOOK

The twelve chapters that make up this volume are organized into four thematic sections, reflecting their respective content. Thus, the book opens with the first section, *Navigating the Digital Economy: Policy, Responsibility, and Future Trends*, which comprises three chapters. Chapter 1, *Exploring the Digital Economy: Regulatory*

Challenges and Implications for Customer Dynamics, offers a critical examination of the shifting dynamics between digital businesses and consumers, particularly in light of existing regulatory gaps. The authors reflect on the factors that have created regulatory obstacles for the digital economy, with a particular focus on FinTech and e-commerce platforms, and analyze the resulting impact on the relationship between businesses and consumers. This first chapter attempts to examine how the rapid adoption of digital technologies is reshaping traditional market architectures, further widening the already evident gap between regulatory frameworks and industries operating under this new paradigm.

In Chapter 2, *The Role of Governments in Corporate Social Responsibility: Effectiveness of Hybrid Instruments*, attention turns to the public policy landscape. Drawing on the case study of the Spanish Corporate Social Responsibility Strategy (EERSE) 2014-2020, the chapter examines the role of hybrid public policy instruments. It highlights challenges such as limited resources and coordination problems, offering valuable insights for policymakers seeking to promote effective corporate responsibility practices.

Chapter 3, *A Bibliometric Approach to Examine the Future Trends in Digital Tourism*, maps the previous research on digital transformation in the tourism sector. Using a bibliometric analysis, the chapter identifies emerging trends in digital tourism and analyzes the contribution of leading authors, institutions, journals, and countries, as well as the most cited articles and authors.

The second section of the book, *Ethics and Governance in Digital Innovation*, comprises three chapters. The ethical implications of digital technologies take center stage in Chapter 4, *Ethical AI and Sustainable Digital Transformation: Building Trust in a Rapidly Digitalized World*. This chapter argues for the integration of structured ethical frameworks within AI initiatives, using case studies to show how good governance, transparency, and trust can be operationalized in organizations. The authors call for a people-centered approach that leverages AI to support environmental sustainability, equity, and long-term resilience.

Continuing with a focus on AI, Chapter 5, *Standardisation for Governance and Ethical Use of Artificial Intelligence and Digital Technology in Organizations*, explores how standardization complements legal regulation in managing AI's ethical and operational risks. Comparing approaches in the USA, China, and the EU, the chapter provides actionable insights for aligning AI governance with broader corporate management systems, while promoting responsible innovation.

Chapter 6, *Does the New European Health Data Space Respect the Principle of Patient Autonomy?*, addresses data governance, with a particular focus on health data, in the context of our increasingly digitalized world. The chapter evaluates the ethical adequacy of informed consent and patient information documents within the EU's health data framework. It proposes a novel methodological tool for assessing the alignment of these documents with the ethical principle of patient autonomy, underscoring the need for sensitivity to human rights in digital health initiatives.

The third section of the book, *People and Organizations in the Digital Age*, comprises four chapters addressing human resource challenges. More in detail, Chapter 7, *Born Digital: How Native Digital Status Shapes Ethical Behavior and Consumer Dissonance*, explores intergenerational differences in ethical consumption behavior in Spain. The findings question prevailing assumptions about digital natives' ethical engagement, showing that digital immigrants often exhibit a stronger alignment between values and actions. The chapter also introduces the DAS BIE scale, offering a practical tool for organizations and educators to address generational gaps in digital ethics.

In Chapter 8, *Does Emotional Capital Influence HRM Decision-Making and Performance?*, the focus shifts to Human Resource Management (HRM). This chapter investigates the role of emotional capital in fostering socially responsible HRM practices and enhancing employee commitment, particularly in Small and Medium-Sized Entreprises (SMEs). By integrating emotional capital theory with organizational performance metrics, the chapter contributes to the literature on people-centered business management and sustainable development goals.

Chapter 9, *Human-Centric Approaches in Industry 5.0: Organizational Strategies and their Influence on Employee Engagement and Productivity*, examines how emerging human-centric technologies and supportive organizational cultures influence employee engagement in Industry 5.0. Based on extensive qualitative and quantitative research, the chapter demonstrates that people-centered strategies enhance inclusiveness, collaboration, and overall productivity, thereby reinforcing the call for ethical innovation.

Chapter 10, *Smart Retention Strategies: Machine Learning Applications in Human Resource Management*, investigates the transformative potential of machine learning in HRM, with a particular focus on talent retention. Through comparative industry analysis, the chapter explores how AI can identify attrition risks, monitor sentiment, and improve performance. Yet, it also highlights significant ethical and technical challenges, underscoring the need for responsible AI integration in HRM systems.

The four and final section of the paper, *Digitalization for Social Development*, comprises two chapters presenting case studies on family and social enterprises. Chapter 11, *Managing Digitalization for the Performance of Family Businesses: Digital Transformation, Flexibility, and Sustainability*, focuses on family businesses navigating the digital transition. This chapter explores the tension between innovation and heritage, offering strategic frameworks for digital transformation that preserve organizational values while driving sustainable growth. It presents a compelling argument for customized, values-based digital strategies in family-owned enterprises.

Chapter 12, *The Use of Mobile Devices by Social Enterprise to Provide Service to Communities in South Africa*, provides a grounded, context-specific case study on the use of mobile technology in social enterprise. By exploring the integration of mobile services through the lens of the technology acceptance model, the chapter identifies key enablers and barriers to digital service delivery in underserved communities in South Africa. The chapter offers critical lessons for social enterprises and policymakers working toward inclusive digital development.

CONCLUSION

As we stand at the intersection of unprecedented digital innovation and pressing global challenges, this book brings together critical insights, research, and perspectives that highlight an overarching truth: technology must be guided by human values and serve people, rather than the reverse.

Each chapter in this book underscores the multifaceted nature of digital transformation—its potential to advance sustainability, equity, and innovation, but also its capacity to deepen divides, disrupt trust, and challenge longstanding ethical frameworks. From AI governance and regulatory policy to digital tourism, healthcare, human resource management, and social enterprise, the chapters collectively call for a more intentional, responsible, and people-centered approach to digital development.

Our goal as editors has been to curate a body of work that not only captures the complexity of ethical and sustainable digital practices but also equips readers with the tools, frameworks, and critical thinking skills necessary to navigate this rapidly evolving landscape. We believe the diverse voices represented in this volume will spark meaningful dialogue and guide future research, practice, and policymaking.

Ultimately, the path forward demands collaboration across disciplines, sectors, and generations. By placing people at the center of digital transformation—protecting their rights, enhancing their well-being, and enabling their active participation—we can ensure that the digital future is not only innovative, but also just, inclusive, and sustainable.

Section 1
Navigating the Digital Economy: Policy, Responsibility, and Future Trends

Chapter 1
Exploring the Digital Economy: Regulatory Challenges and Implications for Customer Dynamics

Ishayu Gupta
https://orcid.org/0009-0006-7622-2269
Christ University, Bengaluru, India

Neelatphal Chanda
Christ University, Bengaluru, India

ABSTRACT

In the setting up of new digital platforms such as FinTech and e-commerce in the world, the most important task that has brought businesses to open up their markets to customers is interaction between the function before and after sale. This chapter thus reflects on the factors that have created regulatory hurdles for the digital economy, along with the effects it has had on the business-consumer relationship. It tries to analyze how the rapid adoption of digital technologies will change the old patterns of market architecture by adding to the already apparent gap between regulation and industries under new design. It also tries to look at how these regulatory issues would be about consumer trust and loyalty, about consumer behavior, and how businesses can adopt a more pragmatic approach to such problems without compromising ethical principles and developing strong consumer relationships. This chapter will show provisions of regulations that would enable innovation to ensure consumer safety, thus giving an appropriate digital marketplace in which a balance is created.

DOI: 10.4018/979-8-3373-0385-7.ch001

INTRODUCTION

The Rise of the Digital Economy

This means that the digital economy comprises those economies where the critical driver is digital technologies. A wide variety of digital sectors such as digital platforms, financial technology (FinTech), e-commerce, etc., comprise the digital economy. Digital platforms including Amazon, Google, and Facebook create a sophisticated platform for interaction between businesses and consumers through algorithms and data analytics, thereby optimizing customer experience and market efficiency (Varian, 2019). FinTech has also innovated in areas like cashless payment systems, blockchain technology, and online banking, thus redefining financial contracts with emphasis on financial inclusion, whereas in some cases, it also raises concerns over the safety of data (Arner, Barberis, & Buckley, 2016). E-commerce has revolutionized the retail world. Cross-border trade has become a possibility through e-commerce, thus reducing available operational costs and providing the consumers with comfort of personalized shopping experience.

Digital transformation is historically just a throw-or-kick for belief change in industry realization and customer interaction towards truly data-driven business organizations. The shift from conventional businesses to digital-first enterprises has altered consumer expectations towards transparency, speed, and personalized experiences (Chaffey, 2022). With the rise of social commerce powered by platforms like Instagram and TikTok, the blurry boundaries between entertainment and shopping have begun to affect buying decisions (Deloitte, 2020). Despite the economic enhancement due to digital transformation, it also poses difficulties in terms of regulatory requirements, which demand regulation to ensure ethical and fair practices are adopted in the digital economy.

Regulatory Landscape in the Digital Era

Regulating digital technologies that evolve so fast is very challenging as they tend to be very dynamic and global. Digital platforms do not function like traditional industries since they operate in a multiplicity of jurisdictions. Most importantly notable, the rapid deployment of AI algorithms and automated decision-making systems raised several issues on accountability, bias, and data ethics (Pasquale, 2015). The gig economy also featured disrupting labor regulations which needed new laws protecting the rights of workers while innovating (De Stefano, 2016).

Such as the General Data Protection Regulation (GDPR) in the European Union and laws such as the California Consumer Privacy Act (CCPA) in the United States, these are existing global regulatory frameworks protecting consumer data through tight rules on collection, storage, and use. Each such antitrust law, particularly directed toward Big Tech, serves to prohibit certain monopolization, anti-competitive acts, and to ensure competition equality (Khan, 2021). Laws may not be effective in this instance, as litigation is often dodged by long arms of these tech giants.

Gaps and inconsistencies in national regulations make things even more complicated. Going forward, while setting the global standard, the GDPR is most definitely heralding a new dawn in data protection; most countries lack similar policies to that effect, leading to regulatory fragmentation at the international sphere (Bamberger & Mulligan, 2015). Developing countries on the verge of stringent digital regulations, like many others, are frustrated by insufficient institutional and infrastructural facilities regarding technology. Also, emerging technologies such as decentralized finance (DeFi) and non-fungible tokens (NFTs) exist in almost totally unregulated environments, thus raising more concerns about consumer protection and the stability of finance.

Implications for Consumer Dynamics

Digital platforms have played a significant role in influencing consumer behaviors and expectations by providing hyper-personalized experiences and seamless transaction processes. Streaming and retail platforms powered by AI, such as Netflix and Amazon, use recommendation engines to mine data on user preferences to recommend content and products through engagement and retention. These are, however, in direct contrast to the interests of consumers, who demand increased transparency and ethical data practices from businesses, citing concerns over data privacy and algorithmic manipulation as just two examples (Acquisti, Taylor, & Wagman, 2016). The advent of digital payment solutions like Apple Pay and PayPal has accelerated the transition from cash to cashless transactions, thereby creating potential cybersecurity risks that incite consumers to look for more secure financial solutions (Kshetri, 2021).

Trust, data privacy, and cybersecurity exert undue influence in shaping consumer relationships with digital businesses. Data breaches impact on the brand and customer loyalty grievously, demonstrated in cases such as the Cambridge Analytica scandal (Cadwalladr & Graham-Harrison, 2018). Legal regimes such as the Right to Be Forgotten in the GDPR, which gives consumers control over their digital footprint, indicates increasing support for digital rights advocacy. Businesses will have to find a balance between regulatory compliance and user experience because too many restrictions on data could negatively impact service personalization and efficiency (Goldfarb & Tucker, 2012).

The challenges for businesses in balancing innovation and regulatory compliance are particularly present when adapting to changing legal requirements while retaining their competitive edge. As interest in the use of ethical AI and data responsible practices increases, companies are starting to implement transparent AI models and privacy-first strategies (Dignum, 2019). The cost of complying with harsh laws could be excessive in particular for small and medium-sized enterprises (SMEs), choking innovation in the process (Calo, 2013). Increased regulatory scrutiny must make ethical consumer business practice and rigorous cybersecurity a priority for firms to engender consumer trust.

THEMATIC DISCUSSION (LITERATURE REVIEW)

'The Digital Economy: what is new and what is not?' is a research study by Bo Carlsson that speaks about one of the widely cherished projects in economics-the so-called 'New Economy'-with substantial discussion regarding the changing forms of productivity transformation brought by digitization and the Internet as well as the market structures and modes of economic growth. In terms of focusing scholarly debate on the issue whether the acceleration in labor and total factor productivity (TFP) growth rates of the late 1990s signals that a basic structural shift is at play or is merely a temporary phenomenon (Baily & Lawrence, 2001). One major element of this debate is the role of general purpose technologies (GPTs) in economic transformation. Historically, GPTs such as electricity and the steam engine have driven economic revolutions by opening entirely new industries and improving productivity in many other sectors (Bresnahan & Trajtenberg, 1995). Digitalization-in conjunction with the Internet-has also been termed as a modern GPT providing innovation facilitation by connecting economic agents and rendering knowledge spillovers possible (Jovanovic & Rousseau, 2005). Connectivity at such higher levels naturally leads to faster diffusion of technology and hence new business models that overthrow traditional economic structures. More empirical phenomena show contributions of digital technologies to productivity. Studies show IT investments-especially in software and communication networks-to be the prerequisite for the attainment of efficiency in numerous industries, majorly retail, finance, and manufacturing (Oliner & Sichel, 2000). On the other hand, some intellectuals critically argue that such developments record clearly at the micro level. However, at the macroeconomic level, measuring them is relatively more difficult due to time lag in generating micro data and improper allocation of resources (Brynjolfsson & Hitt, 2003). The other vital aspect captured with the digital economy is restructuring of economic activity. E-commerce, digital platforms, and automation have greatly disrupted established modes of business, allowing companies to girdle growth while operating at more minor and minor marginal costs (McAfee & Brynjolfsson, 2017). Digital marketplaces like Amazon and Alibaba have revolutionized the traditional retail supply chain through data-driven and artificial intelligence-optimized operations (Goldfarb & Tucker, 2019). Besides these, digital technologies also changed market efficiencies by altering the competitive environment into one whereby network effects and data-driven decision making will ensure who will lead the market. Beyond efficiency and restructuring, market efficiency effects have been researched widely. The decreasing ratios of inventory to shipments in the markets for durable goods will attribute such advances to "just-in-time" production and logistics improvements that digitized tools highly contribute to (Hubbard, 2003). Financial markets also improved a lot in the application of algorithms in trading services and in developing financial technologies or services using blockchain that enhanced the efficiency and liquidity of transactions (Philippon, 2016).

'Defining, Conceptualising and Measuring the Digital Economy', a joint - study carried out by Rumana Bukht & Richard Heeks elucidates on the digital economy has emerged as a major engine of global economic growth, especially in developing countries, but its delineation or measuring remains a matter for heated debate among academics and policymakers alike. Different studies have attempted to put definitions or quantified measurements on the digital economy, and there has been much divergence since these digital activities cross into the traditional economy in many ways. The digital economy may, however, be classified into three kinds of domains: core digital sector; other parts of the digital economy; and the digitized economy. The core digital sector refers to the ICTs and IT industries- the software development, hardware manufacture, telecom services technologies that underlay digital infrastructure (OECD, 2020). The digital economy in its wider sense involves other phenomena-digital platforms, e-commerce, fintech, and so on- that have been witnessing rapid growth as a result of rapid advancement in artificial intelligence, cloud computing, and big data analytics (Mesenbourg, 2001). Finally, in this context, the digitalized economy is whereby digital technologies have found application across all industries-from agriculture, to healthcare, education and logistics- and thus serves to illustrate how digitalization is rendering productivity and innovation enhanced in traditional sectors (Manyika et al., 2016). Nonetheless, a major challenge in the measurement of the digital economy is the lack of defined standards and inconsistency in its data collection. Hence, various studies use GDP contribution, employment statistics, and output from various sectors as key indicators; the downside being that these key indicators underestimate the actual extent of operations in the digital economy due to the informal sector and cross-border digital transactions. The recent estimate shows that the digital economy contributes 5 percent of the world GDP and 3 percent of global employment, with developed countries showing a greater share of the economy than developing countries (OECD, 2020). The digital economy in the global North has witnessed far greater historical growth, benefiting from established technology ecosystems juxtaposed with high digital literacy and considerable R&D investments, while on the other hand, the global South-the new fast track of the entire digital economy-is being held back by a lack of digital infrastructure, regulatory challenges, and a gap in digital skills . Emerging markets in Africa, Asia, and Latin America are witnessing an exponential digital transformation spearheaded by mobile penetration, fintech solutions, and platform-based services (Manyika et al., 2016). Nevertheless, the potential for growth remains substantial; thus, calls for further research to understand the socio-economic impacts of digitalization in developing countries and for the identification of policies capable of fostering digital inclusion, remedial inequality, and maximizing the benefits of digital economic growth.

A study by Robert U. Ayres & Eric Williams titled 'The digital economy: Where do we stand?' explains the rapid advancement of the digital economy has become possible with the convergence of various technological advancements in computing, telecommunications, and networking, which have led to the widespread acceptance of information and communication technologies (ICTs) across all industries (Bresnahan & Trajtenberg, 1995). The underlying innovations such as semiconductor transistors, integrated circuits, personal computers, and graphical interfaces brought about radical changes in the computing domain; while high-speed data transmission, made possible by optical fiber and wireless communication technology, set the stage for digital transformation (Gordon, 2000). The introduction of packet-switching technology and the Worldwide-Web advanced the digital economy since it helped to achieve global interconnectivity, enhanced business processes, and nurtured the development of e-commerce and digital services. After the initial successes in digital innovation, the bursting of the dot-com bubble in the early 2000s exposed several inefficiencies in investment approaches, justifying the need for sustainable applications of technology instead of speculations (Shiller, 2000). As industries emerge from the wreckage, prospects for realizing the new killer applications-mobile communications, digital entertainment, video on demand, and teleconferencing-are underway and may provide the impetus for the next cycle of economic growth. However, with this digital media distribution comes a lot of IPR challenges that will require new normative frameworks that will address the conflicting objectives of nurturing innovation and protecting content ownership (Lessig, 2001). Other infrastructural bottlenecks such as limited capacity for broadband, last-mile connectivity impediments, also obscured by the asymmetries in traditional networking protocols like TCP/IP hinder a seamless digital transformation. The alleviation of these bottlenecks will require investment in broadband infrastructure, DSL technology, and possible enhancements in networking protocols for data transmission effectiveness (Negroponte, 1995). Other factors in society and economy encourage ICT adoption since overoptimism of technological capability often fosters periods of rapid growth followed by stagnation demanding a thorough recalibration of investment and policy arrangements to sustain long-term digital growth (Freeman & Louçã, 2001). While the ICT revolution has greatly improved global connectivity and productivity, the power of digital innovations in sustaining growth in the macroeconomy will depend on the ability to surmount current technical and regulatory barriers.

THE ETHICAL DILEMMAS OF THE DIGITAL ECONOMY

Balancing Innovation with Consumer Rights

The emerging digital economy has enhanced great innovations into remarkably transformed industries and consumer experiences. However, it seems that those innovations are being brought at the cost of consumer rights factors such as privacy, data security, and the provision of informed consent (Acquisti, Taylor and Wagman, 2016). The real challenge will lie in being able to maintain an equilibrium between the needs to promote technology while at the same time ensuring that consumers are not being exploited or manipulated either way. Most of the organizations utilize consumers' data for business intelligence and targeted advertisement, personalized use, but this creates a question of consent and ethical data utilization (Solove, 2013).

A very major ethical concern is using black-box algorithms and artificial intelligence in making decisions. Most of these platforms operate on social networks and e-commerce websites and gather user data to improve their algorithms to give tailor-made experiences (Pasquale, 2015). Although this increases user enhancement, an issue arises regarding the validity of ownership with regard to the customer's little control on how exactly the data is being collected and or used. Most often, businesses utilize dark patterns, i.e., designing tricks to influence consumers without their knowledge consent on being collected through the data collection (Mathur et al., 2019).

In summary, ensuring innovations meet consumer rights entails effort from businesses, regulators, and consumers working collaboratively. Ethical principles of data, transparent AI algorithms, and stricter enforcement of privacy laws will be at a distance between technological advancement and consumer rights protection. It must be with an ethical model that brings consumer interests to the forefront while ensuring sustainable digital innovation.

Ethical Considerations in AI and Data Monetization

AI-driven business models comprise one arm of the digital economy, while ethical debates concerning data monetization and consumer surveillance comprise another. The functioning of an AI system can be fundamentally altered through the availability of enormous datasets. Such reliant arrangements raise discussions surrounding data ownership, consent, and privacy (Eubanks, 2018). Google, Facebook, and Amazon have built an ecosystem of monetizing data collected from users, largely unbeknown to the consumer (Couldry & Mejias, 2019).

Algorithmic bias continues crushing violations of the greatest concern whereby AI systems compound existing biases due to training on bias-laden data. Reports demonstrate facial recognition, predictive policing, and hiring algorithms exhibit racial and gender bias against the ancient symbols of such isolated spatiality and ethical-legal territory (O'Neil, 2016). Transparency is absent from AI decision processes; this adds credence to user grievances regarding their lack of insight into how these systems operate or whether they operate justly.

The second ethical quagmire is due to commodification of personal data. In this context, a business model is created by digital platforms to effectively offer free services in exchange for user data, thus creating a situation where users become the product. Some would claim that this benefits the advertiser and the user alike, who receives personalized experiences. Critics, however, argue that the data do bring in the threat of abuse and exploitation (Andrejevic, 2020). These issues are compounded by cases of data breaches and cyberattacks that put millions of users in jeopardy of identity theft and financial fraud, highlighting the dire need to enforce stronger data protection controls (Schneier, 2015).

The far-reaching economic impacts, on the other hand, grew to consolidate a few players at the apex of the market where technology giants unleashed manipulation of data on huge scales. Having much data on consumers makes it too difficult for other small businesses to compete. Therefore, this gives rise to antitrust contemplation since feasible attempts to monopolize may break competition, hinder innovation, and restrain consumer choice.

Ethical frameworks for AI like bias audits, explainable AI, and consumer-centric data policies need to be adopted by companies to address these pitfalls (Floridi et al., 2018). Regulatory frameworks need to apply incentives that hold organizations responsible for unethical data monetization practices. Setting in motion transparent AI governance frameworks will allow organizations to develop trust among consumers and ensure that AI-led developments stand for virtuous concepts (Danks & London, 2017).

Addressing Misinformation and Digital Manipulation

The conflation and transformations of information such as disinformation are indeed dire issues that besiege the digital economy largely by AI-led dissemination of content and algorithmic amplification. The intensive adoption trend of social media and digital platforms wielded a socially infectious phenomenon characterized by the rapid dissemination of false information that creates public opinion and decision-making processes. This has far-reaching ethical implications, particularly with respect to sectors like politics and public health, consumer behavior.

MoRM creates an increasing concern regarding the model of user engagement-based monetization by digital platforms. That is, social media algorithms favor content that demonstrates higher intensity of user engagement and will often disregard factual matters and instead give preference to sensational or misleading information. This is the reason behind the general use of the terminology 'algorithmic radicalization' to explain the environment which has been accountable for mushrooming conspiracy theories, political polarization, and public distrust in traditional media sources (Benkler, Faris, & Roberts, 2018).

Deepfake technology is being abused to manipulate public perception and includes video, audio, and image content ultimately generated through artificial intelligence. It comprises creating highly realistic but utterly false videos, images, or audio recordings likely to threaten political stability and even reputation of individuals (Chesney & Citron, 2019). Deepfake technology has evolved as a weapon for propagandists, fraud, and terrorist elements in whips by somehow manipulating stock markets and fraudulent transactions, and makes it really difficult to sieve real contents from fake ones.

Such challenges should be approached from multifaceted angles, including complementary regulatory oversight, platform accountability, and public awareness campaigns. It is important for governments and tech companies to come together and formulate policies that will enhance transparency in content moderation and limit the spread of false information. Among the many measures that can be completed are the establishment of fact-checking initiatives, AI-led misinformation detection tools, and digital literacy programs that will raise the critical ability of the consumers in evaluating online content (Lewandowsky, Ecker, & Cook, 2017). Further, the principles of ethical AI must be infiltrated into recommendation systems for content to control unwanted outcomes of algorithmic amplification (Gillespie, 2018).

In summary, misinformation and manipulation are ethical issues that can undoubtedly threaten the integrity of the digital economy. Transparency, promoting digital literacy, and responsible AI governance can ameliorate the harm that misinformation wrought on society. Given that digital platforms are shaping discourse among the citizenry, ethical responsibility should always accompany technological advancement.

CROSS-BORDER REGULATORY CHALLENGES IN THE DIGITAL ECONOMY

The Complexity of International Digital Trade Laws

New challenges in regulating international trade have surfaced with the rapid growth of the digital economy like never before. Digital laws on trade have divergent interpretations from jurisdiction to jurisdiction, making the legal terrain extremely complicated for business operations (Aaronson & Leblond, 2018). Countries have enacted their own laws surrounding digital trade, reflecting the economic policies that are often in contradiction with those of another country, creating a jurisdictional disarray (Bauer et al., 2016). Take, for instance, the setting of the European Union: The General Data Protection Regulation (GDPR) puts forth stringent requirements for data protection; whereas, in the United States, the regulation is simpler and may be affected by various pieces of legislation such as the California Consumer Privacy Act (CCPA). These opposing provisions create challenges of compliance for multinational corporations that conduct digital trade.

Another issue that has arisen is taxation on digital products and services, which becomes a heated discussion in the negotiations of global trade (Becker & Englisch, 2019). Traditional taxation models focus on physical presence, while digital firms move across borders without a physical presence that would allow government taxation to be reasonably imposed (OECD, 2018). OECD proposed guidelines toward fair digital taxation, but implementing the framework has always remained contentious due to some resistant economies benefiting from current tax structures in place (Cockfield, 2018). Consequently, double taxation and loopholes provide an uneven playing field for digital businesses.

The second area is intellectual property rights, which create their own challenges to digital trade due to varying enforcement mechanisms in member states. The rise of digital piracy, unauthorized distribution of content, and differences in copyright enforcement jurisdiction add to the already tenuous international framework for IP protection. Even though conventions like the Berne Convention and WIPO Copyright Treaty attempt to bring some uniformity to IP rules, it is the enforcement mechanisms that will fail to support diffused protection for digital content in the international arena.

These challenges need governments to enter into bilateral and multilateral arrangements for harmonization on digital trade law. The ongoing WTO negotiations on e-commerce aim to harmonize digital trade practices and regulatory cooperation among countries. Without such frameworks, digital businesses will remain with crucial legal uncertainties significantly hampering international digital commerce.

Harmonizing Global Data Protection Standards

The International Digital Economy suffers from a crisis due to the absence of homogeneous data protection laws. National data protection regimes like the European GDPR, the CCPA in the U.S., or the PDPA in Singapore have set localized standards; however, the standards are often contradictory to one another-a fact that exacerbates multinational compliance issues because businesses or individuals are faced with often impossible regulatory hurdles within national jurisdictions (Greenleaf, 2019). The continued unemployment of stricter consent and transfer requirements regarding user data under the GDPR in comparison with looser circumstantial regulations in other countries, has altogether played an aggravated function in creating the competing legal conflicts associated with cross-border transfer of data.

One of the most serious problems delaying harmony is that no nation agrees on principles underlying the adoption of data privacy. The European view considers data protection a human right that is inalienable. In contrast, the American view tends to focus on industry-specific regulation protecting commercial interests first (Solove, 2020). Such divergences hinder the process of agreements on governance at the international level. The EU-U.S. Privacy Shield was ruled invalid by the Court of Justice of the European Union (CJEU), relying on facts about U.S. government surveillance practices (Kuner, 2020). This ruling broke the flow of transatlantic data, at the same time compelling companies to search for alternative compliance mechanisms, such as Standard Contractual Clauses (SCCs) (Hoofnagle et al., 2019).

The second problematic area is that the extraterritorial data protection laws are very often contrary to the principle of national sovereignty (Bennett & Raab, 2020). For example, China and Russia have enacted laws that localize data and so require businesses to store data within national borders, limiting international data flows, and making compliance with such regulations more difficult (Chander & Sun, 2019). Such rules oppose the principles of free movement of data laying down in digital trade agreements such as the Comprehensive and Progressive Agreement for Trans-Pacific Partnership (CPTPP) (Aaronson, 2019).

Yet harmonization of data protection standards is being attempted through multilaterally organized and managed processes like OECD Privacy Guidelines and APEC Cross border Privacy Rules (CBPR) system (OECD, 2021). However, consensus-making becomes difficult with the visibility of geopolitical frictions and economic interests with disabling influence. Unless contradictions are addressed, the multiplicity of data protection with its different conceptions and regulatory approaches will continue posing challenges to businesses and complicating compliance.

The Role of Multilateral Organizations in Digital Governance

Multilateral organizations are actors that play a critical role in shaping the regulatory framework environment created for the digital economy through their engagement and cooperation among nations in issues of digital governance. It is worth mentioning institutions such as the WTO, OECD, and the United Nations Conference on Trade and Development (UNCTAD) and their contribution within frameworks toward the development of international digital trade (Drake et al., 2019). The WTO Joint Statement Initiative on e-commerce, for example, calls for rules across countries related to issues such as cross-border data flow, electronic contracts, and consumer protection by formalizing the notion of digital trade (Aaronson, 2019). Yet, progress has been slow as developed countries establish a broad front against developing countries from which they want to pursue digital trade policies.

The OECD has had a key role in the definition of digital governance, which is to say, through those actions such as Guidelines on Artificial Intelligence (AI) or through principles for data privacy and security (OECD, 2021). These guidelines give recommendations of policies by the government to enhance ethical AI developments and responsible data use. However, compliance with these recommendations, which are not binding, differs among member states, and thus, cannot have much effect in achieving global harmonization at regulatory levels (Bamberger & Mulligan, 2019).

Another aspect of digital governance is that of UNCTAD: digital trade capacity building for developing countries. Through the provision of technical assistance and policy guidance, UNCTAD aims to close the digital gap and ensure that emerging markets benefit from digital transformation. Very largely though, the adoption of best practices in digital governance is crippled by problems of inadequate infrastructure and regulatory capacity (Meltzer, 2020).

However, these organizations have some limitations when propagating digital governance. They are not able to make binding international agreements. Unlike the process for countries drafting trade regulations, those in the development of policies in digital trade usually invoke national security, which makes it difficult for an agreement to be established (Kelsey, 2018). Therefore, the need after this must be that multilateral organizations need to focus on strengthening their collaborative efforts and also on activating more participatory involvement from the stakeholders involved, such as businesses, civil society, and government, attempting to establish truly inclusive and effective digital governance frameworks.

THE FUTURE OF DIGITAL CONSUMERISM AND MARKET TRENDS

Emerging Technologies Reshaping Consumer Experiences

Fast-growing technologies such as artificial intelligence (AI), blockchain, augmented reality (AR), and the Internet of Things (IoT) are beginning to alter the way consumer goods are digitally purchased. With such technologies, the personalization level increases, user engagement grows, and shopping becomes serenely seamless. Hyper-personalized product suggestions enhance user experience through AI-controlled recommendation engines that are able to collect and analyze vast consumer data sets, thereby improving customers' satisfaction and finally generating sales for the company (Chen et al., 2021). AI-driven chatbots and virtual assistants, such as Alexa from Amazon and Google Assistant, for instance, support customers in their business negotiations with instantaneous personalized purchase recommendations (Huang & Rust, 2021).

Blocked yet very crucial for digital consumerism is blockchain—because of the imposition of transparency, security, and trust in online transactions by means of a decentralized, yet immutable record (Pilkington, 2016). Smart contracts on a blockchain in e-commerce actually enable a trustless transaction system, wherein the possibility of fraud is reduced and intermediaries eliminated (Casino et al., 2019). On the other hand, there is the burgeoning influence of cryptocurrencies as a mode of payment online, with permits now all in for companies like Tesla and PayPal, with Bitcoin moving toward a decentralized financial system.

Augmented reality (AR) and virtual reality (VR) are crafting entire new consumer experiences online, especially where shopping involves interaction. IKEA and Sephora utilize AR technology where customers get to imagine where the furniture is placed or try virtual make-up which, in the end, reduce return rates and install confidence in customers' decisions (Hoyer et al., 2020). IoT-smart-retail-powered solutions like Amazon Go, that operate cashier-less stores, make use of "sensor tech" in coinage with AI to help them skip the traditional check-out experience—thus creating a hassle-less experience for shoppers.

Still, despite all the advantages they bring about, skepticism continues to linger around privacy of the consumer, security of data, and the biases of algorithms into play (Acquisti et al., 2016). While AI-based personalization does enhance comfort levels, simple convenience tends to produce some ethical problems due to data exploitation and surveillance capitalism at their hearts. Also, blockchain, along with all its mounting advantages, can also turn unsustainable simply because of the ecological cost associated with its mining operations, caused by energy consumption.

This challenge seems likely to be streamlined through technological development and regulatory interventions (de Vries, 2018).

The Shift Towards Subscription-Based and Platform-Driven Market

Flexibility, convenience, and personalization have pressed digital economies toward a subscription and platform-dependent business model. In terms of entertainment, Netflix, Spotify, and Amazon Prime have set a new trend wherein subscription-based services are displacing ownership by offering access to unlimited content for a flat monthly fee (Lobschat et al., 2021). The trend is spreading in other areas, with similar businesses like software (Microsoft 365, Adobe Creative Cloud), e-commerce (Amazon Subscribe & Save), and automotive services (Tesla's Full Self-Driving subscription).

Certainly, the platform-driven market, where Uber, Airbnb, and Alibaba operate, survives on digital ecosystems that eliminate friction between buyers and sellers (Parker et al., 2016). These platforms leverage the network effects; more users mean better value propositions, thus taking monopolistic shapes in the digital marketplace (Rochet & Tirole, 2003). However, the platforms are under considerable scrutiny by the regulators for lack of visibility, labor exploitation, data monopolization, and unfair competition (Rahman & Thelen, 2019).

In the same spirit, the fledgling "as-a-service" economy has transformed digital habits quite similarly. In fact, cloud computing (Google Drive, Dropbox), gaming (Xbox Game Pass, PlayStation Plus), and even digital fashion, exemplified by Gucci and Balenciaga selling their virtual fashion items for metaverse applications, pretty much underscore this behavior (Dwivedi et al., 2022). Users, although made convenient, may wonder about the long-term cost ramifications and therefore upholding their use in the digital space: in this case, if consumers were to fail to keep up with advancing subscription payments, they would not have anything to show in form of content or service.

Predicting Regulatory Trends for the Next Decade

Digital consumerism going forward, however, requires relevant regulations to face new phenomena such as the promise of consumer privacy, rights, and fairness in the market. For this reason, data protection laws are gaining global traction as the most critical regulatory trend today. The European Union set a global standard for data privacy, and other countries such as Brazil (LGPD), India (DPDP Act), and China (PIPL) followed or adapted as a result of the General Data Protection Regulation (GDPR) (Kuner et al., 2021). Future regulations would probably center around AI governance, algorithmic transparency, and the ethical consumers' data use to dissuade manipulative practices such as dark patterns (Mathur et al., 2019).

Ensuring continued protection from abuse by not monopolizing the provision of services in profit-making by means of antitrust enforcement in the digital economy is also an area of concern. Regulatory agencies in the U.S. and the EU already began investigations into alleged monopolistic dealings in their respective jurisdictions by companies such as Google, Apple, and Amazon (Khan, 2021). Proposed policies like the European Union's Digital Markets Act (DMA) and the U.S. Platform Competition and Opportunity Act are intended to prevent anti-competitive practices by promoting fair market emergence and enhancing platform interoperability.

Consumer protection will also evolve to adapt to the new age where AI and automation will hold sway over the decisions people make. For example, requirements on AI explainability, such as those laid out in the proposed AI Act by the EU, are expected to increase the consumers' ability to grasp and challenge decisions made by AI touching on their finances, health, or employment (Danks & London, 2017). Sustainability laws regarding such areas as digital carbon footprints, e-waste management, and ethical AI creation will also be increasingly popular as governments turn to the digitized economy for addressing important concerns over environmental welfare (Helbing, 2019).

In this sense, technology, coupled with changing business models and a lot of regulations, will define the future of digital consumerism. Emerging technologies will indeed continue to empower the consumer, but the ethics and legislature must also keep pace to make sure that digital markets are indeed fair, transparent, and sustainable.

CORPORATE STRATEGIES FOR NAVIGATING DIGITAL REGULATIONS

Building Compliance-First Business Models

The only way to go would be to have compliance-first models, in which enterprises are willfully kept in navigating a complex regulatory environment made more difficult by digital considerations. An example is where compliance-first business models embrace compliance with regulations as part and status with the strategy of the business rather than just being an afterthought of it (Kuner et al., 2021). Such as those stringent data protection laws, namely- the General Data Protection Regulation (GDPR) of the European Union, the People's Information Protection Law (PIPL) in China, and the Digital Personal Data Protection Act (DPDP) in India, companies must ensure preliminary incorporation of compliance measures within operational frameworks (Tikkinen-Piri et al., 2018).

Another important structure of a compliance-first path is a robust data governance structure. Organizations need to put in place clear mechanisms by which data is collected, stored, and processed to meet the regulations (Solove & Schwartz, 2020). Under the GDPR, for example, companies need to ensure that personal data is collected only where valid and clear user consent has been given to this collection. This compels a redesigning of digital interfaces and applications to make way for clear opt-in mechanisms. Potent penalties can be slapped on companies for non-compliance; thus, Amazon got a fine of €746 million last year for violations under GDPR (Greenleaf, 2022).

Furthermore, compliance technology also refers to applying automated regulatory monitoring systems and AI-based compliance tools to comply with emerging legal requirements (Sartor & Luciano, 2020). Such advancements can help develop machine learning algorithms for tracking legislation updates worldwide and implementing such amendments in the corporation's policy as needed. AI-based transaction monitoring systems are installed by financial institutions to comply with anti-money laundering (AML) and know-your-customer (KYC) regulations. Companies have a competitive edge in reducing legal risks and earning consumers' trust while being proactive in implementing such technologies.

Moreover, compliance-first businesses encourage corporate training programs that focus on developing awareness of the regulatory obligations of employees (Mulligan & Bamberger, 2019). By fostering a culture of compliance, organizations can minimize human errors that lead to data breaches and legal violations. Many multinationals, including Google and Microsoft, conduct periodic employee training on data protection to align staff with the global privacy standard (Hoofnagle et al., 2019).

In the end, it's a model that not only gives birth to reduced uncertainty in regulatory compliance but also polishes the reputation of a business while boosting confidence in consumers. The companies that are proactive in the whole compliance embedded deeply in their core operations are better poised to work within evolving digital regulation while still being competitive in the global marketplace.

The Importance of Corporate Social Responsibility in the Digital Age

Corporate social responsibility (CSR) in today's digital context encompasses ethical data practices, digital inclusion, and environmental sustainability in addition to charity. Since digital businesses today impact the global economies, consumers and stakeholders expect a kind of social responsibility from corporations that reflects society's own values.

Responsible data stewardship is a key tenet of digital CSR. Companies that gather and process vast amounts of consumer data have to be further governed by transparent policies that prioritize the user privacy and the data security of any kind of breach. The enormity of the data breach from the Facebook-Cambridge Analytica scandal elevated the conversation of corporate accountability with regards to data ethics (Isaak & Hanna, 2018). As such, major acts in tech have arisen in the ethical use of data, including Apple's App Tracking Transparency (ATT) framework enabling users to have a say over their data-sharing preferences (Kemp, 2021).

Another critical pillar of CSR in the digital economy is the promotion of digital inclusion and accessibility. With digital services being so mainstream in everyday life, it is imperative that companies respect inclusivity in their platforms for marginalized and underserved communities. A great example of CSR digital inclusion would be Google's Next Billion Users program in finding internet access solutions for emerging global markets. Microsoft equally leads in one of the primary AI-powered accessibility tools for persons living with disabilities, reinforcing CSR in equitable digital innovation (Ladner, 2019).

Another pillar of digital CSR is environmental sustainability. As data centers and related cloud computing infrastructure expand by leaps and bounds, concerns for carbon emissions and energy consumption have risen. In a bid to counteract this, major tech companies like Amazon, Google, and Microsoft have vowed to become carbon neutral through investing in renewable energy and energy-efficient data centers. Google, for example, has promised that by 2030, it will run entirely on carbon-free energy, thus setting the mark for responsible corporate sustainability in the digital industry (Henderson, 2021).

Beyond image-building, digital CSR goes further to encompass corporate advocacy for ethical policy frameworks. Companies taking a front-seat role in promoting digital rights and supporting regulatory initiatives will contribute towards establishing an ethical and inclusive digital space. By prioritizing CSR, digital firms can allocate investment in long-term customer trust, with consumers and policymakers, and an equitable digital economy.

Socio-Political Consequences of Football-Related Policies and Decisions

Cooperation between corporations and regulators is crucial for innovation and compliance in a world undergoing rapid changes due to digitization. Governments across the globe are tightening regulations governing digital services to address issues arising out of data privacy, competition, and cybersecurity. Proactive dialogue between corporations and regulators permits the formation of policies reasonably in restricting illegitimate acts on the one hand and encouraging market growth on the other.

One important enabling feature is that the regulatory sandbox is essentially designed for companies to experiment with their innovative products in a controlled environment under supervisory guard. For instance, sandbox procedures have been active in the context of fintech firms piloting blockchain-based payment solutions while being sure that the rules of their industry are being followed. The British FCA has set up successful sandbox structures for firms to innovate on a relatively safe basis in terms of regulatory requirements as has Singapore with the MAS.

Another facet of the collaboration is co-regulation, in which industry and regulators work jointly to create standards and methods of best practice (Marsden, 2018). Under the example of the European DSA, the Act has taken contributions from industry players in creating content moderation rules for online platforms. By partnering in the discussion of regulatory processes, the industry can keep the practical relevance of policies and ensure that they do not stifle innovation (Hoffmann et al., 2020).

Transparency initiatives constitute a significant area of human-based corporate-regulatory cooperation. Tech giants such as Facebook, Google, and Twitter have implemented transparency reporting to disclose government data requests and content takedown policies (Napoli, 2019). These measures enhance accountability and trust between corporations, regulators, and consumers (Radu, 2020).

Yet legal conflicts remain that hinder cooperation, especially when corporate benefit clashes with government priority. The disputes over digital tax, platform liability, and AI ethics continue to create tensions between regulators and corporations. In fact, to deal with these tensions, corporations should take the initiative in engaging regulators by emphasizing compliance, transparency, and collaboration.

In summary, cooperation among authorities is paramount to creating a fair and sustainable digital economy. Responsibly engaging with policymakers and collaborating in writing regulatory frameworks translates to a business-friendly yet stable regulatory environment that encourages innovation.

CONCLUSION AND DISCUSSION

The rapid development of the digital economy poses considerable regulatory challenges for businesses navigating a disjointed and dynamic legal landscape. For instance, jurisdictional inconsistency in digital trade legislation, regulatory compliance of data privacy, and taxation frameworks all hinder actual and barrier-free international trade. The recent innovations of artificial intelligence (AI), blockchain, and Internet of Things (IoT) add other intricacies for complying with regulations and at the same time provide for more dynamic and adaptive options for policymakers.

A major conclusion of the analysis is that there is an immediate need to harmonize digital trade laws and data protection standards on a global scale. While Europe's General Data Protection Regulation (GDPR) and OECD guidance on digital governance have established important starting points, competing geopolitical and economic interests make a true global regulatory framework virtually impossible to achieve (Solove & Schwartz, 2020). A situation where inconsistent governance policies, such as China's stringent data localization laws versus the U.S. sector-specific approach, lead to compliance burdens for multinational companies is also to be avoided (Kuner et al., 2021).

Business models focusing on compliance will support mitigation of legal risks-a key tenet for sustaining growth in the digital economy-where its stakeholders may deploy resources toward regulatory technology (Mulligan & Bamberger, 2019). Corporate social responsibility will be an increasingly important dimension of digital governance and is expected to give inputs toward ethical data practices, digital inclusiveness, and environmental problems raised by technological growth. Involving companies along with regulators through regulatory sandboxes, co-regulation initiatives, and transparency programs will ensure that the regulatory environment strikes the right balance and nurtures innovation.

Ultimately, the digital economy's future will be determined by how governments, businesses, and multilateral institutions can forge cohesive, adaptable, and forward-looking regulatory frameworks that preserve consumer rights in an environment conducive to technology. If not engaged proactively and cooperatively on an international level, regulatory fragmentation will remain the hurdle for global digital commerce and innovation.

REFERENCES

Aaronson, S. A. (2019). Digital trade agreements: What's on the table? *Journal of International Commerce. Economic Policy*, *10*(2), 1950007.

Aaronson, S. A., & Leblond, P. (2018). Mapping the challenges of digital trade governance. *Journal of International Commerce. Economic Policy*, *9*(2), 1850009.

Acquisti, A., Taylor, C., & Wagman, L. (2016). The economics of privacy. *Journal of Economic Literature*, *54*(2), 442–492. DOI: 10.1257/jel.54.2.442

Andrejevic, M. (2020). *Automated media*. Routledge.

Arner, D. W., Barberis, J., & Buckley, R. P. (2016). The evolution of FinTech: A new post-crisis paradigm? *Georgetown Journal of International Law*, *47*, 1271–1319.

Ayres, R. U., & Williams, E. (2004). The digital economy: Where do we stand? *Technological Forecasting and Social Change*, *71*(4), 315–339. DOI: 10.1016/j.techfore.2003.11.001

Baily, M. N., & Lawrence, R. Z. (2001). Do we have a new e-conomy? *The American Economic Review*, *91*(2), 308–312. DOI: 10.1257/aer.91.2.308

Bamberger, K. A., & Mulligan, D. K. (2015). *Privacy on the ground: Driving corporate behavior in the United States and Europe*. MIT Press.

Bamberger, K. A., & Mulligan, D. K. (2019). Privacy on the books and on the ground. *Stanford Law Review*, *71*(2), 247–313.

Bauer, J. M., Bohlin, E., Welfens, P. J. J., & Yoo, C. S. (Eds.). (2016). *The network code economy: Digital platforms and the governance of the new economy*. Springer.

Becker, J., & Englisch, J. (2019). The OECD approach to addressing the tax challenges of the digitalisation of the economy. *Intertax*, *47*(5), 415–430.

Benkler, Y., Faris, R., & Roberts, H. (2018). *Network propaganda: Manipulation, disinformation, and radicalization in American politics*. Oxford University Press.

Bennett, C. J., & Raab, C. D. (2020). *The governance of privacy: Policy instruments and the public interest in information states*. MIT Press.

Bresnahan, T. F., & Trajtenberg, M. (1995). General purpose technologies: 'Engines of growth'? *Journal of Econometrics*, *65*(1), 83–108. DOI: 10.1016/0304-4076(94)01598-T

Brynjolfsson, E., & Hitt, L. M. (2003). Computing productivity: Firm-level evidence. *The Review of Economics and Statistics, 85*(4), 793–808.

Bukht, R., & Heeks, R. (2017). Defining, Conceptualising and Measuring the Digital Economy. *Research.*manchester.ac.uk. https://research.manchester.ac.uk/en/publications/defining-conceptualising-and-measuring-the-digital-economy

Cadwalladr, C., & Graham-Harrison, E. (2018, March 17). Revealed: 50 million Facebook profiles harvested for Cambridge Analytica in major data breach. *The Guardian.* https://www.theguardian.com

Calo, R. (2013). Consumer subject review boards: A thought experiment. *Stanford Law Review Online, 66*, 97–102.

Carlsson, B. (2004). The Digital Economy: What is new and what is not? *Structural Change and Economic Dynamics, 15*(3), 245–264. DOI: 10.1016/j.strueco.2004.02.001

Casino, F., Dasaklis, T. K., & Patsakis, C. (2019). A systematic literature review of blockchain-based applications: Current status, classification and open issues. *Telematics and Informatics, 36*, 55–81.

Chaffey, D. (2022). *Digital business and e-commerce management: Strategy, implementation, and practice* (8th ed.). Pearson.

Chander, A., & Sun, U. (2019). The romance of cyberlaw in China. *The American Journal of International Law, 113*(3), 519–563.

Chen, L., Mislove, A., & Wilson, C. (2021). Personalization and filter bubbles. *Communications of the ACM, 64*(10), 90–98.

Chesney, R., & Citron, D. (2019). Deepfakes and the new disinformation war. *Foreign Affairs, 98*(1), 147–155.

Cockfield, A. J. (2018). The OECD proposal for taxing the digital economy: A critical evaluation. *Canadian Tax Journal, 66*(4), 859–906.

Couldry, N., & Mejias, U. A. (2019). *The costs of connection: How data is colonizing human life and appropriating it for capitalism.* Stanford University Press.

Danks, D., & London, A. J. (2017). Algorithmic bias in autonomous systems. In *Proceedings of the 26th International Joint Conference on Artificial Intelligence* (pp. 4691–4697). IJCAI.

De Stefano, V. (2016). The rise of the "just-in-time workforce": On-demand work, crowdwork, and labor protection in the gig economy. *Comparative Labor Law & Policy Journal, 37*(3), 471–504.

de Vries, A. (2018). Bitcoin's growing energy problem. *Joule, 2*(5), 801–805.

Deloitte. (2020). The future of social commerce: How digital platforms are shaping retail. *Deloitte Insights.* https://www2.deloitte.com

Dignum, V. (2019). *Responsible artificial intelligence: How to develop and use AI in a responsible way.* Springer.

Drake, W. J., Jørgensen, R. F., & Miège, B. (2019). *Internet governance: Origins, current issues, and future possibilities.* Lynne Rienner Publishers.

Dwivedi, Y. K., Kshetri, N., Hughes, L., Slade, E. L., Jeyaraj, A., Kar, A. K., & Wright, R. (2022). "So you want to talk about the metaverse?": Conceptual underpinnings, synthesis, and research agenda. *Journal of the Association for Information Systems, 23*(5), 1–61.

Eubanks, V. (2018). *Automating inequality: How high-tech tools profile, police, and punish the poor.* St. Martin's Press.

Floridi, L., Cowls, J., Beltrametti, M., Chatila, R., Chazerand, P., Dignum, V., & Vayena, E. (2018). AI4People—An ethical framework for a good AI society: Opportunities, risks, principles, and recommendations. *Minds and Machines, 28*(4), 689–707.

Freeman, C., & Louçã, F. (2001). *As time goes by: From the industrial revolutions to the information revolution.* Oxford University Press.

Gillespie, T. (2018). *Custodians of the internet: Platforms, content moderation, and the hidden decisions that shape social media.* Yale University Press.

Goldfarb, A., & Tucker, C. (2012). Privacy and innovation. *Innovation Policy and the Economy, 12*(1), 65–90.

Goldfarb, A., & Tucker, C. (2019). Digital economics. *Journal of Economic Literature, 57*(1), 3–43.

Gordon, R. J. (2000). Does the "new economy" measure up to the great inventions of the past? *The Journal of Economic Perspectives, 14*(4), 49–74. DOI: 10.1257/jep.14.4.49

Greenleaf, G. (2019). Global convergence of data privacy law: The paths are different. *International Data Privacy Law, 9*(3), 147–172.

Greenleaf, G. (2022). Global data privacy laws 2022: Accelerating coverage but with significant weaknesses. *Privacy Laws & Business International Report*, *176*, 3–16.

Helbing, D. (2019). *Societal self-engineering*. MIT Press.

Henderson, J. (2021, September 14). Google commits to carbon-free energy by 2030. *Utility Dive*. https://www.utilitydive.com

Hoffmann, A. L., Katzenbach, M., & Gollatz, K. (2020). Between coordination and regulation: Finding the governance in data governance. *Internet Policy Review*, *9*(2), 1–16.

Hoofnagle, C. J., van der Sloot, B., & Metzger, A. (2019). The European Union general data protection regulation: What it is and what it means. *Information & Communications Technology Law*, *28*(1), 65–98.

Hoyer, W. D., Kroschke, M., Schmitt, B., Krafft, M., & Shankar, V. (2020). Transforming the customer experience through new technologies. *Journal of Interactive Marketing*, *51*, 57–71.

Huang, M.-H., & Rust, R. T. (2021). Artificial intelligence in service. *Journal of Service Research*, *24*(2), 155–172.

Hubbard, T. N. (2003). Information, decisions, and productivity: On-board computers and capacity utilization in trucking. *The American Economic Review*, *93*(4), 1328–1353.

Isaak, J., & Hanna, M. J. (2018). User data privacy: Facebook, Cambridge Analytica, and privacy protection. *Computer*, *51*(8), 56–59.

Jovanovic, B., & Rousseau, P. L. (2005). General purpose technologies. In Aghion, P., & Durlauf, S. (Eds.), *Handbook of Economic Growth* (Vol. 1, pp. 1181–1224). Elsevier.

Kelsey, J. (2018). Trade, security and sovereignty in the digital economy. *Journal of World Trade*, *52*(6), 947–970.

Kemp, S. (2021). Digital 2021: Global overview report. *DataReportal*. https://datareportal.com/reports/digital-2021-global-overview-report

Khan, L. (2021). Amazon's antitrust paradox. *The Yale Law Journal*, *126*(3), 710–805.

Kshetri, N. (2021). The economics of cybersecurity. *IT Professional*, *23*(1), 42–47.

Kuner, C. (2020). The CJEU's Schrems II decision: Adequacy undermined, SCCs strengthened? *European Data Protection Law Review*, *6*(4), 481–496.

Kuner, C., Cate, F. H., Millard, C., Lynskey, O., & Svantesson, D. (2021). *Transborder data flows and data privacy law*. Oxford University Press.

Ladner, R. D. (2019). *Accessible technology and the developing world*. Oxford University Press.

Lessig, L. (2001). *The future of ideas: The fate of the commons in a connected world*. Random House.

Lewandowsky, S., Ecker, U. K. H., & Cook, J. (2017). Beyond misinformation: Understanding and coping with the "post-truth" era. *Journal of Applied Research in Memory and Cognition*, *6*(4), 353–369.

Lobschat, L., Osinga, E. C., Tompkins, L., & Woratschek, H. (2021). Consumer–brand relationships in the subscription economy: A conceptual framework and research directions. *Journal of the Academy of Marketing Science*, *49*(3), 519–536.

Manyika, J., Chui, M., Farrell, D., Van Kuiken, S., Groves, P., & Doshi, E. A. (2016). *Digital America: A tale of the haves and have-mores*. McKinsey Global Institute.

Marsden, C. T. (2018). *Internet co-regulation: European law, regulatory governance and online services*. Cambridge University Press.

Mathur, A., Acar, G., Friedman, M. G., Lucherini, E., Mayer, J., Chetty, M., & Narayanan, A. (2019). Dark patterns at scale: Findings from a crawl of 11K shopping websites. *Proceedings of the ACM on Human-Computer Interaction, 3*(CSCW), 1–32.

McAfee, A., & Brynjolfsson, E. (2017). *Machine, platform, crowd: Harnessing our digital future*. W. W. Norton & Company.

Meltzer, J. P. (2020). *The impact of the digital economy on developing countries*. Brookings Institution Press.

Mesenbourg, T. L. (2001). *Measuring the digital economy*. U.S. Bureau of the Census.

Napoli, P. M. (2019). *Social media and the public interest: Media regulation in the disinformation age*. Columbia University Press.

Negroponte, N. (1995). *Being digital*. Knopf.

O'Neil, C. (2016). *Weapons of math destruction: How big data increases inequality and threatens democracy*. Crown Publishing.

OECD. (2018). *Tax challenges arising from digitalisation: Economic analysis and evaluation of the impact of the proposals*. OECD Publishing.

OECD. (2020). *The digital economy outlook 2020*. OECD Publishing.

OECD. (2021). *OECD privacy framework*. OECD Publishing.

Oliner, S. D., & Sichel, D. E. (2000). The resurgence of growth in the late 1990s: Is information technology the story? *The Journal of Economic Perspectives*, *14*(4), 3–22.

Parker, G. G., Van Alstyne, M. W., & Choudary, S. P. (2016). *Platform revolution: How networked markets are transforming the economy and how to make them work for you*. W. W. Norton & Company.

Pasquale, F. (2015). *The black box society: The secret algorithms that control money and information*. Harvard University Press.

Philippon, T. (2016). The FinTech opportunity. *NBER Working Paper No. 22476*. https://doi.org/DOI: 10.3386/w22476

Pilkington, M. (2016). Blockchain technology: Principles and applications. In Olleros, X., & Zhegu, M. (Eds.), *Research handbook on digital transformations* (pp. 225–253). Edward Elgar.

Porter, M. E., & Kramer, M. R. (2019). Creating shared value. *Harvard Business Review*, *97*(1), 62–77.

Radu, R. (2020). *Digital sovereignty: The search for power in a data-driven world*. Oxford University Press.

Rahman, S., & Thelen, K. (2019). The gig economy and the future of work: A comparative analysis of labor platforms across sectors and countries. *Comparative Political Studies*, *52*(11), 1652–1680.

Rochet, J.-C., & Tirole, J. (2003). Platform competition in two-sided markets. *Journal of the European Economic Association*, *1*(4), 990–1029.

Sartor, G., & Luciano, F. (2020). Legal reasoning with machine learning: A critical survey. *Artificial Intelligence and Law*, *28*(3), 333–381.

Schneier, B. (2015). *Data and Goliath: The hidden battles to collect your data and control your world*. W. W. Norton & Company.

Shiller, R. J. (2000). *Irrational exuberance*. Princeton University Press.

Solove, D. J. (2013). Privacy self-management and the consent dilemma. *Harvard Law Review*, *126*(7), 1880–1903.

Solove, D. J. (2020). *Understanding privacy*. Harvard University Press.

Solove, D. J., & Schwartz, P. M. (2020). *Privacy law fundamentals* (6th ed.). IAPP.

Tikkinen-Piri, C., Rohunen, A., & Markkula, J. (2018). EU general data protection regulation: Changes and implications for personal data collecting companies. *Computer Law & Security Review*, *34*(1), 134–153.

Varian, H. R. (2019). Artificial intelligence, economics, and industrial organization. In Agrawal, A., Gans, J., & Goldfarb, A. (Eds.), *The economics of artificial intelligence: An agenda* (pp. 399–419). University of Chicago Press.

Chapter 2
The Role of Governments in Corporate Social Responsibility:
Effectiveness of Hybrid Instruments

Orencio Jesús Vázquez Oteo
https://orcid.org/0000-0003-1680-6589
UNED, Spain

Eduardo Soria Cáceres
Observatorio de RSC, Spain

ABSTRACT

This article analyses the role of hybrid public policy instruments based on the case study of the Spanish Corporate Social Responsibility Strategy (EERSE) 2014-2020. Using a mixed methodology with a predominantly qualitative focus, including questionnaires and focus groups with experts, we assess the design, implementation and degree of execution of the Spanish CSR Strategy, as well as its main advances and limitations. The results reveal that, although the EERSE represented a significant effort to institutionalise CSR and was positively valued for its technical and conceptual approach, its impact on the transformation of the business fabric was limited. The main weaknesses detected are related to the lack of follow-up, the scarcity of resources and the low visibility among the actors involved. Likewise, the need for greater inter-institutional coordination, the strengthening of participatory governance structures and the closing of the gap between large companies and SMEs in the effective incorporation of responsible practices are identified as critical challenges.

DOI: 10.4018/979-8-3373-0385-7.ch002

INTRODUCTION

Businesses are no longer merely economic actors but have acquired a decisive role in contemporary political and social relations. The growing offshoring and outsourcing of production processes has weakened the capacity of states to exercise effective control over business activity, without the parallel development of an international institutional architecture capable of adequately controlling it. This vacuum has been filled by large corporations, which have configured global governance networks, exercising a form of "private authority" that transcends the sovereign power of states, influencing public decision-making and assuming traditionally state functions, such as the provision of goods and services (Biersteker and Hall, 2002; Cutler, 2001; Engwall, 2006).

Corporate Social Responsibility (CSR) and corporate sustainability refer to business policies and practices that reflect the commitment of corporations to broader social goals and the management of negative externalities. However, despite the increase in companies promoting CSR actions, negative trends in relation to environmental degradation, unsustainable resource consumption, biodiversity loss and wealth concentration have not been reversed (GRI, 2015; Lu *et al.*, 2019; Gray, 2010). Voluntary initiatives, driven by bodies such as the United Nations or the OECD, while they have helped to frame debates and point to the key elements of CSR, have not substantially changed business practices. The absence of a legal framework and an agreed definition of CSR (Campbell, 2007; Okoye, 2009), together with the proliferation of standards, leads to a lack of systematization in its application (Frynas and Stephens, 2015; Campbell, 2007; Scherer and Palazzo, 2007; Okoye, 2009; Whitehouse, 2003; Dahlsrud, 2008). This makes it difficult to measure results, masks the reality of business practices (Okoye, 2009) and hinders the incorporation of CSR as a market criterion. As a result, self-regulatory mechanisms and codes of conduct have proven to be insufficient. From a critical perspective, it is argued that CSR has been used as an instrument to protect corporate reputation, preserve positions of power (Deegan, 2002; Patten, 2002; Cho *et al.*, 2012), resist regulatory change (Cho *et al.*, 2018) and neutralize criticism of the existing economic system (Shaw, 2009).

Traditionally, CSR has been conceived as an area of voluntary action by companies, often underestimating the importance of governments for CSR (Jette and Moon, 2022) or limiting state intervention to promotion and incentivization, without involving regulatory or sanctioning mechanisms (Utting, 2008; Idemudia and Kwakyemah, 2018). This dichotomous view between CSR and government has been challenged by a growing trend that advocates a relational model, in which governments take a more active role (Steurer *et al.*, 2012; Knudsen and Moon, 2017). In the corporate citizenship approach, responsible corporate action must be guided by legality, integrating four essential dimensions: social contract, collective responsibility, active accountability and legal status (Shaw, 2009). These dimensions require a strong legal framework that provides legitimacy, predictability and enforceability, and in many cases there is a positive coexistence of dichotomous and relational perspectives (Jette and Moon, 2022). Thus, public intervention is essential to establish policies that clearly delineate business obligations and encourage proactive behavior.

This paradigm shift is also reflected in European policy developments. In 2011, the European Commission published the 'Renewed EU Corporate Social Responsibility Strategy 2011-2014' (European Commission, 2011), introducing a vision focused on human rights, business impacts and compliance. While maintaining a balance between voluntary and regulatory measures, the strategy stresses the need for regulations that promote transparency, accountability and responsible consumption, while inviting member states to develop national strategies and implementation plans for the UN Guiding Principles.

Several countries, including Greece, Slovenia, Cyprus, Spain, the Czech Republic, Germany, and Norway, responded to the European Commission's (EC) call by approving plans and strategies. The objectives, levels of development, and policies set out in these plans vary widely. In 2014, Spain's government approved the "Spanish Strategy for Corporate Social Responsibility 2014-2020" (EERSE), which incorporates international standards such as the OECD Guidelines, the Global Compact, the ILO Tripartite Declaration, the UN Guiding Principles, and the Principles for Responsible Investment. Designed and approved by the State Council for Corporate Social Responsibility (CERSE), a quadripartite consultative body that brings together representatives of companies, trade unions, civil society, and public administrations, this strategy is more developed than those of other EU countries.

In academia, CSR research has largely focused on the role of business, with analysis of the role of the state and public policy taking a back seat (Steurer, 2010; Gond, Kang and Moon, 2011; Delannon and Raufflet, 2021; Knudsen and Moon, 2017). Although interest in this field has grown in recent years (Knudsen, Moon and Slager, 2015; Jetten and Moon, 2022), studies tend to classify the relationships between governments and CSR or typify the public instruments employed (Albareda *et al.*, 2008; Steurer, 2010; Steurer *et al.*, 2012), without delving into their effectiveness (Giamporcaro *et al.*, 2020; Idemudia and Kwakyemah, 2018). This shortcoming negatively affects effective policy design (Ji, H and Miao, 2020) and generates conceptual confusion by mixing instruments and issues (Steurer, 2010).

This article analyses the effectiveness of hybrid or adhesive CSR instruments, understood as those that combine different types of public policies. Specifically, it examines the implementation of the Spanish CSR Strategy 2014-2020, developed by the State CSR Council - a collegiate body with representation from business, trade unions, public administration and civil society. Through a mixed approach that combines quantitative indicators with qualitative analysis based on experts, the study offers a comprehensive view of the impact and evolution of the strategy. The motivation of the article is to delve deeper into hybrid instruments within CSR public policies, and to this end we pose the following research question: Are hybrid instruments adequate mechanisms of political action to promote CSR? And through the study of the Spanish case we will try to answer the second research question: What are the factors that determine the effectiveness of hybrid instruments, specifically of the CSR strategy? We start from the following hypothesis: "The National CSR Strategy has contributed significantly to the promotion of CSR in Spain".

This paper offers a twofold contribution: on the one hand, it provides empirical evidence on emerging forms of state intervention through participatory governance mechanisms; on the other, it contributes to the theorization of hybrid instruments as tools for fostering an institutional ecosystem that promotes CSR. At a practical level, the findings are useful for public decision-makers interested in identifying effective policies and understanding the strategic and managerial factors that facilitate their implementation.

Following this introduction, section 2 reviews previous literature on public policy in the field of CSR. Section 3 describes the methodology employed. Section 4 presents the Strategy and the main developments in CSR policy and implementation during its lifetime. Section 5 presents the main results of the two phases of participation in the strategy's diagnosis. Finally, section 6 presents the conclusions and implications of the study.

THE ROLE OF PUBLIC POLICIES IN PROMOTING CSR

CSR can be understood as a broad framework that encompasses various business practices aimed at responsibly managing economic, social and environmental impacts (Frynas and Stephens, 2015). This vision implies an interrelationship with public policy (Frynas and Stephens, 2015), understood as a set of decisions of action or inaction taken by authorities to guide public affairs (Ruggie, 2004). Thus, the link between public authorities and CSR holds both opportunities and risks: while business can contribute to social and environmental goals, there is also the danger of state withdrawal, delegating functions to private actors and favoring regulatory capture.

States can shape business behavior through intervention that strengthens legal, social, political and competition aspects (Etile and Teyssier, 2016; Reinhardt, 1998). In some contexts, it is even governments themselves that encourage irresponsible business practices. Delannon and Raufflet (2021) identify different possible roles for the state: inhibitor of the emergence of CSR, collaborative partner, symbolic promoter or absent actor.

The role of the state as an active driver of sustainability has led to the adoption of policies and regulations aimed at fostering corporate responsibility (Albareda *et al.*, 2007; Moon & Vogel, 2008; Zueva and Fairbrass, 2021). Governments have started to incorporate multi-stakeholder approaches in the design of public policies (Albareda, 2008), considering CSR not only as a governance tool but also as a competitive advantage. From this perspective, Steurer *et al.* (2012) propose three frameworks of state intervention: normative, embedded and agentic, depending on the degree of alignment between public policies and business interests.

However, knowledge on the specific role of governments in CSR remains limited (Delannon and Raufflet, 2021). The debate has focused on "soft regulation", which poses less resistance from business (Albareda *et al.*, 2008; Fox *et al.*, 2002; Steurer, 2010). However, we note that numerous voluntary regulations have been developed in response to evidence of lack of effectiveness and pressure from civil society, in particular NGOs (Guay *et al.*, 2004; Fields *et al.*, 2001), and have led to binding legislation (Steurer, 2010). Recent examples of this approach are Directive 2014/95/EU on non-financial reporting and Directive 2024/1760 on corporate sustainability due diligence, which reflect the evolution towards more demanding public policies (Cerrato and Ferrando, 2020; Kinderman, 2016). Governments can therefore act as facilitators, promoters, but also as regulators of CSR (Fox *et al.*, 2002).

Knudsen and Moon (2017) distinguish between direct intervention - through legislation - and indirect intervention - through trade policies, for example. Indirect intervention is particularly relevant in the context of global supply chains and the environmental and social impact of large corporations. In some cases, CSR has been used by governments as a strategic tool for business differentiation (Hanlon, 2011). Mitchell (1998) highlights the Danish case, where the government acted proactively in the face of controversial business practices, such as those of Shell, promoting a corporate image aligned with environmental values.

In the European context, studies on public CSR policies have been scarce. Cueto and de la Cuesta (2023) classify the public policy models followed in Europe into 4: Continental model or Citizenship based on regulation, social agreement and sustainable development strategies; Mediterranean model or Agora based on the creation of CSR consensus groups; Anglo-Saxon model or Soft intervention based on encouraging the involvement of the company in the community and Nordic model or Partnership based on the development of shared strategies between sectors for socio-labour challenges. Albareda *et al.* (2007, 2008) propose a typology based on the actors involved: governments, business and civil society. Steurer (2010), for his part, proposes a more precise classification of public instruments into five categories: informational, economic, legal, partnership and hybrid. This last group, hybrid instruments, includes policies that combine several approaches, such as national CSR strategies, which are the subject of analysis in this paper.

SPANISH CSR STRATEGY. PROGRESS AND CHALLENGES DURING ITS IMPLEMENTATION

The Spanish Corporate Social Responsibility Strategy (EERSE) 2014-2020 is a public policy framework aimed at promoting responsible and sustainable business management models aligned with the principles of competitiveness, social cohesion and environmental sustainability. Developed within the State Council for Corporate Social Responsibility (CERSE), a four-party consultative body bringing together representatives of business, trade unions, civil society and public administrations, and approved by the Spanish Government, the EERSE represents an attempt to institutionalize social responsibility in public and private organizational practice. The EERSE establishes four strategic objectives: (1) to promote CSR in public and private companies and organizations; (2) to position CSR as an attribute of competitiveness, social cohesion and sustainability; (3) to disseminate the values of CSR in society; and (4) to create a common framework that respects the principles of market unity. To achieve these objectives, the strategy envisages ten lines of action that are deployed in a plan of 60 concrete measures. These lines include: promotion of CSR; integration in education, training and research; promotion of good governance and transparency; responsible management of human capital; socially responsible investment and R&D&I; responsible relations with suppliers; promotion of responsible consumption; respect for the environment; development cooperation; and strengthening coordination and participation.

Within the framework of the evolution of CSR as a fundamental axis in business management and the formulation of public policies, the period of validity of the strategy (2014-2020) has been marked by the implementation of various initiatives aimed at strengthening transparency, sustainability and equity in corporate and financial environments. These initiatives have been promoted by international organizations, the European Union (EU) and the Spanish government, addressing key areas such as the fight against corruption and fraud, corporate governance, human and labor rights, consumer protection, taxation and environmental sustainability.

The most significant progress can be found in the field of sustainability reporting with the approval in 2014 of Directive 95/2014/EU on Non-Financial Reporting and Diversity and its subsequent transposition into the Spanish legal framework through Law 11/2018 on Non- Financial Reporting. Other relevant accountability initiatives include Regulation (EU) 2019/2088 on disclosure of sustainability-related information in the financial services sector and Regulation (EU) 2020/852 on the establishment of a framework to facilitate sustainable Investments, known as the Taxonomy Regulation.

Directive 95/2014/EU, as noted by Aboud et al. (2024), played a significant role in enhancing the quality of corporate sustainability reporting across Europe, while also contributing to narrowing the gap between actual performance and public disclosure. Furthermore, as Papathanassiou and Nieto (2025) emphasize, regulations on non-financial information, due diligence, and taxonomy collectively provide a general regulatory framework that supports the transition towards more sustainable business models and helps prevent practices such as greenwashing. In this context, the incorporation of mechanisms such as double materiality analysis and assurance in the verification of non-financial reports is of critical importance, as these elements strengthen the reliability, objectivity, and comprehensiveness of the information available to various stakeholders

The fight against corruption and fraud has been a priority in the period under review at both European and national level with the adoption of specific programs such as Hercule III and regulations such as Directive (EU) 2015/849, aimed at strengthening financial control mechanisms and the prevention of money laundering. In Spain, the enactment of Law 19/2013 on transparency and Organic Law 3/2015 on the financing of political parties have represented advances in accountability and institutional integrity.

As regards corporate governance, regulatory frameworks have been implemented to improve the oversight of companies and ensure the protection of shareholders and stakeholders rights. Directive 2014/95/EU has introduced mandatory disclosure of non-financial information, while the revisions of the Good Governance Code for Listed Companies in Spain (2015 and revised in 2020) have reinforced transparency standards in the corporate sector. Likewise, the OECD and G20 Principles of Corporate Governance have updated key criteria in terms of oversight, accountability and diversity in management bodies.

The recognition of human and labor rights in the business context has undergone significant development, with initiatives such as the creation of the UN Working Group (2014) for the regulation of transnational corporations, the updating of the ILO Tripartite Declaration, and the adoption of the National Action Plan on Business and Human Rights in Spain. In parallel, the regulation of supply chains through Regulation (EU) 2017/821 has established specific controls on the import of minerals from conflict zones, promoting greater responsibility in international trade.

In the area of consumer and user protection, reforms driven by UNCTAD (2015) have incorporated recommendations on accessibility to essential goods and services, data protection and the regulation of commercial practices. At the European level, Regulation (EU) 2017/2394 has strengthened cooperation between national authorities, while in Spain the enactment of Organic Law 3/2018 on data protection has been a step forward in the regulation of the digital environment and information security.

Tax initiatives have been aimed at combating tax evasion and avoidance by promoting transparency and exchange of information. Directive 2014/107/EU, the EU Corporate Tax Action Plan and the BEPS initiative of the OECD and the G20 have introduced mechanisms to curb base erosion and artificial profit shifting. In this regard, Directive (EU) 2016/1164 (ATAD) has established specific rules against tax avoidance practices, complemented by the listing of tax non-cooperative jurisdictions.

Finally, the development of environmental policies has taken a central role in the CSR agenda, with the updating of international standards such as ISO 14001 (2015) and the adoption of the Paris Agreement as a global framework for the reduction of greenhouse gas emissions. In Europe, the implementation of the European Green Pact, the 2020/852 Regulation known as the Taxonomy Regulation, the Non-Financial Disclosure Regulation and the European and Spanish Circular Economy Strategy have laid the foundations for a transition towards more sustainable production and consumption patterns, complemented by regulations on energy labelling and waste management.

Overall, the initiatives developed between 2014 and 2020 have established a regulatory and institutional framework that reinforces the role of CSR as a key instrument for business sustainability and economic and social development. Companies face a regulatory framework and a society that demands high standards of transparency and corporate responsibility, which puts pressure on them to adopt various commitments to social and environmental sustainability, as well as to business ethics. According to the Spanish Global Compact Network, up to 83% of Spanish companies would be carrying out actions aimed at achieving the SDGs, a figure that rises to 99% in the case of large companies (Spanish Global Compact Network, 2020). However, formal commitments do not always correspond to effective compliance (or information about it) in relation to the different thematic areas considered: research reveals that there is a wide margin for improvement in many areas, and that progress is uneven (Observatorio de Responsabilidad Social Corporativa, 2021; Vázquez, 2024).

We can conclude that, despite progress in the period studied, challenges remain in terms of effective implementation and impact assessment, which requires greater articulation between existing regulations and their adoption by the private sector. On the other hand, future public policies must integrate the regulatory advances that have taken place since 2020, mainly Directive (EU) 2022/2464 on sustainability-related disclosures by companies, which replaced Directive 2014/95/EU, and Directive (EU) 2024/1760 on corporate sustainability due diligence. These regulations, along with Regulation (EU) 2020/852, which establishes a framework to promote sustainable investment and is known as the Taxonomy Regulation, are currently undergoing review through an Omnibus (as of June 2025).

RESEARCH METHOD

In the diagnostic process of the EERSE 2014-2020, representatives of public and private organizations closely linked to the development of CSR in Spain during the period of validity of the Strategy were involved. The approach to collecting information focused on a highly specialized profile, made up of people who played relevant roles in the definition of objectives and design of the EERSE's lines of action, or in its implementation from public institutions with competences in this area. The analysis universe was structured around two main groups:

- Representatives of civil society organizations (business associations, trade unions, consumers, NGOs) with participation in the State Council for Corporate Social Responsibility (CERSE), a body which, due to its plural nature, technical capacity and orientation towards consensus, has played a key role in both the design and institutional articulation of the EERSE.
- Heads of area and technicians with current responsibilities in the definition and execution of public policies related to CSR, both at national and regional level, under the premise that public institutions play a leading role in this area.

Both profiles were included in the two methodologies applied (questionnaires and focus groups).

The research adopts a mixed methodological design with a qualitative predominance, a strategy increasingly used in the evaluation of public policies and social intervention programs, particularly when involving the participation of experts (Creswell & Plano Clark, 2017). This type of design allows, at different levels, from the generation of research questions to the triangulation of results, including the exploratory identification of key issues and the contrast of complementary perspectives (Greene *et al.*, 1989).

Although quantitative approaches are usually based on criteria of statistical representativeness, in this case the limited and specialized nature of the universe of analysis justifies the use of a qualitative approach. This is oriented, on the one hand, towards the selection of actors who, "due to their position in the social structure, best reproduce - through their discourse - the relationships that articulate our field of research" and, on the other hand, towards the identification of "discursive positions, not individuals" (Murillo and Mena, 2006, p. 39).

The sample selection was therefore intentional, considering the knowledge, experience and commitment of the participants to the values of CSR, as well as the need to gather a diversity of perspectives that would allow us to build an overview of the role of key actors in the development of this public policy. These key stakeholders were invited to participate in the study (through questionnaires or focus groups) via formal letters issued by the authors and endorsed by the Ministry of Labor and Social Economy.

The analysis of the qualitative information was conducted through a systematic and comparative reading of the questionnaires and the transcripts of the focus groups, aimed at identifying recurring arguments, shared assessments, and key proposals for the formulation of a new strategy.

Based on the open-ended questions from the questionnaire, the responses were organized according to the strategic lines of the EERSE, grouping comments by thematic similarity and level of consensus. Numerical ratings were examined in terms of their averages and distribution by type of stakeholder, not for inferential purposes, but as a means of supporting the comparison of perceptions.

In the case of the focus groups, representative verbatim quotations were extracted, and the main points of agreement and disagreement among the different participant profiles (public sector, businesses, civil society) were synthesized. This analysis was structured around the axes defined in the research design (progress, limitations, drivers of change, priorities), allowing for the cross-validation of perceptions gathered in both phases and enhancing the validity of the conclusions through triangulation of sources and actors.

Questionnaires

The questionnaire was designed with an in-depth analysis approach, seeking the participation of experts to contribute to the diagnosis of the EERSE. Given the restricted and specialized nature of the study universe, the instrument adopted a mixed format that, while incorporating elements of quantitative assessment, prioritized open-ended responses, thus aligning itself with the characteristics of a semi-structured interview.

Although the numerical assessment of each action line and measure is useful as an indicator of perception, the purpose of the instrument is not limited to a mere assignment of scores. On the contrary, it seeks to understand and interpret the progress, limitations and proposals for improvement from the position that each person occupies with regard to the Strategy and the promotion of CSR. The combination of open and closed response options made it possible to have an individualized assessment of the lines of action, as well as to identify the priority measures for a new EERSE.

The questionnaire was sent to a total of 36 people linked to the CERSE at the time of the design of the strategy. Twelve responses were received from experts with the following profiles and reference organizations:

Table 1. Responses to questionnaires

Type	Description	Position
NGO	Spanish branch of international environmental NGO	Responsible for the private sector
	President of a platform of NGOs promoting CSR	President
Public		Technician Directorate-
Administration		General for the Self-
		Employed, Labour and
	Autonomous Government	Social Economy
	Autonomous Government	Head of CSR and Business
		Model Section
	Autonomous Government	Director General of Labour.
		Ministry of Employment
		and Social Policies
Business associations promoting CSR	Spanish branch of SDG promotion network	Director General
	National association for CSR promotion in business	President
	National large companies association for CSR promotion	Director General
	National association of social economy enterprises	Head of CSR
Trade unions	Largest trade union in Spain	Economist
Investors	Spanish branch of European sustainable investors initiative.	Managing Director
Academics and independents	CERSE	CERSE former participant

Source: own elaboration

The structure of the questionnaire, common to all participants, included the following sections:

- Identification of the person and the organization.
- Assessment of the 10 lines of action: score (0-10), qualitative assessment, suggestion for maintenance, proposal for alternative wording and priority measures.

- Assessment of the 60 measures: score (0-10), qualitative comment, highlighted activities and recommendations.
- Priorities for a new EERSE, including areas and intervention strategies.

While the assessments of the action lines and priorities were mandatory, the assessment of the measures was optional.

The call for responses to the questionnaire was launched in June 2022, and the collection of responses was open until October 2022. Participants completed a virtual questionnaire, with the possibility of saving their answers and returning to them in different sessions, given the characteristics and length of the instrument. The objective of the study and the necessary instructions for its completion were explained in the call for applications.

In addition, the results of this phase served as input to guide the design of the next methodological stage (focus groups), in aspects such as the composition of the groups and the topics of discussion. The analysis of the contributions made it possible to identify key arguments, consensus and preliminary priorities for the design of a new Strategy.

Focus Groups

The aim of the focus groups was to contrast the positions identified from the questionnaires, to deepen the critical aspects of the diagnosis of the 2014-2020 EERSE and to identify key recommendations for the formulation of a new Strategy.

According to Murillo and Mena (2006, p. 99), the focus group "aims to be a situation where the dynamics and potentialities of an everyday conversation occur in a resonance with the peer group (...), while creating an artificial and controlled context that takes advantage of these advantages to respond to research objectives".

The composition of the groups took into account the diversity of institutional positions, as well as the need to ensure fluid interaction based on mutual recognition. This logic responds to the balance between "necessary homogeneity" and "provoked heterogeneity", from which it is possible to analyze how different positions interact with respect to a common object (Zapata Barrero and Sánchez Montijano, 2011). The previous familiarity among some participants - derived from their involvement in spaces such as CERSE - contributed to generating an environment of trust during the sessions.

Table 2. Composition of focus groups

Description	Position	Code	Focus group
National level institution (priority target groups)	Deputy Director, former member of CERSE	SPN01	Public sector
National level institution (human rights and cooperation)	Director	SPN02	Public Sector
National level institution (industry)	Member of the secretariat of the OECD National Contact Point	SPN03	Public sector
Autonomous Institution	Director General for Public Governance, Transparency, Citizen Participation and Agenda 2030	SPA01	Public sector
Autonomous Institution	Director General of Labor Relations	SPA02	Public sector
Autonomous Institution	Deputy Director General for Social Responsibility and Promotion of Self-Governance	SPA03	Public sector
Business organization, generalist	Head of CSR Area	OEM01	Private sector
Business organization, social economy	CSR Manager	OEM02	Private sector
Business organization promoting sustainability	Director General	OES01	Private Sector
Business organization promoting sustainability	Director General	OES02	Private sector
Business organization promoting sustainability	Sustainability Coordinator	OES03	Private sector
Trade Union	Deputy Secretary Trade Union Action. CSR Officer	SIN01	Private Sector
Trade Union	Trade Union Action and Employment Secretary	SIN02	Private Sector
Non-profit organization, civil society	Private Sector Advocacy Officer	CSO01	Private Sector
Sustainable Investment Organization	Deputy Director General	OSC02	Private sector

Source: own elaboration

The call for selected organizations and institutions was launched in October 2022. The two focus groups were held on 17 November 2022, in hybrid format (face-to-face and online). The focus groups were audio-recorded and a summary of their content was subsequently prepared, including the appropriate literal quotes and their attribution.

RESEARCH RESULTS: QUESTIONNAIRES AND FOCUS GROUPS

Questionnaires

The balance of the development of CSR in Spain during the period of validity of the EERSE is positive, however, it is considered that this document has had a low influence on the decisions and initiatives of the institutions and other actors involved in the promotion of CSR. The Strategy is perceived by the participants (experts who were already familiar with the document) as an adequate diagnosis and a sufficiently comprehensive "roadmap": the continuity of the 10 lines of action in a new Strategy has a high acceptance among the respondents, reaching values between 50% and 83% (while non-continuity is preferred by between 10% and 17%).

As determining factors in the progress of CSR in the period studied, the weight of regulatory pressure and the incorporation of certain issues, such as climate change or gender equality, as cross-cutting elements of public policies are recognized.

Coordination at different levels and the participation of different actors appears as a priority area for development, due to its instrumental nature. The CERSE, despite its lack of continuity, is a necessary space that made great contributions in this sense, but it must have adequate planning and resources to properly develop its functions.

Table 3. Assessment of the EERSE according to questionnaires

Positive aspects	Negative aspects
Drafting of a comprehensive strategy, with concrete and timely lines of action and measures.	No compliance indicators. Abstract and generalist objectives, difficult to verify.
Comprehensive strategy in relation to the CSR content included.	Progress in CSR is not due to the EERSE, it has not been a decisive factor. Ambitious in relation to the resources allocated.
CSR values have been strengthened as a cross-cutting element of public policies.	Dispersion and lack of continuity of initiatives, more coordination is needed.
Companies have made progress in incorporating CSR into their business models, there is greater awareness of its advantages.	The incorporation of CSR is uneven: very low in SMEs, questionable in large companies; in many cases it still responds to a corporate image logic.
CERSE as a stakeholder participation structure that favoured stakeholder involvement and was a benchmark.	The CERSE was unable to fulfil the expected function, it was paralysed.

Source: own elaboration based on the questionnaires.

As mentioned above, the assessment of the Strategy as a diagnosis and roadmap is generally positive. Because of its comprehensiveness, it is considered to have anticipated issues that would gain importance during its lifetime, and is even generally perceived as a solid basis for building a new ESSRE.

Table 4. Assessment of the degree of implementation of the action lines and priority measures for the future

Action Line	Assessment	Priority measures
1 Promoting CSR as a driver for more sustainable organisations	6,2	Strengthening of dialogue and cooperation processes between actors. Diversification and increase of incentives for good practices. Accompaniment and training for companies.
2 Integration of CSR in education, training and research.	4,4	Promotion of specialised training pathways. CSR knowledge transfer between companies and universities. CSR as part of the framework of democratic values in formal training.
3 Good governance and transparency as instruments for increasing trust and confidence.	5,6	Guides and resources adapted to different company profiles. CSR competences of managers. Exemplarity of companies and public organisations.
4 Responsible management of human resources and employment development	6,1	Resources to monitor effective compliance with equality and non-discrimination regulations. Development of the regulatory framework for business and human rights. Awareness raising and recognition of the benefits of diversity and inclusion in the workforce.
5 Socially Responsible Investment and R+D+i	7	Coherence of regulations and public policies with international frameworks. Integration of SMEs in SRI. SRI criteria in public investment.
6 Relations with suppliers	6,7	Reinforcement of CSR clauses in public procurement and contracts. Mitigation of the "cascade effect" of regulations for large companies towards SMEs. Proportionality and coherence of requirements towards the value chain with international frameworks.
7 Responsible consumption	5,9	Raising consumer awareness and empowerment. Promote the reliability of product labelling and the visibility of initiatives related to good practices.
		Control and penalise misleading information on social and environmental impact.
8 Respect for the environment	6,5	Ambitious decarbonisation targets aligned with scientific criteria. Common criteria for reporting environmental impacts. Greater inclusion of SMEs and consumers in the promotion of the circular economy, rewarding their good practices.

continued on following page

Table 4. Continued

Action Line	Assessment	Priority measures
9 Development cooperation	7,4	Improved coherence of activities and objectives of external cooperation programmes of institutions at different levels. Strengthening the NCP (OECD) Promotion of public-private partnerships to channel key resources to development cooperation.
10 Coordination and participation	6,1	Reactivation of CERSE Spaces for dialogue and articulation between public institutions with competences related to CSR. Emphasis on the continuity of coordination and participation actions, not limiting them to specific initiatives.

Source: own elaboration based on the questionnaires.

The scores for the different lines of activity are between 4.4 and 7.4 points out of 10, with an average of 6.2. Only the second line (relating to the integration of CSR in education and research) received a score of less than 5 (not for lack of importance, but because of what is perceived as a lack of state protagonism or leadership). It should be noted that these scores are based on the approach or appropriateness of the different lines of action, as well as on the perceived relevance of these lines of action in the work agenda of public institutions during the life of the Strategy. The evaluation of these measures and lines of action takes into account that, although the Ministry of Labor and Social Economy led the design and approval of the EERSE, the measures proposed are based on cross-cutting objectives, involving various institutions beyond the Ministry of Labor.

Table 5. Main developments and constraints in the promotion of CSR during the lifetime of the EERSE

Progress	Constraints
Increasingly comprehensive regulatory framework	Lack of coherence and insufficient interoperability; "cascade effect" on SMEs
State funding of CSR programmes	Insufficient accompaniment outside of financing
CSR-related structures and competences in national and regional public institutions	Heterogeneity, lack of coordination between administrations and common guidelines.
Emergence of numerous multi-stakeholder initiatives and spaces for dialogue.	Dispersion of efforts, lack of continuity, scarce state protagonism.

Source: own elaboration based on the questionnaires.

In summary, the overall assessment of the EERSE 2014–2020 is moderately positive, particularly in terms of its strategic design and capacity to anticipate key CSR trends. However, the findings reveal significant limitations in its implementation, visibility, and influence on institutional decision-making. While regulatory developments and the incorporation of CSR values into public policy frameworks have been acknowledged as important drivers of progress, persistent barriers such as insufficient coordination, limited stakeholder engagement, and uneven uptake—especially among SMEs—continue to hinder systemic advancement.

Results of the Focus Groups

Based on the analysis of the information obtained from the questionnaires, the focus groups were designed to deepen the critical aspects in the diagnosis of the EERSE and the setting of priorities for the future.

The general assessment of the EERSE is similar to that recorded in the questionnaires, although both groups show significant differences in terms of the most salient aspects, as shown in Table 4.

"From a sub-directorate of the Ministry of Labor, it is not possible to act to set global strategies. There is a lack of resources" (OES03).

"The level of knowledge of the Strategy is medium-low. Strategies, projects, plans and so on accumulate, in the end it depends on the personal commitment of the teams" (SPA01).

"A follow-up of the EERSE was planned and would have been necessary" (SPN01).

Table 6. Overall assessment of the development of CSR in Spain during the period of the EERSE 2014-2020

	Public sector	**Private sector**
Degree of progress	Positive, especially in large companies (although not exclusively)	Positive, but insufficient and unequal between SMEs and large companies. Sometimes only in discourse
Main areas of progress	Gender equality, labour rights, climate change	Environment, gender equality, transparency of non-financial information, CSR as a cross-cutting management criterion.
Determinants of progress	Increased awareness in companies, recognition of the advantages of responsible business models	Regulation as main factor, followed by market and investor demands, international initiatives
Constraints to progress	SME/large company gap, lack of awareness of the benefits of CSR	Dispersion of efforts, lack of stakeholder engagement

Source: own elaboration

Public sector actors highlight gender equality, linked to progress on labour rights, and climate Change as the areas where most progress has been made in the strategy period.

"Environmental issues, work-life balance and gender equality are the issues that have evolved the most in the last decade" (PUB06).

In this group, although the importance of regulatory pressure and public policies as factors for progress is recognized, there is a greater discursive prominence of the will of the companies themselves to promote responsible business models; an adaptive response with respect to which a utilitarian vision predominates.

"There is a change in the mentality of the company: due to increasing legislation, but also due to pressure from society and investors... Multinationals have an enormous image risk, so they are more willing and more interested in taking CSR issues into account, but also have more resources to do so" (SPN03).

"Companies have realized that CSR improves their profits, and at the same time society is also evolving in its demands, and public administrations have to support them on both fronts" (SPA02).

The gap between large and small companies appears as the main factor limiting the progress of CSR in Spain, and this issue occupies a significant space in the interventions of the first and subsequent blocks. To a lesser extent, mentions resistance to change or lack of knowledge about CSR as factors limiting its expansion.

"In certain sectors, the 2030 Agenda or CSR itself are perceived as a threat, as a negative impact on their profitability for which they have to be compensated" (SPA01).

There is another "gap" that is mentioned as a constraint, in a more specific but significant way, in the public sector group: the disparity in progress between environmental and social aspects of CSR, which leads to a greater prominence of the former in business strategies.

"For many companies sustainability is limited to the environment, but in social issues perhaps they do not see it so clearly" (SPA01).

Participants from the private sector highlight progress in areas such as environment and equality, and to a lesser extent transparency. On the other hand, stakeholder management and human rights are mentioned. All participants agree on regulation as a key factor in the advancement of CSR and to a lesser extent investor pressure and social awareness. The 2030 agenda is also pointed to as a beacon for companies.

"The degree of progress has been linked to legislation: environmental issues, gender equality... the rest of the issues have advanced but are pending legislation" (OEM01).

"...from 2014 to the present day it seems like a different world, due to the inertia of the regulations and the evolution at an intentional level..." (SIN02)

"...I am skeptical about the progress, which has been basically due to regulation" (OEM02).

Both public and private sector actors coincide in pointing out the persistent gap in the incorporation of CSR between large and small companies: given the importance of SMEs in the Spanish productive fabric, this represents a notable brake in terms of the "capillarity" of progress in this area.

This gap between small and medium-sized enterprises is addressed in greater depth by public sector actors, who, in addition to the aforementioned arguments, allude to insufficient recognition of their own good practices, compared to large companies, which have more systematic CSR strategies and reporting processes.

"The large companies have more structured processes, their reports, their reports... On the other hand, the small companies, although they often have good corporate responsibility practices, they are not planned as such, but are responses that emerge" (SPA01).

The "insufficient impact of promotional strategies" in this area by the public sector in recent years is acknowledged, resulting in a high degree of ignorance about the advantages of incorporating CSR in SMEs.

"There is concern in the public sector about the lack of impact that CSR promotion measures may have on small enterprises" (SPN02).

However, the presence of a growing number of "conscientious" entrepreneurs is seen as positive.

"Spanish SMEs are not doing too badly, there are people who are very aware. But they need more support" (SPN01).

In the group of private sector actors, it was emphasized that the incentives and support processes provided by the public sector had been insufficient during the Strategy's period of validity. In SMEs, more and more CSR-related actions are being carried out, but they do not have specific and structured advocacy plans or strategies:

"Sometimes things are done (CSR-related actions) because they are good for the company, for the business, but not because they see them as appropriate from CSR criteria" (OEM01).

On the issue of CSR in companies and public administrations, the increase and diversification of public sector actors developing relevant CSR-related activities and strategies is seen as positive; but it is questioned that these initiatives have been too focused on their own area of competence, without sufficient knowledge of what other actors (even within the public sector) are doing, or the lack of common criteria:

"Great strides have been made from the public sector. Perhaps what is lacking is a choral vision of CSR, an overall vision of the different administrations" (SPN01).

The degree of progress in the incorporation of CSR in the public sector is uneven, due to the current situation (work overload, insufficient priority or coordination capacity), but above all, depending on the "size" of the administrations and the resources available:

"In large administrations, CSR is more incorporated, they have internalized it and worked on it more, but in smaller institutions, unless there is a special commitment on the part of the person leading them, it is less developed" (SPA01).

With regard to the institutional coordination and articulation of CSR, in both groups, the development of structures linked to CSR in different spheres of activity (ministries) and territorial (national, regional, municipal) is positively valued. However, there is a perception of insufficient coordination, which is attributed to a lack of resources and the proliferation of initiatives at different levels.

"Sometimes in the administration we act as watertight compartments, to be more effective we should move towards greater coordination, concentrate efforts" (SPN02).

"There is a lack of architecture of the sustainability system... there is a lack of harmonization, of addressing standardization. We have many scattered things that together have made us progress but there is no system architecture" (OES03).

"We must move towards a certain syncretism, merge documents or lines of work that are related" (SPA01).

Furthermore, coordination between administrations for the promotion of CSR is not identified as a stable process, but as a contingent one:

"Sometimes it depends on the will or interest of the teams or the person in charge" (SPA01).

It is considered essential to generate spaces for regular dialogue between the heads of the different regional and national administrations. There is a demand from public sector actors for an inter-ministerial and inter-territorial coordination body. One of the objectives of this body should be to publicize what the different actors are doing and to generate links between the different programs:

"There is a lack of inter-ministerial coordination, which was one of the reasons for CERSE, and inter-territorial coordination" (SPN01).

"It would be useful to know what they are doing in other Autonomous Communities, so that we can learn from those who are doing it well" (SPA03).

The role of CERSE during the life of the Strategy (and its future) was raised only in the private sector group. The CERSE "was a breakthrough at the time", with Spain being one of the first countries in the European context to set up such a body. It provided a broad and diverse vision ("with many voices"), and during its first years, it had a positive impact on both the public and private sectors.

"It was useful for everyone, it tried to be a space for exchange" (OES01).

But it was unable to fully develop and stabilize due to a lack of resources and political will. The "paralysis" of CERSE would have meant the loss of an opportunity to represent the interests of various organizations over the years of the strategy's existence, and is a sign of insufficient progress in matters related to citizen participation.

Despite the general pessimism about the current situation and the immediate past of CERSE, its reactivation is considered "urgent and necessary".

"CERSE needs to be reactivated. It can be a very useful tool. How to do it has to be worked out" (OEM01).

"The start-up was highly praised internationally, but it has remained a start-up. The last meeting of the CERSE was in 2012... it would be very interesting for it to act as a consultative body that coordinates all the issues, multifactors that exist in the different ministries" (SIN02).

Among the characteristics that this "new CERSE" should have, the following stand out: 1) use of accumulated experience; 2) sufficient resources; 3) defined functions and activities, focused on results; 4) participatory and plural, transparent; 5) capacity to dynamize and coordinate.

The focus groups addressed 4 thematic areas: transparency and non-financial information, training and awareness-raising, certifications and incentives focused on public procurement.

The issue of transparency and non-financial information was only raised in the group of private sector actors. In general terms, Law 11/2018, which focused on transparency, is highlighted as a milestone. It emerges as a structural component of CSR, serving a dual purpose: internally, it is functional for the company itself by facilitating regulatory compliance and the monitoring of ESG performance; externally, it benefits the stakeholders with whom the company interacts, by providing them with adequate information to act in defense of their legitimate interests in relation to the company's activities. The group emphasized that the development and implementation of regulatory instruments during this period, particularly those promoting greater corporate accountability and sustainability reporting, represented a turning point in aligning business practices with broader ESG goals. However, in practice, there are still gaps in terms of the quality of information, its scope or accessibility.

"A lot of data is being generated, but sometimes it is not accessible, reliable or comparable." (OES02)

This is due to ambiguity in the approach to reporting criteria, which makes it particularly urgent to develop regulations and clear benchmarks to ensure the quality of the information reported:

"There is significant room for improvement in the regulatory development of Law 11/2018" (SPN01).

Regarding training, there is a high degree of agreement in both groups on the need for CSR to be included in the various levels of training and types of education. Both groups question the fact that, during the life of the EERSE, the subjects or training content related to CSR have been dealt with almost exclusively at university level and specifically in business management education.

"I would like to see more CSR training in vocational training, not only at university level" (SPN01).

"CSR issues are developed mainly in business-related faculties, but less so in other faculties that are training professionals who require this type of knowledge: lawyers, journalists, engineers..." (SPA01).

There is therefore a call for greater transversality, providing CSR knowledge to future professionals from other areas in their university studies.

"We must insist on mainstreaming CSR, it is essential to train those who are going to have technical or governance responsibilities in companies" (SPA02).

"There is a training deficit with respect to the complexity and demands of the regulatory context" (SPN03).

This deficit has led to an increase in the supply of specialized training, especially in the private sector. This increase is considered a step forward by both groups, but there is a warning, especially from private sector actors, about the need to establish common criteria, so that the contents can be homologated and do not depend exclusively on the center providing the training.

The issue of certifications as an element of discrimination for consumers, their existence is positively valued; however, it was also underlined that the overabundance of certifications produces undesired effects and is not helping to improve consumer information:

"The consumer issue is complicated, although there has been progress ... there is a lot of greenwhasing. There should be a regulatory body..." (OSC01)

"The accumulation of certifications sometimes leads to overlapping and detracts from their value: the more certifications, the less exclusivity" (SPN03).

"There is an overabundance of certifications and seals, we should have fewer but more concrete ones, with more value" (SPA01).

The need for certifications to have clear and quantifiable criteria, and for them to be auditable, was pointed out. Furthermore, they should not remain mere formal acknowledgements, but should also be used as a reference in public procurement processes or access to funding as assessment criteria. This will promote their practical usefulness and encourage companies to undergo external verification processes.

"There is a huge proliferation of seals, but the opportunity to use them as a reference in procurement documents is being missed. If we had measurable and auditable seals, it would be very positive in that respect" (SPN01).

From the private sector, it was stressed that the lack of common criteria on what is sustainability or CSR on the part of public administrations favors a "sustainability industry" (Oxfam) that offers tools for certification, management or reporting, but not always homologable or sufficient to reflect the company's performance in accordance with stakeholder expectations.

In reference to incentives for CSR mainstreaming, both groups considered public procurement as a priority area for such incentives.

"It is important that ESG aspects are taken into account in procurement and given more weight" (OES02).

In the case of the public sector, it was noted that there is a widespread feeling among SMEs that companies that do not take CSR into account are "rewarded" in tenders and bids:

"The feeling that companies have is that CSR is not rewarded. For example, when they have to go to a public tender, they take on investments to be more sustainable and this reduces their competitiveness in terms of prices; as the scales only take into account the cheapest offer, they feel that the administration does not recognize corporate responsibility" (SPA01).

The focus groups offered a deeper and more nuanced understanding of the dynamics, challenges, and perceptions surrounding CSR development during the implementation period of the EERSE. The insights provided not only validated many of the findings identified through the questionnaires but also highlighted additional tensions, gaps, and opportunities that must be addressed moving forward. These findings provide a valuable basis for formulating strategic recommendations and drawing broader conclusions regarding the design, governance, and implementation of CSR policies in Spain.

The combined analysis of questionnaires and focus groups provides a well-rounded diagnosis of the EERSE's implementation. While the Strategy is valued for its comprehensive design and anticipatory approach, its limited institutional impact and lack of coordination reduced its effectiveness. Key advances—such as regulatory development and increased awareness—coexist with persistent challenges, especially in SME engagement, inter-institutional alignment, and stakeholder participation. These findings inform the strategic considerations outlined in the following conclusions.

CONCLUSIONS

The evolution of CSR in Spain during the period of validity of the EERSE 2014-2020 has been positive, although important challenges and notable asymmetries persist in its degree of Implementation, especially in small and medium-sized enterprises, where the integration of CSR continues to be incipient. Among the factors that have driven this evolution, regulation has played a key role. In this sense, the regulatory framework acts as a driver of change, but it is not the only determining element: the growing pressure from consumers and investors, the expansion of multi-stakeholder CSR promotion spaces and the progress of international initiatives, such as the Sustainable Development Goals (SDGs), have contributed decisively to the progress observed.

The EERSE is positively assessed in terms of its conceptual design, both for its thematic breadth and for the diversity of lines of action and measures proposed. However, its degree of implementation has been limited. Insufficient resources, the absence of systematic monitoring and accountability mechanisms and the low visibility of the Strategy among key actors have reduced its effectiveness and its real impact on the development of CSR.

We can conclude that the initial hypothesis is not fulfilled: "The National CSR Strategy has contributed significantly to the promotion of CSR in Spain". In relation to the research questions, hybrid public policy instruments, such as CSR strategies and plans, to be effective must provide for the articulation of efforts between the public and private sectors as well as adequate inter-institutional coordination, the latter being a critical element for the success of public policies on CSR. Cooperation between administrations must have continuity and stability, and not depend on contingent factors or on the individual will of certain institutional actors. It is essential to consolidate stable mechanisms of inter-administrative and multi- stakeholder coordination, based on systematic processes of dialogue and cooperation. In the case of Spain, the existence of a specialized body responsible for guaranteeing this coordination at inter-ministerial, regional, national and European level is a structural necessity. Another factor conditioning the success of these policies is to provide competent institutions with sufficient material and human resources for this purpose. Finally, Social Responsibility Strategies and Plans must have verifiable objectives, effective compliance mechanisms and demanding accountability processes.

Theoretical Implications

The research contributes with different theoretical and practical contributions to the existing literature on public policy and CSR. On the one hand, it contributes to the scarce literature that studies the implications of government intervention in driving CSR, and delves into the relational model (Steurer, 2010; Knudsen and Moon, 2017). As a contribution to existing studies, the research focuses on assessing the effectiveness of hybrid instruments through the analysis of the Spanish social responsibility strategy which, in its design and approval, involved a multi- stakeholder body with broad representation from civil society (companies, trade unions and

NGOs) and central and regional public administration. Until now, studies have been limited to the analysis of the policies developed without delving into the necessary elements in their design and implementation for them to be effective (Giamporcaro *et al.*, 2020; Idemudia and Kwakyemah, 2018). Moreover, existing work, with the exception of that developed by Steurer *et al* (2012) is descriptive without considering expert opinions involved in policy design and implementation.

Practical Implications

From a practical level, the research result may be useful for regulators. For the regulator: it provides relevant information on the role of governments in fostering an appropriate ecosystem for CSR and which policies are most effective. On the other hand, it provides the keys for the development of a new CSR strategy and the procedures that should accompany the measures proposed. Multi-stakeholder platforms such as CERSE can be a fundamental source of participatory innovation in public policies, but to do so they must have resources, continuity and clear participation and decision-making procedures.

For managers, the study identifies trends in public policy and the implications for business activity. The research can be used to guide decision-making and adapt to future government interventions.

Limitations and Future Lines of Research

The study has limitations stemming from the fact that it is limited to the time frame of the strategy and to the Spanish context with its own cultural, political, economic, legal and administrative factors. On the other hand, since the conclusion of the CSR strategy, progress has been made in terms of enforceability. In order to resolve these issues, we believe that in the future it would be appropriate to look more closely at the impact of pressure from regulators and to undertake a comparative analysis of the effectiveness of the implementation of strategies in other countries.

REFERENCES

Aboud, A., Saleh, A., & Eliwa, Y. (2024). Does mandating ESG reporting reduce ESG decoupling? Evidence from the European Union's Directive 2014/95. *Business Strategy and the Environment, 33*(2), 1305–1320.

Albareda, L., Lozano, J. M., Tencati, A., Midttun, A., & Perrini, F. (2008). The changing role of governments in corporate social responsibility: drivers and responses. *Business ethics: a European review, 17*(4), 347-363. https://doi.org/DOI: 10.1111/j.1467-8608.2008.00539.x

Albareda, L., Lozano, J. M., & Ysa, T. (2007). Public Policies on Corporate Social Responsibility: The Role of Governments in Europe. *Journal of Business Ethics, 74*, 391–407. DOI: 10.1007/s10551-007-9514-1

Biersteker, T. J., & Hall, R. B. (2002). 10 Private authority as global governance. *The emergence of private authority in global governance*, 85, 203.

Campbell, T. (2007). The normative grounding of corporate social responsibility: a human rights approach. In D. McBarnet, A. Voiculescu, & T. Campbell (Eds.), *New Corporate Accountability: Corporate Social Responsibility and the Law* (1 ed., pp. 529-564). [18] Cambridge University Press.

Cerrato, D., & Ferrando, T. (2020). The Financialization of Civil Society Activism: Sustainable Finance, Non-Financial Disclosure and the Shrinking Space for Engagement. *Accounting, Economics, and Law : A Convivium, 10*(2), 1–28. DOI: 10.1515/ael-2019-0006

Cho, C. H., Laine, M., Roberts, R. W., & Rodrigue, M. (2018). The frontstage and backstage of corporate sustainability reporting: Evidence from the Arctic National Wildlife Refuge Bill. *Journal of Business Ethics, 152*, 865–886. DOI: 10.1007/s10551-016-3375-4

Cho, C. H., Laine, M., Roberts, R. W., & Rodrigue, M. (2018). The frontstage and backstage of corporate sustainability reporting: Evidence from the Arctic National Wildlife Refuge Bill. *Journal of Business Ethics, 152*, 865–886. DOI: 10.1007/s10551-016-3375-4

Creswell, J. W., & Clark, V. L. P. (2017). *Designing and conducting mixed methods research*. Sage publications.

Cueto Cedillo, C., & De la Cuesta González, M. M. (2023). *La Administración Pública de la responsabilidad social corporativa y la sostenibilidad. Fundamentos, políticas y herramientas de gestión*. Editorial UNED.

Cutler, A. C. (2001). Critical reflections on the Westphalian assumptions of international law and organization: A crisis of legitimacy. *Review of International Studies, 27*(2), 133–150. DOI: 10.1017/S0260210500001339

Dahlsrud, A. (2008). How corporate social responsibility is defined: An analysis of 37 definitions. *Corporate Social Responsibility and Environmental Management, 15*(1), 1–13. DOI: 10.1002/csr.132

Deegan, C. (2002). Introduction: The legitimising effect of social and environmental disclosures–a theoretical foundation. *Accounting, Auditing & Accountability Journal, 15*(3), 282–311. DOI: 10.1108/09513570210435852

Delannon, N., & Raufflet, E. (2021). Impeding corporate social responsibility: Revisiting the role of government in shaping business—Marginalized local community relations. *Business Ethics, the Environment & Responsibility, 30*(4), 470–484. DOI: 10.1111/beer.12378

Engwall, L. (2006). Global enterprises in fields of governance. In Djelic, M., & Sahlin-Andersson, K. (Eds.), *Transnational Governance: Institutional Dynamics of Regulation* (pp. 161–179). Cambridge University Press., DOI: 10.1017/CBO9780511488665.009

Etilé, F., & Teyssier, S. (2016). Signaling Corporate Social Responsibility: Third-Party Certification versus Brands. *The Scandinavian Journal of Economics, 118*(3), 397–432. DOI: 10.1111/sjoe.12150

Fields, T. D., Lys, T. Z., & Vincent, L. (2001). Empirical research on accounting choice. *Journal of Accounting and Economics, 31*(1-3), 255–307. DOI: 10.1016/S0165-4101(01)00028-3

Fox, T., Ward, H., & Howard, B. (2002). *Public sector roles in strengthening corporate social responsibility: A baseline study*. World Bank.

Frynas, J., & Stephens, S. (2015). Political Corporate Social Responsibility: Reviewing Theories and Setting New Agendas. *International Journal of Management Reviews: IJMR, 17*(4), 483–509. DOI: 10.1111/ijmr.12049

Giamporcaro, S., Gond, J.-P., & O'Sullivan, N. (2020). Orchestrating Governmental Corporate Social Responsibility Interventions through Financial Markets: The Case of French Socially Responsible Investment. *Business Ethics Quarterly, 30*(3), 288–334. DOI: 10.1017/beq.2019.40

Global Reporting Iniciative. (2015). *Sustainability and Reporting Trends in 2025.* Disponible en https://www.globalreporting.org/resourcelibrary/Sustainability-and-Reporting-Trends-in-2025-1.pdf

Gond, J. P., Kang, N., & Moon, J. (2011). The government of self-regulation: On the comparative dynamics of corporate social responsibility. *Economy and Society*, *40*(4), 640–671. DOI: 10.1080/03085147.2011.607364

Gray, R. (2010). Is accounting for sustainability actually accounting for sustainability… and how would we know? An exploration of narratives of organisations and the planet. *Accounting, Organizations and Society*, *35*(1), 47–62. DOI: 10.1016/j.aos.2009.04.006

Greene, J. C., Caracelli, V. J., & Graham, W. F. (1989). Toward a Conceptual Framework for Mixed-Method Evaluation Designs. *Educational Evaluation and Policy Analysis, 11*(3), 255-274. https://doi.org/ (Original work published 1989) DOI: 10.3102/01623737011003255

Guay, T., Doh, J., & Sinclair, G. (2004). Non-Governmental Organizations, Shareholder Activism, and Socially Responsible Investments: Ethical, Strategic, and Governance Implications. *Journal of Business Ethics*, *52*(1), 125–139. DOI: 10.1023/B:BUSI.0000033112.11461.69

Hanlon, R. J. (2011). Engineering corporate social responsibility: Elite stakeholders, states and the resilience of neoliberalism. *Contemporary Politics*, *17*(1), 71–87. DOI: 10.1080/13569775.2011.552689

Idemudia, U., & Kwakyewah, C. (2018). Analysis of the Canadian national corporate social responsibility strategy: Insights and implications. *Corporate Social Responsibility and Environmental Management*, *25*(5), 928–938.

Jette, S. K., & Moon, J. (2022). Corporate social responsibility and government: The role of discretion for engagement with public policy. *Business Ethics Quarterly*, *32*(2), 243–271. DOI: 10.1017/beq.2021.17

Ji, H., & Miao, Z. (2020). Corporate social responsibility and collaborative innovation: The role of government support. *Journal of Cleaner Production*, *260*, 121028. DOI: 10.1016/j.jclepro.2020.121028

Kinderman, D. (2016). Time for a reality check: Is business willing to support a smart mix of complementary regulation in private governance? *Policy and Society*, *35*(1), 29–42. DOI: 10.1016/j.polsoc.2016.01.001

Knudsen, J. S., & Moon, J. (2017). *Visible hands: Government regulation and international business responsibility*. Cambridge University Press.

Knudsen, J. S., Moon, J., & Slager, R. (2015). Government policies for corporate social responsibility in Europe: A comparative analysis of institutionalisation. *Policy and Politics*, *43*(1), 81–99. Retrieved July 15, 2025, from. DOI: 10.1332/030557312X656016

Lu, J., Ren, L., Qiao, J., Yao, S., Strielkowski, W., & Streimikis, J. (2019). Corporate social responsibility and corruption: Implications for the sustainable energy sector. *Sustainability, 11*(15), 4128. DOI: 10.3390/su11154128

Mitchell, J. V. (Ed.). (1998). Companies in a World of Conflict: NGOs, Sanctions and Corporate Responsibility; *Papers from a Workshop Organized in Oslo by the Royal Institute of International Affairs, April 1997*. Earthscan.

Moon, J., & Vogel, D. (2008). Corporate social responsibility, government, and civil society. In Crane, A. (Eds.), *The Oxford Handbook of Corporate Social Responsibility*., DOI: 10.1093/oxfordhb/9780199211593.003.0013

Murillo, S., & Mena, L. (2006). *Detectives y camaleones: el grupo de discusión: una propuesta par la investigación cualitativa*. Talasa.

Observatorio de Responsabilidad Social Corporativa. (2021), *La responsabilidad social corporativa en las memorias anuales de las empresas del IBEX 35, análisis del ejercicio 2019*. Disponible en: https://observatoriorsc.org/inicio/que-hacemos/estudios/)

Okoye, A. (2009). Theorising corporate social responsibility as an essentially contested concept: Is a definition necessary? *Journal of Business Ethics*, *89*, 613–627. DOI: 10.1007/s10551-008-0021-9

Papathanassiou, C., & Nieto, M. J. (2025). Different shades of green: EU corporate disclosure rules and their effectiveness in limiting "greenwashing". *ECB Occasional Paper*, (2025/370).

Patten, D. M. (2002). The relation between environmental performance and environmental disclosure: A research note. *Accounting, Organizations and Society*, *27*(8), 763–773. DOI: 10.1016/S0361-3682(02)00028-4

Reinhardt, F. (1998). Environmental product differentiation: Implications for corporate strategy. *California Management Review*, *40*(4), 43. DOI: 10.2307/41165964

Ruggie, J. G. American Exceptionalism, Exemptionalism and Global Governance (February 6, 2004). Available at *SSRN*: https://ssrn.com/abstract=517642 or http://dx.doi.org/DOI: 10.2139/ssrn.517642

Scherer, A., & Palazzo, G. (2007). Toward a Political Conception of Corporate Responsibility: Business and Society Seen from a Habermasian Perspective. *Academy of Management Review*, *32*(4), 1096–1120. DOI: 10.5465/amr.2007.26585837

Shaw, W. H. (2009). Marxism, business ethics, and corporate social responsibility. *Journal of Business Ethics*, *84*, 565–576. DOI: 10.1007/s10551-008-9725-0

Steurer, R. (2010). The role of governments in corporate social responsibility: Characterising public policies on CSR in Europe. *Policy Sciences*, *43*, 49–72. DOI: 10.1007/s11077-009-9084-4

Steurer, R., Martinuzzi, A., & Margula, S. (2012). Public policies on CSR in Europe: Themes, instruments and regional differences. *Corporate Social Responsibility and Environmental Management*, *19*, 206–227. DOI: 10.1002/csr.264

Utting, P. (2008). The struggle for corporate accountability. *Development and Change*, *39*(6), 959–975.

Whitehouse, L. (2003). Corporate Social Responsibility, Corporate Citizenship and the Global Compact. *Global Social Policy*, *3*(3), 299–318. DOI: 10.1177/146801810300330

Zueva, A., & Fairbrass, J. (2021). Politicising Government Engagement with Corporate Social Responsibility: "CSR" as an Empty Signifier. *Journal of Business Ethics*, *170*, 635–655. DOI: 10.1007/s10551-019-04330-5

Chapter 3

A Bibliometric Approach to Examine the Future Trends in Digital Tourism

Anil Kumar
https://orcid.org/0009-0000-8565-9522
Graphic Era Hill University, India

Sakshi Pandey
Pal College of Technology and Management, India

Vipin Chandra Kurais
Graphic Era Hill University, India

ABSTRACT

The growth of tourism has piqued the interest of political leaders, prompting them to market their countries as popular tourist destinations. Recognizing tourism's potential as a significant economic engine, authorities in certain nations have begun to focus on international relations tactics to improve their country's image and earn a portion of global tourist income. The present study is a bibliometric approach to examine the future trends in digital tourism through a review approach using R tool. The study examines the contribution of top authors, institutions, journals and countries and also examined the top cited articles and authors. Scopus database is used to extract the dataset as it is the largest repository of published articles. The thematic map technique is used to examine the trends in digital tourism to pave the way for future research directions for academicians and researchers.

DOI: 10.4018/979-8-3373-0385-7.ch003

INTRODUCTION

Tourism has long been recognized as one of the world's most important economic industries. In 2018, it contributed both directly and indirectly to 10.4% of the global GDP (World Travel & Tourism Council [WTTC], 2019). This industry has contributed significantly to job creation, revenue generation in local communities, and the expansion and development of linked sectors. The growth of tourism has piqued the interest of political leaders, prompting them to market their countries as popular tourist destinations. Recognizing tourism's potential as a significant economic engine, authorities in certain nations have begun to focus on international relations tactics to improve their country's image and earn a portion of global tourist income (Shafiee et al., 2019).

The expansion of the tourist business has coincided with advances in information and communication technologies (ICTs), which have transformed the tourism experience (Xiang & Fesenmaier, 2017). ICTs enable visitors to make more informed decisions by providing better access to information (Gretzel et al., 2015). Many governments are making significant investments in smart city programs and smart tourist destinations (Gretzel et al. 2016). In many nations, the idea of "smart tourism" has become well-known as a calculated strategy to boost the growth of the travel industry. For example, countries in Asia are working on smart tourism initiatives, including South Korea, Taiwan, and China (Zhang et al., 2012; Zhu et al., 2014) (Hwang et al., 2015). Smart city projects are the source of many smart tourism efforts in Europe (Caragliu et al., 2011). Political leaders around the world recognize the revolutionary power of smart technologies, not just for their economic advantages but also for their capacity to improve the social and experiential elements of travel (Gretzel et al., 2015). The use of these technologies by the tourist sector encourages innovation and creativity as well as competitiveness among locations (Gretzel et al., 2016). Tourism destinations can improve the quality of their services, provide more pleasurable experiences for passengers, and attract tourists by utilizing smart technologies through the development of tourism-oriented information technology (Minghetti & Buhalis, 2010). Despite arguments that smart tourism technologies have greatly accelerated innovation in the travel industry (Tu & Liu, 2014), researchers have not thoroughly examined these technologies (Gretzel et al., 2015). There is a lot of promise for these technologies to help underdeveloped nations grow their tourism sectors. But since much of the research in this field has been conducted in rich countries, there is a knowledge vacuum about how smart infrastructures and technologies operate and are implemented in less developed areas. According to the World Economic Forum's (WEF) 2024 Travel and Tourism Development Index (TTDI), India is ranked 39th out of 119 nations. The report highlights India's advancements in three key areas: boosting tourism and travel, strengthening security and safety, and advancing sanitation and health. According to the UNWTO Barometer for May 2024, India accounted for 1.47% of the global inbound tourism sector in 2022, receiving 14.3 million of the 975 million foreign tourists globally. Additionally, India accounted for 15.66% of all international tourists to the Asia-Pacific region in that same year. (PIB, 2024). Technological innovations have had a considerable influence on the tourist business in recent years, with the use of smart technologies becoming more popular among numerous players in the sector.

Historically, travel has been defined as the process of discovering new or uncharted territory (Arthur & Nuenen, 2019; Ashcroft, 2015). But this viewpoint has been altered by centuries of technological progress, from steam trains to cars to airplanes, which have made travel considerably simpler and more accessible (Löfgren, 1999). According to Salazar (2010), the development in "cosmobility" or global movement can be attributed to the expanding middle classes in industrialized nations having more access to international travel in recent decades. We now live in a "world of flows" (Franklin & Crang, 2001), where tourism, labor migration, commuting, and the international exchange of commodities and services are all intertwined, as Franklin and Crang also note in Tourist Studies. Over the past two decades, mobility has emerged as a significant area of study in the social sciences, with tourism playing a major role (Hannam, 2009; Hannam et al., 2014; Sheller & Urry, 2004; Vannini, 2010). Mobility has become a normal aspect of life (Franklin & Crang, 2001). To uncover the publication trends in the field of Digital Tourism, this study aims to identify the most influential journals, authors, countries, and articles that are shaping academic work in this area. Additionally, the study seeks to explore emerging topics and themes within the academic literature related to Digital Tourism. By examining these aspects, the research will also aim to uncover the social network among authors, countries, and institutions actively contributing to the field of Digital Tourism.

LITERATURE REVIEW

Role of Tourism in Fostering Growth

Despite ongoing technological advancements, the tourist business has grown to be a significant worldwide industry (Kontogianni & Alepis, 2020). Both wealthy and emerging nations must modify their approaches to remain competitive in the global market as the demand for tourism rises. As a result, tourist locations have a number of difficulties in keeping up with the quick changes in technology (Iunius et al., 2015). Technology is changing the travel industry, impacting the competitiveness of travel agencies and destinations, and changing their strategies (Buhalis,

2020). The tourism industry is now driven by information technology (Januszewska et al., 2015). Information and communication technology (ICT) has had a huge impact on tourism over the last 20 years, changing how travelers perceive their trip experiences (Xiang & Fesenmaier, 2017). ICT provides prospects for greater data and insights into travel behavior and allows travelers to access tourism products in new ways (Gretzel et al., 2015).

Technology and Tourism

E-tourism is a contemporary approach to travel product distribution in which service or product suppliers reach clients online, wherever they may be. It facilitates quicker customer service, increases profitability, lowers expenses, and lets travelers look up information about travel-related goods and locations. This procedure frequently promotes information sharing among travelers (Buhalis & Deimezi, 2004). E-tourism also makes it easier for people to share their thoughts and experiences about places on social media.

Modern communication technologies give tourists the means to become knowledgeable travelers. They can look up places to visit, weigh their alternatives, and gain insight from other people's travel experiences and choices (Wang et al., 2016; Snellen & de Hollander, 2017). Websites, travel blogs, advisory systems, online communities, and mobile technology are some of the platforms that enable this. Before, during, and after their travels, visitors' experiences are influenced by information and communication technologies (ICTs) (Wang et al., 2016).

Since 2010, the emergence of Web 2.0 and its focus on interaction, as well as developments in areas like search engines, social media, the Internet of Things (IoT), and mobile technologies, have made a more sophisticated framework for tourism management necessary. The collecting and analysis of data enabled by the integration of ICT infrastructure with interconnected systems facilitates better decision-making based on common knowledge. This approach improves quality of life and operational efficiency. The Internet of Things is crucial to building a smart technological environment because it connects digital and physical infrastructures (Atzori et al., 2010). People can work together and communicate toward common objectives thanks to technologies like mobile devices, sensors, and radio frequency identification (RFID). According to Miorandi et al. (2012), these Internet-connected technologies aid in bridging the gap between the real and virtual worlds. The growth of big data analytics has made businesses, cities, and organizations more capable of meeting the demands of their communities (Xiang & Fesenmaier, 2017). New networking and communication techniques made feasible by contemporary technology infrastructures have allowed for deeper insights into the travel experience (Xiang et al., 2015). Additionally, mobile communication has increased due to improvements in location-based technology, which influences passengers' behavior by encouraging freedom and creativity (Wang et al., 2012). According to researchers, these advancements mark the beginning of a new era of "smart tourism" (Gretzel et al., 2015).

Enhancing access to online sharing and interactive services is largely dependent on the use of mobile devices and the Internet of Things (IoT) for resource and information sharing (Wang et al., 2013; Dickinson et al., 2014), as well as smartphones and online platforms for information exchange (Wang et al., 2012; Dickinson et al., 2014). Furthermore, the accessibility of these services is greatly impacted by the value of utilizing social networks and content channels (Xiang & Gretzel, 2010; Leung et al., 2013; Zeng & Gerritsen, 2014). At tourist locations, promoting the availability of interactive services and online sharing might increase demand for digital solutions.

Digital tourism technology have advanced, yet there are still a number of unanswered questions. One major problem that underserves emerging economies is the unequal accessibility to tools like social networks, mobile devices, and the Internet of Things, which are mostly available in industrialized countries. Furthermore, there aren't many thorough research looking at how users' experiences with social networks affect their enjoyment and judgment. It can be difficult to integrate digital solutions with traditional tourism services, especially in locations with poor technology infrastructure, and little is known about how promoting digital tourism affects society and the environment, including concerns about digital equity, data privacy, and energy use. This study aims to fill existing gaps by analyzing the evolution of digital tourism research, identifying significant authors, and exploring novel subjects including sustainability and inclusivity. Another objective is to map the networks of cooperation among authors, institutions, and countries. By focusing on the effects of interactive and online-sharing services on the travel and tourism industry, the study seeks to provide significant insights into addressing current challenges while promoting innovation and furthering inclusivity.

Research Objectives

1. To uncover the publication trend in the area of Digital Tourism.
2. To uncover the most influential journals, authors, countries, articles shaping the academic work in Digital Tourism.
3. To identify the emerging topics, and emerging themes related to Digital Tourism within the academic literature.
4. To uncover the social network among authors, countries and institutions working in the field of digital tourism

MATERIAL AND METHODOLOGY

This study employed bibliometric analysis to visualize global research trends and future research directions in Digital Tourism. Bibliometric analysis is a quantitative method for analyzing scientific literature and identifying patterns, trends, and structures within a specific research field. The data was extracted from the Scopus database, one of the most comprehensive and widely used bibliometric databases.

Search Strategy

The search strategy was designed to identify relevant literature by using specific keywords and search terms related to Digital Tourism. The search terms included:

TITLE-ABS-KEY (“Digital Tourism” OR “E-tourism” OR “Electronic Tourism” OR “online tourism” OR “smart tourism” OR “smart-tourism”) AND PUBYEAR > 1999 AND PUBYEAR < 2025 AND (LIMIT-TO (LANGUAGE, “English”)) AND (LIMIT-TO (SUBJAREA, “BUSI”) OR LIMIT-TO (SUBJAREA, “SOCI”) OR LIMIT-TO (SUBJAREA, “ECON”) OR LIMIT-TO (SUBJAREA, “ARTS”)) AND (LIMIT-TO (DOCTYPE, “ar”) OR LIMIT-TO (DOCTYPE, “re”))

Data Collection

These terms were applied to the title, abstract, and keywords fields to ensure a comprehensive retrieval of relevant publications. The search period was set from 2000 to 2024 to encompass recent developments. The subject areas included Business, Management and Accounting, Economics, Econometrics and Finance, Social Sciences, and Arts and Humanities. Only articles and review papers published in English were considered to maintain consistency and quality. Initially, the search identified 2852 papers. Filtering by Year range the number remain 2845, by applying Language filter it came to 2754. subject area reduced the number to 1515 papers. Further refinement to include only articles and reviews resulted in 988 papers. The final count included in our study therefore is 988 articles.

DATA ANALYSIS

The extracted data was analyzed using bibliometric technique. The Bibliometric R tool was employed for data processing, visualization, and analysis. This software is widely recognized for its capability to handle large bibliometric datasets and generate insightful visualizations. Descriptive analysis was first conducted to outline the basic characteristics of the data, including publication trends over time, distribution by country, and leading journals in the field. Citation analysis followed, identifying highly cited papers, influential authors, and prominent institutions. Co-occurrence analysis of keywords was conducted to identify major research themes and topics, and thematic map and thematic evolution was used to uncover the trending theme whereas social network analysis was performed to uncover the collaboration network.

Table 1. Selection criteria and selection of article

Selection Criteria and article selection	Exclude	Include
Filtering Criteria		
Search Engine- Scopus		
Search Date- 6 September 2024		
Search Term- TITLE-ABS-KEY ("Digital Tourism" OR "E-tourism" OR "Electronic Tourism" OR "online tourism" OR "smart tourism" OR "smart-tourism")		2852
Period of Publication2000-2024	7	2845
Language: English	91	2754
Subject area "Business, management and accounting, Economics, Econometrics and Finance, Social sciences and Arts and Humanities"	1239	1515
Document type: ''Articles'' and ''Reviews''	527	988

Source: Author Elaboration

DESCRIPTIVE ANALYSIS

Table 1 provides a brief summary of the dataset used for analyzing Digital Tourism in the academic scenario during 2000-2024. A total of 327 sources produced 988 documents during this period with an annual growth rate of more than 20 percent. The average age of document was 4.32 year with average citation per document being 35.77. A total of 53469 references were analyzed with 1433 keywords plus and 2991 author keywords. Total authors in our analysis were 2196 out of which authors who contributed as single author in a document were 94. The international co-authorship percentage was less than 30% which indicate that there is wide scope for foreign collaboration in this academic piece of work. Out of the 988 total documents, 937 were research papers while 51 were review papers.

Table 2. Summary of dataset

Description	Results
MAIN INFORMATION ABOUT DATA	
Timespan	2000:2024
Sources (Journals, Books, etc)	327
Documents	988
Annual Growth Rate %	22.03
Document Average Age	4.32
Average citations per doc	35.77
References	53469
DOCUMENT CONTENTS	
Keywords Plus (ID)	1433
Author's Keywords (DE)	2991
AUTHORS	
Authors	2396
Authors of single-authored docs	94
AUTHORS COLLABORATION	
Single-authored docs	101
Co-Authors per Doc	3.1
International co-authorships %	28.14
DOCUMENT TYPES	
article	937
review	51

Source: Author Compilation

Figure 1 Shows the annual scientific production or the article production over time in the context of Digital Tourism from the year 2000 till 2024. Figure 1 clearly reflects that there is an increasing trend in the publication pattern in this research area. This trend reflects the importance of this field in the academic literature. As we can see that from 2000 till 2006 there was constant rate of publication of one or three articles which triggered in the year 2007 from where we can see a constant increase in the annual publication with some dips in between in the year 2021. In the year 2023 the article production was highest with 175 articles. As we can see that till date in the year 2024 there are 119 articles that have been published in the field of Digital Tourism and we have more to come in the remaining time period.

Figure 1. Annual production over time

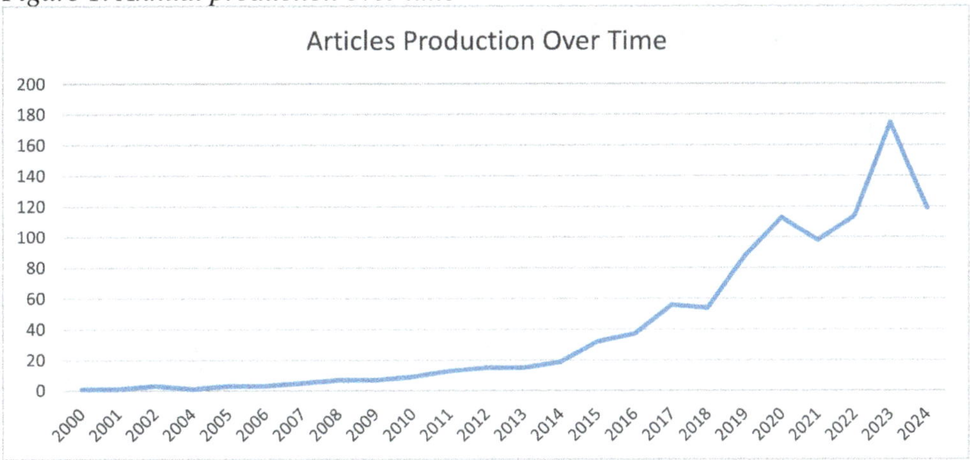

(Author Creation)

Figure 2 represents "Average Citations per Year" plots the average number of citations received by scientific articles from 2000 to 2024. The y-axis measures the average citations, and the x-axis represents time in years. Figure 2 is showing ups and downs in the citation trend throughout the years from the very commencement in the Average Citations since 2000. In the year 2000 the AC was 0.6 which was 1.1 in 2001 and till 2005 there was an increasing trend. The first major decline came in te year 2006 when the average citation came to 0.7. the average citations reached highest in 2010 with AC of 15.9. following that there was sharp decline till 2015 when it reached second highest average citations of 15.3. there was a sudden fall in this and till date there is ups and down in this aspect reflecting that somehow digital tourism is being explored in some years and in some durations very less importance is assigned to this phenomenon. The graph shows that while there were periods of high citation impact, overall, there seems to be a downward trend in recent years.

Figure 2. Average citations per year

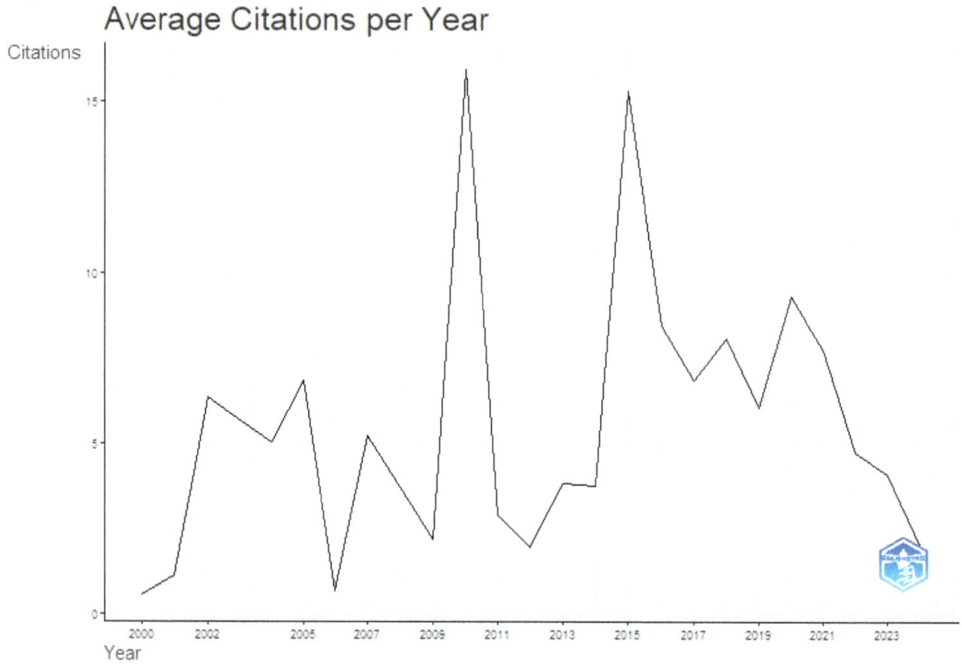

(Author Creation)

Figure 3 is a three-field plot that visualizes the interconnections between countries, authors, and keywords within a body of academic literature. The leftmost column comprises of the most active sources working in context of Digital Tourism. The middle column comprises of most prolific keywords and the rightmost column comprises of the most active countries. We found that Smart Tourism, Tourism, E-Tourism, Smart Tourism Destination and Social Media were the prominent keywords in these years. Sustainability (Switzerland) is the prominent journal that is working on smart tourism and is highly promoted by Spain and Korea. Smart Tourism Destination is a major theme in Sustainability (Switzerland) that is explored in Italy and Spain the most. E-Tourism is a major theme in China, Italy and Spain which is published majorly by Information Technology and Tourism.

Figure 3. Three field plot

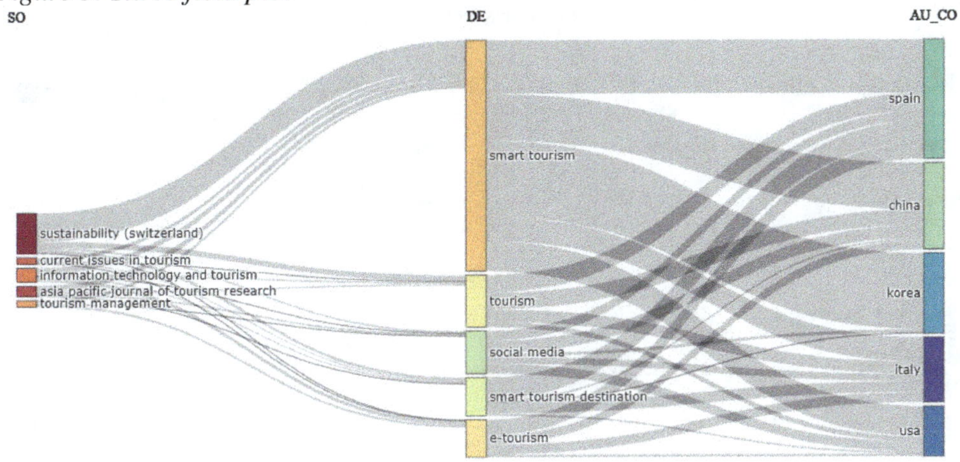

(Author Creation)

Figure 4 presents a bubble chart titled "Most Relevant Sources," displaying the distribution of articles published across various academic journals and conference series within a specific field. The x-axis, labeled "No. of documents," indicates the number of articles, while the y-axis lists the names of the sources, such as journals and conference proceedings. Each bubble's size correlates with the number of articles published in that source.

Figure 4. Most relevant sources

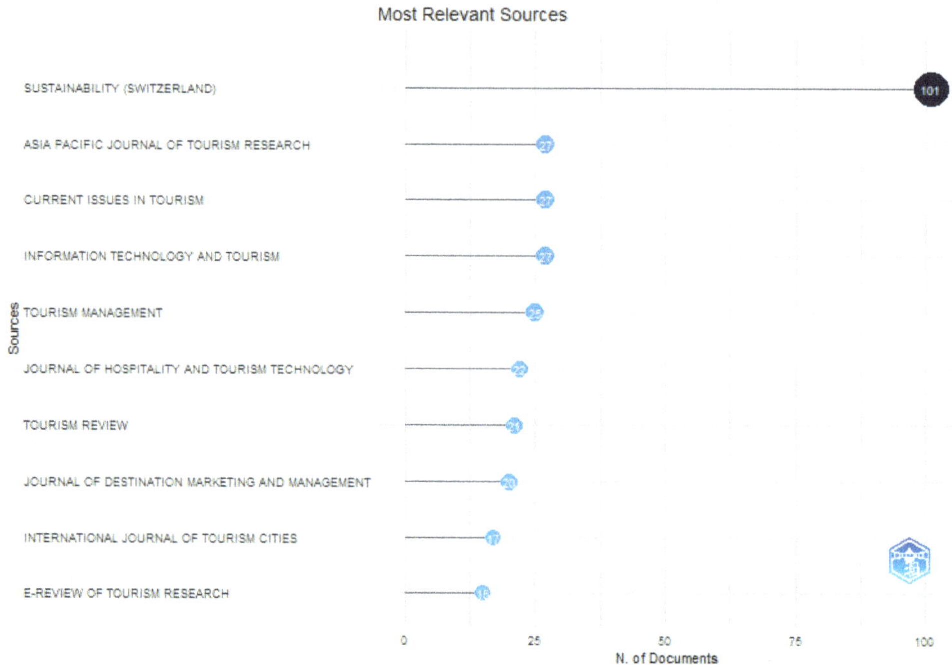

(Author Creation)

Sustainability (Switzerland) is the most relavant source with highest publication of 101 articles, Asia Pacific Journal of Tourism Research is the second most productive journal followed by Current Issues in Tourism with 27 article each. These leading sources suggest a strong focus on Climate risk and financial resilience within the dataset. Figure 5 provides a list organized by Bradford's Law, categorizing sources into three distinct zones based on their productivity in a given field. Zone 1, the core zone, includes sources with the highest number of articles, such as "Sustainability (Switzerland)" with rank 1 and "Asia Pacific Journal of Tourism Research" holding rank 2 "Current Issues in Tourism" holding the rank 3, 'Information technology and tourism' holding 4th rank and "Tourism Management" ranked 5th in this law. Suggesting these are the most influential or most commonly referred to in the research area. These sources form the core or essential publications in the field.

Figure 5. Bradford's law

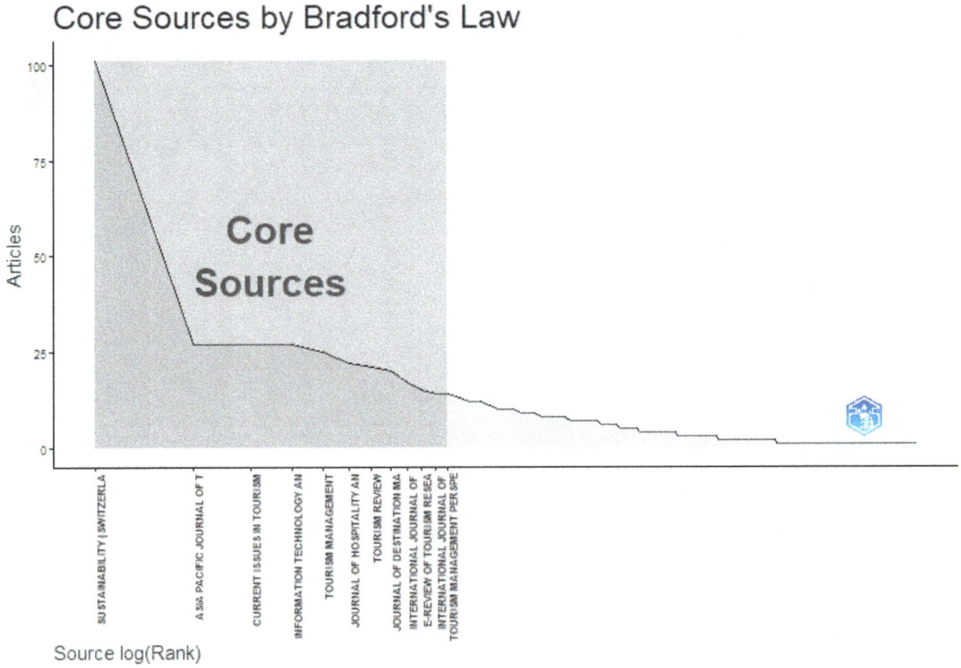

(Author Creation)

As we move to Zones 2 and 3, the frequency of articles per source diminishes, which aligns with Bradford's Law, indicating that fewer articles are published in a larger number of sources. The distribution suggests a typical pattern where a few core journals publish most of the articles, and as one moves to less productive journals, the number of articles per journal decreases. This pattern is useful for identifying which journals are most central to a research area and guiding literature search strategies for researchers.

Source of Impact

Source impact is how impactful a journal is in context to the area of study and the h-index is a metric that aims to capture both the productivity and citation impact of the publications within these sources. Figure 6 depicts that Sustainability (Switzerland) is at the top in this list with an H-index of 32 followed by 'Tourism Management' with an H-Index of 22. Information Technology and Tourism is the third most impactful source with an H-Index of 17 followed by Asia Pacific Journal of Tourism Research, Current Issues in Tourism and Journal of Destination Marketing and Management with H-Index of 14 each.

Figure 6. Sources' of local impact by H index

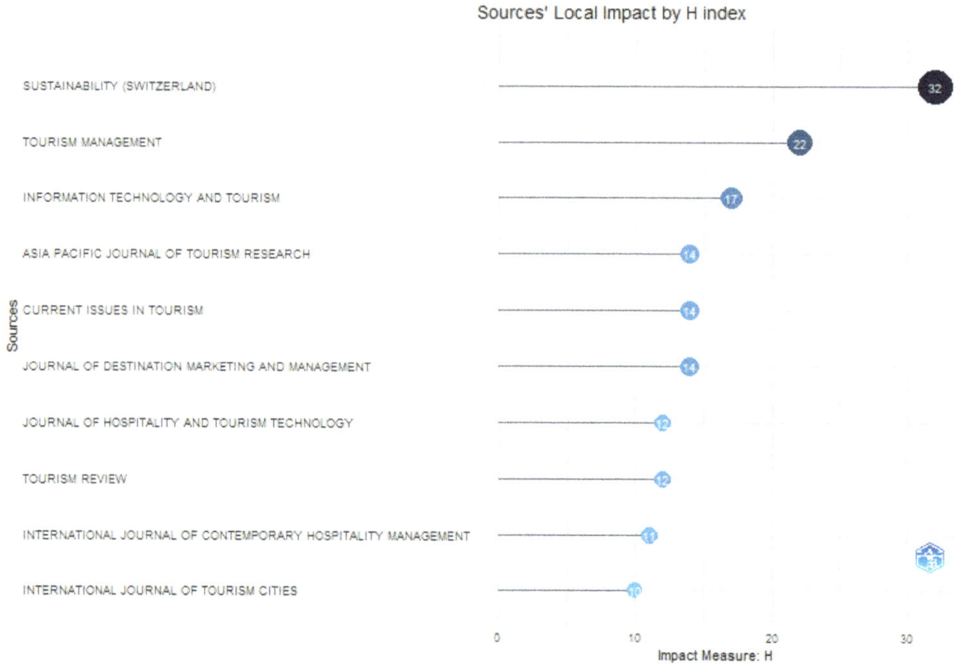

(Author Creation)

Higher h-index values suggest that the publications from those sources are frequently cited and are influential in the field. 'Sustainability (Switzerland) stand out as the most impactful sources with the highest h-index values, indicating they are likely to be key outlets for research dissemination in the field. The variation in h-index among these sources helps researchers identify where to find the most seminal and potentially influential work in their area of study, and also to discern the key outlets for disseminating their own research to reach a broad and engaged audience.

Figure 7 shows "Sources' Production over Time" depicts the cumulative publications from different sources from around 2000 to 2024. Each line represents a different academic source, and the steepness of the line indicates the rate of publication over time. From the said graph, we see that "Sustainability (Switzerland)" is the leading source in context to Digital Tourism but the first article focusing on this aspect was published in the year 2002 in the journal "Current Issues in Tourism' and in 'Tourism Management' as per the data extracted. This was followed by 'Asia Pacific Journal of Tourism Research' and 'Information Technology and Tourism' which published their first article in this aspect in the year 2015. Sustainability (Switzerland) started publishing articles in Digital Tourism in the year 2016 and there onwards the productivity is the highest among all these top five sources.

Figure 7. Sources' local impact by H index

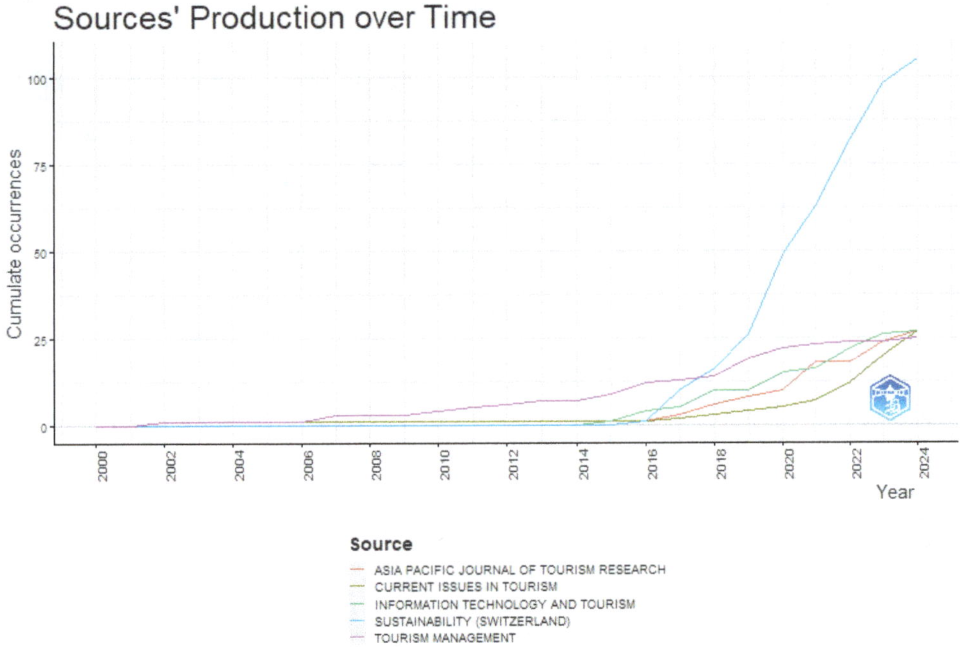

(Author Creation)

Most Relevant Authors

The graph of "Most Relevant Authors" visualizes the academic output of various authors, measured by the number of articles published (Figure 8). The y-axis lists the names of the authors, while the x-axis likely represents the h-index or another metric of publication impact, though it's not labeled here.

Figure 8. Most relevant authors

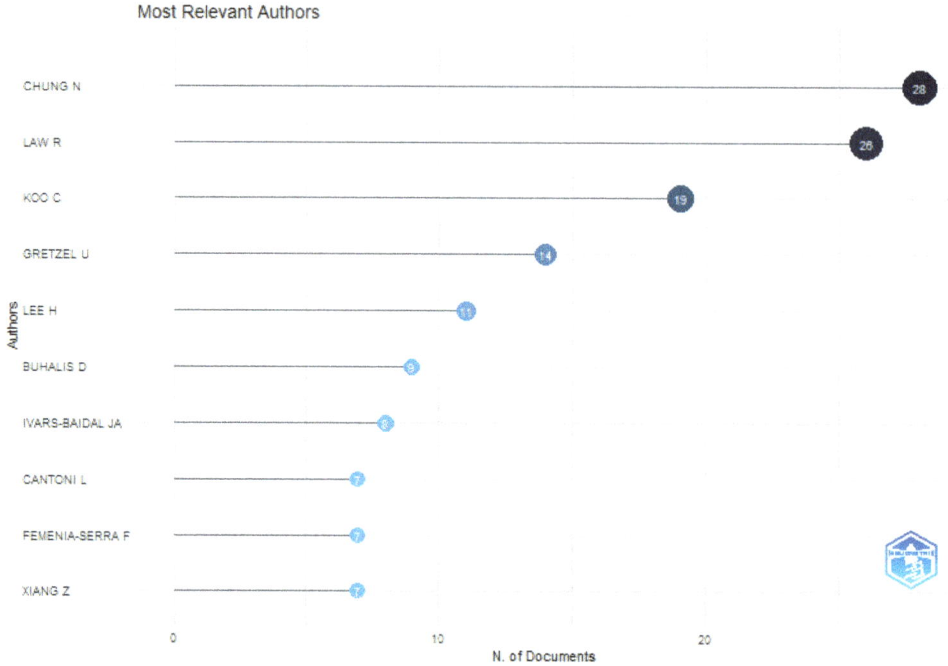

(Author Creation)

Based on the number of publications by each author to find the most productive author Figure 8 represents an idea to it Chung N is the most relevant author in the domain of digital marketing with 28 articles till date followed by Law R with 26 articles and Koo C with 19 articles.

Figure 9 shows the author's production over time. This analysis is important from various aspects. Firstly it talks about the journey of an author as when an author started producing articles in any domain and on the same time the citation the article got during specific duration of time. The bubble size reflects the total number of publication by any author and the color of the bubble represent the number of citation received by the article. The darker the circle the more the number of citation received by any article in the dataset analyzed in the study by the author.

Figure 9. Author's production over Time

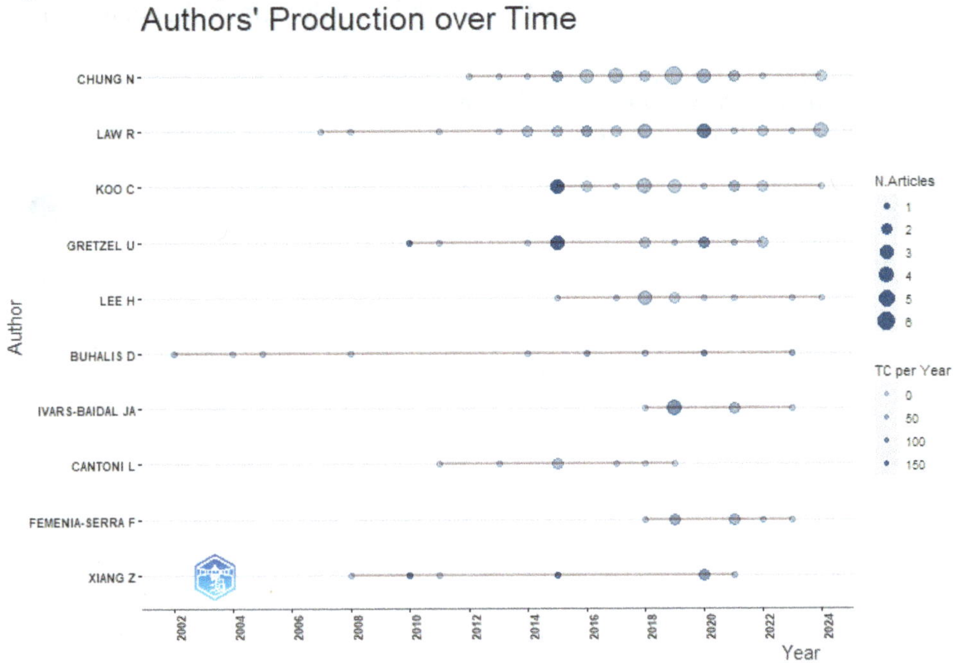

(Author Creation)

Buhalis D first published in the domain of digital tourism in the year 2002 with an total citation per year of 17.78, the author is producing continuously over the years and the last work as per the data extracted is in the year 2023 with total citation per year of 46. The article produced by any author reflects the most prolific author as the author is contributing in the domain of Digital tourism, whereas the citation is reflecting the importance the article of the author has received in the academic literature as the citation is considered as getting recognition in academia. Law R is one of a consistent author with 26 articles produced over the year at increasing pace and the citation average per year is also increasing with highest as 114 in 2020. Chung N is one of the prolific author with 28 articles over the years with highest 6 articles in 2019 and last work in 2024.

Authors local impact is one of the measure to assess impactful author over the period of time. In this study H-Index is used as a measure to assess the author's impact (Figure 10). Chung N and Law R are the most impactful authors with H-index of 18 in the domain of digital tourism. Gretzel U is at third place with an H-index of 12 followed by Koo, C with H-index of 11. Buhalis D is at 5th Position with H-index of 9 followed by Ivars JA and Lee H with H-index of 8. The top ten authors are in the h-index range of 6 to 18 which is a good count as all authors included in this list are somehow impactful with their work in the domain of digital tourism.

Figure 10. Author's local impact by H-index

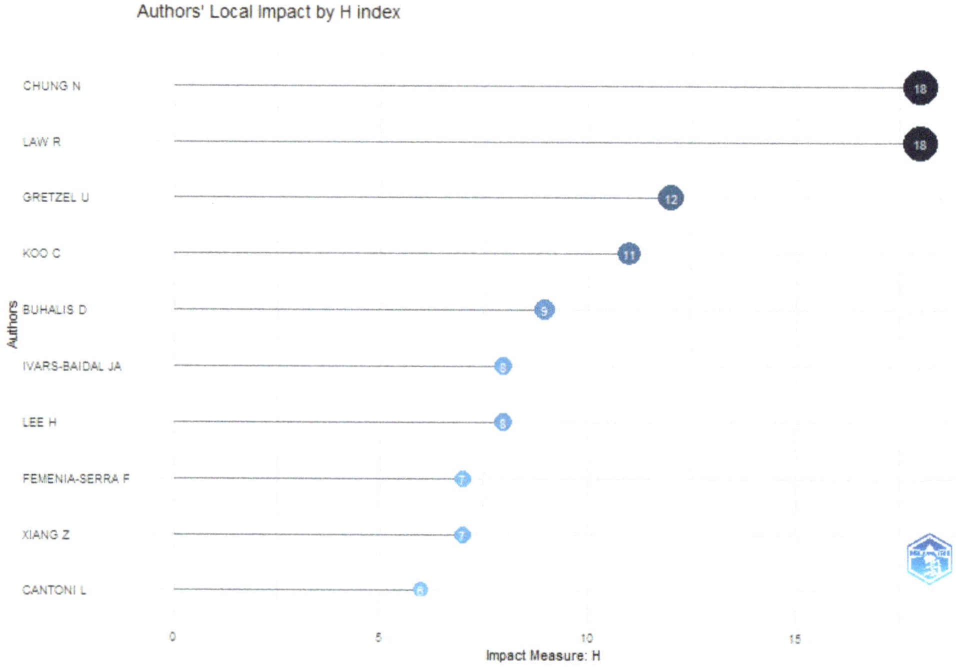

(Author Creation)

Institutions relevance is reflected in Figure 11 as it shows "Most Relevant Affiliations," each bubble represents an academic or research institution's contribution to the literature in terms of the number of articles published. The position of the bubble along the horizontal axis suggests the quantity of articles, while the vertical positioning corresponds to different institutions. The institution with the largest bubble appears to have produced 102 articles, indicating a significant level of research activity and output. This could suggest a leading role in the respective field, possibly due to robust funding, a large number of active researchers, or a focus on prolific publishing practices.

Figure 11. Most relevant affiliations

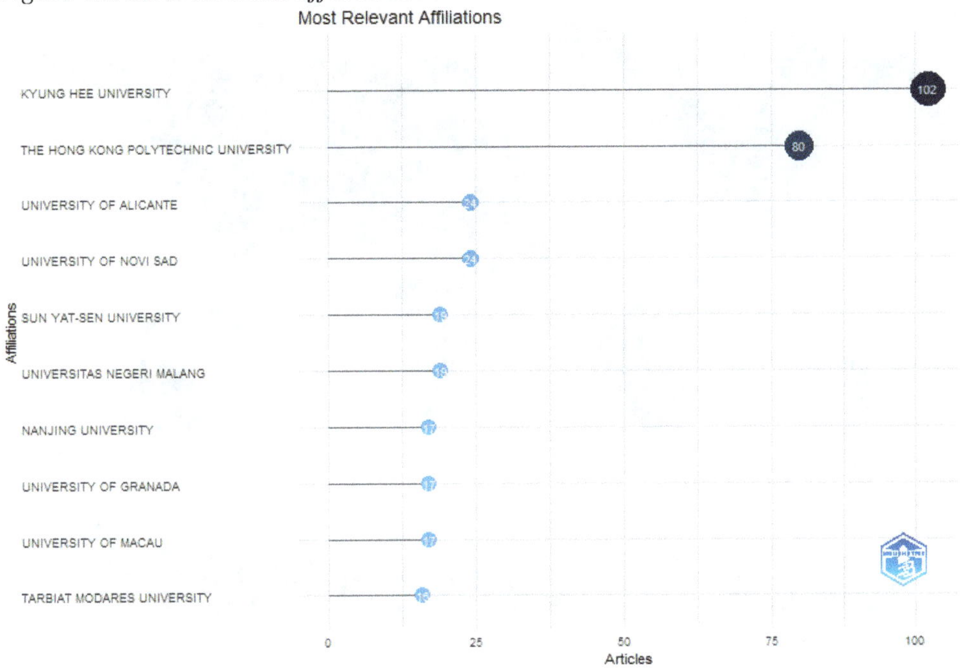

(Author Creation)

Kyung Hee University is the most prolific affiliation with 102 articles in the dojmain of digital tourism. The Hong Kong Polytechnic University is with 80 articles followed by University of Aucante and University of Sovi Nad is with 24 articles each. This reflects that South Korea, Hong Kong and Spain are promoting research in this domain as these universities are located in the respective countries.

In context to article production over time by the affiliations, The Hong Kong Polytechnic University published the first article in domain of digital tourism in 2008 and in 2024 it published 80 article till date. followed by Kyung Hee University of Spain which published first article in 2012 and in 2024 it has 102 articles till date. The Sun-Yat Sen University of China in 2014 published the first article and in 2024 it has 19 articles which shows that compared to the former ones, this university is publishing at a slower pace.

Assessing the countries scientific production visualized that China is the most productive country in the domain of digital tourism as can be seen in Figure 12 with 400 publication till date. It is followed by Spain with 296 articles, South Korea with 220 articles, USA with 168 articles and Italy with 164 articles as top 5 productive nations. India is also at 8th position with 94 articles in its name indicating that digital tourism is now being explored well by India.

Figure 12. Country's scientific production

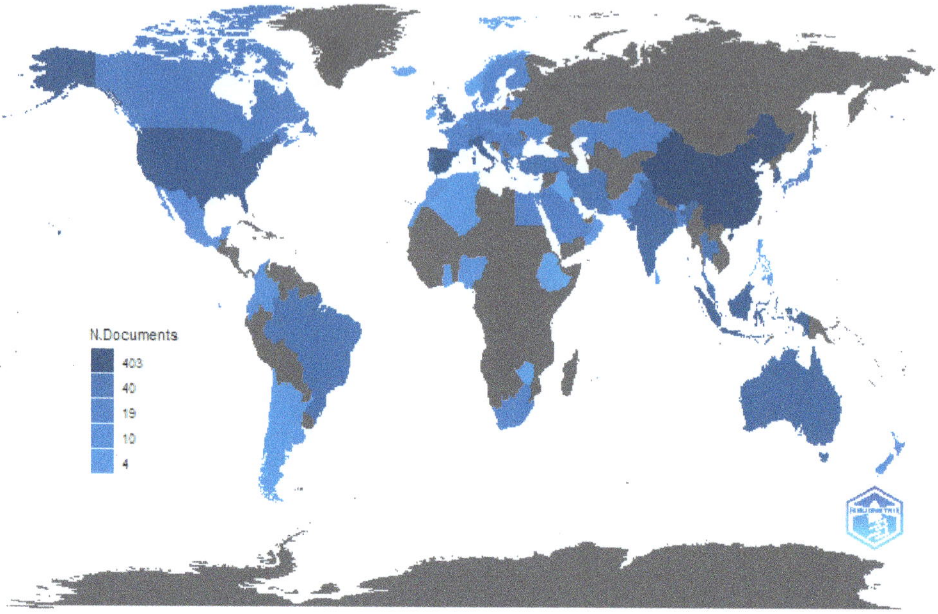

(Author Creation)

In context to country's production over time to assess which country produced first and how the growth in the productivity emerged during the years, it can be seen from Figure 13 that Korea published its first article in the year 2002 and till 2012 the publication rate was low but since 2013 there is a surge in the production and in 2024 it got highest publication of 220. USA published the first article in 2004 and since then the publication growth is rising upward with 168 publications as highest in 2024. Italy published first article in 2007 but till 2013 the growth was low and after 2014 there is an upward trend with highest publication of 164 in 2024.

Figure 13. Country's production over time

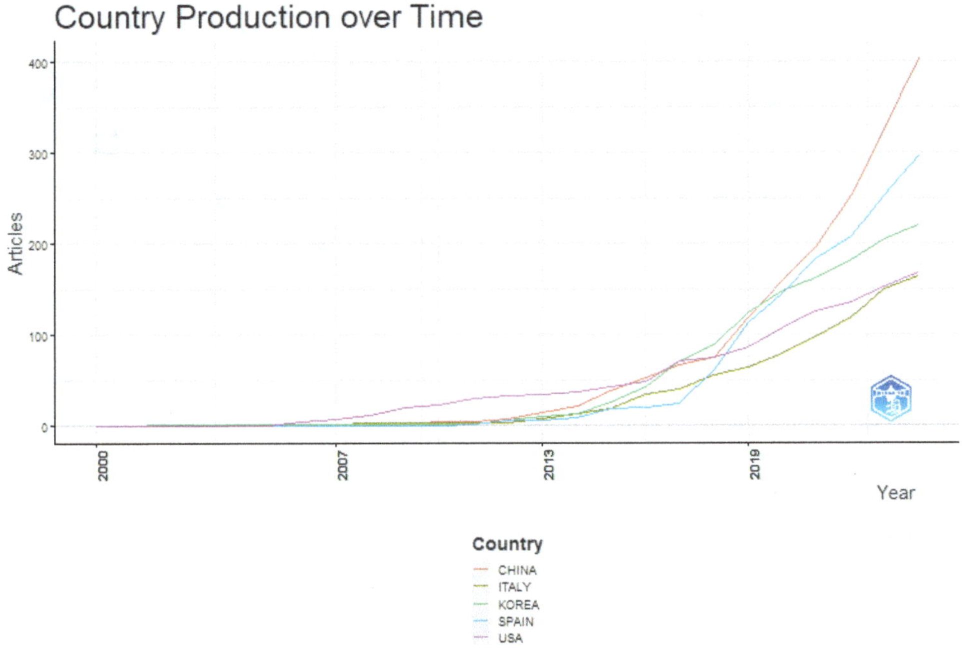

(Author Creation)

In context to most cited countries, USA is the most impactful country with 4348 citations followed by Korea with 4028 citations and is the second most impactful country. China is at third position with 3287 citations, Spain is with 2778 citation and is at fourth place in most impactful nation. UK with 2449 citations is the 5th place in context to most cited nation followed by Italy with 1964 citations followed by Hong Kong with 837 citations. This indicates that along with productivity these nations are also getting recognition as articles produced in these articles are getting good citations.

Figure 14. Most cited countries

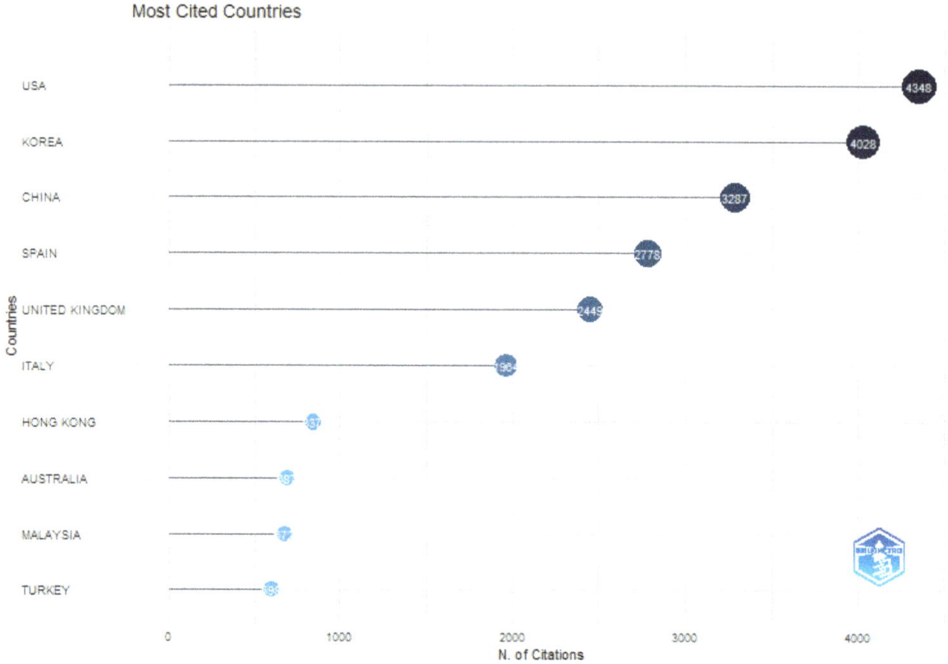

(Author Creation)

Global citation is used in Figure 15 to analyze the most relevant document in the present study to study the academic literature of Digital Tourism. Global citations are the total citations received by any article from all domains in the total time span of the article which makes this an important aspect to consider while studying the most relevant document. The vertical axis consists of author name with year of publication while the horizontal axis consist of total global citation received. Xiang Z "Role of Social Media in Online Travel Information Search" which was published in 2010 is the highly globally cited article with 1950 Total Citation and an average annual citation of 130. The article examined the extent to which social media appears when someone search for travel related aspects. Study results indicated that social media appears frequently as travelers search for travel related aspects and indicate that social media and travel have a relationship. Lu J published article "Recommender System Application Development: A Survey" in 2015 that examined how users can get personalized services in travel. Results indicated that recommender service offers great assistance in this. The article received 1242 citations and average annual citation of 124.20. Gretzel U published article in 2015 which got 1154 total citation and titled "Smart Tourism: Foundations and developments". In this study smart tourism was defined with its various forms and it was found that being a new phenomenon this can assist travelers and industry to promote new form of tourism.

Figure 15. Most global cited documents

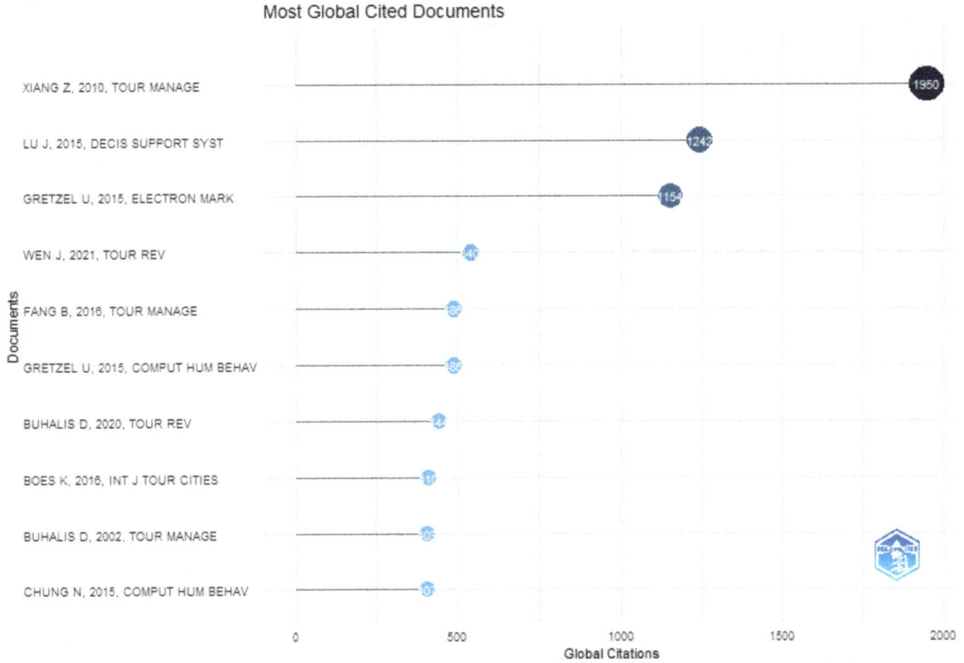

(Author Creation)

Keyword analysis is one of the important tool to gain insight regarding trending topics in any domain. Author keywords refer to the keywords as specified by the author in their article while submitting the final manuscript for submission. Figure 16 (Most Relevant Words) likely plots keywords on a two-dimensional plane, with the x-axis representing the number of documents a particular keyword appears in (its occurrence), and possibly the y-axis representing the strength of the relationship between keywords (measured by a metric like the co-occurrence or a weighted occurrence score).

Figure 16. Most relevant words

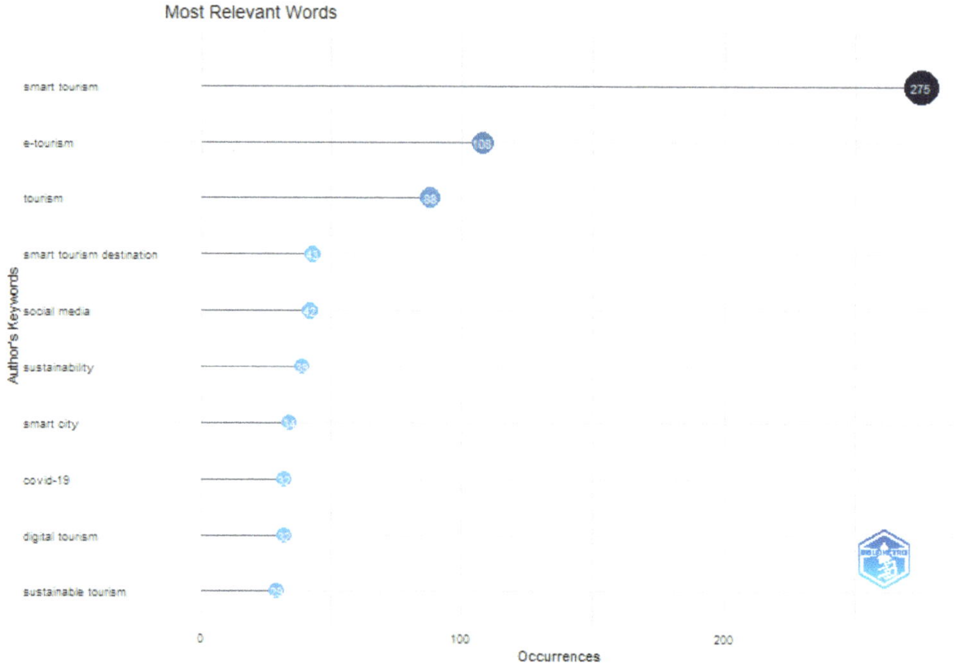

(Author Creation)

"Smart Tourism" appeared in 275 documents denoting the topmost relevance of the word in context of the present study and indicating that how this topic is in exploration in the academic literature. The word "e-tourism" occurred 108 times and indicate that digital tourism is one of the main theme that is/has emerged. This indicates a high volume of research and discussions for exploring new form of tourism and to fulfil the needs of modern day travelers is being synthesized and suggested by academic writers. These influential words are followed by "tourism", "Smart Tourism Destination", "Social Media", "Sustainability", "Smart City", "Covid-19", "Digital Tourism", "Smart Tourism", "Sustainable Tourism". This analysis highlights that sustainability and social media are some of the other major themes that are being explored in context to digital tourism.

Word Cloud

Word cloud is a feature in biblioshiny that allows to visualize the most frequent words by making them a central point in the visualization. In context of Digital Tourism by using author keywords and keeping 50 minimum keywords, word occurrence by frequency, it can be clearly noticed that "Smart-Tourism", 'E-tourism',

'tourism', 'Smart Tourism Destination', 'Sustainability', 'Smart Destination', and 'Social Media' are some of the major words that are being shown as the most impactful keywords in context to the research in Digital Tourism. This puts light in the fact that researchers in this domain are majorly working on these topics and also it highlights the future trending keywords. This also focuses as how various aspects of Digital Tourism is being explored by researchers in the academic front nowadays.

Figure 17. Word cloud

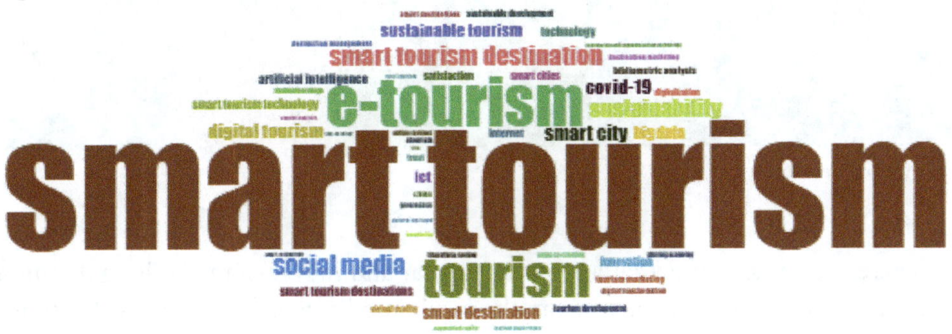

(Author Creation)

TreeMap graphically (Figure 18) represents the relative frequency of various keywords in a dataset, likely from academic research or publications. In this treemap, each keyword is allocated a space proportional to its frequency, with 'Smart Tourism' being the most prominent, indicating it is the most frequently occurring or studied topic within the context of the data, occupying 38% of the occurrences. Following Smart Tourism, the term 'E-Tourism' holds 15% visibility, suggesting significant attention towards various aspects of digital tourism aspects. 'Tourism', 'Smart Tourism Destination;, 'Social Media', occupy 12%, 6% and 6% visibility. 'Sustainability' and 'Smart City' occupy 5% visibility each followed by 'Covid-19', 'Digital Tourism' and 'Sustainable Tourism' holding 4% visibility each.

Figure 18. Tree map

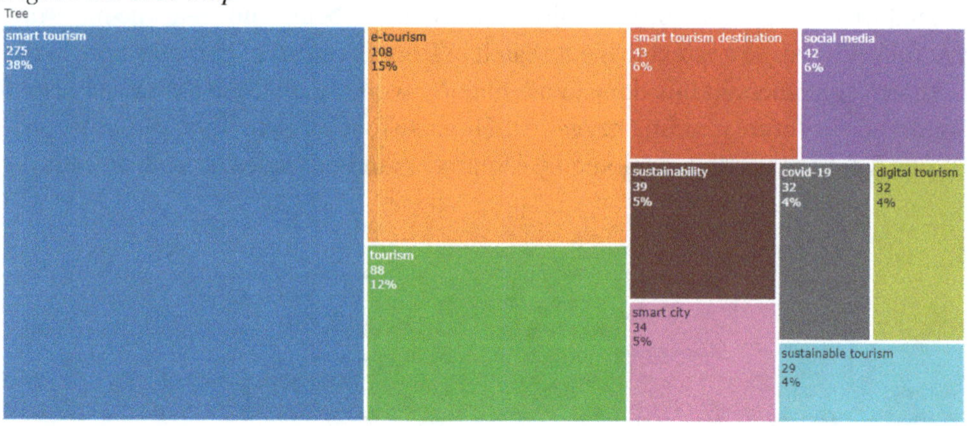

(Author Creation)

There are some words that appear in an year and may sustain for long duration and some words may disappear from the academic literature. Figure 19 illustrates the words frequency over time which demonstrates as how these words are being evolved and sustained in the progressive course of action with many advancement in research in Digital Tourism. The graph demonstrates that 'Smart Tourism' firstly appeared in the year 2013 with 1 occurrence and since 2016 the graph has surged with an increasing rate with 275 occurrences in the year 2024 which is the highest till date. This shows that this aspect is being now explored and is a major theme today in the academic literature. The word frequency is a major technique in biblioshiny to explore the trend in words from its evolution in specific domain to know that what aspect is evolving at present in that domain. 'E-tourism' which occurred first in year 2004 evolved trough these years and has a continues occurrence in the academic literature over the years showing that this theme is still adopted by many researchers even getting 108 occurrences in 2024. 'Social Media' in context to tourism was first used in the year 2010 and since then there is a continues growth and in past five years this occurrence has got great surge. 'Smart Tourism Destination' which appeared for the first time in 2014 is one of the trending topic in the academic literature on digital tourism which is being promoted nowadays. 'Sustainable Tourism' appeared for the first time in 2007 which shows that this trend of sustainability in tourism evolved way back past decade and still one of the prominent topic.

Figure 19. Words' frequency over time

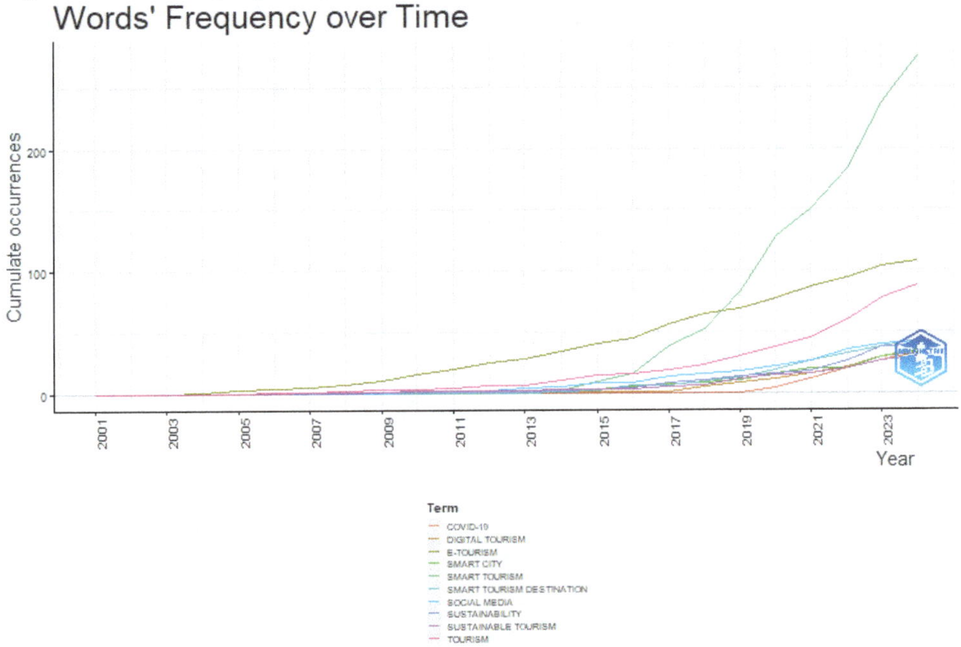

(Author Creation)

To further examine the trending topics in the context of Digital Tourism, an analysis of author keywords was conducted with time span from 2000 till 2024. The size of the bubbles represents the term frequency, while their position on the horizontal axis indicates the time of occurrence, by setting timespan ranging from 2000 to 2024 considering minimum 5 occurrences and 2 words per year, the results indicates the various aspects. The term 'Semantic Web', 'User Experience', 'E-commerce', 'E-services' were trending topics between 2008-2013, 'e-tourism', 'ict', 'Recommender Systems', 'Technology acceptance model' were some of the trending topics between 2014-2019. 'Big Data', 'Smart Tourism', 'Sustainability', 'Smart Tourism Technology', 'Artificial Intelligence', 'Digital Transformation' are trending topic since 2019 . This indicate that now this topic is much explored.

Figure 20. Trending topics

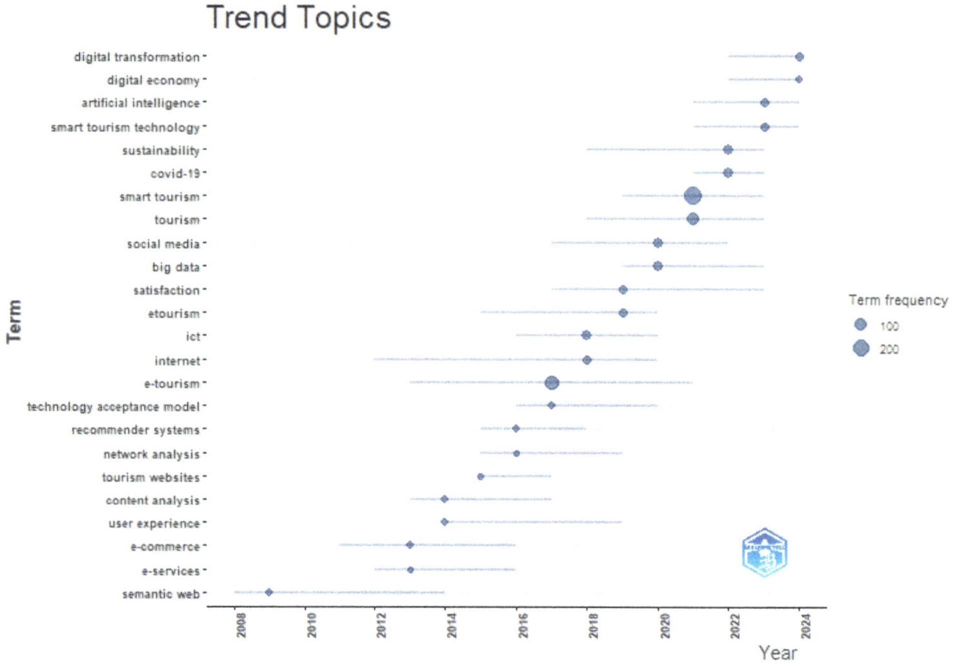

(Author Creation)

In addition, our study employs the keyword co-occurrence using author keywords to gain insights into the field of Digital Tourism. Keyword Co-occurrence Network (KCN) analysis draws the links between the keywords used in the literature that provides deep insights regarding knowledge structure (Esfahani et al., 2019). Notably, some keywords seem to have a greater impact on a network. For example, a close examination of these keywords from its color code suggests that a bigger keyword represented by their width are cohesively connected to other smaller keywords.

Figure 21 shows node-link diagram, highlighting the interconnectivity between various terms related to Digital Tourism. In this network, the nodes (represented by dots or circles) stand for terms or concepts, and the links (the lines connecting the nodes) illustrate the relationships or associations between these terms. The figure represents direct as well as indirect linkages between various keywords that have been also a part of highly cited keywords or trending topics and here in the co-occurrence keyword network diagram they are linked to guide scholars towards some themes in which potential for exploration is there. The co-occurrence network diagram clearly showing that 'Digital Tourism' is directly linked with 'Big Data' and 'Smart Tourism Destination' as these co-occurred frequently as the bubbles are joined with a thick node. There we can observe five colors of bubbles (Red,

Green, Blue, yellow and Violet). Cluster 1 (Red) consists of nineteen keywords which are interrelated to one another but the word 'Smart Tourism' is connected to all words and is the main or major theme in the cluster and closely with 'Big Data' and 'Sustainability'. Cluster 2 (Blue) consist of 13 keywords with 'E-tourism' as a main theme and major co-occurrence with 'Internet'. Cluster 3 (Green) consist of 8 keywords of which 'Tourism' seems to be the major theme linked with all other keywords and high co-occurrence with 'Technology'. Cluster 4 (Violet) consist of 7 keywords of which 'Smart tourism destination' is a major theme and the only direct link with 'Smart City'. The final cluster 5 (Yellow) consist of 3 keywords of which high linkage is between 'Smart tourism Technology' and 'Destination Image'.

Figure 21. Co-occurrence network of keywords

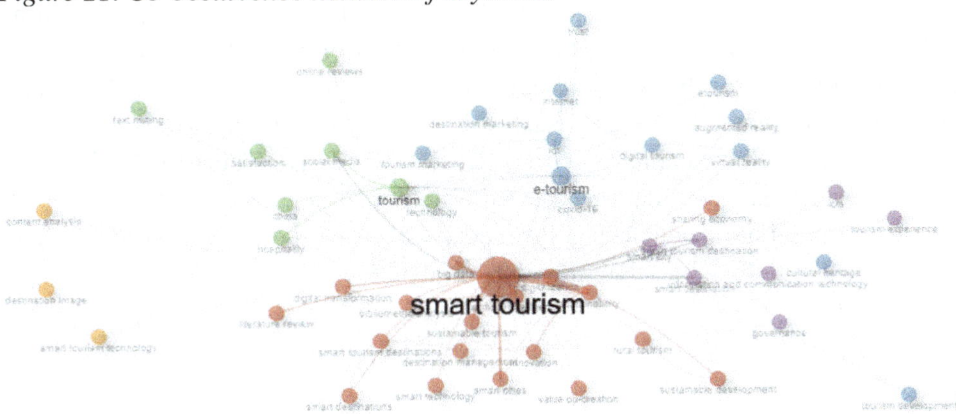

(Author Creation)

Thematic Map

A Thematic map is a two dimensional plot which plots the typological themes on the basis of centrality and density (Cobo et al., 2011). In this, clusters are identified based on the co-word analysis and then the themes in each cluster is generated in research domain. These themes can be classified into four quadrants on the basis of density and centrality. Each theme is represented in the map with a bubble. Centrality is plotted on X-axis whereas the density is plotted on the Y axis. Centrality is a measure of inter-cluster interaction among the keywords and it denotes as to which extent one topic is connected or related to other topic in a domain. Density on the other hand refers to the intra-cluster interactions of keywords to develop a theme of that cluster. The top right quadrant contains motor themes with high centrality and density denoting to those themes that are well developed as well as are core to the research domain. The lower right quadrant refers to Basic theme with high centrality and low density denoting themes that are important and can impact other themes but are less developed internally. Themes in the lower left quadrant refers to emerging or disappearing themes as they have low centrality as well density and are less explored. The upper left quadrant consist of niche themes that are having high density but low centrality and are well developed internally but less discussed widely.

The upper right quadrant in Figure 22 consist of Motor themes that are highly discussed and are highly developed in the research domain due to which they are the core themes including 'Smart Tourism', 'Big Data', 'Artificial Intelligence'. The upper left quadrant that consist of the Niche themes that are well developed internally but have wide scope of discussion in the research domain consist of keywords such as 'Destination Marketing', 'Tourism 4.0', 'Tourism Motivation', 'Social Media', 'Online Reviews', 'Destination Image', 'Smart Tourism Technology', 'Text Mining', 'Satisfaction'. The lower right quadrant consist of basic themes which are of utmost importance for the development of the research field but are less developed internally and includes keywords such as 'E-tourism', 'Digital Tourism', 'ICT', 'Sustainability', 'Sustainable Tourism', 'Covid-19', 'Smart Tourism Destination', 'Smart City', 'Smart Destination'. The lower left quadrant consist of themes which are either emerging or which may disappear with time include keywords such as 'Tourism', 'Digitalization', 'Bibliometric Analysis'.

Figure 22. Thematic map

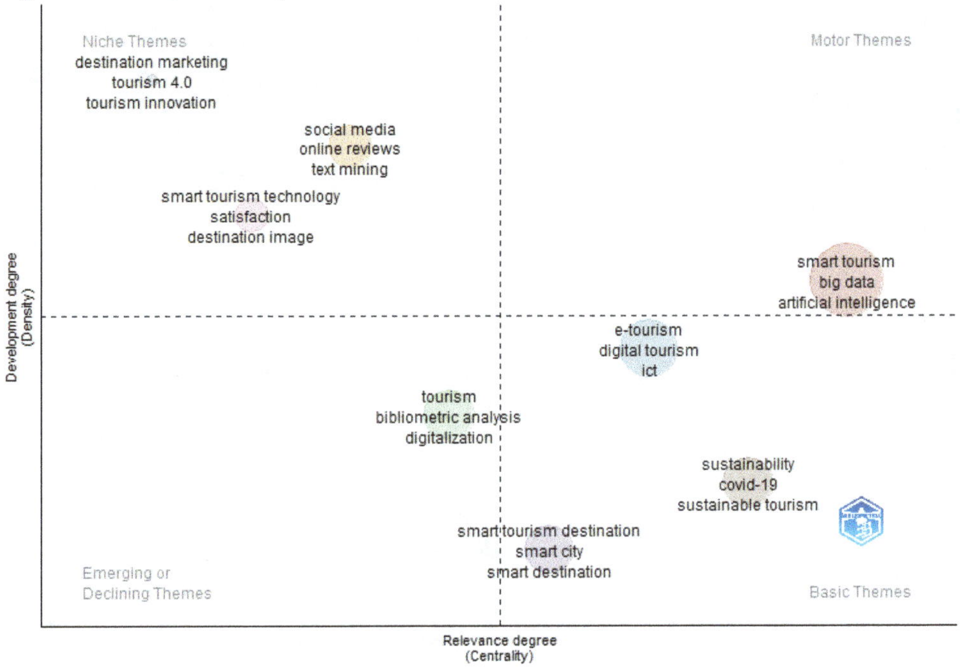

(Author Creation)

Thematic Evolution

The thematic evolution demonstrates the evolution of themes in a broad manner over a time period by dividing the entire time span into time slices with various cut points. Thematic evolution assist scholars in exploring themes based on centrality and density. With 100-word count in author keyword field,, thematic evolution, over four time slices with cut points of 2006, 2012, 2018 and 2024 is shown in Figure 23-26.

Figure 23. Time slice 1: Thematic evolution 2000-2006

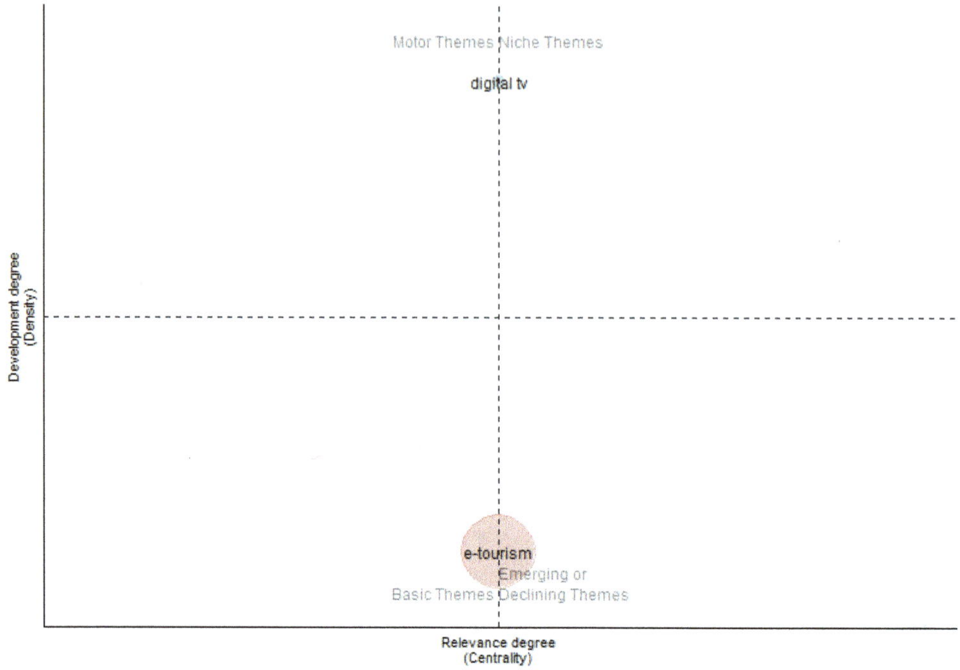

(Author Creation)

Figure 24. Time slice 2: Thematic evolution 2007-2012

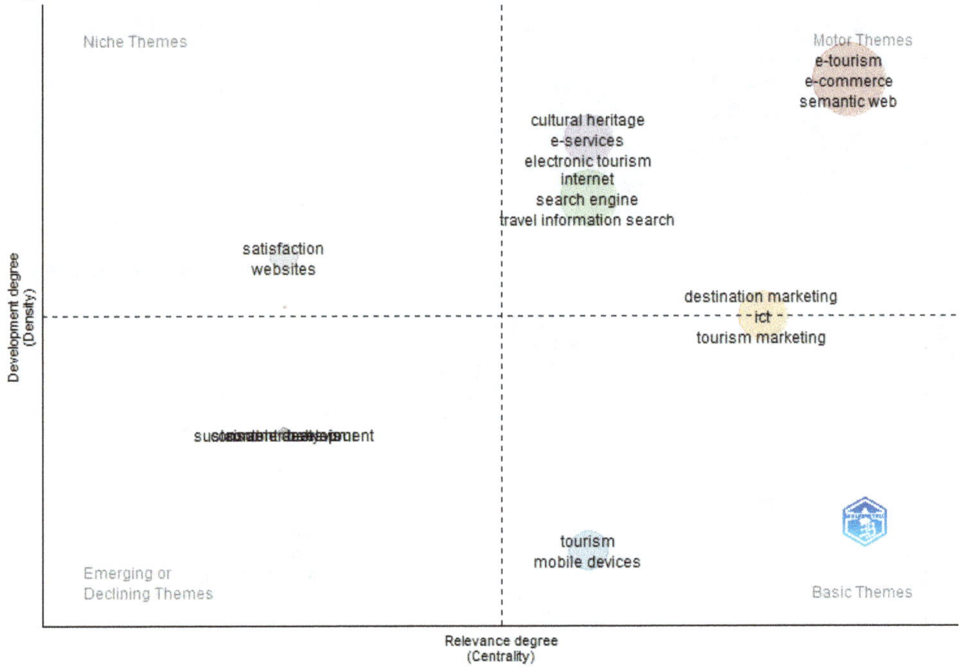

(Author Creation)

Figure 25. Time slice 3: Thematic evolution 2013-2018

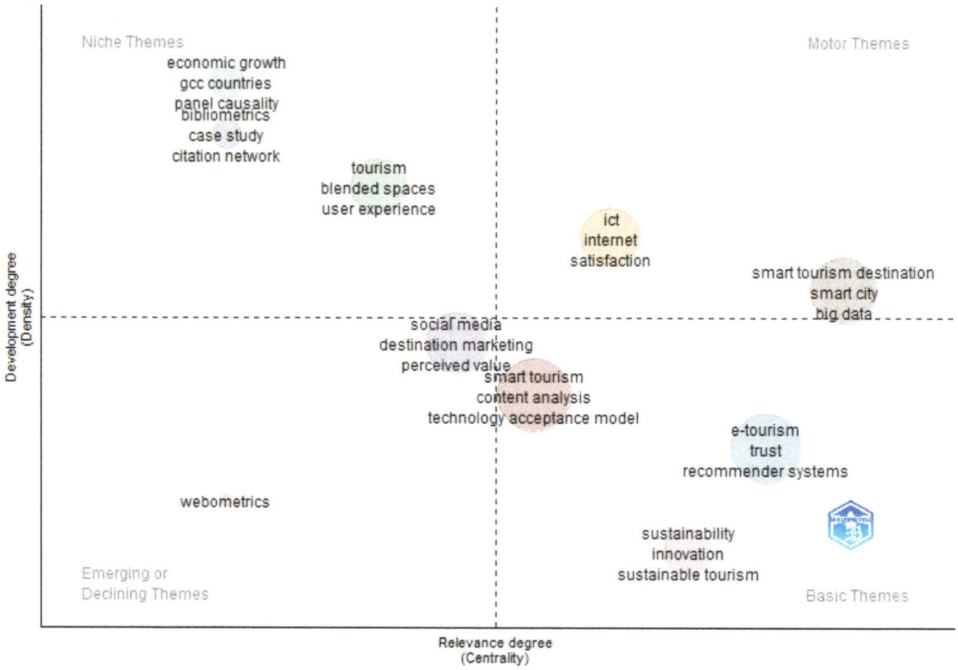

(Author Creation)

Figure 26. Time slice 4: Thematic evolution 2019-2024

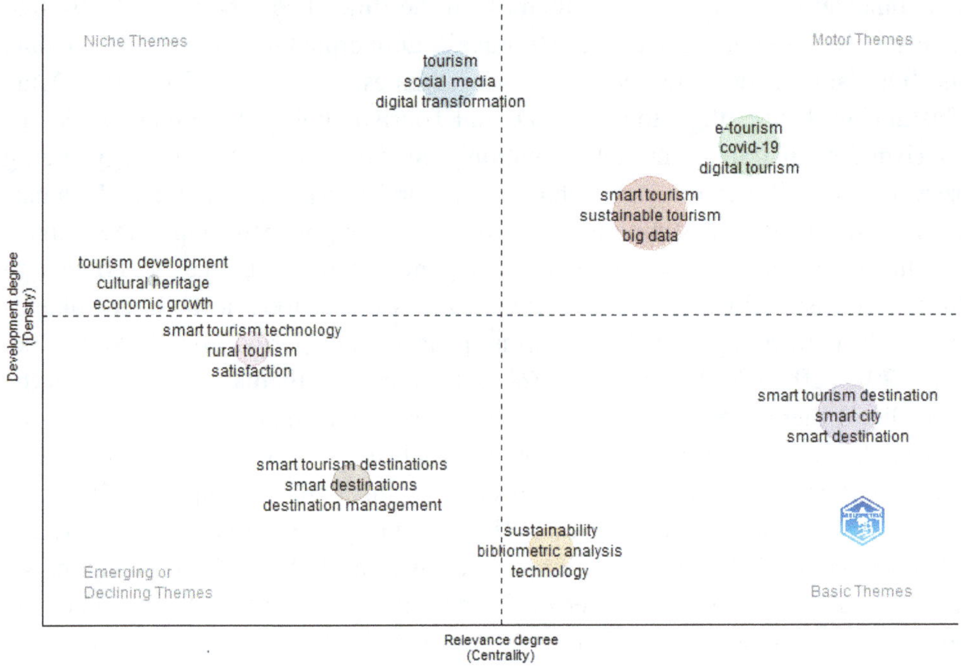

(Author Creation)

In the time slice 1 thematic evolution it can be seen that 'Digital TV' lies between niche theme and motor theme indicating that this topic was either a new aspect or a core theme for academicians while 'E-tourism' lies between emerging or basic theme which also indicate the same in 2000-2006. In the time slice 2 between 2007-2012, 'Satisfaction' and 'websites' were niche themes indicating work on tourist satisfaction and focus on website development for tourism as niche aspect. 'cultural heritage', 'e-services', 'electronic tourism', 'internet', 'search engine' and 'travel information search', 'e-tourism', 'e-commerce', 'semantic web' were the motor themes and core concepts. 'Destination Marketing', 'Tourism Marketing', 'ICT' lies between motor and basic theme indicating these topics as core as well as important. 'tourism' and 'mobile devices' were basic themes. 'Sustainable Development', 'Consumer Behavior' were emerging concept in this time slice. In the time slice 3 between 2013-2018 we can observe new themes growing such as 'User Experience', 'economic growth' related studies were focused using bibliometric analysis as these keywords also appear as niche theme. 'ICT', 'Satisfaction', 'Smart Tourism Destination', 'Smart City', and 'Big Data' were the core themes. 'Webometrics', 'Social Media', 'Destination Marketing' and Perceived Value' were emerging or disappearing themes along with 'Smart Tourism', 'Content Analysis', 'Technology acceptance model', 'e-tourism', 'recommender system', 'sustainability', 'sustainable tourism', 'trust', and 'Innovation' being the basic themes. In the time slice 4 between 2019-2024 'Tourism Development', 'Cultural Heritage', 'Economic Growth', 'Social Media', and 'Digital transformation' were the niche themes. 'Smart Tourism', 'Big Data', 'Sustainable Tourism', 'E-tourism', 'Digital Tourism' being motor themes. 'Smart Tourism Destination', 'Smart Destination', 'Sustainability', 'Technology' being basic themes. 'Smart tourism technology', 'rural tourism', 'satisfaction', 'smart tourism destination', 'destination management' in emerging or disappearing themes.

The three field plot captured the emergence of broad themes in context to Digital Tourism which is shown in Figure 27. A closer look at the inter-linkages among the themes separated by four-time spans, namely period from 2000 to 2006, 2007–2012, 2013–2018 and 2019-2024 underscores the thematic evolution. In the time slice 1 there is only one concept which emerged as major themes namely 'E-Tourism'. 'Consumer Behaviour', 'Content Analysis', 'E-services', 'Social Media', 'Cultural Heritage; emerged as trending and evolving themes during 2007-2012. All themes except e-services and Cultural Heritage merged in e-tourism. 'E-tourism', 'also merged in 'Destination Branding', 'Destination Marketing', and 'E-learning'. 'E-services' merged in 'Consumer Preference' in the year 2013-18 and some new prolific themes 'Trust', 'Smart Tourism', 'Sustainability', 'Perceived value' emerged. In recent years in time slice 2019-2024 'Smart Tourism', 'Smart Tourism Technology', 'Online Tourism', 'Smart City', 'Social Media', and 'Smart Destinations' are the major evolving themes.

Figure 27. Thematic evolution

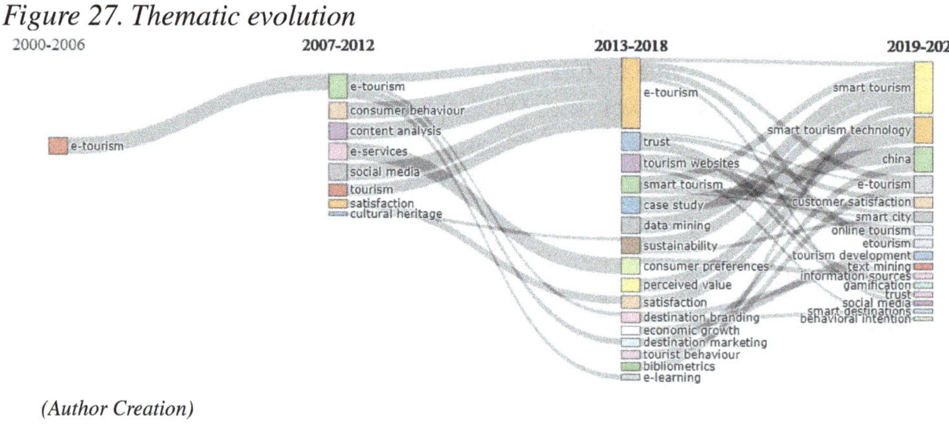

(Author Creation)

Social Network Analysis

The social network analysis in bibliometric study assist in developing knowledge that which authors, universities or countries work together in the respective domain of study. Collaboration map of authors, countries and affiliation are shown in Figure 28 to Figure 30 that reflect author, country and institution collaboration respectively. Law R, Chung N, Koo C are the major collaborating authors in this domain. 'China', 'Korea', 'Spain', 'USA' are the major collaborating countries in digital tourism. 'Kyung Hee University', 'The Hong Kong Polytechnic University' are the major collaborating universities in digital tourism.

Figure 28. Author collaboration network

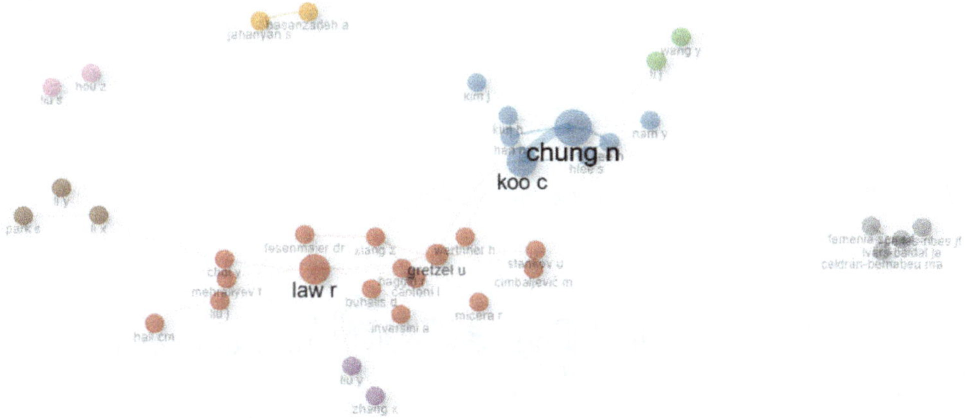

(Author Creation)

Figure 29. Country's collaboration network

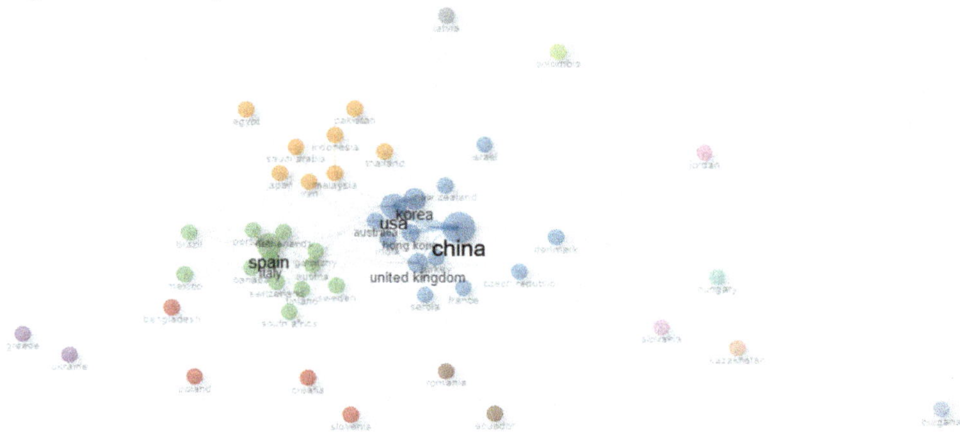

(Author Creation)

Figure 30. Institutions collaboration network

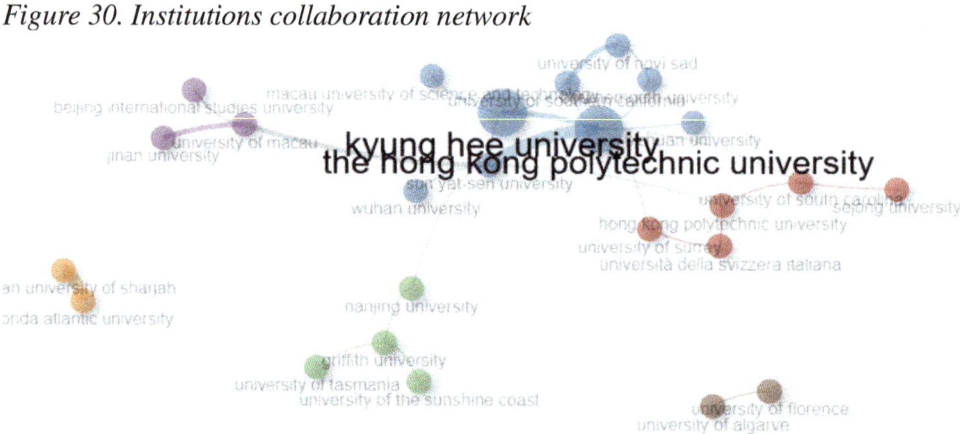

(Author Creation)

CONCLUSION

This study employed bibliometric analysis to visualize global research trends and future research directions in Digital Tourism. The search period was set from 2000 to 2024 to encompass recent developments. A total of 988 documents were included in performing the final analysis. The Bibliometric R tool was employed for data processing, visualization, and analysis. Descriptive analysis was first conducted to outline the basic characteristics of the data, including publication trends over time, distribution by country, and leading journals in the field. Descriptive analysis reflected that A total of 327 sources produced 988 documents during this period with an annual growth rate of more than 20 percent. The average age of document was 4.32 year with average citation per document being 35.77. A total of 53469 references were analyzed with 1433 keywords plus and 2991 author keywords. Total authors in our analysis were 2196 out of which authors who contributed as single author in a document were 94.

In context of annual scientific production there is an increasing trend in the publication pattern in this research area. The average citations recorded ups and downs in the citation trend throughout the years from the very commencement in the Average Citations since 2000. We found that Smart Tourism, Tourism, E-Tourism, Smart Tourism Destination and Social Media were the prominent keywords in these years. Sustainability (Switzerland) is the prominent journal that is working on smart tourism and is highly promoted by Spain and Korea. Smart Tourism Destination is a major theme in Sustainability (Switzerland) that is explored in Italy and Spain the most. E-Tourism is a major theme in China, Italy and Spain which is published majorly by Information Technology and Tourism. Sustainability (Switzerland) is the most relavant source with highest publication of 101 articles, Asia Pacific Journal of Tourism Research is the second most productive journal followed by Current Issues in Tourism with 27 article each. In context of impact, Sustainability (Switzerland) is at the top in this list with an H-index of 32 followed by 'Tourism Management' with an H-Index of 22. Information Technology and Tourism is the third most impactful source with an H-Index of 17. Based on the number of publications by each author to find the most productive author figure 8 represents an idea to it Chung N is the most relevant author in the domain of digital marketing with 28 articles till date followed by Law R with 26 articles and Koo C with 19 articles. Buhalis D first published in the domain of digital tourism in the year 2002 with an total citation per year of 17.78, the author is producing continuously over the years and the last work as per the data extracted is in the year 2023 with total citation per year of 46. Chung N and Law R are the most impactful authors with H-index of 18 in the domain of digital tourism. Kyung Hee University is the most prolific affiliation with 102 articles in the domain of digital tourism. The Hong Kong Polytechnic University is with 80 articles followed by University of Aucante and University of Sovi Nad is with 24 articles each. China is the most productive country in the domain of digital tourism with 400 publication till date. It is followed by Spain with 296 articles, South Korea with 220 articles. USA is the most impactful country with 4348 citations followed by Korea with 4028 citations and is the second most impactful country. China is at third position with 3287 citations. Xiang Z "Role of Social Media in Online Travel

Information Search" which was published in 2010 is the highly globally cited article with 1950 Total Citation and an average annual citation of 130. The article examined the extent to which social media appears when someone search for travel related aspects. Study results indicated that social media appears frequently as travelers search for travel related aspects and indicate that social media and travel have a relationship. "Smart Tourism" appeared in 275 documents denoting the topmost relevance of the word in context of the present study and indicating that how this topic is in exploration in the academic literature. The word "e-tourism" occurred 108 times and indicate that digital tourism is one of the main theme that is/has emerged. This indicates a high volume of research and discussions for exploring new form of tourism and to fulfil the needs of modern day travelers is being synthesized and suggested by academic writers. The term 'Semantic Web', 'User Experience', 'E-commerce', 'E-services' were trending topics between 2008-2013, 'e-tourism', 'ict', 'Recommender Systems', 'Technology acceptance model' were some of the trending topics between 2014-2019. 'Big Data', 'Smart Tourism', 'Sustainability', 'Smart Tourism Technology', 'Artificial Intelligence', 'Digital Transformation' are trending topic since 2019 . This indicate that now this topic is much explored. The co-occurrence network diagram clearly showing that 'Digital Tourism' is directly linked with 'Big Data' and 'Smart Tourism Destination' as these co-occurred frequently as the bubbles are joined with a thick node. There we can observe five colors of bubbles (Red, Green, Blue, yellow and Violet). Cluster 1 (Red) consists of nineteen keywords which are interrelated to one another but the word 'Smart Tourism' is connected to all words and is the main or major theme in the cluster and closely with 'Big Data' and 'Sustainability'. Cluster 2 (Blue) consist of 13 keywords with 'E-tourism' as a main theme and major co-occurrence with 'Internet'. Cluster 3 (Green) consist of 8 keywords of which 'Tourism' seems to be the major theme linked with all other keywords and high co-occurrence with 'Technology'. Cluster 4 (Violet) consist of 7 keywords of which 'Smart tourism destination' is a major theme and the only direct link with 'Smart City'. The final cluster 5 (Yellow) consist of 3 keywords of which high linkage is between 'Smart tourism Technology' and 'Destination Image'. The three field plot captured the emergence of broad themes in context to Digital Tourism. A closer look at the inter-linkages among the themes separated by four-time spans, namely period from 2000 to 2006, 2007–2012, 2013–2018 and 2019-2024 underscores the thematic evolution. In the time slice 1 there is only one concept which emerged as major themes namely 'E-Tourism'. 'Consumer Behaviour', 'Content Analysis', 'E-services', 'Social Media', 'Cultural Heritage; emerged as trending and evolving themes during 2007-2012. All themes except e-services and Cultural Heritage merged in e-tourism. 'E-tourism', 'also merged in 'Destination Branding', 'Destination Marketing', and 'E-learning'. 'E-services' merged in 'Consumer Preference' in the year 2013-18 and some new prolific themes 'Trust', 'Smart Tourism', 'Sustainability', 'Perceived value' emerged. In recent years in time slice 2019-2024 'Smart Tourism', 'Smart Tourism Technology', 'Online Tourism', 'Smart City', 'Social Media', and 'Smart Destinations' are the major evolving themes. Law R, Chung N, Koo C are the major collaborating authors in this domain. 'China', 'Korea', 'Spain', 'USA' are the major collaborating countries in digital tourism. 'Kyung Hee University', 'The Hong Kong Polytechnic University' are the major collaborating universities in digital tourism.

This study provided various results which indicated how digital tourism evolved and what future potential it provides. But along with this there are some limitations that exist. The search criteria and the keywords used in this study have determined the research's sample and consequently all the results. The study incorporated Scopus database to analyze the results, in future studies web of science can also be incorporated along with Scopus database to make the study results more reliable. The future research work can also include systematic literature review along with bibliometric analysis to enhance the qualitative analysis. The study offers policy makers and practitioners a useful baseline for developing policies and strategies to promote tourism digitally through its various forms.

REFERENCES

Arthur, P. L., & Nuenen, T. (2019). Travel in the Digital Age. In Das, N., & Youngs, T. (Eds.), *The Cambridge History of Travel Writing* (pp. 504–518). Cambridge University Press.

Ashcroft, B. (2015). Travel and Utopia. In Kuehn, J., & Smethurst, P. (Eds.), *New Directions in Travel Writing Studies* (pp. 249–262). Palgrave Macmillan.

Atzori, L., Iera, A., & Morabito, G. (2010). The Internet of things: A survey. *Computer Networks*, *54*(15), 2787–2805. DOI: 10.1016/j.comnet.2010.05.010

Buhalis, D. (2020). Technology in tourism-from information communication technologies to eTourism and smart tourism towards ambient intelligence tourism: A perspective article. *Tourism Review*, *75*(1), 267–272. DOI: 10.1108/TR-06-2019-0258

Buhalis, D., & Deimezi, O. (2004). E-tourism developments in Greece: Information communication technologies adoption for the strategic management of the Greek tourism industry. *Tourism and Hospitality Research*, *5*(2), 103–130. DOI: 10.1057/palgrave.thr.6040011

Caragliu, A., Del Bo, C., & Nijkamp, P. (2011). Smart cities in Europe. *Journal of Urban Technology*, *18*(2), 65–82. DOI: 10.1080/10630732.2011.601117

Dickinson, J. E., Ghali, K., Cherrett, T., Speed, C., Davies, N., & Norgate, S. (2014). Tourism and the smartphone app: Capabilities, emerging practice and scope in the travel domain. *Current Issues in Tourism*, *17*(1), 84–101. DOI: 10.1080/13683500.2012.718323

Franklin, A., & Crang, C. (2001). The Trouble with Tourism and Travel Theory? *Tourist Studies*, *1*(1), 5–22.

Gretzel, U., Sigala, M., Xiang, Z., & Koo, C. (2015). Smart tourism: Foundations and developments. *Electronic Markets*, *25*(3), 179–188. DOI: 10.1007/s12525-015-0196-8

Gretzel, U., Zhong, L., & Koo, C. (2016). Application of smart tourism to cities. *International Journal of Tourism Cities*, *2*(2), 216–233. DOI: 10.1108/IJTC-04-2016-0007

Hannam, K. (2009). 'The End of Tourism? Nomadology and the Mobilities Paradigm', Philosophical Issues in Tourism 37: 101–114. Hannam, K., G. Butler and C. M. Paris (2014) 'Developments and Key Issues in Tourism Mobilities'. *Annals of Tourism Research*, *44*(1), 171–185.

Hwang, J., Park, H.-Y., & Hunter, W. C. (2015). Constructivism in smart tourism research: Seoul destination image. *Asia Pacific Journal of Information Systems, 25*(1), 163–178. DOI: 10.14329/apjis.2015.25.1.163

Iunius, R. F., Cismaru, L., & Foris, D. (2015). Raising competitiveness for tourist destinations through information technologies within the newest tourism action framework proposed by the European commission. *Sustainability, 7*(9), 12891–12909. DOI: 10.3390/su70912891

Januszewska, M., Jaremen, D. E., & Nawrocka, E. (2015). The effects of the use of ICT by tourism enterprises. Zeszyty Naukowe Uniwersytetu Szczecińskiego. Scientific Journal. *Supervisory Management, 16*, 65–73. DOI: 10.18276/smt.2015.16-07

Kontogianni, A., & Alepis, E. (2020). Smart tourism: State of the art and literature review for the last six years. *Array (New York, N.Y.), 6*, 100020. DOI: 10.1016/j.array.2020.100020

Koo, C., Joun, Y., Han, H., & Chung, N. (2016). A structural model for destination travel intention as a media exposure: Belief-desire-intention model perspective. *International Journal of Contemporary Hospitality Management, 28*(7), 1338–1360. *Scopus*. Advance online publication. DOI: 10.1108/IJCHM-07-2014-0354

Law, R., Chan, I. C. C., & Wang, L. (2018). A comprehensive review of mobile technology use in hospitality and tourism. *Journal of Hospitality Marketing and Management, 27*(6), 626–648. *Scopus*. Advance online publication. DOI: 10.1080/19368623.2018.1423251

Leung, D., Law, R., Van Hoof, H., & Buhalis, D. (2013). Social media in tourism and hospitality: A literature review. *Journal of Travel & Tourism Marketing, 30*(1-2), 3–22. DOI: 10.1080/10548408.2013.750919

Löfgren, O. (1999). *On Holiday: A History of Vacationing*. University of California Press.

Lu, A. C. C., & Gursoy, D. (2015). A conceptual model of consumers' online tourism confusion. *International Journal of Contemporary Hospitality Management, 27*(6), 1320–1342. *Scopus*. Advance online publication. DOI: 10.1108/IJCHM-04-2014-0171

Minghetti, V., & Buhalis, D. (2010). Digital divide in tourism. *Journal of Travel Research, 49*(3), 267–281. DOI: 10.1177/0047287509346843

Miorandi, D., Sicari, S., De Pellegrini, F., & Chlamtac, I. (2012). Internet of things: Vision, applications and research challenges. *Ad Hoc Networks, 10*(7), 1497–1516. DOI: 10.1016/j.adhoc.2012.02.016

Salazar, N. B. (2010). *Envisioning Eden: Mobilizing Imaginaries in Tourism and Beyond*. Berghahn Books., Available at https://books.google.nl/books?id=Vx85TX9T3h0C

Shafiee, S., Ghatari, A. R., Hasanzadeh, A., & Jahanyan, S. (2019). Developing a model for sustainable smart tourism destinations: A systematic review. *Tourism Management Perspectives*, *31*, 287–300. DOI: 10.1016/j.tmp.2019.06.002

Sheller, M., & Urry, J. (2004). *Tourism Mobilities: Places to Play, Places in Play*. Routledge.

Sun, Y., Ma, H., & Chan, E. H. W. (2018). A model to measure tourist preference toward scenic spots based on social media data: A case of Dapeng in China. *Sustainability (Switzerland)*, *10*(1). *Scopus*. Advance online publication. DOI: 10.3390/su10010043

Tu, Q., & Liu, A. (2014). Framework of smart tourism research and related progress in China. In A. Kong (Ed.), International conference on management and engineering (CME 2014) (pp. 140-146). Shanghai, China.

Vannini, P. (2010). Mobile Cultures: From the Sociology of Transportation to the Study of Mobilities. *Sociology Compass*, *4*(2), 111–121.

Wang, D., Li, X. R., & Li, Y. (2013). China's "smart tourism destination" initiative: A taste of the service-dominant logic. *Journal of Destination Marketing & Management*, *2*(2), 59–61. DOI: 10.1016/j.jdmm.2013.05.004

Wang, D., Park, S., & Fesenmaier, D. R. (2012). The role of smartphones in mediating the touristic experience. *Journal of Travel Research*, *51*(4), 371–387. DOI: 10.1177/0047287511426341

Wang, D., Xiang, Z., & Fesenmaier, D. R. (2016). Smartphone use in everyday life and travel. *Journal of Travel Research*, *55*(1), 52–63. DOI: 10.1177/0047287514535847

World Travel & Tourism Council. (2019). Economic impact. https://wttc.org/Research/Insights

Xiang, Z., & Fesenmaier, D. R. (2017). Big data analytics, tourism design and smart tourism. In Xiang, Z., & Fesenmaier, D. R. (Eds.), *Analytics in smart tourism design* (pp. 299–307). Springer., DOI: 10.1007/978-3-319-44263-1_17

Xiang, Z., & Gretzel, U. (2010). Role of social media in online travel information search. *Tourism Management*, *31*(2), 179–188. DOI: 0.1016/j.tourman.2009.02.016

Xiang, Z., Wang, D., O'Leary, J. T., & Fesenmaier, D. R. (2015). Adapting to the Internet: Trends in travelers' use of the web for trip planning. *Journal of Travel Research*, *54*(4), 511–527. DOI: 10.1177/0047287514522883

Zeng, B., & Gerritsen, R. (2014). What do we know about social media in tourism? A review. *Tourism Management Perspectives*, *10*, 27–36. DOI: 10.1016/j.tmp.2014.01.001

Zhang, L.-y., Li, N., & Liu, M. (2012). On the basic concept of smarter tourism and its theoretical system. *Luyou Xuekan*, *27*(5), 66–73.

Zhu, W., Zhang, L., & Li, N. (2014). Challenges, function changing of government and enterprises in Chinese smart tourism. In Z. Xiang, & I. Tussyadiah (Eds.), Short paper proceedings of the ENTER 2014 conference on information and communication technologies in tourism. https://ertr.tamu.edu/enter-2014-volume-4-research-notes/

Section 2
Ethics and Governance in Digital Innovation

Chapter 4

Ethical AI and Sustainable Digital Transformation: Building Trust in a Rapidly Digitalized World

Ana Cristina Saraiva
https://orcid.org/0000-0002-6989-5274
APEE, Portugal & UNA Portugal, Portugal

Maria A. Rodrigues
https://orcid.org/0000-0002-7858-5358
ISCAL, Portugal

ABSTRACT

This chapter explores the integration of ethics and sustainability into AInitiatives amidst rapid digital transformation. Emphasizing the centrality of ethical governance and sustainable practices, it examines how organizations can address critical ethical, social, and environmental challenges associated with AI technologies. Through a detailed analysis of the Ai.ethics program developed by the APEE and the UNA PT, the chapter demonstrates how structured frameworks such as Good Governance, Explainability, and Trust can enhance stakeholder confidence and organizational accountability. It underscores the significance of a people-centered approach, highlighting AI's potential to promote organizational efficiency, environmental sustainability, and socio-economic equity.

DOI: 10.4018/979-8-3373-0385-7.ch004

INTRODUCTION

We are currently undergoing a period of exponential digitalization, wherein the need to align technological progress with ethical and sustainable frameworks has become not only necessary but critically urgent. As digital technologies increasingly shape economic, social, and political systems, ethical and sustainable practices must move to the forefront of innovation strategies to prevent negative consequences and foster responsible progress.

Among these transformative technologies, Artificial Intelligence (AI) stands out as particularly influential, significantly reshaping economic activity and offering innovative solutions to a wide range of complex societal and industrial challenges.

However, the widespread uptake of AI technologies has also surfaced pressing ethical, social, and environmental concerns that cannot be overlooked. As Floridi (2020) wrotes, without responsible governance, AI risks reinforcing existing inequalities, infringing on privacy rights, and contributing to environmental degradation. For AI to serve as an enabler of societal well-being, it is essential that organizations embed ethical values, sound governance structures, and sustainability principles in technological development and implementation. Achieving this equilibrium is not only necessary for risk mitigation but for ensuring that AI technologies contribute positively, inclusively, and responsibly to society.

The accelerated deployment of AI and related technologies has driven to several issues in the center of academic, corporate, and policy discussions. These issues include algorithmic discrimination, privacy loss, gaps in accountability, and the environmental costs associated with energy-intensive machine learning models. Left unchecked, such challenges threaten to wear down public trust and intensify social disparities. Therefore, good governance is essential—not only to prevent harm but also to guarantee that AI operates all for the public interest. Ethics must be inserted into the very fabric of technological systems from the outset, not treated as an afterthought. This calls for proactive frameworks that ensure transparency, fairness, and human-centric design principles across the entire AI lifecycle.

In this context, in Portugal, the Ai.ethics program, jointly developed by the Portuguese Business Ethics Association (APEE) and the United Nations Association Portugal (UNA - PT), represents an initiative that embodies the principles of responsible digital transformation. Located in Portugal, the program aims to build trust in AI through a structured system of ethical recognition seals—*Good Governance*, *Explainability*, and *Trust*. Each seal means a foundational pillar of ethical AI and collectively addresses major ethical dilemmas while promoting confidence among the stakeholders. This initiative provides a concrete, operational example of how values-driven digital governance can be implemented in practice.

Other iniciatives presented in this chapter are:

- *"Autonomous AI in Diabetic Retinopathy Screening",* where an autonomous AI system, without human intervention, is designed to detect diabetic retinopathy, the leading cause of blindness globally;
- the *"AI-Powered Predictive Analytics in Elderly Care",* where a UK healthcare company uses AI to predict health deteriorations in elderly patients from home visit data;
- *the "AI in Urban Mobility Management*", where we see the ethical considerations of several European cities who has adopted AI-driven systems to manage urban mobility, reducing congestion and environmental impact;
- and the *"AI for Environmental Monitoring".* In Singapore, AI technologies are used to monitor environmental parameters such as air quality and waste management. These systems enable real-time responses to environmental issues, promoting sustainability.

With these case studies, we will try to show which are the ethical considerations of the using of AI in the diverse areas of a society.

This chapter, therefore, explores the dynamic interplay between AI, ethics, and sustainability, underscoring the significance of people-centered approaches in guiding digital transformation.

The need for ethics in AI development has never been more needing. AI can be broadly defined as a collection of computational systems designed to perform tasks that typically require human cognitive functions—such as learning, perception, reasoning, and decision-making (Brynjolfsson & McAfee, 2017).

As AI systems become deeply integrated into societies and in modern economies, their impact continues to expand. Recent technological breakthroughs have revolutionized various industries, enabling new levels of efficiency, accuracy, and productivity. From healthcare diagnostics and personalized treatment plans to automated financial services, autonomous vehicles, and intelligent manufacturing systems, AI is profoundly altering the ways in which goods and services are produced, distributed, and consumed (Agrawal, 2019).

Alongside these transformative opportunities, come substantial ethical challenges that require careful attention. Prominent among these are algorithmic bias, data privacy violations, the displacement of workers due to automation, and the environmental implications of increasingly data and energy intensive AI applications. These concerns have become central themes in scholarly discourse and policymaking, highlighting the necessity of critically examining the ethical implications and societal trade-offs associated with AI deployment (Pasquale, 2015).

As a result, the integration of ethical considerations into AI development is no longer a complement but a prerequisite for ensuring that technological innovation supports long-term societal goals.

Developing ethical AI requires a firm commitment by organizations to design, implement, and manage AI systems in ways that safeguard human rights, promote fairness and justice, and uphold principles of accountability and transparency throughout their operational lifecycle (Jobin et al., 2019).

The academic literature supports the view that ethical AI requires comprehensive governance mechanisms, interdisciplinary collaboration, and continuous, inclusive stakeholder engagement. These elements collectively serve to mitigate potential risks and amplify the benefits of AI for society (Hagendorff, 2020).

In this regard, this chapter seeks to deepen the understanding of the interconnected dimensions of AI, ethics, and sustainability by advocating for people-centered approaches to technological transformation. Such approaches prioritize the protection of human dignity, the promotion of social inclusion, and the empowerment of individuals and communities.

Rather than functioning as a disruptive force, AI should be guided by principles that enhance human capabilities and ensure that technology serves the broader public good (Zuboff, 2019). The academic consensus also affirms that aligning the innovation with the ethical values not only contributes to economic growth but also to sustainable development in terms of social equity, ecological preservation, and cultural resilience (Schwab & Davis, 2020).

Furthermore, this chapter critically engages with ongoing global debates surrounding AI governance, with particular emphasis on issues such as transparency, fairness, data protection, and environmental sustainability.

These themes have become central to recent international policy frameworks and international standards, such as the European Union's proposed AI Act and UNESCO's Recommendation on the Ethics of Artificial Intelligence (European Commission, 2021; UNESCO, 2021). These developments reflect a growing international consensus that ethical AI governance is essential for regulatory compliance and for fostering organizational resilience, innovation, and alignment with societal values.

So, organizations must cultivate a culture of governance based on openness, anticipatory risk management, and a commitment to continuous ethical improvement.

Just as crucial is the active inclusion of diverse stakeholder voices, like academia, civil society, industry, and policymakers, in shaping the design, deployment, and evaluation of AI systems (Crawford & Calo, 2016).

This inclusive approach fosters more just, effective, and context-aware technological outcomes.

Ultimately, this chapter presents a forward vision for sustainable digital transformation: one in which ethics and technology are not treated as separate spheres but are deeply and necessarily intertwined.

Ethical AI emerges not only as a societal priority but also as a strategic asset for organizations aiming to build trust, resilience, and global relevance.

By integrating ethical principles across every stage of technological innovation, organizations can help ensure that digital transformation serves as a driver of human development, social progress, and environmental responsibility.

ETHICS IN DIGITAL TRANSFORMATION

In the current era of rapid and pervasive technological advancement, digital transformation must be firmly anchored in robust ethical principles to effectively mitigate emerging risks while maximizing opportunities. As digital systems (like AI) increasingly saturate the social, economic, and political fabric of contemporary society, the demand for ethical governance has become both indispensable and non-negotiable in ensuring responsible innovation and societal benefit.

The UNESCO Recommendation on the Ethics of Artificial Intelligence (2021), reinforces this global responsibility by emphasizing that organizations must develop and manage AI systems that are not only effective and secure but also transparent, accountable, and firmly grounded in the protection of human rights, democratic values, and the public interest.

Achieving a meaningful alignment between innovation and ethical integrity requires more than surface-level compliance with technical standards. It demands the adoption of comprehensive, multidimensional governance frameworks that actively embed normative principles into the design, deployment, oversight, and evaluation of AI systems. In this sense, ethical AI cannot be reduced to a checklist or legal formality, but it must be recognized as a strategic cornerstone for establishing institutional legitimacy, promoting long-term sustainability, and cultivating trust within an increasingly interconnected and digitally mediated world.

Good Governance serves as the foundational pillar for ethics in digital transformation, requiring organizations to institutionalize ethical practices through comprehensive internal mechanisms and in their corporate strategy. These may include risk assessments, algorithmic audits, stress-testing protocols, privacy safeguards, and transparent decision-making processes, each of which plays a critical role in ensuring that AI systems operate reliably, fairly, and in alignment with human rights standards (Eitel-Porter, 2021). In an increasingly dynamic and uncertain regulatory landscape, effective governance must be iterative and adaptive, responding to both technological advancements and evolving societal expectations. It must also promote a culture of ethical vigilance, where continuous evaluation and improvement are the norm rather than the exception.

As AI systems grow more advanced, their internal logic becomes increasingly inaccessible to both users and regulators. This presents a significant barrier to accountability, trust, and informed decision-making. Explainability thus emerges as a vital ethical and practical requirement for enabling individuals to understand, challenge, and contextualize the outcomes produced by AI systems.

Advances in model interpretability, such as LIME (Local Interpretable Model-Agnostic Explanations) and SHAP (SHapley Additive exPlanations), offer promising pathways for making otherwise opaque models more transparent and accessible (Ribeiro et al., 2016). Explainability is not simply about technical transparency; it is a vehicle for ensuring procedural justice, informed consent, and user empowerment in AI-mediated decision environments.

So, Trust in AI is not inherent—it must be earned and continuously maintained through the demonstration of ethical conduct, transparent communication, and consistent stakeholder engagement. It is a socially constructed and context-sensitive phenomenon, shaped by how well organizations align their technological practices with societal values and expectations. In this regard, trust becomes a central enabler of technology acceptance, policy compliance, and institutional resilience, particularly in a world marked by growing public skepticism, rapid change, and technological disruption (Siau & Wang, 2018).

The centrality of ethics in digital transformation reflects an alignment with international regulatory trends, particularly the European Union's proposed AI Act (2021), which adopts a risk-based approach to AI regulation. This framework emphasizes key ethical principles including human agency, transparency, technical robustness, and accountability. Organizations that voluntarily embrace such comprehensive frameworks are not only better equipped to meet regulatory requirements but also position themselves as ethical pioneers in the evolving digital economy. This strategic positioning can yield a wide range of competitive advantages, from improved stakeholder trust and market differentiation to enhanced brand reputation and increased investor confidence (European Commission, 2021).

Digital technologies are not value-neutral. They embed the priorities, perspectives, and blind spots of their developers and deploying organizations. Consequently, the growing reliance on AI systems brings with it pressing ethical questions, about fairness, accountability, human autonomy, and environmental sustainability. These concerns are not hypothetical; they are playing out in real-world scenarios where biased algorithms influence loan approvals, opaque AI systems determine medical treatment pathways, and unregulated data harvesting challenges fundamental rights to privacy and consent.

As Saraiva and Silva (2024) argue, ethical leadership in the digital world is not about compliance alone, it is about strategic foresight and institutional responsibility.

Trust, therefore, emerges not only as a desired outcome but as a structural requirement for ethical digital governance. It is cultivated through transparency, inclusiveness, and consistent ethical oversight—elements that Saraiva (2023) underscores in her analysis of global regulatory frameworks and Portugal's national

AI strategies. In this context, ethics becomes the cornerstone that binds innovation with democratic legitimacy and human dignity.

Furthermore, a growing body of empirical research demonstrates that organizations perceived as ethical, transparent, and socially inclusive are more likely to attract socially responsible investment, retain high-quality talent, and build lasting relationships with customers and partners (Binns, 2018). These factors are increasingly recognized as essential drivers of sustainable innovation and organizational success. In this light, embedding ethics into the core of digital transformation is not a peripheral consideration, but a strategic imperative—one that enables organizations to navigate complexity, safeguard legitimacy, and foster systems of shared value in an AI-driven world.

Ultimately, ethics in the digital world is not an obstacle to innovation—it is its most essential foundation. By embedding ethical reflection, stakeholder engagement, and institutional integrity into AI systems, societies can unlock the transformative potential of digital technologies while safeguarding democratic values and human rights.

It is also crucial to recognize that digital transformation is not a purely technical undertaking. Rather, it is a deeply sociotechnical process that reconfigures institutional structures, labor markets, organizational cultures, and even public discourse. As such, ethical considerations must occupy a central role in shaping the strategic objectives and implementation practices of digital transformation. Ethical digital transformation compels us to ask not only what technology *can* do, but what it *should* do — and for whom. It demands constant reflection on how values are embedded within and influenced by digital systems.

Ultimately, as AI continues to reshape global economies and redefine the contours of institutional capability, organizations must recognize that ethical stewardship is not optional. It is essential. The future of digital transformation will belong not to those who adopt technology fastest, but to those who do so with the foresight, integrity, and inclusivity required to earn and sustain public trust.

AI AND SUSTAINABLE DEVELOPMENT

The role of people in the digital transformation process is foundational and cannot be overstated. As technological innovation accelerates across sectors and societies, there is a growing consensus that digital transformation must be guided by human-centered principles - principles that prioritize well-being, dignity, and equity over mere efficiency or profit maximization. A people-centered approach to the development and implementation of AI emphasizes the intrinsic value of human life and agency, ensuring that digital technologies function as tools for empowerment, not as instruments of control, surveillance, or social displacement (Zuboff, 2019).

This human-centric philosophy not only complements the ethical imperatives outlined in previous chapters but also forms a conceptual bridge to the discussion of sustainability. When AI is framed within a people-first paradigm, its alignment with sustainable development becomes clear. Sustainability, as defined in global frameworks such as the United Nations Sustainable Development Goals (SDGs), is rooted in a balance between economic growth, social inclusion, and environmental protection. Ethically governed AI is uniquely positioned to support this agenda, to provided its design and deployment are approached with intention, foresight, and responsibility (UN, 2015).

Organizational Sustainability

Organizational sustainability encompasses not only the long-term operational and financial viability of institutions but also their capacity to cultivate ethical work environments that uphold labor rights, support employee well-being, and contribute to social responsibility. AI systems can play a transformative role in enhancing organizational sustainability by increasing decision-making accuracy, reducing operational inefficiencies, and driving data-informed innovation. However, this potential must be pursued without compromising the dignity of workers or excluding vulnerable groups from participating in the digital transformation process (Schwab & Davis, 2020).

For example, AI technologies are increasingly being used to streamline internal functions such as human resource management, through predictive analytics for workforce planning, performance evaluation, and skills development. Yet, these tools must be implemented with concern. If poorly designed, they may unintentionally reinforce biases or undermine worker autonomy. Ensuring fairness, transparency, and explainability within these systems is vital, not only to mitigate harm but also to build trust among employees and other organizational stakeholders (Binns, 2018).

Moreover, organizations have an ethical responsibility to promote digital literacy among their employees. Equipping employees with the skills necessary to engage with emerging technologies is essential for innovation. This ensures that all individuals (not just those with technical expertise) can benefit from the AI-driven transformation (Eubanks, 2018).

Environmental Sustainability

AI and related digital technologies hold vast potential in addressing the pressing environmental challenges of our time. Through advanced data analytics, predictive modeling, and optimization capabilities, AI can be leveraged to support sustainable resource management and accelerate the transition toward circular, regenerative economic models.

For instance, machine learning algorithms can be applied to monitor and forecast ecological phenomena such as deforestation, biodiversity loss, and climate change. These tools provide environmental agencies and policymakers with actionable insights that enable a more efficient allocation of resources (Pappas et al., 2021).

In urban environments, AI systems can be used to improve energy efficiency, manage grids, optimize transportation, and monitor the air quality. Similarly, in agriculture, AI-powered image and acoustic recognition tools support real-time biodiversity monitoring and environmental protection (Rolnick et al., 2019).

Nevertheless, the environmental benefits of AI must be weighed against its own ecological costs. The development of large-scale AI models require substantial computational resources, leading to significant energy consumption and a lot of carbon emissions.

This paradox underscores the importance of transitioning toward "Green AI" - a research and design paradigm that emphasizes energy-efficient models, resource-aware architectures, and environmental responsibility (Schwartz et al., 2020).

Sustainable digital transformation must account for both the enabling and extractive impacts of AI on the planet.

Socio-Economic Sustainability

Socio-economic sustainability refers to the equitable distribution of the benefits of technological progress, the inclusion of all communities in digital development, and the promotion of social justice. AI, when developed and governed ethically, can be a powerful enabler of inclusive innovation, extending access to services in education, healthcare, finance, and employment for marginalized or underserved populations (Raji et al., 2020).

In education, adaptive AI platforms can personalize learning pathways based on individual needs, enhancing accessibility and equity in diverse learning environments.

In healthcare, AI diagnostic tools, predictive models, and medicine applications are improving care delivery, particularly in remote areas. Yet, these advancements must be accompanied by safeguards to protect sensitive data, ensure algorithmic fairness, and prevent the replication of existing inequalities (Veale & Binns, 2017).

Financial inclusion is another domain where AI should be concerned. Innovative credit scoring systems that use alternative data can provide remote populations with access to financial services. However, these systems require regular auditing to avoid perpetuating socio-economic biases (Barocas et al., 2019).

In short, socio-economic sustainability in AI joints on intentional design and governance. This involves embedding principles of equity, justice, and accountability from the earliest stages of development. It also requires robust mechanisms for bias detection, community engagement in co-design, and interdisciplinary collaboration to ensure that technological outcomes are aligned with public values and with the world needs.

Integrating AI into the SDG Framework

Aligning AI development with the Sustainable Development Goals (SDGs) enables organizations to ensure that their technological initiatives support inclusive, equitable, and sustainable global progress. A people-centered approach to AI not only addresses ethical and regulatory obligations but also responds to a broader societal vision rooted in human rights and collective well-being.

Some clear alignments between AI applications and the SDG agenda include:

- SDG 3 (Good Health and Well-Being): AI-driven diagnostic tools, predictive healthcare models, and medicine platforms.
- SDG 4 (Quality Education): Personalized learning technologies and digital accessibility tools.
- SDG 8 (Decent Work and Economic Growth): Workforce upskilling through AI-enhanced training programs and productivity tools.
- SDG 10 (Reduced Inequalities): AI systems designed for inclusive service delivery and equitable access to finance and resources.
- SDG 13 (Climate Action): Climate modeling, energy optimization, and environmental monitoring through AI.

By embedding people-centered principles into AI design and aligning with the SDG framework, organizations can transform ethical aspirations into measurable outcomes. This alignment not only enhances social legitimacy but also positions organizations as a contributors for sustainability efforts.

Adopting sustainability and a people-centered approach to AI development is both a moral imperative and a strategic advantage.

This will allows organizations to lead responsibly in an era of rapid digital transformation, ensuring that innovation serves as a catalyst for human flourishing, ecological stewardship, and equitable growth. In doing so, they help realize a vision of technological progress that is just, inclusive, and sustainable for all.

CASE STUDIES

The Ai.ethics Recognition Program

The Ai.ethics program, a joint initiative developed by the Portuguese Business Ethics Association (APEE) and the United Nations Association Portugal (UNA PT), serves as a leading example of how ethical principles can be operationalized within the governance of AI.

It is built upon a proactive vision for trustworthy AI, emphasizing that the rapid integration of AI into public and private sectors must be accompanied by a commitment to ethics, transparency, and accountability. The program seeks to raise awareness about the ethical dimensions of AI while providing practical tools and institutional mechanisms for ensuring that AI systems serve the common good.

Rooted in internationally recognized standards such as the *UNESCO Recommendation on the Ethics of Artificial Intelligence* and the *G7 Code of Conduct for Advanced AI Systems*, the Ai.ethics program offers a structured framework that enables organizations to validate and demonstrate their alignment with ethical best practices. Central to this framework are three recognition seals—Good Governance, Explainability, and Trust—each representing a core dimension of responsible AI. These seals function as both internal benchmarks and external signals of credibility, certifying that an organization's AI practices are ethically sound, socially responsible, and aligned with sustainable development goals.

The Ai.ethics seals address the complex landscape of ethical AI by distilling it into three actionable categories. These categories help organizations break down abstract ethical principles into practical governance objectives:

Good Governance

This seal is awarded to organizations that demonstrate robust internal governance mechanisms for the ethical development, deployment, and monitoring of AI systems. Good Governance entails the presence of clear policies, inclusive decision-making processes, and ongoing risk assessments. It incorporates algorithmic audits, human oversight, and a commitment to compliance with both national and international regulations (Fjeld et al., 2020). This foundational pillar ensures that AI systems are not only technically sound but also institutionally accountable.

Explainability

Recognizing the challenges posed by increasingly complex algorithmic systems, this seal focuses on ensuring that AI models are interpretable and transparent to relevant stakeholders. Explainability is particularly critical for high-risk applications in healthcare, finance, and criminal justice, where opaque decision-making can have serious consequences. AI systems should be designed to allow end-users and auditors to understand their functioning, limitations, and rationale. This is crucial for procedural fairness, regulatory compliance, and fostering informed consent (Gilpin et al., 2018).

Trust

This seal is granted to organizations that integrate transparency, risk prevention, and ethical foresight across the AI lifecycle. Trust is not a static achievement but an evolving outcome of sustained ethical performance. It reflects public perception, institutional integrity, and the perceived legitimacy of AI systems (Floridi & Cowls, 2019). Building trust requires not only technical safeguards but also effective communication, inclusive design practices, and responsiveness to stakeholder concerns.

Together, these three seals form a comprehensive model for ethical AI governance that aligns with the principles advocated by international institutions such as the European Commission, OECD, and UNESCO. Their interdependence ensures that organizations address ethical challenges holistically rather than piecemeal.

The certification process designed by Ai.ethics provides a replicable and transparent mechanism for embedding ethics into organizational practices. It includes five systematic stages:

Submission of the Application

Organizations initiate the process by submitting a formal application indicating their interest in ethical certification. This step includes a preliminary declaration of adherence to the principles defined by the Ai.ethics program.

Preliminary Acceptance

The application undergoes a screening process to determine eligibility. Criteria include the existence of deployed or in-development AI systems and a baseline commitment to ethical principles.

Self-Assessment

Approved applicants conduct an in-depth self-evaluation using a standardized questionnaire developed by the Ai.ethics committee. This tool is designed to assess current practices across dimensions such as governance, transparency, stakeholder engagement, and risk management.

External Audit

To ensure credibility and objectivity, an independent ethics audit is conducted. External evaluators verify the claims made during the self-assessment, conduct interviews with internal teams, and review relevant documentation.

Jury Deliberation and Final Decision

A multidisciplinary panel of experts—comprising ethicists, technologists, legal scholars, and industry practitioners—reviews the audit findings and determines whether the applicant qualifies for the seal(s). If successful, the organization receives certification and permission to display the Ai.ethics seal.

This rigorous and multidimensional process not only enhances the legitimacy of the recognition seals but also functions as a catalyst for organizational learning. It encourages continuous improvement and adaptive governance, thereby enabling organizations to stay ahead of ethical, regulatory, and societal expectations.

Strategic and Societal Impacts

The Ai.ethics recognition program creates value on multiple fronts. For organizations, it offers a clear pathway to ethical compliance and a competitive advantage in increasingly regulated markets. Ethical certification signals reliability to customers, investors, regulators, and the broader public, enhancing reputational capital and trustworthiness.

At the societal level, the program contributes to broader efforts to promote responsible AI. It encourages ethical literacy among stakeholders, supports public dialogue, and fosters cross-sectoral collaboration. Moreover, it complements existing European and global regulatory frameworks by providing an operational model that bridges the gap between high-level principles and organizational practice (European Commission, 2021).

The Ai.ethics program also anticipates future developments in the global AI governance landscape. By aligning with the Sustainable Development Goals (SDGs), it situates AI not as a neutral tool but as a transformative force that must be directed toward shared human values and global well-being. In doing so, it serves as a replicable model for other national and regional contexts seeking to institutionalize AI ethics in a pragmatic and scalable manner.

In a rapidly digitalizing world, ethical governance of AI is no longer optional—it is imperative. The Ai.ethics program exemplifies how high-level ethical principles can be translated into actionable standards that guide both public and private institutions. Through its recognition seals and rigorous certification process, the program provides a roadmap for operationalizing trust, accountability, and sustainability in AI.

By adopting such frameworks, organizations can not only future-proof their technologies but also contribute to a more just, transparent, and human-centered digital society. The Ai.ethics program thus represents a pioneering effort in the global movement toward ethical, responsible, and sustainable AI.

Ethical AI Applications in Healthcare

Case Study: Autonomous AI in Diabetic Retinopathy Screening

Diabetic retinopathy is a leading cause of blindness globally. Early detection through regular screening is crucial but often hindered by limited access to specialists. To address this, Digital Diagnostics developed LumineticsCore (formerly IDx-DR), an autonomous AI system designed to detect diabetic retinopathy. In 2018, it became the first autonomous AI system cleared by the U.S. Food and Drug Administration (FDA) to provide diagnostic decisions without human intervention.

Ethical Considerations:

- Patient Safety and Accuracy: The system underwent rigorous clinical trials to ensure its diagnostic accuracy matched or exceeded that of human specialists, prioritizing patient safety.
- Accountability: Clear guidelines were established delineating the responsibilities of the AI developers, healthcare providers, and the institutions implementing the technology, ensuring accountability in case of errors.arXiv+2The Guardian+2IFPMA+2
- Transparency: Efforts were made to make the AI's decision-making process interpretable to clinicians, fostering trust and understanding.

Case Study: AI-Powered Predictive Analytics in Elderly Care

Cera Care, a UK-based healthcare company, employs AI algorithms to analyze data collected during home visits to predict health deteriorations in elderly patients. Their Hospitalisation Predict-Prevent tool forecasts over 80% of health risks in advance, facilitating timely interventions and reducing hospital admissions by up to 70% (Tapper, 2024).

Ethical Considerations:

- Privacy and Consent: Cera ensures that patient data is handled with strict confidentiality, obtaining informed consent and complying with data protection regulations.
- Bias and Fairness: Continuous monitoring for biases in the AI system is conducted to prevent disparities in care recommendations across different demographic groups (Jha, 2025).
- Human Oversight: AI-generated alerts are reviewed by healthcare professionals before action, maintaining a balance between technological assistance and human judgment.

Ethical AI Applications in Smart Cities

Case Study: AI in Urban Mobility Management

Several European cities have implemented AI-driven systems to manage urban mobility, aiming to reduce congestion and environmental impact. For instance, Barcelona's use of AI to optimize traffic flow has led to significant improvements in air quality and commute times (Lungu, 2024).

Ethical Considerations:

- Surveillance and Privacy: Deploying AI systems in public spaces raises concerns about surveillance. Measures such as data anonymization and strict access controls are implemented to protect citizens' privacy.
- Public Participation: Engaging the community in the planning and implementation phases ensures that the AI solutions align with the needs and values of the residents.
- Transparency: Providing clear information about how data is collected, used, and stored fosters public trust and acceptance of AI initiatives.

Case Study: AI for Environmental Monitoring

In Singapore, AI technologies are utilized to monitor environmental parameters like air quality and waste management. These systems enable real-time responses to environmental issues, promoting sustainability (Olawade, 2024).

Ethical Considerations:

- Data Integrity: Ensuring the accuracy and reliability of environmental data is critical for informed decision-making and public safety.
- Equity: AI applications are designed to benefit all communities, preventing the exacerbation of existing inequalities.

- Regulatory Compliance: Adhering to environmental laws and standards is essential to maintain ethical and legal integrity.

The integration of AI into healthcare and smart cities offers transformative potential. However, it necessitates meticulous attention to ethical considerations, including patient safety, privacy, accountability, transparency, and fairness. The case studies highlighted demonstrate that with responsible design and implementation, AI can significantly enhance societal well-being while upholding ethical standards.

ETHICAL CHALLENGES IN AI IMPLEMENTATION

While AI holds transformative potential across sectors ranging from healthcare and education to logistics and climate science, its implementation introduces a host of complex ethical challenges that must be addressed by organizations. These challenges are not confined to technical concerns alone; they extend deeply into societal, legal, and ecological dimensions, implicating fundamental questions about fairness, accountability, transparency, and sustainability.

As AI systems increasingly mediate decision-making in high-stakes environments, from medical diagnoses to judicial assessments and financial evaluations, the urgency of developing ethical governance frameworks becomes paramount.

This section explores four key ethical challenges:

- transparency and explainability;
- bias and fairness;
- privacy and data protection;
- environmental impact

Each of which demands context-sensitive, interdisciplinary, and forward-looking strategies for mitigation and ethical alignment.

Transparency and Explainability

A foundational ethical concern in contemporary AI practice is the lack of transparency in algorithmic decision-making, particularly in systems powered by deep learning and other complex machine learning architectures. These systems often function as "black boxes", generating outputs without offering clear insights into the internal mechanisms that produced them (Burrell, 2016).

This opacity undermines the principles of accountability and due process, complicates oversight by regulators, and erodes trust among users and stakeholders.

Addressing this challenge requires a concerted investment in explainability frameworks - approaches that render AI outputs comprehensible to a range of users, from regulators to impacted individuals.

Model agnostic techniques such as LIME (Local Interpretable Model-Agnostic Explanations) and SHAP (SHapley Additive exPlanations) have gained traction as effective tools for generating interpretable explanations of model behavior (Ribeiro, 2016).

In high-risk domains such as healthcare, criminal justice, and finance, explainability is not merely a technical feature, it is a legal and ethical necessity that underpins informed consent, procedural fairness, and institutional legitimacy.

Moreover, the emerging paradigm of contextual explainability emphasizes that explanations should be tailored to users' needs, levels of expertise, and the context of application (Gilpin, 2018).

As regulatory bodies (including those shaping the EU's proposed AI Act) begin to mandate explainability in certain risk categories, organizations must proactively develop capabilities for ethically aligned, interpretable AI design and deployment.

Bias and Fairness

AI systems are not immune to the biases embedded in their training data or development pipelines. In fact, they often reflect and magnify existing social inequalities, leading to discriminatory outcomes in domains such as recruitment, lending, predictive policing, and public service allocation (Eubanks, 2018).

Bias can enter at multiple points in the AI lifecycle (during data collection, preprocessing, model selection, training, and even interpretation) and can disproportionately impact already marginalized communities.

Mitigating algorithmic bias requires a multifaceted and proactive approach. Organizations must incorporate practices such as regular algorithmic audits, fairness benchmarking, and participatory design processes that include input from affected stakeholders. Technical solutions, including adversarial debiasing, reweighing, and disparate impact analysis, can be employed to reduce inequities in model outcomes (Feldman et al., 2015).

However, these tools must be complemented by governance structures that prioritize inclusion and justice.

Importantly, fairness is not a universal or static concept. It varies across cultural, legal, and contextual dimensions. This variability calls for a pluralistic and context-aware ethical stance, in which affected communities play an active role in defining what constitutes fairness and in shaping AI systems to reflect shared values and localized norms.

Privacy and Data Protection

AI's effectiveness is largely derived from its capacity to analyze vast datasets, many of which contain sensitive personal information. This data dependency introduces substantial risks related to privacy, surveillance, autonomy, and data security. Without adequate safeguards, AI systems can be leveraged for invasive tracking, unauthorized profiling, and data exploitation, undermining individual freedoms and democratic accountability.

In response, organizations must comply with evolving data protection regulations, most notably the General Data Protection Regulation (GDPR) in the European Union, which protect principles such as data minimization, informed consent, purpose limitation, and the right to explanation (Voigt & Von dem Bussche, 2017). However, ethical AI design goes beyond regulatory compliance, requiring proactive privacy integration into system architecture.

Emerging techniques in privacy-preserving machine learning offer promising pathways. Federated learning, for example, enables decentralized model training without transferring raw data, thereby reducing exposure to privacy breaches. Differential privacy techniques introduce controlled statistical noise into datasets to obscure individual data points while preserving analytical integrity (Dwork et al., 2014). These methods reflect a growing commitment to privacy by design, an approach that embeds data ethics into the very foundation of AI development.

Environmental Impact

While often underrated in mainstream ethical discussions, the environmental footprint of AI technologies represents a critical concern. Training large-scale models, especially in natural language processing and computer vision, requires significant computational resources. These processes contribute substantially to energy consumption and to carbon emissions. One study found that developing a single deep learning model can emit as much CO_2 as five cars over their entire lifespans (Strubell et al., 2019).

To address these ecological costs, the movement toward "Green AI" advocates for the creation of more energy-efficient algorithms, reduced computational complexity, and the use of renewable energy sources in data center operations. Techniques such as model pruning, quantization, and knowledge distillation help reduce the energy demands of models without sacrificing performance (Schwartz, 2020).

Incorporating sustainability metrics into AI evaluation frameworks is essential for ensuring that environmental considerations are placed alongside performance, fairness, and safety.

Organizations should adopt sustainability AI development practices, assessing trade-offs not just in technical terms but in relation to climate impact and resource consumption. As the scale of AI infrastructure grows, environmental ethics must become a core consideration in responsible innovation.

In sum, the ethical deployment of AI requires a multidimensional governance approach that addresses transparency, fairness, privacy, and sustainability in a balanced manner. These challenges are not isolated, they intersect with one and with another, shaping the broader social, legal, and ecological ecosystem in which AI operates.

Organizations that engage with these interdependencies will be better positioned to deal with the complexities of ethical AI, build public trust, and ensure that technological progress genuinely contributes to inclusive, accountable, and sustainable futures.

In the table below, we see a sum up of the ethical challenges in AI implementation.

Table 1. Ethical challenges in AI implementation

ETHICAL CHALLENGE	KEY RISKS	MITIGATION STRATEGIES
Transparency & Explainability	Opaque "black-box" models reduce trust and accountability	Use LIME, SHAP, contextual explainability
Bias & Fairness	Algorithmic discrimination reinforces societal inequalities	Conduct audits, apply fairness-aware algorithms
Privacy & Data Protection	Inadequate safeguards risk data breaches and inequalitys	Adopt GDPR, use federated learning and differential
Environmental Impact	High computational demand increases carboon footprints	Apply Green AI methods, use different architectures

Source: Own elaboration

This table outlines the four major ethical challenges in AI implementation—transparency and explainability, bias and fairness, privacy and data protection, and environmental impact presented in this point.

Each challenge is associated with specific risks, such as reduced trust due to opaque models, algorithmic discrimination, data breaches, and high carbon emissions. To mitigate these risks, the table recommends strategies including interpretability tools (e.g., LIME, SHAP), fairness audits, compliance with data protection laws (e.g., GDPR), privacy-preserving techniques (e.g., federated learning, differential privacy), and environmentally sustainable practices through Green AI and energy-efficient model architectures.

BUILDING TRUST THROUGH GOVERNANCE AND COLLABORATION

Trust constitutes a foundational pillar for the ethical and sustainable integration of AI into society. As AI systems increasingly mediate decisions in critical areas such as healthcare, justice, finance, and education, the presence or absence of trust significantly influences public acceptance, policy legitimacy, and long-term societal impact. Trust in AI is not merely an abstract aspiration or a static condition, it is a tangible and dynamic outcome, continually shaped by the ethical quality of design choices, the transparency of organizational practices, and the inclusivity of governance frameworks (Floridi & Cowls, 2019).

Figure 1. Business organizations reasons for adopting artificial intelligence worldwide, as of 2017

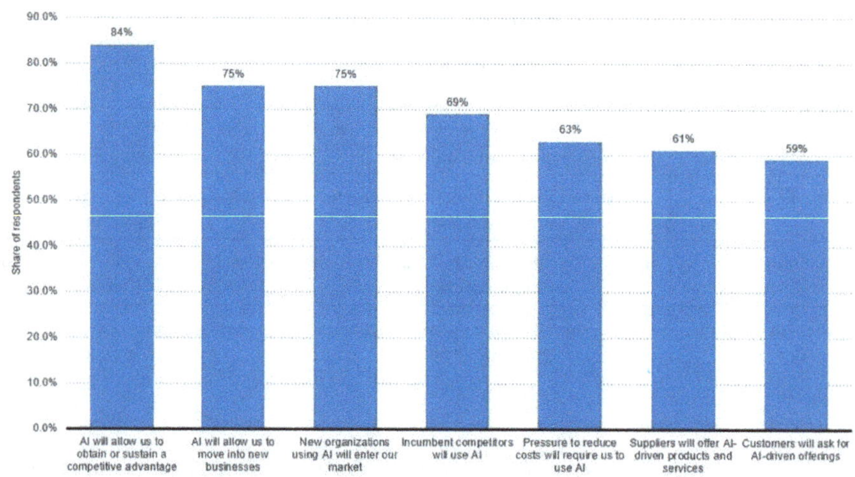

(Statista, 2017)

As we can see in the graph above, the main reason for business organizations to adopt AI is because they believe that AI will allow them to obtain or sustain a competitive advantage. 84% of the companies believe that this technology system is a real competitive vantage for the business, and also will help them to "move into new businesses" (75%) or to help "new organizations to enter their market" (also 75%). Furthermore, 69% of the companies believe that "incumbent competitors will use AI in their organizational strategie and that this technology will help them to reduce costs (63%). For last, "only" 59% of the business organizations believe that customers will ask for AI-driven offerings and a little bit above that the "suppliers" will offer AI-driven products and services (61%). This graph enhances the importance of trust in AI.

Building trust in AI demands more than technical reliability or compliance with regulations. It requires a comprehensive, a multidimensional strategy that integrates ethical reflection, institutional accountability, and continuous stakeholder engagement. Governance structures must be designed to ensure ethical oversight and risk mitigation; transparency must be embedded to make AI systems understandable and accountable; and collaboration must involve a diverse range of stakeholders, including affected communities, experts, and regulators.

These three pillars—governance, transparency, and collaboration—are not alone elements. They are mutually reinforcing, working together to enhance the legitimacy, reliability, and societal alignment of AI technologies.

When implemented in concert, they contribute to the formation of trustworthy AI systems that respect human dignity, foster public confidence, and support long-term, inclusive digital transformation.

Also, that trust in AI is notably higher in emerging economies such as India and China, while more developed nations exhibit greater skepticism. These variations may stem from differing cultural attitudes towards technology, levels of public awareness, and the extent of AI integration into daily life (Statista, 2022).

Figure 2. In AI we trust

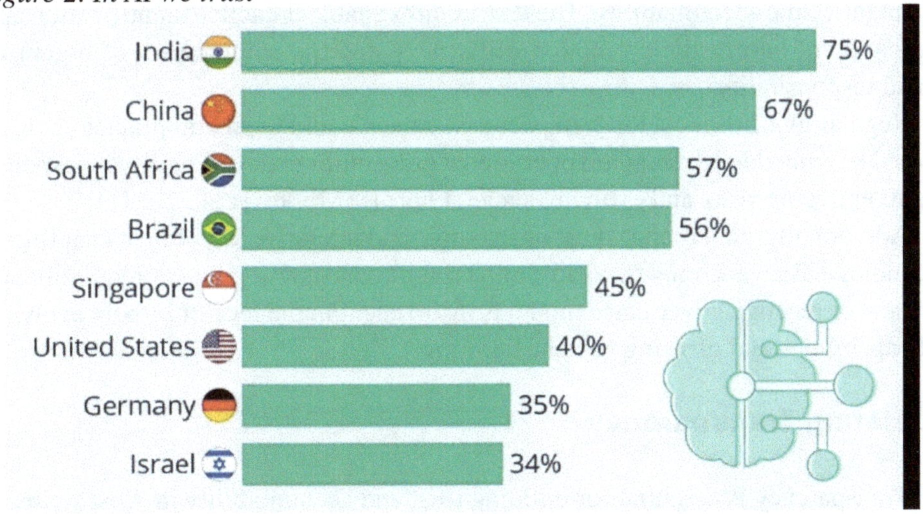

In the graph above, we see a pertinent example is the global survey conducted by KPMG International, which highlights varying levels of trust in AI across different countries.

As we can see, India (75%) and China (67%) lead in public trust, followed by South Africa (57%) and Brazil (56%), indicating a generally higher openness toward AI in emerging economies.

In contrast, developed countries like the United States (40%), Germany (35%), and Israel (34%) exhibit more cautious attitudes towards trust.

This divergence suggests that public trust in AI is influenced not only by exposure to and dependence on digital technologies but also by cultural, economic, and regulatory factors.

In this point, we´re going to try to understand in which ways we can build trust through governance and collaboration, where steps like "adopting effective governance frameworks", "fostering transparency", "engaging stakeholders through collaboration" and "enroll with collaborative platforms" are essential and crucial.

Adopting Effective Governance Frameworks

The cornerstone of trustworthy AI is the implementation of strong, adaptable governance frameworks that span the entire AI lifecycle. From data acquisition and model training to deployment, monitoring, and continuous improvement. Effective governance ensures that AI systems operate in alignment with ethical principles, legal mandates, and public expectations.

Such frameworks must include mechanisms for ethical oversight, risk assessment, and algorithmic accountability. These structures enable proactive identification and mitigation of harms, the promotion of fairness, and the enforcement of organizational responsibility.

Regular algorithmic audits, impact assessments, and legal compliance reviews should be embedded as standard operational procedures to ensure agility in responding to emerging risks and evolving societal norms (Morley et al., 2021).

Additionally, governance must be dynamic and interative, capable of adapting to technological advancements, socio-political shifts, and new regulatory requirements. A static or reactive governance model is insufficient in the face of rapidly evolving AI capabilities and growing societal scrutiny.

Fostering Transparency

Transparency is essential for building trust and accountability in AI systems. It enables stakeholders (from users and regulators to affected individuals) to understand how AI models function, what data they use, and how decisions are made.

In high-stakes applications, this is critical for safeguarding rights, maintaining fairness, and ensuring institutional accountability.

Organizational transparency involves both technical and procedural dimensions. On the technical side, it includes making AI models more interpretable, documenting data sources, disclosing algorithmic logic, and publishing performance metrics where appropriate. Procedurally, it encompasses open communication about decision-making processes, the rationale behind system outputs, and the known limitations or uncertainties of AI predictions (Ananny & Crawford, 2018).

Emerging legal frameworks, such as the European Union's Artificial Intelligence Act (2021), are now codifying transparency as a legal obligation, particularly for high-risk systems.

This regulatory standards highlights that transparency is not only an ethical preference but a mandatory aspect of responsible AI.

Moreover, it facilitates informed consent, regulatory compliance, and human oversight, reinforcing the public trust.

Engaging Stakeholders through Collaboration

Stakeholder engagement is vital to the ethical development and deployment of AI. While technical robustness is critical, social legitimacy depends on the inclusion of diverse voices in the AI development process. Collaborating with academic institutions, industry experts, civil society organizations, and policymakers provides a broader ethical lens and fosters democratic accountability (Crawford & Calo, 2016).

Such collaboration allows organizations to anticipate and address potential risks, including social biases, discriminatory impacts, and unintended consequences. Participatory mechanisms such as workshops, consultations, and stakeholder working groups have emerged as the best practices for embedding the user perspectives and the ethical values into AI systems (Voelsen, 2021).

This inclusive approach strengthens procedural justice, ensuring that those most affected by AI systems have a voice in their development. It also enhances the credibility of AI governance frameworks by demonstrating a commitment to openness, fairness, and responsiveness.

The Role Collaboratives Platforms

In the pursuit of ethical, trustworthy, and sustainable AI, collaborative platforms play a critical role in bridging the gap between high-level ethical principles and their concrete, operational implementation. As AI systems grow increasingly complex, opaque, and influential, no single actor (be it a company, government, or academic institution) can effectively address the ethical, legal, and social implications of AI in isolation.

The governance of AI must therefore be treated as a shared societal responsibility, requiring collective action, mutual learning, and inclusive dialogue across sectors and disciplines.

Collaborative platforms function as multi-stakeholder ecosystems, bringing together actors from public institutions, private industry, academia, civil society, and regulatory bodies. These platforms facilitate critical dialogue, promote interdisciplinary cooperation, and create opportunities for the co-creation of ethical guidelines, governance mechanisms, and technical standards.

By integrating expertise from different domains (like technological, legal, social, and ethical), they help ensure that AI systems are not only technically sound but also socially aligned and democratically accountable.

In addition to fostering knowledge exchange, policy experimentation, and capacity building, collaborative platforms provide a neutral space for surfacing emerging risks, sharing best practices, and aligning governance approaches with both global frameworks and local priorities.

Through working groups, roundtables, certification schemes, public consultations, and open-access tools, these platforms help stakeholders translate broad ethical aspirations into actionable and context-sensitive solutions.

A leading example of this approach, in Portugal, is the Ai.ethics platform, that we´ve talked previous in this chapter.

This initiative exemplifies how a localized, yet globally informed, collaborative framework can promote ethical digital transformation. Through its system of recognition seals (Good Governance, Explainability, and Trust), Ai.ethics supports organizations in evaluating their ethical AI practices. It also acts as a hub for interdisciplinary dialogue, providing a space for technical experts, policymakers, and civil society to converge and co-develop standards aligned with international norms such as those of UNESCO, the OECD, and the European Commission.

At the international level, several other collaborative initiatives further reinforce this ecosystem of responsible AI development:

- The OECD AI Policy Observatory provides a platform for data sharing, policy analysis, and international benchmarking, helping governments and stakeholders align AI policies with the OECD's Principles on AI;
- The Partnership on AI (PAI) brings together major tech companies, academic institutions, and non-profits to explore critical issues such as algorithmic fairness, labor impacts, and responsible AI deployment. PAI emphasizes transparency and inclusive participation, fostering multi-sectoral collaboration on global AI challenges;

- The AI Commons initiative seeks to democratize AI by providing open access to tools, data, and resources that support socially beneficial applications. It emphasizes cross-border cooperation and aligns with the United Nations Sustainable Development Goals (SDGs);
- The Global Partnership on Artificial Intelligence (GPAI), supported by the OECD and backed by member governments, is a multilateral initiative aimed at bridging the gap between theory and practice in AI governance. GPAI supports research and applied projects on responsible AI, data governance, innovation, and the future of work.

These platforms, among others, illustrate that ethical AI governance cannot be siloed within national boundaries or individual institutions.

Instead, it must emerge from collaborative networks that are inclusive, transparent, and adaptable. Such platforms provide the infrastructure for sustainable governance ecosystems that evolve with technological change while remaining grounded in human rights, democratic values, and societal needs.

So, collaborative platforms are essential enablers of trustworthy AI. They foster the conditions under which shared norms can be defined, contested, and refined through inclusive engagement. As AI continues to reshape the global digital landscape, the role of these platforms will be central in ensuring that innovation is not only cutting-edge but also ethically resilient, socially beneficial, and globally equitable.

Also, building trust in AI systems is neither a one-time effort nor the responsibility of a single actor. It requires robust governance structures, transparent processes, and active the above offer a compelling blueprint for how multi-stakeholder engagement can drive responsible innovation and ensure that AI technologies serve the public good. As AI becomes more deeply embedded in societal infrastructure, this collaborative, ethically grounded approach will be indispensable for ensuring that its benefits are broadly shared and its risks are responsibly managed.

CONCLUSION

In the context of accelerating digital transformation and growing societal reliance on AI, trust has emerged as a central pillar of ethical, sustainable, and inclusive technological development.

This chapter has argued that trust in AI is neither incidental nor automatic, it is a deliberate and dynamic outcome, shaped through the ongoing interplay of governance, transparency, and collaboration.

Far from being an abstract aspiration, trust represents the collective confidence that AI systems will act in ways that are aligned with public values, human rights, and long-term societal goals.

Establishing and maintaining this trust requires an integrated approach. First, robust governance frameworks are essential to ensure ethical integrity across the entire AI lifecycle (from data acquisition and model design to deployment and post-deployment monitoring).

Second, transparency must be embedded into both technical systems and institutional practices, enabling accountability, informed consent, and meaningful oversight.

Third, stakeholder engagement (particularly through collaborative platforms) must be institutionalized to reflect diverse perspectives, prevent harm, and co-create socially legitimate solutions.

Importantly, the ethical governance of AI must not be perceived as a constraint on innovation, but rather as an enabler of sustainable progress.

Addressing critical risks such as algorithmic opacity, systemic bias, data exploitation, and environmental degradation requires anticipatory, adaptive, and transparent governance mechanisms.

Platforms like Ai.ethics help operationalize these mechanisms through tools such as independent audits, participatory assessments, and value-based certification systems.

Real-world applications illustrate that ethics on AI is not only feasible but highly impactful. From diagnostic tools in healthcare and predictive analytics in elderly care to AI systems supporting urban sustainability and environmental monitoring, ethically grounded AI is already delivering measurable societal value. These examples reaffirm that ethics is not just theoretical - it is a practical imperative for a responsible innovation.

Crucially, the chapter has emphasized that ethical AI is fundamentally people-centered.

It is grounded in the idea that digital technologies should augment human capabilities, promote social justice, and support ecological resilience. This perspective aligns seamlessly with the objectives of the United Nations Sustainable Development Goals (SDGs), reinforcing the notion that AI, when ethically designed and governed, can contribute meaningfully to global development and intergenerational equity.

As international institutions (including the European Commission, OECD, and UNESCO) continue to refine the ethical and legal architecture for AI, organizations are increasingly called upon to move from reactive compliance to proactive ethical leadership.

In this landscape, ethical excellence is becoming a strategic differentiator, by enhancing institutional credibility, stakeholder trust, long-term adaptability, and market competitiveness in an ever-evolving global ecosystem.

Moreover, some empirical studies can consistently show us that organizations perceived as ethical, transparent, and socially responsible are more likely to attract investment, retain top talent, and foster innovation-friendly cultures.

In this sense, ethical AI is not only a social good but a core driver of resilience and innovation in the digital age.

Ultimately, the insights presented throughout this chapter promote for a paradigm shift in how digital transformation can be implemented.

Rather than focusing narrowly on speed, efficiency, or profit maximization, organizations must embrace a broader vision: one in which technological advancement is guided by an ethical purpose.

Ethics should not be seen as a brake or a stop on progress but as the very foundation upon which inclusive, equitable, and sustainable futures are built.

In sum, achieving sustainable digital transformation is not solely a technological challenge; it is an ethical responsibility. Only through the careful, intentional integration of ethics into every stage of the innovation process can we ensure AI technologies fulfill their highest potential: to advance human flourishing, social equity, and global sustainability.

Furthermore, as highlighted by Rodrigues and Morais (2021), integrating sustainability into corporate reporting through frameworks like Integrated Reporting (<IR>) enhances organizational transparency and accountability, fostering greater stakeholder trust.

Similarly, Saraiva (2023) emphasizes the importance of ethical considerations in e-commerce, advocating for consumer-centric models that prioritize privacy and fairness. These perspectives underscore the necessity of embedding ethical principles across all technological domains to achieve truly sustainable digital transformation.

By embedding principles of transparency, accountability, and human dignity into the core of AI systems, and by supporting institutional mechanisms like collaborative platforms, we can shape digital ecosystems that are not only intelligent but also just. We presented some programs and platforms that can offer us a tangible and probably some adaptable model for navigating this path, a path that can reaffirm the potential of AI to serve humanity, enhance democratic values, and protect the planet.

In sum, achieving sustainable digital transformation is not solely a technological challenge, it is an ethical responsibility.

And it is only through the careful, intentional integration of ethics into every stage of the innovation process that we can ensure AI technologies fulfill their highest potential: to advance human flourishing, social equity, and global sustainability.

Above, we have a figure representing the chapter as an image. As we can see, is a cycle, where the digital transformation is accelerated by the AI, that must be guided by Ethics, which should be operationalized through (1) Good Governance, (2) Explainability, (3) Trust. Here, this three concepts should be defined by (4)

Transparency, (5) Accountability, (6) Stakeholder Inclusion, which, in this case, should be embedded in frameworks like (7) UNESCO Recommendation, (8) EU AI Act, (9) International Standards, enabling:

1 - Responsible Innovation;
2 – And People-Centered Design;
3 – With Digital Transformation.

Figure 3. Visual synthesis of the chapter

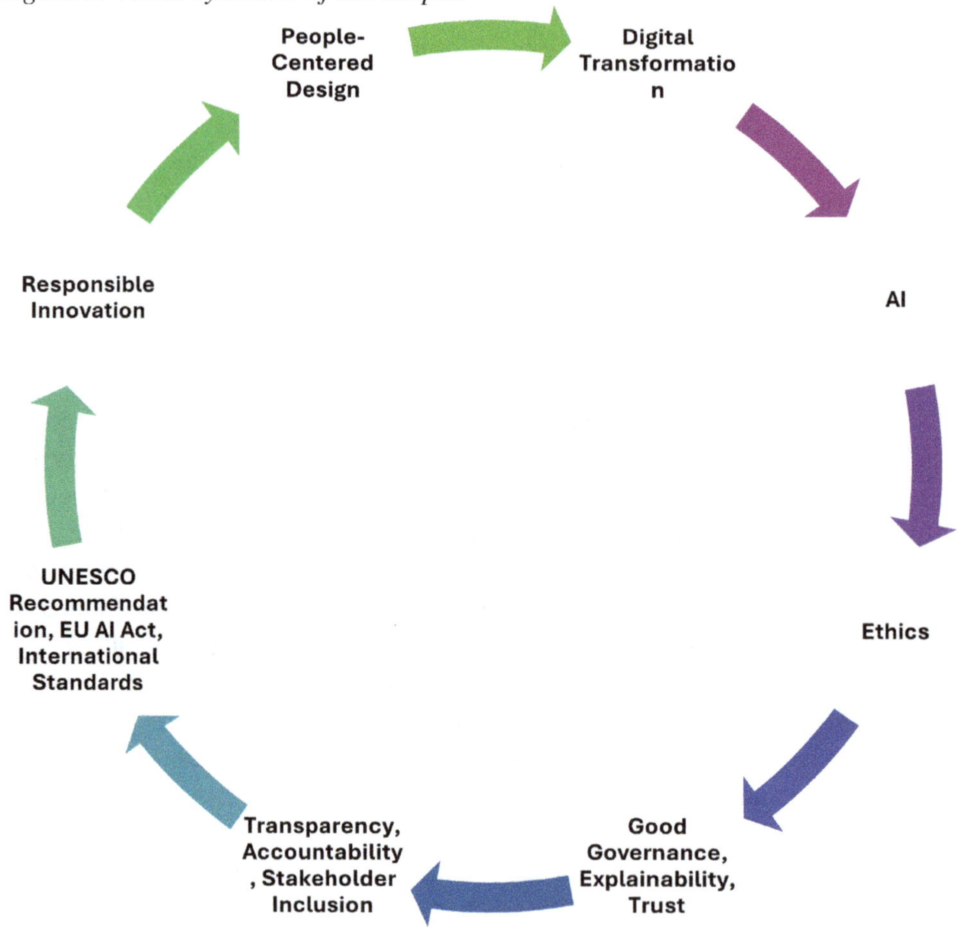

This circular model reinforces the idea that ethical AI is not a linear or one-time achievement—it is an ongoing, iterative process that requires vigilance, flexibility, and continuous stakeholder engagement. By cycling through these stages, organizations can foster AI systems that are more just, sustainable, and trusted by society. This model also aligns well with the values discussed in this chapter.

REFERENCES

Agrawal, A., Gans, J., & Goldfarb, A. (2019). The Economics of Artificial Intelligence: An Agenda. University of Chicago Press. Available in: https://press.uchicago.edu/ucp/books/book/chicago/E/bo35780726.html

Ananny, M., & Crawford, K. (2018). Seeing without knowing: Limitations of the transparency ideal and its application to algorithmic accountability. New Media & Society, 20(3), 973–989. Available in: https://journals.sagepub.com/doi/10.1177/1461444816676645

Barocas, S., Hardt, M., & Narayanan, A. (2019). Fairness and Machine Learning: Limitations and Opportunities. Available in: https://fairmlbook.org

Binns, R. (2018). Fairness in machine learning: Lessons from political philosophy. Proceedings of the 2018 Conference on Fairness, Accountability, and Transparency. Available in: https://proceedings.mlr.press/v81/binns18a.html

Brynjolfsson, E., & McAfee, A. (2017). The Second Machine Age: Work, Progress, and Prosperity in a Time of Brilliant Technologies. W. W. Norton & Company. Available in: https://wwnorton.com/books/the-second-machine-age/

Burrell, J. (2016). How the machine 'thinks': Understanding opacity in machine learning algorithms. Big Data & Society, 3(1). Available in: https://journals.sagepub.com/doi/abs/10.1177/2053951715622512?utm_source=chatgpt.com

Crawford, K., & Calo, R. (2016). There is a blind spot in AI research. Nature, 538(7625), 311-313. DOI: . Available in: https://www.nature.com/articles/538311aDOI: 10.1038/538311a

Dwork, C., Roth, A., ... (2014). The algorithmic foundations of differential privacy. Foundations and Trends® in Theoretical Computer Science, 9(3–4), 211–407. DOI: . Available in: https://www.nowpublishers.com/article/Details/TCS-042DOI: 10.1561/0400000042

Eubanks, V. (2018). Automating Inequality: How High-Tech Tools Profile, Police, and Punish the Poor. St. Martin's Press. Available in: https://us.macmillan.com/books/9781250074317/automatinginequality

European Commission. (2021). Proposal for a Regulation laying down harmonised rules on artificial intelligence (Artificial Intelligence Act). Available in: https://digital-strategy.ec.europa.eu/en/library/proposal-regulation-laying-down-harmonised-rules-artificial-intelligence

Feldman, M., Friedler, S. A., Moeller, J., Scheidegger, C., & Venkatasubramanian, S. (2015). Certifying and removing disparate impact. Proceedings of the 21st ACM SIGKDD International Conference on Knowledge Discovery and Data Mining. DOI: . Available in: https://dl.acm.org/doi/10.1145/2783258.2783311DOI: 10.1145/2783258.2783311

Fjeld, J., Achten, N., Hilligoss, H., Nagy, A. C., & Srikumar, M. (2020). *Principled artificial intelligence: Mapping consensus in ethical and rights-based approaches to principles for Artificial Intelligence.* Berkman Klein Center Research Publication.

Floridi, L., & Cowls, J. (2019). A unified framework of five principles for Artificial Intelligence in society. *Harvard Data Science Review, 1*(1). Advance online publication. DOI: 10.1162/99608f92.8cd550d1

Gilpin, L. H., Bau, D., Zoran, D., Pan, Y., Bajwa, A., & Explainable Artificial Intelligence team. (2018). Explaining explanations: An overview of interpretability of machine learning. arXiv preprint arXiv:1806.00069.

Hagendorff, T. (2020). The Ethics of Artificial Intelligence Ethics: An Evaluation of Guidelines. *Minds and Machines, 30*(1), 99–120.

Jobin, A., Ienca, M., & Vayena, E. (2019). The global landscape of Artificial Intelligence ethics guidelines. *Nature Machine Intelligence, 1*(9), 389–399. DOI: 10.1038/s42256-019-0088-2

Morley, J., Floridi, L., Kinsey, L., & Elhalal, A. (2021). From what to how: An initial review of publicly available Artificial Intelligence ethics tools, methods and research to translate principles into practices. *Science and Engineering Ethics, 27*(4). Advance online publication. DOI: 10.1007/s11948-019-00165-5 PMID: 31828533

Pappas, I. O., Mikalef, P., Giannakos, M. N., Krogstie, J., & Lekakos, G. (2021). Big data and business analytics ecosystems: Paving the way towards digital transformation and sustainable societies. *Information Systems and e-Business Management, 19*(4), 885–902. 10.1007-s10257-018-0377-z

Raji, I. D., Gebru, T., Mitchell, M., Buolamwini, J., Lee, J., & Denton, E. (2020). Saving face: Investigating the ethical concerns of facial recognition auditing. *Proceedings of the AAAI/ACM Conference on Artificial Intelligence, Ethics, and Society.* DOI: DOI: 10.1145/3375627.3375820

Ribeiro, M. T., Singh, S., & Guestrin, C. (2016). Why should I trust you? Explaining the predictions of any classifier. *Proceedings of the 22nd ACM SIGKDD International Conference on Knowledge Discovery and Data Mining.* DOI: DOI: 10.1145/2939672.2939778

Rodrigues, M. A. B., & Morais, A. I. (2021). How to Challenge University Students to Work on Integrated Reporting and Integrated Reporting Assurance. *Sustainability*, *13*(19), 10761. DOI: 10.3390/su131910761

Rolnick, D., Donti, P. L., Kaack, L. H., ... (2019). Tackling Climate Change with Machine Learning. arXiv preprint arXiv:1906.05433. Available in: https://arxiv .org/abs/1906.05433

Saraiva, A. (2023). Ethics and Responsibility in Artificial Intelligence: A Global Perspective and Portugal's AI Governance. 186. Call for AI – GEE Papers. GOV. Available in: https://www.gee.gov.pt/pt/estudos-eseminarios/gee-papers-category/ 33900-ethics-and-responsibility-in-artificial-intelligence-a-global-perspectiveand -portugal-s-ai-governance

Saraiva, A., & Silva, M. (2024). Governance and Transparency: Ethical Leadership in the information age. In Machado, A., Sousa, M., Pequeira, A., Brambila, A., & Alavaro, A. (Eds.), *Environmental, Social And Governance And Digital Transformation In Organizations*. Springer.

Schwab, K., & Davis, N. (2020). *Shaping the Future of the Fourth Industrial Revolution*. Currency. DOI.

Schwartz, R., Dodge, J., Smith, N. A., & Etzioni, O. (2020). Green Artificial Intelligence. *Communications of the ACM*, *63*(12), 54–63. DOI: 10.1145/3381831

Siau, K., & Wang, W. (2018). Building trust in artificial intelligence, machine learning, and robotics. Cutter Business Technology Journal, 31(2), 47–53. Available in: https://www.cutter.com/article/building-trust-artificial-intelligence-machine -learning-and-robotics-498981

Strubell, E., Ganesh, A., & McCallum, A. (2019). Energy and policy considerations for deep learning in NLP. *Proceedings of the 57th Annual Meeting of the Association for Computational Linguistics*. DOI: DOI: 10.18653/v1/P19-1355

UNESCO. (2021). Recommendation on the Ethics of Artificial Intelligence. Available in: https://unesdoc.unesco.org/ark:/48223/pf0000380455

United Nations (UN). (2015). Transforming our world: The 2030 Agenda for Sustainable Development. Available in: https://sdgs.un.org/2030agenda

Veale, M., & Binns, R. (2017). Fairer machine learning in the real world: Mitigating discrimination without collecting sensitive data. *Big Data & Society*, *4*(2). Advance online publication. DOI: 10.1177/2053951717743530

Voelsen, D. (2021). Democracy and Digital Technology. German Institute for International and Security Affairs. Available in: https://www.swp-berlin.org/10.18449/2021RP03/

Voigt, P., & Von dem Bussche, A. (2017). *The EU General Data Protection Regulation (GDPR): A Practical Guide*. Springer., DOI: 10.1007/978-3-319-57959-7

Zuboff, S. (2019). *The Age of Surveillance Capitalism: The Fight for a Human Future at the New Frontier of Power*. PublicAffairs.

Chapter 5
Standardisation for Governance and Ethical Use of Artificial Intelligence and Digital Technology in Organizations

Juan-Pablo Peñarrubia Carrión
https://orcid.org/0009-0005-1707-2929
Universidad de Valencia, Spain

ABSTRACT

This chapter explains the role and value of standardisation for governance and ethical use of artificial intelligence and information technologies in organizations. This aproach is based on complementarity between legal regulation and standardisation, providing a coherent and viable scenario for governance and ethical use in practice at the organizational level. The main international models of AI governance and ethics are presented: United States of America, China and European Union. To understand both their differences and the leading role that standardization plays in all of them. It addresses how organizations can make AI governance viable in an integrated way with the rest of corporate management systems, and also how to materialize an applied ethics of AI in the company through practical tools and standards. Finally, some proposals are made to improve the usefulness and effectiveness of standardization for governance and the responsible and people-centered use of information technologies in organizations.

DOI: 10.4018/979-8-3373-0385-7.ch005

INTRODUCTION

In a normative society such as ours, a society of law, all human activity is essentially governed by a combination of legal regulation and self-regulation (Peñarrubia, 2022b).

Legal regulation consists of normative regulation through laws that affect a certain activity; both general purpose laws (which typify modes, administrative requirements, potential crimes, etc.), and specific laws directly oriented to said activity or the sector in which it is framed. The legal regulation is mandatory.

Self-regulation is deployed in several dimensions, in particular: professional, sectoral and ethical. Dimensions that, although dependent and intersecting with each other, have an entity in themselves and allow complementary developments, particularly in the field of standardization.

Professional self-regulation is materialized especially through: a) the creation of professional bodies; b) standardization through formal standards: both recognized international standards (CEN, ISO, IEEE...), and professional standards (chartered professional bodies standards); c) professional ethics, in its dual deontological and ethical aspects.

Sectoral self-regulation is that relating to the ecosystem of all companies and professionals in a given field of activity. It is materialized in particular through: a) the creation of sectoral organizations; b) standardization through formal standards, quality seals, certifications of conformity, etc.; c) also sectoral ethics: business ethics, professional ethics...

Ethics materializes pervasive self-regulation and also acts as an integrator of the set of conditioning elements of a given activity, both legal regulation and self-regulation. Ethics is understood as its general conception, and of a non-normative nature: professional, business, public, political, citizen Including instruments and mechanisms of applied ethics, such as Ethics Committees, mechanisms for reporting potential ethical conflicts, ethical dialogue (including customers, consumers, citizens...), etc.

On the other hand, self-regulation could be seen as essentially constituted: a) on the one hand normative, but not mandatory from the point of view of law. That is, regulations of voluntary assumption for whatever reasons: search for excellence, market interests, sector, technological compatibility, corporate culture, image... This part includes: general standardisation rules, professional or business standards, codes of ethics, guidelines and procedures of professional bodies, etc. b) and on the other hand, ethics, also of a voluntary nature: ethical guidelines, corporate values, ethical committees, etc. and in general all non-deontological and normative ethics. There is another alternative view in which ethics can be considered globally and separated from self-regulation. That is, considering Ethics as a third element along with Legal Regulations and Self-Regulation. In this case, Ethics would also include codes of ethics or any other ethical element of a normative nature. In any case, they are alternative maps of the same territory.

Communicating Vessels

It is important to understand that the aforementioned elements (legal regulation, self-regulation and ethics) are not silos separated from each other, but rather are communicating vessels (Peñarrubia, 2022b). For example, a certain practice may not be legally obligatory but it may be part of professional ethics and deontology and over time its proven value becomes a legal requirement. This would be the case of informed consent in the field of health. Also in the field of self-regulation through standardization in the technological field, with standards initially assumed by professionals and specialized companies and over time considered legal requirements. This has happened on multiple occasions, especially in the field of engineering and building.

Standardization and Competitiveness

Traditionally, the first value sought in standardization by companies has been their contribution to competitiveness. Firstly, in emerging activities there are no clear technical frameworks for their materialisation in the economic and social sphere. In addition, in fully consolidated activities, standardization, especially international standardization, is a business mechanism to show excellence and quality against its competitors. In other words, it is another element of competitiveness, both to demonstrate excellent operation at a technical level, and to provide a high-quality image to potential customers and society.

Standardization is an essential mechanism in professional culture, not only in the field of professional excellence, but also in the field of deontology and professional ethics. It is common for professional bodies to establish standards that are included as part of their professional deontology. That is, not necessarily recognized or international standards, but even standards established at the regional level, or in relation to a certain very specific activity in the professional field. An archetypal case is expert or forensic actions, which are usually part of the deontology of professional associations due to their use in the judicial field and their consequent impact on the general interest.

In addition, standardisation at the sectoral level helps professionals and companies to agree on technical aspects (to facilitate the compatibility of devices, products, installations, etc.), or to agree on essential aspects (requirements) such as mechanisms for ensuring basic criteria of technical effectiveness and reliability (indirectly quality). In short, standardisation is a mechanism for boosting the sectors of activity by allowing companies and professionals to work on the same activities and products, ensuring the final quality and the ability to maintain the results regardless of the professionals or companies that execute them. Last but not least, standardization is an efficiency mechanism because it provides companies and professionals with common methodologies and criteria to address multiple situations or needs, avoiding that each one has to reinvent the wheel. With the consequent saving of time and resources, and as if that were not enough, ensuring that the measures adopted are recognised and shared in the associated sector of activity.

Similarly, standardization is especially relevant in emerging or innovative business activities. Especially at the beginning of the journey in new sectors of activity, standardization serves to reduce risks of technological incompatibility and additionally move from an emerging scenario of isolated companies to a scenario of sectoral business fabrics or ecosystems. In other words, standardization fosters economic growth. To illustrate this with an example that is understandable to any reader, think of the field of home automation, in which an infinite number of devices, systems and services for the "smart home" can be illuminated. In this sector, it has been necessary to move from the initial phase of effervescent and very divergent innovation to a certain progressive consensus in relation to both electronic devices and their installation, since it is clear that it is not desirable or appropriate that each possible innovative solution (lighting, television, air conditioning, blinds...) requires a different installation and technologies without a certain degree of integration that allows not only their adequate maintenance, but also their proper maintenance. but also its adequate safety and sustainability.

Obviously, the aforementioned emerging or innovative aspect is present in the incessant proposals for products and services in the field of computer technologies. Therefore, standardization is an instrument of very high value. In particular, we are witnessing it today in the field of artificial intelligence and the enormous effort in international standardization committees both at European and global level. Respectively, the CEN-CENELEC Joint Technical Committee (European Committee for Standardisation - European Committee for Electrotechnical Standardisation), CEN/CLC/JTC 21 "Artificial Intelligence", and the Joint Technical Committee ISO/IEC JTC 1 "Information technology" and its multiple subcommittees, such as SC 42 "Artificial Intelligence", some of whose contributions we will see later in the field of AI governance and ethics. As of the date of writing this document, the ISO/IEC JTC 1/SC 42 committee has published 34 standardization documents and has 42 in progress, and CEN/CLC/JTC 21 has published 11 standardization documents and has 32 in progress.

Along with the aforementioned general benefits of standardization for companies, we will explain later in detail how standardization can also contribute to AI governance and the handling of ethical AI issues.

Ethics, Regulation and Self-Regulation in the IT Industry

As an epilogue to the relationship between ethics and regulation in the IT sector, it is worth noting the argument of "sectoral self-regulation" as an alternative to legal regulation in the field of digital products and services. The mantra of sectoral self-regulation has been the argument used for decades to justify "the jungle of non-regulation" in the IT field, along with the supposedly inevitable penalization of innovation or competitiveness that any legal regulation would generate. It has taken notorious scandals, including the loss of human lives, to rescue the need and political will for adequate regulation. We will highlight: the Volkswagen case of manipulation of the emission control software of its engines (2015)[1]; the Facebook-Cambridge Analytica case of collection and massive use of citizens' data for political propaganda purposes (2015)[2]; and finally the Boeing 737 MAX case, after two accidents in October 2018 and March 2019 that killed 346 people. A poor design of the software and the automatic tilt control system of the aircraft, as well as the audit and certification processes in this regard, was confirmed, and that put one of the main US multinationals at risk of bankruptcy[3].

These scandals, together with numerous and continuous incidents of foreign interference, social destabilization and malicious interference in electoral processes, led to the turning point of the so-called "death of self-regulation" and the beginning of an attitude of necessary legal regulation. Even authors such as Luciano Floridi have spoken out in this regard: "The time has come to acknowledge that, much as it might have been worth trying, self-regulation did not work. So, to use the words of the Gospel, now that the invitation has not been accepted, the alternative is "to force them [companies] to enter" (Luke 14:23). Self-regulation needs to be replaced by the law; the sooner, the better." (Floridi, 2021)

AI GOVERNANCE

An initial reflection is worth understanding what we mean when we talk about AI governance. AI governance has at least two levels of interpretation: 1) At the business level, that is, at the level of the direction and action of a company or organization in general to achieve its objectives; 2) And at the social level, that is, the action of public authorities (governments, legislators, justice...), individuals and social actors (companies, associations, organizations of all kinds, etc.).

In the governance of AI at the societal level, there are also at least two relevant scales: the level of states and the international or global level. In the materialization of both, the vision adopted for legal regulation and the ethical impact on people and society as a whole is especially relevant.

At present, at the societal level, there is no governance of AI on a global global scale. On the other hand, this is not surprising, since it is the equally fragmented starting point of the regulation and governance of information technologies in general. As it could not be otherwise, with AI we start from the same regulatory and ethical place where we were at the level of computing in general. But, despite regulatory shortcomings, uncertainty and even some calls for a moratorium on the use of AI systems[4], society is not going to wait for the era of hard digital regulation, nor for desirable regulatory consensus, much less for ethical consensus to use AI systems. (Domingo and Peñarrubia, 2024). Regulatory, ethical and cultural differences generate different approaches to AI governance in the states, below, some fundamental aspects of the approach in the United States, China and the European Union will be presented.

AI Governance in the United States

The regulation and governance of AI in the United States has its first high-level milestone in the Blueprint for an AI Bill of Rights (White House, 2022), which is presented as a guide for future industry and government policies. To this end, it defines five central principles that must be considered for the development of AI that respects the civil rights of citizens.

The American vision of AI governance is based on an orientation to the management of the risks associated with AI systems, together with respect for freedoms and promoting innovation and the use of new technological possibilities. This last aspect is especially relevant as it materializes in a greater interest in highly practical instruments as opposed to legal instruments, that is, promoting standardization over regulation.

In line with this vision, another important milestone in AI governance is the leading role assigned to the National Institute of Standards and Technology (NIST), under the Department of Commerce. With important lines of work and short- and long-term results:

- NIST follows the lines of action established in the Plan for Federal Engagement in AI Standards and Related Tools and coordinates the different federal agencies through the Interagency Committee on Standards Policy (ICSP).

- The Artificial Intelligence Risk Management Framework (AI RMF 1.0) published in January 2023, as a voluntary framework for action, is formulated to help organizations and companies manage the possible risks posed by the use of AI systems. It embodies the essential concern for risk management in AI systems, being a key contribution not only in the United States but internationally. (NIST, 2023)
- Creating a Resource Center: Trustworthy and Responsible AI Resource Center
- Trustworthy AI in Law and Society, whose focus is the application of ethics and human rights in the development of these new technologies. Co-founded by NIST with the U.S. National Science Foundation (NSF)

Another major initiative to promote AI was the National Artificial Intelligence Research and Development Strategic Plan, focused on promoting research and technology, with an update in 2023. (White House, 2023). It includes the line of action: Definition of standards and evaluation and benchmarking systems. Standards that must be aligned with the Blueprint for an AI Bill of Rights and the AI RMF.

Additionally, in 2024 the government published in 2024 Advancing Governance, Innovation, and Risk Management for Agency Use of Artificial Intelligence (White House, 2024) It establishes recommendations for the adoption of AI tools by federal agencies, based on both the indications established in the Blueprint for an AI Bill of Rights and in the AI RMF. It focuses on three main areas of action, one of them being to improve governance.

However, the vision explained in the months prior to the writing of this document is witnessing some changes in the regulation and governance of AI in the United States.

In the initial weeks of the new presidency, in January 2025 Donald Trump revoked a 2023 executive order signed by Joe Biden oriented to reduce the risks that artificial intelligence poses to consumers, workers and national security[5].

Few weeks after, during high level international AI summit hel in Paris, Vice President J.D. Vance rejected current vision about AI regulation because of supposed negative incidence on innovation and adoption. In fact, in another sign of divergence on AI governance, the United States did not sign up to the final statement of this international AI summit, while at least 60 countries including China had done so. Statement saying AI should be inclusive, open, ethical and safe[6].

More details on the governance and regulation of AI in the United States can be found at (ICEX, 2025)

AI Governance in China

The Chinese government's big push for artificial intelligence came with the Next Generation Artificial Intelligence Development Plan presented in 2017 (China, 2017). The plan lays out a three-stage strategy with the ultimate goal of positioning China as a global leader in AI by 2030. The first stage (2018-2020) focuses on China equalling the leading powers in AI, both in scientific research and in key technologies. The second stage (2021-2025) seeks for AI to become the main engine of economic growth in China, with applications in key sectors such as security, health and education. Finally, from 2025 to 2030, the goal is for China to be a world leader in AI models, technologies, and applications, and to be a leader in innovation in this field.

In terms of regulation, on March 1, 2022, the Provisions on the Management of Algorithmic Recommendations in Internet Information Services (China, 2022) came into force. It promotes the transparency and accountability of algorithms used to make recommendations on the internet, even forcing companies to disclose key information about their operation. The approach is not based on a classification of risk levels like the European AI regulation, but rather prioritises direct state supervision. The literal of Article 1 says "to carry forward the Core Socialist Values, preserve national security and the societal public interest, protect the lawful rights and interests of citizens, legal persons, and other organizations, and promote the healthy and orderly development of internet information services."

Interim Measures for the Management of Generative Artificial Intelligence Services: Vigente desde agosto de 2023, establece directrices éticas y técnicas para sistemas de IA generativa. Aunque las peculiaridades culturales y políticas recogen aspectos muy cuestionados desde los países basados en democracias abiertas al considerarlos mecanismos de contrl social y de limitación de derechos fundamentales. El literal del artículo 4 dice The provision and use of generative AI services shall "Uphold the Core Socialist Values; content that is prohibited by laws and administrative regulations such as that inciting subversion of national sovereignty or the overturn of the socialist system, endangering national security and interests or harming the nation's image, inciting separatism or undermining national unity and social stability, advocating terrorism or extremism, promoting ethnic hatred and ethnic discrimination, violence and obscenity, as well as fake and harmful information"

Guide for the AI Industry: Which includes a clear roadmap for AI standardization in China, although very much oriented towards fostering technological self-sufficiency rather than towards global interoperability or international collaboration as approaches to standardization are common in most countries.

Some bodies involved in AI governance in China:

- Ministry of Industry and Information Technology. Through the issuance of technical guidelines and regulations, it ensures that AI technologies are safe, efficient, and adapted to national priorities
- The Central Commission for Cybersecurity and Informatization.. It is responsible for regulating data security and cross-border information flows.
- The ministry of Scence and Technology Ministry plays a crucial role in promoting and funding AI research. It leads strategic programs such as IA 2030, which aims to promote the development and application of AI in key sectors of the economy.
- Standardization Administration of China. Created in March of 2018, is the body in charge of establishing and defining specific standards for AI, ensuring that these are aligned with national interests and objectives. Defining national standards helps to create a coherent and competitive technological environment. And at the same time, in order to ensure international technological alignment, China participates in international AI standardization committees, especially the International Standardization Organization (ISO)

On the other hand, it is necessary to add that China goes beyond AI strategy and governance with a clear vision on the strategy and governance of IT as a whole. Of course, including AI, but also quantum computing, etc. in its latest 14th Five-Year Plan for National Informatization (China, 2021a) Nothing less than the fourteenth already. In this understanding of the strategic importance of computing, and its associated policies in a sustained way for decades, it is necessary to contextualize China's great advance in the field of computing, including the aforementioned Next Generation Artificial Intelligence Development Plan launched in 2017 of which we are currently witnessing the results.

More details on the governance and regulation of AI in China can be found in (ICEX, 2024; Sheehan, 2023)

European Vision of AI Governance

The governance of AI in the European Union is based on the regulatory vision of AI with two components: legal regulations, with special mention of the AI Regulation, and AI standardization regulations.

The materialization of AI governance is implemented through a cycle with three essential elements: the provisions of the AI regulatory regulation (both legal standards and standardization standards), the action of regulatory compliance control authorities, and the action of social actors: citizens and organizations in general in their different AI roles (ISO, 2022a), including companies and public sector entities.

This action, in turn, feeds back into the improvement and updating of regulatory regulation, both legal and standardization.

Understanding this governance model is essential to put it into practice in a viable and valuable way for companies and organizations in general, especially when it comes to AI producers or AI providers. And in this implementation, the key element for organizations will be AI standardization regulations, among other reasons because:

- The legal provisions establish requirements and guidelines for companies, more or less succinctly, and generally do not go into detail about their practical implementation. Of course, it is possible for each organization to design how to implement legal provisions, but it is also highly inefficient in a technical context such as that of AI systems. In fact, this would make the oversight functions of AI regulators very costly, and perhaps even unfeasible. In this context, the essential value of standardization standards is understood to specify what practical measures must be implemented in the sense of compliance with technical or corporate requirements established in the legal regulation. Standardization standards serve in many cases to bridge the gap between the brief declaration of a legal obligation and its detailed practical materialization in organizations. It is a matter of moving from the brief sentence or paragraph with legal guidance to a detailed specification of a possible adequate practical materialization with the necessary documentary length. In this way, the standardization standard ensures that the organization has a clear understanding of the scope, resources and practical implications for compliance with a certain requirement or guideline, with the added advantage of doing so in a standardized and uniform way, which facilitates the performance of related professionals and managers, as well as the sectoral practices in this regard (audits, certifications...). On the other hand, it is also relevant that this standardization helps to comply with the supervisory and control functions of regulatory authorities in the field of AI, which are greatly facilitated by being associated with standards and not having a particular case for each organization.
- As if that were not enough, in European AI governance the idea is that compliance with standardisation standards is considered a presumption of compliance with the requirements set out in the AI Regulation. In other words, the standardization regulations detail to organizations and professionals how to practically implement the generic obligations established in the AI Regulation, both at the technological, organizational and documentary levels.

- They collect good practices from industry and professionals, resulting in the excellence and reliability of the corresponding AI systems and better governance of AI at the organizational level.
- They guide the implementation of measures in relation to AI systems even when they are not a legal requirement, but for standardised uses, which will increase productivity, generate higher quality AI systems and facilitate the integration of different systems and the mobility of professionals familiar with these standardized practices.

To materialize this governance model, the European Commission formulates "*standardization requests*" in the aspects it considers necessary to complement and implement the legal provisions, including obligations, information, documentation, controls, etc. (As stated in the EU AI Act[7]). For this reason, in parallel to the preparation of the AI Regulation, the European Commission made an standardization request in AI in May 2023 (European Commission, 2023), which includes the first batch of standardization standards that are considered a priority and essential to complement the provisions of the European AI regulation.

This is the list of new European Standards and European standardisation deliverables to be drafted. Standardisation request reference information (European Commission, 2023):

1. European standard(s) and/or European standardisation deliverable(s) on risk management systems for AI systems
2. European standard(s) and/or European standardisation deliverable(s) on governance and quality of datasets used to build AI systems
3. European standard(s) and/or European standardisation deliverable(s) on record keeping through logging capabilities by AI systems
4. European standard(s) and/or European standardisation deliverable(s) on transparency and information provisions for users of AI systems
5. European standard(s) and/or European standardisation deliverable(s) on human oversight of AI systems
6. European standard(s) and/or European standardisation deliverable(s) on accuracy specifications for AI systems
7. European standard(s) and/or European standardisation deliverable(s) on robustness specifications for AI systems
8. European standard(s) and/or European standardisation deliverable(s) on cybersecurity specifications for AI systems
9. European standard(s) and/or European standardisation deliverable(s) on quality management systems for providers of AI systems, including post-market monitoring processes

10. European standard(s) and/or European standardisation deliverable(s) on conformity assessment for AI systems

This set of standardization standards is materialized by a Joint Technical Committee CEN-CENELEC, specifically the CEN/CLC/JTC 21 – Artificial Intelligence committee, in which Spain is represented by the Spanish Association for Standardization (UNE). The scope of this committee is: "The JTC shall produce standardization deliverables in the field of Artificial Intelligence (AI) and related use of data, as well as provide guidance to other technical committees concerned with Artificial Intelligence. The JTC shall also consider the adoption of relevant international standards and standards from other relevant organizations, like ISO/IEC JTC 1 and its subcommittees, such as SC 42 Artificial intelligence. The JTC shall produce standardization deliverables to address European market and societal needs and to underpin primarily EU legislation, policies, principles, and values."[8]. The timetable associated with the materialization of this standardization request is aligned with the timetable of the AI Regulation, published in June 2024, but which establishes a progressive timetable for the entry into force of the different provisions until 2026. The desired objective is that the set of standards resulting from the standardization request will be available throughout 2025 or 2026.

On the other hand, as is well known, the European approach to the legal regulation of AI systems, and therefore to a large extent to their governance, is a risk-based approach. The AI Act defines 4 levels of risk for AI systems:

1. Unacceptable risk. All AI systems considered a clear threat to the safety, livelihoods and rights of people are banned. The AI Act prohibits eight practices: harmful AI-based manipulation and deception; harmful AI-based exploitation of vulnerabilities; social scoring; individual criminal offence risk assessment or prediction; untargeted scraping of the internet or CCTV material to create or expand facial recognition databases; emotion recognition in workplaces and education institutions; biometric categorisation to deduce certain protected characteristics; real-time remote biometric identification for law enforcement purposes in publicly accessible spaces.
2. High risk systems: AI use cases that can pose serious risks to health, safety or fundamental rights are classified as high-risk.
3. Limited risk AI systems: AI sytems with sècific transparency obligations
4. Minimal risk AI systems: The AI Act does not introduce rules for AI that is deemed minimal or no risk.

Regarding the authorities for the governance of AI in the European Union, the AI Regulation specifies the legal compliance authorities for AI and some complementary bodies for the governance of AI in the European Union (European Commission, 2024):

- The European Office for Artificial Intelligence, which has the task of developing European Union expertise and capabilities in the field of AI and contributing to the implementation of European AI legislation.
- The European Council on Artificial Intelligence, composed of representatives of Member States, should support the Commission to promote AI literacy tools, public awareness and understanding of the benefits, risks, safeguards, rights and obligations in relation to the use of AI systems
- Group of independent scientific experts, aimed at supporting compliance assurance activities in their more technical aspect or in the face of future innovations.
- Consultative forum to facilitate stakeholder input on the implementation of European AI standards. Including representatives of European standardization organizations.
- National competent authorities. Each Member State shall have at least one notifying authority and at least one market surveillance authority as national AI competent authorities

The latest developments in relation to the governance and development of AI in the European Union are: the publication of various guidelines and codes of good practice, as established in the EU IA Act: Guidelines on AI system definition9; Guidelines on prohibited artificial intelligence practices10; General-Purpose AI Code of Practice11. A d the presentation of the AI Continent Action Plan, presented in February 2025 in the context of the AI Action Summit, set to transform Europe's strong traditional industries and its exceptional talent pool into powerful engines of AI innovation and acceleration, with the ultimate goal for Europe to become a global leader in artificial intelligence12. Including lines of action for greater AI adoption and regulatory simplification, perhaps to some extent as a result of the United States' divergence in the previous weeks on AI governance.

Latest News on Global Social Governance of AI

Despite the various state approaches to AI governance, the desirable goal of a certain global governance of AI is not discarded. The latest high-level sample is the document on the subject by the Organisation for Economic Co-operation and Development (OECD), Futures of Global AI Governance: Co-Creating an Approach for Transforming Economies and Societies, of October 2024 (OECD, 2024). The document identifies three possible scenarios:

An ideal scenario based on inclusive governance and shared prosperity: With a vision of an AI revolution in which the human being is at the centre, supported by an inclusive and multilateral governance ecosystem for decisive progress towards the sustainable development goals.

A suboptimal scenario labeled as "Fast and Furious", with proliferation of low-cost AI models, tools and services that drive an explosion of innovation, but in which the capabilities of AI overwhelm advances in its supervision and reliability.

A scenario described as the worst possible scenario, in which AI advances are counterproductive. With an escalation of geopolitical tensions that leads governments to a race to develop the most advanced AI systems, while cutting back on security and accountability and restricting technology transfer.

With the main conclusion that the decisions that governments around the world will make in the coming years on AI governance that will be decisive in shaping the global AI governance ecosystem. There is an urgent need for international collaboration to build coherent and holistic mechanisms for global and multilateral AI governance that balance competing priorities and meaningfully include all stakeholders.

Roles of the Organization with Respect to AI

To materialize the corporate governance of AI, there will be great differences depending on the role of the organization in relation to AI systems. It is easy to understand that the needs and practices of a company in the IT sector dedicated to the development and production of AI systems for third parties will be different from a company in any sector that is only a user of an AI system.

On the other hand, it must be taken into account that organizations will often have several simultaneous roles. And not only for companies in the IT industry. For example, a generalist company (in the financial, automotive, health sector... of any sector other than IT) does not have to be just a user of third-party AI systems, but your IT department may have developed additional AI systems for use by the company itself. In other words, in this case the company would be simultaneously a user of AI systems and a developer of AI systems.

There is no exhaustive list of AI roles but there is a reference taxonomy that includes figures such as: AI provider, AI producer, AI customer, AI user, AI collaborator, AI system integrator, AI evaluator, AI auditor, AI subject, relevant AI authority, etc. This taxonomy for identifying organizational roles in relation to AI is included in the International Standard ISO/IEC 22989:2022 Information technology — Artificial intelligence — Artificial intelligence concepts and terminology[13] (ISO,

2022a), which provides and defines an illustrative relationship of AI stakeholder roles and subroles.

In addition to the impact on AI governance, these roles of the company or any other actor (suppliers, customers, users, regulators, etc.) will greatly influence when it comes to evaluating and managing the ethical impact of the use of AI. In the case of organizations, especially to determine their needs and practical mechanisms to develop and materialize a corporate ethics of AI systems. For example, for a producer of AI systems, it will be essential to equip itself as a company, and to provide its professional developers, with specific knowledge and practical mechanisms to manage and make decisions on ethical issues of AI systems when they arise at any stage of the AI system's life cycle (conception, development, exploitation...), and both with an internal or external corporeal origin of a customer or user.

On the other hand, the terms used are not only relevant to understand the different roles, but also these denominations are frequently used in sectoral documents or even legal regulation of AI. For example, this is the case in the wording of European Regulation on Artificial Intelligence (EU AI Act) (European Commission, 2024), e.g.: AI system producer, AI system provider, AI system user....

AI Governance in the Enterprise

Regarding the governance of AI in companies and organizations in general, it is essential to understand that organizations need to understand and specify at a technical, material and organizational level how to carry out regulatory compliance and corporate governance of AI. While this is particularly relevant for organisations producing or providing AI systems, it should also be considered by organisations that use AI systems or any other AI role.

The use of AI must necessarily be managed and integrated into the overall management and governance of organizations, not only for organizational convenience but also for the potential responsibilities and due diligence in relation to the peculiarities of AI. And both at the managerial level, and of the company as a whole, both in relation to its employees and internal sphere, as well as to its customers, suppliers, consumers and external sphere in general.

Standards for AI Governance in the Enterprise

As explained, in all models of legal regulation and social governance of AI (United States, China, Europe, etc.), standardization plays a leading role for companies. In the European case, it is the most accentuated, as compliance with standardization standards is considered as a presumption of compliance with the requirements established in the European AI Regulation.

In other words, standardization is the guide for companies to implement at a practical level the obligations established in the legal regulation on AI, whether at a technological, organizational, documentary level...

Here are some key rules for the implementation of AI governance in organizations:

- ISO/IEC 42001:2023 Information technology — Artificial intelligence — Management system (ISO, 2023b): Published in 2023. It specifies the requirements and provides guidance for establishing, implementing, maintaining, and continuously improving an AI management system in the context of an organization. It facilitates the organization to develop, provide or use AI systems responsibly in the achievement of its objectives and to comply with the applicable requirements, including the relationship with stakeholders. Applicable to any organization, regardless of size, type, and nature, that provides or uses products or services that use AI systems. The importance of this standard is central to the governance of AI in organizations since it applies to all AI roles and that, as it is a management system standard, it is coherently integrated with other management system standards widely known and used by organizations (e.g. ISO 9001 Quality Management System, ISO 27001 Information Security Management System, etc.)
- ISO/IEC 23894:2023 Information technology — Artificial intelligence — Guidance on risk management (ISO, 2023a): Published in 2023. It provides guidance on how organizations that develop, produce, deploy, or use products, systems, and services that use AI can manage AI-specific risk. It should also serve organizations to integrate risk management into their AI-related activities and functions. It should be used in conjunction with ISO 31000:2018 Risk management. Guidelines.
- ISO/IEC 38507:2022 Information technology — Governance of IT — Governance implications of the use of artificial intelligence by organizations (ISO, 2022b): Published in 2022. It provides guidance to members of an organization's governing bodies to enable and govern the use of AI, in order to ensure its effective, efficient, and acceptable use within the organization. It also provides guidance to managers, professionals in any field, business associations, professional associations, public authorities, service providers, auditors, etc. Applicable to the governance of current and future uses of AI, as well as the implications of such use for the organization itself. Applicable to any organization, and of any size, including public and private companies, government entities, and non-profit organizations.

- ISO/IEC 5339:2024 Information technology — Artificial intelligence — Guidance for AI applications (ISO, 2024a): Publicado en 2024. Provides guidance on AI applications, emphasizing stakeholder engagement and the AI application life cycle. It aims to enhance multi-stakeholder communication and acceptance by offering a framework that includes the make, use, and impact perspectives of AI systems.
- ISO/IEC TR 24030:2024 Information technology — Artificial intelligence (AI) — Use cases (ISO, 2024b): Publicado en 2024. It is not propoerly a internatina standard but a Technical Report ofering orientation on AI use cases across various domains. It encompasses an extensive range of applications, illustrating the applicability and potential of AI in different sectors.
- ISO/IEC 42005: 2025 Information technology — Artificial intelligence — AI system impact assessment (ISO, 2025a): Under publication14. Provides guidance for organizations performing AI system impact assessments for individuals and societies that can be affected by an AI system and its intended and foreseeable applications. It includes considerations for how and when to perform such assessments and at what stages of the AI system lifecycle, as well as guidance for AI system impact assessment documentation. Additionally, this guidance includes how this AI system impact assessment process can be integrated into an organization's AI risk management and AI management system. This document is intended for use by organizations developing, providing, or using AI systems. This document is applicable to any organization, regardless of size, type and nature.
- ISO/IEC AWI TS 25568 Information technology — Artificial Intelligence — Guidance on addressing risks in generative AI systems (ISO, 2025c): Under development. Technical specification providing guidance on addressing risks in generative AI systems. It includes: the objectives of generative AI systems when identifying risks; the risk sources and the stakeholders facing the risks in generative AI systems throughout its life cycle; guidance for risk analysis, risk treatment and controls of addressing risks in generative AI systems.

In conclusion, standardization is a key element for AI governance in companies. Not only does it provide significant competitive benefits, but it also materializes practical compliance with AI regulatory obligations and guidelines. In addition, it promotes sectoral excellence in the governance of AI systems, including the integration of components such as ethics and corporate social responsibility for the use of AI systems. On the other hand, standardization facilitates integrated corporate governance of the multiple business aspects that are widely adopted in companies: quality management, risk management, information systems security management, etc. Incorporating AI governance into corporate governance necessarily involves knowing and considering the standards that have an impact on it and facilitate its integration into the company's organization and operation as a whole.

BUILDING APPLIED ETHICS OF AI AND INFORMATION TECHNOLOGIES

The ethical aspect is one of the most transcendental issues of the impact of information technologies. However, in the past decades, this dimension was often left as a pending issue in the face of the dazzle of continuous computer innovations and their potential and incessant demand in the form of products or services in all spheres of human activity. In fact, the main cause of this lack has been in the alleged paradigm of self-regulation of computer products, services and activities, promoted for decades by the big technology giants. Once the jungle of legal non-regulation was allowed, the even more complex aspect of ethical impact was automatically excluded from the priorities in the development and use of information technologies. This scenario began to change fueled by two key factors (Peñarrubia, 2024):

- Firstly, notorious media scandals that brought to the fore the ethical aspect of computer products and services. For example, the Volkswagen case of manipulation of the emission control software of its engines15; the Facebook-Cambridge Analytica case of collection and massive use of citizens' data for political propaganda purposes16; and the Boeing 737 MAX case, after two accidents in October 2018 and March 2019 and the death of 346 people17.
- And on the other hand, the observation, without hesitation, of the malicious uses of computer technologies to influence social processes (presidential elections in the US18, BREXIT referendum19 or in Spain the Russian action with the Catalan independence movement20...), promote disinformation through fake news and processes of artificial viralization, social unrest... In short, harmful uses for destabilization and social manipulation, especially in open democratic societies. Often the result of actions from totalitarian foreign states, with techniques that are currently considered cyberwarfare tactics.

Latest innovations in AI have acted as a catalyst for the unresolved concerns regarding the ethical impact of computing. AI has crystallised the "social trigger" to demand measures to regulate and control information technologies after decades of growing concern in relation to the computer products and services that have built current digital society: helplessness, opacity, lack of responsibility, objectification, threat to the foundations of society... (Peñarrubia, 2023) We are witnessing a change of vision, to put the importance of people-centered and ethical impact of information technologies in the foreground, liquidating the paradigm of self-regulation and promoting the paradigm of necessary regulation and ethics (Floridi, 2021). In the aspect of necessary regulation, for the first time, a regulation with two aspects is addressed: legal regulations and standardization regulations, with the ambition of reconciling the guarantee of fundamental rights and some systemic foundations such as security and real democracy, with the promotion of innovation. At the European level, it is a variant of the so-called smart regulation . In this new context, the ethical dimension of AI, and by extension of any information technology, is put in the foreground, on the one hand permeating regulatory developments both at the legal and standardization levels, and secondly promoting measures for an applied ethics of AI that materializes key values such as equity, reliability or transparency. Always with the horizon of people-centered IT.

Impossibility of a Single Ethical Approach

But the ethical vision of AI is not uniform at the global level. The ethical foundation depends on the social group concerned: culture, tradition, ideology... This leads to an ethical foundation susceptible to different variants, as is being reflected in the different regulatory and ethical approaches to AI at a global level: the US, the USA, China... (Domingo y Peñarrubia, 2024; 2025)

To illustrate this, and in contrast to the European ethical vision explained below, let us look at some distinctive brushstrokes of China's approach. As noted in the section on AI governance, the Chinese approach considers appropriate obligations with profound ethical implications (uphold the Core Socialist Values, prohibition of content considered inciting subversion or the overturn of the socialist system, or harming the nation's image, or undermining social stability...) This conception has become evident in the implementation, for example, of the Ernie chatbot application or Deepseek, which are reluctant to answer questions about COVID-19, Chinese political leaders or Tibet[21].

On other occasions, the collision of different ethical views occurs at the level of states, for example, in relation to the personal data collection practices of applications such as Tik Tok or Deepseek[22].

In the Chinese context, measures such as these are aligned with the government's usual action, so they are not perceived by the bulk of Chinese citizens as something new, significant, or with a relevant ethical impact, but as part of the ways of doing things in Chinese society. On the contrary, the vision of the European media highlights the ideologization and impact on basic freedoms and the right to information, openly speaking of censorship.

On the other hand, China has promoted specific ethical measures in the field of AI, such as Ethical Norms for New Generation Artificial Intelligence Released, in 2021 (China, 2021b), which also includes several references to standardization.

Given the impossibility of a single ethical foundation, the promotion of an applied ethics linked to common references on a global scale is key. That is, even though there may be differences, a certain common framework is taken into consideration. This common global framework, in the first instance, would be given by the ethics linked to the protection of the rights contained in the Universal Declaration of Human Rights[23]. At the European level, the common reference is the Charter of Fundamental Rights of the European Union, which goes beyond the declaration of human rights by collecting civil, political and social rights of the citizens of the European Union[24].

It should be noted, in this context, that when we speak of the Universal Declaration of Human Rights, we are dealing with at least two dimensions: Firstly, the pure ethical aspect linked to respect for the rights contained in the Charter, and on the other hand, the legal aspect derived from the fact that a state signs an international treaty, in this case the Universal Declaration of Human Rights. This entails an obligation, but the bills of rights do not specify or detail the mechanisms for its implementation or the consequences of non-compliance. Therefore, although it is a great advance at the international level, development is necessary for its systemic practical impact on the day-to-day life of states and societies. In the case at hand, for the transfer of these rights to AI systems. And just as importantly, the control mechanisms and the consequences of non-compliance. This field of practical application is the great challenge: both at the level of legal regulation and applied ethics in general, which is deployed beyond legal obligations strictly speaking, and in all social areas: companies, public administration, professionals, citizens... Ethics without practical application is mere academicism, or what is worse in the technological field: from toasts to the sun to self-interested demagoguery.

Ethics of AI Systems in the EU

An essential and distinctive element of the European vision for AI is the achievement of ethical use of AI systems. In fact, this spirit is explicitly reflected in the European Artificial Intelligence Regulation (hereinafter the AI Regulation): "this Regulation supports the objective of promoting the European human-centred approach to AI and of being a world leader in the development of safe, trustworthy and ethical AI, as indicated by the European Council, and guarantees the protection of ethical principles, as specifically requested by the European Parliament" (European Commission, 2024)

With this objective at the level of legal regulation and governance of AI, the European Commission promoted a study on what the ethical guidelines should be for trustworthy AI that respects the Charter of Fundamental Rights of the European Union. The 2019 report "Ethical Guidelines for Trustworthy AI" by the European Commission's Independent High-Level Expert Group on Artificial Intelligence, sets out a non-exhaustive set of requirements for trustworthy AI[25]. All requirements are considered to be of equal importance, support each other, and should be met and evaluated throughout the entire lifecycle of an AI system. (AI-HLEG, 2019) These same requirements are assumed as the "ethical principles" that guide the AI Regulation: "The seven principles include human agency and oversight; technical robustness and safety; privacy and data governance; transparency; diversity, non-discrimination and fairness; societal and environmental well-being and accountability. Without prejudice to the legally binding requirements of this Regulation and any other applicable Union law, those guidelines contribute to the design of coherent, trustworthy and human-centric AI, in line with the Charter and with the values on which the Union is founded." .../... "All stakeholders, including industry, academia, civil society and standardisation organisations, are encouraged to take into account, as appropriate, the ethical principles for the development of voluntary best practices and standards." (European Commission, 2024)

Note that in the European vision, these principles not only form the backbone of the legal regulation contained in the AI Regulation, but are also considered essential for the reliability of AI in the development of "voluntary best practices and standards". This is very relevant for the ethical field in the broad sense which, as has been explained, extends beyond the strict legal obligation. And also for the field of standardization organizations, as producers of sectoral standards that, even if they are of voluntary use, constitute a powerful tool for industry governance linked to any technology.

Standardization for Actionable AI Ethics in Bussiness

To materialize an applied ethics of AI, it must be taken to the management and updating of organizations. In other words, the ethics of artificial intelligence must be integrated into the life cycle of AI systems, and indeed of all computer products in general. It is not a matter of a company "being ethical or not", but rather making it possible to address ethical issues during the life cycle of a system as well as any other type of technical aspect, for example, performance, design, usability, reliability, etc. That is, considering each of the stages of an ethical issue as part of the life cycle: appearance; analysis; decision-making; and implementation of decisions.

It is necessary to put in place concrete mechanisms and tools to make the ethics of artificial intelligence and computer systems in general actionable in organizations. In two ways: on the one hand, in the life cycle and day-to-day life of computer products and on the other hand in the progressive construction of an ethical culture of artificial intelligence and computing in general. Additionally, also as part of corporate ethics and corporate social responsibility in general in the context of the digital society. Some examples of these tools are: AI Ethics Committee; AI Ethics Panel; AI Codes of Good Practice; AI Ethical dialogue; - AI Ethical Canvas; Deliberative methods for new AI systems; AI focus group; AI Ethics Review Board, Public AI ethics reporting channel; Internal AI ethics reporting channel, etc. A description of these tools and additional examples can be found in (Domingo y Peñarrubia, 2024; 2025)

In addition to the broad ethical foundation of the European legal regulation embodied in the AI Regulation, standards are being promoted to materialise an applied ethics of AI systems. In short, to bring the treatment of ethical AI issues to the day-to-day life of companies, administrations, consumers, citizens and society as a whole. These are standardisation standards that are being carried out at European level in the Joint Standardisation Committee CEN/CLC/JTC 21 - Artificial Intelligence. Below are some ongoing initiatives with special importance or impact in the field of AI ethics at European level[26]:

- AI trustworthiness framework: Under development. Primarily aimed at organizations that commercialize or commission AI systems. It provides a framework for the reliability of AI systems that contains terminology, concepts, horizontal requirements, guidance, and a method for contextualizing them specifically to stakeholders, domains, or applications. High-level horizontal requirements address the fundamentals and characterization of the reliability of AI systems. Availability forecast in mid-2026.
- Competence requirements for AI ethicists professionals: Provides a systematized framework for the competencies of AI ethicists, categorizing them into knowledge, skills, and attitudes related to the specific activities and tasks of the role. It identifies requirements and recommendations necessary for individuals to effectively perform as AI ethicists. Availability forecast in 2025 or 2026.
- Guidelines on tools for handling ethical issues in AI system life cycle:Under development. Provides specification and guidelines for a set of tools (instruments, activities, procedures) for the practical handling of social and ethical concerns throughout AI systems life cycle: from the emergence of a new issue to the corresponding decision-making. This document offers a list of tools along a minimum set of requirements and guidance that enable organisations to put them into practice. As a general principle, tools provided are independent from any concrete ethical foundation. This document is applicable to all organisations, with any AI stakeholder role, including customers and users. However, it is primarily intended to assist AI systems producers and providers in practical handling of societal concerns and ethical consider-

ations issues during the AI systems life cycle. Availability forecast in 2027. This initiative is very relevant for companies, as the availability of practical tools enables professionals within AI provider organizations to integrate the resolution of ethical issues as an additional category of operational requirements throughout the AI system lifecycle. In doing so, AI providers will be able to adopt a model of corporate ethics specifically applied to AI systems in a manner that is both viable and sustainable. (Domingo y Peñarrubia, 2024)

- Guidance for upskilling organisations on AI ethics and social concerns: Under development. Will provide guidance for upskilling on AI ethics and social concerns in organisations. The document will complement existing standards related to AI ethics and social concerns. Its ultimate objective is to enable organisations to enhance their basic capabilities and culture regarding AI ethics and social concerns, both at the individual level (for employees in any position, excepted AI ethics professionals) and at the organisational level (including AI development teams, departments, board, managers, etc.) In particular, but not limited, to develop continuous learning programs that could include basic capabilities on AI ethics and social concerns in all organisations regardless of their AI stakeholder role. Availability forecast in 2027.

In addition, it is worth mentioning other ongoing developments of standardization standards with special importance or incidence in the field of AI ethics at a global global level, in the ISO/IEC JTC 1/SC 42 Artificial intelligence committee. Sometimes these are parallel *developments* (CEN/CLC – ISO/IEC), i.e. they result in both European and global standards. And in other cases it is a question of global developments that can be adopted at the European level, either literally or with the incorporation of European specificities. This last possibility is very interesting to promote global standardization standards and at the same time consistent with the European model of legal regulation and ethical foundation.

- ISO/IEC TR 24368:2022 Information technology — Artificial intelligence — Overview of ethical and societal concerns (ISO, 2022c): High-level overview of the ethical and societal issues associated with AI. In addition: it provides information regarding the principles, processes and methods in this area; it is intended for technologists, regulators, interest groups and society in general; it does not claim to defend any specific value system. Published in 2022.
- ISO/IEC AWI TS 22443 – Information technology — Artificial intelligence — Guidance on addressing societal concerns and ethical considerations (ISO, 2025b): Provides guidance on how an organization can identify and address societal concerns and ethical considerations during the cycle of AI systems that can potentially harm people and society. Applicable to all types

of organizations that develop or use AI systems, regardless of their size, type, and nature. Availability forecast in 2026.

Finally, alongside the ethical aspects directly linked to AI systems, there are broader ethical implications linked to the potential uses of AI in embedded systems, especially in its interaction with people. Special mention in this field is the application of AI in robotics, whether it is avatars, or software robots in general, or physical robots. Beyond the ethical aspects associated with the functionalities themselves, individuals can perceive a "personality" where there is only one machine (material or virtual), which can lead to the generation of emotional bonds, with unusual potential repercussions. Especially in virtual environments, such as video games, or in ambitious initiatives such as the metaverse, ethical measures by design are necessary that, for example, make it possible to know at all times whether a person is interacting with another human being or with an integrated AI system.

Improvements in the Management and Handling of AI Ethical Issues in the Company: Ethics and Trustworthiness

One aspect that can be improved by current attempts to standardize trustworthiness is that they are currently essentially focused on the technical reliability of the products themselves. Of course, this is fundamental and must be the first area of action, and in this case of standardization in relation to trustworthiness. But in the context of artificial intelligence systems and computer systems in general, it seems necessary to include within the characterization of trustworthiness the handling of ethical issues as part of the life cycle of the artificial intelligence system or the computer system in general. In other words, it is a technical aspect related not to a specific technology but to the whole of the technical management of the system: from its mere conception, to its design, commissioning, maintenance, evolution, until its withdrawal from the market. In other words, it could be said that it is a technical aspect related to the approach of computer engineering in relation to products and services. Whether it is software products and services, physical products, or even hybrid products, i.e. the integration of physical components and software components into the same product or service. The latter typology has become increasingly frequent to take advantage of the infinite possibilities of computer technologies in general in any field of application.

This technical aspect of the life cycle can be characterized and evidenced for its incorporation as part of the trustworthiness characterization of artificial intelligence systems or computer products in general. On a practical level, it would be a matter of incorporating specific mechanisms and tools into the operation of the organization to handle any ethical issue that may arise during the life cycle of a system. This incorporation must have at least three aspects: the first, the assurance of effective channels so that any interested party can raise an ethical issue in relation to a given system (both internal stakeholders, i.e. developers, computer engineers or any employee of the organization, as well as externally: customers, suppliers, users or citizens in general). Secondly, the existence of the aforementioned tools. Not only with a theoretical existence but with the necessary training of the people interested internally. For example, there must be developers, computer engineers, product managers, etc. who have received the necessary training in the use of these tools: for example, participating in an ethics panel, or an ethical dialogue with stakeholders, or an ethics committee... And thirdly, that the possible solution proposals that are the result of the aforementioned tools be considered for their implementation in the life cycle of the systems concerned. This is what we are talking about when we talk about applied AI ethics or true ethical AI culture in the company. A key element for people-orientes AI and IT technologies.

There is currently little receptivity to this proposal in the environment of organizations in the IT industry. But it is necessary to understand that it is inconsistent to talk about trustworthiness in relation to an artificial intelligence system or a computer system in general when this does not include the consideration of ethical issues as part of the life cycle of the system itself. Talking about the ethics of artificial intelligence and trustworthiness in artificial intelligence systems without at least including this aspect as part of the life cycle of the systems is an obvious shortcoming. Some would go further and say that it is nonsense and completely wrong. In other words, it is inappropriate to speak of Responsible AI or trustworthy AI if it does not necessarily include the aspect of ethical issues as part of the life cycle of such systems.

It is necessary to point out that although there is talk of handling ethical issues, no concrete ethical foundation is being considered, nor is it being thought that there has to be a certain scale of values agreed upon, concrete. In other words, it would be a matter of organizations having effective tools for decision-making regardless of the set of values or the specific ethical foundation that the company takes into account for ethical analysis and decision-making. It should be borne in mind that not only are there variants of ethical foundation from the society in which the company operates, but that the organization itself will provide variants when it has declarations of corporate values, corporate codes of ethics, corporate social responsibility commitments, etc. that will have an impact on the case.

Thus, it is proposed to include the handling of ethical issues during the life cycle of AI systems as a necessary element in frameworks on trustworthiness of AI systems. In particular in the international standards proposed by Frameworks and trustworthiness of AI systems. In addition, it is proposed to extend this to all computer systems in general. In fact, it has been this type of ethical shortcoming in the past decades that has brought to us the numerous and very diverse negative side effects of the use of the set in technologies and computer systems in general (misinformation, cognitive biases, loss of attention, and psychological impact on minors, uninformed consent, etc.). generalized lack of responsibility, malicious influence in electoral processes, impact on vulnerable groups, cybercrime, cyberwar, etc.)

An ethical use of artificial intelligence and computer science in general will be impossible as long as the management of ethical issues is not part of the day-to-day life cycle of systems. On the other hand, as long as this is not the case, we cannot speak of a true applied ethics of artificial intelligence and computer systems in general. Without reaching the milestone of making ethics actionable in the field of computer science again. In the beginnings of corporate computing, from the 50s until the advent of the personal computer, ethics continued to be part of the activity and the culture of responsibility of computer professionals. The explosion of computer programming in all areas from personal to business imposed enormous pressure on professionals and companies providing IT solutions to implement as quickly as possible the mere functionality demanded by customers. This pressure had a negative impact on key aspects of professional responsibility, such as safety requirements and ethical issues. Aspects that progressively lost weight in the life cycle of computer products and services. Only if we recover this ground will we achieve a humanized and sustainable digital society (Peñarrubia, 2022a, 2022b).

CONCLUSION

Corporate Social Responsibility is also based in the key reference of the international standard ISO 26000:2010 Guide on social responsibility, which establishes worldwide voluntary guidance on social responsibility for organisations.

This standard was published in 2010 with a very different scenario on social concerns and ethical considerations about information technologies impact. There is a notorious lack of awareness of the impact of information technologies. Neither in the internal dimension of companies, nor in the external dimension of society because of IT products and services produced by companies.

Current awareness of the pervasive effect and impact of AI and information technologies, open the debate about the importance of technology in corporate social responsibility. Even the convenience of an updated version of the ISO 26000 (2018) standard that further develops the aspect of responsible use of technology. Especially in relation to AI in any of its roles and considerations for companies in the IT industry in general in the face of the impact of computer products and services on people and society as a whole, including its systemic elements at the political and fundamental rights level. After fifteen years of the ISO 26000:2010 standard, perhaps the time has come for its revision to evaluate a Corporate Social Responsibility 2.0 in the context of the explosion in the use of artificial intelligence systems.

Therefore, standards are an essential tool to make the ethics of AI systems in the company actionable. To implement an applied ethics of AI and IT systems in companies. Both at the level of corporate management, and in the day-to-day life cycle of AI systems. The latter is especially important in organizations that produce or distribute AI systems, which must promote a true culture of ethical and responsible use of AI. This culture will not be real if it does not materialize as a mechanism and concrete practical tools that can be used by human teams during the life cycle of the systems. And additionally, tools that, if standardized, can facilitate the participation of users of AI systems and stakeholders in general to address ethical issues.

Usual handling of ethical issues and social concerns in organizations is a key point to implement a trustworthy and people-oriented AI and IT systems.

REFERENCES

AI-HLEG. (2019) Ethics guidelines for trustworthy AI. High-Level Expert Group on Artificial Intelligence (AI-HLEG). Publication Office of the European Union. 2019. Brussels. ISBN 978-92-76-11994-4. doi:. Available on https://data.europa.eu/doi/10.2759/346720. (Accessed 10 March 2024)DOI: 10.2759/14078

China (2017) China's State Council Notice on the Issuance of the Next Generation Artificial Intelligence Development Plan. 20 July 2017. Traslation Aavailable on https://digichina.stanford.edu/work/full-translation-chinas-new-generation-artificial-intelligence-development-plan-2017/ Original available on https://www.gov.cn/zhengce/content/2017-07/20/content_5211996.htm (Accessesd 22 March 2025)

China (2021a) China's 14th Five-Year Plan for National Informatization. The Central Commission for Cybersecurity and Informatization. 28 December 2021. Traslation Aavailable on https://digichina.stanford.edu/work/translation-14th-five-year-plan-for-national-informatization-dec-2021/ Original available on https://www.gov.cn/xinwen/2021-12/28/5664873/files/1760823a103e4d75ac681564fe481af4.pdf (Accessesd 22 March 2025)

China (2021b) Ethical Norms for New Generation Artificial Intelligence Released. Traslation of Ethical Norms for New Generation Artificial Intelligence Released. The National New Generation Artificial Intelligence Governance Specialist Committee. Ministry of Science and Technology. Center for Security and Emerging Technology. 21 Octiber 2021. Traslation Aavailable on https://cset.georgetown.edu/publication/ethical-norms-for-new-generation-artificial-intelligence-released/. Original available on https://www.most.gov.cn/kjbgz/202109/t20210926_177063.html (Accessesd 22 March 2025)

China (2022) China's Provisions on the Management of Algorithmic Recommendations in Internet Information Services. 1 April 2022. The Central Commission for Cybersecurity and Informatization. Traslation Aavailable on https://www.chinalawtranslate.com/en/algorithms/ Original available on https://www.gov.cn/zhengce/zhengceku/2022-01/04/content_5666429.htm (Accessesd 22 March 2025)

Domingo, A., & Peñarrubia, J. P. (2024) Faros en la niebla: Herramientas de ética aplicada para sistemas de IA. Conferencia en XXV World Congress of Philosophy: "Philosophy across Boundaries". 1-8 August 2024. Roma. Congress web site https://wcprome2024.com

Domingo, A., & Peñarrubia, J. P. (2025) Proposal of tools for the practical development of ai ethics in business. Ramon Llull Journal of Applied Ethics, 2024, núm. 16, 2025. In press, accepted for publication 3 February 2025. ISSN paper: 2013-8393. ISSN electrònic: 2938-4362. Available on https://raco.cat/index.php/rljae

European Commission. (2023) C(2023)3215 – Standardisation request M/593 commission implementing decision of 22.5.2023 on a standardisation request to the European Committee for Standardisation and the European Committee for Electrotechnical Standardisation in support of Union policy on artificial intelligence. vailable on https://ec.europa.eu/growth/tools-databases/enorm/mandate/593_en (Accessed 2 April 2025)

European Commission. (2024) Regulation (EU) 2024/1689 of the European Parliament and of the Council of 13 June 2024 laying down harmonised rules on artificial intelligence and amending Regulations (EC) No 300/2008, (EU) No 167/2013, (EU) No 168/2013, (EU) 2018/858, (EU) 2018/1139 and (EU) 2019/2144 and Directives 2014/90/EU, (EU) 2016/797 and (EU) 2020/1828 (Artificial Intelligence Act) Official Journal of the European Union, DO L, 2024/1689, 12.7.2024. Available on https://eur-lex.europa.eu/eli/reg/2024/1689/oj (Accessed 2 April 2025)

Floridi, Luciano. (2021) The End of an Era: from Self-Regulation to Hard Law for the Digital Industry Philosophy and Technology 34 (4), 619–622 https://doi.org/ DOI: 10.1007/s13347-021-00493-0

ICEX (2024) El ecosistema de la Inteligencia Artificial (AI) en China 2024. Oficina Económica y Comercial de España en Pekín. . 20 de diciembre de 2024 . Editado por ICEX España Exportación e Inversiones, E.P.E. NIPO: 224240096

ICEX (2025) Esquema regulatorio e institucional en inteligencia artificial de los EE. UU. Oficina Económica y Comercial de la Embajada de España en Washington. 31 de enero de 2025. Washington. Editado por ICEX España Exportación e Inversiones, E.P.E. NIPO: 224240096

ISO. (2018) Discovering ISO 26000. International Organization for Standardization – ISO. Ginebra. Available on https://www.iso.org/files/live/sites/isoorg/files/store/en/PUB100258.pdf (Accessed 11 April 2024)

ISO. (2022a) ISO/IEC 22989:2022 Information technology — Artificial intelligence — Artificial intelligence concepts and terminology. International Organization for Standardization – ISO. Geneva. Available on https://standards.iso.org/ittf/PubliclyAvailableStandards/ISO_IEC_22989_2022_ed.1_id.74296_Publication_PDF_(en).zip (Accessed: 10 March 2025)

ISO. (2022b) ISO/IEC 38507:2022 Information technology — Governance of IT —Governance implications of the use of artificial intelligence by organizations. International Organization for Standardization – ISO. Ginebra. Disponible en: https://www.iso.org (Accessed 11 April 2024)

ISO. (2022c) ISO/IEC TR 24368:2022 Information technology — Artificial intelligence — Overview of ethical and societal concerns. International Organization for Standardization – ISO. Ginebra. Disponible en: https://www.iso.org (Accessed 10 March 2025)

ISO. (2023a) ISO/IEC 23894:2023 Information technology — Artificial intelligence — Guidance on risk management. International Organization for Standardization – ISO. Geneva. Available in: https://www.iso.org (Accessed 10 March 2025)

ISO. (2023b) ISO/IEC 42001:2023 Information technology — Artificial intelligence — Management system. International Organization for Standardization – ISO. Geneva. Available in: https://www.iso.org (Accessed 10 March 2025)

ISO. (2024a) ISO/IEC 5339:2024 Information technology — Artificial intelligence — Guidance for AI applications. International Organization for Standardization – ISO. Geneva. Available in: https://www.iso.org (Accessed 10 March 2025)

ISO. (2024b) ISO/IEC TR 24030:2024 Information technology — Artificial intelligence (AI) — Use cases. International Organization for Standardization – ISO. Geneva. Available in: https://www.iso.org (Accessed 10 March 2025)

ISO. (2025a) ISO/IEC 42005: 2025 Information technology — Artificial intelligence — AI system impact assessment. International Organization for Standardization – ISO. Geneva. Available in: https://www.iso.org (Accessed 10 March 2025)

ISO. (2025b) ISO/IEC AWI TS 22443 Information technology — Artificial intelligence — Guidance on addressing societal concerns and ethical considerations. International Organization for Standardization – ISO. Ginebra. Disponible en: https://www.iso.org (Accessed 10 March 2025)

ISO. (2025c) ISO/IEC AWI TS 25568 Information technology — Artificial Intelligence — Guidance on addressing risks in generative AI systems. International Organization for Standardization – ISO. Ginebra. Disponible en: https://www.iso.org (Accessed 10 March 2025)

NIST. (2023) National Institute of Standards and Technology (NIST) Artificial Intelligence Risk Management Framework (AI RMF 1.0) Available on https://nvlpubs.nist.gov/nistpubs/ai/nist.ai.100-1.pdf (Accessed 20 March 2025)

OECD. (2024) Futures of Global AI Governance: Co-Creating an Approach for Transforming Economies and Societies. 2024 OECD Global Strategy Group. Organisation for Economic Co-operation and Development OECD October 2024. Paris. JT03551355. Available on https://www.oecd.org/content/dam/oecd/en/about/programmes/strategic-foresight/GSG%20Background%20Note_GSG(2024)1en.pdf/_jcr_content/renditions/original./GSG%20Background%20Note_GSG(2024)1en.pdf (Accessed 20 March 2025)

Peñarrubia, J. P. (2022a) Etica profesional TIC para una sociedad digital sostenible. Conference on XXIX Congress European Business Ethics Network - EBEN España. 25-27 May 2022. ESIC University. Pozuelo de Alarcón.

Peñarrubia, J. P. (2022b) El papel de la ética profesional de la ingeniería informática como elemento necesario para la construcción y la sostenibilidad de la sociedad digital. Communication on VI International Congress on Bioethics / Congreso Internacional de Bioética: Bioética y Democracia ante el reto de la Inteligencia Artificial. 24-28 October 2022. University of Costa Rica. San José. In press, accepted for publication 25 August 2022.

Peñarrubia, J. P (2024) ¿Quién cuida el jardín?: Cuidado humanizador de los cimientos individuales y sociales ante el impacto de las tecnologías digitales. SCIO Revista de Filosofía, n.º 26, Julio de 2024, 123-149, ISSN: 1887-9853 DOI: https://doi.org/DOI: 10.46583/scio_2024.26.1155

Sheehan, M. (2023) China's AI Regulations and How They Get Made Carnegie Endowment for International Peace. Available on https://carnegieendowment.org/research/2023/07/chinas-ai-regulations-and-how-they-get-made (Accessed 22 March 2025)

White House. (2022) Blueprint for an AI Bill of Rights. White House Office of Science and Technology Policy (OSTP). October 2022. Available on https://www.whitehouse.gov/wp-content/uploads/2022/10/Blueprint-for-an-AI-Bill-of-Rights.pdf (Accessed 25 March 2025)

White House. (2023) National artificial intelligence research and development strategic plan: 2023 update. The White House Office of Management and Budget. Available on https://www.whitehouse.gov/wp-content/uploads/2023/05/National-Artificial-Intelligence-Research-and-Development-Strategic-Plan-2023-Update.pdf (Accessed 20 March 2025)

White House. (2024) Advancing Governance, Innovation, and Risk Management for Agency Use of Artificial Intelligence. The White House Office of Management and Budget. Available on https://www.whitehouse.gov/wp-content/uploads/2024/03/M-24-10-Advancing-Governance-Innovation-and-Risk-Management-for-Agency-Use-of-Artificial-Intelligence.pdf (Accessed 20 March 2025)

KEY TERMS AND DEFINITIONS

AI Stakeholder Roles: In the context of artificial intelligence an organisation can have one or several stakeholder roles related to an AI system. There is no exhaustive list of AI roles but there is a reference taxonomy stablished by an intrenational standard that includes figures such as: AI provider, AI producer, AI customer, AI user, AI collaborator, AI system integrator, AI evaluator, AI auditor, AI subject, relevant AI authority, etc.

AI System Trustworthiness: Trustworthiness of AI systems is defined by a set of characteristics which help relevant stakeholders understand whether the AI system meets their expectations, for instance, reliability, availability, resilience, security, privacy, safety, accountability, transparency, integrity, authenticity, quality and usability.

Standardisation Request: In the context of the European Union, it is a procedure by which the European Commission establishes certain areas on which it wishes standardisation to be carried out as a complementary instrument to legal regulation, and commissions a standardisation body for its implementation in a certain period of time.

CEN/CLC/JTC 21: Joint Technical Committee between CEN (European Committee for Standardisation) and CENELEC (European Committee for Electrotechnical Standardisation) that shall produce standardization deliverables in the field of Artificial Intelligence (AI) to address European market and societal needs and to underpin primarily EU legislation and policies. It is the responsible of the development of the European Commission Standardisation Request on AI to complement EU AI Act.

ISO/IEC JTC 1 SC 42: Is an standardisation unit with the form of Subcommitte inside of Joint Technical Committee 1 (ISO/IEC JTC 1 "Information technology") between ISO (International Organization for Standardization) and IEC (International Electrotechnical Commission). With the objective of providing standardisation deliverables in the specific field of Artificial Intelligence at global international level.

ISO 26000: International standard on social responsibility, which establishes worldwide voluntary guidance on social responsibility for organisations. It based on 7 criteria or core issues to promote the integration of social responsibility on these issues in the operation of companies and organisations in general.

ISO/IEC 42001: International standard providing the requirements and guidance for establishing, implementing, maintaining, and continuously improving an AI management system in the context of an organization. It is a key reference for AI governance in organisations since it applies to all AI roles and that, as it is a management system standard, it is coherently integrated with other management system standards widely known and used by organizations (e.g. ISO 9001 Quality Management System, ISO 27001 Information Security Management System, etc.)

ENDNOTES

1 Volkswagen emissions scandal – Dieselgate - Emissionsgate https://en.wikipedia.org/wiki/Volkswagen_emissions_scandal

2 Facebook–Cambridge Analytica data scandal https://en.wikipedia.org/wiki/Facebook%E2%80%93Cambridge_Analytica_data_scandal

3 Boeing 737 MAX groundings https://en.wikipedia.org/wiki/Boeing_737_MAX_groundings

4 Pause Giant AI Experiments: An Open Letter. March 2023. https://en.wikipedia.org/wiki/Pause_Giant_AI_Experiments:_An_Open_Letter

5 Trump revokes Biden executive order on addressing AI risks. Reuters. 21 January 2025. Available on https://www.reuters.com/technology/artificial-intelligence/trump-revokes-biden-executive-order-addressing-ai-risks-2025-01-21/

6 Vance tells Europeans that heavy regulation could kill AI. 11 February 2025. Available on https://www.reuters.com/technology/artificial-intelligence/europe-looks-embrace-ai-paris-summits-2nd-day-while-global-consensus-unclear-2025-02-11/

7 EU IA Act: Article 40 Harmonised standards and standardisation deliverables "2.In accordance with Article 10 of Regulation (EU) No 1025/2012, the Commission shall issue, without undue delay, standardisation requests covering all requirements set out in Section 2 of this Chapter and, as applicable, standard-

isation requests covering obligations set out in Chapter V, Sections 2 and 3, of this Regulation. The standardisation request shall also ask for deliverables on reporting and documentation processes to improve AI systems' resource performance, such as reducing the high-risk AI system's consumption of energy and of other resources during its lifecycle, and on the energy-efficient development of general-purpose AI models. When preparing a standardisation request, the Commission shall consult the Board and relevant stakeholders, including the advisory forum."

8 Web site CEN/CLC/JTC 21 – Artificial Intelligence: https://standards.cencenelec.eu/dyn/www/f?p=205:22:0::::FSP_ORG_ID,FSP_LANG_ID:2916257,25&cs=1827B89DA69577BF3631EE2B6070F207D

9 The Commission publishes guidelines on AI system definition to facilitate the first AI Act's rules application. 4 February 2025. https://digital-strategy.ec.europa.eu/en/library/commission-publishes-guidelines-prohibited-artificial-intelligence-ai-practices-defined-ai-act

10 Commission publishes the Guidelines on prohibited artificial intelligence (AI) practices, as defined by the AI Act. 4 February 2025. https://digital-strategy.ec.europa.eu/en/library/commission-publishes-guidelines-prohibited-artificial-intelligence-ai-practices-defined-ai-act

11 Third Draft of the General-Purpose AI Code of Practice published, written by independent experts. 11 March 2025. https://digital-strategy.ec.europa.eu/en/library/third-draft-general-purpose-ai-code-practice-published-written-independent-experts

12 European Commission. 9 abril. Press release Apr 9, 2025 Brussels. Commission sets course for Europe's AI leadership with an ambitious AI Continent Action Plan. https://ec.europa.eu/commission/presscorner/detail/en/ip_25_1013

13 International Standard ISO/IEC 22989:2022 Information technology — Artificial intelligence — Artificial intelligence concepts and terminology has been released for public use by ISO. It is available at no acquisition cost at the link indicated in the bibliography.

14 At the time of writing, the ISO/IEC 42005 standard is in the publication phase, so the year has been included in the title: ISO/IEC 42005: 2025

15 Volkswagen emissions scandal – Dieselgate - Emissionsgate https://en.wikipedia.org/wiki/Volkswagen_emissions_scandal

16 Facebook–Cambridge Analytica data scandal https://en.wikipedia.org/wiki/Facebook%E2%80%93Cambridge_Analytica_data_scandal

17 Boeing 737 MAX groundings https://en.wikipedia.org/wiki/Boeing_737_MAX_groundings

18 Russian interference in the 2016 United States elections https://en.wikipedia.org/wiki/Russian_interference_in_the_2016_United_States_elections

19 Russian interference in the 2016 Brexit referendum https://en.wikipedia.org/wiki/Russian_interference_in_the_2016_Brexit_referendum

20 US Senate report condemns Russian interference in Catalan referendum https://english.elpais.com/elpais/2018/01/11/inenglish/1515667883_820857.html

21 Elusive Ernie: China's new chatbot has a censorship problem. https://www.bbc.com/news/world-asia-66727459 Ernie, the Chinese artificial intelligence trained with information censorship. https://www.lavanguardia.com/tecnologia/actualidad/20230525/8990969/china-censura-propio-chatbot-inteligencia-artificial-pmv.html) Chinese AI chatbot DeepSeek censors itself in realtime, users report. The Guardian. 28 January 2025. https://www.theguardian.com/technology/2025/jan/28/chinese-ai-chatbot-deepseek-censors-itself-in-realtime-users-report

22 South Korea spy agency says DeepSeek 'excessively' collects personal data https://www.reuters.com/technology/artificial-intelligence/south-korea-spy-agency-says-deepseek-excessively-collects-personal-data-2025-02-10/ DeepSeek 'shared user data' with TikTok owner ByteDance 18 February 2025. https://www.bbc.com/news/articles/c4gex0x87g4o

23 Universal Declaration of Human Rights. Available on https://www.un.org/en/about-us/universal-declaration-of-human-rights

24 Charter of Fundamental Rights of the European Union. Available on https://eur-lex.europa.eu/EN/legal-content/summary/charter-of-fundamental-rights-of-the-european-union.html

25 These requirements have their origin in the Charter of Fundamental Rights of the European Union

26 Excerpt from the titles and scope of some standardization initiatives at the time of writing this publication.

Chapter 6
Does the New European Health Data Space Respect the Principle of Patient Autonomy?
Methodological Proposal for the Design of a Validation Tool

Ana Fayos
https://orcid.org/0000-0003-1124-3772
University of Valencia, Spain

Carlos Andres
Valencian Oncology Institute, Spain

ABSTRACT

The creation of this European Health Data Space is part of a regulatory development that takes into account habeas data and the right to data protection of personal data. This normative regulation is insufficient if ethical aspects such as the protection of the patient's freedom and right to autonomy, expressed through the informed consent (IC) and the patient information sheet (PIS), are not taken into account in this great project. The present work aims to provide tools to assess the greater or lesser respect of these documents for patient autonomy, by quantifying the degree of sensitivity of the informed consent and the patient information sheet to the concept of patient autonomy from an ethical point of view.

DOI: 10.4018/979-8-3373-0385-7.ch006

INTRODUCTION

The concept of autonomy is rooted in the Judeo-Christian conception of the human being. Man is created in the image and likeness of his Creator, and therefore endowed with the capacity for choice—even the choice to disobey God and assert moral autonomy, potentially culminating in the ontological death of the person:

> *[1:26] Then Elohim said, "Let us make humankind in our image, according to our likeness; and let them have dominion over the fish of the sea, and over the birds of the air, and over the cattle, and over all the wild animals of the earth, and over every creeping thing that creeps upon the earth." [1:27] So Elohim created humankind in his image, in the image of Elohim he created them; male and female he created them. (Bereshit)*

Elsewhere in the Mediterranean, the Greek world developed the concept of *autos* (self) and *nomos* (law) to refer to the legislative autonomy of city-states. Thus, each autonomous city enjoyed its own laws and currency—or chose not to have one, like Sparta, where the possession of money was considered abominable. Aristotle restricted the concept of autonomy to those who belonged to the *polis*; "He who is without a city through nature rather than chance is either a mean sort or superior to man," (*Pol. I,* 1253a3), "One who is incapable of participating or who is in need of nothing through being self-sufficient is no part of a city, and so is either a beast or a god" (*Pol. I,* 1253a27). In an ideal *polis*, citizens are virtuous agents who exercise autonomy because they are capable of giving themselves their own laws. However, a political authority still determines what should be done. First, the citizen must know what ought to be done, and there must be an institutional framework that helps ensure that individual deliberations are not distorted by private influences (*Pol. VII*).

Kant (1797) likewise defines autonomy as the capacity of the person to transform their own will into law for themselves: "The autonomy of the will is the property the will has of being a law unto itself (independently of any property of the objects of volition). The principle of autonomy is thus: to choose only in such a way that the maxims of one's choice are included simultaneously in the same volition as a universal law" (Kant, 1797). He therefore proposes an autonomous ethics, in contrast to *hetero-nomos* ethics—where some external element dictates what one must do in order to achieve a particular desire. According to Kant's autonomous ethics, it is the individual who decides on their behavior because it is good in itself. The practice of this autonomous ethics allows one to achieve the common good. It is therefore a universal ethics, applicable to any individual deliberation, implemented through the practical use of reason—capable of formulating true judgments, which Kant called *a priori synthetic judgments*.

Later, in the modern era, J.S. Mill (2014) grants autonomy the status of a necessary condition for achieving human happiness: "You probably know from my *Essay on

Liberty*, in what sense and within what limits I understand our common principle, that of individual autonomy. I recognize this autonomy as a strict rule in matters that concern only the individual himself." (*Letter to John Elliot Cairnes*, XVII: 1831–2). He advocates individual autonomy: "Actions are right in proportion as they tend to promote happiness, wrong as they tend to produce the reverse of happiness." (Mill, 2014). For Mill, happiness is pleasure—the exercise of intellectual faculties characteristic of a free, enlightened, and dignified being, where dignity means self-respect. Mill's principle of utility aims to achieve qualified pleasures to produce self-satisfied and self-developed individuals. Pleasure is not to be measured as something purely material or physical; the value of a moral action must not be judged merely by quantity. Mill's concept of happiness is based on what a human being is and ought to be: a morally developed, autonomous person, who respects both themselves and others. A happy society is one in which individuals are autonomous and possess full moral and spiritual development. The greatest happiness of the person lies in the greatest happiness of all. Society as a whole can only be happy if each person is treated as an autonomous and free being. Moral and political progress must be directed toward this end. A good government should enhance capacities for autonomy, self-development, uniqueness, and originality in order to foster the dignity of each member of society and the achievement of individual freedom (*On Liberty*).

Beauchamp and Childress (1998) summarize most existing theories of autonomy into two common conditions: liberty and agency. The first, liberty, involves acting independently of controlling influences. The second, agency, involves the capacity to act intentionally. Generally, autonomy theories describe characteristics an autonomous person should have, including the ability for self-governance—comprising understanding, reasoning, reflection, and independent choice. At this point, the authors add a necessary third condition: autonomous choice, which refers more to governance itself than to the capacity for it. Thus, autonomous actions are analyzed based on their agents, who must act intentionally, with understanding, and in the absence of external influences attempting to control or determine the action. The first condition holds absolute value, while the other two are relative—allowing for varying degrees of autonomy in actions. They also emphasize the difference between *being autonomous* and *being respected* as an autonomous agent. Respecting an autonomous agent means recognizing their right to hold their own views and to choose and act in accordance with them—and that respect must be active, not just an attitude. Respecting another's autonomy means not only respecting their opinions and tendencies and refraining from interference, but also ensuring the conditions necessary for them to make an autonomous choice (Beauchamp & Childress, 1998).

EUROPEAN HEALTH DATA SPACE (EHDS)

In the spring of 2024, the European Parliament and the Council reached a political agreement on the European Commission's proposal for the European Health Data Space (EHDS). The EHDS Regulation aims to establish a common framework for the use and exchange of electronic health data across the EU. It enhances individuals' access to and control over their personal electronic health data, while allowing certain data to be re-used for public interest, policy support and scientific research purposes. It promotes a health data environment that supports an internal market for digital health services and products. In addition, the Regulation establishes a harmonized legal and technical framework for electronic health record (EHR) systems, fostering interoperability, innovation and the smooth functioning of the internal market.

The EHDS will:

- empower individuals to access, control and share their electronic health data across borders for the healthcare delivery (primary use of data);
- enable the secure and trustworthy reuse health data for research, innovation, policy-making, and regulatory activities (secondary use of data);
- foster a single market for electronic health record (EHR) systems, supporting both primary and secondary use.

To this end, a catalogue of health data categories will be established, including data from medical histories, clinical trials, etc., which will be provided by the data holders, at the discretion of each State, subject to their informed consent. It will provide a consistent, reliable and efficient system for the secondary use of health data in research, innovation, policy and regulatory activities. A catalogue of health data categories will be established, including clinical history data, clinical trial data, etc., to be provided by data holders. Informed consent may be required at the discretion of each Member State. The concept of "data holders" is broad and includes natural persons or, where appropriate, healthcare institutions or researchers. Various purposes are foreseen for access to health data, ranging from public health and health planning to AI-driven innovation and personalized medicine.

The EHDS will also include opt-out provisions:

- Primary use: Member States may offer a total opt-out from infrastructures built under the EHDS.
- Secondary use: The regulation includes opt-out provisions seeking a balance between patient preferences and ensuring access to relevant data for public interest purposes.

For example, the General Data Protection Regulation (RGPD) explicitly states: (13) It may be the case that natural persons do not wish to allow access to some parts of their personal electronic health data, while allowing access to other parts. This selective sharing of personal electronic health data needs to be supported. As a matter of principle, personal electronic health data should only be processed on the basis of the vital interests of another natural person if it is not obvious that the processing can be based on another legal basis. Member States need to provide in national legislation more specific legal provisions on restriction mechanisms imposed by the natural person on parts of his or her personal electronic health data. As the non-availability of restricted personal electronic health data may affect the provision or quality of health services received by the individual, the individual must take responsibility for the fact that the health care provider cannot take the data into account when providing health care services.

And in the Data Governance Law (DGA): (15), where appropriate, public sector agencies must facilitate, through the appropriate technical means, the reuse of data based on the consent of the interested parties or the permission of the holders of that data so that their data is reused. In this regard, the public sector agency must do everything possible to provide assistance to the potential reuse to obtain consent or permission by establishing technical mechanisms that allow transmitting the appropriate requests of the reuses asking for consent or permission, when it is feasible in practice. Contact data should not be provided that allow reuses to go directly to interested parties or data holders. If the public sector agency transmits a request for consent or permission, it must ensure that the interested party or the data holder is clearly informed of the possibility of refusing to give their consent or permission.

With all the precautions, it is possible to anticipate certain trends that are already being lived can be a deviation or disability of the principle of autonomy are already being the nature of the transfer of data for secondary, generic or indiscriminate use, confusion between the confidentiality of the data and ownership of the data, or conflicts with the right to privacy, understood as what is established by the law of autonomy of the patient.

WHAT IS SECONDARY CLINICAL DATA FOR RESEARCH USE?

Secondary data is defined by the Royal Spanish Academy as 'information about something specific that allows for precise knowledge or helps deduce consequences'. This suggests that it encompasses more than mere numerical or textual values, but rather constitutes the foundation for constructing knowledge. Therefore, it is important to understand this concept, as a structured set of information allows us to infer new knowledge.

Medical data's true value lies in its interrelationship with other factors, not isolated values. Researchers care little about anonymization; the interconnectivity that allows information to be obtained matters more. Patients should be aware that the value of their data comes from this interrelationship, and that anonymization alone does not fully protect autonomy.

The “data seeker” generally cares little whether the data are anonymized, pseudo-anonymized or identifiable, and is willing to accept whatever is proposed in this regard, because what he or she really values is the relationship between the data. For this very reason, the patient who generates the data should be aware that, regardless of the degree of anonymity with which they are exploited, it is this value of interrelationship that makes their data coveted by research and the pharmaceutical industry, despite the fact that on many occasions when the data are referred to, informed consent is focused solely on the protection of confidentiality.

As a consequence of the foregoing, the interrelationship among the data that constitute the “datum” itself should be duly recognized and valued, and ownership of such data should be rightfully restored to its legitimate source—the patient. Though challenging, mechanisms must be found to reconcile data accessibility with patient rights. Upholding human dignity requires investment and sincerity in the exercise of bioethical principles.

INFORMED CONSENT

The source of the problem—and at the same time, its potential solution—lies in the formulation of Informed Consent (IC) and the Patient Information Sheet (PIS). Initially, IC was considered a method to reduce the potential harm to participants in research projects. More recently, the main justification for IC has shifted to the protection of autonomous choice. IC safeguards patients’ rights, especially their right to autonomy.

Informed Consent is meant to allow patients to approve or reject:

- Clinical interventions within the context of clinical trials or research projects
- Use of data resulting from clinical procedures or regular healthcare follow-up
- Use of biological samples derived from clinical interventions
- Use of personal data to varying degrees

This occurs after receiving sufficient information to allow the individual to consent knowledgeably and freely.

Traditionally, explicit or informed consent has been regarded as the basic paradigm of autonomy in healthcare. Other valid forms include tacit IC, expressed passively through omission; implicit IC, derived from behavior; or presumed IC, based on what is known about the individual.

According to current regulations, two types of IC should be considered that do not contradict the principle of autonomy:

- **Specific informed consent.** For a particular study
- **Broad informed consent.** The large informed consent covers the variety of future uses in the investigation for which the consent occurs. Broad informed consent is not a general consent. On the contrary, broad informed consent should impose certain limitations:
    - Present yourself in an initial study with specific consent.
    - Cover only future studies in the same pathology and with the same object of study (drug, health product, technique ...)

ELEMENTS OF INFORMED CONSENT (IC)

The gradation of autonomy in actions, as proposed by Beauchamp and Childress (1998), helps distinguish sufficient from insufficient informed consent. Within the context of the healthcare sector, the Informed Consent (IC) can be interpreted as a metric of patient autonomy. It is important to note that IC should be understood as a temporal process—a joint decision-making dialogue between physician and patient—not merely a signed form. This understanding serves to refute the notion that the document which is signed by both parties constitutes the basis of IC. It is important to note that, as a temporal process, the IC can be interrupted at any given moment. In addition, it is important to distinguish between the exchange of information regarding the potential for selection of the various medical interventions and the approval and authorization of a specific intervention.

Within the framework of the IC, two fundamental components are identified: the informative component and the component of consent. Within the medical and legal domains, five fundamental elements have been identified for the implementation of informed consent: competence, disclosure, comprehension, voluntariness, and consent. Beauchamp and Childress (1998) propose a substitute model for the traditional five-component model of CI, distinguished by the integration of a sixth and seventh element: Decision (in favor of a plan) and Authorization (of the chosen plan)

This is also a conventional classification that does not align with contemporary interests. It is being superseded by the proliferation of novel technologies that necessitate substantial real-world databases for their enhancement. New types of broad consent are emerging. The practical interest in implementing a comprehensive consent model is derived from the entity in question (the health institution) rather than an individual (e.g., a physician) or within the context of a specific clinical trial. This interest stems from a nebulous definition of intervention, which encompasses a range of actions undertaken on the patient's behalf that yield "data."

Accordingly, the following categories of broad consent are hereby presented for consideration:

- Withdrawal from any specific study.
    - Anonymized data
    - Coded data
- Associated with a first study:
    - Reuse of anonymized data.
        - Optional
        - Mandatory
        - Telematic consultation
    - Reuse of coded data in any study:
        - Optional
        - Mandatory
        - Telematic consultation
    - Reuse of coded data in studies with the same pathology, same drug/health product/technique, same conditions of confidentiality, protection and use of the data.
        - Optional
        - Mandatory
        - Telematic consultation

CRITERIA FOR ASSESSING RESPECT FOR PATIENT AUTONOMY

Beauchamp and Childress 91998) ask: *Must we respect others?* Returning to the concept of autonomy, Kant (1797) argues that it arises from recognizing each person as having unconditional value and the capacity to determine their own destiny. Disregarding autonomy means treating individuals as mere means rather than ends.

Beauchamp and Childress (1998) raise the question: Should we respect others? In relation to the concept of respect for autonomy, Kant (1797) argues that this respect stems from recognizing the inherent, unconditional value of each person and their capacity to determine their own destiny. Failing to respect an individual's autonomy means treating them merely as a means to an end, disregarding their own objectives in favor of those of others. This constitutes a fundamental moral violation, as every autonomous person is an end in themselves, capable of determining their own path. Kant (1797) invokes the moral imperative to treat people as ends, not merely as means. On the other hand, J.S. Mill (2014) defines autonomy as the individuality of the person. He argues that every citizen should be allowed to develop according to their personal convictions, provided these do not interfere with the freedom of others. Mill demands not only a prohibition on interference but also an active reinforcement of the expression of autonomy.

To achieve the objectives of the previously mentioned projects, it is necessary to either forgo the informed consent process (IC) or to establish a broad consent model that minimizes the need for obtaining consent for each project utilizing these databases. Consequently, various models of broad informed consent are generated. We propose three key dimensions to assess the level of respect for autonomy of the patient:

Generic Consent (GC)

This is given to the patient when he/she comes to the hospital, in the form of a generic consent, or even as a more or less brief message sent to his/her cell phone, informing him/her and/or requesting that his/her health data may be used for the development of unspecified research. This type of consent, based on a dubious legal basis, can be given as an exemption from subsequent specific consents, or at best open the door to subsequent specific consents for subsequent studies.

Secondary Use with Data Reuse Option (ORD)

In this case, when the patient is offered the possibility of participating in an initial survey, he/she is presented with a specific IC for that study, which opens the door to a secondary use of his/her data in subsequent studies, in a generic way or limited to different scenarios. Thus, we can find:

- ORD in the same pathology
- ORD with the same drug/technique/medical device as appropriate
- ORD with the same confidentiality as in the initial survey
- ORD with the same data protection as in the initial survey
- ORD with the same work system as in the initial survey
- Or with a combination of these limits, generally the first two: same pathology and same drug/technique/medical device.

There are other parameters whose evaluation describes the greater or lesser consideration that the study sponsor has for the patient's autonomy:

Comprehensibility

Intelligibility

The degree of intelligibility of the informed consent and the Patient Information Sheet (PIS) is a clear indicator of the degree to which the patient's decision to participate in the trial is free and therefore autonomous. Unfortunately, this parameter is not always satisfactory (Mariscal-Crespo et al., 2017).

Length

The HIP and the IC should be long enough to develop all the areas that make up these documents (Shah, 2025), and at the same time not too long so that the patient can read them comfortably in a reasonable time, and of sufficient length to provide the reasonably complete information that the patient needs to know in order to make an autonomous decision.

ASSESSMENT TOOL

In order to assess the greater or lesser respect of these IC and PIS documents for patient autonomy, we propose a tool that allows us to quantify the degree of respect of IC/PIS sensitivity with respect to the concept of patient autonomy.

The tool allows for a four-part assessment as described in the previous sections. These four criteria would be evaluated in the IC process, each with a specific weight, resulting in a final score from 0 to 10. This specific weight can be defined for each specific case by consensus of the evaluation group. Thus, the same tool would be useful for the different ethics committees evaluating research projects and trials.

These four criteria are:

1. Data Use Option (DUO)
2. Generic Consent (GC)
3. Initial Survey with Data Reuse Option (DRO)
    a. ORD in the same pathology
    b. ORD with the same drug/technique/medical device
    c. ORD with the same confidentiality
    d. ORD with the same data protection

    e. ORD with the same work system
4. Comprehensibility
    a. Intelligibility
    b. Length

Primary use is assessed via the degree of data anonymization and whether consent is generic or properly informed. Reuse assessment checks whether data reuse is optional or mandatory, and under what limitations.

The second point already presupposes the existence of an initial study with its corresponding consent, in which the subject participant is given the possibility of consenting to the reuse of the data or is denied this possibility, making it obligatory that if the patient wants to participate in the first study, he/she must necessarily consent to the reuse of the data in subsequent projects. The ideal scenario respects autonomy by allowing patients to consent voluntarily to future research use within the same pathology, same methods, and under consistent privacy protections.

The third point relates to the specific aspects that allow us to define in concrete terms the ideal situation in which consent for re-use should be considered, in order to make it compatible with the normative daughter-in-law and, on the other hand, to allow us to respect the principle of patient autonomy. Thus, we found that the ideal situation is one in which the patient can voluntarily consent to the re-use of data in the context of future research related to the same pathology, the same drug, test or procedure, and under conditions of privacy, protection and systematic use of data similar to those of the first study.

Finally, under the heading of comprehensibility, two aspects were referred to that determine the possibility of making a truly informed choice. These are legibility and the length of the patient information sheet, since excessive length can lead to difficulties in understanding, while excessive parsimony can lead to incomplete or biased information.

CONCLUSION

The nature of health data starts with a clinical contact, either in routine clinical practice or in a clinical trial setting. The unique origin of these data is always the patient: their anatomy, physiology, pathology, pharmacokinetics and pharmacodynamics of the drug in that patient. It is debatable whether the data should generate a measurement (blood pressure, height, weight, etc.), a typification (ICD classification of diseases), a gradation (autism, epilepsy, alcoholism, cancer, etc.), additional information that would be generated in the clinical act, etc. Subsequently, the raw data are also useless and a cleaning of the databases is required for their use as secondary data. This process involves other professionals, not necessarily linked to the health sector, and analysis tools that facilitate the process. Finally, the secondary data with which it is marketed is the result of an accumulation of means and actions that allow it to be alienated from the patient.

All research must respect patient autonomy. This also applies to the use of secondary data. Ethics committees are a fundamental tool to ensure that this premise is respected in clinical practice. Providing experts with the tools to make an objective assessment ensures compliance with this premise.

The tool enables a four-part assessment: primary use of data, possibility of data reuse, scope of reuse (specificity of consent to future research), and comprehensibility of information. This tool provides a structured and practical approach for ethics committees to evaluate how well patient autonomy is respected in research proposals. From the development of this assessment tool, we conclude that informed consent should be seen as a process—not a single document—but a combination of resources: digital communication, the PIS, the IC form, supporting materials, and verbal dialogue. From this point on, further studies are needed to validate the tool within the ethics committees, to verify its usefulness in the actual performance of their functions and whether it should be modified or extended. Further validation in real settings is encouraged.

We are fully aware of the challenges involved in reconciling the return of data ownership to the patient with the ease of data accessibility. However, it would be desirable to at least engage in honest reflection and acknowledge that in many cases the underlying motive is to reduce research costs - often at the expense of respecting patient autonomy. On the other hand, if there really is a social will to uphold this bioethical principle, today's technological means offer feasible ways of doing so without undue difficulty. But let us not deceive ourselves: respect for human dignity has its price. The crucial question is whether we value that dignity enough to invest the resources necessary to protect it.

REFERENCES

Aristotle, The Politics. Book I, part II, 1253a27-29. Book VII, part I, 1323a-1324a.

Beauchamp, T. L., & Childress, J. F. (1998). *Principios de ética biomédica*. Ed. Masson, 1999. Cap. 3.

Kant, I. 1797. *Metaphysics of Morals*. A87.

Mariscal-Crespo, M. I., Coronado-Vázquez, M. V., & Ramirez-Duran, M. V. (2017). Global analysis of the readability of informed consent documents used in public hospitals in Spain. *Revista de Calidad Asistencial*, *32*(4), 200–208. PMID: 28268150

Mill, J. S. (2014). On Liberty. Akal Publishing. *Letter to John Elliot Cairnes, XVII*, 1831–1832.

Section 3
People and Organizations in the Digital Age

Chapter 7
Born Digital:
How Native Digital Status Shapes Ethical Behavior and Consumer Dissonance

Julieta Díez-Hernández
https://orcid.org/0000-0001-9935-077X
University of Burgos, Spain

Paula Antón-Maraña
https://orcid.org/0000-0003-1299-1385
University of Burgos, Spain

ABSTRACT

This chapter examines the impact of digital nativeness and generational identity on ethical values and responsible consumption behaviours in Spain. Through a data-driven analysis of six generational cohorts, the findings reveal significant intergenerational differences in both the strength of ethical values and the consistency of ethical behaviour. Notably, digital immigrants demonstrate higher ethical commitment and more responsible consumption than digital natives. Accordingly, the former presents a stronger coherence between intention and behaviour, although there is no cognitive dissonance on any of the groups. The study validates key ethical consumption theories and introduces the DAS BIE scale as a novel tool for assessing generational differences. Practical implications highlight the need for targeted educational initiatives, ethical marketing strategies, and digital tools that align values with actions. This research underscores the need of a people-centred digital transformation to bridge generational disparities and foster a more sustainable, ethically engaged society..

DOI: 10.4018/979-8-3373-0385-7.ch007

INTRODUCTION

From 2018 onwards, teenagers around the world, with Greta Thunberg as their spokesperson, led a weekly demonstration, demanding adults, ruling the world and their lives, paying attention to the climate crisis, and taking action (e.g. Stephen Stromberg, 2019). Three aspects stood out in Fridays for the Future protests: the striking youth of the demonstrators, who voiced strong ethical concerns about the planet's future; the rise of an intergenerational conflict (Higgs & Gilleard, 2015) which was then magnified in the times of COVID-19 (Ellerich-Groppe et al., 2021) and the pivotal role of new technologies and social media in rapidly replicating these protests worldwide.

While these demonstrations highlighted the power of youth-led movements and the catalytic role of digital platforms, they also raised a fundamental question: how can technological advancement be reconciled with the ethical imperatives demanded by younger generations? In this context, ensuring that digital transformation places people—and the values they defend—at its core becomes essential. Technology must remain a means to enhance human dignity and social responsibility, rather than an end in itself. Achieving this alignment is crucial if we are to leverage digital innovation in ways that promote sustainability, equity, and collective well-being (Hartley et al., 2024; Wallimann-Helmer et al., 2021).

Generation Z, to which most of those demonstrators belonged, has been raised in the digital world, hyperaware of global news on injustice and climate disasters, and exposed to online hate speeches, infinite information sources, and raging activism (Tiainen, 2024). Nevertheless, Gen Z, considered as a completely 'digital native' generation (Naci Çoklar & Tatli, 2021), and well-known for their ethical and conscientious values (Djafarova & Foots, 2022) is the main consumer of unsustainable ultra-fast fashion, moved by materialistic motivations, yet feeling a mild sense of responsibility for their purchases (Zimand-Sheiner & Lissitsa, 2024). This sole example reflects a predisposition towards higher cognitive dissonance (Festinger, 1957) than the previous generations, attributed to the limits caused by the frugality of their current stage of life (Djafarova & Foots, 2022).

Transformations in core values throughout generations has shaped the way in which individuals, as consumers (Nakova, 2024), but also as citizens (Cho et al., 2020), interact with one another, and with the non-human beings (Bonifacio et al., 2024; Otegui Carles et al., 2023). The younger generations have topped the previous ones in environmental awareness (Stephen Stromberg, 2019), they show higher compassion for non-human beings that any generation before had shown (Nakova, 2024; Otegui Carles et al., 2023), however younger generations are also frequently portrayed in a negative light, being labelled as excessively consumer-oriented and harmful to the environment (Diprose et al., 2019). Moreover, They have surpassed any other generation in antisocial behaviours (Nagata et al., 2023), suicide ideation (Twenge et al., 2019) and materialism (Gentina & Tang, 2024; Zimand-Sheiner & Lissitsa, 2024).

This research aims at pinning down the effect that generational cohorts have on ethical values and consumer behaviours, building on Muncy & Vitell (1992) concept of "consumer ethics" and the works of philosopher Adela Cortina (2002), on the ethical values of consumers in a globalised society, the cognitive dissonance is studied for every different generations from the Silent Generation (born between 1928 and 1945) to Generation Z (born from 1997 to 2013). Besides, this study innovatively traces the effect of digital nativeness on such dissonance and includes environmental consciousness into the equation.

To analyse the effect of being born and raised in a digital-led environment, it is vital to study the consumer's decision-making process, in which cognitive dissonance, or the imbalance between ideas and actions, plays a major role. While this dissonance has been studied for consumers' sustainable behaviours, for instance, individuals may advocate for sustainability yet purchase non-sustainable products due to convenience or cost constraints (García-Allen, 2015; Marron, 2020), it has never been conceptualized from an intergenerational perspective, considering the impacts of digitalization on consumers' values and behaviours.

Aligned with prior research (Ivanova et al., 2019; Lazarevic, 2012), generational segmentation aims not to account for individual differences but to highlight common values within a group while avoiding oversimplified generalizations. Consequently, this chapter aims to examine how digital nativeness and generational identity shape ethical values and responsible consumption behaviours in a digitally mediated society. By analysing intergenerational differences across ethical constructs—such as solidarity, sustainability, social justice, responsibility, and respect—it explores how people of different ages and digital experiences internalize and enact ethics in their everyday consumer choices. Situated within the Spanish context, the study contributes to the broader conversation on how digital transformation intersects with value systems, revealing both challenges and opportunities for fostering ethical and sustainable practices across generations.

For studying these relationships, a survey was conducted collecting a sample of 937 responses from Spain. The results show that digital immigrants (Silent Generation, Baby Boomers, and Generation X) score significantly higher on ethical values and demonstrate more consistent responsible consumption behaviours than digital natives (Millennials, Zillennials, and Generation Z). Furthermore, while both groups show a positive correlation between values and behaviours, the predictive strength is notably weaker among digital natives, suggesting a growing intention-behaviour gap.

The main contributions of this chapter are as follows. First, it offers empirical validation of the influence of digital nativeness on consumer ethics, highlighting the need to move beyond traditional generational segmentation and consider digital experience as a key dimension in ethical behaviour. Second, it combines Cortina's ethics of consumption with the Theory of Reasoned Action and the Muncy and Vitell (1992) model to explain behavioural inconsistencies and ethical decision-making processes, particularly among younger, digitally native cohorts. Third, by incorporating sociodemographic factors such as income, education, and gender, it provides a multidimensional view of the structural and motivational elements that shape ethical engagement. Finally, the chapter addresses the urgent need for inter-generational dialogue and inclusive policy design by revealing ethical tensions across digital generations. In doing so, it contributes to a more equitable, human-centred vision of sustainability, where technological progress supports ethical awareness, social justice, and responsible consumption.

The chapter is structured as follows: first, the theoretical background is presented, including relevant literature on generational theory, consumer ethics, and consumer behaviours. It ends with the definition of the study's hypotheses. Next, the methodology is detailed, including the measurement scales and the characteristics of the sample. Then, the results are presented and discussed in relation to the existing literature and theoretical framework. Finally, the chapter concludes by summarising the key findings, highlighting the academic and practical contributions, and suggesting directions for future research.

LITERATURE REVIEW AND HYPOTHESES FORMULATION

Generational Cohorts and Digital Nativeness

The Generational Cohorts Theory (Inglehart, 1977) proposes a framework that clusters individuals in groups following the idea that those who experienced similar social, economic, cultural and political views in their youth would end up having similar beliefs, values, attitudes and behaviours for the rest of their lives. In this line Generational Cohorts are conceptualised groups of individuals born during the same timeframe who experience life together, going through similar events in their teenage and young adulthood years (Baigorri, 2008; Strauss & Howe, 1991), the effect that these events cause in their personalities remains for their lifetime, shaping their collective identity's attitudes, values, buying behaviours and expectations (Schewe & Meredith, 2004). Nevertheless, the semantic sense in which generations should be conceptualised, must not be limited to demographic cohorts, but should include course of life, life cycle, life span and life stages (Alwin, 2012; Caballero & Baigorri, 2019).

Digital nativeness was firstly defined by Prensky (2001), considering that those born after 1980s share the common trait of being raised surrounded by technology, and therefore relying on digital tools and information technologies for the development of their lives. Figure 1 presents some of the best-known Information technology popularisation in relation to the different generations born around the same years.

Figure 1. Information technology diffusion and generational cohorts

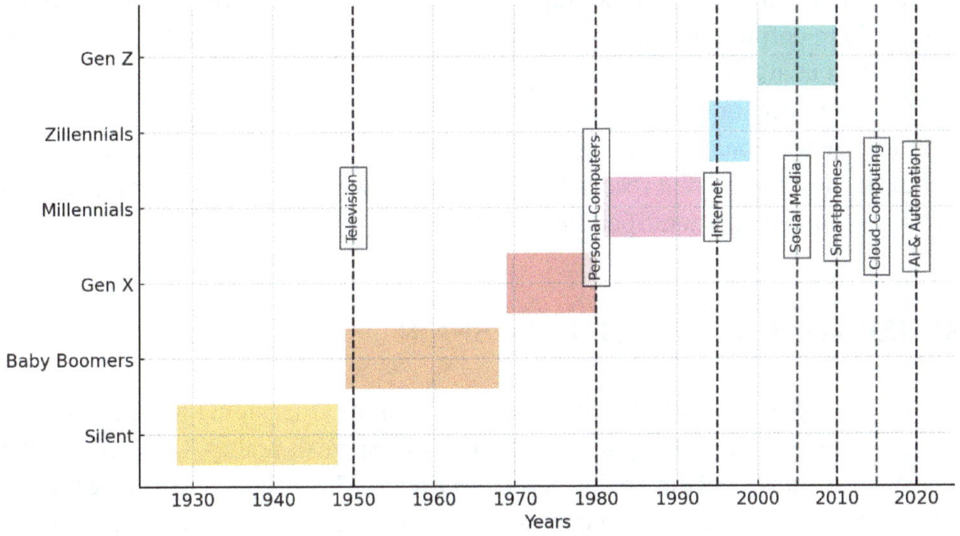

This concept, as a basis for generational change, has been questioned because of the lack of empirical evidence (Bennett et al., 2008; Bennett & Maton, 2011). Nevertheless, recent studies have considered the breach existing between digital natives and digital immigrants for analysing differences in teaching and learning environments (Aavakare & Nikou, 2020a; Bristow, 2010), in creative industries and workers digital literacy (Nikou et al., 2020), in organisational studies (Wang et al., 2013), marketing strategies (Cabeza-Ramírez et al., 2022; Munsch, 2021) or in banking decisions (Agárdi & Alt, 2022; Park et al., 2024).

However, considering the inclusion of other socioeconomic and demographic criteria for identifying generational shifts, digital natives and digital immigrants have been studied extensively in the context of their identities, attitudes, values, buying behaviours, and expectations. In terms of buying behaviours and consumer attitudes, digital natives show distinct characteristics, according to literature they are more likely to rely on digital media for product information, while mastering the avoidance of digital advertising (Chang & Chang, 2023; Munsch, 2021). Generation Z, responding positively in particular to short, humorous digital marketing with music and social media influencers (Munsch, 2021). Additionally, digital natives show a greater inclination to use mobile payment systems and to perceive less financial risk when doing so (Agárdi & Alt, 2022), while digital immigrants are more influenced by perceived ease of use and subjective norms when adopting new technologies (Agárdi & Alt, 2022).

Some authors have criticised this theory as it assumes that the two groups are dichotomised, while evidence show that digital nativeness is closer to falling in a continuum in which other demographical, cultural, social and psychological traits play a role in defining technological literacy (Aavakare & Nikou, 2020a; Bristow, 2010; Wang et al., 2013).

In order to account for the different semantic subtleties and opposing theories regarding generational shifts and the existence of a digital breach independent to digital fluency, the current research has been narrowed to a analysing the potential effects in a single country. Specifically, in Spain.

GENERATIONAL COHORTS IN SPAIN

Caballero & Baigorri (2019) considered the multidimensional nature of generations to glocalise the theory and adapt it to the Spanish reality. Considering the year-of-birth biological dimension based on Ortega y Gasset concept of "date areas", but also the social, cultural and economic dimension, the authors built a model to address the social phenomenon of generation for putting into analysis the specificities of the contemporaneous generations coexisting during the 20th Century in the Spanish society (Caballero & Baigorri, 2019), as shown in Table 1.

Table 1. Caballero & Baigorri (2019) localisation of the generational theory to the Spanish contemporary reality

Name	Year of birth	Events shaping their generational identity
Silenced generation	1914–1928	Political instability, poverty, and authoritarian rule shaped a generation that later fought in the Civil War and was silenced by the ensuing dictatorship.
Francoist Generation	1929–1943	This generation was marked by political instability, the Civil War, and National Catholicism. The generations shaped by war and repression later played roles in both Franco's regime and the democratic transition, creating lasting divisions and obstacles for future generations.
Generation of protest or the Baby boom	1944–1958	This generation experienced the post-war hardships and the early benefits of economic recovery. Coming from poorer regions, they shifted from rationing to slight increases in consumption. Few attended universities, but by the late 1960s, many joined opposition movements against Franco. Rejecting previous ideologies, they embraced new values like pacifism, feminism, environmentalism, and anti-bureaucracy.

continued on following page

Table 1. Continued

Name	Year of birth	Events shaping their generational identity
Generation X	1959–1973	pain's economic growth, fuelled by development plans, led to urban migration and modernization. This generation grew up with more material security but still faced traditional education and values. Many attended university, and women gained full access to the workforce. Their youth in the 1980s was marked by social changes, a cultural boom, and the impact of mass unemployment, alongside a rise in drug use that cost many lives.
Generation Y	1974–1988	a global economic crisis and political instability marked Spain's transition to democracy. After the Moncloa Pacts and Spain's 1986 entry into the EEC, the country stabilized. The Millennial generation grew up under democracy, benefiting from new freedoms and social policies, with secular education and exposure to personal computers and video games. However, a new economic crisis delayed their independence, leaving them frustrated by unfulfilled promises and a stagnant job market.
Generation Z	1989–2003	At the end of the century, Spain's economy expanded until the 2008 recession. The Maastricht Treaty and the adoption of the Euro marked this period. This generation grew up without material struggles, immersed in globalisation, multiculturalism, and expanded rights. They experienced diverse family structures, attended schools managing cultural diversity, and were raised in a consumer-driven society. As digital natives, they adapted quickly to new technologies like computers, video games, and the internet.

This approximation, differs slightly from Strauss & Howe (1991) distinction of four generations – the Silent Generation (1925-1942), the Baby Boomers (1943-1960); Generation X (1961-1981) and Generation Y (1982-2000) – and its more recent reconfiguration by (McCrindle, 2014) – Boomers (1946–1964); Gen X (1965–1979), Gen Y (1980–1994), Gen Z (1995–2010), and Gen Alpha (2010-present).

For this study an integrative approach straddling the different classifications have been developed, in order to catch the nuances of the contemporary Spanish society, while respecting an integrative nomenclature and timeframes.

Besides, another generation has been included between Gen Y and Gen Z, this is the Zillennial or Cusper Generation (Fullscreen, 2019; Llanos Anaya & Paredes Quenta, 2023), born at the cusp of the century, the state of development of the technologies during their upbringing justifies its differences from other generations, conceiving a "micro-generation" (Cheong, 2023; Elmore, 2022; Napoli, 2020). As children, they experienced the shift from analogue to digital. They recall a childhood without pervasive internet but adapted swiftly to emerging technologies during their adolescence (Peralta, 2024). They are more likely cohort to self-identify as person of colour, minority, LGBTQ or another intersectional identity (Fullscreen, 2019). They are less wealthy than Gen Z, but more economically stable (PYMNTS, 2023). They have more disposable income than the previous generation and are less price sensible than Millennials, showing a higher loyalty towards brands (Siu, 2023). These differences serve as a basis for studying whether there is a significant difference between this micro-generation's personal values and ethical behaviours and the other digital natives' generations.

Ethical Consumption Theory

Individual ethical consumption is rooted in personal and sociocultural values, as highlighted by philosopher Adela Cortina. She posits that the need for an ethics of consumption arises from the social repercussions of individual acts. Economic crises, according to Cortina, stem from a lack of ethics in consumption, economic management, and corporate social responsibility, leading to consumerism and undermining sustainability. She proposes an ethics of consumption based on values such as freedom, equality, solidarity, and happiness, emphasizing the selection of ethical criteria and lifestyles aligned with these values (Cortina, 2002).

Cortina introduces the concept of the *Homo consumens Era,* a time in which humanity focuses on consumerism and its relationship with happiness and social progress. However, she observes a shift towards more rational and responsible consumption, highlighting the importance of autonomy and justice, emphasizing virtues like prudence and wisdom to balance consumption. Her advocacy for autonomous consumers uniting in groups with common goals links her theory with Ballestero Izquierdo (2011) theory for developing social ethics for individual consumption. Expands upon Cortina's theory by advocating for co-responsibility and happiness as fundamental aspects of consumption ethics.

Ethical consumption is based on reciprocity and decisions that do not harm others or the environment, promoting sustainable lifestyles and collective defence of interests. Ballestero Izquierdo proposes a social ethics of consumption that supports environmentally respectful practices and coherence between ethical principles and consumption actions, cautioning against ethical consumption becoming an elitist trend (2011). Collectively, Cortina's ethical consumption theory is founded on autonomy, justice, co-responsibility, and happiness, supplemented by sustainability and coherence, to prevent the proposed system from failing when applied in an unsustainable environment with inconsistent consumers (Cortina, 2002). Based on her theory, a set of five underlying ethical values are defined, namely, solidarity, sustainability, justice, responsibility and respect.

Solidarity

Cortina and Ballesteros highlight an ethical framework based on highly consolidated values among which they talk about solidarity. The current conception of the term solidarity is closely connected to the French *fraternité,* which carrying political connotations (Ellerich-Groppe et al., 2021). Durkheim et al. (2014) differentiates two types of solidarity, a mechanical conception prominent in archaic societies based on homogeneity, tradition and shared life worlds, and a modern organic solidarity, tending to functionality and individualisation. Ellerich-Groppe et al. (2020) reduce all the different implications and connotations of the term solidarity to three overarching conceptual elements: (1) belonging to a group with shared characteristics, (2) commitment requirement among its members, and (3) willingness to bear costs for the benefit of the collective, balancing resources and values. The concept of intergenerational solidarity has gained prominence in public discourses, especially in the context of the COVID-19 pandemic, highlighting the complex dynamics of social cohesion in late-modern societies (Ellerich-Groppe et al., 2021). With demographic aging widespread in Western societies, the discussion on social security systems' long-term sustainability has usually been accompanied by claims of overaging population and scapegoating the elders (Fealy et al., 2012; Gee & Gutman, 2000), considered as burdening younger cohorts (A. Walker, 2012).

From a generational cohorts' perspective, research indicates varying perceptions of solidarity across generations. A survey conducted in Switzerland, Germany and France revealed that 65% of respondents believe younger individuals are too self-focused, a sentiment shared by 70% of Millennials and Generation X participants, 52% of Millennials feel that older generations benefit at their expense, although the majority of Baby boomers and older generations disagree with this assessment, highlighting intergenerational tensions regarding mutual support (Swiss Life, 2016). Other studies highlighted the different stances of different cohorts, concluding that in times of recession, solidarity values are reduced, and highlighting that whereas Generation X showed a more socio-democratic type of solidarity towards citizens, Millennials usually present a liberal type of solidarity towards the poor (Helve, 2023).

Sustainability

The term sustainability has been used to the point of exhaustion in ecology and development literature (Ruggerio, 2021). However, it is worth remembering that its most literal meaning relates to maintenance over time (Grober, 2007). In the same way that sustainable development refers to a type of development that does not compromise the resources of future generations while meeting the needs of the present (Brundtland, 1987), sustainability as a value refers to resilience (Ruggerio, 2021; Walker et al., 2006), to the ability to maintain certain lifestyles over time. Opposed to these ideas of maintenance over time, is the materialist consumerism values that overshadows the risk of unsustainability (Isham et al., 2022).

From generational cohorts' perspectives different attitudes relating to resilience have been identified in literature, with Gen Z showing lower resilience than Gen X (Harari et al., 2022), or with different perceptions on lack of sustainability risks differing among generations (Divasson-J et al., 2025). Shiel et al. (2020) refers to the term "generativity" defined as the concern for the future, determining that age is a relevant variable that influences generativity which dramatically increase in elder groups.

Justice

Cortina (2002) refers to Kantian ethics, and their principles of individual freedom as the core for moral behaviours and universality for making a norm fair and just. Cortina makes justice a key element for an ethical consumption framework, alongside happiness, autonomy and responsibility. As it refers to universal justice towards peers, it has been named as social justice. Justice has been studied from a generational perspective, as a matter of resource allocation, highlighting the intergenerational conflict predicted by Preston (1984) derived from economic downturns which benefited present-day baby-boomers' advantages at the expense of younger cohorts with more restricted education, employment and social rights, and less redistributive trends (Higgs & Gilleard, 2015).

Responsibility

Both Cortina (2002) and Ballestero Izquierdo (2011) consider mutual responsibility, or co-responsibility as a key value for ethical consumption. While responsibility and its counterpart accountability, are usual in organisational studies, in the sense of roles' enforcement and duties recognition (Grossi et al., 2007; Wood & Winston, 2007), these terms have been also conceptualised in a broad sense, pinning accountability as a universal feature of decision-making, present in everyday choices (Mendez, 2009; Tetlock, 1985), for Tetlock et al. (1989) accountability serves as an essential enforcement mechanism for rules and norms that highlights the social psychological connection between individual thinkers and the social systems they belong to. From a generational perspective, responsibility has been studied in the sense of mutual obligations. While the Silent Generation felt family, and marital obligations as part of their identity and responsibility (Galea, 2012), especially in widowed women (Longoria, 2022), Baby boomers do not want to label themselves as caregivers or adhere to family responsibilities as a defining trait for their identities (Guberman et al., 2012). For younger generations, research on responsibility is limited to workplace dynamics (Kuron et al., 2015; Ng et al., 2010) and corporate social responsibility (Dave & Parikh, 2022; Divasson-J et al., 2025; Narayanan, 2022; Uche, 2018), reflecting a shift toward a more institutional and professional understanding of accountability rather than personal or familial obligations (Ng et al., 2010). This evolution suggests that while responsibility remains a core ethical value, its interpretation and application vary across generations, shaped by social, economic, and cultural changes.

Respect

Cortina (2002) notion of respect relies on the idea of autonomy and freedom of choice, as according to her theory, societies where autonomous will is respected and taken into consideration in decision-making achieve the basis for individual happiness (Ballestero Izquierdo, 2011).

Respect has been studied in generational studies for organisational and institutional contexts to analyse differences in institutional loyalty, respect towards authority and rule-following attitudes (Singh & Prakash, 2020), these values were reported high for Baby Boomers, but reduce their strength for Gen X and Millennials, specially in work-related environments (Singh & Prakash, 2020). In the sense of autonomy versus dependency in decision-making, it was studied in life-stage cohorts by Luszcz & Fitzgerald (1986) concluding that middle-aged cohorts are more autonomous than elders and adolescents, being younger cohorts the least autonomous, at least from the other generations' perspectives. Therefore, there are diverting perspectives regarding the idea that respect and its related concepts depend on the stage of life rather than on the generation (Jecker, 2021).

The literature review on generational cohorts and Cortina (2002) values for ethical consumption hint that there is an underlying characterisation of the values in relation to environmental, social and institutional stances as institutional roles are often discussed in literature on solidarity (Ellerich-Groppe et al., 2020), respect (Singh & Prakash, 2020) and justice (Higgs & Gilleard, 2015). Environmental awareness and considerations in sustainability (Divasson-J et al., 2025; Isham et al., 2022) and responsibility (Narayanan, 2022; Uche, 2018), and social considerations in all of the described values (e.g. Divasson-J et al., 2025; Ellerich-Groppe et al., 2021; Singh & Prakash, 2020).

In order to acknowledge this influence, a Triple Bottom Line (Elkington, 1998) approach has been followed to study the nuances in values' recognitions among generations in the present study. This approach has been employed for developing the questionnaire regarding ethical values, including items that reflect the conceptualisation of each of the values from a social, environmental and economic or institutional point of view (Diprose et al., 2019).

Translating Values to Behaviors

The Theory of Reasoned Action (TRA) proposed by Ajzen & Fishbein (1980) identifies three key considerations that shape human actions. First, "behavioural beliefs" involve the perceptions of possible outcomes associated with a specific behaviour, which in turn influence whether one holds a positive or critical attitude toward it. Second, "normative beliefs" relate to the social expectations and behaviours of others, creating social pressures or subjective norms. Third, "control beliefs" refer to the perceived factors that can either enable or hinder certain behaviours, thereby affecting an individual's sense of control or self-efficacy (Bosnjak et al., 2020). It posits that individual intention to engage in a behaviour is the most immediate predictor of its actual execution (Ivanova et al., 2019; Toleikienė et al., 2020). It is considered a suitable theoretical basis for evaluating individuals' attitudes towards ethical behaviours (De Pelsmacker & Janssens, 2007; Fukukawa, 2003) and sustainable consumption patterns (Jebarajakirthy et al., 2024).

However, literature is divided regarding the adequacy of TRA to analyse ethical consumption, as there is not consistent evidence of beliefs translating into behaviours in responsible or pro-environmental consumption (Carrington et al., 2014; Zaikauskaitė et al., 2022). While environmentally consciousness has been conceptualised in consumer behaviour studies as a synonym to moral behaviour (Markowitz & Shariff, 2012), and the responsible consumer as motivated by moral beliefs (Crane et al., 2019), literature has shown that there is an existing gap between the beliefs, values and attitudes the consumers adhere to, and the behavioural patterns they ascribe (Zaikauskaitė et al., 2022).

This gap, referred to as the intention-behaviour gap (Carrington et al., 2014; Zaikauskaitė et al., 2022), portrays the existence of cognitive dissonance (Festinger, 1957). Literature has shown that there exist an inconsistency between values or attitudes and behaviours, which is exceptionally pronounced in environmental choices' scenarios (Zaikauskaitė et al., 2022)

Consumer Behavior and Generational Cohorts

Consumption behaviour has been studied regarding different generational cohorts. Authors as Pekerti & Arli (2017) have documented a change in the last decades in generational values which is affecting consumer behaviours.

While there is mixed evidence on age and generations affecting responsible consumption, with some authors concluding that consuming responsible alternatives as fair trade or eco-labelled products does not vary significantly among age cohorts (Brécard et al., 2012; Doran, 2009; Lange et al., 2015).

There have been plenty of examples in literature that present behaviours differing significantly between cohorts, with Baby Boomers producing higher emissions than younger generations in France (Chancel, 2014). In the context of sustainable and green product purchases, environmental concern and perceived consumer effectiveness have been discovered to be strong antecedents of sustainable purchase behaviour across Gens X, Y and Z (Casalegno et al., 2022). For responsible consumption, a comparison of Gen X and Y showed that there were significant difference among the generations in the intention to purchase environmentally responsible products, regarding perceived consumer effectiveness, their ability to influence in environmental outcomes which is more pronounced for Xers, and media exposure which influences Millennials more (Ivanova et al., 2019). Younger generations perceive higher values and are more prone to buy second-hand clothing than older cohorts, with Gen Y showing the strongest resistance (Liang & Xu, 2018). Digital natives' generations are more prone to use online banking services and contactless payment methods (Agárdi & Alt, 2022).

Environmental citizenship (defined as the active participation or willingness to participate in environmental organisations), only influence younger generations (Y and Z) purchase behaviour, while collectivism influences sustainable purchase behaviour solely for Gen Z (Casalegno et al., 2022).

Morality, Muncy-Vittel, and Ethical Consumption

Marketing research has adopted a framework based on moral philosophy for ethical behaviours developed by Hunt & Vitell (1986) according to which morality serves as a core parameter for decision-making in consumption. While the theory has been validated on organisational and mass consumer studies (S. D. Hunt & Laverie, 2004; S. J. Vitell et al., 2001). However, there have been not many studies linking the Hunt-Vittel theory to green consumption (Arikan & Jiang, 2018; Lu et al., 2015; Nimri et al., 2021; Zaikauskaitė et al., 2022). Based on this theory, Muncy and Vittel developed a scale of unethical consumer behaviours (Muncy & Vitell, 1992; S. J. Vitell & Muncy, 2005), difining a taxonomy of actions that conceptualise unethical consumption behaviours (Ramos-Hidalgo et al., 2022). These authors defined consumer ethics as the moral principles and norms that influence how individuals or groups acquire, utilize, and discard goods and services (Sharma, 2022).

Muncy and Vittel works has previously been employed in generational studies. Grzesiuk & Wanat (2010) analysed the differences in results for the Muncy-Vittel scale original sample of US students and Polish students, concluding the relevance of the age group, their hypothesis was that young students would achieve lower scores compared to older ones, which was partially accepted. Mladjan & Marković (2021) studied the generational responsibility in consumption for responding to economic crises, considering generational responsibility as a phenomenon dependent on community solidarity, they build on Muncy and Vitell (2005) scale, which determined that consumers' ethical behaviour is closely linked to their environmental consciousness and willingness to engage in post-consumption activities, considering that the attitude consumers hold toward ethical consumption, which contributes to resource preservation for future generations, varies based on the consumption context (Mladjan & Marković, 2021). Van Kenhove et al., (2001) used their framework to understand how ethical beliefs and ideology influenced Dutch-speaking customers considering different age groups. Sharma (2022) qualitatively examined the ethical behaviours of Millennials based on different ethical consumption theories, concluding that Millennials consider ethics as relative, they are sceptical about them, and while they understand how consumption can contribute to a degrading environment their willingness to change consumption behaviour was weak. Comparing unethical consumer behaviour, following Muncy-Vittel scale, in French and Chinese Gen Zers and the traits that are behind their materialism show differences in the traits that influence the unethical behaviours regarding self-esteem and power (Gentina & Tang, 2024).

Hypotheses Formulation

To understand how these differences affect generations' actual buying predisposition, Cortina's (2002) work on the values that influence ethical consumption have been employed, namely solidarity, sustainability, social justice, responsibility, and respect, have been analysed as core ethical values. While analysing behavioural patterns, a scale was designed based on Vitell and Muncy (2005), clustering unethical behavioural patterns in consumer actions. These have been characterized and transformed into a construct for responsible behaviour.

Four hypotheses were developed based on the theoretical framework and research gaps identified in literature (Figure 2). Two generational clusters have been differentiated: Digital Immigrants, encompassing those pertaining to the Silent, Baby Boom and X generations, and Digital Natives, gathering the Millennials, Zillenials and Z Generation.

Figure 2. Conceptual model

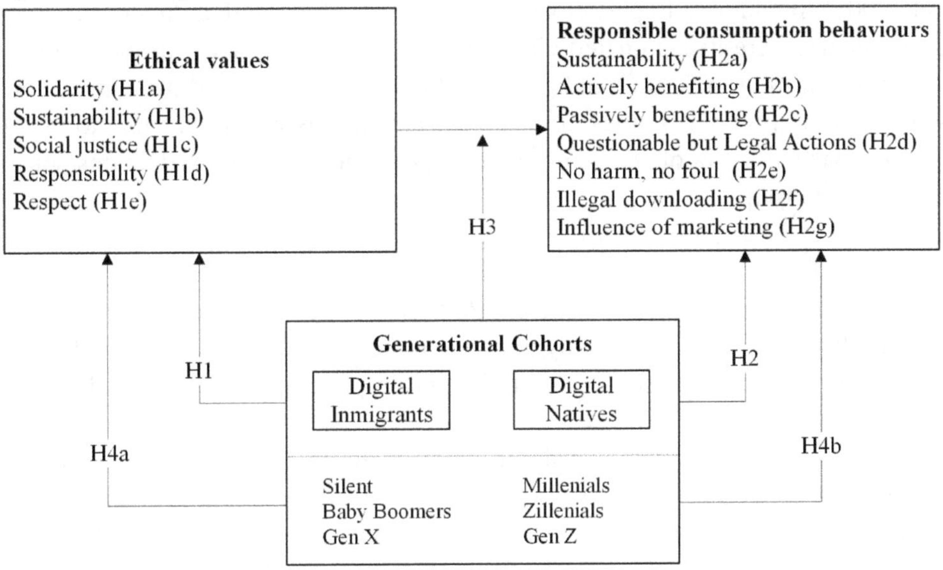

H1: Digital immigrants and natives differ in ethical values: solidarity (H1a), sustainability (H1b), social justice (H1c), responsibility (H1d), and respect (H1e).

H2: Digital Immigrants and Digital natives differ in responsible consumption behaviours regarding sustainability (H2a), actively benefiting (H2b), passively benefiting (H2c), engaging in questionable but legal actions (H2d), actions based on "no harm, no foul" (H2e), illegal downloading (H2f), and the influence of marketing (H2g).

H3: There is no cognitive dissonance between ethical values and responsible consumption behaviour among Digital Immigrants (H3a), but there is cognitive dissonance among digital natives (H3b).

H4: The six generational cohorts differ in ethical values (H4a) and responsible behaviour (H4b).

MEANS AND METHODS

Data Collection

This study employed a web-based self-administered survey to collect data from consumers across six generational cohorts. A structured questionnaire was designed and distributed online, leveraging the benefits of digital surveys such as reduced response time, cost efficiency, and broader accessibility (Green et al., 2004; Ilieva et al., 2002). Invitations to participate in the survey, along with a direct link to the questionnaire, were disseminated via WhatsApp, leveraging its widespread usage for communication in Spain. Additionally, the survey was shared through various associations, old people's homes, companies, high schools, and universities to ensure a diverse participant pool. This approach helped reach diverse participants across different age groups.

The data collection took place in Burgos, a mid-sized Spanish city with a population of 148,862. To ensure representativeness, the minimum sample size was calculated based on statistical parameters (Table 2). Participants were selected using the snowball sampling technique. This study aimed to collect data from 661 respondents in Spain, covering six generational cohorts. The target population included individuals born between 1928 and 2007, encompassing Silent, Baby Boomers, X, Millenials, Zillenials and Z Generations. In order to preserve the peculiarities surrounding the consumption of people born between 1995 and 1999, a generation halfway between the Gen Z and the Millenials, groups with very specific consumption patterns, we have resorted to studying this generation, Zillenials, separately (Hontañon Pombo, 2023; Peralta, 2024; PYMNTS, 2023). The primary goal was to obtain a minimum sample size per generational cohort to ensure representativeness. However, given that a snowball sampling method was employed, controlling the exact number of participants for each cohort was challenging.

Table 2. Generational distribution of the target

Generation	Age in 2023	Born in	Inhabitants	Minimum sample size for it to be representative [1]
Z	16-23	2000 - 2007	13,916	62
Zillenials	24-29	1994 - 1999	9,730	43
Millenials	30-42	1981 - 1993	26,060	116
X	43-54	1969 - 1980	32,600	145
Baby Boomers	55-74	1949 - 1968	45,877	204
Silent	>75	1928 - 1948	20,679	92
Total			**148,862**	**661**

Following Aavakare & Niko (2020) critique of the concept of Digital Native responses from a single country and region were collected, as the authors pointed out that not only does generation should count for considering someone as Digital Immigrant or Native, but other characteristics as their cultural background, socio-economic status, and overall their relationship with digital technologies should also be considered (Aavakare & Nikou, 2020a). Consequently, limiting the study to a single country could reduce potential biases existing when more heterogeneous backgrounds are considered.

Participants were informed about the voluntary nature of their participation, and consent was obtained before they proceeded with the survey[2]. To enhance response rates, respondents were assured of the confidentiality and anonymity of their data. They were also given the option to exit the survey at any point without any obligation. The questionnaire was structured to ensure clarity and ease of response, guiding participants to consider their overall digital experiences rather than a single digital interaction. Data collection was carried out during the autumn of 2023, using a cloud-based survey platform that facilitated efficient response gathering and management.

As the response rate dropped after a collection period of 5 weeks, it was determined that the collection window be closed and reaching a total of 959 completed questionnaires (43% over the minimum sample size required for it to be representative). To ensure data quality, a cleaning process was conducted, and responses were reviewed for inconsistencies. A total of 22 surveys were removed based on the following criteria: (a) evidence of random answering patterns (e.g., straight-lining responses), (b) incomplete surveys with more than half of the key research questions unanswered, or (c) responses with illogical or contradictory answers (e.g., providing similar responses to opposing questions). After filtering out these cases, 937 valid responses were retained for analysis.

Instrument

To gather information to prove or deny the already presented hypothesis, a questionnaire was developed, divided into four differentiated parts, and structured into 47 questions. The first measured consumer demographics: age, educational attainment, gender, annual income, and current occupation.

Second, to measure consumers' ethical values, Cortina (2002) and Alberto Ballestero's (2011) philosophy-infused Theory of a Socially Ethical Consumption was used as a basis, associating five ethical values with responsible consumption: solidarity, sustainability, social justice, responsibility, and respect. Three questions were used to assess each value considering a Triple Bottom Line perspective (Elkington, 1998) using a 5-point Likert scale (1: not at all identified, 2: somewhat identified, 3: moderately identified, 4: quite identified and 5: totally identified) and building ad hoc a new scale titled DAS BIE (Table 3).

Table 3. The DAS BIE scale

Statements	1	2	3	4	5
Solidarity					
I believe it is necessary to work together to address global environmental challenges.					
I contribute to the well-being of my social environment (family, work, education, etc.).					
I believe institutions should invest in community support programs.					
Sustainability					
I believe it is essential to ensure a healthy future for the planet.					
My decisions are more influenced by the future than by the present.					
I prefer to save for the future rather than consume in the present.					
Social Justice					
I believe all countries should have the same environmental regulations.					
I care about citizens living in precarious conditions.					
I value living in a society that guarantees equal rights and opportunities					
Responsibility					
I consider environmental impact when making decisions.					
I do not like others making decisions for me.					
I value the government implementing and fulfilling its proposals.					
Respect					
I contribute to respecting the environment (recycling, reusing, etc.).					
I believe it is important to treat all people with dignity and respect, regardless of their background or condition.					
I demand transparency and integrity in institutional and corporate practices.					

The development of the DAS BIE scale followed a rigorous and participatory process to ensure conceptual clarity, empirical robustness, and relevance to diverse consumer realities. The scale was co-produced through an intergenerational focus group that brought together participants of varying ages and socio-demographic backgrounds, including secondary students, university students, working adults, and retirees. This inclusive approach allowed the research team to capture a wide range of perceptions and interpretations of ethical values, ensuring that the items were contextually meaningful and generationally sensitive.

In addition, the scale underwent expert validation through a panel of university scholars in the fields of marketing, ethics, and sustainability. These academic experts provided feedback on the clarity, theoretical coherence, and applicability of each item, helping refine the language and structure of the scale. The iterative development process culminated in a measurement instrument that is both theoretically grounded and empirically informed, tailored to assess ethical value identification across generational cohorts in a robust and interdisciplinary manner.

In the last two sections, the Muncy-Vitell Ethical Consumer Behaviour Scale (Vitell & Muncy, 2005) was used to measure consumers' predisposition to engage in unethical consumer behaviour and sustainable consumer behaviour, building the responsible behaviour construct, the scale was modified through the same focus group that co-produced the DAS BIE scale to allow a correct translation and adaptation to current consumer ethical dilemmas. The Muncy-Vitell Scale introduces a taxonomy of actions in which consumers may behave better or worse. Table 4 presents situations in which consumers may actively benefit from a situation at the expense of others, passively benefit, engage in questionable but legal actions, participate in so-called "no harm, no foul" actions, engage in actions related to illegal downloading and piracy, let advertising influence their behaviour.

A 5-point Likert scale was used, as the scale was originally created to identified non-ethical behaviours the scale corresponds to the frequency of the unethical behaviour. 1 corresponding to "I never do it and/or I would never do it"; 2 corresponding to "I rarely do it and/or I would rarely do it"; 3, to "I sometimes do it and/or I would sometimes do it"; 4, "I often do it and/or I would often do it" and 5 corresponds to "I always do it and/or I would always do it".

Table 4. Adaptation of the scale for ethical consumption developed by Muncy-Vittel (1992)

Behaviours	1	2	3	4	5
Actively benefitting (ACT)					
Drinking or eating a product in a store without paying for it.					
Cheating an insurance company, for example, by reporting a lost item as stolen.					
Lying about the age of a family member (child, sibling, cousin, etc.) to get a lower price.					
Passively benefiting (PAS)					
Realising that you have not been charged for a product and saying nothing.					
Receiving too much change and saying nothing.					
Seeing someone stealing discreetly in a shop (e.g. by putting things in their bag) and pretending nothing.					
Questionable but Legal Actions (QUEST)					
Hiding information you know when selling a second-hand product.					
Taking a "souvenir" from a hotel or vacation rental.					
Signing up for trial periods of services, clubs, or newsletters just to get free products.					
Accidentally breaking a product in a supermarket and leaving without saying or doing anything.					

continued on following page

Table 4. Continued

Behaviours	1	2	3	4	5
No harm, no foul (NOH)					
Returning an item after discovering it is now on sale and you can get it cheaper.					
Weighing fruit in the supermarket, labelling its price, and then adding more to the bag.					
Using a shared password to access a streaming service (e.g., sharing a Netflix profile).					
Using unpaid software, such as pirated Windows or Spotify.					
Illegal Downloading (DL)					
Downloading music or books from the internet instead of buying them.					
Buying counterfeit products instead of purchasing the original brands from manufacturers.					
Influence of Marketing (MK)					
Buying a product just because an influencer or celebrity recommended it on social media (Instagram, Facebook, TikTok, etc.).					
Buying a product you don't need just because an ad caught your attention.					

Finally, a set of statements (Table 5) regarding actions related to sustainability and sustainable behaviours was considered. These were presented separately to avoid confusion, as the polarity of the responses was inversed. For the development of this last set of questions, Vitell & Muncy (2005) scale REC category was taken as a basis and adapted considering the works by Rodriguez-Rad & Ramos-Hidalgo (2018) and Vitell et al. (2018).

Table 5. Adaptation of the Muncy-Vittel (2005) scale for responsible consmuption

Behaviours	1	2	3	4	5
Sustainability (SUST)					
I buy products labelled as environmentally friendly, even if they do not perform as well as competing products.					
I buy products made from recycled materials, even if they are more expensive.					
When purchasing products, I check that their ingredients are biodegradable.					
When buying cosmetics, I make sure they are cruelty-free, meaning they do not involve animal testing or experimentation.					
I avoid buying products that are harmful to the environment or very difficult to recycle.					
I stop buying products from companies that relocate their production abroad to reduce costs.					
I stop purchasing from a company after unethical practices in its production system come to light.					
I try to buy sustainable and/or second-hand clothing					

Once gathered, the questionnaire responses were tabulated and codified to then be inputted into the statistical analysis software SSPS, through which different tests were conducted to test the hypotheses, leading to the following results.

RESULTS

Sample Profile

A general overview of the sample profile (Table 6) was obtained via a descriptive analysis of the data. The study included 937 respondents across six generational cohorts: Silent, Baby Boomers, Generation X, Millennials, Zillenials, and Generation Z. The sample sizes varied across cohorts, with Generation Z, representing the largest group (328 respondents, 35%), followed by Baby Boomers (211 respondents, 23%) and Generation X (171 respondents, 18%). The remaining groups included Millennials (97 respondents, 10%), Zillenials (88 respondents, 9%), and the Silent generation (42 respondents, 4%). Due to the snowball sampling technique, the distribution among cohorts was not perfectly proportional to the population. Furthermore, the minimum sample size was exceeded for all generations except for the Silent Generation sample, exhibiting that this generation is the most difficult to reach through digitally distributed questionnaires.

Table 6. Sample profile

	Silent		Baby Boomers		X		Millenials		Zillenials		Z		Total	
	Count	%	Count	%	Count	%	Count	%	Count	%	Count	%	Count	%
Age														
16 - 23 years old											328	100%	328	35%
24 - 29 years old									88	100%			88	9%
30 - 42 years old							97	100%					97	10%
43 - 54 years old					171	100%							171	18%
55 - 74 years old			211	100%									211	23%
> 75 years old	42	100%											42	4%
Gender														
Female	23	55%	130	62%	117	68%	75	77%	56	64%	208	63%	609	65%
Male	15	36%	80	38%	51	30%	22	23%	31	35%	107	33%	306	33%
I prefer not to answer	2	5%	1	0%	3	2%	-	-	-	-	5	2%	11	1%
Other gender identity	2	5%	-	-	-	-	-	-	1	0%	8	2%	11	1%

continued on following page

Table 6. Continued

	Silent		Baby Boomers		X		Millenials		Zillenials		Z		Total	
	Count	%	Count	%	Count	%	Count	%	Count	%	Count	%	Count	%
Training														
Primary studies	20	48%	12	6%	-	-	-	-	-	-	13	4%	45	5%
Secondary studies	9	21%	27	13%	5	3%	3	3%	3	3%	66	20%	113	12%
Undergraduate studies	6	14%	33	16%	7	4%	3	3%	4	5%	143	44%	196	21%
Vocational studies	3	7%	40	19%	28	16%	6	6%	16	18%	57	17%	150	16%
Degree studies	2	5%	75	36%	91	53%	34	35%	25	28%	46	14%	273	29%
Postgraduate studies	2	5%	24	11%	40	23%	51	53%	40	45%	3	1%	160	17%
Income (gross per year)														
< 15,000 €	9	21%	30	14%	18	11%	12	12%	27	31%	57	17%	153	16%
15,000 € - 21,999 €	14	33%	39	18%	39	23%	25	26%	21	24%	4	1%	142	15%
22,000 € - 31,999 €	12	29%	70	33%	69	40%	28	29%	11	13%	2	1%	192	20%
> 32,000 €	5	12%	61	29%	38	22%	28	29%	7	8%	1	0%	140	15%
No income	2	5%	11	5%	7	4%	4	4%	22	25%	264	80%	310	33%
Occupation (multiple question)														
Unemployed	-	-	17	8%	9	5%	5	5%	7	8%	6	2%	44	5%
Student	1	2%	1	0%	4	2%	11	11%	39	44%	323	98%	379	40%
Retired	40	95%	109	52%	2	1%	-	-	-	-	-	-	149	16%
Employed person	-	-	27	13%	79	46%	53	55%	49	56%	37	11%	245	26%
Self-employed	-	-	8	4%	10	6%	3	3%	1	1%	5	2%	27	3%
Official servent	-	-	45	21%	70	41%	36	37%	9	10%	1	0%	161	17%
Unpaid domestic work	3	7%	7	3%	2	1%	1	1%	1	1%	2	1%	16	2%

Regarding gender composition, the majority of respondents were female (65%), while males represented 33% of the total sample. A small percentage (1%) identified with another gender identity or preferred not to answer. Across the generational cohorts, Millennials had the highest proportion of female respondents (77%), whereas Generation X had a slightly higher proportion of males (30%) compared to other groups.

The educational background of the sample indicated a relatively high level of formal education. Overall, 32% of respondents had completed a university degree, while 15% had pursued postgraduate studies (Master's or Ph.D.). However, there were differences across generations. Older generations (Baby Boomers and Generation X) had the highest percentage of respondents with vocational or degree studies, while Millennials and Zillenials showed an increasing trend in postgraduate education (35% and 45%, respectively). The Generation Z cohort had the highest proportion of respondents still in secondary or undergraduate education (44%), reflecting their younger age profile.

In terms of income levels, 30% of respondents reported having no income, a trend particularly pronounced among Generation Z (60%) and Zillenials (25%), likely due to their status as students or early-career professionals. Among those with income, 16% earned less than 15,000€ per year, while 21% earned between 22,000€ and 31,999€ per year, and 14% reported earnings above 32,000€ per year. The higher-income brackets were more prevalent in the older cohorts, with Baby Boomers and Generation X having the highest proportion of respondents earning over 32,000€ per year (29% and 16%, respectively).

The occupational distribution varied significantly across generational cohorts. While most Silent and Baby Boomer respondents were retired, a large percentage of Millennials, Zillenials, and Generation Z identified as students. Among working-age respondents, employment was the most common status, with a mix of employed individuals, self-employed professionals, and official servants

Overall, the sample provided a diverse representation of different generational cohorts, balancing gender, education, income, and occupational status, allowing for meaningful generational comparisons in the study.

Hypotheses Testing

Reliability assessments were performed on the multi-item constructs. As stated by Nunnally and Bernstein (1994), a coefficient alpha score above 0.50 is generally considered an acceptable indicator of scale reliability. The standardized Cronbach's alpha values for all of the measured constructs were above this threshold, demonstrating adequate internal consistency (Table 7).

Table 7. Reliability assessment

Construct	Cronbach's alpha
Solidarity	0.780
Sustainability	0.693
Social Justice	0.669
Responsibility	0.515
Respect	0.792

continued on following page

Table 7. Continued

Construct	Cronbach's alpha
Actively benefitting	0.814
Passively benefiting	0.770
Questionable but Legal Actions	0.794
No harm, no foul	0.758
Illegal Downloading	0.632
Influence of Advertisement	0.831
Sustainability	0.903

Two independent samples Student's t-tests were carried out to test whether H1: Digital immigrants and natives differ in ethical values: solidarity (H1a), sustainability (H1b), social justice (H1c), responsibility (H1d), and respect (H1e); and to test whether H2: Digital Immigrants and Digital natives differ in responsible consumption behaviours regarding sustainability (H2a), actively benefiting (H2b), passively benefiting (H2c), engaging in questionable but legal actions (H2d), actions based on "no harm, no foul" (H2e), illegal downloading (H2f), and the influence of marketing (H2g). The results are shown in Table 8 and Table 9, respectively.

Table 8. ANOVA results of ethical values

Ethical values	Digital groups	N	Average	Standard Deviation	Mean standard error	Levene's test		T-student	Group comparisions
						F	Sig.	Sig.	
Solidarity	Inmigrants	424	4.30	0.82	0.04	0.669	0.414	0.000	Inmigrants > Natives*
	Natives	513	4.07	0.82	0.04				
Sustainability	Inmigrants	424	3.76	0.83	0.04	0.919	0.338	0.176	Inmigrants > Natives
	Natives	513	3.68	0.80	0.04				
Social Justice	Inmigrants	424	4.09	0.80	0.04	5.455	0.020*	0.000	Inmigrants > Natives*
	Natives	513	3.83	0.87	0.04				
Responsibility	Inmigrants	424	4.17	0.77	0.04	2.763	0.097	0.000	Inmigrants > Natives*
	Natives	513	3.86	0.68	0.03				
Respect	Inmigrants	424	4.49	0.78	0.04	11.284	0.001*	0.000	Inmigrants > Natives*
	Natives	513	4,17	0,85	0,04				

Notes: All the items are measured on a 5-point Likert Scale with 1 = not at all identified and 5 = totally identified. * Indicates significant at p value of .05.

After performing Levene's test for equality of variances, equal variances are assumed for all constructs except social justice and respect (if $p<0.05$, there is no homogeneity of variances). Significant differences were detected between the two groups (digital immigrants and natives) in all ethical value constructs with digital immigrants scoring significantly higher on average, except for sustainability. Therefore, hypotheses H1a, H1c, H1d, and H1e were accepted.

According to Figure 3, digital immigrants tend to hold stronger ethical values in solidarity, social justice, responsibility, and respect compared to digital natives. The lack of significant differences in sustainability suggests a shared perception regarding environmental responsibility between both groups. The observed differences reinforce the idea that digital immigrants have a more developed ethical framework in these areas, whereas digital natives may display more variation in their ethical perspectives.

Figure 3. Comparison of averages between ethical values by digital groups

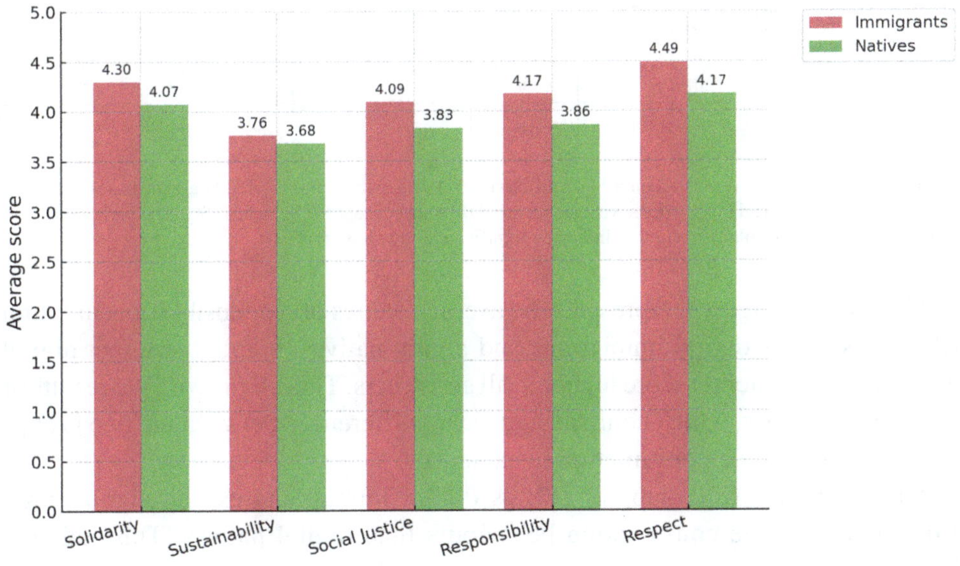

After performing the Levene test for equality of variances for responsible consumption behaviours (Table 9), it is assumed that there is no homogeneity of variances ($p<0.05$) for all constructs except SOST, NOH and DL. Additionally, significant differences were also identified in constructs related to responsible consumption behaviours, with digital immigrants again showing higher averages. Thus, H2 was fully supported.

Table 9. ANOVA results of responsible consumption behaviours

Responsible consumption behaviours	Digital groups	N	Average	Standard Deviation	Mean standard error	Levene's test		T-student	Group comparisions
						F	Sig.	Sig.	
SUST	Inmigrants	424	3.05	0.92	0.04	0.210	0.647	0.000	Inmigrants > Natives*
	Natives	513	2.52	0.89	0.04				
ACT	Inmigrants	424	4.60	0.81	0.04	44.059	0.000	0.000	Inmigrants > Natives*
	Natives	513	4.17	0.98	0.04				
PAS	Inmigrants	424	3.86	1.03	0.05	20.327	0.000	0.000	Inmigrants > Natives*
	Natives	513	3.16	1.15	0.05				
QUEST	Inmigrants	424	4.17	0.90	0.04	28.795	0.000	0.000	Inmigrants > Natives*
	Natives	513	3.34	1.05	0.05				
NOH	Inmigrants	424	3.95	0.99	0.05	0.148	0.701	0.000	Inmigrants > Natives*
	Natives	513	2.91	0.98	0.04				
DL	Inmigrants	424	3.49	1.08	0.05	0.419	0.517	0.000	Inmigrants > Natives*
	Natives	513	2.61	1.09	0.05				
MK	Inmigrants	424	4.37	0.95	0.05	53.731	0.000	0.000	Inmigrants > Natives*

Notes: All the items are measured on a 5-point Likert Scale. Since the Muncy-Vitell Scale measures unethical behaviour, in the analytical calculations we have inverted the scale except for Sustainability. The higher the figure, the more responsible behaviour. * Indicates significant at p value of .05.

The graph in Figure 4 represents the average values of responsible consumption behaviours across digital immigrants and digital natives, highlighting that digital immigrants consistently score higher in all constructs. This aligns with the results of the Student's t-tests, which confirm significant differences between the two groups across all responsible consumption behaviours.

These findings fully support H2, as digital immigrants exhibit significantly stronger responsible consumption behaviours than digital natives. This suggests that digital immigrants not only perceive ethical values more strongly but also translate them into more responsible consumer actions. The lower scores among digital natives may indicate a weaker commitment to responsible consumption or greater inconsistency in their behaviours.

Figure 4. Comparison of averages between responsible consumption behaviours by digital groups

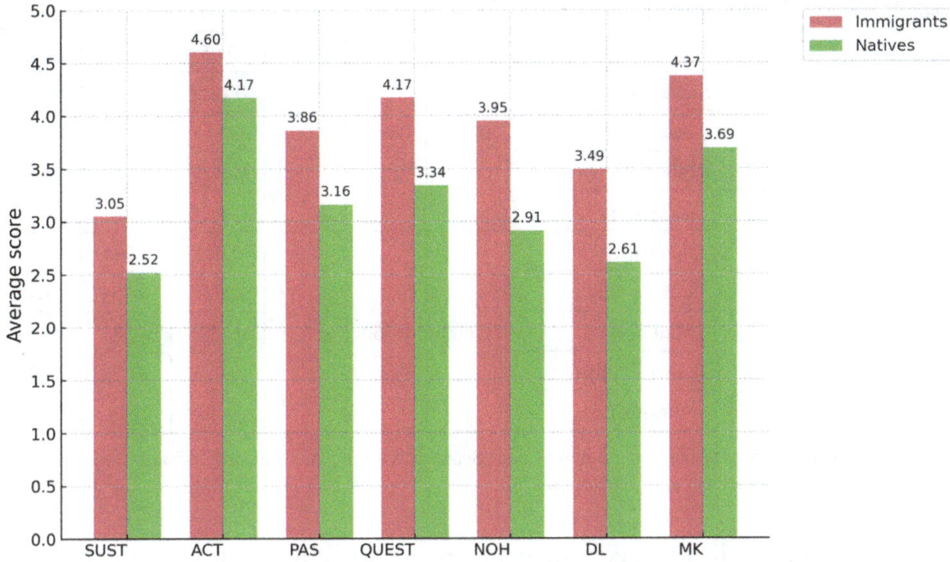

Two multiple regression analyses were conducted, on the one hand, to test whether there is no cognitive dissonance between ethical values and responsible consumption behaviour among Digital Immigrants (H3a), and on other hand, to test whether there is cognitive dissonance among digital natives (H3b). Responsible consumption behaviour (which is the arithmetic mean of all items) is considered as the dependent variable and the constructs of ethical values as the independent variable.

According to the results shown in Table 10, a strong positive correlation was observed between ethical values and responsible consumption behaviours among both digital immigrants (R = 0.741) and digital natives (R = 0.600). In addition, 54.9% of the dependent variance is explained by independents, in the case of immigrants, and 36% in the case of natives.

In the former case, sustainability, responsibility, and respect values significantly and positively influence responsible consumption behaviours. Therefore, we can conclude that there is no cognitive dissonance as there is a link between what digital migrants think and how they act in terms of social responsibility. This leads us to accept H3a.

For digital natives, the significant independent variables were social justice and respect values. Hence, we can also conclude that there is no cognitive dissonance and therefore reject H3b, as there is no significant negative influence between values and responsible behaviour.

Table 10. Results of multiple regression analyses, with Responsible consumption behaviour as the dependent variable

Digital groups	Independent variables	R	R^2	Sig.	Beta	*t*	Sig.
Inmigrants	Solidarity	0.741	0.549	<.001	-0.058	-1.015	0.311
	Sustainability				0.235*	4.589	0.000
	Social Justice				0.106	1.856	0.064
	Responsibility				0.101*	1.959	0.051
	Respect				0.442*	7.847	0.000
Natives	Solidarity	0.600	0.360	<.001	0.015	0.248	0.804
	Sustainability				0.024	0.468	0.640
	Social Justice				0.139*	2.583	0.010
	Responsibility				0.050	1.092	0.276
	Respect				0.436*	7.436	0.000

Notes: All the items are measured on a 5-point Likert Scale with 1 = not at all identified and 5 = totally identified. * Indicates significant at p value of .05.

These findings indicate no cognitive dissonance for either group since their ethical values positively influence their responsible consumption behaviours. However, the weaker relationship among digital natives (lower R-value and lower explanatory power of independent variables) suggests that their ethical values may not translate into responsible behaviour as strongly as in digital immigrants. Moreover, only two of the five ethical values have an influence on their responsible behaviour.

According to Figure 5, the comparatively lower score in responsible consumption behaviours for digital natives may further indicate a gap between their ethical stance and their actual behaviour, even though it is not classified as cognitive dissonance.

Figure 5. Comparison of averages between ethical values and responsible consumption behaviour by digital groups

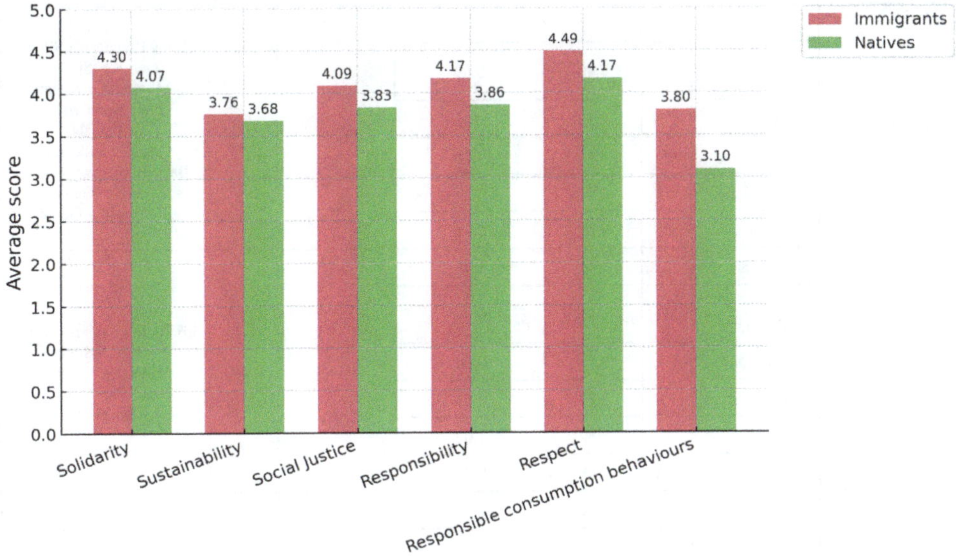

Finally, multiple one-way ANOVA (MANOVA) was conducted to test H4, regarding the differences among the six generational cohorts in their ethical values (H4a) (Table 11) and in their responsible behaviour (H4b) (Table 12). Considering that the Box's test indicates that covariance matrices are not equal across cohorts, we observe the significance of Pillai's Trace, which is 0.000 (< 0.05) in all the constructs. Therefore, significant differences were found in all ethical value and responsible consumption behaviour variables across the cohorts. Therefore, H4 is supported. Subsequently, a post hoc test was conducted to identify the groups that differed for each variable. The Games-Howell statistic was used for multiple comparisons, as variances were found to be nonhomogeneous according to Levene's test.

Table 11. Results of multiple one-way ANOVA (MANOVA) in ethical values

Ethical values	Digital groups	N	Average	Standard Deviation	Levene's test	Sig.	Significant differences in cohorts
Solidarity	Silent	42	3.39	1.40	0.000	0.000	Baby Boomers > Silent Gen X > Silent Millenials > Silent Baby Boomers > Zillenials Gen X > Zillenials Baby Boomers > Gen Z Gen X > Gen Z Millenials > Gen Z
	Baby Boomers	211	4.40	0.69			
	Gen X	171	4.39	0.63			
	Millenials	97	4.34	0.66			
	Zillenials	88	4.01	1.13			
	Gen Z	328	4.00	0.75			
Sustainability	Silent	42	2.99	1.35	0.000	0.000	Baby Boomers > Silent Gen X > Silent Millenials > Silent Gen Z > Silent Baby Boomers > Gen Z
	Baby Boomers	211	3.93	0.74			
	Gen X	171	3.73	0.66			
	Millenials	97	3.77	0.64			
	Zillenials	88	3.59	1.02			
	Gen Z	328	3.68	0.77			
Social Justice	Silent	42	3.39	1.28	0.000	0.000	Baby Boomers > Silent Gen X > Silent Baby Boomers > Zillenials Baby Boomers > Gen Z Gen X > Gen Z
	Baby Boomers	211	4.18	0.76			
	Gen X	171	4.15	0.61			
	Millenials	97	3.93	0.75			
	Zillenials	88	3.83	1.04			
	Gen Z	328	3.80	0.85			
Responsibility	Silent	42	3.60	0.99	0.001	0.000	Baby Boomers > Silent Gen X > Silent Baby Boomers > Zillenials Gen X > Zillenials Baby Boomers > Gen Z Gen X > Gen Z Millenials > Gen Z
	Baby Boomers	211	4.26	0.76			
	Gen X	171	4.20	0.65			
	Millenials	97	4.05	0.56			
	Zillenials	88	3.92	0.73			
	Gen Z	328	3.79	0.68			
Respect	Silent	42	3.68	1.45	0.000	0.000	Baby Boomers > Silent Gen X > Silent Millenials > Silent Zillenials > Gen X Baby Boomers > Gen Z Gen X > Gen Z Millenials > Gen Z
	Baby Boomers	211	4.56	0.73			
	Gen X	171	4.60	0.40			
	Millenials	97	4.47	0.65			
	Zillenials	88	4.20	1.11			
	Gen Z	328	4.08	0.80			

Notes: All the items are measured on a 5-point Likert Scale with 1 = not at all identified and 5 = totally identified.

For ethical values, significant pairwise differences were observed between the Silent Generation and, on the other side, the Boomers, Gen X, and Millennials, with the latter groups always scoring higher on values as solidarity, sustainability, and respect. Notably, there was a significant difference between the Silent Generation and Gen Z regarding sustainability, with Gen Z scoring higher on average. No significant differences were found in any ethical value among Baby Boomers, Gen X, and Millennials. However, they differed significantly from those of Gen Z. The most pronounced differences were observed between Boomers and the Silent Generation, as well as between Boomers and Gen Z, with boomers demonstrating higher ethical standards overall. Millennials differ from Gen Z in solidarity, responsibility, and respect.

Table 12. Results of multiple one-way ANOVA (MANOVA) in responsible consumption behaviours

Responsible consumption behaviours	Digital groups	N	Average	Standard Deviation	Levene's test	Sig.	Significant differences in cohorts
SUST	Silent	42	2.30	1.22	0.000	0.000	Baby boomers > Silent Gen X > Silent Baby Boomers > Gen X Baby Boomers > Millenials Baby Boomers > Zillenials Baby Boomers > Gen Z Gen X > Gen Z
	Baby Boomers	211	3.27	0.85			
	Gen X	171	2.95	0.79			
	Millenials	97	2.64	0.88			
	Zillenials	88	2.74	0.98			
	Gen Z	328	2.43	0.85			
ACT	Silent	42	2.76	0.94	0.000	0.000	Baby boomers > Silent Gen X > Silent Millenials > Silent Zillenials > Baby Boomers Gen X > Zillenials Gen Z > Baby Boomers Gen X > Gen Z Millenials > Gen Z
	Baby Boomers	211	3.83	1.40			
	Gen X	171	4.66	0.76			
	Millenials	97	4.73	0.53			
	Zillenials	88	4.54	0.71			
	Gen Z	328	4.20	1.14			
PAS	Silent	42	3.18	1.62	0.000	0.000	Gen X > Silent Baby Boomers > Zillenials Gen X > Zillenials Millenials > Zillenials Baby Boomers > Gen Z Gen X > Gen Z Millenials > Gen Z
	Baby Boomers	211	3.88	0.95			
	Gen X	171	4.01	0.86			
	Millenials	97	3.74	0.93			
	Zillenials	88	3.27	1.21			
	Gen Z	328	2.96	1.14			

continued on following page

Table 12. Continued

Responsible consumption behaviours	Digital groups	N	Average	Standard Deviation	Levene's test	Sig.	Significant differences in cohorts
QUEST	Silent	42	3.35	1.51	0.001	0.000	Baby boomers > Silent Gen X > Silent Baby Boomers > Millenials Gen X > Millenials Baby Boomers > Zillenials Gen X > Zillenials Millenials > Zillenials Baby Boomers > Gen Z Gen X > Gen Z Millenials > Gen Z
	Baby Boomers	211	4.27	0.81			
	Gen X	171	4.26	0.68			
	Millenials	97	3.89	0.92			
	Zillenials	88	3.43	1.16			
	Gen Z	328	3.16	1.00			
NOH	Silent	42	3.43	1.56	0.000	0.000	Baby Boomers > Gen X Baby Boomers > Millenials Gen X > Millenials Baby Boomers > Zillenials Gen X > Zillenials Baby Boomers > Gen Z Gen X > Gen Z Millenials > Gen Z
	Baby Boomers	211	4.16	0.91			
	Gen X	171	3.82	0.85			
	Millenials	97	3.15	0.92			
	Zillenials	88	2.87	1.01			
	Gen Z	328	2.85	0.99			
DL	Silent	42	3.37	1.70	0.000	0.000	Silent > Gen Z Baby Boomers > Millenials Baby Boomers > Zillenials Gen X > Zillenials Millenials > Zillenials Baby Boomers > Gen Z Gen X > Gen Z Millenials > Gen Z
	Baby Boomers	211	3.63	1.01			
	Gen X	171	3.35	0.95			
	Millenials	97	3.07	1.16			
	Zillenials	88	2.53	1.17			
	Gen Z	328	2.50	1.01			
MK	Silent	42	3.49	1.59	0.000	0.000	Baby boomers > Silent Gen X > Silent Baby Boomers > Zillenials Gen X > Zillenials Baby Boomers > Gen Z Gen X > Gen Z Millenials > Gen Z
	Baby Boomers	211	4.49	0.87			
	Gen X	171	4.44	0.71			
	Millenials	97	4.13	1.19			
	Zillenials	88	3.61	1.30			
	Gen Z	328	3.58	1.10			

Notes: All the items are measured on a 5-point Likert Scale. Since the Muncy-Vitell Scale measures unethical behaviour, in the analytical calculations we have inverted the scale except for Sustainability. The higher the figure, the more responsible behaviour.

Regarding responsible consumption behaviours, notable differences were observed between the Silent Generation and both Boomers and Gen X, particularly in acting sustainably, actively benefiting, questionable but legal actions, and the influence of advertising. Additionally, the Silent Generation differs from Gen Z in terms of illegal downloading. In this context, significant differences were found between Baby Boomers and the rest of the generations in most behaviours, especially with Gen Z, with Boomers demonstrating more responsible behaviour overall. Each generation tends to differ significantly from the generations that follow, with older generations displaying more responsible consumption behaviours than their successors. Notably, there were significant differences between millennials and Gen Z.

DISCUSSION

The findings of this study provide robust empirical support for the influence of generational membership and digital nativeness on ethical values and responsible consumer behaviours. Drawing upon the theoretical frameworks of Generational Cohort Theory (Inglehart, 1977; Strauss & Howe, 1991), Cortina's (2002) Ethical Consumption framework, the Theory of Reasoned Action (Ajzen & Fishbein, 1980), and Muncy & Vittel (1992) Theory of Responsible Consumption the results clarify how values and behaviours diverge across age cohorts and how these are shaped by broader socio-technological contexts. The results support all the hypotheses, confirming significant differences in ethical values and responsible behaviours across generations, and revealing distinct patterns based on digital nativeness.

A central finding is that digital immigrants (i.e., Silent Generation, Baby Boomers, and Generation X) consistently demonstrated higher levels of ethical values across solidarity, social justice, responsibility, and respect compared to digital natives (Millennials, Zillennials, and Generation Z). This aligns with prior research indicating that older generations often display a more consolidated ethical framework, shaped by life experiences, institutional trust, and collective memory of social and economic transitions (Caballero & Baigorri, 2019). For instance, Baby Boomers, who came of age during democratic transitions and social movements, scored highest on most ethical constructs, particularly solidarity and justice, consistent with their documented engagement in values-based activism (Helve, 2023).

Despite being raised in a hyper-connected, information-rich digital environment, digital natives did not exhibit stronger ethical convictions than their predecessors. This contradicts expectations derived from recent literature portraying Gen Z as environmentally conscious and ethically inclined (Djafarova & Foots, 2022; Tiainen, 2024). Instead, their ethical self-perception appears weaker or, at best, ambivalent. One possible explanation is that the abundance of information and consumer choice in digital environments generates moral fatigue or desensitization, diluting the impact of ethical appeals (Carrington et al., 2014; Zaikauskaitė et al., 2022).

The discussion of the value of respect requires special consideration. Literature suggests diverging perspectives on whether respect and autonomy are more dependent on generational identity or life stage. While older cohorts may be perceived as more respectful due to traditional norms, Jecker (2021) argues that these differences may instead reflect age-related shifts in autonomy rather than generational values *per se*. The present findings—showing significant differences in respect across generations—may support both interpretations, depending on the context.

Regarding responsible consumption behaviours, digital immigrants again outperformed digital natives across all categories, including sustainable consumption, active and passive ethical breaches, and digital piracy. These findings suggest that older generations not only endorse ethical values more strongly but also enact them more consistently in their consumer choices. Interestingly, sustainability was the only ethical value where no statistically significant differences were found between digital groups, indicating that environmental concerns might be more evenly distributed across cohorts, albeit manifested differently in practice.

Nonetheless, some nuances emerge. Zillennials, often defined as a micro-generation between Millennials and Gen Z, performed significantly better than Baby Boomers in the "Actively Benefitting" dimension, which includes behaviours such as eating or drinking a product in a store without paying, cheating an insurance company, or lying about the age of a family member to obtain a discount. This suggests that certain forms of unethical behaviour—particularly those involving direct deception or opportunism—may be less prevalent among younger digital natives than often assumed, especially within this intermediary cohort.

The regression analysis revealed that while ethical values predict responsible behaviours in both groups, the strength of association is notably higher among digital immigrants ($R = 0.741$ vs. $R = 0.600$). Among immigrants, sustainability, responsibility, and respect had the greatest predictive power, suggesting a value system anchored in future-oriented, autonomous decision-making and institutional integrity. In contrast, for digital natives, only social justice and respect significantly predicted behaviour, potentially reflecting a more individualised and socially driven ethics, yet less consistent in its behavioural application.

Crucially, the analysis rejected the hypothesis of cognitive dissonance among digital natives. Although they scored lower in values and behaviours, the positive correlation between them indicates internal consistency. However, the weaker relationship and lower overall scores might still signal a behavioural-intention gap (Carrington et al., 2014), where ethical intent exists but is not effectively translated into action due to economic constraints, social pressures, or decision-making fatigue typical of younger cohorts (Isham et al., 2022).

Sociodemographic variables provided further insight. Gender distribution showed higher female participation, especially among Millennials (77%). This overrepresentation may reflect a greater predisposition among women to participate altruistically in studies related to ethics and social values, as previously observed in research on survey participation and civic engagement (Pullen & Vachhani, 2021). Income disparities across generations revealed that Gen Z and Zillennials, who had the highest proportion of participants with no income, scored lowest in responsible behaviours. This reinforces the literature linking economic precarity to materialistic or inconsistent ethical practices (Zimand-Sheiner & Lissitsa, 2024). Educational attainment also played a role: younger cohorts had higher postgraduate education rates, yet this did not necessarily translate into stronger ethical behaviour, indicating a possible decoupling between formal education and value enactment.

A notable limitation of the study lies in the underrepresentation of the Silent Generation. This shortcoming is not only methodological but also illustrative: it reveals an important generational gap in digital literacy and access. Since the main instrument for data collection was an online questionnaire, participation required a minimum level of digital competence, a skill less prevalent in older generations. As such, the limited input from the Silent Generation underscores the very technological divide this study seeks to explore.

Overall, the results support the notion that generational differences in ethical values and behaviours are not merely chronological but deeply embedded in sociohistorical and digital experiences. The study advances the literature by empirically validating the relevance of digital nativeness as a moderating variable in ethical consumption, providing a nuanced, intergenerational understanding of the evolving ethics of consumption in the digital era. It also highlights the importance of addressing the structural and economic limitations that may hinder ethical behaviour, particularly among younger consumers, to bridge the gap between values and practices.

CONCLUSIONS

This chapter has explored the influence of digital nativeness and generational identity on ethical values and responsible consumption behaviours, offering a nuanced, data-driven analysis of how consumers across six generational cohorts in Spain internalize and enact ethical principles. The results confirm all four proposed hypotheses, revealing significant intergenerational differences both in the strength of ethical values and in the consistency of ethical behaviour.

A key finding is that digital immigrants—comprising the Silent Generation, Baby Boomers, and Generation X—consistently report higher levels of ethical values and demonstrate more responsible consumption behaviours than digital natives. While both groups exhibit a positive correlation between ethical values and behaviours, the predictive strength is significantly lower among digital natives, suggesting a widening intention-behaviour gap. Notably, values such as respect and social justice remain significant predictors of behaviour across groups, while others—like responsibility and sustainability—show generational variation in their impact. These insights advance the literature on consumer ethics by highlighting the importance of digital experience, not just age, in shaping moral decision-making.

From a theoretical perspective, this chapter contributes to the growing body of work that integrates ethical consumption theory (Cortina, 2002; Ballestero, 2011), the Theory of Reasoned Action (Ajzen & Fishbein, 1980), and the Muncy and Vitell (1992) model of consumer ethics. It empirically validates the cognitive dissonance described in the literature and positions digital nativeness as a key explanatory variable for behavioural inconsistency. Moreover, the development and validation of the DAS BIE scale represents a valuable methodological contribution, enabling more granular assessment of ethical values across generations using a co-produced, interdisciplinary, and socially grounded instrument.

Practically, these findings have clear implications for policy, education, and marketing. First, they suggest the urgent need for intergenerational dialogue and targeted interventions to strengthen ethical engagement among digital natives. Second, educational initiatives that foster critical reflection on values and decision-making, particularly in digital environments, may help reduce cognitive dissonance. Third, marketing strategies should consider the ethical sensitivities of different generational cohorts, especially when promoting sustainability-oriented products or services. Businesses must avoid superficial appeals to ethical branding and instead engage consumers in authentic, transparent, and inclusive ways. Additionally, it is crucial to promote digital tools that reinforce the alignment between ethical values and consumption patterns—particularly among younger generations. Encouraging the use of collaborative consumption platforms and sharing economy applications can serve as a practical bridge between the ethical values promoted in educational environments and real-world behaviours. In this way, technology becomes not only a medium for consumption but also a tool for ethical empowerment.

Nonetheless, the study presents some limitations. The use of a non-probabilistic, snowball sampling method, although mitigated by representativeness in most cohorts, limits the generalisability of the results. The underrepresentation of the Silent Generation also highlights a persistent digital divide, not only in behaviour but in accessibility to digital research tools. Furthermore, the reliance on self-reported data may introduce social desirability bias, particularly in ethical domains. Future studies should explore mixed-methods designs and longitudinal approaches to deepen our understanding of how digital nativeness interacts with life stage, socio-economic background, and cultural context in shaping ethical behaviour.

In conclusion, this chapter underscores the complexity of ethical consumption in the digital age. While younger generations express awareness and concern for sustainability and justice, their actions often fall short of their stated values. Bridging this gap requires not only better tools and education, but also systemic support for ethical lifestyles. A people-centred digital transformation must actively consider these generational differences if it is to foster a more equitable, sustainable, and ethically engaged society.

REFERENCES

Aavakare, M., & Nikou, S. (2020a). Challenging the Concept of Digital Nativeness. In M. Cacace, R. Halonen, H. Li, T. P. Orrensalo, C. Li, G. Widén, & R. Suomi (Eds.), *Well-Being in the Information Society. 8th International Conference, WIS 2020* (Vol. 1270). Springer. https://doi.org/DOI: 10.1007/978-3-030-57847-3

Aavakare, M., & Nikou, S. (2020b). Challenging the Concept of Digital Nativeness. In M. Cacace, R. Halonen, H. Li, T. P. Orrensalo, C. Li, G. Widén, & R. Suomi (Eds.), *Well-Being in the Information Society. 8th International Conference, WIS 2020* (Vol. 1270). Springer. https://doi.org/DOI: 10.1007/978-3-030-57847-3

Agárdi, I., & Alt, M. A. (2022). Do digital natives use mobile payment differently than digital immigrants? A comparative study between generation X and Z. *Electronic Commerce Research, 24,* 1463–1490. DOI: 10.1007/s10660-022-09537-9

Ajzen, H., & Fishbein, M. (1980). *Understanding attitudes and predicting social behavior*. Prentice-Hal.

Alwin, D. F. (2012). Integrating Varieties of Life Course Concepts. *The Journals of Gerontology: Series B*, *67B*(2), 206–220. DOI: 10.1093/geronb/gbr146

Arikan, R. H., & Jiang, C. (2018). An expectancy model of green product consumption and green brand equity. *Back to the Future: Using Marketing Basics to Provide Customer Value: Proceedings of the 2017 Academy of Marketing Science (AMS) Annual Conference*, 685–696.

Baigorri, A. (2008). ¿De la generación del 98 a la Chiki Chiki? *El País*. https://elpais.com/diario/2008/06/08/sociedad/1212876003_850215.html#?prm=copy_link

Ballestero Izquierdo, A. (2011). Notas Para Una Ética Social Del Consumo Individual. *Estudios Filosóficos*, *60*(175), 551–559.

Bennett, S., & Maton, K. (2011). Intellectual field or faith-based religion: Moving on from the idea of "digital natives." *Deconstructing Digital Natives: Young People, Technology, and the New Literacies, January 2011*, 169–185.

Bennett, S., Maton, K., & Kervin, L. (2008). The "digital natives" debate: A critical review of the evidence. *British Journal of Educational Technology*, *39*(5), 775–786. DOI: 10.1111/j.1467-8535.2007.00793.x

Bonifacio, R. A., Baui, A. F., Uy, M. Y. T., Bandojo, A. J., & Etrata, A. (2024). Generation Z's Purchasing Intention of Cruelty-free Cosmetic Products: The Moderating Role of Environmental and Animal Welfare Concerns. *International Business Education Journal, 17*(1), 118–132. DOI: 10.37134/ibej.Vol17.1.10.2024

Bosnjak, M., Ajzen, I., & Schmidt, P. (2020). The Theory of Planned Behavior: Selected Recent Advances and Applications. *Europe's Journal of Psychology, 16*(3 SE-Special Thematic Section), 352–356. https://doi.org/DOI: 10.5964/ejop.v16i3.3107

Brécard, D., Lucas, S., Pichot, N., & Salladarré, F. (2012). *Consumer Preferences for Eco, Health and Fair Trade Labels. An Application to Seafood Product in France. 10*(1). https://doi.org/doi:10.1515/1542-0485.1360

Bristow, P. (2010). *The digital divide: Is it an age old question?* https://doi.org/DOI: 10.1109/ITICT.2009.5405933

Brundtland, G. H. (1987). Our common future - Call for action. *Environmental Conservation, 14*(4). Advance online publication. DOI: 10.1017/s0376892900016805

Caballero, M., & Baigorri, A. (2019). Glocalising the theory of generations: The case of Spain. *Time & Society, 28*(1), 333–357. DOI: 10.1177/0961463X18783374

Cabeza-Ramírez, L. J., Fuentes-García, F. J., Cano-Vicente, M. C., & González-Mohino, M. (2022). How Generation X and Millennials Perceive Influencers' Recommendations: Perceived Trustworthiness, Product Involvement, and Perceived Risk. In *Journal of Theoretical and Applied Electronic Commerce Research* (Vol. 17, Issue 4, pp. 1431–1449). https://doi.org/DOI: 10.3390/jtaer17040072

Carrington, M. J., Neville, B. A., & Whitwell, G. J. (2014). Lost in translation: Exploring the ethical consumer intention–behavior gap. *Journal of Business Research, 67*(1), 2759–2767. https://doi.org/https://doi.org/10.1016/j.jbusres.2012.09.022

Casalegno, C., Candelo, E., & Santoro, G. (2022). Exploring the antecedents of green and sustainable purchase behaviour: A comparison among different generations. *Psychology and Marketing, 39*(5), 1007–1021. DOI: 10.1002/mar.21637

Chancel, L. (2014). Are younger generations higher carbon emitters than their elders?: Inequalities, generations and CO2 emissions in France and in the USA. *Ecological Economics, 100*, 195–207. https://doi.org/https://doi.org/10.1016/j.ecolecon.2014.02.009

Chang, C. W., & Chang, S. H. (2023). The Impact of Digital Disruption: Influences of Digital Media and Social Networks on Forming Digital Natives' Attitude. *SAGE Open, 13*(3), 1–10. DOI: 10.1177/21582440231191741

Cheong, C. (2023). How to spot a "zillennial" in the wild, according to TikTok. *Business Insider*. https://www.businessinsider.com/spotting-zillennials-millenial-gen-z-tiktok-2023-7

Cho, A., Byrne, J., & Zoe, P. (2020). Digital civic engagement by young people. In *UNICEF Office of Global Insight and Policy*. https://www.unicef.org/globalinsight/reports/digital-civic-engagement-young-people

Cortina, A. (2002). Por una ética del consumo:la ciudadanía del consumidor en un mundo global. In *Pensamiento: Vol. 2ª* (pp. 1–119; 265–349). https://ibdigital.uib.es/greenstone/collect/cd2/index/assoc/consumca.dir/consumcat0001.pdf

Crane, A., Matten, D., Glozer, S., & Spence, L. J. (2019). *Business ethics: Managing corporate citizenship and sustainability in the age of globalization*. Oxford university press.

Dave, D., & Parikh, A. (2022). Preferences of Gen Z for Investing in Socially Accountable Funds. *Journal of Social Commerce*, *2*(4), 154–166.

De Pelsmacker, P., & Janssens, W. (2007). A model for fair trade buying behaviour: The role of perceived quantity and quality of information and of product-specific attitudes. *Journal of Business Ethics*, *75*(4), 361–380. DOI: 10.1007/s10551-006-9259-2

Diprose, K., Valentine, G., Vanderbeck, R. M., Liu, C., & McQuaid, K. (2019). Building common cause towards sustainable consumption: A cross-generational perspective. *Environment and Planning E*, *2*(2), 203–228. DOI: 10.1177/2514848619834845

Divasson-J, A., Aguayo-Mendoza, A., Quesada, C., Casado-Mansilla, D., & Borges, C. E. (2025). Climate change from B to Z: A cross-generational perception study in Spain. *Frontiers in Environmental Science*, *13*(February), 1–10. DOI: 10.3389/fenvs.2025.1511398

Djafarova, E., & Foots, S. (2022). Exploring ethical consumption of generation Z: Theory of planned behaviour. *Young Consumers*, *23*(3), 413–431. DOI: 10.1108/YC-10-2021-1405

Doran, C. J. (2009). The Role of Personal Values in Fair Trade Consumption. *Journal of Business Ethics*, *84*(4), 549–563. DOI: 10.1007/s10551-008-9724-1

Durkheim, E., Lukes, S., & Halls, W. D. (2014). The division of labor in society. In *TA - TT* - (Free Press). Free Press. https://doi.org/LK - https://worldcat.org/title/876277501

Elkington, J. (1998). Partnerships from cannibals with forks: The triple bottom line of 21st-century business. *Environmental Quality Management*. Advance online publication. DOI: 10.1002/tqem.3310080106

Ellerich-Groppe, N., Pfaller, L., & Schweda, M. (2021). Young for old—Old for young? Ethical perspectives on intergenerational solidarity and responsibility in public discourses on COVID-19. *European Journal of Ageing*, *18*(2), 159–171. DOI: 10.1007/s10433-021-00623-9

Ellerich-Groppe, N., Schweda, M., & Pfaller, L. (2020). #StayHomeForGrandma – Towards an analysis of intergenerational solidarity and responsibility in the coronavirus pandemic. *Social Sciences & Humanities Open*, *2*(1), 100085. https://doi.org/https://doi.org/10.1016/j.ssaho.2020.100085

Elmore, T. (2022). *A new kind of diversity: Making the different generations on your team a competitive advantage*. Simon and Schuster.

Fealy, G., McNamara, M., Treacy, M. P., & Lyons, I. (2012). Constructing ageing and age identities: A case study of newspaper discourses. *Ageing and Society*, *32*(1), 85–102. https://doi.org/DOI. DOI: 10.1017/S0144686X11000092

Festinger, L. (1957). Social comparison theory. *Selective Exposure Theory*, *16*(401), 3.

Fukukawa, K. (2003). A theoretical review of business and consumer ethics research: Normative and descriptive approaches. *The Marketing Review*, *3*(4), 381–401.

Fullscreen. (2019). Cuspers: Creative, Stressed, Impulsive - Fullscreen Generational Study Shines Light on the Unique Life Stage Between Millennials and Gen Z. *Business Wire*. https://www.businesswire.com/news/home/20190617005597/en/Cuspers-Creative-Stressed-Impulsive-----Fullscreen-Generational-Study-Shines-Light-on-the-Unique-Life-Stage-Between-Millennials-and-Gen-Z

Galea, P. (2012). Grandparenting and Extended-Family Support: The Silent Generation. *Int'l J. Jurisprudence Fam.*, *3*, 283.

García-Allen, J. (2015). *Disonancia cognitiva: la teoría que explica el autoengaño*. Psicología y Mente. https://psicologiaymente.com/psicologia/disonancia-cognitiva-teoria-autoengano

Gee, E. M. T., & Gutman, G. (2000). *The Overselling of Population Ageing: Apocalyptic Demography, Intergenerational Challenges, and Social Policy*. https://api.semanticscholar.org/CorpusID:153842482

Gentina, E., & Tang, T. L. P. (2024). Youth materialism and consumer ethics: Do Gen Z adolescents' self-concepts (power and self-esteem) vary across cultures (China vs. France)? *Ethics & Behavior*, *34*(2), 120–150. DOI: 10.1080/10508422.2022.2151012

Green, P. E., Johnson, R. M., & Neal, W. D. (2004). In Wind, Y., & Green, P. E. (Eds.), *The Journal of Marketing Research: Its Initiation, Growth, and Knowledge Dissemination BT - Marketing Research and Modeling: Progress and Prospects: A Tribute to Paul E. Green* (pp. 245–264). Springer US., DOI: 10.1007/978-0-387-28692-1_12

Grober, U. (2007). Deep roots: A conceptual history of 'sustainable development' (Nachhaltigkeit). *WZB Discussion Paper P 2007-002, February*, 1–30. http://skylla.wz-berlin.de/pdf/2007/p07-002.pdf

Grossi, D., Royakkers, L., & Dignum, F. (2007). Organizational structure and responsibility. *Artificial Intelligence and Law*, *15*(3), 223–249. DOI: 10.1007/s10506-007-9054-0

Grzesiuk, A., & Wanat, T. (2010). Consumer ethics: Some evidence from young consumers from Poland. *Proceedings on the 9th International Marketing Trends Conference, Venice-Paris, ESCP Europe*.

Guberman, N., Lavoie, J.-P., Blein, L., & Olazabal, I. (2012). Baby Boom Caregivers: Care in the Age of Individualization. *The Gerontologist*, *52*(2), 210–218. DOI: 10.1093/geront/gnr140

Harari, T. T., Sela, Y., & Bareket-Bojmel, L. (2022). Gen Z during the COVID-19 crisis: A comparative analysis of the differences between Gen Z and Gen X in resilience, values and attitudes. *Current Psychology (New Brunswick, N.J.)*, •••, 1–10. DOI: 10.1007/s12144-022-03501-4

Hartley, N., Kunz, W., & Tarbit, J. (2024). The corporate digital responsibility (CDR) calculus: How and why organizations reconcile digital and ethical trade-offs for growth. *Organizational Dynamics*, *53*(2), 101056. https://doi.org/https://doi.org/10.1016/j.orgdyn.2024.101056

Helve, H. M. (2023). Values and Solidarity of Young Finnish Millennials and Generation X. In *Youth* (Vol. 3, Issue 1, pp. 401–413). https://doi.org/DOI: 10.3390/youth3010027

Higgs, P., & Gilleard, C. (2015). In Torp, C. (Ed.), *Generational Justice, Generational Habitus and the 'Problem' of the Baby Boomers BT - Challenges of Aging: Pensions, Retirement and Generational Justice* (pp. 251–263)., DOI: 10.1057/9781137283177_13

Hontañon Pombo, R. (2023). Los Zillenials y su relación con las marcas. Así es la micro-generación más reciente. *PuroMarketing*. https://www.puromarketing.com/88/212041/zillennials-relacion-marcas-micro-generacion-reciente

Hunt, S. D., & Laverie, D. A. (2004). Experiential learning and the Hunt-Vitell theory of ethics: Teaching marketing ethics by integrating theory and practice. *Marketing Education Review*, *14*(3), 1–14.

Hunt, S. D., & Vitell, S. (1986). A General Theory of Marketing Ethics. *Journal of Macromarketing*, *6*(1), 5–16. DOI: 10.1177/027614678600600103

Ilieva, J., Baron, S., & Healey, N. M. (2002). Online Surveys in Marketing Research. *International Journal of Market Research*, *44*(3), 1–14. DOI: 10.1177/147078530204400303

Inglehart, R. (1977). *The silent revolution: Changing values and political styles among Western publics*. Princeton University Press.

Isham, A., Verfuerth, C., Armstrong, A., Elf, P., Gatersleben, B., & Jackson, T. (2022). The Problematic Role of Materialistic Values in the Pursuit of Sustainable Well-Being. *International Journal of Environmental Research and Public Health*, *19*(6). Advance online publication. DOI: 10.3390/ijerph19063673

Ivanova, O., Flores-Zamora, J., Khelladi, I., & Ivanaj, S. (2019). The generational cohort effect in the context of responsible consumption. *Management Decision*, *57*(5), 1162–1183. DOI: 10.1108/MD-12-2016-0915

Jebarajakirthy, C., Sivapalan, A., Das, M., Maseeh, H. I., Ashaduzzaman, M., Strong, C., & Sangroya, D. (2024). A meta-analytic integration of the theory of planned behavior and the value-belief-norm model to predict green consumption. *European Journal of Marketing*, *58*(4), 1141–1174. DOI: 10.1108/EJM-06-2021-0436

Jecker, N. S. (2021). The time of one's life: Views of aging and age group justice. *History and Philosophy of the Life Sciences*, *43*(1), 24. DOI: 10.1007/s40656-021-00377-8

Kuron, L. K. J., Lyons, S. T., Schweitzer, L., & Ng, E. S. W. (2015). Millennials' work values: Differences across the school to work transition. *Personnel Review*, *44*(6), 991–1009. DOI: 10.1108/PR-01-2014-0024

Lange, C., Combris, P., Issanchou, S., & Schlich, P. (2015). Impact of information and in-home sensory exposure on liking and willingness to pay: The beginning of Fairtrade labeled coffee in France. *Food Research International*, *76*, 317–324. https://doi.org/https://doi.org/10.1016/j.foodres.2015.06.017

Lazarevic, V. (2012). Encouraging brand loyalty in fickle generation Y consumers. *Young Consumers*, *13*(1), 45–61. DOI: 10.1108/17473611211203939

Liang, J., & Xu, Y. (2018). Second-hand clothing consumption: A generational cohort analysis of the Chinese market. *International Journal of Consumer Studies*, *42*(1), 120–130. DOI: 10.1111/ijcs.12393

Llanos Anaya, P. M., & Paredes Quenta, F. K. (2023). *Creación de contenido para Instagram utilizando inteligencia artificial (IA) en la marca weCOOL, enfocado en la generación Zillennial* [Universidad Peruana de Ciencias Aplicadas]. http://hdl.handle.net/10757/670777

Longoria, B. C. (2022). The widowed identity: Identity transformations of the silent generation and the influence of time. *Journal of Women & Aging*, *34*(6), 773–784. DOI: 10.1080/08952841.2021.1948790

Lu, L.-C., Chang, H.-H., & Chang, A. (2015). Consumer personality and green buying intention: The mediate role of consumer ethical beliefs. *Journal of Business Ethics*, *127*, 205–219.

Luszcz, M. A., & Fitzgerald, K. M. (1986). Understanding cohort differences in cross-generational, self, and peer perceptions. *Journal of Gerontology*, *41*(2), 234–240. DOI: 10.1093/geronj/41.2.234

Markowitz, E. M., & Shariff, A. F. (2012). Climate change and moral judgement. *Nature Climate Change*, *2*(4), 243–247. DOI: 10.1038/nclimate1378

Marron, D. (2020). *50 Teorías económicas sugerentes y desafiantes*. Blume.

McCrindle, M. (2014). *The ABC of XYZ: Understanding the Global Generations* (Issue October). McCrindle Research. https://mccrindle.com.au/resources/The-ABC-of-XYZ_Chapter-1.pdf

Mendez, E. N. (2009). *Intergenerational Responsibility and Accountability*. Royal Roads University.

Mladjan, M. M., & Marković, D. Z. (2021). Generational responsibility in consumption as a response to global economic crises. *Sustainability*, *13*(6), 3329.

Muncy, J. A., & Vitell, S. J. (1992). Consumer ethics: An investigation of the ethical beliefs of the final consumer. *Journal of Business Research*, *24*(4), 297–311. DOI: 10.1016/0148-2963(92)90036-B

Munsch, A. (2021). Millennial and generation Z digital marketing communication and advertising effectiveness: A qualitative exploration. *Journal of Global Scholars of Marketing Science*, *31*(1), 10–29. DOI: 10.1080/21639159.2020.1808812

Naci Çoklar, A., & Tatli, A. (2021). Examining the Digital Nativity Levels of Digital Generations: From Generation X to Generation Z. *Shanlax International Journal of Education, 9*(4), 433–434. DOI: 10.34293/education.v9i4.4224

Nagata, J. M., Chu, J., Ganson, K. T., Murray, S. B., Iyer, P., Gabriel, K. P., Garber, A. K., Bibbins-Domingo, K., & Baker, F. C. (2023). Contemporary screen time modalities and disruptive behavior disorders in children: A prospective cohort study. *Journal of Child Psychology and Psychiatry, and Allied Disciplines, 64*(1), 125–135. https://doi.org/https://doi.org/10.1111/jcpp.13673

Nakova, R. (2024). Generational differences in grocery shopping behaviour. *Industrial Growth Conference 2024*, 376–385. https://doi.org/DOI: 10.53656/igc-2024.32

Napoli, C. (2020). Zennials: The In-Between Generation. *WGSN*. https://www.wgsn.com/insight/p/article/88103?lang=en

Narayanan, S. (2022). Does Generation Z value and reward corporate social responsibility practices? *Journal of Marketing Management, 38*(9–10), 903–937.

Ng, E., Schweitzer, L., & Lyons, S. (2010). New Generation, Great Expectations: A Field Study of the Millennial Generation. *Journal of Business and Psychology, 25*, 281–292. DOI: 10.1007/s10869-010-9159-4

Nikou, S., Cavalheiro, S., & Widén, G. (2020). In Sundqvist, A., Berget, G., Nolin, J., & Skjerdingstad, K. I. (Eds.), *Digital Natives and Digital Immigrants in the Creative Economy BT - Sustainable Digital Communities* (pp. 343–362). Springer International Publishing.

Nimri, R., Dharmesti, M., Arcodia, C., & Mahshi, R. (2021). UK consumers' ethical beliefs towards dining at green restaurants: A qualitative evaluation. *Journal of Hospitality and Tourism Management, 48*, 572–581.

Nunnally, J. C., & Bernstein, I. H. (1994). *Psychometric theory* (3rd ed.). McGraw-Hill.

Otegui Carles, A., Brea, J. A., & Araújo, N. (2023). The Ethical Attitudes of Generation Z in Spain Toward Animal-Based Tourism Attractions. *Tourism (Zagreb), 71*, 285–300. DOI: 10.37741/t.71.2.4

Park, J., Yoo, J. W., Cho, Y., & Park, H. (2024). Understanding switching intentions between traditional banks and Internet-only banks among Generation X and Generation Z. *International Journal of Bank Marketing, 42*(5), 1114–1141. DOI: 10.1108/IJBM-06-2023-0338

Pekerti, A. A., & Arli, D. (2017). Do Cultural and Generational Cohorts Matter to Ideologies and Consumer Ethics? A Comparative Study of Australians, Indonesians, and Indonesian Migrants in Australia. *Journal of Business Ethics*, *143*(2), 387–404. DOI: 10.1007/s10551-015-2777-z

Peralta, A. (2024). ¿Millenials, Generación Z o Zillennials? Te decimos a cuál perteneces según éstas características. *Milenio*. https://www.milenio.com/cultura/entre-la-generacion-z-y-los-millenias-se-encuentran-los-zillenials?utm_source=chatgpt.com

Prensky, M. (2001). Nativos e Inmigrantes Digitales. *Cuadrenos SEK 2.O*, 21.

Preston, S. H. (1984). Children and the elderly in the US. *Scientific American*, *251*(6), 44–49.

Pullen, A., & Vachhani, S. J. (2021). Feminist Ethics and Women Leaders: From Difference to Intercorporeality. *Journal of Business Ethics*, *173*(2), 233–243. DOI: 10.1007/s10551-020-04526-0

PYMNTS. (2023). *The ConnectedEconomy Monthly Report: Meet the Zillenials.* https://www.pymnts.com/study/the-connectedeconomy-monthly-report-zillennials-generation-trends/

Ramos-Hidalgo, E., Diaz-Carrion, R., & Rodríguez-Rad, C. (2022). Does sustainable consumption make consumers happy? *International Journal of Market Research*, *64*(2), 227–248. DOI: 10.1177/14707853211030482

Rodriguez-Rad, C. J., & Ramos-Hidalgo, E. (2018). Spirituality, consumer ethics, and sustainability: The mediating role of moral identity. *Journal of Consumer Marketing*, *35*(1), 51–63. DOI: 10.1108/JCM-12-2016-2035

Ruggerio, C. A. (2021). Sustainability and sustainable development: A review of principles and definitions. *The Science of the Total Environment*, *786*, 147481. DOI: 10.1016/j.scitotenv.2021.147481

Schewe, C. D., & Meredith, G. (2004). Segmenting global markets by generational cohorts: Determining motivations by age. *Journal of Consumer Behaviour: An International Research Review*, *4*(1), 51–63.

Sharma, S. (2022). How ethical are my millennials? A qualitative study. *Journal of Information. Communication and Ethics in Society*, *20*(4), 531–545.

Shiel, C., do Paço, A., & Alves, H. (2020). Generativity, sustainable development and green consumer behaviour. *Journal of Cleaner Production*, *245*, 118865. https://doi.org/https://doi.org/10.1016/j.jclepro.2019.118865

Singh, S., & Prakash, N. (2020). Are Values A Differentiation Criterion for Generational Cohorts? International Journal of Current Advanced Research. *International Journal of Current Advanced Research, 9*(12), 23505–23510. DOI: 10.24327/ijcar.2020.23510.4655

Siu, A. (2023). What marketers need to know about 'Generation Zennial,' from social media to buying habits. *Digiday*. https://digiday.com/marketing/what-marketers-need-to-know-about-generation-zennial-from-social-media-to-buying-habits/

Strauss, W., & Howe, N. (1991). *Consumer Behaviour*. The Dryden Press.

Stromberg, S. (2019, September 17). Why baby boomers' grandchildren will hate them. *The Washington Post*. https://www.washingtonpost.com/opinions/2019/09/17/why-baby-boomers-grandchildren-will-hate-them/

Swiss Life. (2016). *Study intergenerational solidarity*. https://www.swisslife.com/en/home/blog/intergenerational-solidarity.html

Tetlock, P., Skitka, L., & Boettger, R. (1989). Social and Cognitive Strategies for Coping With Accountability: Conformity, Complexity, and Bolstering. *Journal of Personality and Social Psychology, 57*, 632–640. DOI: 10.1037//0022-3514.57.4.632

Tetlock, P. E. (1985). Accountability: A social check on the fundamental attribution error. *Social Psychology Quarterly, 48*(3), 227–236. DOI: 10.2307/3033683

Tiainen, L. (2024). *Unmasking Greenwashing : An Examination of Generation Z 's Perception of Sustainable Business* [LAB University of Applied Sciences]. https://www.theseus.fi/handle/10024/852630

Toleikienė, R., Balciunas, S., & Juknevičienė, V. (2020). Youth Attitudes Towards Intolerance to Corruption in Lithuania. *Scientific Papers of the University of Pardubice, Series D. Faculty of Economics and Administration, 28*, 1–13. DOI: 10.46585/sp28020109

Twenge, J. M., Cooper, A. B., Joiner, T. E., Duffy, M. E., & Binau, S. G. (2019). Age, period, and cohort trends in mood disorder indicators and suicide-related outcomes in a Nationally Representative Dataset, 2005 – 2017. *Journal of Abnormal Psychology, 128*(3), 185–199. https://doi.org/https://dx.doi.org/10.1037/abn0000410

Uche, S. C. (2018). *Generation Z and corporate social responsibility*. Syracuse University.

Van Kenhove, P., Vermeir, I., & Verniers, S. (2001). An Empirical Investigation of the Relationships between Ethical Beliefs, Ethical Ideology, Political Preference and Need for Closure e of Dutch-Speaking Consumers in Belgium. *Journal of Business Ethics*, *32*, 347–361. DOI: 10.1023/A:1010720908680

Vitell, S., Ramos-Hidalgo, E., & Rodríguez-Rad, C. (2018). A Spanish perspective on the impact on religiosity and spirituality on consumer ethics. *International Journal of Consumer Studies*, *42*(6), 675–686. https://doi.org/https://doi.org/10.1111/ijcs.12438

Vitell, S. J., & Muncy, J. (2005). The Muncy-Vitell consumer ethics scale: A modification and application. *Journal of Business Ethics*, *62*(3), 267–275. DOI: 10.1007/s10551-005-7058-9

Vitell, S. J., Singhapakdi, A., & Thomas, J. (2001). Consumer ethics: An application and empirical testing of the Hunt-Vitell theory of ethics. *Journal of Consumer Marketing*, *18*(2), 153–178.

Walker, A. (2012). The New Ageism. *The Political Quarterly*, *83*(4), 812–819. https://doi.org/https://doi.org/10.1111/j.1467-923X.2012.02360.x

Walker, B., Gunderson, L. H., Kinzig, A., Folke, C., Carpenter, S., & Schultz, L. (2006). A Handful of Heuristics and Some Propositions for Understanding Resilience. *Ecology and Society*, *11*(1), 13.

Wallimann-Helmer, I., Terán, L., Portmann, E., Schübel, H., & Pincay, J. (2021). An Integrated Framework for Ethical and Sustainable Digitalization. *2021 Eighth International Conference on EDemocracy & EGovernment (ICEDEG)*, 156–162. https://doi.org/DOI: 10.1109/ICEDEG52154.2021.9530972

Wang, Q., Myers, M. D., & Sundaram, D. (2013). Digital natives and digital immigrants: Towards a model of digital fluency. *Business & Information Systems Engineering*, *5*(6), 409–419. DOI: 10.1007/s12599-013-0296-y

Wood, J., & Winston, B. (2007). Development of three scales to measure leader accountability. *Leadership and Organization Development Journal*, *28*, 167–185. DOI: 10.1108/01437730710726859

Zaikauskaitė, L., Butler, G., Helmi, N. F. S., Robinson, C. L., Treglown, L., Tsivrikos, D., & Devlin, J. T. (2022). Hunt–Vitell's General Theory of Marketing Ethics Predicts "Attitude-Behaviour" Gap in Pro-environmental Domain. *Frontiers in Psychology*, *13*(March), 1–19. DOI: 10.3389/fpsyg.2022.732661

Zimand-Sheiner, D., & Lissitsa, S. (2024). Generation Z - factors predicting decline in purchase intentions after receiving negative environmental information: Fast fashion brand SHEIN as a case study. *Journal of Retailing and Consumer Services, 81*, 103999. https://doi.org/https://doi.org/10.1016/j.jretconser.2024.103999

KEY TERMS AND DEFINITIONS

Cognitive Dissonance: A psychological state experienced when there is a conflict between personal values and actual behaviours. In consumer ethics, it refers to the inconsistency observed when individuals endorse ethical principles yet fail to reflect them in their consumption practices. This concept is used as a synonym of the term "intention-behaviour gap" throughout the chapter.

DAS BIE Scale: A novel measurement instrument developed in this study to assess ethical value identification across generations. It includes five core values—solidarity, sustainability, social justice, responsibility, and respect—using a triple-bottom-line approach.

Digital Immigrants: Individuals who were born before the widespread adoption of digital technologies and who have had to adapt to the digital environment later in life. Their relationship with technology is often shaped by prior analogue experiences, which may influence their ethical reasoning, information processing, and consumer behaviour in distinct ways.

Digital Nativeness: A generational condition characterised by growing up in a digitally saturated environment, which shapes individuals' cognitive frameworks, communication habits, and access to information, as well as their ethical awareness and modes of social interaction.

Ethical Consumption: A value-driven approach to consumer behaviour where individuals consider the social, environmental, and moral consequences of their purchasing decisions, aiming to minimise harm and promote justice, sustainability, and solidarity.

Ethical Values: Core moral principles that orient individual attitudes and behaviours toward what is considered just, responsible, and respectful in social life. Drawing on Adela Cortina's (2002) framework of a socially ethical consumption, these values—solidarity, sustainability, social justice, responsibility, and respect—provide a foundation for ethical reasoning and guide decision-making in both individual and collective spheres, particularly within consumer practices.

Generational Cohorts: Socially constructed groups defined by shared historical, cultural, and technological experiences during formative years. These cohorts tend to display common attitudes, values, and consumption behaviours.

Responsible Consumption: The act of making conscious, informed, and ethically guided consumption choices that consider long-term social, environmental, and economic consequences. Grounded in models such as Muncy and Vitell's (1992) framework of consumer ethics, responsible consumption involves avoiding harmful or dishonest behaviours and aligning personal actions with broader societal values, such as fairness, sustainability, and accountability.

ENDNOTES

1 At a 99% confidence level and a 5% margin of error.

2 In the presentation of the questionnaire, the anonymity, voluntariness and confidentiality of the answers were clarified. In addition, the link to the Informed Consent was included as a question to verify its reading and acceptance (if not accepted, it is not possible to send the questionnaire), in compliance with Regulation (EU) 2016/679 on the protection of individuals with regard to the processing of personal data and on the free movement of such data.

3 In addition, all respondents were over 16 years old, which is the minimum age required for them to consent to the processing of their personal data and participate in the survey without needing the consent of their legal guardians, according to art. 7 of Organic Law 3/2018, of 5 December, on the Protection of Personal Data and guarantee of digital rights.

Chapter 8
Does Emotional Capital Influence HRM Decision-Making and Performance?

Jesus Barrena Martinez
https://orcid.org/0000-0002-5501-742X
Universidad de Cadiz, Spain

Maria-José Foncubierta-Rodriguez
https://orcid.org/0000-0003-3231-5261
Universidad de Cadiz, Spain

Dara Hernández-Roque
Universidad de Cadiz, Spain

María del Carmen Peces-Prieto
https://orcid.org/0000-0003-4043-6549
UCLM, Spain

ABSTRACT

The field of human resource management (HRM) has seen a growing body of research emphasizing the conceptualization of intellectual capital and its various dimensions. In response to increasing calls from the scientific community to deepen research in this area, the aim of this project is to analyze the role of emotional capital in fostering a socially responsible orientation in HRM decision-making. This process, in turn, could be key to building more committed and productive human capital within organizations. As emphasized in the literature, these practices are vital to the success of SMEs. This chapter sets out to explore two specific sub-objectives: to examine the effect of emotional capital on socially responsible HRM decisions and analyze whether socially responsible HRM decisions influence employee commit-

DOI: 10.4018/979-8-3373-0385-7.ch008

ment and productivity levels. Main theories and articles which combine emotional capital and HRM are examined, providing implications for SDGs, conclusions and future research lines.

INTRODUCTION

People are the most important asset that companies possess, serving as the core drivers of innovation, productivity, and strategic advantage. Their influence on organizational success has long been acknowledged, not only from an economic standpoint but also through their intrinsic connection to human, social, and organizational capital (Becker, 1964; Nahapiet & Ghoshal, 1998). Human capital reflects employees' skills, knowledge, and abilities; social capital encompasses the quality of relationships and networks within and outside the organization; and organizational capital refers to the institutionalized knowledge embedded in routines, processes, and culture (Subramaniam & Youndt, 2005). The synergistic interaction among these forms of capital enhances an organization's adaptive capacity and long-term performance (Youndt et al., 2004). This still remains one of the main concerns of current organizations.

Numerous studies have focused on developing strategies to improve employee performance, satisfaction, commitment, and engagement as mechanisms to strengthen these intangible assets (Albrecht et al., 2015; Saks, 2006). Research in strategic human resource management (SHRM) has shown that investing in people-centric policies—such as inclusive leadership, continuous learning, emotional support, and ethical climate—significantly contributes to positive organizational outcomes, including innovation, resilience, and sustainable growth (Wright & McMahan, 2011; Guest, 2017). Moreover, fostering a work environment that values psychological and emotional resources promotes not only individual well-being but also collective effectiveness and organizational citizenship behaviors (Luthans et al., 2007; Cameron et al., 2003).

However, the management of emotions—a fundamental concept in psychology—has been relatively underexplored in the fields of Organizational Management and Human Resource Management (HRM), despite its potential implications for individual performance, group decision-making, reduced absenteeism, the development of cohesive teamwork, and overall improvements in organizational behavior (Brammer et al., 2007; Fahr et al., 2012).

In response to this gap, the present project aims to analyze, from the perspective of Organizational Management, the significance of emotional capital in HRM decisions. Specifically, it seeks to determine whether a higher stock of emotional capital positively influences the development and implementation of more socially responsible decisions by the HR function.

Conceptually, emotional capital can be defined from both the employee's and the organization's viewpoints. Given that this project focuses on HRM, the most appropriate definition considers emotional capital as "the aggregated feelings of goodwill toward the company and the way it operates," representing a set of emotion-based assets that the organization has developed and manages over time with its employees (Huy & Shipilov, 2012: 74). Therefore, emotional capital constitutes an asset in which to invest resources with future expectations, necessitating the specification of its measurement and causal relationship with organizational outcomes.

Researchers Huy and Shipilov (2012) argue that emotional capital can be built through the actions of managers—a role that, in this chapter, corresponds to the HR manager. It is essential to study whether their decisions can enhance the quality of the emotional connection between the company and its employees.

Regarding its classification, emotional capital can be considered a specific dimension of social capital, complementing the structural, cognitive, and relational dimensions (Nahapiet & Ghoshal, 1998). It can be measured through four interconnected dimensions:

- *Feelings of Authenticity*: Perceived by employees when they observe alignment between what the company and its leaders say and what they actually do.
- *Pride at Work*: Felt when employees' achievements are recognized by the company, especially publicly.
- *Attachment to Work*: Arises when employees feel they belong to a community with shared values and interests within the company.
- *Joy*: Experienced by employees when engaging in new situations or procedures at work (Huy & Shipilov, 2012).

These dimensions are crucial for analyzing their individual and combined effects on socially responsible decisions made within HRM, aiming to improve employee productivity and commitment.

To explain the emotional exchanges and contributions between the company and employees, Social Exchange Theory, developed by Blau (1964), provides a coherent foundation. This theory posits that employees conduct a cost-benefit analysis of their relationship with the organization, perceiving stability as a process of negotiated exchanges between both parties. Positive exchanges lead employees to increase their efforts and performance to achieve greater interaction with the company, while negative exchanges may prompt thoughts of leaving the organization.

Various studies have considered this theoretical approach suitable for examining the relationship between social capital and other significant HR variables, such as organizational culture, levels of organizational citizenship, and the support employees receive from managers (Melé, 2003; Wayne et al., 1997). However, few studies specifically examine emotional capital and how its dimensions affect HRM, highlighting the novelty of this project.

Empirically, to examine these theoretical premises in practice, the study will be conducted in Small and Medium-sized Enterprises (SMEs). Although their revenue may be lower than that of large companies in Spain, SMEs contribute more to the country's Gross Domestic Product (GDP), specifically 62% (Instituto Nacional de Estadística, 2022). According to the January 2023 SME Figures Report, SMEs represent 99.83% of companies registered with Social Security (2.921.650), employing 10,749.229 people (63,80%) of total registered workers. This positions SMEs as a strategic focus for professional and scientific analysis, aligning with the challenges of the European macro-project Horizon-Europe 2021-2027 where SMEs play a special role.

Following the recommendations of Regulation (EU) No. 651/2014 of the European Commission, SMEs are categorized based on the number of employees, turnover, and balance sheet total. Since this project focuses on HRM, SMEs are categorized by the number of employees as follows:

Microenterprises (1–9 employees): In Spain represents 93.60% of the SME population and employ 46.59%.

Small Enterprises (10–49 employees): Account for 5.50% of the SME population and generate 29.41% of SME employment in Spain.

Medium-sized Enterprises (50–249 employees): Although they constitute only 0.89% of the SME population, they generate 24% of employment.

Additionally, it is presumed that Small and Medium-sized Enterprises have more structured HRM processes than Microenterprises, making them the focus of this analysis for both reasons.

Having clarified the sample selection and the measurement of emotional capital through four dimensions, the next step is to select key variables of organizational behavior and performance to obtain relevant project results and report them to the participating companies. Literature indicates that companies developing a responsible culture in HRM can achieve improvements in variables such as commitment, sense of belonging, and task involvement (Brammer et al., 2007).

Specifically, this chapter uses the following performance variables due to their importance in HRM:

- *Perception of Affective and Continuance Commitment*: As perceived by the HR manager regarding their employees (Allen & Meyer, 1990).

- *Annual Average Turnover Rates and Absenteeism Rates*: As key indicators of employee productivity (Huselid, 1995).
- *Organizational Citizenship Behavior*: As a primary outcome of socially responsible decisions (Wayne et al., 1997).
- *Development of Greater Transparency*: As another key outcome (Rawlins, 2008).

This division of behavioral and performance variables, in terms of economic productivity and social performance, provides more comprehensive results for the study, allowing an assessment of whether the HR function plays a socially responsible role in analyzing emotional capital within SMEs.

CONNECTING EMOTIONAL INTELLIGENCE AND HRM THROUGH HUMAN-CENTERED APPROACH

In today's dynamic and interconnected business environment, emotional intelligence (EI) plays a critical role in fostering ethical, sustainable, and human-centered organizations. Emotional intelligence—the capacity to recognize, understand, and manage one's own emotions and those of others—is foundational to ethical leadership and people-centered strategies (Goleman, 1995; Salovey & Mayer, 1990).

A Human-Centered Approach (HCA) focuses on designing systems, cultures, and strategies around the real needs, values, and aspirations of people—employees, customers, and communities (Norman, 2013). Leaders with high emotional intelligence are more empathetic, responsive, and collaborative, making them well-suited to implement HCA principles in decision-making and innovation (Boyatzis, 2018). Meanwhile, business ethics calls for organizations to go beyond legal compliance, prioritizing respect, fairness, transparency, and the long-term well-being of all stakeholders (Crane & Matten, 2016). Emotional intelligence enhances moral awareness and sensitivity to the consequences of decisions, supporting ethical behavior in complex, high-stakes situations (Treviño, Weaver, & Reynolds, 2006). Integrating EI, HCA, and ethical principles enables organizations to: (a) Develop more inclusive, compassionate, and resilient workplace cultures; (b) Build trust-based relationships with stakeholders through transparent and empathetic communication; (c) Consider the social and emotional dimensions of strategic decisions; and (d) Align innovation with human and environmental sustainability. Ultimately, putting people at the center of strategic decision-making is not just a design principle—it is a moral and emotional commitment. It requires emotionally intelligent leadership and a strong ethical foundation to ensure that organizations serve not only their shareholders, but also society at large in a meaningful and sustainable way.

In the current landscape of organizational management, the interplay between business ethics and human-centered approaches has emerged as a critical foundation for fostering responsible decision-making and promoting sustainable business practices. These two concepts, while distinct, are deeply interwoven and collectively shape the moral and cultural compass of modern organizations. Business ethics, broadly defined, refers to the application of moral principles and standards to business behavior and decision-making (Ferrell, Fraedrich, & Ferrell, 2021). It encompasses elements such as fairness, transparency, accountability, and respect for stakeholders. Meanwhile, a human-centered approach prioritizes the experiences, needs, and well-being of individuals — particularly employees and customers — in the design and implementation of business strategies (Norman & Verganti, 2014).

When these frameworks converge, organizations are better equipped to make responsible decisions that consider not only economic outcomes but also the human and societal implications of their actions. For example, a decision to automate a process might be economically sound but could also displace workers. A business that integrates ethical reasoning and human-centered thinking might instead choose a strategy that includes reskilling programs or phased transitions, demonstrating a commitment to both innovation and social responsibility. Ethical and human-focused practices directly influence several core dimensions of employee experience and organizational performance. Notably, they impact commitment, absenteeism, turnover, and engagement — all of which are critical indicators of organizational health.

Commitment

Organizational commitment refers to the emotional attachment and loyalty employees feel toward their organization. Studies show that ethical leadership and people-first cultures are strongly associated with higher levels of affective commitment (Meyer & Allen, 1997; Treviño & Nelson, 2021). When employees perceive their organization as fair, respectful, and values-driven, they are more likely to identify with its mission and goals, reinforcing long-term dedication.

Absenteeism

Workplace absenteeism is often linked to stress, dissatisfaction, and a lack of psychological safety. Human-centered organizations that prioritize employee well-being — through flexible policies, mental health support, and inclusive environments — tend to experience lower absenteeism rates (Grawitch et al., 2006). Ethical leadership further enhances this effect by building trust and fairness, reducing the emotional strain that often leads to absentee behavior.

Turnover

Employee turnover, especially when high, can be both financially and culturally damaging to organizations. Research suggests that unethical organizational cultures are a significant driver of voluntary turnover, as employees disengage from environments that lack integrity or inclusivity (Valentine, Godkin, & Lucero, 2002). Conversely, businesses that embed human-centered ethics into their management practices often enjoy stronger retention, as workers feel respected and supported.

Engagement

Employee engagement — the degree to which individuals are emotionally and cognitively invested in their work — is heavily influenced by ethical treatment and a sense of purpose. A human-centered and ethical workplace provides autonomy, recognition, and meaningful work, all of which enhance engagement (Kahn, 1990; Saks, 2006). Ethical behavior from leaders also serves as a model, reinforcing a culture of trust and psychological ownership.

Integrating ethics and a human-centered mindset is not merely a moral choice — it is also a strategic imperative. As organizations face increasing pressure to address social, environmental, and psychological concerns, those that adopt values-driven leadership and inclusive organizational design will be better positioned to navigate complexity and build resilience.

Such integration signals a shift from transactional, profit-centered thinking to a holistic, purpose-oriented paradigm where business success is measured not just by financial returns, but by human impact and long-term sustainability.

The chapter presented has as its main objective to measure and evaluate the stock of emotional capital in Spanish Small and Medium Enterprises (SMEs), examining its influence on socially responsible decision-making by Human Resources Management. This objective is divided into three specific sub-objectives:

The first sub-objective is to analyze the interplay of connections among emotional capital and HRM, as well as the main approaches followed. In this regard, two possible situations could be understood: First, that in small companies, due to the closeness and greater contact established between employees, the stock of emotional capital might be higher than in medium-sized companies; or second, that having a greater number of employees in medium-sized companies could generate an accumulation effect of emotional capital, making it more extensive than in small or micro-enterprises. These aspects will be empirically addressed in the project.

The second sub-objective aims to examine the effect of emotional capital on the socially responsible decisions made by HR Management, trying to discern whether higher levels of emotional capital help in implementing more responsible decisions in economic, social, or ethical terms for the workers, with the purpose of preserving the existing emotional capital within the company. In this sub-objective, understanding human resources management or leadership processes plays a vital role, where the aforementioned social exchange approach must be thoroughly reviewed to form a logical theoretical framework for the research. This could help determine whether a socially responsible HR function is currently part of the roles performed by SMEs.

The third sub-objective will attempt to analyze whether the socially responsible decisions made by HR Management affect workers' levels of commitment and productivity. To this end, key variables such as the degree of commitment, turnover, absenteeism levels, the development of organizational citizenship behavior among employees, and the existence of greater informational transparency will be examined. All the performance variables selected for the research have been widely tested and validated in other contexts, so the study adds as its main value the knowledge of these variables applied to the Spanish SME environment.

The objectives of the project are illustrated in Figure 1.

Figure 1. Conceptual figure

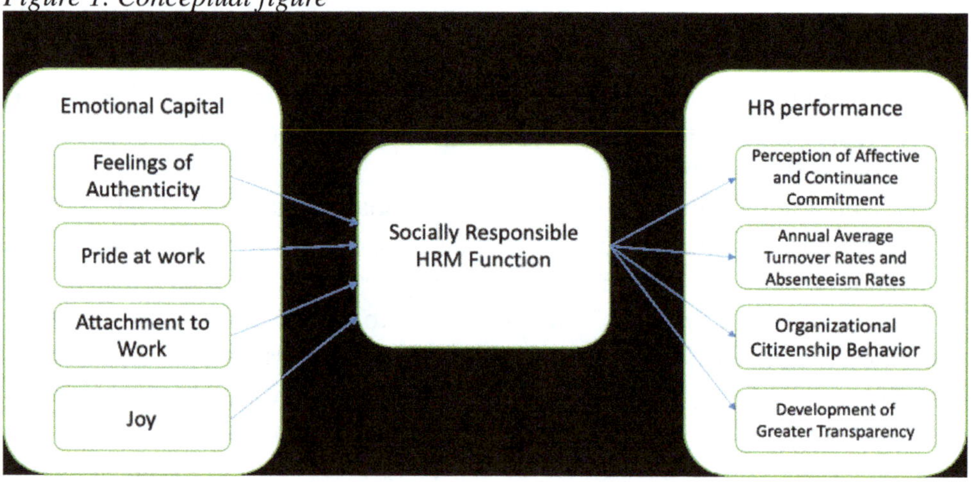

Literature Review in Databases

We conducted two reviews in Web of Science (WoS) and Scopus Databases. The first search in Web of Science that includes the terms "emotional capital" and "HRM", only reported 12 results. Figure 2.

Figure 2. (Web of Science, 05.06.2025)

Despite the report only includes 12 publications, 5 of theM accumulated 312 citations (Figure 3) were in the last 12 years.

Figure 3. (Web of Science 05.06.2025)

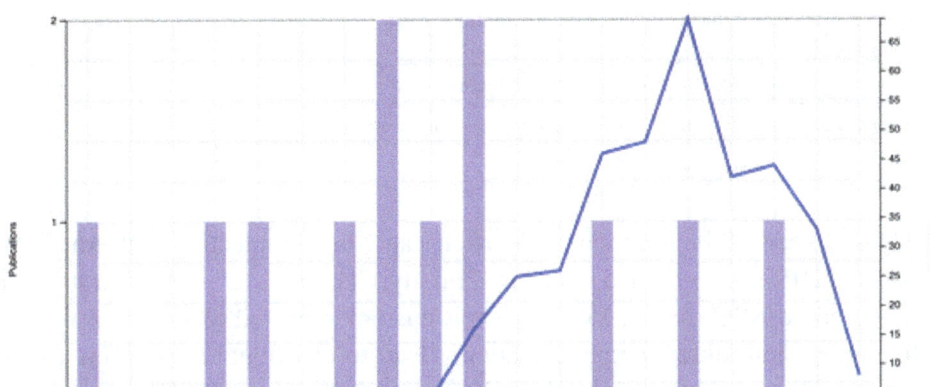

Table 1 reported the complete and detailed articles, including 12 articles.

*Table 1. Articles which include "emotional capital" and "HRM" terms**

Article	Authors	Citations
Testing the stressor-strain-outcome model of customer-related social stressors in predicting emotional exhaustion, customer orientation and service recovery performance	Choi, C.H., Kim, T.T., Lee, G., Lee, S.K.	173
Enhancing the employer-employee relationship through corporate social responsibility (CSR) engagement	Supanti, D., Butcher, K., Fredline, L.	91
People Make the Difference: An Explorative Study on the Relationship between Organizational Practices, Employees' Resources, and Organizational Behavior Enhancing the Psychology of Sustainability and Sustainable Development	Manuti, A., Giancaspro, ML	48
Holistic approach to human resources and organizational acceleration	Pluta, A., Rudawska,A.	35
High commitment HRM and burnout of frontline food service employees: a moderated mediation model	Teo, STT; Nguyen, D; Bentley, T	13
Antecedents and Moderators of Software Professionals' Performance	Prasad, HCS; Suar, D and Taraban, R	6
The secret of reducing turnover intention: Evidence from Indonesia	Yusuf, FA and Widodo, W.	3
Human Resource Management and Perceived Performance: The Role of Worker-Organization Relationship in Portuguese Hospital Workers	Martins, M.	0
The influence of human resource management and communities of practice on the management of knowledge: a case study of two malaysian firms	Muktar, S. N.	0
Personal networks in russian business: structure, rules, trust	Chen, G.	0
Perspectives of emotional work - On HRM practice in service sector	Fu, H	0

Source: author's own elaboration.

The synthesis of the following five articles and their connection with emotional capital and HRM are provided as follows. Firstly, Choi et al. (2014) tests a stressor-strain-outcome (SSO) model, exploring how customer-related social stressors (e.g., verbal aggression, unrealistic expectations) lead to emotional exhaustion among service employees. Emotional exhaustion negatively impacts customer orientation and service recovery performance. This article reinforces the importance of emotional capital — the emotional energy and resilience employees possess — in high-contact service roles. From an HRM perspective, managing stressors through training, supportive leadership, and mental health resources can protect emotional capital and sustain service quality.

Secondly, Supanti et al. (2015). This research demonstrates that CSR engagement strengthens the employer–employee relationship by increasing trust, organizational identification, and perceived organizational support. Employees involved in CSR initiatives report greater loyalty and positive affective responses. Regarding the link between emotional capital and HRM, CSR becomes a form of emotional enrichment — boosting pride, connection, and morale. From an HRM lens, CSR is not just external reputation-building, but an internal strategy for emotional engagement and retention.

Thirdly, Manuti & Giancaspro (2019). This paper explores how sustainable HRM practices (e.g., lifelong learning, well-being programs) enhance employee psychological resources (self-efficacy, optimism), which in turn support sustainable organizational behavior. In this manuscript, emotional capital is explicitly addressed as part of employee resources. Sustainable HRM builds this capital by creating environments that nurture psychological strength, contributing to both personal resilience and collective organizational sustainability.

Fourthly, Pluta & Rudawska (2016). The authors argue for a holistic HRM approach, integrating strategic and operational dimensions to drive organizational change and performance. Emphasis is placed on agility, adaptability, and alignment of human capital with dynamic environments. While not explicitly labeled as such, emotional capital is embedded in the model — through adaptability, employee empowerment, and readiness for change. Holistic HRM includes emotional resilience as a core lever for sustainable transformation.

Finally, Teo et al. (2021). This study finds that high-commitment HRM (e.g., developmental opportunities, participative leadership) can reduce burnout, but only when the job context supports it. Without supportive conditions, the pressure to perform may even amplify emotional strain. High-commitment HRM has the potential to build emotional capital by affirming employees' value and supporting their growth. However, HR strategies must be contextually sensitive to avoid unintended emotional depletion, particularly in high-stress environments.

Across these studies, several unifying themes emerge. Emotional capital highlights like the capacity to manage and invest emotional energy — is critical for sustainable performance, resilience, and service quality. HRM plays a pivotal role in protecting, developing, and leveraging this emotional capital through policies that promote well-being, purpose, and alignment with organizational values. Practices like CSR engagement, supportive leadership, high-commitment HRM, and stress management are not "soft" tools, but strategic levers that directly impact engagement, burnout, and performance. Emotional capital is also a collective resource, influencing not only individual experiences but the broader emotional climate of the organization — a key factor in service industries and dynamic environments.

The same search in Scopus Database provided 8 results with predominance of business and management, like in WoS database. These documents accumulated 305 citations.

Subject area ↓	Documents ↓
Business, Management and Accounting	6
Arts and Humanities	2
Decision Sciences	2
Economics, Econometrics and Finance	2
Social Sciences	2
Environmental Science	1

The first three articles, are also some of the same registered in WOS (Choi et al. 2014; Supanti et al. 2015; Pluta & Rudawska 2016). Additionally, we found the manuscript Tabouli et al. (2016), which finds that HRM practices (e.g., performance appraisals, training) enhance employee organizational commitment, which in turn improves individual performance. Commitment acts as a mediating variable in HRM-performance linkage. The article concludes that organizational commitment is deeply tied to emotional attachment, identity, and motivation — all aspects of emotional capital. HRM's role in fostering psychological safety and belonging is highlighted.

The article of Pandey (2018), discusses how HR can proactively manage emotional labor demands in service industries through training, policy support, and leadership development. Finally, in their connection between emotional capital and HRM, emotional labor, if unsupported, depletes emotional capital. HRM should act to replenish emotional resources, ensure role clarity, and provide recovery mechanisms to sustain performance and well-being.

The work of Prasad et al. (2014), identifies personal (e.g., motivation) and contextual (e.g., leadership support) antecedents that influence job performance among software professionals, highlighting the role of moderators like work environment. It also suggests that emotional states (like confidence or frustration) are critical to knowledge-based performance. HR must cultivate emotional capital through recognition, developmental support, and positive work climates.

Yusuf & Widodo (2023), examines key organizational factors that lower turnover intention, such as job satisfaction, leadership style, and perceived fairness. As a main result, it highlights that retaining talent depends on affective commitment and emotional connection to the workplace. HRM policies that address employee feelings of justice, purpose, and recognition are vital in retaining emotional capital.

Vanka et al. (2023), discusses how sustainable HRM can be a force for societal change. It emphasizes well-being, ethics, environmental stewardship, and long-term thinking in people management. This book provides a broad systemic framework where emotional capital is not just a workforce asset but also a social and sustainability imperative. Advocates for HRM that respects human dignity and psychological development as core values.

Along both searchs, the main theories and approaches that links emotional capital and HRM are eight. Firstly, emotional capital theory (Gendron, 2004), in which emotional capital refers to the reservoir of emotional resources (e.g., empathy, trust, motivation, resilience) that individuals or organizations accumulate and can draw upon in social or work interactions. The application of this approach, said that HR practices such as leadership development, emotional labor management, or CSR programs help build and maintain emotional capital within teams and individuals. Secondly, Conservation of Resources (COR) Theory (Hobfoll, 1989), posits that individuals strive to acquire and preserve resources, including emotional energy, and that stress occurs when these resources are threatened or depleted. In its application to HRM, emotional exhaustion from emotional labor or poor HR support reduces emotional capital. Positive HR practices (e.g., support, autonomy, training) help conserve and replenish emotional capital. Thirdly, job demands-resources (JD-R) model (Bakker & Demerouti, 2007).

The JD-R model argues that every job has demands (stressors) and resources (supportive factors). When job resources are high, employees can cope better with demands, protecting emotional energy. Regarding application in HRM, human resources can shape job design, provide support systems, and foster engagement, thus building emotional capital. Fourthly, affective events theory (AET), explains how workplace events trigger emotional reactions, which in turn affect job satisfaction, performance, and well-being. In this line, positive HR practices (e.g., recognition, inclusion) influence the frequency and impact of affective events, helping cultivate emotional capital.

On the other hand, Social Exchange Theory (SET), (Blau, 1964), posits that relationships are built on reciprocal exchanges of resources—emotional or material. When employees perceive organizational support, they reciprocate with loyalty and performance. In this matter, HR strategies that invest in employee well-being and emotional recognition foster strong emotional bonds (emotional capital). Moreover, Positive Organizational Scholarship (POS) (Cameron et al. 2003) focuses on strengths, virtues, and positive capacities in individuals and organizations—such as hope, compassion, and resilience. POS provides a lens to design HR practices that build psychological and emotional capital, leading to thriving workplaces. A similar approach that relates a closer concept, like Psychological Capital (PsyCap) (Luthans et al. 2007), comprises self-efficacy, optimism, hope, and resilience—resources that closely relate to emotional capital. Regarding the application into HRM, interventions (e.g., coaching, development programs) that target these dimensions enhance employees' emotional capital and coping capacity. Finally, the approach we selected for our chapter, Humanistic HRM / Human-Centered Management, emphasizes employee dignity, autonomy, and well-being as central to management and organizational success (Ghoshal, 2005). Human-centered HRM practices build emotional trust, engagement, and purpose—core aspects of emotional capital.

All of these eight approaches are shown in Table 2, using as main support for the objective of this research the Humanistic/People-Centered HRM.

Table 2. Synthesis table: theories connecting emotional capital and HRM

Theory/Approach	Core Concept	Emotional Capital Mechanism
Emotional capital theory	Emotional resources as key intangible assets.	Accumulated through trust, empathy, belonging.
Conservation of resources	Stress from resource loss.	HRM helps protect emotional energy.
Job demands–resources model	Balance between demands and supports.	HR can buffer emotional strain and support capacity building.
Affective events theory	Impact of daily events on emotions.	HR creates positive emotional experiences.
Social exchange theory	Reciprocity in relationships.	Emotional capital grows through perceived support.
Positive organizational scholarship	Flourishing through strengths and positivity.	Develops emotional richness via compassion, hope, and meaning.
Psychological capital	Optimism, efficacy, resilience, hope.	Foundation for emotional strength in workforce.
Humanistic/People-centered HRM	People over profits.	Emotionally intelligent systems lead to sustainable commitment.

METHODS

To identify the population of Small and Medium-sized Enterprises (SMEs) to which the research will be directed, the SABI database (Iberian Balance Sheet Analysis System) will be used, for which the University of Cádiz holds a license. The main filters established are: i) companies with registered office in Spain; ii) active companies; iii) number of employees between 10 and 249; iv) companies with directors/administrators who perform the function of human resources; and v) companies with directors/administrators whose directors are natural persons.

Since the research is framed within the scope of Human Resources Management (HRM), the survey will be addressed to the person responsible for human resources in the Spanish companies classified as SMEs, given their degree of knowledge and understanding of the human resources actions carried out. Applying the six filters described above, a total of 34,932 companies are obtained in SABI, which constitute the population under study.

To obtain statistical inferences that can reliably support the theoretical foundations of the research, it is necessary to extract from the total population of companies (N) a specific number of observations (n) that, by fulfilling the condition of representativeness, allows the characteristics found in these companies to be extrapolated to the general population. This subgroup is called the sample. Following the recommendations of Pérez-López (2009) and Morales-Vallejo (2011), who warn about the necessity to apply statistical laws in order to accurately determine the minimum sample size that guarantees the condition of representativeness, the following mathematical equation will be applied:

$p \cdot q$= Population variance;

N= Total population;

e= Sample error;

z= Confidence level;

Thus, assuming a margin of error of 10% and a confidence level of 95%, it can be observed in Table 3 that a minimum sample size of 96 observations will be required to guarantee the representativeness of this research.

Thus, assuming a margin of error of 10% and a confidence level of 95%, it can be observed in Table 1 that a minimum sample size of 96 observations will be necessary to guarantee the representativeness of this research.

Table 3. Minimum theoretical sample according to confidence interval and assumed margin of error

Sample criteria						
Margin or error (α)	**5%**	**6%**	**7%**	**8%**	**9%**	**10%**
Sample (confidence level 95%)	382	266	195	150	118	96

With the intention of selecting the representative number of companies (n) from the population under study, a simple random sampling (SRS) method without replacement (each selected element is discarded for subsequent selection) was chosen (Scheaffer et al., 2006).

EXPECTED RESULTS AND CONCLUSIONS

The intersection between emotional capital and Human Resource Management (HRM) highlights the importance of managing emotional and psychological resources to foster sustainable, resilient, and high-performing organizations. Emotional Capital—comprised of empathy, trust, emotional resilience, and engagement—is increasingly recognized as a strategic asset that HRM can develop through thoughtful, people-centered practices.

Theories such as emotional capital theory, conservation of resources (COR), and the job demands–resources (JD-R) model provide the conceptual backbone for understanding how emotional resources are accumulated, preserved, and depleted in organizational settings. Social exchange theory (SET) and affective events theory (AET) further explain the dynamic and reciprocal nature of emotional experiences in the workplace.

Psychological capital and positive organizational scholarship expand this understanding by integrating concepts like hope, optimism, and resilience, offering pathways to cultivate emotional capital through HRM interventions. Finally, the humanistic or People-Centered HRM approach reinforces the ethical and strategic imperative to design systems that support employee dignity, autonomy, and emotional well-being.

In sum, these theories collectively emphasize that emotional capital is not only a personal or social resource but also an organizational one, deeply influenced by HRM policies and practices. Organizations that invest in building emotional capital through strategic HRM gain a sustainable advantage in employee engagement, well-being, and performance.

Regarding empirial expected results, the study is expected to yield several key outcomes:

- Identification of key HR decision-makers in SMEs. By targeting SMEs with defined HR responsibilities, the research anticipates a more accurate understanding of how HR decisions are currently made in small and medium-sized firms in Spain.
- Insights into emotional capital as a strategic asset. The research aims to highlight the presence and perceived importance of emotional capital—defined as the collective emotional resources (e.g., trust, empathy, motivation, emotional intelligence) within an organization—as a contributing factor to effective HRM.
- Empirical validation of emotional capital's value. The study expects to find correlations between firms with high emotional capital and better HRM outcomes such as employee engagement, retention, and adaptability to change.
- Statistical representativeness of findings. With a robust sampling method and a statistically representative sample of 96 SMEs, the findings will be generalizable to a broader population of similar companies, thereby supporting the theoretical framework with empirical evidence.

CONCLUSIONS FOR HRM PRACTITIONERS

Regarding the main conclusions, emotional capital should be consider as a new strategic sesource. This research reinforces the idea that emotional capital is not merely a "soft" asset but a measurable and impactful form of capital. HR practitioners should recognize it as an essential factor in enhancing organizational value and strategic decision-making.

Secondly, the approach of human-centered decision-making is essential in new scenarios. Practitioners are encouraged to incorporate emotional awareness into their decision-making frameworks. Doing so can result in more adaptive, resilient, and engaged teams—especially critical in SMEs where interpersonal relationships are often central to organizational functioning.

Thirdly, the measurement of emotional capital. The study underscores the need to develop tools and metrics that can assess emotional capital within organizations, enabling HR professionals to monitor and enhance this intangible asset systematically.

Fourthly, HRM can act as a driver of sustainable growth. By acknowledging emotional capital, HRM can shift from a reactive administrative function to a proactive strategic driver. HR professionals will be better equipped to contribute to sustainable business growth by aligning emotional intelligence with organizational goals.

Finally, leadership and emotional intelligence are essential variables to be combined. HR leaders should invest in developing emotionally intelligent leadership throughout the organization. Leaders who model empathy, trust, and emotional regulation can significantly strengthen emotional capital across teams.

Alignment with the Sustainable Development Goals (SDGs)

The integration of business ethics and a human-centered approach is not only essential for internal organizational health but also strongly supports several of the United Nations Sustainable Development Goals (SDGs). These global objectives aim to promote prosperity, protect the planet, and ensure peace and justice for all by 2030. Companies that embed ethical behavior and human-focused practices into their strategies contribute meaningfully to this vision. Below are the most relevant SDGs that connect to the themes explored in this chapter (See Figure 4):

SDG 3: Good Health and Well-being

By fostering ethical workplaces that prioritize employee well-being, mental health, and safety, organizations directly support SDG 3. Reduced absenteeism, lower stress, and healthier work environments result from practices that value individuals as more than mere economic inputs.

SDG 5: Gender Equality

Human-centered approaches inherently promote diversity, equity, and inclusion, helping eliminate gender-based discrimination and creating more equitable access to leadership and development opportunities. Ethical companies also implement policies that ensure equal pay and protection against harassment.

SDG 8: Decent Work and Economic Growth

Ethical labor practices, employee engagement, fair wages, and safe working conditions all align with the aim of SDG 8 to ensure inclusive and sustainable economic growth, full and productive employment, and decent work for all. Lower turnover and higher engagement contribute to long-term economic resilience.

SDG 10: Reduced Inequalities

Human-centered decision-making is rooted in recognizing and addressing inequality. Inclusive hiring, accessibility initiatives, and ethical leadership all contribute to reducing disparities within and across organizations, directly supporting SDG 10.

SDG 12: Responsible Consumption and Production

Organizations that adopt ethical frameworks often expand their responsibility beyond the internal workforce to include sustainable sourcing, ethical supply chains, and reduced environmental impact. This supports SDG 12, which promotes responsible production and corporate accountability.

SDG 16: Peace, Justice and Strong Institutions

Corporate ethics play a crucial role in supporting transparent, accountable, and inclusive institutions. Companies with integrity-based cultures and strong ethical leadership serve as models of ethical governance, aligning with SDG 16's emphasis on justice and institutional trust.

Figure 5. SDGs affected by research

(Author's elaboration with Artificial Inteligence)

Future Research Lines and Connection with the Reality of the Companies

To deepen the understanding of emotional capital and its influence on organizational performance, future research should explore several promising avenues that integrate both conceptual and empirical inquiry.

Operationalization and Contextualization of Emotional Capital

Future studies should aim to refine the operational definition of emotional capital within different organizational contexts. This includes delineating its components—such as empathy, trust, emotional resilience, and belonging—and examining how these elements vary across sectors and cultures (Gendron, 2004). Context-sensitive models are needed to better capture the interplay between emotional capital and industry-specific stressors or relational dynamics.

Development of Multilevel Measurement Instruments

There is a need for validated tools that can measure emotional capital at the individual, team, and organizational levels. While existing frameworks such as Emotional Intelligence Scales (Mayer et al., 2000) and the Psychological Capital Questionnaire (Luthans et al., 2007) offer foundational insights, future research should adapt or extend these tools to assess emotional capital holistically and longitudinally. Mixed-method approaches combining surveys, interviews, and digital analytics may enhance reliability and depth.

Empirical Linkages with HRM Practices and Organizational Outcomes

Further empirical work should investigate how emotional capital interacts with specific HRM systems—such as high-commitment practices, emotional labor policies, and employee well-being programs—and how these relationships influence key outcomes such as engagement, burnout, service quality, and turnover intention (Bakker & Demerouti, 2007; Teo et al., 2021). Longitudinal studies and cross-lagged panel models would help identify causality and directional effects.

Integration with Strategic People Analytics and Technology

Research should explore how emerging HR analytics tools and artificial intelligence can be leveraged to track and interpret emotional capital indicators in real time (Angrave et al., 2016). For instance, natural language processing techniques may be applied to communication datasets to detect emotional tone and cohesion within teams, opening novel avenues for predictive analytics.

Examination of Emotional Capital in Leadership and Organizational Culture

Another fruitful line of inquiry is the role of leadership in cultivating emotional capital. Studies should assess how emotionally intelligent or servant leadership styles influence the development and sustainability of emotional capital across hierarchical levels (Cameron et al., 2003). Similarly, psychological safety, inclusive practices, and values-based management can be investigated as cultural enablers of emotional resource accumulation (Edmondson, 1999).

Cross-Cultural and Cross-Sectoral Comparative Studies

Given the increasing globalization of work, future research should undertake cross-cultural and cross-sectoral comparisons to evaluate how emotional capital is conceptualized, valued, and utilized across different environments. Comparative case studies could illuminate how emotional capital operates in collectivist versus individualist societies, or in service-oriented versus production-driven sectors.

REFERENCES

Albrecht, S. L., Bakker, A. B., Gruman, J. A., Macey, W. H., & Saks, A. M. (2015). Employee engagement, human resource management practices and competitive advantage: An integrated approach. *Journal of Organizational Effectiveness: People and Performance, 2*(1), 7–35. DOI: 10.1108/JOEPP-08-2014-0042

Allen, N. J., & Meyer, J. P. (1990). The measurement and antecedents of affective, continuance and normative commitment to the organization. *Journal of Occupational and Organizational Psychology, 63*(1), 1–18.

Angrave, D., Charlwood, A., Kirkpatrick, I., Lawrence, M., & Stuart, M. (2016). HR and analytics: Why HR is set to fail the big data challenge. *Human Resource Management Journal, 26*(1), 1–11. DOI: 10.1111/1748-8583.12090

Bakker, A. B., & Demerouti, E. (2007). The Job Demands–Resources model: State of the art. *Journal of Managerial Psychology, 22*(3), 309–328. DOI: 10.1108/02683940710733115

Becker, G. S. (1964). *Human capital: A theoretical and empirical analysis, with special reference to education*. University of Chicago Press.

Blau, P. M. (1964). *Exchange and power in social life*. Wiley.

Boyatzis, R. E. (2018). *The competent manager: A model for effective performance*. John Wiley & Sons.

Brammer, S., Millington, A., & Rayton, B. (2007). The contribution of corporate social responsibility to organizational commitment. *International Journal of Human Resource Management, 18*(10), 1701–1719.

Cameron, K. S., Dutton, J. E., & Quinn, R. E. (2003). *Positive organizational scholarship: Foundations of a new discipline*. Berrett-Koehler Publishers.

Choi, C. H., Kim, T. T., Lee, G., & Lee, S. K. (2014). Testing the stressor-strain-outcome model of customer-related social stressors in predicting emotional exhaustion, customer orientation and service recovery performance. *International Journal of Hospitality Management, 36*, 272–285. DOI: 10.1016/j.ijhm.2013.10.009

Crane, A., & Matten, D. (2016). *Business ethics: Managing corporate citizenship and sustainability in the age of globalization* (4th ed.). Oxford University Press.

Crane, A., & Matten, D. (2016). *Business ethics: Managing corporate citizenship and sustainability in the age of globalization* (4th ed.). Oxford University Press.

Edmondson, A. C. (1999). Psychological safety and learning behavior in work teams. *Administrative Science Quarterly, 44*(2), 350–383. DOI: 10.2307/2666999

Ferrell, O. C., Fraedrich, J., & Ferrell, L. (2021). *Business Ethics: Ethical Decision Making and Cases* (13th ed.). Cengage Learning.

Gendron, B. (2004). *Why emotional capital matters in education and in the labour market: Toward an optimal use of human capital and knowledge management. Centre for Educational Research and Innovation (CERI).* OECD., DOI: 10.1787/870020048750

Ghoshal, S. (2005). Bad management theories are destroying good management practices. *Academy of Management Learning & Education, 4*(1), 75–91. DOI: 10.5465/amle.2005.16132558

Goleman, D. (1995). *Emotional intelligence: Why it can matter more than IQ.* Bantam Books.

Grawitch, M. J., Gottschalk, M., & Munz, D. C. (2006). The Path to a Healthy Workplace: A Critical Review Linking Healthy Workplace Practices, Employee Well-Being, and Organizational Improvements. *Consulting Psychology Journal, 58*(3), 129–147. DOI: 10.1037/1065-9293.58.3.129

Guest, D. E. (2017). Human resource management and employee well-being: Towards a new analytic framework. *Human Resource Management Journal, 27*(1), 22–38. DOI: 10.1111/1748-8583.12139

Hobfoll, S. E. (1989). Conservation of resources: A new attempt at conceptualizing stress. *The American Psychologist, 44*(3), 513–524. DOI: 10.1037/0003-066X.44.3.513

Huselid, M. A. (1995). The impact of human resource management practices on turnover, productivity, and corporate financial performance. *Academy of Management Journal, 38*(3), 635–672.

Huy, Q., & Shipilov, A. (2012). The key to social media success within organizations. MIT Sloan Management Review, 54(1), 73. Melé, D. (2003). Organizational humanizing cultures: Do they generate social capital? *Journal of Business Ethics, 45*(1), 3–14.

Kahn, W. A. (1990). Psychological Conditions of Personal Engagement and Disengagement at Work. *Academy of Management Journal, 33*(4), 692–724. DOI: 10.5465/256287

Luthans, F., Youssef, C. M., & Avolio, B. J. (2007). *Psychological capital: Developing the human competitive edge.* Oxford University Press.

Manuti, A., & Giancaspro, M. L. (2019). People make the difference: An explorative study on the relationship between organizational practices, employees' resources, and organizational behavior. *Sustainability, 11*(5), 1499. DOI: 10.3390/su11051499

Mayer, J. D., Salovey, P., & Caruso, D. R. (2000). Emotional intelligence as zeitgeist, as personality, and as a mental ability. In Bar-On, R., & Parker, J. D. A. (Eds.), *The handbook of emotional intelligence* (pp. 92–117). Jossey-Bass.

Meyer, J. P., & Allen, N. J. (1997). *Commitment in the Workplace: Theory, Research, and Application*. Sage Publications.

Nahapiet, J., & Ghoshal, S. (1998). Social capital, intellectual capital, and the organizational advantage. *Academy of Management Review, 23*(2), 242–266. DOI: 10.5465/amr.1998.533225

Norman, D. A. (2013). *The design of everyday things: Revised and expanded edition*. Basic Books.

Norman, D. A., & Verganti, R. (2014). Incremental and Radical Innovation: Design Research vs. Technology and Meaning Change. *Design Issues, 30*(1), 78–96. DOI: 10.1162/DESI_a_00250

Pandey, J. (2018). Managing emotional labor for service employees: An HRM-based approach. *Human Resource Management International Digest, 26*(4), 1–4. DOI: 10.1108/HRMID-03-2018-0044

Pluta, A., & Rudawska, A. (2016). Holistic approach to human resources and organizational acceleration. *Journal of Organizational Change Management, 29*(2), 293–309. DOI: 10.1108/JOCM-04-2015-0060

Prasad, H. C. S., Suar, D., & Taraban, R. (2014). Antecedents and moderators of software professionals' performance. *SAGE Open, 4*(1), 1–11. DOI: 10.1177/2158244014522633

Rawlins, B. (2008). Measuring the Relationship Between Organizational Transparency and Employee Trust. *The Public Relations Journal, 2*(2), 1–21.

Saks, A. M. (2006). Antecedents and Consequences of Employee Engagement. *Journal of Managerial Psychology, 21*(7), 600–619. DOI: 10.1108/02683940610690169

Salovey, P., & Mayer, J. D. (1990). Emotional intelligence. *Imagination, Cognition and Personality, 9*(3), 185–211. DOI: 10.2190/DUGG-P24E-52WK-6CDG

Subramaniam, M., & Youndt, M. A. (2005). The influence of intellectual capital on the types of innovative capabilities. *Academy of Management Journal, 48*(3), 450–463. DOI: 10.5465/amj.2005.17407911

Supanti, D., Butcher, K., & Fredline, L. (2015). Enhancing the employer-employee relationship through corporate social responsibility (CSR) engagement. *International Journal of Contemporary Hospitality Management*, *27*(7), 1479–1498. DOI: 10.1108/IJCHM-06-2014-0286

Tabouli, E. M. A., Habtoor, N. A., & Nashief, S. M. (2016). The impact of human resources management on employee performance: Organizational commitment mediator variable. *Asian Social Science*, *12*(9), 176–192. DOI: 10.5539/ass.v12n9p176

Teo, S. T. T., Nguyen, D., Meurer, M., & Bentley, T. (2021). High commitment HRM and burnout of frontline food service employees: A moderated mediation model. *Employee Relations*, *43*(6), 1342–1361. DOI: 10.1108/ER-10-2020-0484

Treviño, L. K., & Nelson, K. A. (2021). *Managing Business Ethics: Straight Talk About How to Do It Right* (8th ed.). Wiley.

Treviño, L. K., Weaver, G. R., & Reynolds, S. J. (2006). Behavioral ethics in organizations: A review. *Journal of Management*, *32*(6), 951–990. DOI: 10.1177/0149206306294258

Valentine, S., Godkin, L., & Lucero, M. (2002). Ethical Context, Organizational Commitment, and Person–Organization Fit. *Journal of Business Ethics*, *41*(4), 349–360. DOI: 10.1023/A:1021243117958

Vanka, S., Rao, M. B., Singh, S., & Pulaparthi, M. R. (2023). *Sustainable Human Resource Management: Transforming Organizations, Societies and Environment*. Routledge., DOI: 10.4324/9781003258220

Wayne, S. J., Shore, L. M., & Liden, R. C. (1997). Perceived organizational support and leader-member exchange: A social exchange perspective. *Academy of Management Journal*, *40*(1), 82–111.

Wright, P. M., & McMahan, G. C. (2011). Exploring human capital: Putting 'human' back into strategic human resource management. *Human Resource Management Journal*, *21*(2), 93–104. DOI: 10.1111/j.1748-8583.2010.00165.x

Wright, P. M., & Ulrich, M. D. (2017). A Road Well Travelled: The Past, Present, and Future Journey of Strategic Human Resource Management. *Annual Review of Organizational Psychology and Organizational Behavior*, *4*(1), 45–65.

Youndt, M. A., Subramaniam, M., & Snell, S. A. (2004). Intellectual capital profiles: An examination of investments and returns. *Journal of Management Studies*, *41*(2), 335–361. DOI: 10.1111/j.1467-6486.2004.00435.x

Yusuf, F. A., & Widodo, W. (2023). The secret of reducing turnover intention: Evidence from Indonesia. *Cogent Business & Management*, *10*(2), 2202026. DOI: 10.1080/23311975.2023.2202026

Chapter 9
Human-Centric Approaches in Industry 5.0:
Organizational Strategies and Their Influence on Employee Engagement and Productivity

A. Ayyoob
https://orcid.org/0009-0003-2839-3598
University of Calicut, India

Aparna Sajeev
https://orcid.org/0000-0001-5642-5460
University of Calicut, India

ABSTRACT

This study examines the effects of a human-centric approach in Industry 5.0 on employee productivity and engagement focusing on human-centric technologies, organizational culture, and organizational support. The development of Industry 5.0, which emphasizes human-machine interaction rather than automation, has brought about changes in the workplace ecosystem but the impacts of such factors on employee engagement are understudied. This study uses a qualitative approach composed of interviews with HR managers, organizational leaders, industry specialists, and a broader quantitative survey of 264 employees. Findings indicate that human-centric technologies, favourable organizational culture, and supportive leadership positively impact employee engagement. These practices increase collaboration, inclusiveness, and employee empowerment, leading to higher job

DOI: 10.4018/979-8-3373-0385-7.ch009

satisfaction and productivity. The study concludes that there is a need to adopt more human-centric strategies for improving worker's health and organizational performance in the context of Industry 5.0.

INTRODUCTION

The rise of Industry 5.0 marks a shift in the paradigm of how organizations harness modern technology in tandem with human intelligence, with an aim to developing a system where productivity and human well-being is enhanced through innovation. Different from the previous phase 4.0 which concentrated on automation and operational effectiveness, Industry 5.0 focuses on human-machine synergies, hence, more emphasis is placed on human workforce in 5.0 (Khanna et al., 2024; Kanchan & Mugdha, 2024). This shift goes beyond technology to rethinking the definition of work to include creativity, emotional intelligence, and nuanced decision making in addition to efficiency (Ibrahim & Amjad, 2024). At the core of Industry 5.0 is human-machine collaboration. Technologies like collaborative robots (cobots), for example, are specially designed to augment human abilities, not replace them (Khanna et al., 2024). These systems complement human employees, fostering an environment of integrated human and technological skills. This synergy goes further to enhance not only safety at the workplace, but also satisfaction and engagement at work (Singh & Cohen, 2024). Automating work processes empowers employees to concentrate on complex tasks like innovation, problem solving, and creativity, which increases motivation and self-fulfilment (Kanchan & Mugdha, 2024).

Furthermore, besides the technological perspective, Industry 5.0 emphasizes focus on organizational culture and leadership as key elements deciding the level of employee engagement. Strong organizational culture that fosters inclusion, well-being, and teamwork is fundamental to the effective execution of human-centric initiatives (Madzik et al., 2024). Cultures that cultivate emotional agility further enhance goal alignment between employees and the organization, enabling easier implementation of human-centered technologies (Singh & Cohen, 2024). Equally important is leadership. Human-centric change requires strong support from leaders who nurture trust and collaboration. Such leaders have greater capability to harness employee engagement and commitment (Ibrahim & Amjad, 2024). Additionally, leadership that advances other concerns like social responsibility and sustainability strengthens the overarching vision of Industry 5.0 by transforming organizations into places where employees truly feel appreciated and empowered to share their ideas (Kanchan & Mugdha, 2024). The challenges include sectors that continue to rely on manual labour and low-tech processes. Moreover, usually lack of motivation, limited skills, workforce apathy, and even aged systems can obstruct progress. This study aims to the human strategies make towards employee engagement no less in neglected domains. The goal is to show the relationship among human-centric technologies, organizational culture, leadership support, and their impact in guiding organizations towards engaging employees in the transitions to Industry 5.0.

Statement of the Problem

The focus shifts towards more human-centric aspects such as employee focus, wellbeing, and productivity improvement through organizational culture, advanced technologies, and integrated leadership as organizations adopt the tenets of Industry 5.0. There is growing interest in those strategies but scant literature documenting the impact. Even though the impact of technology and organizational culture is well documented, the support from leadership towards human-centric initiatives and organizational culture to employee engagement within Industry 5.0 remains underexplored. This study aims to address this gap by analysing the connections human-centric technologies, organizational culture, support from leadership, and employee engagement. The study will analyse the dynamics of these factors towards fostering a more engaged and productive workforce which, in turn, enhances organizational performance within the framework of Industry 5.0. Following are the research questions

1. In what ways does the application of human-centric technologies affect employee engagement in Industry 5.0 compliant organizations?
2. What is the nexus between organizational culture and employee engagement in relation to human-centric involvement?
3. How significant is the effect of leadership's support for human-centric policies on employee engagement in organizations transitioning to Industry 5.0?

Significance of the Study

This study is important in attempting to bridge the gap regarding the effect of human-centric frameworks and employee engagement concerning Industry 5.0 technologies. With the integration of sophisticated technologies and human-machine collaboration, organizations need to evaluate the impacts on employee engagement, to improve organizational success and productivity. The relationship between technologies related to humans and employee engagement provides value within the context of integrating collaborative robots and other sophisticated tools to enhance productivity and job satisfaction. Their attention is appreciated more as organizations seek to devise these work settings where employees use their human-specific competencies such as creativity and problem-solving (Khanna et al., 2024; Ibrahim & Amjad, 2024).

The role of culture in organizational engagement has also been studied. By looking at the impact of emotional intelligence and adaptability on engagement to organizational culture, the study offers direction on how to construct supportive and resilient workplaces (Kanchan & Mugdha, 2024; Singh & Cohen, 2024). Moreover, the emphasis on nurturing change through human-centric approaches deepens the conversation on social responsibility and ethical business conduct. Investigating the role of human-centric approaches to sustainability in Industry 5.0 underlines the ethical aspect of business for enduring organizational efficacy (Kanchan & Mugdha, 2024; Madzik et al., 2024). Thus, the study is important for business executives, policy strategists, and scholars who focus on the shifts brought about by industry 5.0 principles.

Objectives of the Study

Objective 1

- ✓ To explore the perceived impact of human-centric technologies, cultural influences, and leadership strategies on employee engagement in the context of Industry 5.0, highlighting their role in fostering job satisfaction, autonomy, and productivity.

Objective 2

- ✓ To analyse employee perceptions of human-centric technologies, organizational culture, leadership support, and employee engagement through descriptive statistics, highlighting key trends and variations in responses to assess the effectiveness of Industry 5.0 initiatives.

Objective 3

- ✓ To examine gender and generational differences in employee engagement, human-centric technologies, organizational culture, and leadership support

Hypotheses

- H01-H04: There is no significant difference in gender characteristics of respondents towards the employee engagement, human-centric technologies, organizational culture, and leadership support

- H05-H08: There is no significant difference in the generations of respondents towards the employee engagement, human-centric technologies, organizational culture, and leadership support

Objective 4

✓ To analyze the relationship between human-centric technologies, organizational culture, and leadership support in influencing employee engagement.

Hypotheses

- H09-H011: There is no significant relationship between employee engagement and human-centric technologies, organizational culture, and leadership support

Variables for the Study

Dependent Variable

Employee Engagement (EE): Represents the enthusiasm and commitment of the employees towards the organization and their work which can be affected by human-centric policies.

Independent Variables

1. Implementation of Human-Centric Technologies (HCT): The relative degree of application of technologies aimed at improving human welfare and productivity within the organization, such as AI personalized learning modules and ergonomic furniture.
2. Organizational Culture (OC): The extent to which the organization promotes collaboration, inclusivity, and the overall wellness of its employees. This has an effect on the acceptance of human-centric strategies and their effectiveness within the organization.
3. Leadership Support for Human Initiatives (LS): Support and commitment of the leadership to human-centric initiatives, such as policies focused towards the employees, which may determine the success of these strategies.

REVIEW OF LITERATURES

Human-Machine Collaboration in Industry 5.0

Moving from Industry 4.0 to Industry 5.0 marks a distinct change in focus to human-centric attributes like sustainability, resilience, and well-being of stakeholders. This change is incorporating collaborative robots, also called cobots, that work with human workers to optimize workflow, productivity, and safety in the workplace (Darwish, 2024). Furthermore, in Industry 4.0, The human-centric technology focus is collaborative but subordinate to the existing human work structures, while in Industry 5.0, the focus shifts to complimentary collaboration that enhances human abilities. This evolution greatly improves the work experience, creating a culture of empowerment and appreciation (Vajravelu et al., 2024).

In the collaborative model, advanced technologies like digital twins and cobots have particular importance. Cobots are built specifically to work closely with people; the machines possess advanced algorithms and sensors that make them safe and efficient operators. They enhance the performance of employees by taking over physically straining and complex tasks that allow workers to concentrate on creative and strategic work (Krupas et al., 2024). Enhancing given decision processes with data and predictive analytics is done with virtual models that replicate real processes: digital twins.

These innovations bolster consistent collaboration, advance versatility, and adjust organizational techniques with the objectives of Industry 5.0 (Darwish, 2024; Krupas et al., 2024). Enthusiastic insights (EI) moreover play a basic part in encouraging human-machine collaboration. Machines prepared with counterfeit passionate insights can decipher and react to human feelings, cultivating believe and viable communication. This interaction upgrades the collaboration between people and machines, driving to more noteworthy development and efficiency (Singh et al., 2024). At the same time, sincerely cleverly representatives are superior prepared to explore these intuitive, guaranteeing agreeable and effective workflows (Patil & Kulkarni, 2024).

Investigate advance highlights the significance of engaging representatives through abilities improvement, ethical hones, and supportability activities. Abilities improvement programs prepare representatives with the ability required to utilize progressed advances successfully. Ethical hones, counting straightforward usage of innovation, fortify believe and engagement inside the workforce. Also, sustainability-focused methodologies adjust organizational destinations with broader societal values, cultivating worker commitment and upgrading working environment elements (Vajravelu et al., 2024; Patil & Kulkarni, 2024).

In conclusion, the move from Industry 4.0 to Industry 5.0 underscores the transformative potential of human-machine collaboration. By joining progressed advances like cobots and computerized twins, cultivating enthusiastic insights, and prioritizing ethical and economical hones, organizations can make locked in, inventive, and flexible working environments. This approach adjusts efficiency objectives with the broader goals of maintainability and well-being, checking a noteworthy progression in mechanical advancement (Darwish, 2024; Singh et al., 2024; Krupas et al., 2024).

Organizational Culture and Representative Engagement

A survey of the writing highlights the basic relationship between organizational culture and representative engagement, especially within the setting of human-centric work environments. Components such as incorporation, collaboration, passionate insights, and flexibility are foundational to cultivating an environment that underpins engagement (Hidayat et al., 2024). These social components adjust with organizational behavior hypotheses, which emphasize the part of shared values and hones in forming worker states of mind and behaviors. This arrangement makes a propelled workforce able of contributing definitively to organizational goals (Ritu, 2024).

Within the setting of Industry 5.0, organizational culture and representative engagement play an essential part in supporting a human-centric approach that upgrades efficiency and advancement. Investigate recommends that a solid organizational culture, combined with transformational administration, altogether impacts representative engagement. This engagement, in turn, impacts organizational commitment and advances citizenship behaviors, which are basic for supporting competitive advantage (Hidayat et al., 2024). Transformational authority cultivates a sense of vision and reason, propelling workers to adjust their individual objectives with organizational targets (Saputra, 2024).

Successful administration styles and steady organizational societies are fundamental in driving higher levels of worker engagement. For occurrence, authority improvement programs, acknowledgment activities, and work-life adjust techniques have been appeared to essentially upgrade engagement levels, progressing by and large organizational execution (Ritu, 2024). These techniques illustrate the expanding significance of representative engagement as a determinant of organizational victory within the cutting-edge working environment (Adisa et al., 2024).

The integration of maintainable HRM hones with progressed innovations has encourage changed organizational culture. Maintainable HRM hones center on cultivating versatility, collaboration, and inclusivity, which are pivotal for adjusting worker engagement with broader supportability goals (Narayana, 2023). Advances such as AI-driven stages and digital collaboration apparatuses upgrade communication, expertise advancement, and cooperation, advancing a culture of development (Adisa et al., 2024). These practices help organizations flourish within the energetic scene of Industry 5.0 by adjusting their workforce with both innovative and supportability objectives.

In conclusion, the transaction between organizational culture and worker engagement is central to accomplishing human-centric working environments in Industry 5.0. A solid culture emphasizing consideration, collaboration, and flexibility combined with transformational administration and economical HRM hones drives engagement and development (Hidayat et al., 2024; Ritu, 2024). By leveraging these components, organizations can upgrade efficiency, versatility, and maintainability, guaranteeing long-term victory in an advancing mechanical environment (Saputra, 2024; Narayana, 2023).

Leadership Support for Human-Centric Activities

Authority plays a central part in progressing human-centric methodologies in Industry 5.0, centering on harmonizing human insights with progressed advances to cultivate work environments that prioritize worker well-being. Investigate highlights that transformational and worker authority styles are especially viable in upgrading representative inspiration, engagement, and strengthening. These authority approaches empower a steady organizational culture that empowers consistent collaboration between people and machines, subsequently cultivating advancement and flexibility (Patil & Kulkarni, 2024; Khanna et al., 2024).

Passionate insights may be a basic quality for pioneers in Industry 5.0, empowering them to explore the complexities of human-robot intelligent. Pioneers with tall enthusiastic insights can superiorly get it and address worker concerns, cultivating a climate of believe and collaboration (Thomas et al., 2024). Furthermore, successful administration includes problem-solving aptitudes and a solid commitment to maintainability, guaranteeing that the integration of advances upgrades laborer well-being and advances persistent learning. This human-centric approach underscores the need of recognizing workers as key supporters to organizational victory (Patil & Kulkarni, 2024; Thomas et al., 2024).

Systems and information graph-based approaches give down to earth instruments for pioneers to actualize human-centric fabricating forms. SMSD encourages creation of frameworks that optimize efficiency whereas defending worker well-being through made strides collaboration and security measures (Peruzzini et al., 2023). Essentially, information graph-based frameworks permit pioneers to streamline organizational forms by mapping and coordination human and machine information, assist improving productivity and flexibility (Nagy et al., 2024). These systems emphasize the part of administration in adjusting mechanical progressions with human-centric objectives.

As Industry 5.0 advances, authority must prioritize the human component inside organizations by cultivating versatile societies that adjust to developing challenges. Pioneers play a critical role in engaging workers, advancing expertise improvement, and adjusting organizational objectives with broader supportability targets (Khanna et al., 2024). human-centric authority approach recognizes the significance of workers as drivers' development and maintainability, guaranteeing that organizations stay competitive in progressively complex scene (Thomas et al., 2024; Patil & Kulkarni, 2024).

In conclusion, administration in Industry 5.0 is basic for joining progressed advances with human well-being. Through candidly brilliantly administration styles, the application of systems like SMSD, and a commitment to cultivating versatile and steady organizational societies, pioneers can drive efficiency and development whereas guaranteeing maintainability. These procedures highlight the significance of authority in forming the human-centric working environments of long term (Peruzzini et al., 2023; Nagy et al., 2024; Khanna et al., 2024).

RESEARCH METHODOLOGY

This paper uses a mixed-methods research design to assess the effects of human-centric methods in Industry 5.0 on employee engagement within the organization. It collects and integrates both qualitative and quantitative data to comprehensively address the research problem. The qualitative component describes participants' experiences, while the quantitative component provides empirical evidence to support and test the qualitative findings. This approach examines the influences of human-centric technologies, organizational culture, and leadership support toward employees' organizational engagement at all levels.

This study's data was obtained through two key sources. First, qualitative data was captured through semi-structured interviews with human resource executives, organizational strategists, and other industry specialists who understand firsthand the human-centric technology, organizational culture, and leadership within the context of Industry 5.0. These people were chosen through purposive sampling, which made sure the participants had direct knowledge of the subject. Second, quantitative data was collected through a structured questionnaire sent to a sample of 264 employees and managers from different industry sectors. The survey's focus was on capturing the respondents' perceptions regarding the adoption of human-centric technologies, organizational culture, leadership relations, and their impact on employee engagement. To achieve sample representativeness across different demographic and organizational hierarchies, stratified random sampling was utilized.

In terms of tools for collecting data, qualitative data was collected primarily through conducting semi-structured interviews. Along the salient themes captured during the literature review, a diagnostic interview guide was developed to explore participants' human-centric technology experiences and organizational culture and leadership structures in terms of influence on employee engagement. The interviews were recorded and then transcribed so that they could be analyzed using thematic analysis to identify relevant themes and patterns. During the quantitative phase, participants' perceptions of human-centric technologies, organizational culture, leadership support, and employee engagement were assessed using a custom developed Likert scale survey. A pilot study was conducted for the survey where respondents were asked to provide feedback on the relevance and clarity of the questions. That version was then made final and shared electronically with all respondents.

The qualitative data was analyzed through thematic analysis by coding the transcripts of the interviews to extract themes in relation to the research variables. This particular approach helped the study to understand better the participants' insights regarding the contribution of human approach toward increasing employee engagement. In the quantitative part, descriptive statistics were used first to summarize the survey data, followed by correlation analysis to examine relationships among the variables. Then, a multiple regression analysis was used to assess the degree and significance of the relations between human-centered technologies, organizational culture, leadership support, and employee engagement. The regression model used in the analysis is as follows:

In this case, the regression model to be used is designed to evaluate the effect of human oriented technologies, organizational culture, leadership support and employee engagement in the context of multiple regression analysis with emphasis in this study is as stated above.

The regression equation demonstrates utilized within the examination is as takes after:

$$Y = \alpha + \beta 1x1 + \beta 2x2 + \beta 3x3 + \varepsilon$$

Where:

- Y= Dependant Variable (Employee Engagement)
- α is the intercept term.
- X1 (human-centric technologies), X2 (organizational culture), and X3 (leadership support) are the independent variables
- $\beta 1$, $\beta 2$, $\beta 3$ are the coefficients that represent the magnitude and direction of the relationship between each independent variable and employee engagement.

- ϵ is the error term, capturing other factors that may influence employee engagement but are not included in the model.

The structure of this model permits testing hypotheses regarding the effects of human-centric technologies, organizational culture, and leadership support on employee engagement as a dependent variable while controlling for other variables already incorporated into the model. Significance testing is performed to evaluate the intensity and reliability of the relationships stated before.

Ethics were of utmost importance in the planning and conducting phases of the research. Each participant of the study was fully informed of the purpose of the research, their expected contributions to it, and the option to withdraw from the study at any stage, prior to enrolling in the study. In order to protect the confidentiality and anonymity of the participants, no identifying details were included in the final dataset. All data were securely stored, cleaning them from potential misuse. Participants were guaranteed that there would be no adverse consequences for them and were free to choose whether or not to take part in the study, which was emphasized as voluntary. Moreover, the applicable data protection legislation was respected by ensuring that the information gathered from participants was solely for research purposes.

By using a mixed-methods approach, this study aims to provide a robust and comprehensive understanding of how human-centric approaches in Industry 5.0 can enhance employee engagement and productivity, offering both qualitative insights and empirical evidence that contribute to the growing body of research in this area.

FINDINGS AND DISCUSSIONS

Thematic Analysis

Perceived Impact of Human-Centric Technologies on Employee Engagement

Topical investigation is a compelling approach to understanding employees' recognitions of how human-centric innovations such as AI instruments, ergonomic workspaces, and collaborative robots (cobots) impact their engagement. Through this examination, key topics like expanded work fulfillment, upgraded independence, and moved forward work execution develop, which are necessarily to the objectives of Industry 5.0. These advances prioritize laborer well-being whereas adjusting mechanical progressions with human-centric organizational methodologies (Shchepkina et al., 2024; Vajravelu et al., 2024).

Investigate underscores the noteworthy effect of these innovations on efficiency and work fulfillment. For case, joining AI devices with enthusiastic insights capabilities has been appeared to extend efficiency by 35.5% and move forward work fulfillment by 20.6%, illustrating the transformative benefits of such headways in cultivating a locked in and spurred workforce (Shchepkina et al., 2024). Additionally, actively including representatives within the arrangement of AI instruments advances a sense of proprietorship and guarantees the arrangement of mechanical headways with organizational and social maintainability objectives. Case ponders from the broadcast communications division demonstrate that participatory approaches to AI sending improve arrangement between representative desires and organizational destinations, contributing to a more locked in workforce (Haipeter et al., 2024).

Human-centric HRM hones moreover play an urgent part in driving engagement and improving labor efficiency. Organizations in major Asian economies that emphasize employee-focused techniques such as personalized expertise improvement, adaptable work situations, and the utilize of AI-powered analytics report noteworthy enhancements in labor efficiency and work execution (Cooke et al., 2023). These hones not as it were boosting representative engagement but to emphasize the part of workers within the organization's victory. This arrangement of innovation with human needs strengthens Industry 5.0's accentuation on making work environments where workers are seen as central to development and efficiency.

Besides, the integration of cobots and ergonomic workspaces advance upgrades representative independence and diminishes working environment weakness, contributing to a more locked in and profitable workforce. These human-centric advances specifically back the broader objectives of Industry 5.0, including supportability and advancement, guaranteeing that innovative headways adjust with representative well-being whereas at the same time boosting organizational execution (Vajravelu et al., 2024). Study about too highlights how receiving worker-centric approaches encourages more noteworthy collaboration between human and technological capabilities, cultivating versatility within the quickly changing mechanical scene (Haipeter et al., 2024; Shchepkina et al., 2024).

In conclusion, human-centric advances have a significant impact on representative engagement by making strides work fulfillment, independence, and efficiency. Topical investigation uncovers that joining these innovations with participatory HRM hones and supportability destinations not as it were benefits person workers but too upgrades in general organizational execution. These discoveries emphasize the significance of receiving human-centric procedures in Industry 5.0, to construct a versatile, locked in workforce competent of flourishing in an energetic innovative environment (Cooke et al., 2023; Vajravelu et al., 2024; Haipeter et al., 2024).

Cultural Influences on Employee Engagement

Organizational culture plays an urgent part in forming representative engagement, especially within the setting of Industry 5.0, where human-centric approaches take priority. Topics such as "cooperation," "working environment security," "collaboration over offices," and "representative strengthening" give basic bits of knowledge into how social elements impact employees' encounters and their levels of engagement.

Authority styles and organizational culture are broadly recognized as basic variables that straightforwardly influence worker engagement. Considers have illustrated that comprehensive and steady administration cultivates higher levels of representative inspiration, commitment, and arrangement with organizational objectives (Saputra, 2024). Social standards and values altogether affect worker demeanors and behaviors, cultivating a committed workforce that's irreplaceable for organizational victory (Nambiar & Parmar, 2024).

Moreover, a positive organizational culture contributes to moved forward work fulfillment and work-life adjust, which are key to keeping up maintained representative engagement. Investigate appears that representatives who see their working environment culture as strong and engaging are more likely to illustrate tall levels of efficiency and organizational devotion (Munawar & Suriyanti, 2024). For illustration, emphasizing work environment security and cultivating cross-departmental collaboration can fortify employees' sense of having a place, improving by and large engagement.

The appropriation of culture-conscious Human Resource Management (HRM) techniques is additionally imperative in advancing consideration, advancement, and value. These methodologies are especially compelling in tending to challenges such as imbued predispositions and cultivating a collaborative environment over assorted working environments (Shah & Sarif, 2023). By joining these approaches, organizations can adjust social hones with broader supportability goals, ensuring their pertinence within the industry 5.0 period.

Eventually, developing a strong organizational culture is significant for upgrading worker engagement and efficiency. Organizations that prioritize social components such as consideration, collaboration, and well-being are way better prepared to adjust to the challenges of the advancing mechanical scene. These endeavors not as it were boost worker fulfillment but moreover make a resilient and imaginative workforce balanced for long-term victory (Lakshmi et al., 2024).

Leadership's Role in Promoting Human-Centric Strategies

The topical examination of leadership's part in advancing human-centric techniques inside Industry 5.0 may reveal a few designs that shape how workers see administration back for these activities. Key topics such as "authority perceivability," "commitment to development," "believe in authority," and "communication of organizational objectives" are basic in deciding whether leadership's back for human-centric procedures is seen as viable. These subjects offer assistance evaluate the degree to which administration impacts representative engagement and efficiency, particularly in situations where human capabilities are coordinates with progressed innovations.

Administration is vital in advancing human-centric methodologies inside Industry 5.0, which emphasizes the integration of human well-being, ability advancement, and collaboration with cutting-edge advances. As the center of Industry 5.0 shifts from insignificant robotization to upgrading human capabilities, pioneers are anticipated to cultivate situations that prioritize representative engagement and efficiency. This will be accomplished through transformational authority styles that rouse and propel workers, in this manner improving work fulfillment, possession, and a sense of reason all of which are basic for moved forward efficiency (Thomas et al., 2024

Viable communication and strengthening are urgent authority hones that offer assistance develop a strong organizational culture. These hones empower laborers to flourish in a collaborative environment where advanced advances are utilized to increase human potential. Enabled workers feel more esteemed and are more likely to lock in completely with the organization's targets (Alves et al., 2023; Kumari et al., 2024). For occasion, when pioneers clearly communicate organizational objectives and adjust them with employees' individual development and improvement, it cultivates a culture of shared believe and collaboration.

Besides, adjusting authority procedures with human-centric standards can make flexible, feasible generation frameworks that advantage not as it were the representatives but moreover drive the by and large victory of the organization. Study about highlights that when pioneers embrace human-centric approaches, organizations are superior situated to explore challenges, upgrade representative fulfillment, and accomplish long-term victory (Onyemelukwe et al., 2023; Kumari et al., 2024). Through the dynamic advancement of advancement, communication, and believe, authority can play a conclusive role in forming a lock in and beneficial working environment within the industry 5.0 setting.

Empirical Analysis

Sample Profile

Table 1 presents the distribution of gender across three generational categories: Generation X, Baby Boomers, and Millennials. Among male respondents, 31 belong to Generation X, 21 to Baby Boomers, and 83 to Millennials, totaling 135 males.

For females, 20 are from Generation X, 21 from Baby Boomers, and 88 from Millennials, totaling 129 females. The largest generational group is Millennials, with a higher proportion of males compared to females. The overall sample consists of 264 respondents, with Millennials making up the majority.

*Table 1. Gender * generation crosstabulation*

		Generation			Total
		Generation X	Baby boomers	Millennials	
Gender	Male	31	21	83	135
	Female	20	21	88	129
Total		51	42	171	264

Source: Field data, 2024

Descriptive Statistics

Table 2 presents the descriptive statistics for various statements related to human-centric technologies, organizational culture, leadership support, and employee engagement. The results show a generally positive response across all items. The statement "The organization fosters an inclusive environment where all employees' ideas are valued" received the highest mean score of 3.99 (SD = 0.823), indicating strong agreement.

Table 2. Descriptive statistics

	Mean	Std. Deviation
The organization provides technologies that support employee well-being and productivity.	3.58	.837
The use of collaborative robots (cobots) has enhanced my ability to perform my tasks efficiently.	3.30	.793
Human-centric technologies have helped create a safer work environment.	3.39	.851
The technologies used in my workplace promote creativity and problem-solving.	3.34	.871
I believe the organization effectively integrates technology to improve employee engagement.	3.26	1.029
Implementation of Human-Centric Technologies	**3.3735**	**.60848**
The organization fosters an inclusive environment where all employee's ideas are valued.	3.99	.823
Collaboration and teamwork are encouraged within the organization.	3.94	.794
The company prioritizes employee well-being in its policies and practices.	4.00	.848
There is a strong culture of emotional intelligence and adaptability within the organization.	3.86	.850
Organizational values emphasize mutual respect and trust among colleagues.	3.89	.870
Organizational Culture	**3.9356**	**.54061**

continued on following page

Table 2. Continued

	Mean	Std. Deviation
The leadership actively supports initiatives that promote employee well-being.	3.10	.911
Leaders encourage the use of technology to enhance employee engagement.	3.93	.882
Leadership provides clear direction on the importance of human-centric strategies in the workplace.	3.76	.939
The leadership team is committed to fostering a collaborative work environment.	3.91	.824
Leaders demonstrate a strong commitment to sustainability and ethical business practices.	3.90	.864
Leadership Support for Human-Centric Initiatives	**3.7197**	**.51935**
I feel enthusiastic about my work and the projects I am assigned to.	3.71	.838
I am fully committed to the success of my organization.	3.35	.956
I find my work meaningful and aligned with my personal values.	3.33	.959
I actively seek ways to contribute to the organization's goals.	3.84	.705
I feel motivated to perform at my best every day.	3.56	.782
I believe my contributions are recognized and valued by my organization.	3.50	.804
Employee Engagement	**3.5492**	**.50231**

Source: Field data, 2024

Similarly, "Collaboration and teamwork are encouraged within the organization" and "The company prioritizes employee well-being in its policies and practices" also received high mean scores of 3.94 (SD = 0.794) and 4.00 (SD = 0.848), respectively. In terms of technology and employee well-being, the statement "The organization provides technologies that support employee well-being and productivity" scored a mean of 3.58 (SD = 0.837), reflecting a favorable perception, while "The use of collaborative robots (cobots) has enhanced my ability to perform my tasks efficiently" had a lower mean of 3.30 (SD = 0.793), suggesting moderate agreement. For leadership support, the statement "Leadership provides clear direction on the importance of human-centric strategies in the workplace" scored a mean of 3.76 (SD = 0.939), demonstrating a positive yet slightly less pronounced response.

Lastly, regarding employee engagement, the item "I feel enthusiastic about my work and the projects I am assigned to" received a mean score of 3.71 (SD = 0.838), while "I actively seek ways to contribute to the organization's goals" had a higher mean of 3.84 (SD = 0.705), indicating strong motivation. Overall, the mean scores for the dimensions of Organizational Culture, Implementation of Human-Centric Technologies, Leadership Support for Human-Centric Initiatives, and Employee Engagement ranged from 3.37 to 3.94, demonstrating overall positive employee perceptions towards these constructs.

Gender and Employee Engagement, Human-Centric Technologies, Organizational Culture, and Leadership Support

Table 3. Descriptive statistics and independent sample t test

					Levene's Test for Equality of Variances		t-test for Equality of Means			
	Gender	**N**	**Mean**	**Std. Deviation**	**F**	**Sig.**	**t**	**df**	**Sig. (2-tailed)**	**Decision**
EE	Male	135	3.5086	.50055	.346	.557	-1.346	262	.180	H_{01} Failed to reject – difference is not significant
	Female	129	3.5917	.50258						
HCT	Male	135	3.3081	.63045	.237	.627	-1.792	262	.074	H_{02} Failed to reject – difference is not significant
	Female	129	3.4419	.57916						
OC	Male	135	3.9333	.53755	.032	.857	-.070	262	.944	H_{03} Failed to reject – difference is not significant
	Female	129	3.9380	.54589						
LS	Male	135	3.6667	.50844	.500	.480	-1.703	262	.090	H_{04} Failed to reject – difference is not significant
	Female	129	3.7752	.52679						

Source: Field data; 2024

Table 3 presents the group statistics for gender differences across various variables: employee engagement (EE), implementation of human-centric technologies (I), organizational culture (OC), and leadership support (LS). Females had slightly higher mean scores than males in all areas: employee engagement (females: 3.59, males: 3.51), human-centric technologies (females: 3.44, males: 3.31), organizational culture (females: 3.94, males: 3.93), and leadership support (females: 3.78, males: 3.67). The standard deviations and standard error means were similar across both genders.

Table 3 also shows the results of the independent samples t-test for equality of means. For employee engagement (EE), implementation of human-centric technologies (I), organizational culture (OC), and leadership support (LS), the significance values (p-values) are all above 0.05, indicating no significant differences between males and females for these variables. Specifically, EE had a p-value of 0.180, I had a p-value of 0.074, OC had a p-value of 0.944, and LS had a p-value of 0.090. Therefore, while females had higher mean scores across these variables, the differences were not statistically significant.

Generations and Employee Engagement, Human-Centric Technologies, Organizational Culture, and Leadership Support

Tables 4 provides descriptive statistics and ANOVA results for the variables: employee engagement (EE), implementation of human-centric technologies (I), organizational culture (OC), and leadership support (LS) across different generations (Generation X, Baby Boomers, and Millennials).

Table 4. Descriptive statistics and one way ANOVA

		Descriptives			Test of Homogeneity of Variances		ANOVA		Decision
		N	Mean	Std. Deviation	Levene Statistic	Sig.	F	Sig.	
EE	Generation X	51	3.578	.479	.320	.727	.673	.511	H_{05} Failed to reject – difference is not significant
	Baby boomers	42	3.468	.572					
	Millennials	171	3.560	.491					
	Total	264	3.549	.502					
HCT	Generation X	51	3.415	.616	.092	.912	.151	.860	H_{06} Failed to reject – difference is not significant
	Baby boomers	42	3.361	.632					
	Millennials	171	3.363	.603					
	Total	264	3.373	.608					
OC	Generation X	51	3.972	.520	1.680	.188	.229	.796	H_{07} Failed to reject – difference is not significant
	Baby boomers	42	3.957	.453					
	Millennials	171	3.919	.567					
	Total	264	3.935	.540					
LS	Generation X	51	3.725	.499	.300	.741	.138	.871	H_{08} Failed to reject – difference is not significant
	Baby boomers	42	3.681	.570					
	Millennials	171	3.727	.514					
	Total	264	3.719	.519					

Source: Field data; 2024

For employee engagement, Millennials had the highest mean (3.56), followed by Generation X (3.58) and Baby Boomers (3.47). Regarding the implementation of human-centric technologies, Generation X had the highest mean (3.42), while Millennials had the lowest (3.36). Organizational culture scores were similar across generations, with Generation X showing the highest mean (3.97) and Millennials the lowest (3.92). Leadership support scores were relatively consistent, with Millennials and Generation X having similar means (3.73 and 3.73, respectively), while Baby Boomers had a slightly lower mean (3.68).

Levene's test indicates that the variances across generations are homogeneous for all variables, with significance values greater than 0.05: employee engagement (0.727), implementation of human-centric technologies (0.912), organizational culture (0.188), and leadership support (0.741). The p-values for all variables are above the 0.05 threshold, indicating no statistically significant differences between the generations for employee engagement ($p = 0.511$), implementation of human-centric technologies ($p = 0.860$), organizational culture ($p = 0.796$), and leadership support ($p = 0.871$). Therefore, while the mean scores vary slightly across generations, these differences are not significant.

Relationship of Employee Engagement with Human-Centric technologies, Organizational Culture, and Leadership Support

Table 5 presents the descriptive statistics and correlation analysis between employee engagement (EE) and three key variables: the implementation of human-centric technologies (I), organizational culture (OC), and leadership support for human-centric initiatives (LS).

Table 5. Descriptive statistics and multiple correlation

		Implementation of Human-Centric Technologies	**Organizational Culture**	**Leadership Support for Human-Centric Initiatives**
Employee Engagement	N	264	264	264
	Mean	3.3735	3.9356	3.7197
	Std. Deviation	.60848	. 54061	. 51935
	Pearson Correlation	.544**	.485**	.353**
	Sig. (2-tailed)	**.000**	**.000**	**.000**
	Testing Hypotheses	H_{09}	H_{10}	H_{11}
	Decision	Rejected	Rejected	Rejected
	Results	Correlation is significant	Correlation is significant	Correlation is significant

Note: **. Correlation is significant at the 0.01 level (2-tailed).
Source: Field data; 2024-2025

The results show significant positive correlations between employee engagement and all three variables. Specifically, the implementation of human-centric technologies is strongly correlated with employee engagement ($r = 0.544$, $p < 0.001$), suggesting that enhanced technological support improves engagement. Similarly, organizational culture ($r = 0.485$, $p < 0.001$) and leadership support for human-centric initiatives ($r = 0.353$, $p < 0.001$) are also positively correlated with employee engagement, indicating that a supportive and inclusive work environment, along with strong leadership commitment, foster higher employee engagement. Descriptive statistics reveal that the mean scores for these variables are 3.37 for employee engagement, 3.94 for organizational culture, and 3.72 for leadership support, with moderate variability in responses as indicated by their standard deviations of 0.61, 0.54, and 0.52, respectively. These findings highlight the significant role of technology, culture, and leadership in driving employee engagement.

Influence of Human-Centric Technologies, Organizational Culture, and Leadership Support on the Employee Engagement

Table 6, 7, and 8 present the results of a regression analysis investigating the factors that influence employee engagement (EE), with a focus on leadership support for human-centric initiatives, the implementation of human-centric technologies, and organizational culture.

Model Summary (Table 6) reveals that the predictors leadership support for human-centric initiatives, implementation of human-centric technologies, and organizational culture together explain 44% of the variance in employee engagement ($R^2 = 0.440$). The adjusted R^2 value of 0.433 indicates that the model has a strong fit to the data, with a low standard error of the estimate (0.37807). The Durbin-Watson statistic of 1.991 suggests no significant autocorrelation in the residuals, indicating that the assumptions of the regression analysis are met.

Table 6. Model summary[b]

Model	R	R Square	Adjusted R Square	Std. Error of the Estimate	Durbin-Watson
1	.663[a]	.440	.433	.37807	1.991

Source: Field data, 2024

a. Predictors: (Constant), Leadership Support for Human-Centric Initiatives, Implementation of Human-Centric Technologies, Organizational Culture

b. Dependent Variable: Employee Engagement

Table 7. ANOVA

Model		Sum of Squares	df	Mean Square	F	Sig.
1	Regression	29.196	3	9.732	68.084	.000[b]
	Residual	37.164	260	.143		
	Total	66.360	263			

Source: Field data, 2024

a. Dependent Variable: Employee Engagement

b. Predictors: (Constant), Leadership Support for Human-Centric Initiatives, Implementation of Human-Centric Technologies, Organizational Culture

Table 8. Coefficients[a]

Model		Unstandardized Coefficients		Standardized Coefficients	t	Sig.
		B	Std. Error	Beta		
1	(Constant)	.690	.217		3.178	.002
	Implementation of Human-Centric Technologies	.354	.040	.429	8.777	.000
	Organizational Culture	.316	.047	.340	6.772	.000
	Leadership Support for Human-Centric Initiatives	.113	.049	.117	2.302	.022

Source: Field data, 2024

a. Dependent Variable: Employee Engagement

ANOVA (Table 7) tests the overall significance of the regression model. The F-value of 68.084 with a significance value of 0.000 indicates that the model is statistically significant, meaning the independent variables collectively have a strong influence on employee engagement. Coefficients (Table 8) provide a detailed look at the individual contributions of the predictors. The unstandardized coefficients show the magnitude of change in employee engagement for each unit change in the predictors. Specifically, the implementation of human-centric technologies has the largest impact ($B = 0.354$, $p < 0.001$), followed by organizational culture ($B = 0.316$, $p < 0.001$). Leadership support for human-centric initiatives also has a significant effect ($B = 0.113$, $p = 0.022$), though to a lesser degree. The standardized coefficients (Beta) confirm that the implementation of human-centric technologies has the strongest relationship with employee engagement ($\beta = 0.429$), followed by organizational culture ($\beta = 0.340$) and leadership support ($\beta = 0.117$). These results underline the importance of human-centric technologies, organizational culture, and leadership support in driving employee engagement.

A one-unit increase in the implementation of human-centric technologies is expected to lead to a 0.354 unit increase in employee engagement. Similarly, a one-unit improvement in organizational culture will result in a 0.316 unit increase in employee engagement. Lastly, a one-unit increase in leadership support for human-centric initiatives will contribute to a 0.113 unit rise in employee engagement. These findings highlight the significant role each of these factors plays in fostering higher levels of engagement among employees.

Discussion

This study inspected how human-centric methodologies beneath Industry 5.0 impact representative engagement inside Indian associations. Drawing on interviews over IT, fabricating, and benefit segments, three center subjects risen: The changing nature of work and ability requests; the part of administration in cultivating a human-centric culture; and the interaction of hierarchical back and representative independence. These discoveries offer important bits of knowledge into how worker engagement can be improved through astute integration of innovation, human values, and ethical leadership-an approach central to the industry 5.0 vision (European Commission, 2021; Thomas et al., 2024).

A key finding was that the nature of work has moved altogether, with representatives encountering an increment in important, inventive, and savvy people invigorating assignments. Respondents related the integration of human-centric advances such as collaborative robots and AI-driven apparatuses with decreased dullness, empowering them to lock in in more vital and value-driven work. This bolsters existing writing that accentuates Industry 5.0's potential to reestablish the human part in innovatively progressed settings (Khanna et al., 2024; Vajravelu et al., 2024). Such change adjusts with Deci and Ryan's (2000) self-determination hypothesis, which states that independence and competence are pivotal to cultivating inherent inspiration and engagement. Representatives in This study detailed improved self-worth, certainty, and creativity-traits that are broadly related with tall levels of engagement (Macey & Schneider, 2008).

The think about moreover affirmed that ability advancement and ceaseless learning are crucial components of human-centric procedures. Members recognized the developing significance of advanced familiarity and cognitive adaptability, showing that engagement was closely connected to the accessibility of upskilling openings. This adjusts with Cooke et al. (2023), who contend that associations grasping Industry 5.0 must contribute in supported learning and flexibility. Strikingly, workers accentuated the esteem of experiential learning and hands-on introduction instead of routine classroom training-highlighting a require for HRM hones to advance in arrangement with grown-up learning standards and energetic work situations (Haipeter et al., 2024).

Vitally, the researcher found that administration hones play a central part in forming engagement inside the industry 5.0 worldview. Representatives communicated those strong, compassionate, and straightforward pioneers contributed to their sense of having a place, reason, and mental security. Pioneers who illustrated ethical duty, recognized person commitments, and made an comprehensive culture were seen as enablers of engagement. This finding echoes Thomas et al. (2023), who set that within the setting of Industry 5.0, administration must organize passionate insights, inclusivity, and shared decision-making. It moreover reverberates with the discoveries of Patil and Kulkarni (2024), who contend that ethical authority acts as a key driver in adjusting innovative progresses with human values.

Workers especially acknowledged authority hones that went past specialized supervision to grasp enthusiastic well-being and social back. This reflects the industry 5.0 accentuation on all-encompassing esteem creation, where social and passionate perspectives of work are considered as vital as financial results (European Commission, 2021). The nearness of such authority not as it were spurred representatives but too empowered knowledge-sharing, trust-building, and common respect-all of which are foundational to supported engagement (Mone & London, 2018).

Another critical subject was the steady authoritative culture that organizes independence, adaptability, and inclusivity. Representatives who experienced more prominent flexibility in how they drawn nearer their work, had input in decision-making forms, and were trusted with duties detailed essentially higher levels of engagement. These discoveries assert the contention of Hidayat et al. (2024), who fight that the victory of Industry 5.0 depends on implanting believe and mental strengthening inside authoritative frameworks. Moreover, the think about underscores the part of customisation and personalisation in upgrading engagement-when workers feel seen and esteemed as people, their inspiration to contribute seriously increments (Deci & Ryan, 2000; Macey & Schneider, 2008).

Be that as it may, the researcher moreover distinguished obstructions to engagement within the setting of Industry 5.0. A few representatives communicated concerns with respect to the need of clarity and conflicting usage of human-centric methodologies. The nonappearance of shared understanding among pioneers, misalignment between vision and hone, and a need of inter-departmental collaboration were highlighted as variables that lessened the potential benefits of Industry 5.0. These discoveries fortify earlier writing recommending that shallow selection of modern advances or separated endeavors without vital arrangement can lead to separation and resistance (Cooke et al., 2023; Ritu, 2024).

Besides, they consider highlighted the require for more noteworthy partner association in forming human-centric procedures. Representatives communicated a want to be counseled in decision-making, especially with respect to the plan and execution of advances that affect their parts. The need of participatory components frequently cleared out workers feeling prohibited, which is counterproductive to the comprehensive soul of Industry 5.0 (Haipeter et al., 2024). This proposes that future human-centric activities must be co-created, with clear structures for worker input and engagement.

In conclusion, the discoveries from This study demonstrate that representative engagement within the industry 5.0 time is profoundly affected by the interaction between innovation, authority, and culture. Associations that grasp a systemic, human-centred approach-grounded in ethical authority, adaptable work plan, and inclusive organisational practices-are more likely to cultivate locked in, spurred, and versatile workers. These experiences contribute to the developing body of prove supporting Industry 5.0 as a pathway not fair to innovative headway, but too to human and societal well-being (European Commission, 2021; Khanna et al., 2024). For Indian associations exploring this change, adjusting human-centric methodologies with engagement objectives isn't fair alluring, but fundamental for long-term versatility and supportability.

THEORETICAL AND PRACTICAL IMPLICATIONS

This study offers noteworthy hypothetical commitments to the understanding of Industry 5.0, especially by joining human-centric approaches into worker engagement systems. By looking at the parts of human-centric advances, organizational culture, and authority bolster, the researcher improves existing speculations on human-machine collaboration, worker strengthening, and organizational culture, amplifying them to the setting of Industry 5.0. The investigate enhances hypothetical models by highlighting how these components collectively shape representative engagement and organizational results, especially in situations where innovation and human collaboration are central. Furthermore, this researcher contributes to the hypothetical talk on enthusiastic insights and flexibility, emphasizing their parts in cultivating steady work situations. Besides, the study about bridges holes in understanding the crossing point between human-centric procedures and supportability, advertising novel experiences into how ethical hones and social duty impact both representative engagement and in general organizational execution.

From a viable point of view, the discoveries give profitable experiences for organizations looking to actualize Industry 5.0 standards successfully. The consider underscores the significance of human-centric advances, such as collaborative robots, in boosting worker engagement and efficiency. Organizations can use these bits of knowledge to optimize the integration of such advances, guaranteeing they complement and adjust with human asset procedures. The accentuation on organizational culture highlights the require for companies to develop a steady work environment that values enthusiastic insights and flexibility, eventually upgrading representative engagement and fulfillment. Also, the think about emphasizes the essential part of administration in supporting human-centric activities. By understanding the impact of administration on representative engagement, organizations can create focused on methodologies to cultivate administration hones that back and maintain human-centric approaches. In general, this researcher gives down to earth suggestions for commerce pioneers, HR experts, and policymakers looking for to form locks in, feasible, and flexible organizational situations inside the system of Industry 5.0.

LIMITATIONS AND SCOPE FOR FUTURE RESEARCH

This study, whereas giving profitable bits of knowledge into the effect of human-centric approaches on worker engagement within the setting of Industry 5.0, has a few restrictions that ought to be considered when deciphering the comes about. To begin with, the investigate depends on self-reported information from representatives, which may be subject to inclinations such as social attractive quality or self-perception predispositions. This may influence the precision of the discoveries with respect to representative engagement, Leadership Support, and organizational culture. Moment, the test measure, whereas satisfactory, is restricted to a particular geological locale and industry, which may confine the generalizability of the comes about to other settings or divisions. Further, the think about centers fundamentally on the viewpoints of workers, and the incorporation of administration or organizational leaders' sees might have given a more comprehensive understanding of how human-centric approaches impact representative engagement from a top-down point of view.

The scope for assist investigates in this region is wide. Future considers seem address the impediments of This study by utilizing longitudinal plans to survey the long-term impacts of human-centric advances and administration on representative engagement and organizational results. Also, investigate seem investigate the effect of human-centric approaches over distinctive businesses and social settings to get it how these components may shift. Exploring the part of management's point of view and how their authority behaviors adjust with worker engagement might to give valuable insights. Besides, future considers may look at the interaction between human-centric methodologies and other organizational factors, such as development, execution, and supportability, to develop our understanding of the broader suggestions of Industry 5.0. At long last, investigating the potential challenges and boundaries organizations confront when executing human-centric innovations and authority hones would give down to earth direction for overcoming these obstacles.

CONCLUSION

This study examined the impact of human-centric approaches in Industry 5.0 with regards to transforming employee engagement and productivity. The emergence of human-centric technologies, organizational culture, and leadership support for human-centric initiatives were identified as critical drivers for employee engagement in Industry 5.0. The research indicates the application of collaborative technologies like cobots and AI tools enhances employee engagement by shifting the focus from mundane, repetitive tasks to more creative, meaningful endeavors. Employees feel more empowered and valued in work environments where human-machine interaction, powered by non-displacive technologies, fosters holistic appreciation of human efforts. Such conditions improve job satisfaction, engagement, and organizational productivity.

In addition, the study outlines the human-supporting aspects of organizational culture on employee engagement. Engagement is better supported by collaboration and inclusion-oriented culture with emotional intelligence and change readiness. Such human-centric organizational culture enhances not only employee engagement but also contribute towards an organizational atmosphere that is more conducive to innovation and sustainability, enabling organizations to remain resilient in a rapidly evolving industrial landscape. Leadership support emerged as another key factor impacting employee engagement within the context of Industry 5.0. Transformational leadership stood out as particularly effective in enhancing employee motivation, and building trust, as well as in properly humanizing concern strategies throughout the organization. Those leaders who are most concerned about the employees' welfare and use emotional intelligence are more likely to realize success and sustainability for the organization.

As a final point, humanistic elements within Industry 5.0 provide a new direction towards deepening engagement and productivity while promoting sustainable and adaptable organizational culture. The interplay among sophisticated technologies, organizational culture, and supportive leadership can be synergized to give rise to an organizational setting that responds to emerging changes and motivates employee participation in broader goals of sustainability, innovation and harnessing them. The progression of the world brings about opportunities for the incorporation of human intellect with sophisticated technologies, and this is what Industry 5.0 seeks to achieve for the growth of the organization in future.

REFERENCES

Alves, J., Lima, T. M., & Gaspar, P. D. (2023). Is Industry 5.0 a Human-Centred Approach? A Systematic Review. *Processes (Basel, Switzerland), 11*(1), 193. DOI: 10.3390/pr11010193

Cooke, F. L. (2023). Nikolai Rogovsky, Premilla D'Cruz, Kubo, K., Lee, B.-H., Nho, Y., & Noronha, E. (2023). The Human-Centered Approach to Increasing Workplace Productivity. *Proceedings - Academy of Management*, (1). Advance online publication. DOI: 10.5465/amproc.2023.11052symposium

Darwish, D. (2024). Human-AI Collaboration in Industry 5. *Advances in Computational Intelligence and Robotics Book Series*, 44–70. https://doi.org/DOI: 10.4018/979-8-3693-6806-0.ch003

Haipeter, T., Manfred Wannöffel, Daus, J.-T., & Schaffarczik, S. (2024). Human-centered AI through employee participation. *Frontiers in Artificial Intelligence, 7*. Advance online publication. DOI: 10.3389/frai.2024.1272102 PMID: 38496830

Hidayat, C., Asep Hermawan, & Dita Oki Berliyanti. (2024). The influence of organizational culture, transformational leadership on organizational citizenship behaviors, and organizational commitment through employee engagement. *Indonesian Journal of Education and Social Science, 3*(2), 100–120. DOI: 10.56916/ijess.v3i2.635

Khanna, P., Kumari, J., & Karim, R. (2024). Human-Centric PHM in the Era of Industry 5.0. *PHM Society European Conference, 8*(1), 7–7. https://doi.org/DOI: 10.36001/phme.2024.v8i1.4121

Krupas, M., Kajati, E., Liu, C., & Zolotova, I. (2024). Towards a Human-Centric Digital Twin for Human–Machine Collaboration: A Review on Enabling Technologies and Methods. *Sensors (Basel), 24*(7), 2232. DOI: 10.3390/s24072232 PMID: 38610442

Kumari, P., Anand, A., Praveen, P., Verma, A.R., & Godiyal, A. (2024). Infrastructure Potential and Human-Centric Strategies in the Context of Industry 5.0. *Advances in Web Technologies and Engineering Book Series*, 199–214. https://doi.org/DOI: 10.4018/979-8-3693-0782-3.ch012

Madzik, P., & Falat, L., Jum'a, L., Vrábliková, M. & Zimon, D. (2024). Human-centricity in Industry 5.0 – revealing of hidden research topics by unsupervised topic modeling using Latent Dirichlet Allocation. *European Journal of Innovation Management*. Advance online publication. DOI: 10.1108/ejim-09-2023-0753

Munawar, M., & Suriyanti, S. (2024). The Effect of Organizational Culture, Work-Life Balance, and Job Satisfaction on Non-Commercial Employee Work Engagement. *Golden Ratio of Human Resource Management*, *4*(1), 53–66. DOI: 10.52970/grhrm.v4i1.452

Nagy, L., Abonyi, J. & Ruppert, T. (2024). Knowledge Graph-Based Framework to Support Human-Centered Collaborative Manufacturing in Industry 5.0. *Applied Sciences (Basel, Switzerland)*, *14*(8), 3398–3398. DOI: 10.3390/app14083398

Nambiar, R., & Parmar, N. (2024). A Study on Impact of Culture on Creating an Engaged Workforce. *International Journal of Research Publication and Reviews*, *5*(4), 2161–2165. DOI: 10.55248/gengpi.5.0424.0956

Narayana, A. (2023). Futuristic HRM and the Implications of Integration with Industry 5.0 for Sustainable Business. *Management Insight*, *19*(01), 71–78. DOI: 10.21844/mijia.19.1.7

Onyemelukwe, I. C., Ferreira, J. A. V., & Ramos, A. L. (2023, July). Exploring human centricity in industry 5.0: a systematic review. In *Proceedings of the International Conference on Industrial Engineering and Operations Management.*

Patil, K. P., & Kulkarni, M. S. (2024). Harmonising human and robotic workforces in Industry 5.0: Creating a resilient, human-centric, and sustainable organisational ecosystem. In *Modern Technologies and Tools Supporting the Development of Industry 5.0* (pp. 179–208). CRC Press.

Peruzzini, M., & Prati, E., & Pelicciari, M. (2023). A framework to design smart manufacturing systems for Industry 5.0 based on the human-automation symbiosis. *International Journal of Computer Integrated Manufacturing*, •••, 1–18. DOI: 10.1080/0951192x.2023.2257634

Ritu, R. (2024). A Comprehensive Study On Employee Engagement Strategies. *Educational Administration: Theory and Practice*, 5894–5899. https://doi.org/DOI: 10.53555/kuey.v30i4.2309

Saputra, W. (2024). Pengaruh Gaya Kepemimpinan dan Budaya Organisasi Terhadap Keterlibatan Karyawan. *Indo-Fintech Intellectuals: Journal of Economics and Business*, *4*(4), 1559–1567. DOI: 10.54373/ifijeb.v4i4.1662

Shah, S., & Suhaimi Mhd. Sarif. (2023). Building a Culture-Conscious Workforce. *International Journal of Culture and Education*, *1*(3). Advance online publication. DOI: 10.59600/ijcae.v1i3.15

Shchepkina, N., Ramnarayan, Dhaliwal, N., Ravikiran K, & Nangia, R. (2024). Human-Centric AI Adoption and Its Influence on Worker Productivity: An Empirical Investigation. *BIO Web of Conferences, 86*, 01060–01060. https://doi.org/DOI: 10.1051/bioconf/20248601060

Singh, D., & Cohen, V. (2024). Socio-economic dimensions and human centricity in Industry 5.0: A study on manufacturing sectors in central and Eastern European economies. *Journal of Economic Studies (Glasgow, Scotland)*. Advance online publication. DOI: 10.1108/jes-02-2024-0067

Singh, S., Rai, M., Pandey, J. K., & Saxena, A. K. (2024). Emotional Intelligence and Collaborative Dynamics in Industry 5.0 for Human-Machine Interactions. *Advances in Computational Intelligence and Robotics Book Series*, 190–204. https://doi.org/DOI: 10.4018/979-8-3693-6806-0.ch010

Thomas, A., Chawla, Y., Varma, A., & Szleter, P. (2024). The Role of Business Leaders in Industry 5.0. *Springer Proceedings in Complexity*, 629–640. https://doi.org/DOI: 10.1007/978-3-031-44721-1_47

Vajravelu, A., Thanikachalam, Y., Abd Wahab, M. H. B., Jamil, M. M. B. A., & Sivaranjani, S. (2024). Human-Machine Collaboration and Emotional Intelligence in Industry 5.0. In Human-Machine Collaboration and Emotional Intelligence in Industry 5.0 (pp. 220-232). IGI Global.

Chapter 10
Smart Retention Strategies:
Machine Learning Applications in Human Resource Management

Dolores Botella-Carrubi
https://orcid.org/0000-0002-3947-6490
Universitat Politècnica de València, Spain

Al Anoud Saad Al-Naemi
https://orcid.org/0009-0001-5083-7226
Universitat Politècnica de València, Spain

ABSTRACT

Machine learning (ML) continues to gain attention for its role in retaining talent across various industrial sectors.This chapter examines how ML systems help organizations retain employees by identifying departures, measuring worker sentiment, and monitoring performance.A research objective is to study these applications' effectiveness through industry comparisons.ML systems enhance retention by delivering customized methods and automatic departure alerts, along with continuous sentiment tracking.These approaches lead to better workforce performance and higher employee satisfaction.However, they face major obstacles including ethical concerns, data protection, and integration issues.Research highlights ML's transformative potential for talent retention, but organizations need ethical solutions and simple implementation methods to achieve optimal results.The research adds knowledge that advances the understanding of artificial intelligence applications in human resource management fields.

DOI: 10.4018/979-8-3373-0385-7.ch010

INTRODUCTION

Organizations achieve stability and success by maintaining the stable retention of their employees. Organizations face substantial difficulties when turnover rates remain high because they must handle multiple financial expenses together with missed growth chances and decreased staff spirit. Understaffing situations force organizations to lose potential business deals and trigger productivity reduction (Brown-Crawford, 2022). Business operations become slower in essential periods because poor retention rates cause critical staff to leave positions that help manage crises and capitalize on emerging business opportunities. Business sustainability becomes at risk when companies lose their seasoned workers because this results in the disappearance of important organizational experience and specialized expertise.

The integration of machine learning and artificial intelligence technologies has produced a major change within employee lifecycle assessment systems. The combination of modern technological solutions provides companies with extended perspectives into their workforce engagement metrics, retention patterns, and individual performance data (Marvin et al., 2021). The combination of AI analytics produces individualized development approaches according to employee needs, thus producing a content and satisfied workforce. Through predictive capabilities, ML enables organizations to detect emerging workforce concerns so they can prevent their growth into major complications (InbuiltData, 2024). AI and ML technologies are developing toward transforming employee metrics assessment, which will ensure organizations respond better to their staffing requirements.

Food service and hospitality, together with warehousing transportation, demonstrate excessively high rates of employee turnover (Dwesini, 2019). The nature of these industries depends on temporary employees and youth workers along with minimum-wage personnel, which leads to both worker disconnection and regular job switching. Customers generate high stress for the hospitality industry because of overcrowded venues in addition to challenging workplace conditions. Workers in warehousing and transportation roles struggle to retain staff because their jobs require physical labor. Many hourly wage workers decide to switch jobs for better positions or secure income steadiness, which raises employee turnover. High-turnover industries need to establish comprehensive approaches for worker engagement and appreciation in order to preserve their motivated staff.

A lot of current employee retention programs fail to deal with the difficult aspects that cause employees to leave their positions. The movement of employees in industries that experience high turnover requires special characterization. Today's organizations continue using outdated retention approaches that fail to consider what employees seek in their professional roles in addition to modern technological developments. The implementation of ML in HRM Using ML in systems creates organizations that face complicated dual advantages and obstacles. ML solutions yield valuable data findings yet create problems during implementation challenges as well as privacy and algorithmic bias concerns. The analysis must include Multiple businesses in various sectors to evaluate the effectiveness of ML-based solutions in their operations. Healthcare establishments must evaluate their distinct workforce characteristics to determine appropriate employee retention programs.

Human capital analytics leverages ML techniques that bring about two main benefits. Evaluation of employee departure risk together with workforce planning customization constitute the main advantages of this approach planning method according to research. The combination of employee behavioral patterns with sentiment analysis and engagement metrics enables ML algorithms to achieve accurate predictions, according to research findings of Garg et al. (2021) and Venugopal et al. (2024). Employee attrition prediction depends on research conducted by Garg et al. (2021) and Venugopal et al. (2024). ML-driven talent retention models function at Google as part of their strategic deployment along with IBM and Amazon, according to Rajuroy (2024). Positive workforce happiness results and reduced employee turnover emerged from the partnership between IBM and Amazon. Rajuroy (2024) found that employee departure cuts accompanied these studies.

The existing research lacks sufficient data about how companies from different market sectors should utilize ML tactics for maximum success. The research concerning ML adoption in HR focuses primarily on individual sectors, which reduces the ability to generalize results between various industries. Research on ML still lacks solutions for algorithmic fairness in HR decisions, as well as workforce acceptance of AI-based policies and compliance with labor regulations (Samson et al., 2024; Rashid & Kausik, 2024). Organizations face insufficient evidence about the implementation methods that merge artificial intelligence analytics into human-focused human resource practices to maintain ethical practices and inclusive workforce management.

This book chapter undertakes a cross-sectoral examination that identifies successful retention practices through ML applications and their individual obstacles and ethical requirements for AI-based Human Resource Management systems.

This chapter answers fundamental research questions, which include:

1. **How does the adoption of machine learning in HRM influence employee retention rates across different industries, and what factors contribute to its effectiveness or limitations in various sectors?**

The question investigates the effect of ML-based HR strategies throughout technology implementation and management in addition to financial services and healthcare alongside production facilities. The study investigates three specific retention-enhancing methods of predictive analytics with sentiment analysis and engagement models. The chapter explores particular obstacles within each industry field, which include regulatory hurdles alongside ethical complications and staff reactions toward artificial intelligence for decision processes.

2. **What are the key challenges and ethical considerations associated with ML implementation in workforce retention, and how can organizations balance AI-driven decision-making with human-centric HR approaches?**

This question addresses the problems of AI system prejudice as well as AI database security and AI operational transparency in management. The investigation studies methods for organizations to merge AI analytical information with human supervision to develop inclusive retention approaches. This evaluation examines necessary policy systems as well as governance structures for the ethical deployment of AI in employee retention practices.

The investigation presents findings about machine learning (ML) effects on employee retention throughout different industries while examining successful and failed conditions with adjustments to workforce administration through ML-based job satisfaction improvement and prediction of employee turnover tendencies. The research surveys obstacles as well as moral and regulatory restrictions that emerge with ML implementation in HRM systems and presents actionable recommendations for organizations.

ML-based employee retention approaches lead to substantial performance gains in workforce retention rates in organizations that handle large datasets, particularly in the technology and finance sectors. Sentiment analysis and predictive analytics allow HR professionals to find unengaged staff members so they can make early interventions to prevent turnover. Certain sectors face obstacles when utilizing ML-based solutions because of privacy concerns and governmental rules that restrict implementation, along with the need for human staff in human resource decisions (Bekbolatova et al., 2024).

A better system for retention came from the adoption of ML. However, public agencies experience key limitations partly because employees raise ethical doubts about HR AI systems, mainly because of algorithmic bias risks and skepticism about AI decision processes. Research reveals that workforce retention solutions attain ethical and effective results whenever AI joins forces with human oversight, as found in studies conducted.

The chapter examines how machine learning systems improve talent retention throughout various industries through an analysis of predictive analytics, employee sentiment analysis, and performance monitoring applications. This research collects information from multiple business sectors to find successful methods and difficulties faced in employee retention. This chapter investigates machine learning theory applied to talent retention through several sections about research methodologies and findings from industry comparison studies. It also provides recommendations for future research along with implications for businesses in the final segment.

THEORETICAL FRAMEWORK

Theoretical Foundations

Organizational stability relies heavily on employee retention because it determines business achievement along with financial outcomes and employee happiness levels. High employee turnover creates multiple substantial difficulties because it affects production efficiency, and organizations lose valuable institutional expertise while spending more on hiring new staff (Brown-Crawford, 2022). Human Capital Theory, together with Motivation Theories and Social Exchange Theory, serve organizations as frameworks to study employee conduct and retention patterns. The use of machine learning technology in human resources management enhances current applications through data-based methods for predicting and reducing employee departure rates.

Human Capital Theory

An organization's prolonged success depends on employee assets, as stated by Human Capital Theory (HCT) because employees bring valuable skills, expertise, and experience (Winterton & Cafferkey, 2019). Organizations spend funds on workforce development by providing training along with educational programs and career advancement endeavors to build their human resource capacity. AI and ML technologies amplify HCT by providing tools to generate predictive workforce analytics, according to Alowais et al. (2023). ML algorithms use career trajectory analyses together with performance trends and employee engagement data to assist organizations in finding out which workers show signs of leaving (Basnet, 2024). Analysis capabilities through human capital technologies help HR professionals deliver career development opportunities and specific training sessions along with employee retention measures that match individual employee goals, thus promoting long-term commitment and lower resignations.

Motivation Theories

Staff motivation stands as a vital determinant in maintaining employee loyalty because psychological sciences provide multiple frameworks that explain why workers stay committed to their companies (Kanfer, 2010). The workplace motivational models, which consist of Maslow's Hierarchy of Needs and Herzberg's Two-Factor Theory, demonstrate an extraordinary influence on motivational research. Theoretical evidence presented by Maslow demonstrates that employee needs evolve through five stages, from physiological to self-actualization status (Pardee, 1990). Herzberg's Two-Factor Theory differentiates between hygiene factors, including salary and job security, along with motivators like recognition and career growth, as organizations need to address both to keep employees (Pardee, 1990). The application of sentiment analysis technology powered by ML and employee feedback analytics now provides organizations with innovative measurement methods and improvement solutions for motivation (Basnet, 2024). Upon decision-making, systems recognize frustration signals in workplace analytics along with performance data to generate specific programs that boost staff involvement levels.

Social Exchange Theory

Social Exchange Theory (SET) describes employee retention by understanding the mutual relationships that exist between employers and their staff. Employee retention increases when people believe their organization deals fairly with rewards and provides proper recognition with opportunities to advance their careers (Meira & Hancer, 2021). Organizations that do not establish fair compensation relationships will encounter employee departures when competitors present improved motivational benefits. HR tools powered by artificial intelligence use predictive analytics to measure employee attitudes and recognize employee disengagement symptoms, which leads to satisfaction-improving recommendations (Thakkar, 2021). Organizations that actively solve compensation issues along with workload challenges and professional acknowledgment problems can boost employee retention and establish robust employer-employee bonds, according to Timsina (2024). Understanding the function of machine learning in workforce analytics forms the basis for studying predictive models. Predictive analytics helps organizations retain talent because it forecasts employee attrition rates so measures can be taken in advance. The subsequent analysis examines various predictive approaches that different sectors use to develop their retention strategies.

Machine Learning in HRM

The implementation of artificial intelligence (AI) and machine learning (ML) has completely transformed human resource management while developing modern workforce management systems that operate based on data analysis. The use of ML capabilities enables HR professionals to analyze extensive workforce data collections to recognize employee disengagement signals before predicting personnel departure, thus allowing specific intervention strategies to boost retention rates (Marvin et al., 2021). Organizations gain prompt employee behavioral insights from ML-driven analytics instead of using traditional periodic surveys and managerial, psychological assessments for workforce management.

Predictive analytics stands as a major success of ML in HRM because it examines employee records to recognize patterns of departure along with risk indicators. Research on performance records, employee engagement, and work history alongside external labor market trends allows predictive models to generate customized retention strategies that meet the personal needs of staff members as well as organizational objectives (Garg et al., 2021). For employee sentiment analysis, NLP technology activates the systematic interpretation of survey answers as well as internal workplace messages and feedback emails to determine workplace satisfaction and employee morale (Sammu & Joy, 2024).

HRM uses clustering algorithms as a fundamental ML approach to divide employees based on their engagement data, their career goals, and the potential risk of leaving the organization. The HR team achieves better outcomes when they break employees into custom groups because this matching-based approach creates tailored retention initiatives that benefit individual staff demographics, according to Rahman (2023). Deep learning models, together with neural networks, extend the analysis by recognizing understated employee disengagement signals through monitoring workplace performance and social engagement changes (Garg, Kiwelekar, et al., 2021).

Workforce instability prevention can be achieved through AI-powered HRM systems, which allow organizations to make decisions early on. Businesses obtain numerous advantages from AI-based workforce analytics that lead organizations to experience reduced worker departures while improving workforce engagement and producing steady workforce units. Organizations face complex challenges because of AI model bias, workforce privacy concerns, and worker resistance against AI-based human resource decisions, although they achieve system performance enhancements. The combination of ethical AI governance together with transparent decision-making systems enables businesses to unlock all possible advantages of ML in HRM and build workplaces that are both trustworthy and inclusive. The analysis of workforce sentiment is equally important as predictive analytics for employee turnover prediction. The study of workforce feedback across behavioral indicators provides live emotional measurements of employee satisfaction together with worker engagement. The following section demonstrates implementation methods of sentiment analysis that organizations use to enhance workplace culture while improving retention.

Industry-Specific Talent Retention Challenges

Different complicated operational industries need customized employee retention methods to handle specific workforce retention issues that surface in their sectors. The retention problems vary between industries because of workplace issues and regulatory needs, as well as professional development demands and employee expectations.

Technology employs extremely costly recruitment measures because essential skills expire rapidly, and its workers face constant burnout due to aggressive competitor recruitment. Employee retention remains difficult because specialized workers' market demand surpasses the available job positions. Workplace transition becomes common for professionals since project-based work and demanding norms create worker burnout (Lin et al., 2021).

Healthcare institutions face workforce retention issues because their staff must work through physically challenging environments along with long shifts while caring for numerous patients. The healthcare field observes medical staff, including nurses and doctors, moving on because of stress burnout and institutional support inadequacy (Lin et al., 2021). The current deficit of healthcare staff has worsened the situation because institutions must prioritize employee retention solutions.

Employees in financial services leave their roles at high rates due to demanding regulations as well as workload intensity and inadequate work-life balance policies. Numerous financial professionals choose career changes because they find their workplaces too stressful and need better compliance management coupled with fewer restrictions on career advancement (Brown-Crawford, 2022). Business organizations that neglect these difficulties face the threat of losing their best employees to companies that provide superior work conditions and better payment packages.

Manufacturing operations face two major issues: employees encounter unstable employment conditions and worry about future automation systems. Staff members worry about AI and robotic job replacements, which results in lower workplace morale and employee focus. Limited career advancements, together with repetitive job duties, cause many employees to leave, according to Holzer (2022). Organizations in this sector should dedicate resources to professional development initiatives that will help their staff stay committed in an automated workplace.

Employment turnover rates at hospitality services and warehousing facilities rise because workers face challenging positions, inconsistent work schedules, and unstable labor situations. Employees in these sectors pursue different positions because they give access to higher wages together with more stable working hours and better benefits (Dwesini, 2019). The industries face ongoing difficulties in developing effective solutions to keep their seasonal and temporary employees because they depend heavily on such workers.

Single bonuses and salary adjustments alone do not provide enough motivation for employees to stay in industries with high turnover rates. Businesses need to use machine learning (ML) solutions to study workplace engagement patterns alongside risk indicators for employee retention and create specialized strategies for workforce retention problems (Suriati et al., 2024). HR departments leveraging AI solutions create retention programs that solve industry-specific issues by strengthening their sustainability in employee engagement. The ongoing assessment from performance monitoring systems helps organizations find both successful workers who deserve more help and staff members who excel at their jobs. Machine learning applications in performance evaluation systems generate data-based decisions because of their analytical capabilities. This piece looks at how assorted industries make use of machine learning techniques for workforce productivity enhancement while keeping their staff member.

Applications of ML in Talent Retention

Talent retention through machine learning depends on two main factors: real-time workplace sentiment analysis and employee welfare surveillance. Organizations utilize ML algorithms to monitor employee engagement challenges at their early stages before determining staff retention factors to ultimately attain enhanced staff maintenance results.

Predictive modeling functions as an ML-based system that allows the HR team to examine employee attrition risks by analyzing organizational personnel records. Organizations achieve strategic worker performance intelligence through the implementation of logistic regression models, decision trees, and support vector machines (SVM) together with recurrent neural networks (RNNs) to analyze worker performance data alongside sentiments about workplace atmosphere and worker participation (Rathore & Rathore, 2024). The models enable prevention strategies to develop as HR managers can identify employee problems ahead of work abandonment through these systems.

Multiple worldwide companies, led by Google, Amazon, and IBM, use ML-based HRM approaches to boost workforce loyalty so that their senior HR leaders continue working for the company.

- Google employs sentiment analysis technology to track workplace morale through its internal communications and employee feedback surveys, as explained by Rajuroy (2024). The real-time workforce sentiment analysis allows Google to create specific HR policies that improve personnel satisfaction and office experience.

- IBM develops targeted activities to improve staff retention after using predictive modeling to identify which employees are most likely to leave. Predictive HR analytics helps IBM retain its prized talent by enabling the company to provide professional advancement options along with customized incentives.
- Amazon applies ML to workforce management to develop better employee relationships and decrease employee departures. AI-powered systems control work hours and conduct work distribution while tracking staff health parameters, thus resulting in superior employee retention (AWS, 2024).

These practical systems showcase how artificial intelligence in human resource management transforms existing workforce retention methods. Organizations that use predictive analytics sentiment analysis along with personalized engagement tools built on ML systems will decrease employee departures and build job satisfaction to establish a robust workforce.

The implementation success of ML-driven retention solutions requires organizations to follow ethical AI practices alongside providing algorithmic transparency to gain employee trust. The implementation of AI-driven HRM needs organizations to establish procedures that minimize biases in AI decisions while guaranteeing fairness in human resources management. These organizations must tackle data privacy issues and discriminatory algorithms as well as establish proper AI management processes. The implementation of clear and honest AI-based HR models allows organizations to establish enduring workforce stability combined with enduring employee retention.

Comparative Studies on ML Adoption

Research on machine learning implementation in company retention approaches shows large differences between various industries. Technology companies adopt AI systems for career development and specific learning models, which retain valuable staff members by preventing their skills from becoming outdated (Sun & Jung, 2024). Healthcare establishments use the predictive power of machine learning to forecast medical staff burnout while providing individualized wellness initiatives (Lin et al., 2021). The financial sector depends on predictive data analysis for assessing employee contentment and building work-life balance programs to improve worker performance. AI-powered analysis helps factories and hotels improve their workplace environments by creating efficient shift patterns and decreasing physical workloads while resolving staff issues ahead of escalation (Meira & Hancer, 2021). Some challenges exist that prevent the widespread adoption of machine learning technology within the field of human resource management. The general adoption of machine learning faces obstacles such as data privacy challenges together with complex integration processes, while algorithmic biases and lack of resources hinder its wide implementation (Samson et al., 2024). The implementation of AI decision-making affects many organizations that have difficulties finding an equilibrium between ethical considerations and compliance with labor regulations and managing employee resistance to technological HR practice adoption (Murire, 2024). Workforce retention can achieve maximum benefits through addressing these important implementation challenges.

Research Gaps and Hypothesis Development

Machine learning has established advanced ability for talent retention, yet more research needs to be conducted to fill existing gaps. Recent research indicates minimal investigation of how AI retention methods permanently change organizational cultures and work environment quality (Basnet, 2024). A deficiency exists in research that conducts a thorough evaluation between machine learning interventions for attrition reduction and traditional human resources practices (Guerranti & Dimitri, 2022). More studies must be conducted into AI ethical issues in HRM because predictive algorithms demonstrate potential biases in their decision-making processes. Future studies need to evaluate AI workforce management implementation at multiple levels of organizational structure and measure the general effects of integrating AI technology in workforce operations (Chowdhury et al., 2023). The available literature provides key assumptions that researchers can derive. The adoption of predictive analytics powered by machine learning indicates it will minimize employee departure rates because it allows proactive human resource action (Mishra, 2025). Expert opinion stands that sentiment analysis coupled with natural language processing will enhance the identification of employee disengagement at its early stages. AI approaches within HR management systems will raise employee total satisfaction rates through customized personal encounters and tailored career progression paths. The personalized career recommendations from AI models enhance both employee devotion and workplace loyalty, thus creating a steady team of committed employees, according to Sari et al. (2020). Unresolved research areas will uncover fundamental insights about the current transformations of AI and machine learning applications within employee retention methods and human resource management systems.

METHODOLOGY

The research relies on expert opinions and second-hand data analysis to quantify the effect of ML technology on retention rates using a qualitative research model. Within the framework, the methodology derived from human capital theory and social exchange theory builds workforce investment relationships and commitment factors for retention practices. The study benefits from additional secondary research methods that process industrial reports with case studies and existing data to supplement primary data collection because this study lacks those methods. Further, the study employs a quantitative approach using regression analysis to quantify the statistical relationship between employee turnover reduction and ML implementation.

The data used in the study is gathered from different sources, including:

- **Expert Opinions:** Research data was obtained from scholarly academic papers, white papers, and HR industry reports about AI-driven HRM applications and talent retention methods. These sources provide statistical evidence about how ML applies theoretically and practically to workforce retention.
- **Industry Reports:** Leading consulting firms, including McKinsey, Deloitte, and the Society for Human Resource Management (SHRM), present significant information about ML adoption trends during this period and provide both industry-specific implementations and implementation challenges.
- **Case Studies:** A systematic evaluation of practical ML deployments in human resources management occurs among technology enterprises, financial organizations, healthcare institutions, and manufacturing companies. The examined case studies show direct examples of how ML affects employee retention efforts.

Further, these analytical procedures were used to guarantee both methodical and thorough analysis:

- **Content Analysis**: The study used this technique to isolate common elements in studies about ML usage in HRM. This method detects recurring patterns, making expert opinions and secondary data sources easier to understand.
- **Trend Analysis**: This method assessed how ML adoption has transformed over time while documenting its effect on keeping talents within organizations and identifying proven implementation methods.
- **Comparative Analysis:** The research materials cover ML sector variances by investigating the unique needs and business advantages within different fields.
- **Thematic Synthesis:** This approach leads to a complete understanding of ML-driven HRM strategies, emerging from unified research results because it preserves the consistency between theoretical knowledge and secondary evidence.
- **Regression Analysis:** The regression modeling identifies industry-based effects of ML adoption by interpreting significance values and coefficient

evaluations. Through this approach, the study can confirm empirical data that demonstrate how ML-based retention methods lead to better results.

The study ensures validity by sourcing data from well-established academic and industry publications. Multiple diverse research sources help achieve reliable insights by allowing different viewpoints about ML adoption in HRM to be cross-compared. The method has limitations because it uses secondary data sources that might overlook fresh industry progress and internal corporate plans. Expert evaluations bring meaningful information, but their value exceeds direct observation and interaction between employees and HR practitioners using Machine Learning technologies in Human Resource systems. Future studies should add original field data from interviews with direct stakeholders who work with ML applications in HRM to build a detailed understanding of its function.

The approach creates a robust foundation for supporting the analysis and research findings through evaluated academic literature and enabling future practical and empirical studies.

RESULTS

The research demonstrates crucial information regarding ML adoption trends, how processes affect retention levels, and what obstacles stand in the way of successful implementation. This section provides practical implementation guidelines for businesses that seek to adopt AI-based retention solutions by analyzing these vital findings. The analysis explores sector-specific use cases and identification of barriers, demonstrating methods to optimize ML-based HRM strategies for improved workforce connection and decreased employee departures.

Figure 1. ML adoption rates by industry

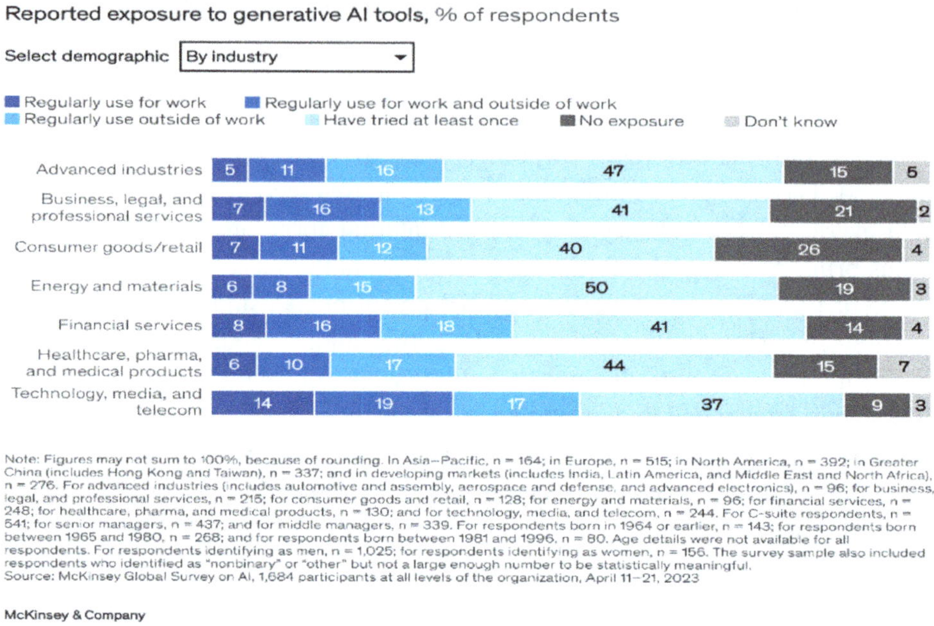

(McKinsey & Company, 2023)

The data presented in Figure 1 indicates that technology and finance widely embrace ML solutions, yet healthcare and manufacturing experience slow growth mainly due to strict regulatory frameworks. Industry research indicates that global companies will implement AI technology for operational enhancement, reaching above 80% in 2023. The Middle of April 2023 survey established that business professionals had a substantial interest in Gen AI while experimenting with new organizational tools (McKinsey & Company, 2023). 79.9% of workplace personnel have experienced AI applications at work or outside work settings, while regular AI application usage rates approach 22%. Technology professionals based in North America use AI technology at the highest rate.

Figure 2. Trend line showing increase in ML adoption (2017-2022) across industries

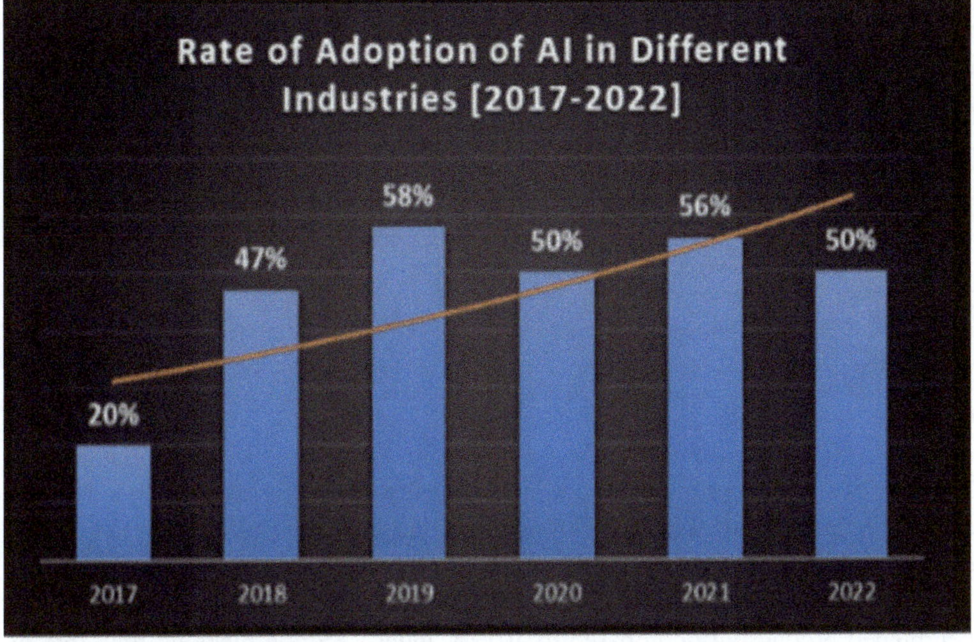

(McKinsey & Company, 2023)

Figure 2 shows McKinsey's report that documented 20% of organizations had implemented AI into their business operations as well as their product offerings for the year 2017. In the previous years, the adoption rate of this data has exploded, resulting in a peak value of 58% adoption in 2019. The adoption and utilization of AI reached 50-56% stability during 2022 after experiencing quick growth from 2020 through 2022 (McKinsey & Company, 2023). The survey findings show that generative AI deployment exists in at least one business area for 60% of organizations, while another 40% plans additional AI spending because of generative AI technology. Until now, marketing and sales functions, together with product and service development and service operations, have proven to be the most frequent business applications of these tools. Software engineering, together with these areas, holds the capability to generate 75% of the total yearly value from generative AI applications.

Table 1. AI adoption by companies per industry

	HR	Manufac-turing	Marketing & Sales	Product/ Service Develop-ment	Risk	Service Oper-ations	Strategy & Corporate Finance	Supply Chain Management
All Industries	11%	8%	5%	10%	19%	19%	21%	9%
Profession-al Services	11%	10%	9%	8%	16%	20%	19%	12%
Retail	14%	4%	3%	4%	15%	31%	29%	11%
Financial Services	1%	8%	7%	31%	17%	24%	23%	2%
Healthcare	15%	7%	2%	4%	22%	12%	8%	8%
High Tech	6%	6%	4%	7%	38%	21%	25%	8%

Overview of various industries that utilize AI in their operations in multiple functions and approaches (Cardillo, 2024)

More businesses within different industrial sectors embrace AI since it delivers expense reduction and faster development while increasing profitability. Businesses utilize AI applications at a rate of 35%, while 42% of organizations conduct AI research (Rashid & Kausik, 2024). Moreover, 92.1% of businesses experience heightened productivity compared to 2017 standards. Stone picks up that 26% of legal services organizations now use generative AI platforms for their operations. AI implementation by retail stores reaches 40% due to its ability to create improved customer interactions and support prices in real-time and customer data research.

The increasing adoption of AI continues to transform multiple business sectors, including retail businesses, finance operations, healthcare institutions, and healthcare organizations. AI technology supports retail operations at Sephora along with the North Face decorator and Taco Bell provider, while Lowes, Walgreens, Walmart, and Amazon use AI to improve their retail environments (McKinsey & Company, 2023). The Generative AI in Financial Services market will increase to $9.48 billion in 2032 as it demonstrates a compound annual growth rate of 28.1% from 2022 to 2032. AI has enabled financial organizations to use it for fraud detection while also executing mobile banking features, digital loans, and insurance services alongside asset administration solutions. Healthcare organizations have experienced rapid growth in adoption rate because of COVID-19, resulting in a $15.4 billion market in 2022.

Multiple industries employ machine learning (ML) technology at different levels, but the tech and finance sectors demonstrate the highest level of integration (Cardillo, 2024). The technology field demonstrates the highest level of ML acceptance while applying predictive models to analyze staff numbers, improve recruiting practices, and maintain valuable personnel. The finance industry utilizes machine learning tools to detect fraud and conduct risk evaluation, as well as automate customer service operations. Industrial healthcare and manufacturing operations fall behind other sectors because of regulatory and structural impediments (Bekbolatova et al., 2024). The adoption of AI technologies in healthcare increased dramatically after COVID-19; however, ML implementation for workforce retention proves difficult because of ethical issues, patient data requirements, and specialized professional scarcity (Mennella et al., 2024). The adoption of ML techniques is slower in the manufacturing sector because of standard manufacturing operations combined with the difficulty of digitizing human resource administration. Three key components of artificial intelligence solutions for employee retention consist of predictive analytics together with personalized employee experience and automated performance monitoring. Research investigating regulatory modifications and specialized ML approaches for different industries should aim to sustain talent retention in these business sectors.

Table 2. Regression coefficients (impact of ML on turnover reduction)

Industry	Coefficient	P-Value	Impact on Turnover Reduction (%)
Technology	-0.72	0.001**	25%
Finance	-0.65	0.002**	22%
Manufacturing	-0.30	0.045*	10%
Healthcare	-0.40	0.030*	15%

*Significant at 0.05 level, **Significant at 0.01 level
(McKinsey & Company, 2023)

Regression analysis (Table 2) shows a significant correlation between ML implementation and reduced employee turnover, particularly in data-intensive sectors. Research indicates that Machine Learning (ML) achieves outstanding results in employee turnover prediction across data-based fields such as technology alongside finance (Adeusi et al., 2024). Predictive models based on machine learning have demonstrated their ability to detect important risk indicators for employee attrition through regression analysis, thus enabling organizations to develop early prevention strategies. A table shows regression coefficients that explain how ML applications decrease turnover frequency in organizations.

Predictive modeling through ML analytics leads to reduced turnover, specifically within technology and finance, that allows companies to address the concerns of their employees proactively. Manufacturing shows inconsistent results regarding employee retention because traditional workforce management methods complain of resistance in addition to structural rigidity. Healthcare struggles to integrate ML methodologies smoothly because data privacy and ethical challenges and the improvement of employee retention achieved through scheduling optimization limit the process.

Figure 3. Word cloud of common challenges

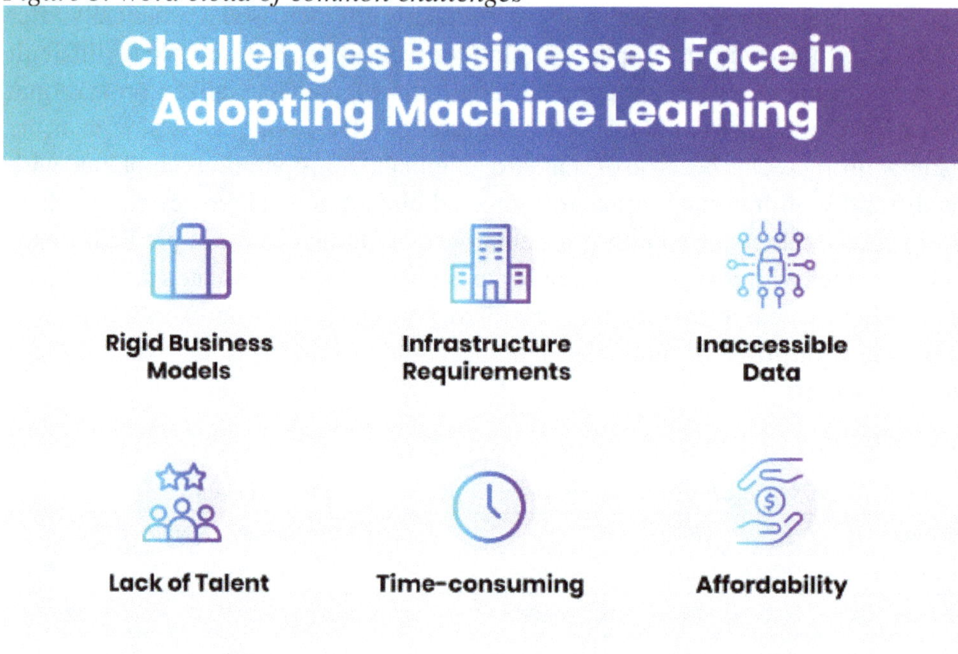

(Maruti Techlabs, 2020)

Figure 3 presents a word cloud analysis reveals three main challenges: privacy concerns about data protection, refusal to implement AI-based human resources decisions, and ethical concerns. The effectiveness of using ML for talent retention depends on three key elements: reliable data systems, powerful executive backing, and respectful rules for AI operations. Organizations using robust ML framework integration can better manage their workforce and experience less employee turnover (Venugopal et al., 2024). The challenges remain apparent because of qualitative interview data that produced this word cloud. High-quality data infrastructure stands as an essential success factor because it makes ML models train effectively for deployment (Gardas & Narwane, 2024). The commitment of executive leaders guarantees that artificial intelligence human resource strategies support the organizational targets. The establishment of ethical AI policies serves to protect employee fairness and reduce algorithmic bias while securing trust among staff members. The high price of implementation stands as a significant challenge above all other barriers, especially for businesses that have constrained technological funding resources (Pasipamire & Muroyiwa, 2024). The resistance shown by HR personnel against ML creates additional barriers because they believe the implementation of ML threatens their current roles in HR functions. The presence of algorithmic bias in ML models creates essential concerns about achieving fairness and inclusivity during decision-making procedures.

Table 3. Comparison of ML approaches used in different industries

Industry	Primary ML Approach	Use Case
Technology	Deep Learning & NLP	Employee Sentiment Analysis
Finance	Predictive Analytics	Attrition Risk Scoring
Healthcare	Machine Learning on EHR Data	Workforce Scheduling
Manufacturing	IoT-Driven Workforce Analytics	Productivity & Safety Analysis

(Adeusi et al., 2024)

Table 3 illustrates how various industries benefit from ML-driven retention solutions by applying numerical data analysis across different sectors. Every industry utilizes machine learning models that meet their exclusive workforce requirements. Figure 4 illustrates an analysis includes a table comparing ML implementation across different sectors, along with a heatmap showing ML accuracy metrics with success metrics in focus.

Figure 4. Heatmap showing ML model accuracy across industries

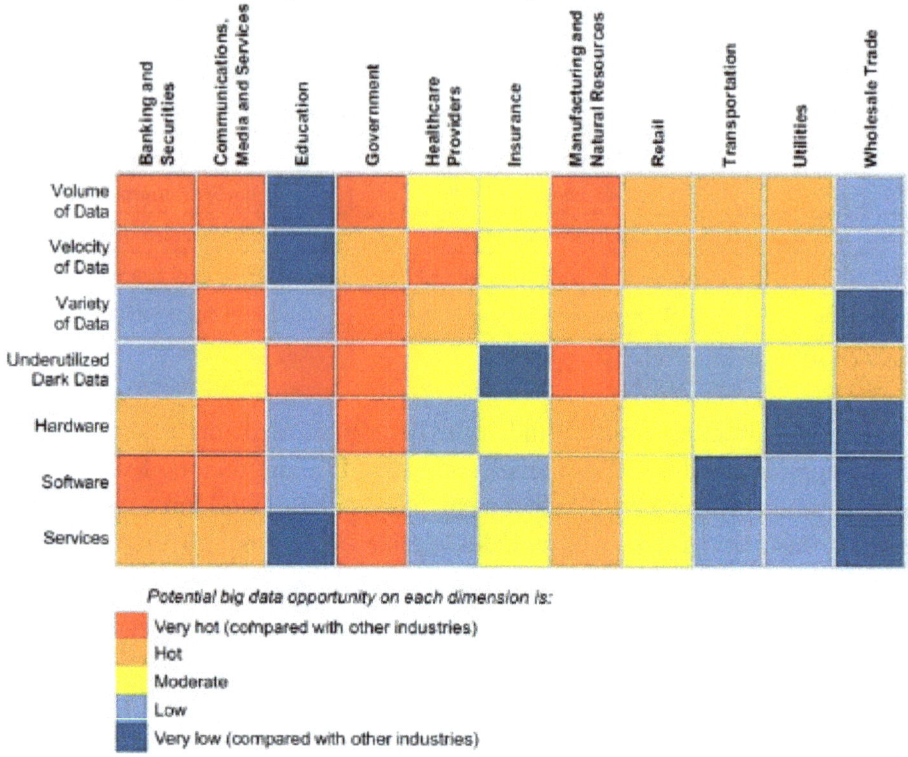

(Cha et al., 2015)

Technological companies put great financial resources into deep learning and Natural Language Processing (NLP) technology for employee sentiment analysis through AI-driven feedback systems that boost employee engagement (Rane et al., 2024). Predictive analytics serves as the main tool for finance businesses to measure employee retention risks, which enables them to create specific retention strategies, according to Broby (2022). Healthcare organizations experience challenges when they try to integrate ML because of strong privacy laws and the requirement to maintain human involvement in HR decisions (Gerke et al., 2020). The manufacturing sector implements workforce analytics through IoT systems, which monitor sensors and automate tasks rather than using predictive ML approaches for a different strategy in workforce optimization (Visconti et al., 2024).

Figure 5. Flowchart showing ML's role in talent retention strategy development

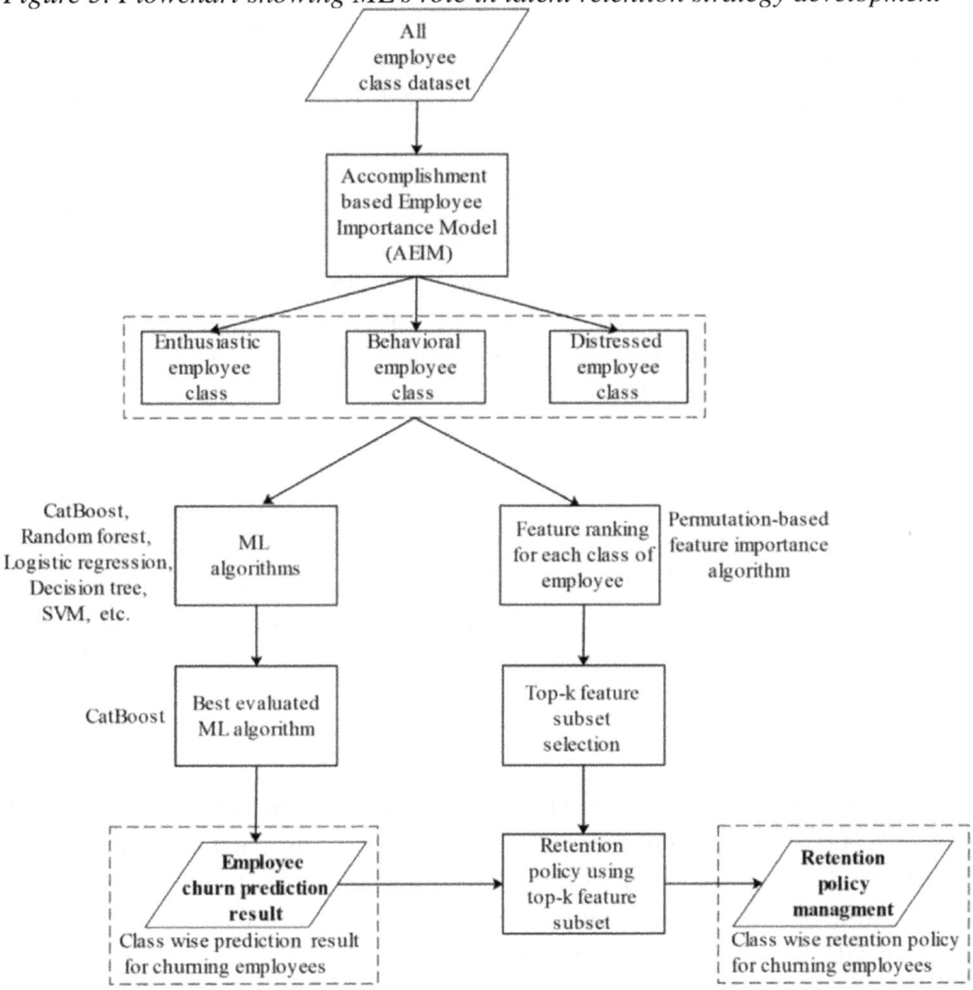

(Jain et al., 2020)

Table 4. Summative depiction of theoretical alignment of ML in talent retention (HR theories vs. ML impact)

HR Theory	ML Impact
Human Capital Theory	ML optimizes HR investments and workforce productivity.
Social Exchange Theory	AI decisions may lack a human touch, affecting employee-employer relationships.
Resource-Based View	ML strengthens HR capabilities as a strategic asset.

(Hassan, 2016; Venugopal et al., 2024)

The implementation of Machine Learning in talent retention approaches matches essential HR principles and remodels established methods of human resource management (Venugopal et al., 2024). Figure 5 presents ML's path for developing talent retention strategies, and table 4 connects ML applications to HR theoretical frameworks. Human Capital Theory finds theoretical support in ML because the technology allows companies to maximize their human resources spending to build more productive teams that demonstrate increased job satisfaction (Hassan, 2016). The adoption of distributed management encounters difficulties with Social Exchange Theory since the theory relies on mutual employee-employer relationships. The use of automated HR decision systems needs to maintain human interaction to cultivate commitment and loyalty, which might otherwise fade due to AI-driven automation (Venugopal et al., 2024).

The central lesson for managers in retaining employees involves ML implementation while human workers maintain active participation. Organizations should utilize AI tools to strengthen human intuition while making decisions because AI systems must enhance human abilities rather than replace them. The retention rates of employees depend on their understanding and trust in HR decisions that utilize AI technology since sustainable organizational outcomes are based on this factor.

DISCUSSION

According to existing literature, this section examines research results to understand their connection with proven empirical knowledge regarding machine learning (ML) approaches to employee retention. This segment examines extensive implications for industrial sectors related to ML implementation through the delivery of specific recommendations to handle current hindrances.

Comparison with Theoretical Framework

Research findings prove that Machine Learning provides organizations with better tools to keep their employees because it creates accurate workforce attrition forecasting, personalized employee engagement initiatives, and advanced human resources management approaches. Studies confirm Human Capital theory because organizational investments in workforce retention strategies create higher performance levels and productivity achievement (Winterton & Cafferkey, 2019). The findings from the study prove that predictive analytics using ML technology delivers superior data-centric retention solutions, which help HR professionals detect employee disengagement behaviors and direct their resources optimally (Basnet, 2024). The research demonstrates both the strengths and the disadvantages of using ML models independently because these technological tools fail to capture the entire scope of employee loyalty together with motivation and workplace dynamics of human interaction.

Social exchange theory receives partial backing from the study because it demonstrates the importance of mutual employer-employee bonds for employee retention (Meira & Hancer, 2021). Information technology-enabled human resources management systems improve workforce analytics but simultaneously break down personal bonds between workers and leaders, thus decreasing staff perceptions of organizational support. The application of AI decision systems in HRM shows research evidence of workforce relation dehumanization that generates trust issues and impacts employee engagement and the workplace atmosphere. Staff members tend to view HR retention methods powered by artificial intelligence as strictly automated processes when AI systems eliminate instead of supporting the human approach to management.

The investigation confirms that AI functions better together with HRM systems based on human connection. Organizations should focus on the psychological contracts between staff and their employers when implementing ML for decision systems. Organizations achieve equilibrium retention results through the combination of AI with human oversight, so they protect employee trust and satisfaction and organizational dedication. Organizations can achieve better employee retention outcomes and stable workforce retention through the deployment of AI analytics in workforce management systems used for human employees, which improves workforce engagement.

Alignment with ML Applications in HRM

Human resource management received an improvement through machine learning algorithms that enabled predictive analytics, sentiment analysis, and clustering algorithms to improve employee retention methods. The predictions from machine learning-based predictive models excel at attrition forecasting, according to Marvin et al. (2021) and Garg et al. (2021), thus enabling HR professionals to predict departure risks. These tools enable businesses to develop specific decision-oriented employee retention solutions through detailed analysis of historical employee performance data alongside performance records as well as worker participation ratings.

The HR departments of Google and IBM use real-time sentiment analysis from machine learning to detect employee satisfaction changes that help them prevent staff dissatisfaction from becoming employee turnover (Venugopal et al., 2024). These companies use NLP algorithms to read both workplace documents and employee internal communication to generate insights about employee sentiment that improve human resource policy development.

Multiple ongoing obstacles prevent ML-driven HRM systems from becoming universally applied in organizations. UST workforce analytics face multiple strong barriers to employee participation because workers fear algorithmic discrimination and worry about data safety as well as privacy breaches. Research by Samson et al. (2024) and Murire (2024) establishes that employees develop skepticism about AI systems because they cannot comprehend the decision-making logic when AI systems affect human resource development strategies, compensation schemes, and retention decisions. Employee understanding of AI recommendations is crucial because a lack of information leads them to perceive ML-driven HRM as discriminatory and unfair, promoting both engagement decline and resistance to AI adoption.

Organizations will obtain maximal benefits from Machine Learning in Human Resource Management by executing these three essential organizational elements in their implementation:

1. Organizations need to use bias detection models together with fairness audits for objective identification of discrimination caused by AI system operations.
2. Organizations should accept explainable AI (XAI) frameworks to provide employees with an understanding of how AI affects workforce management decisions.
3. AI Tools for human resources must match worldwide labor laws and ethical AI principles to guarantee the safety of employee information along with their rights.

Businesses that tackle these obstacles will establish trust in artificial intelligence-led human resource approaches, which will create an open, transparent worker retention system built on fairness.

Industry-Specific ML Retention Trends

Cardillo (2024), together with McKinsey & Company (2023), discovered broad industry variations in HRM ML adoption because of specific business challenges and workforce composition together with regulatory limitations. The AI-powered workforce management activities prosper primarily in technology and finance industries because they possess extensive structured repositories of data together with high digital readiness and data-oriented decision-making culture (Broby, 2022). Industries that implement AI predictive analytics along with attrition risk modeling systems have achieved major employee retention improvements by effectively reducing staff turnover rates.

Healthcare, together with manufacturing, operates with lower AI adoption rates because structural barriers and regulatory constraints limit the deployment of AI-driven human resource solutions. The strict adherence to data privacy rules that healthcare organizations must follow, such as HIPAA in the U.S. and GDPR in Europe, makes implementing AI-driven employee analytics systems complex, according to multiple studies (Gerke et al. 2020 and Bekbolatova et al. 2024). Predictive analytics models have lower effectiveness in medical roles because retention strategies need to understand long work hours combined with emotional burnout and staff shortages in these fields.

AI presents retention challenges to manufacturers because their work depends primarily on manual labor skills, while employee unions regulate operations and staff members fear machine automation across workplaces. Most personnel in this industry believe that artificial intelligence presents a threat to their job stability, thus resisting HR management strategies based on AI (Holzer, 2022). Small businesses operating in healthcare and manufacturing must deal with more limited budgets, resulting in reduced capacity to adopt AI solutions compared to large enterprises.

The unique needs of every industry require specialized AI-driven HRM solutions because of these existing difficulties. A general approach toward AI implementation fails to work. Hence, organizations need to use custom-made ML models that consider both regulatory needs and workplace characteristics and industrial-specific employee retention issues.

Effectiveness of ML in Employee Retention

The study confirms through regression analysis that ML technology effectively decreases employee turnover rates in data-oriented industries, including technology and finance. The analysis demonstrates that ML-based retention tools decrease employee departure rates by twenty-five percent among technology employees and twenty-two percent among finance workers, according to Rathore and Rathore (2024). Predictive analytics becomes more effective when labor data is available at high volumes to companies operating in these industrial sectors.

The healthcare and manufacturing industries do not benefit to the same extent as other sectors because their ML efficiency achieves only 10% and 15% turnover reductions, respectively. AI implementation success in HRM depends on two main factors that emerge from the research:

1. Limited workforce access to data affects the precise implementation of ML-based predictive models in such sectors.
2. The staff retention needs of healthcare, together with manufacturing, require human supervision because artificial intelligence systems that operate without human involvement fail to manage complex workforce demands.

The research demonstrates the effectiveness of adopting a combined human and artificial intelligence approach to human resource management. The hybrid model of AI-human HR strategy increases AI efficiency in workforce management and upholds employee trust together with ethical practices and organizational adaptability.

Challenges and Future Considerations

Machine learning (ML) adoption for human resource management (HRM) experiences multiple obstacles that prevent its extensive deployment. Workforce retention strategies based on AI systems will reach their full potential only when we solve three main problems: data infrastructure quality and executive financial and ethical AI challenges.

Organizations face one of their most challenging hurdles in managing poor data infrastructure and low-quality information systems. To produce precise predictive outcomes, ML models require data from a high-quality workforce structure. Gardas and Narwane (2024) discovered that numerous organizations face problems with inadequate data management systems, which decreases the value of HR solutions powered by AI. AI models that lack accurate data administration or operate with unmanaged datasets will generate wrong predictions concerning employee retention, which leads organizations to introduce inefficient human resources interventions and potentially creates performance issues with workforce management. A reliable and precise operation of ML-driven HR systems depends on complete data management structures that organizations need to develop through strategic capital investments.

Executive organizations, along with financial limitations, act as major barriers to successful implementation. Businesses need funding combined with executive backing to integrate ML into their HRM systems. Small and mid-level organizations that want to adopt AI encounter budgetary constraints and uncertainty about their investment return (ROI). Organizations that resist investing in artificial intelligence for human resource management face a disadvantage in accessing strategic predictive analytics benefits, according to Pasipamire & Muroyiwa (2024). Businesses should establish exact ROI forecasts that will help them show how AI leads to better employee retention rates, decreased hiring expenses, and stronger employee connections. The successful implementation of ML-driven workforce strategies requires both funding and organizational backing, which can only be obtained through executive backing.

The adoption of machine learning (ML) for human resource management (HRM) encounters multiple barriers that block its general usage. Workforce retention strategies based on AI systems will reach their full potential only when we solve three main problems: data infrastructure quality and executive financial and ethical AI challenges.

The most immediate problem affecting machine learning implementation is poor data quality, together with inadequate data infrastructure. To produce precise predictive outcomes, ML models require data from a high-quality workforce structure. Gardas and Narwane (2024) discovered that numerous organizations face problems with inadequate data management systems, which decreases the value of HR solutions powered by AI. AI models that lack accurate data administration or operate with unmanaged datasets will generate wrong predictions concerning employee retention, which leads organizations to introduce inefficient human resources interventions and potentially creates performance issues with workforce management. A reliable and precise operation of ML-driven HR systems depends on complete data management structures that organizations need to develop through strategic capital investments.

Executive organizations, together with financial restrictions, form the main hurdles to successful implementation. Businesses require financial backing from executives and leaders who support the integration of ML into their HRM technological systems. Budgetary restrictions, together with unclear ROI predictability, pose challenges for organizations of small and mid-size scale who wish to introduce AI solutions. Organizations that deny artificial intelligence investments for human resource management reduce their access to strategic predictive analytics benefits, thus creating disadvantageous conditions, according to Pasipamire and Muroyiwa (2024). Challengers demand that businesses show long-term gains by demonstrating both estimated returns on investment and providing better retention rates while reducing staffing expenses and increasing employee involvement. Obtaining executive support stands as an absolute necessity for organizations that seek access to funding and organizational adoption of ML-driven workforce tactics.

The application of Machine Learning (ML) in workforce management enhances Employee Retention strategies through predictive analysis and workforce clustering as it combines them with sentiment data assessments. The study confirms how AI transforms human resource management practices and demonstrates key industrial limitations of AI implementation in practice. The research demonstrates that ML practices match HR principles, but society requires strict ethical standards to maintain human intervention when using AI.

The long-term sustainability of AI-driven human resources interventions requires further research through time-based assessment studies. Analyzing how artificial intelligence transforms organizational culture and employee psychological contracts will grant an improved understanding of its extensive HRM effects. The effectiveness of AI-driven retention strategies in industries depends on successful bias prevention in algorithms as well as greater AI explanation capabilities and improved regulatory frameworks.

CONCLUSION

The acceptance of machine learning (ML) within human resource management (HRM) struggles with multiple obstacles that obstruct its total adoption. Workforce retention strategies based on AI systems will reach their full potential only when we solve three main problems: data infrastructure quality and executive financial and ethical AI challenges.

The challenge of poor data infrastructure, together with data quality, ranks as a leading difficulty in the field. To produce precise predictive outcomes, ML models require data from a high-quality workforce structure. Gardas and Narwane (2024) discovered that numerous organizations face problems with inadequate data management systems, which decreases the value of HR solutions powered by AI. AI models that lack accurate data administration or operate with unmanaged datasets will generate wrong predictions concerning employee retention, which leads organizations to introduce inefficient human resources interventions and potentially creates performance issues with workforce management. A reliable and precise operation of ML-driven HR systems depends on complete data management structures that organizations need to develop through strategic capital investments.

Executive organizations, along with financial limitations, act as major barriers to successful implementation. Businesses need funding combined with executive backing to integrate ML into their HRM systems. Small and mid-level organizations that want to adopt AI encounter budgetary constraints and uncertainty about their investment return (ROI). Organizations that resist investing in artificial intelligence for human resource management face a disadvantage in accessing strategic predictive analytics benefits, according to Pasipamire & Muroyiwa (2024). Businesses need to create precise ROI forecasts while demonstrating extended advantages of AI implementation that include raised staff retention numbers, lowered recruitment expenses, and improved workforce participation. Acquiring executive backing represents an essential requirement to obtain both funds and organizational backing needed for implementing ML-driven workforce strategies.

Theoretical Implications

Machine learning (ML) adoption in human resource management (HRM) encounters multiple implementation barriers that restrict its general use. Workforce retention strategies based on AI systems will reach their full potential only when we solve three main problems: data infrastructure quality and executive financial and ethical AI challenges.

Data infrastructure and quality issues stand as the most crucial barriers to overcome when implementing machine learning in human resource management. To produce precise predictive outcomes, ML models require data from a high-quality workforce structure. Gardas and Narwane (2024) discovered that numerous organizations face problems with inadequate data management systems, which decreases the value of HR solutions powered by AI. AI models that lack accurate data administration or operate with unmanaged datasets will generate wrong predictions concerning employee retention, which leads organizations to introduce inefficient human resources interventions and potentially creates performance issues with workforce management. A reliable and precise operation of ML-driven HR systems depends on complete data management structures that organizations need to develop through strategic capital investments.

Executive organizations, along with financial limitations, act as major barriers to successful implementation. Businesses need funding combined with executive backing to integrate ML into their HRM systems. Small and mid-level organizations that want to adopt AI encounter budgetary constraints and uncertainty about their investment return (ROI). Organizations that resist investing in artificial intelligence for human resource management face a disadvantage in accessing strategic predictive analytics benefits, according to Pasipamire & Muroyiwa (2024). AI adoption requires precise ROI forecasts and evidence that shows the future advantages, which include better employee retention combined with lower hiring expenses and better staff involvement. Executive support is a fundamental necessity to attain funding and an organizational endorsement for deploying ML-based workforce strategies.

Practical Implications for HRM

Organizations need to develop strong governance systems regarding AI data and ethics because they enable fairness in AI-based Human Resource Management. AI model bias creates discriminatory behavior, which damages employee faith and violates legal requirements. Organizations should adopt exceptional bias mitigation approaches together with AI inspection systems along with specific ethical AI governance systems to prevent unwanted discrimination while increasing trust in artificial intelligence's decision-making processes (Sivarajah et al., 2021).

The combination of human personnel with AI systems forms essential models that ensure transparent observation and ethical control in human resources management. The task of making final workforce decisions requires human operators to step in after machine learning determines employee engagement and attrition levels. By keeping decision power with the workforce, this model secures both compliance with ethical standards and workforce agreement (Hamilton & Davison, 2021).

Organizations need industry-specific machine learning implementation strategies to succeed with their artificial intelligence-based human resources improvements. Industries that include healthcare, together with manufacturing, operate under strict regulatory requirements and require diverse workforce management, which forces them to include both AI models built for regulatory compliance and adaptive workforce analytics systems (Nankya et al., 2024). The implementation of these retention strategies through AI technologies ensures their effectiveness and legal compliance for different sectors of operation.

Successful application of ML demands that HR professionals must understand the basics of AI concepts. The majority of HR leaders do not have sufficient knowledge of the technical aspects needed to translate and use AI-generated workforce intelligence properly. Organizations need to establish AI-focused learning programs that train their HR professionals to utilize data-based workforce information for making decisions while maintaining ethical standards of AI deployment (Rodgers et al., 2022).

Organizations must implement comprehensive measures to boost worker trust in AI management systems if they want their workforce to accept HR policies guided by AI. Labor force members commonly exhibit worries regarding AI-generated decisions because they fear unconscious biases along with job uncertainties and discriminatory treatment. XAI models should become a part of organizational operations to demonstrate to employees how their AI-driven retention choices are computed according to Chowdhury et al. (2023). The implementation of transparent AI management policies by Clear AI leads to workforce confidence improvements and reduces the resistance toward HRM systems using artificial intelligence.

Study Limitations

The research features several drawbacks that researchers should consider. The research framework mainly depends on information from existing sources. The research bases its findings on industry reports, academic studies, and case studies, but these sources limit the ability to verify AI-driven HRM strategies empirically (Sivarajah et al., 2021). Future research should conduct field investigations through surveys and interviews with HR professionals and employees to acquire firsthand knowledge about the effects of ML on workforce retention.

Sector-specific variations exist as a limiting factor that affects the adoption of ML technologies. AI readiness regulatory limitations and workforce structures among different industries pose challenges for creating a general AI-driven HRM framework (Nankya et al., 2024). The rapid implementation of artificial intelligence retention solutions occurs mostly in technology fields along with finance. However, healthcare and manufacturing face major barriers because of regulatory restrictions and demanding workforce specifications. Future investigations must conduct examinations with individual industries because they demonstrate how Automl gaining traction progresses differently between distinct work environments.

The investigation lacks information about the extended timeframe effects that ML implementation brings to HRM management. By nature, employee retention requires sustained efforts, yet the early response to AI-based retention methods might not display their full-time results. Research needs to develop over time to observe the lasting effects of ML-driven HRM practices over prolonged periods, thus measuring workforce stability and employee retention and AI trend changes (Bergin, 2018).

Future Research Directions

Several unrevealed research areas demand additional investigation for the development of AI-driven workforce retention knowledge. Research teams should perform empirical case studies on AI retention models to determine how ML implementation affects employee stability across time intervals. Sequential research studies enable the evaluation of ML-based HR program benefits by determining their ability to create lasting workforce maintenance outcomes or whether these advantages fade as time progresses.

The research needs to focus intensely on the ethical facets of using AI alongside algorithmic fairness within human resource management operations. The lack of AI solution monitoring allows discriminatory practices to use discriminatory biases to become stronger. Advanced research needs to develop and test new methods that eliminate bias in AI workforce analysis systems without affecting their unbiased operation (Jan et al., 2023).

Research investigators examine the employees' understanding of artificial intelligence implementation within HR management systems. The benefits of AI technology toward operational efficiency increase while employers face job security risks alongside privacy concerns and equal treatment needs of human employees. Research investigations must study how workers interact with AI Human Resources tools in their work environments and which elements create trust and acceptance, according to Shneiderman (2020).

Future research should study the methods to develop explainable AI (XAI) frameworks for their employment in human resources management practices. The confidence level of employees towards AI decision-making arises from how transparent the underlying AI system functions are. Research must evaluate how explainable artificial intelligence models improve both workforce maintenance and human resource transparency, as well as ethical artificial intelligence implementation (Chowdhury et al., 2023).

Research teams must study machine learning-based talent retention models that have been tailored for particular industries. AI-driven human resources solutions require specific development for particular workforce requirements because different sectors operate according to their unique operational needs. Future investigations must determine proper adjustments to ML systems applications in the healthcare, manufacturing, and public administration sectors to preserve industry-relevant limitations.

Final Remarks

Predictive solutions from ML systems enhance employee retention strategies while producing proactive HRM tools that use data analysis. However, its success hinges on ethical AI governance, industry-specific adaptation, and the integration of AI with human-centric HR approaches. AI optimization demands organizations to use human supervisors for system monitoring to verify that AI solutions boost workforce engagement methods while improving their performance.

The full potential of ML in workforce retention becomes possible when organizations manage ethical issues toward data regulation and build trustworthy worker relationships. Organizations that implement AI-based employee retention systems with proper execution will gain market superiority and attain stable staff along with structures built for employee success.

REFERENCES

Adeusi, N. K. B., Amajuoyi, N. P., & Lucky, N. (2024). Utilizing machine learning to predict employee turnover in high-stress sectors. *International Journal of Management & Entrepreneurship Research, 6*(5), 1702–1732. DOI: 10.51594/ijmer.v6i5.1143

Alowais, S. A., Alghamdi, S. S., Alsuhebany, N., Alqahtani, T., Alshaya, A., Almohareb, S. N., Aldairem, A., Alrashed, M., Saleh, K. B., Badreldin, H. A., Yami, A., Harbi, S. A., & Albekairy, A. M. (2023). Revolutionizing Healthcare: The Role Of Artificial Intelligence In Clinical Practice. *BMC Medical Education, 23*(1). Advance online publication. DOI: 10.1186/s12909-023-04698-z PMID: 37740191

AWS. (2024). *Artificial Intelligence and Machine Learning: Now is the Time to Invest in Skilling Your Workforce | AWS Executive Insights*. Amazon Web Services, Inc. https://aws.amazon.com/executive-insights/content/artificial-intelligence-and-machine-learning-now-is-the-time-to-invest-in-skilling-your-workforce/

Basnet, S. (2024). The Impact of AI-Driven Predictive Analytics on Employee Retention Strategies. *International Journal of Research and Review, 11*(9), 50–65. DOI: 10.52403/ijrr.20240906

Bekbolatova, M., Mayer, J., Ong, C. W., & Toma, M. (2024). Transformative Potential of AI in Healthcare: Definitions, Applications, and Navigating the Ethical Landscape and Public Perspectives. *Health Care, 12*(2), 125–125. DOI: 10.3390/healthcare12020125 PMID: 38255014

Broby, D. (2022). The use of predictive analytics in finance. *The Journal of Finance and Data Science, 8*(1), 145–161. ScienceDirect. https://doi.org/DOI: 10.1016/j.jfds.2022.05.003

Brown-Crawford, D. (2022). The Effects of Leadership Organizational Culture on Employee Performance Resulting in High Turnover, Low Morale, and Decreased Productivity. *Doctoral Dissertations and Projects*. https://digitalcommons.liberty.edu/doctoral/3676/

Cardillo, A. (2024, March 4). *How Many Companies Use AI? (New Data)*. Exploding Topics. https://explodingtopics.com/blog/companies-using-ai#companies-using-ai-percentage

Cha, J.-m., Shin, J., & Yeom, C.-S. (2015). A Review on Applicability of Big Data Technology in Nuclear Power Plant: Focused on O&M Phases. *Transactions of the Korean Nuclear Society Spring Meeting*. https://www.researchgate.net/publication/278329620_A_Review_on_Applicability_of_Big_Data_Technology_in_Nuclear_Power_Plant_Focused_on_OM_Phases

Chowdhury, S., Dey, P., Joel-Edgar, S., Bhattacharya, S., Rodriguez-Espindola, O., Abadie, A., & Truong, L. (2023). Unlocking the Value of Artificial Intelligence in Human Resource Management through AI Capability Framework. *Human Resource Management Review*, *33*(1), 100899. DOI: 10.1016/j.hrmr.2022.100899

Dwesini, N. (2019). Causes and prevention of high employee turnover within the hospitality industry: A literature review. *African Journal of Hospitality, Tourism and Leisure*, *8*(3), 1–15. https://www.ajhtl.com/uploads/7/1/6/3/7163688/article_38_vol_8_3__2019.pdf

Gardas, R., & Narwane, S. (2024). An analysis of critical factors for adopting machine learning in manufacturing supply chains. *Decision Analytics Journal*, *10*, 100377. DOI: 10.1016/j.dajour.2023.100377

Garg, R., Kiwelekar, A. W., Netak, L. D., & Ghodake, A. (2021). I-Pulse: A NLP-Based Novel Approach for Employee Engagement in Logistics Organization. *International Journal of Information Management Data Insights*, *1*(1), 100011. DOI: 10.1016/j.jjimei.2021.100011

Garg, S., Sinha, S., Kar, A. K., & Mani, M. (2021). A Review of Machine Learning Applications in Human Resource Management. *International Journal of Productivity and Performance Management*, *71*(5), 1590–1610. DOI: 10.1108/ijppm-08-2020-0427

Gerke, S., Minssen, T., & Cohen, G. (2020). Ethical and Legal Challenges of Artificial Intelligence-driven Healthcare. *Artificial Intelligence in Health*, *1*(1), 295–336. DOI: 10.1016/B978-0-12-818438-7.00012-5

Guerranti, F., & Dimitri, G. M. (2022). A Comparison of Machine Learning Approaches for Predicting Employee Attrition. *Applied Sciences (Basel, Switzerland)*, *13*(1), 267. DOI: 10.3390/app13010267

Hamilton, R. H., & Davison, H. K. (2021). Legal and Ethical Challenges for HR in Machine Learning. *Employee Responsibilities and Rights Journal*, *34*(1). Advance online publication. DOI: 10.1007/s10672-021-09377-z

Hassan, R. (2016). The Role of Human Capital Management in Enhancing Engagement and Retention Among Top Talent in Organization: A Critical Literature Revie. *Journal of Emerging Economies and Islamic Research*, *4*(4), 54. DOI: 10.24191/jeeir.v4i4.9103

Holzer, H. (2022, January 19). *Understanding the Impact of Automation on workers, jobs, and Wages*. Brookings. https://www.brookings.edu/articles/understanding-the-impact-of-automation-on-workers-jobs-and-wages/

InbuiltData. (2024, October 6). *AI-Powered Predictive Analytics for Workforce Planning*. Linkedin.com. https://www.linkedin.com/pulse/ai-powered-predictive-analytics-workforce-planning-inbuiltdata-qld9c

Jain, N., Tomar, A., & Jana, P. K. (2020). A novel scheme for employee churn problem using multi-attribute decision-making approach and machine learning. *Journal of Intelligent Information Systems*. Advance online publication. DOI: 10.1007/s10844-020-00614-9

Jan, Z., Ahamed, F., Mayer, W., Patel, N., Grossmann, G., Stumptner, M., & Kuusk, A. (2023). Artificial intelligence for industry 4.0: Systematic review of applications, challenges, and opportunities. *Expert Systems with Applications*, *216*(216), 119456. DOI: 10.1016/j.eswa.2022.119456

Kanfer, R., (2010). Kanfer Motivation Theory in Handbook Indus Orgl Psych.

Lin, R., Lin, Y., Hsia, Y., & Kuo, C. (2021). Long working hours and burnout in health care workers: Non-linear dose-response relationship and the effect mediated by sleeping hours—A cross-sectional study. *Journal of Occupational Health*, *63*(1). Advance online publication. DOI: 10.1002/1348-9585.12228 PMID: 33957007

Marvin, G., Jackson, M., & Alam, Md. G. R. (2021). A Machine Learning Approach for Employee Retention Prediction. *2021 IEEE Region 10 Symposium (TENSYMP)*. https://doi.org/DOI: 10.1109/tensymp52854.2021.9550921

McKinsey & Company. (2023, August 1). *The state of AI in 2023: Generative AI's breakout year*. Mckinsey. https://www.mckinsey.com/capabilities/quantumblack/our-insights/the-state-of-ai-in-2023-generative-ais-breakout-year

Meira, J. V. de S., & Hancer, M. (2021). Using the Social Exchange Theory to Explore the Employee-organization Relationship in the Hospitality Industry. *International Journal of Contemporary Hospitality Management*, *33*(2), 670–692. DOI: 10.1108/ijchm-06-2020-0538

Mennella, C., Maniscalco, U., Pietro, G. D., & Esposito, M. (2024). Ethical and regulatory challenges of AI technologies in healthcare: A narrative review. *Heliyon*, *10*(4), e26297–e26297. DOI: 10.1016/j.heliyon.2024.e26297 PMID: 38384518

Mishra, A. (2025). The Impact of Predictive Analytics on Employee Engagement and Turnover in Knowledge-based Teams: A Systematic Literature Review. SSRN *Electronic Journal*. https://doi.org/DOI: 10.2139/ssrn.5038568

Murire, O. T. (2024). Artificial Intelligence and Its Role in Shaping Organizational Work Practices and Culture. *Administrative Sciences*, *14*(12), 316. DOI: 10.3390/admsci14120316

Nankya, M., Mugisa, A., Usman, Y., Upadhyay, A., & Chataut, R. (2024). Security and Privacy in E-Health Systems: A Review of AI and Machine Learning Techniques. *IEEE Access : Practical Innovations, Open Solutions*, *12*, 148796–148816. DOI: 10.1109/access.2024.3469215

Pardee, R. L. (1990, February). *Motivation Theories of Maslow, Herzberg, McGregor & McClelland. A Literature Review of Selected Theories Dealing with Job Satisfaction and Motivation.* Ed.gov; ERIC. https://eric.ed.gov/?id=ED316767

Pasipamire, N., & Muroyiwa, A. (2024). Navigating algorithm bias in AI: Ensuring fairness and trust in Africa. *Frontiers in Research Metrics and Analytics*, *9*. Advance online publication. DOI: 10.3389/frma.2024.1486600 PMID: 39512269

Rahman, M. A. (2023, December 20). *HR Analytics: Association with Big Data and Machine Learning Algorithms. An Empirical Study*. https://doi.org/DOI: 10.13140/RG.2.2.35545.49768

Rajuroy, A. (2024, December 22). *AI-Driven Solutions for Monitoring and Addressing Employee Engagement in High-Stress IT Roles*. https://www.researchgate.net/publication/387312543_AI-Driven_Solutions_for_Monitoring_and_Addressing_Employee_Engagement_in_High-Stress_IT_Roles

Rane, N. L., Desai, P., Rane, J., & Mallick, S. K. (2024). *Using artificial intelligence, machine learning, and deep learning for sentiment analysis in customer relationship management to improve customer experience, loyalty, and satisfaction*. Using Artificial Intelligence, Machine Learning, and Deep Learning for Sentiment Analysis in Customer Relationship Management to Improve Customer Experience, Loyalty, and Satisfaction., DOI: 10.70593/978-81-981367-4-9_7

Rashid, A. B., & Kausik, A. K. (2024). AI Revolutionizing Industries Worldwide: A Comprehensive Overview of Its Diverse Applications. *Hybrid Advances*, *7*(100277), 100277–100277. DOI: 10.1016/j.hybadv.2024.100277

Rathore, R., & Rathore, S. P. S. (2024). Machine Learning Applications in Human Resource Management: Predicting Employee Turnover and Performance. *International Journal for Global Academic & Scientific Research*, *3*(2), 48–59. DOI: 10.55938/ijgasr.v3i2.77

Rodgers, W., Murray, J. M., Stefanidis, A., Degbey, W. Y., & Tarba, S. Y. (2022). An artificial intelligence algorithmic approach to ethical decision-making in human resource management processes. *Human Resource Management Review*, *33*(1), 100925. DOI: 10.1016/j.hrmr.2022.100925

Sammu, J., & Joy, J. (2024, November 22). *Predictive Analytics in Employee Retention and Engagement Strategies*. ResearchGate; unknown. https://www.researchgate.net/publication/386050620_Predictive_Analytics_in_Employee_Retention_and_Engagement_Strategies

Samson, B., None Olukunle Oladipupo Amoo, None Akoh Atadoga, Abrahams, O., None Femi Osasona, & None Oluwatoyin Ajoke Farayola. (2024). Ethical AI in practice: Balancing technological advancements with human values. *International Journal of Science and Research Archive*, *11*(1), 1311–1326. DOI: 10.30574/ijsra.2024.11.1.0218

Sari, R. E., Min, S., Purwoko, H., Furinto, A., & Tamara, D. (2020). Artificial Intelligence for a Better Employee Engagement. *International Research Journal of Business Studies*, *13*(2), 173–188. DOI: 10.21632/irjbs.13.2.173-188

Shneiderman, B. (2020). Bridging the Gap between Ethics and Practice. *ACM Transactions on Interactive Intelligent Systems*, *10*(4), 1–31. DOI: 10.1145/3419764

Sivarajah, U., Kamal, M. M., Irani, Z., & Weerakkody, V. (2021). Critical analysis of big data challenges and analytical methods. *Journal of Business Research*, *70*(1), 263–286. https://www.sciencedirect.com/science/article/pii/S014829631630488X

Sun, Y., & Jung, H. (2024). Machine Learning (ML) Modeling, IoT, and Optimizing Organizational Operations through Integrated Strategies: The Role of Technology and Human Resource Management. *Sustainability*, *16*(16), 6751–6751. DOI: 10.3390/su16166751

Suriati, S., Ibrahim, M. B. H., Irawan, A., Akbar, M. A., & Yendra, Y. (2024). Effective Strategies for Retaining and Nurturing Employees in Organizations. *Advances: Jurnal Ekonomi & Bisnis*, *2*(3), 151–162. DOI: 10.60079/ajeb.v2i3.191

Thakkar, D. (2021). Leveraging AI to Transform Talent Acquisition. *ResearchGate*. https://doi.org/DOI: 10.13140/RG.2.2.27746.54722

Timsina, S. (2024). Employee Turnover and Engagement Programs for Retention. *Theseus.fi, 1*(1). https://www.theseus.fi/handle/10024/851623

Venugopal, M., Madhavan, V., Prasad, R., & Raman, R. (2024). Transformative AI in human resource management: Enhancing workforce planning with topic modeling. *Cogent Business & Management*, *11*(1). Advance online publication. DOI: 10.1080/23311975.2024.2432550

Visconti, P., Rausa, G., Del-Valle-Soto, C., & Velázquez, R., Donato Cafagna, & Fazio, R. D. (2024). Machine Learning and IoT-Based Solutions in Industrial Applications for Smart Manufacturing: A Critical Review. *Future Internet*, *16*(11), 394–394. DOI: 10.3390/fi16110394

Winterton, J., & Cafferkey, K. (2019). Revisiting human capital theory: progress and prospects. *Elgar Introduction to Human Resources and Employment Relations Theories*, 218–234. https://doi.org/DOI: 10.4337/9781786439017.00023

ADDITIONAL READING

Cafferkey, K., Harney, B., Townsend, K., & Winterton, J. (2021). Guest editorial: Human capital, high involvement, and well-being: assessing progress and advancing understanding. *Employee Relations: The International Journal*, *43*(4), 829–841. DOI: 10.1108/er-06-2021-545

Chauhan, A. S. (2024). The Role Of Artificial Intelligence In HRM: Opportunities, Challenges, And Ethical Considerations. *Educational Administration Theory and Practice Journal, 30*(4), 7427–7435. https://www.researchgate.net/publication/380784083_The_Role_Of_Artificial_Intelligence_In_HRM_Opportunities_Challenges_And_Ethical_Considerations

Davenport, T. H. (2018, January 30). *Artificial Intelligence for the Real World.* Harvard Business Review. https://hbr.org/webinar/2018/02/artificial-intelligence-for-the-real-world

Didem Ozkiziltan, & Hassel, A. (2021). *Artificial Intelligence at Work: An Overview of the Literature*. ResearchGate; Elsevier BV. https://www.researchgate.net/publication/349854588_Artificial_Intelligence_at_Work_An_Overview_of_the_Literature

Gasana Kayitesi Mugisha, & Kiu Publication Extension. (2024). The Impact of Artificial Intelligence on Human Resource Management. *The Impact of Artificial Intelligence on Human Resource Management, 3*(2), 14–18. https://www.researchgate.net/publication/383084162_The_Impact_of_Artificial_Intelligence_on_Human_Resource_Management

Lepri, B., Oliver, N., Letouzé, E., Pentland, A., & Vinck, P. (2017). Fair, Transparent, and Accountable Algorithmic Decision-making Processes. *Philosophy & Technology*, *31*(4), 611–627. DOI: 10.1007/s13347-017-0279-x

Nyathani, R. (2023). AI-Driven HR Analytics: Unleashing the Power of HR Data Management. *Journal of Technology and Systems*, *5*(2), 15–26. DOI: 10.47941/jts.1513

Shrestha, Y. R., Ben-Menahem, S. M., & von Krogh, G. (2019). Organizational Decision-Making Structures in the Age of Artificial Intelligence. *California Management Review*, *61*(4), 66–83. DOI: 10.1177/0008125619862257

Tsiskaridze, R., Reinhold, K., & Jarvis, M. (2023). Innovating HRM Recruitment: A Comprehensive Review Of AI Deployment. *Marketing and Management of Innovations*, *14*(4), 239–254. DOI: 10.21272/mmi.2023.4-18

Visconti, P., Rausa, G., Del-Valle-Soto, C., & Velázquez, R., Donato Cafagna, & Fazio, R. D. (2024). Machine Learning and IoT-Based Solutions in Industrial Applications for Smart Manufacturing: A Critical Review. *Future Internet*, *16*(11), 394–394. DOI: 10.3390/fi16110394

KEY TERMS AND DEFINITIONS

AI Ethics: The framework for responsible AI decision-making consists of rules and guidelines that maintain transparent procedures and fair processes coupled with comprehensive supervision.

Algorithmic Bias: Dependable errors in algorithmic decision systems produce unequal treatment of particular employee groups because training data is biased or algorithmic designs are flawed.

Employee Retention: Various work strategies coupled with practices utilized by Companies to cut employee turnover through satisfaction improvement, job engagement advancement, and career enhancement opportunities.

Human Resource Management (HRM): A strategic method for managing employees within organizations that encourages maximum performance through decision-making about appointments, employee development, pay levels, and staff member retention practices.

Machine Learning (ML): ML is a subset of AI that makes computers generate predictions and recognize patterns in unprogrammed systems through data analysis. The ML method in HRM helps organizations forecast workforce developments while measuring employee retention risks through predictive analytics.

Predictive Analytics: The technique of predicting future events using data. To identify patterns that might forecast future behavior, the procedure makes use of statistical models, machine learning, artificial intelligence, and data analysis.

Workforce Engagement: An organization's workforce shows two levels of allegiance toward their workplace, which destroys their job satisfaction and productivity.

Section 4
Digitalization for Social Development

Chapter 11
Managing Digitalization for the Performance of Family Businesses:
Digital Transformation, Flexibility, and Sustainability

Badr Bentalha
https://orcid.org/0000-0003-1339-542X
National School of Business and Management, Sidi Mohammed Ben Abdellah University, Morocco

ABSTRACT

Digital transformation has become imperative for business survival and competitiveness in today's rapidly evolving economic landscape. While digitalization offers unprecedented opportunities through technologies it presents unique challenges for family businesses that must balance innovation with tradition. This chapter examines the multifaceted nature of digital transformation. It specifically addresses the distinctive challenges faced by family businesses, where the integration of digital technologies must be reconciled with preserved heritage and stakeholder relationships. The discussion outlines frameworks for implementing digital transformation while maintaining organizational values and emphasizes a human-centered approach. The chapter demonstrates how these organizations can leverage technological advancement for sustainable growth while preserving their distinctive identity and core values by providing practical strategies for family businesses to navigate this digital transition.

DOI: 10.4018/979-8-3373-0385-7.ch011

INTRODUCTION

All industries are undergoing change and transformation as a result of the digital revolution. But the digital revolution brought about by innovations like blockchain artificial intelligence and the Internet of Things (IoT) also comes with significant drawbacks.

A high rate of investment and risk associated with organizational culture and the human variable in businesses necessitates a high degree of flexibility. Thus effective management of this technological shift is essential to guaranteeing a robust and fruitful digital transformation. For businesses and all organizations digitization and computerization mark a significant shift. The way businesses function is changing as a result of this digital innovation upending established models. This digitization affects data as well as processes. Utilizing strategic data to maximize business operations is another aspect of it. Nowadays its thought that improving the customer experience or increasing market share requires digital transformation.

A family business has many obstacles to overcome. Strong family values and a strong sense of cultural identity appear to be associated with these particular entities. These organizations can differentiate themselves and modernize their management through digital transformation. Finding a careful balance between innovation and maintaining family customs and culture is difficult. The difficulty is increased by the risk of upending established procedures and siding with important stakeholders such as family members coworkers and important clients.

In order for family businesses to stay up to date with the latest advancements in digital transformation this chapter looks at the managerial opportunities they can take advantage of. Our goal is related to how this migration affects family businesses ethical sustainable and human elements. Family businesses can use digital tools to increase their flexibility competitiveness and long-term viability by cultivating a culture of resilience and adaptability. This chapter offers a fresh strategy for using digital transformation to support family businesses expansion adaptability and long-term success.

THEORETICAL AND CONCEPTUAL FRAMEWORK

Digitalization: Definition, Levels and Evolution

Digitization according to Brennen and Kreiss (2016) is the process of socio-technical restructuring that shifts activities relationships and structures from analog to digital. . The mainstreaming of numerical technologies has enabled a profound transformation of relationships processes and modes of operation (Bounfour 2016).

Businesses have been able to completely reevaluate their business models by adopting digital transformation. This has made it possible for them to use e-commerce to reach new markets create cutting-edge services by utilizing AI and current digital tools and streamline their entire supply chain (Boudri et al. 2024). Today's digital giants, such as GAFAM (Google, Apple, Facebook, Amazon, Microsoft), are the most striking examples of this. These companies have disrupted many traditional sectors. For example, Amazon has revolutionized retailing with its online sales platform, threatening traditional physical retail chains.

Digital transformation entails a profound cultural change that impacts all aspects of the company: strategy, processes, work organization, skills, customer relations, etc. To succeed in this transformation, companies need to adopt more agile operating modes, place data at the heart of their strategy, develop new skills and raise awareness of digital issues among all employees. This digital acculturation is essential to ensure a successful transition and to maximize the benefits of digitalization.

The beginnings of digitization date back to the 1950s, with the emergence of the first computers and digital data processing systems. However, the development of the Internet and web technologies in the 90s enabled digitization to take off. The advent of cell phones and connected devices accelerated the digitization process, enabling ubiquitous access to digital information and services. At the same time, the emergence of cloud computing, big data analysis and artificial intelligence (AI) has opened up new prospects for digitizing processes and creating new business models (Bouhtati et al., 2023). Today, digitization affects the majority of aspects of life, from healthcare and education to commerce, transport and financial services (Meziane et al., 2025). It is completely transforming ways of living, producing, consuming and interacting, offering new opportunities, but also posing new challenges in terms of trust, the defense of sensitive or commercial data, and social impacts.

In today's world, digitalization has become a central issue for all players in contemporary society. It has become an inescapable necessity if we are to remain competitive, meet consumer expectations, exploit technological advances and meet today's societal challenges. Indeed, digitalization is an essential driver of innovation, enabling companies to develop new offers and more competitive business models (Bounfour, 2016). It plays a key role in the transformation of organizations and economic sectors, opening the way to unprecedented opportunities.

Automation and process optimization, made possible by digital technologies, enable organizations to significantly increase productivity and efficiency (Bentalha, 2025). This increases their ability to compete in markets that are becoming more demanding (Degryse 2016). Digitalization is also encouraging the development of new business models that rely on data online services and digital platforms. Innovations in modern technology are radically changing the dynamics of competition and opening up previously unheard-of market opportunities (Schwab 2016). Businesses that resist this change risk becoming outdated in this rapidly changing landscape. In order to sustain economic and social functions digitization is essential as demonstrated by the recent global health emergency. Through online conferencing tools e-commerce and remote working arrangements organizations with established digital capabilities have continued to operate (Papadopoulos et al. 2020). Organizations with little digital integration however have a lot of operational difficulties. Because of this circumstance the significance of digital transformation in addressing upcoming disruptions and enhancing organizational sustainability has become more apparent (Saadat et al. 2020). Because of digital tools customers expect experiences that are connected integrated and customized (Heller et al. 2019). Innovative working practices such as remote collaboration and digitally connected teams are being encouraged by the digital landscape (Degryse 2016). Digitalization raises concerns about inequalities in access to technology even as it opens doors for greater economic participation (Ragnedda and Muschert 2018). A complex picture of fewer jobs and new career paths is presented by workforce automation. Established organizational structures are under threat from the proliferation of flexible decentralized employment models. Digital platforms independent contracts remote work and virtual collaboration are all examples of emerging trends. Although these arrangements provide more flexibility and autonomy in terms of scheduling they also bring up significant issues regarding benefits workplace norms and employment laws (Huws et al. 2019). In addition, digitization is encouraging more responsive organizational frameworks such as networked entities, virtual companies and platform-based business structures (Bounfour, 2016). This evolution requires fundamental changes in institutional culture and leadership approaches.

Contemporary technological breakthroughs generate both opportunities and complexities (Gens et al., 2016). Expanding wireless infrastructure, advanced mobile networks and wearable technologies enable universal connectivity. The expansion of digital infrastructure has significant implications for space and resources (Belkhir & Elmeligi, 2018). Information security and protection have become key concerns involving cybersecurity, privacy and digital trust.

Digitization raises ethical and societal questions, particularly in terms of accessibility, digital inclusion, surveillance and respect for human rights. Although digital technologies have a significant environmental impact, digitization is also seen as an indispensable lever for achieving the sustainable development propelled by the United Nations and non-governmental organizations (Freitag et al., 2021).

Family Businesses: Contours and Specifics

Family businesses are a specific type of company with unique characteristics. These characteristics are linked to the presence of the family in the company and the importance attached to intergenerational transmission.

According to the European Commission's Expert Report (2009), a company is family-owned if the majority of voting rights are held by the founder or his descendants, and one of the family members is invested in the governance system. According to Comblet & Colot (2006), a family business is a broad construct, and its definition needs to be aggregated. It must meet at least two criteria:

- a family holds at least 50% of the company's shares;
- a family has a decisive influence on the company's strategy and on decisions concerning the transfer of the company (this criterion will be identified by the fact that the majority of management members are family members);
- the majority of board members are family members.

Family businesses demonstrate distinctive characteristics that necessitate specialized management approaches addressing the interconnected dynamics between family and business domains. Family-business proximity represents a fundamental trait of these enterprises. This closeness can generate strong cohesion and deep commitment to the business but may simultaneously trigger conflicts when family priorities clash with business imperatives.

Family businesses have distinctive features. The cross-generation aspect has a significant effect on management decisions. Family values and culture are often the focus of these organizations which helps employees feel like they belong. However when traditions are over-preserved it can occasionally stifle creativity. Families typically maintain strong control over operations and strategy and ownership structures tend to stay concentrated. Closeness strengthens trust in management relationships but it can also lead to resistance to necessary changes which can make it more difficult to adapt to changing market conditions. Family businesses tend to take a cautious approach to financing hesitant to bring in outside capital that might weaken family control and limit their ability to grow. Despite these governance concerns family businesses have important advantages that can set them apart from the competition particularly because of the strong loyalty and involvement shown by family members. Financial difficulties can also hinder the growth of family businesses especially when it comes to their reluctance to reduce family ownership through outside funding. Ownership and management separation frequently causes issues possibly leading to conflicts in governance and conflicts of interest.

The Family Businesss Digital Transformation: Obstacles and Opportunities

Business operations in all industries have changed as a result of the technological revolution (Furr and Shipilov 2016). Every organizational dimension is changing as a result of these technological advancements (Rachinger et al. (2018).

Digital transformation has significantly reconfigured family business operations. Previously manual processes have been automated, enabling these traditional businesses to operate with greater flexibility and responsiveness thanks to digital solutions (Brynjolfsson & McAfee, 2012; Fichman et al., 2014).

Regardless of a company's age or scale, successful transformation into a digital enterprise requires the acquisition of new skill sets and talents among employees, embedded in an entrepreneurial organizational culture that embraces the power of digital technologies (Mihardjo et al., 2019). Such a culture encourages innovative and risky ideas, even if they initially seem incompatible with current business activities or risk cannibalizing existing revenue streams. Companies that fail to recognize the importance of new technologies run the risk of suffering unexpected competition and becoming irrelevant to their customers (Soluk, 2018). Thus, a key success factor for digital business transformations lies in cultivating the right organizational culture.

While family businesses are measured against similar challenges to their non-family counterparts, several unique characteristics influence the success rate of their digital transformations. One of these key differentiating factors is the role of the owning family, particularly in shaping organizational culture (Dyer, 1986) and in building a lasting family legacy through commercial focus (Ward, 2004; Lumpkin et al., 2010).

In family businesses, the owning family instills organizational routines, structures and values, which are then adopted by senior managers, who in turn decide how to orchestrate the resources available within the business (Sirmon et al., 2011). Traditionally, family businesses have long management mandates, often with family managers who have limited experience outside the family business and, consequently, limited exposure to how digital technologies are applied in other businesses. In addition, family businesses often find it difficult to deviate from their core business, as it represents the source of their success (König et al., 2013). This makes it difficult not only to alter their core business model, but especially to make radical changes to it (De Massis et al., 2018). Finally, tradition plays a key role for family businesses - tradition as a value, as well as tradition in organizational structures and processes. The ability to leverage tradition while embracing necessary change is particularly challenging for an owner family (De Massis et al., 2016).

A key differentiating feature of family businesses is their long-term focus on building multigenerational wealth (Lumpkin et al., 2010; Ward, 2004). This extended time horizon colors both investment decisions and the management of corporate resources. Family businesses are often willing to commit significant resources to longer-term initiatives such as redesigning systems or exploring new business models, with a multi-year vision (Kraus et al., 2019). Family businesses have unique characteristics. Even if they are not immediately profitable their ability to think strategically allows them to make technological investments. Paradoxically though this same trait may make it more difficult for them to adapt to the quick changes in technology (Weismeier-Sammer 2011). Adoption of disruptive technologies may be slowed down by strong emotional attachments to conventional business models potentially resulting in lost growth opportunities. Since these organizations frequently see traditional methods as essential to their identity and past success De Massis et al. (2016) found significant resistance to change. The process of transformation is made more difficult by generational differences. According to research by Kellermanns et al. (2012) younger family members who grew up in digital environments view digital technologies as crucial to future viability while older generations that make decisions typically doubt their worth. In addition many family businesses struggle with a lack of technical know-how. According to Kraus et al. (2019) small businesses are ill-prepared for technological complexity because they lack the funds to invest in digital training programs or hire technology specialists. Adoption of potentially advantageous cloud solutions or managed services is also constrained by family businesses emphasis on control and confidentiality which makes them reluctant to share data with outside parties (Diéguez-Soto et al. 2018). Family businesses must foster cultures that encourage innovation and digital entrepreneurship in order to successfully undergo digital transformation (Mihardjo et al. in 2019). This cultural change needs to make room for ideas that go against the grain and for measured risk-taking. Family traditions can be used as competitive advantages during the digital transformation rather than as barriers. Digital initiatives can be implemented consistently with the support of core values like responsibility loyalty and commitment. While typically flatter hierarchical structures encourage efficient team communication and collaboration concentrated ownership structures facilitate efficient decision-making in line with digital goals (Carlock and Ward 2010). According to Seethamraju and Krishna Sundar (2013) ERP systems can automate a large number of manual tasks lowering errors and freeing up family members to concentrate on strategic priorities. Ates et al., 2013 note that family businesses typically depend on experience and intuition. (2013) have demonstrated how operating metrics customer preferences and sales trends can be analyzed using data analytics tools to make better decisions. Chrisman et al. (2021) described how digital tools improve every stage, from procurement to distribution reducing costs while improving delivery times and customer satisfaction.

While family businesses experience digitization in unique ways due to their distinctive characteristics, it is essential for these businesses to recognize both specific challenges and unique strengths to succeed in digital transformation (Matt et al., 2015; Soluk & Kammerlander, 2021; Sachse, 2022).

RESEARCH METHODOLOGY

There are two main approaches to social science research: quantitative and qualitative methods. The qualitative approach focuses on collecting verbal data, such as interviews or observations, rather than quantifiable data. The information gathered is then interpretatively analyzed to understand the meanings and nuances of the phenomenon under study.

In this work, we used a qualitative approach. The survey was developed through a series of semi-structured interviews and an analysis of the digitization effort. Qualitative research involves direct, individual experience. A qualitative approach can be defined as complex, methodical work that analyzes textual languages to give meaning and interpretation to reality. It involves analyzing words rather than numbers (Evrard et al., 2009). The aim of these studies is contextualized comprehension.

A qualitative paradigm therefore has several theoretical underpinnings. The first is the analysis of words and texts. Qualitative research deals with data that is difficult to quantify. The second is the analysis of data in the real-life context of the subjects. These methods are considered more natural, as they are closer to real life (Bentalha & Alla, 2024). Finally, it also implies the approval of an undeniable subjectivity on the part of the researcher, who is involved in the process of data extraction and analysis. Qualitative research has a flexible approach to life habits, behaviours, and attitudes. Qualitative research can adapt to divergent thinking, tracking changes in thinking and extracting data from responses.

To collect qualitative data, we have chosen to conduct semi-structured interviews with actors linked to the theme under study. The aim is to understand, explore and analyze, through discussions and interviews, the basic variables involved in the digitalization of family businesses. A semi-structured interview is a variant of interviews marked by the presence of open-ended questions. The semi-structured interview encourages communication (Kallio et al., 2016) and enables the collection of open-ended responses from participants.

Interviews are conducted between April and October 2024. The average interview lasts 32 minutes. To conduct these interviews, we used an Interview Guide. Respondents were given the freedom to discuss, and we tried to focus discussions around the study's problematic. Respondents also had diverse and complementary profiles, to gain a global view of the phenomenon under study (Table 1).

Table 1. Profiles of semi-structured interview respondents

Respondent	Gender	Position	Seniority	Workforce
1	Women	Chartered accountant	8	120
2	Male	Managing director	12	2500
3	Male	Sales manager	4	400
4	Women	Manager	6	480
5	Women	Accountant	18	90
6	Male	Sales	16	12
7	Male	Purchasing manager	13	80
8	Male	Owner-manager	9	140

Source: Personal elaboration

In our case, we interviewed people involved in the digitalization and digitalization projects of the family business. Thus, the number of respondents we interviewed was eight. The interviewees have varied profiles in terms of age, sector, region, and level of education. The interviews were recorded verbally (with the explicit agreement of the respondent) and then transcribed, word by word, to retain the richness of the qualitative data. The themes discussed during the interviews related to the chosen research question, i.e. the digitalization of the family business. We chose four related and coordinated themes:

- Theme 1: Criteria for digitizing family businesses
- Theme 2: Digitization objectives for family businesses
- Theme 3: The obstacles to digitizing family businesses
- Theme 4: Effects of digitizing family businesses on performance

Qualitative data processing begins with word-by-word transcription of the interviews in a single file. The first step is to read, structure, and categorize the various themes in the text file. The analysis begins with an in-depth reading of the data collected, by going back and forth between the theoretical data collected and the qualitative interview data. Computer-assisted textual analysis can be decisive at this stage, as it enables certain tasks to be performed automatically, making it easier to observe patterns and obtain unexpected information.

RESULTS AND DISCUSSION

Whether extracting keywords or entities, or classifying text according to sentiment, subject or intent, text analysis tools help researchers and practitioners achieve their respective goals. There are many different types of text analysis software. There is a wide variety of these tools in terms of free availability, speed, purpose and functionality. Statistical analysis of the interviews carried out has brought to light a collection of essential elements for our study. Thus, the first point relating to the presentation of the results of the qualitative study will be linked to the most frequent words (Table 2).

Table 2. Occurrence of the main items linked to the digitalization of family businesses

Items	Occurrence
Digitalization	110
Companies	93
Family	70
Process	31
Time	28
Objectives	24
Performance	22
Management	20
Transformation	17
Software	14
Sector	14
Brakes	11
Tasks	11
Digital	10
Efficiency	10
Change	9
Management	8
Costs	8

Source: Qualitative study

Theme 1: Criteria for Digitizing Family Businesses

The first point discussed in this theme concerns the criteria for digitizing family businesses. Respondents discussed the importance of defining clear objectives for digitization according to business area, positioning, size and sales volume, as well as the importance of using the right working methods. It is also important to ensure that the right resources are deployed, with limited budgets (time and deployment costs) in family-run businesses, and internal resources and skills in family-owned businesses. Finally, the criteria selected must take into account resistance to change in family businesses and the lack of leadership involvement in family businesses.

As a result, digitalization is an important issue for family businesses, as it enables them to increase productivity and operational efficiency, meet the demands of customers and regulatory authorities, and remain competitive on a national and international scale. Factors identified by respondents as favoring digitalization in family businesses include external pressure, such as that exerted by customers or regulatory authorities, management's desire to increase productivity and operational efficiency, investment in the right digital solutions tailored to the business, and the involvement of all teams in the digitalization process.

Here are some Verbatims that illustrate this category of words:

> "some project owners, who are generally public administrations, require all companies to digitalize all operations with them."
>
> "This procedure must define the precise stages of digital transformation and the actions to be taken for each stage."
>
> "Another essential criterion is management's willingness to increase productivity and operational efficiency by digitizing key processes."

Theme 2: Digitization Objectives for Family Businesses

Family businesses seek to achieve several objectives through digitization, notably to improve productivity and operational efficiency by automating certain time-consuming tasks and streamlining the flow of information and data within the company, and to increase the competitiveness and growth of family businesses by being faster, more responsive, and having greater visibility over their operations. There is also the objective of improving traceability and quality monitoring of products/services throughout the production/service cycle, and of better controlling the company by providing key performance indicators in real time, giving an accurate idea of profitability at any given moment. Some respondents spoke of the aim of decentralizing decisions and responsibilities within the family business, so that not all decisions rest solely with the head of the company, and of facilitating the management of resources, such as the equipment pool, by optimizing the use and maintenance of equipment, leading to a reduction in operating costs and an improvement in profitability. Finally, digitization improves communication and coordination between different departments and teams within the company (Beddaa & Bentalha, 2025).

Digitization objectives are also aligned with the company's vision and family values, reinforcing transparency and accountability. By providing key performance indicators in real time, digitization supports informed, decentralized decision-making, enhancing the trust and autonomy of team members. It also improves operational efficiency, enabling the company to remain competitive while respecting its values of sustainability and innovation. Digitization facilitates more collaborative management, while preserving the family spirit and traditional values. Digitization makes it possible to structure and automate processes, reducing the risk of errors and fraud, and the management of resources, such as equipment, can be optimized to improve utilization and maintenance, leading to lower operating costs and improved profitability. Last but not least, digitization enables coordination between different teams, and information sharing can be improved.

Here are some Verbatims that illustrate this category of words:

> "Companies are looking to take advantage of the time-saving benefits of digitization and track the status and situation of each deal."
>
> "Another important objective is to empower managers to make decisions and take responsibility according to their role, based on key data derived from digitization."
>
> "It improves operational efficiency, enabling the company to remain competitive while respecting its values of sustainability and innovation."

Theme 3: Obstacles to the Digitalization of Family Businesses

According to respondents, the main obstacles encountered by family businesses in their digitalization drive are related to the reluctance to change of some managers or employees, who fear losing autonomy and grey areas with greater digital transparency, and to the lack of in-house digital skills and the need to train teams, which can slow down or compromise digitalization projects. Some also point to the financial investment required to acquire the right tools and solutions, and to be supported in their implementation, which can be an obstacle for many family-run SMEs with limited resources.

These obstacles to digitization can be overcome by making managers understand that digitization is not simply a cost, but a long-term strategic investment that will rapidly translate into gains in productivity, efficiency, and competitiveness for their company, and by presenting digitization as a progressive approach, starting with the most critical processes and adapting the pace to the company's resources. Also, an effort must be made to offer step-by-step support and well-managed change management, to support family businesses in their digital transition, and to provide concrete examples of success stories in their sector, to demonstrate the potential gains in terms of profitability and productivity. Last but not least, we need to keep up to date with technological advances to avoid falling behind our competitors.

Delayed deployment of new digital technologies and processes will create poor implementation of digital tools and solutions, which may not meet business needs, and a loss of competitiveness for the company, which may be overtaken by the competition.

To encourage managers to overcome these obstacles, it is important to make them understand that digitalization is a long-term investment that can generate significant benefits, such as improved operational efficiency, long-term cost reduction, and improved competitiveness in the marketplace, and to provide concrete examples of success stories in their sector, to demonstrate the potential gains in terms of profitability and productivity. Presenting digitization as a gradual process, adapting the pace to the company's resources and offering step-by-step support and assessment of the company's needs and priorities, will help motivate managers to take the path of digitizing family businesses.

Here are some Verbatims that illustrate this category of words:

> "There are also managers who have a phobia of digitalization and the structured organization it imposes. These executives may resist change, which slows down the digitization process."
>
> "Among the challenges of digitizing companies, the purchase of expensive software and the time required for this transformation are often mentioned."
>
> "It's also useful to provide concrete examples of success stories in their sector, demonstrate the potential gains in terms of profitability and productivity, and stress the importance of staying up to date with technological advances."

Theme 4: The Impact of Digitalization on the Performance of Family Businesses

The impact of digitization on the performance of family businesses is significant, positive, and is felt in different aspects of the business. Indeed, respondents discussed digitization and its role in operational efficiency, reducing costs and increasing productivity. Digitization can also improve the flexibility and sustainability of family businesses. The impact of digitization on performance is not limited to financial gains, but also includes improved decision-making, greater customer satisfaction and new business opportunities.

Digitization is essential for the survival of family businesses in today's competitive marketplace. Companies that fail to digitize risk falling behind and losing their competitive edge. Finally, digitization can help companies innovate and stay ahead of the game.

The main challenges of digitization for family businesses are the cost of implementing new technologies, the lack of digital skills among employees and the need to change the culture and mindset of the business, it can be difficult for family businesses to convince their employees to adopt new technologies and family businesses can also struggle to find the digital solutions that best suit their specific needs and budget.

Here are some Verbatim that illustrate this word category:

> "digitization minimizes many expenses over time."
>
> "digitalization benefits from the use of analytical informations and detailed reports on all aspects of the business."
>
> "Having a real-time view and reliable data on your operations enables you to make better strategic and commercial decisions to gain in competitiveness."

So, after this analysis of qualitative data, we have a global vision of the problem studied. We propose an action plan based on 5 components: strategic, commercial, managerial, human resources, and financial. Table 3 & Figure 1 summarizes the proposed action plan.

Table 3. Digitization action plan for the family business

Levels	Actions
Strategic	- Define a digital strategy - Map the processes to be digitized - Plan technological investments - Draw up financial forecasts - Define an investment strategy - Manage cash flow
Commercial	- Redesigning the digital customer journey - Developing digital marketing - Digital competitive intelligence - Negotiate customer/supplier payment terms - Competitor analysis - Define sales objectives
Managerial	- Digitizing project management - Optimizing digital processes - Digital performance dashboards - Plan flexibility - Administrative control of objectives - Improve internal communication

continued on following page

Table 3. Continued

Levels	Actions
Human Resources	- Digital training strategy - Change management - Recruiting digital profiles - Training and skills development - Attractive remuneration - Employee/management communication
Financial	- Digital business model - Digital cost/benefit analysis - Digital financing options - Cash flow forecasting - Cash management - Tax planning - Project profitability analysis

Source: Personal elaboration

Figure 1. Digitization transformation framework for the family business

(Personal elaboration)

The "Operational Actions" foundation at the bottom recognizes that strategic planning must ultimately translate to daily implementation across departments, an area where family businesses often excel due to their typically flatter hierarchies and stronger cross-functional communication. This framework serves as both a diagnostic tool to identify gaps in current digital transformation efforts and a roadmap for developing comprehensive digital initiatives that leverage the unique strengths of family business structures.

Following the development of this action plan, and after analyzing the results of the qualitative study, here are some recommendations for developing the digitalization of the family business. First of all, management must be involved, and there must be real strategic support for change management: digital transformation represents a profound change for the company. To succeed, it's essential to have the support and involvement of senior management and the executive committee. They must be the first ambassadors of change, embodying the vision and communicating the challenges and expected benefits. Their role will be to mobilize all teams around the project. The next step is to set measurable objectives and key performance indicators to monitor the transformation: Defining SMART (Specific, Measurable, Achievable, Realistic, Time-bound) objectives from the outset will enable the transformation to be managed in concrete terms. Key indicators such as the rate of adoption of new tools, productivity gains and customer satisfaction need to be monitored regularly to ensure that the desired results are being achieved. In addition, a culture of data and transparency must be fostered via the digital tools deployed: data and digital tools deployed must enable a fluid flow of information at all levels for rapid, factually-informed decision-making. Encouraging this culture of data and transparency internally is fundamental. We also need to empower field teams in the use of new solutions: Capitalize on the business expertise of field teams by involving them in the deployment of digital solutions. Their empowerment and appropriate training in these new tools will ensure optimal adoption and use. Finally, we need to consider remuneration models that encourage the adoption of the new tools: to ensure optimal adoption of the new tools by teams, variable remuneration mechanisms could be envisaged, linking part of the bonus to the effective use of the solutions deployed.

This wave of digitalization represents a lever for growth and sustainability, provided that all the human, technological and financial challenges are mastered. It's an ambitious but achievable challenge, provided the whole organization is fully committed to the adventure.

CONCLUSION

This research demonstrates the crucial importance of digital transformation for family businesses in the current economic climate. While digitalization offers major opportunities in terms of growth, efficiency and competitiveness, it also represents a major challenge for these companies, which have to reconcile modernity with the preservation of their heritage.

Theoretical research has enabled us to define the conceptual and operational issues involved in driving this digital transformation within family businesses. Specific factors such as multi-generational governance, preservation of corporate culture and a long-term vision must be taken into account if this transition is to be successful. This research underlines that far from being a threat to family businesses, digitalization represents a tremendous opportunity for transformation, development and sustainability for these structures, provided it is approached strategically. By embracing digitalization while preserving their roots and founding values, family businesses can resolutely embrace the modernity and competitiveness of the 21st century. The flexibility and sustainability of their unique model will thus be strengthened to meet the entrepreneurial challenges of tomorrow.

This research into digitization and the performance of family businesses has produced some rich and enlightening conclusions. Nevertheless, as with any study, there are several avenues to be explored. Firstly, additional case studies of family businesses that have undergone digital transformation would provide a broader panel of experiences, in different sectors and countries. This would refine and consolidate the models and best practices identified. An in-depth quantitative and qualitative analysis of the key success factors and potential obstacles to the digitalization of these companies would also be a valuable complement. In addition, the development of a detailed, formalized model of the digitization process in family businesses, in the form of a methodological framework or benchmark, would represent a major contribution. Such a model would reinforce both the theoretical and operational aspects of the work carried out.

REFERENCES

Ates, A., Garengo, P., Cocca, P., & Bititci, U. (2013). The development of SME managerial practice for effective performance management. *Journal of Small Business and Enterprise Development, 20*(1), 28–54.

Beddaa, M., & Bentalha, B. (2025). Optimizing Local Attractiveness Through Territorial Digital Communication. In Sustainable and Intelligent Territorial Marketing and Entrepreneurship (pp. 159-192). IGI Global.

Belkhir, L., & Elmeligi, A. (2018). Assessing ICT global emissions footprint: Trends to 2040 & recommendations. *Journal of Cleaner Production, 177*, 448–463.

Bentalha, B. (2025). A Prospective Analysis for Robotic Mobile Fulfillment Systems: Assessing the Benefits of Automated Logistics. In Digital Transformation and Innovation in Emerging Markets (pp. 251-278). IGI Global.

Bentalha, B., & Alla, L. (2024). Revealing the subtleties: The art of qualitative studies in science and management. In *Applying qualitative research methods to management science* (pp. 1–21). IGI Global.

Boudri, R., Bentalha, B., & Benjelloun, O. (2024). Phygital marketing and the pain of paying: An Amazon Go netnographic case study. In *AI and data engineering solutions for effective marketing* (pp. 348–363). IGI Global.

Bouhtati, N., Alla, L., & Bentalha, B. (2023). Marketing big data analytics and customer relationship management: A fuzzy approach. In *Integrating intelligence and sustainability in supply chains* (pp. 75–86). IGI Global.

Bounfour, A. (2016). *Digital Futures, Digital Transformation: From Lean Production to Acceluction*. Springer International Publishing.

Brennen, J. S., & Kreiss, D. (2016). Digitalisation. The International Encyclopedia of Communication Theory and Philosophy, 1-11.

Brynjolfsson, E., & McAfee, A. (2012). *Race against the machine: How the digital revolution is accelerating innovation, driving productivity, and irreversibly transforming employment and the economy*. Brynjolfsson and McAfee.

Carlock, R. S., & Ward, J. L. (2010). *When family businesses are best: The parallel planning process for family harmony and business success*. Palgrave Macmillan.

Chrisman, J. J., Chua, J. H., De Massis, A., Minola, T., & Vismara, S. (2021). Management processes and strategy execution in family firms: From "what" to "how". *Small Business Economics, 56*(3), 1085–1122.

De Massis, A., Frattini, F., Kotlar, J., Petruzzelli, A. M., & Wright, M. (2016). Innovation through tradition: Lessons from innovative family businesses and directions for future research. *The Academy of Management Perspectives, 30*(1), 93–116.

De Massis, A., Frattini, F., Majocchi, A., & Piscitello, L. (2018). Family firms and the circular economy's entry and extension strategies in biology-based markets. *Journal of Business Research, 82*, 345–355.

Degryse, C. (2016). *Digitalisation of the Economy and its Impact on Labour Markets. European Trade Union Institute*. ETUI.

Diéguez-Soto, J., López-Delgado, P., & Rojo-Ramírez, A. A. (2018). Identifying and classifying family businesses. *Review of Managerial Science, 12*(4), 983–1023.

Dyer, W. G. (1986). *Cultural change in family firms: Anticipating and managing business and family transitions*. Jossey-Bass.

Evrard, Y., Pras, B., Roux, E., Desmet, P., Dussaix, A.-M., & Gary, L. (2009). *Market - Fondements et méthodes des recherches en marketing*. Dunod.

Fichman, R. G., Dos Santos, B. L., & Zheng, Z. E. (2014). Digital innovation as a fundamental and powerful concept in the information systems curriculum. *Management Information Systems Quarterly, 38*(2), 329–353.

Freitag, C., Berners-Lee, M., Widdicks, K., Knowles, B., Blair, G. S., & Friday, A. (2021). The real climate and transformative impact of ICT: A critique of estimates, trends, and regulations. *Patterns (New York, N.Y.), 2*(9), 100340. PMID: 34553177

Furr, N., & Shipilov, A. (2016). Digital doesn't have to be disruptive. *Harvard Business Review, 94*(7-8), 94–103.

Gens, F., Levitas, D., & Pone, S. (2016). The Digital Universe in 2020: Big Data, Bigger Digital Shadows, and Biggest Growth in the Far East. IDC iView.

Heller, J., Chylinski, M., de Ruyter, K., Mahr, D., & Keeling, D. I. (2019). Embracing digital technology: Clients' perspective on future affordances of makerspaces. *Futures, 109*, 82–97.

Huws, U., Spencer, N. H., & Coates, M. (2019). *The platformisation of work in Europe: Results from research in 13 European countries*. Foundation for European Progressive Studies.

Kallio, H., Pietilä, A. M., Johnson, M., & Kangasniemi, M. (2016). Systematic methodological review: Developing a framework for a qualitative semi-structured interview guide. *Journal of Advanced Nursing, 72*(12), 2954–2965. PMID: 27221824

Kellermanns, F. W., Eddleston, K. A., Sarathy, R., & Murphy, F. (2012). Innovativeness in family firms: A family influence perspective. *Small Business Economics, 38*(1), 85–101.

König, A., Kammerlander, N., & Enders, A. (2013). The family innovator's dilemma: How family influence affects the adoption of discontinuous technologies by incumbent firms. *Academy of Management Review, 38*(3), 418–441.

Kraus, S., Fink, M., & Rössl, D. (2019). From family succession to incubation: A perspective shift in the study of entrepreneurship. *International Journal of Entrepreneurial Behaviour & Research, 25*(6), 1183–1187.

Lumpkin, G. T., Brigham, K. H., & Moss, T. W. (2010). Long-term orientation: Implications for the entrepreneurial orientation and performance of family businesses. *Entrepreneurship and Regional Development, 22*(3-4), 241–264.

Matt, C., Hess, T., & Benlian, A. (2015). Digital transformation strategies. *Business & Information Systems Engineering, 57*(5), 339–343.

Meziane, B., Alla, L., & Bentalha, B. (2025). Transformational Trends of Territorial Economic Intelligence Strategies in the Digital Era: A Systematic Theoretical Exploration. In Utilizing Technology to Manage Territories (pp. 455-490). IGI Global.

Mihardjo, L. W. W., Jeremic, J., & Shahriari, S. (2019). The digital transformation of SMEs. In *Proceedings of the 2019 International Conference on Information Technology & Systems* (pp. 277-286). Springer.

Papadopoulos, T., Baltas, K. N., & Balta, M. E. (2020). The use of digital technologies by small and medium enterprises during COVID-19: Implications for theory and practice. *International Journal of Information Management, 55*, 102192. PMID: 32836646

Rachinger, M., Rauter, R., Müller, C., Vorraber, W., & Schirgi, E. (2018). Digitalization and the labour market: Theoretical knowledge and empirical project findings. *International Journal of Environmental and Science Education, 13*(7), 537–556.

Ragnedda, M., & Muschert, G. W. (Eds.). (2018). *Theorizing digital divides*. Routledge.

Saadat, S., Rahmati, D., & Lahooti, V. (2020). The underlying paradigms of industry 4.0-based societies. *IEEE Access : Practical Innovations, Open Solutions, 8*, 173825–173836.

Sachse, U. (2022). Digital transformation in family firms: An exploratory analysis. *Journal of Business Research, 144*, 143–162.

Schwab, K. (2016). The Fourth Industrial Revolution. World Economic Forum.

Seethamraju, R., & Krishna Sundar, D. (2013). Influence of ERP systems on business process agility. *IIMB Management Review*, *25*(3), 137–149.

Sirmon, D. G., Arregle, J. L., Hitt, M. A., & Webb, J. W. (2011). Resource orchestration to create competitive advantage: Breadth, depth, and life cycle effects. In Corbett, A. C., & Katz, J. A. (Eds.), *Insights to a Changing World* (Vol. 2, pp. 63–88). Emerald Group Publishing Limited.

Soluk, J. (2018). How digitalization is changing today's business. *European Scientific Journal*, *14*(13), 59–66.

Soluk, J., & Kammerlander, N. (2021). Digital transformation in family-owned Mittelstand firms: A dynamic capabilities perspective. *European Journal of Information Systems*, *30*(6), 636–671.

Ward, J. L. (2004). *Perpetuating the family business: 50 lessons learned from long-lasting, successful families in business*. Palgrave Macmillan.

Chapter 12
The Use of Mobile Devices by Social Enterprise to Provide Service to Communities in South Africa

William Howard Olivier
https://orcid.org/0000-0003-2641-1169
Cape Peninsula University of Technology, South Africa

Tiko Iyamu
https://orcid.org/0000-0002-4949-094X
Cape Peninsula University of Technology, South Africa

ABSTRACT

This study investigates the factors influencing the integration of mobile technology and services of Social Enterprise, to communities in South Africa. The Case study approach was employed using a South African community. We conducted a qualitative study involving semi-structured interviews with Social Enterprise (SE) employees and members of a community in South Africa. The technology acceptance model (TAM) was applied in the analysis of the data. Our analysis revealed seven key factors: connectivity, network infrastructure, capabilities, affordability, accessibility, contextualisation, language translation, and knowledgeability. The study reveals how various factors interact in complex ways to shape the integration of mobile technology with SE services in the community. The study contributes to literature by providing a nuanced understanding of how mobile technology can be integrated with

DOI: 10.4018/979-8-3373-0385-7.ch012

SE services, highlighting the potential implications and consequences. The study has significant impact on SEs, community members, and IT specialists including those involved in policymaking.

INTRODUCTION

Social Enterprise within the Western Cape of South Africa seeks to provide services to communities to improve their well-being and contribute to poverty alleviation. Despite information and technology communication (ICT) advancements, Social Enterprises (SEs) within the Western Cape have not been able to integrate their operations with ICT functions. This lack of integration leads to a disconnect between many communities and those who provide the services. As a result, services, such as the distribution of messages and information related to social, economic growth, and opportunities for communities, are hindered. Thus, this study aimed to develop a framework to integrate mobile technology into the operations of Social Enterprise for service improvisation.

Social Enterprise within the Western Cape of South Africa seeks to provide services to communities to improve their well-being and contribute to poverty alleviation. Currently, there is a lack of ICT integration within the operations of Social Enterprises within the Western Cape, even though there have been many technological advancements. This lack of integration leads to a disconnect between many communities and those who provide the services. As a result, services, such as the distribution of messages and information related to social, and economic growth, and opportunities for communities, are hindered (Nxele, 2018). The problem is that no framework helps Social Enterprises with the integration of ICT within their service delivery to these communities.

Information and Communication Technology (ICT) continues to draw attention as a key enabler for innovation and employment (Bilbao-Osorio & Dutta, 2014). There is a strong connection between ICT adoption, economic development, and social change. Thus, organisations (like Social Enterprises) agree on the importance of adopting ICT to support their social mission and business operations (Tauringana & Afrifa, 2013). ICT is essential in mediating relationships between communities and government (Sofyani et al., 2020). Because of this, SE can also benefit from the use of ICT in its service delivery to communities.

In achieving the study's aim, objectives were formulated: (1) To examine and understand the factors that influence how SE uses the information to provide services to communities; and (2) To investigate how mobile technologies can facilitate ease of access to information and service distribution. In the process of achieving the research objective, the qualitative methods were employed. The case study was applied, based on which a Social Enterprise organisation was selected using a set of criteria. Data was collected from the SE using the semi-structured interview technique. The data was analysed following the interpretive approach, which was guided using the Technology Acceptance Model (TAM) as a theoretical lens.

LITERATURE REVIEW

Many communities face socioeconomic challenges such as poverty, inequality, and unemployment (Adenke, 2021; Ngubane et al., 2023). Government agencies cannot always address these socioeconomic challenges; thus, living conditions in many communities remain unchanged (Bazoobandi, 2020; Saka, 2024). These demands and challenges have given rise to organisations aiming to address these socioeconomic challenges within their communities. Non-profit organisations (NPOs) and non-government organisations (NGOs) continue to focus on providing the necessary services (Cortis, 2017). Social enterprises (SE) are also among these organisations that seek to make a societal impact.

Social Enterprises (SE) are organisations that employ commercial practices while focusing on making an environmental and societal impact (Ureche, 2023). SE differs from traditional NGOs and NPOs because they drive to be financially viable while supporting their social goals (Jayawardhana et al., 2022). What distinguishes SE from commercial enterprises is their prioritisation of social value creation over economic value creation (Bansal et al., 2023). SE focuses on providing services in social care and agriculture (Halsall et al., 2022; Park & Park, 2024). Laha et al. (2024) highlighted how SE supports smallholder organic farmers to further sustainable agriculture. Maksum et al. (2020) and Castro & Vanclay (2020) explain the impact of SE on small and medium enterprise empowerment and sustainable rural development.

Community development and socioeconomic improvements have been the focus of both government and civic organisations. SE has been the backbone of socioeconomic change in many communities over the last two decades (Suriyankietkaew et al.,2022). The same sentiments are also shared by Bozhikin et al. (2019), who recognise SE's role in achieving sustainable development. The social mission and market-oriented approach of SEs have placed them at the intersection between civil society, government, and the marketplace (Choi & Park, 2024). SE has also become an essential social partner to governments who rely on them to deliver on many of the UN's SDGs by 2030 (Esua & Tengeh, 2022). Many studies have highlighted the importance of SE within community development (Chundu et al., 2022). For example, Kajiita (2022) highlights SE's role in community development in a South

African context. This study reflects how the operations of SE facilitated job creation, reduction of inequality, and social inclusion.

While aiming to be impactful, many SEs still face challenges that could lead to them being unable to address socioeconomic challenges and even closing (Esua & Tengeh, 2022). The notable challenges that weaken SE interventions to address social ills in communities include a lack of funding, a lack of qualified employees, and a lack of support from the government (Dzomonda, 2021). Another challenge is balancing being socially responsible and wanting to be financially viable. Hynes (2009) believes that where social values are dominant, adopting more informal strategies can lead to commercial neglect, which could make the SE less financially viable. Growing the organisation in terms of quantity and quality becomes a challenge if the balance is not kept between being socially responsible while employing business strategies (Verver et al., 2024).

The term "community" is widely used within different settings. Community is commonly used to denote a group of people and where they are physically located (Han et al., 2016). Although a distinction can be made between a community that refers to locality (geographical communities) and a community that refers to a group of interest (community of practice), the meaning is changing to be more relationship-specific (Lo et al., 2015). A community of practice refers to a group of people identified by their shared interest and commitment which is not limited to a group within the same location (Hansson & Wihlborg, 2016).

TECHNOLOGY ACCEPTANCE MODEL

Based on the objectives of this study, as presented in section 1 above, the Technology Acceptance Model (TAM) was used to underpin this research. TAM focuses on how technology acceptance affects individuals and groups (Guner & Acarturk, 2018). Using the two main determinants, namely perceived ease of use and perceived usefulness, TAM has been widely used to predict ICT adoption in many areas (Teeroovengadum et al., 2017). It is also noted that TAM has frequently been used in investigating users' acceptance or rejection of information technology systems (Granic & Marangunic, 2015).

Figure 1. Technology acceptance model

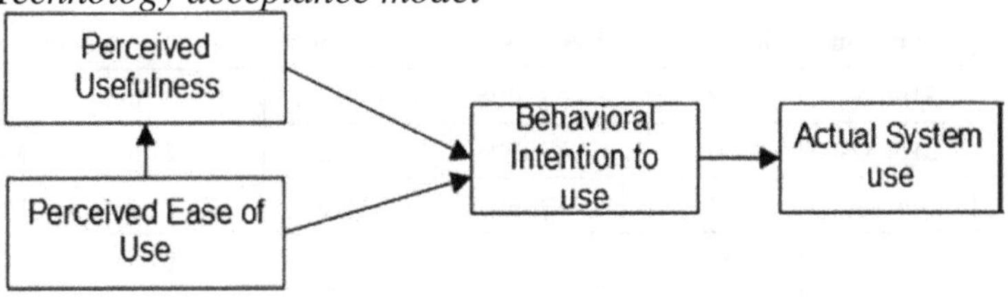

(Davis, 1989)

As an information systems theory, TAM models the way users accept technology and how they make use of that technology. TAM key constructs are shown in Figure 1, and they include *perceived usefulness (PU), perceived ease of use* (PEOU), *behavioural intention* (BI) and *actual usage* (AU). Alharbi and Drew (2014) explain the relationships between and effects of each of these constructs upon each other. Here, they explain that PU and PEOU have an impact on BI; and PEOU has a direct impact on PU.

RESEARCH METHODOLOGY

Semi-structured interviews were conducted with 25 participants: 15 and 10 from the SE and community, respectively. The interviews were stopped at a point of saturation. As shown in Table 1, the participants were assigned pseudonyms and included users, managers, project coordinators, IT specialists, fieldworkers, and community members. The interview data were analysed using thematic analysis.

Table 1. List of participant interviews

Interview#	Duration	RespID	PseudoName	Gender	Designation
1	22m 22s	C101	ACSE01	Male	Project Coordinator
2	30m 43s	C102	ACSE02	Female	Administrator / Manager
3	23m 7s	C103	ACSE03	Female	IT Specialist / Manager
4	35m 15s	C104	ACSE04	Male	Project Coordinator
5	14m 21s	C105	ACSE05	Male	IT Specialist
6	38m 5s	C201	WGSE01	Male	Fieldworker / User
7	40m 28s	C202	WGSE02	Female	Field Worker / User
8	57m 15s	C203	WGSE03	Female	Field Worker / User
9	4m 41s	C204	WGSE04	Male	Community Member

continued on following page

Table 1. Continued

Interview#	Duration	RespID	PseudoName	Gender	Designation
10	31m 19s	C205	WGSE05	Female	AdministratorUser
11	31m 52s	C206	WGSE06	Female	Community Member
12	9m 31 s	COM07	WGSE07	Male	Community Member
13	8m 04 s	COM08	WGSE08	Male	Community Member
14	4m 46 s	COM09	WGSE09	Female	Community Member
15	6m 06 s	COM10	WGSE10	Female	Community Member
16	13m 36s	COM11	WGSE11	Male	Community Member
17	15m 06s	COM12	WGSE12	Female	Community Member / User
18	9m 07s	COM13	WGSE13	Male	Community Member / User
19	9m 15s	COM14	WGSE14	Female	Field Worker / User
20	10 m 00s	COM15	WGSE15	Male	Community Member
21	30 m 42	C216	WGSE16	Male	Project Coordinator
22	58m 47s	C217	WGSE17	Female	Manager
23	37m 54s	C218	WGSE18	Male	Field Worker
24	27m 13s	C219	WGSE19	Female	Administrator
25	21m 25s	C220	WGSE20	Female	Fieldworker / User

Thematic analysis is used in qualitative research to search for themes and patterns within the collected qualitative data (Naeem et al., 2023). The thematic technique is used to systematically for analysing textual data to uncover themes. The identified themes describe the social realities listed in the qualitative data and, in this way, organise related ideas into groups (Vaismoradi et al., 2016). The thematic analysis allowed the researcher to understand the underlying meanings and perspectives shared by participants. Through subjective reasoning and an interpretive process, thematic technique for analysis helped develop themes (Terry et al., 2017). TAM was used as a lens to guide thematic technique in the analysis of the data. In employing TAM, the main tenets of the theory, namely perceived usefulness (PU), perceived ease of usefulness (PEOU), behavioural intention (BI), and actual use (AU), as shown in Figure 1, were followed.

The data were coded for analysis purposes, including ease of readability and clarifications. Each interview with a participant formed a document. Each document is assigned a code name to avoid disclosure of participants' identities. A format was adopted and used to reference the text from the data. For the SE, an example of the referencing format is ACSE01,12:232. For the community, COM01,12,232 is an example of the referencing format. This represents the following:

- ACSE refers to the name of the Social Enterprise (e.g. Assist Community Social Enterprise)
- COM refers to the community that receives services from the SE,
- 01 refers to the number allocated to the participant at the organization or community,
- 12 refers to the page number in the data document which is the transcribed interviews.
- 232 refers to the line number in the data document.

ANALYSIS OF THE DATA

Perceived Usefulness

In Tam, perceived usefulness (PU) is the degree to which a person believes that the technology can be useful to help accomplish a certain task (Davis, 1989). At ACSE, mobile phones were perceived as useful even before they were used to serve the community. One of the participants highlights the importance of using mobile phones to share information as follows:

> *"We share information via email. If the Mayor resigns on Thursday, I will send that via email. If there is a new policy or document where I think others can make submissions, this is emailed or sent via WhatsApp, a call, or text. This information is important for our partners" (ACSE01,4,183).*

The perception is influenced by various factors from both technical (technology) and nontechnical perspectives. From a technical perspective, perceived usefulness is influenced by both the physical aspects of a mobile device and the device's software features. For example, older people are used to the older type of mobile phones. Older mobile devices are more straightforward, and navigating to the functionalities makes them useful. One participant noted that some community members find older mobile phones useful for what they want to accomplish.

> *"We have also had some projects where they provide farmers with mobile phones, which has also been very helpful because not all the farmers got smartphones. Accessibility to adequate devices is also important. Some people do have smart-phones, but the older versions do not work as well" (WGSE,17,1065).*

From a non-technical perspective, people find mobile devices useful because of the ease they bring to their daily tasks. Both the community and those who provide a service communicate with each other by sending SMSes. Farmers can send an SMS with a list of their produce to retailers. It also establishes relationships between the farmers as food producers and retailers as distributors. This reality is demonstrated in the input from one of the participants:

"We also engage with farmers through SMS. We also have an SMS database, and we use an SMS portal to distribute bulk SMSs when needed" (WGSE,01,875).

Technical and non-technical factors influence people's perception of the usefulness of technology because they relate to the experience a user might have with the particular technology. A technical factor like the user interface of an application or the available options in the application might influence a person's perception of the usefulness of the application. A non-technical factor like software training or user support on the application could also affect how people perceive a system to be useful or not. This is still an assumption because a particular technical or non-technical factor might not influence some people.

From a technical standpoint, features and functions embedded in mobile devices are acclaimed to be useful for the services the SE provides to society. For example, using an application called Kobo helps the SE to collect information about the community's farming activities. *Kobo is an internationally developed open-source software. It focuses on humanitarian crisis management, such as floods, fire disasters and food shortages.* According to one of the participants:

"The organisation needs to coordinate resources for humanitarian purposes if there's a tsunami. It is available for anybody to use, and our team uses it extensively when they are out in the field. They can collect data without the need for connectivity" (WGSE17,21-22,972).

Another example of the usefulness of a technical feature involves communication. A group of people is formed. Within the group, the WhatsApp application is used to disseminate information for important events such as training. Additionally, the application is important in two ways. First, it allows sending bulk messages. Secondly, it is cost-effective for both the senders (service providers) and recipients. Thus, all recipients receive useful information partaking to your services.

"If people come here for the 3-day basic training course, they will leave their cell numbers with us, and we will create a WhatsApp group for that group of attendees. We would also create their WhatsApp groups. Every group that comes here also creates its own WhatsApp group, where they would share information" (WGSE18,31,1355).

Community members like-wise perceive technical features like WhatsApp messaging to be useful. Information about upcoming training does reach community members through those who have attended training and, in turn, spread the message by 'word of mouth' to others in the community. These 'words of mouth' make other community members think that the use of mobile devices and WhatsApp applications will be useful to them in the context of accessing vital information about SE services.

"When we announce the next training course to these groups, they will inform their neighbours or friends of the training course that will take place and that

it would be interesting for them to attend. That is how the information about the training is shared" (WGSE18,31,1359).

However, the WhatsApp application cannot be downloaded or used with all types of mobile devices (phones). Currently, the application can only be used with smartphones. Due to its perceived usefulness, some community members who are not interested or cannot avoid a mobile device make a plan to acquire one. This adds a financial burden to some members of the community.

From a non-technical perspective, both service providers (SE) and some community members perceive mobile device use as useful. The SE perception was that it fosters inclusion by allowing them to connect with more community with more community members. However, the SE was not aware of the members of the community's access to mobile devices with WhatsApp applications. Also, the SE does lack evidence of community members who are literate enough to read and write using mobile devices. Thus, makes the choice of language or translator important. Therefore, language impacts the usefulness of mobile technology in providing a service to the community. One of the participants shares their view as follows:

"..it's a very active WhatsApp group where they share. We don't curate that in any way. They share posts, and it becomes like a community sharing ideas and tips around farming" (WGSE17,17,789).

Also, training positively impacts the community and the perceived usefulness of mobile devices. Community members would not have known about the training offered by the SE. The announced training also allowed home gardeners to improve their gardening skills. However, the factors that primarily influence the perceived usefulness of mobile devices are language and access to the devices. Some community members miss out on some services because of either of these factors, as explained above.

Perceived Ease of Use (PEOU)

The perceived ease of use has to do with whether someone believes that using technology for some activity is easy to use for that purpose (Davis, 1989). Technical or non-technical functions or needs often influence users' perceptions of whether a technology is easy to use. Users would regard a system (technology) as easy to use if the features are easily accessible and allow the user to perform the required task. This is an assumption if the technology has not been used or tried by the user. Thus, in the context of TAM, PEOU is about people perceiving whether a technology is easy to use or not even before using the system. This perception could be influenced by system features that have been communicated to them.

PEOU can be observed in the aspect of communication within SE organisations. Communication at ACSE occurs mostly by sending and receiving emails, which is important for the organisation's operations. For staff members, it is thus important to always check their emails for critical information and respond promptly. Being able to access emails and other communication channels using their smartphones becomes an important capability for work efficiency. However, some people who have not used mobile phones for email purposes do not perceive it to be of ease of use. One of the participants pointed out as follows:

"I receive information that is communicated to me via emails, which I access through my cellular phone when I am in the field" (ACSE,01,173).

The ability to easily navigate to mobile device features creates a perception that the system is easy to use. If a person perceives the use of certain device features as easy to use, it creates a sense that their work-related tasks can be accomplished with ease. If this is the case with email features being easily assessable, it could lead to improved work performance as far as tasks that involve sending and receiving emails.

The organisation's fieldworkers also express their dependency on mobile phones and the features that allow them to capture important data while doing fieldwork (such as checking if farmers need help with their gardens). Tasks like capturing pictures while doing fieldwork are made easy with smartphones and the necessary software that allows them to edit and store images for reporting purposes. This was a perception that smartphones do offer camera features that would enhance the ability to capture pictures and thus help perform critical work-related functions. One participant explained as follows:

"I use my mobile phone to capture pictures, and recordings and share this with community leaders in various WhatsApp groups" (ACSE,01,165)

Not having access to mobile phone features to take pictures and store them, such as taking images makes the task of providing a service to farmers and reporting on their progress very difficult. This was an assumption that such a technology could ease farmers' tasks. To assist their workers, WGSE has provided their staff with the necessary devices and capabilities to provide a service to the community and report on their activities. The provision of the devices and the features have pointed out the necessity of easy-to-use technology for accomplishing work-related tasks, which was also a perception. This is only a perception because some might have other ways to accomplish a task that might not require a technological device. One of the participants briefly explained:

"On mobile phones - all my staff have been provided with mobile phones to have and download the Kobo app. We have been using that for the last two years" (WGSE,17,1060).

Farmers and community members also find it difficult to provide images of their crops for either requiring assistance from the SE or selling their crops. This is caused by two things. Firstly, some farmers perceived that mobile devices cannot be used for the dissemination of such information. The second aspect is that those who perceived the capability of mobile devices had the type of devices that did not have the required features. To compensate for this, they send their produce list using the short message service (SMS) function. For many of the farmers, this is a preferred way of making contact with retailers and other buyers of their crops. The reasons for this choice are that they do not have smartphones with WhatsApp capabilities and also because they find older devices easy to use. This was an assumption because the view was not tested. The assumption could be attributed to a lack of knowledge about the devices. According to one of the participants:

"Some farmers prefer using SMS services for communication. The SMSes are mainly for us to distribute information" (WGSE,17,887).

Despite the challenges that both SE and community members experience, they still find a way of making their current mobile device features work in their favour. This was not the case for all members because some continued to perceive the use of mobile devices for such tasks was not as easy as claimed. This could be attributed to a lack of knowledge (or illiteracy) about the devices. Also, some people seem to be intimidated by the sophistication of the technological devices. A factor that stands out when it comes to providing a service to the community is the ability to communicate and do so using the necessary technology.

Notwithstanding this vital need for communication, there were positive and negative perceptions about using technology. Both service providers and community members improvise using what they have at their disposal. Those who do not find it easy to use their mobile devices optimally miss out on important information being shared by the SE as a service provider.

The implication for missing out on important information is that community members might not find the help they need with the gardening projects. Although information about training and gardening tips is shared via WhatsApp, those who perceive the system as not easy to use will not have access to this information. As a result, they lack the necessary knowledge for gardening, leading to them not growing the crops they expect. Furthermore, food security and lack of nutrition remain problems in the community. Community gardeners hoping to supplement their income through the sale of their produce would also be the consequence of not being able to access information about gardening being unable to access gardening information.

Behavioural Intention

In TAM, behavioural intention (BI) is the degree to which a person is ready to carry out a particular behavior (Alambaigi & Ahangari, 2016). When individuals or groups of people are presented with new technology, they reach a point where they develop an intention to use or not to use the technology. Such a point of intentionality (BI) is influenced by certain factors. Some of the factors could be access, know-how (knowledge), affordability or both. Additionally, affordability is influenced by the scale of preference. One of the participants briefly explained as follows:

"I think I will google for information, but right now I do not have a mobile phone. When I have it, I will search and access the information via Google" (COM,12,265).

From an organisation and a community perspective, behavioural intentions are influenced by both technical and non-technical factors. From a community perspective, technical factors include the physical aspects of a mobile phone, which some community members were not accustomed to. As such, they lacked knowledge of the technology. Consequently, these groups of community members show no intention to use WhatsApp applications for communication purposes, whether receiving or sending messages (information). This is attributable to being accustomed to the older model mobile phones, which did not have or could not use WhatsApp applications. They, therefore, prefer to receive and send messages using the SMS application. As one of the participants stated:

"My mobile phone cannot use WhatsApp because it is not a smartphone. " (COM, 11, 187).

Although, in many instances, older people received services from SE, their knowledge of the technical aspects of mobile phones was limited. However, this group of older people in the community intended to use mobile phones. This is evident as they continued to request help from younger family members who were more knowledgeable about the use of smartphones. The community's interest in showing intention to use the technology is because of the service they receive from SE, like gardening tips, information about upcoming training and information on how they can sell their produce. One of the community members shared their experience as follows:

Less than half of our people are not that comfortable to use with WhatsApp. I'd say it might be 30% of people. They get help from either another farmer or a younger family member. (WGSE,17,821)

From the SE perspective, employees of the organisation showed an intention to use mobile phones to share their services and communicate with community members. This is attributed to the capability of mobile technology, which enabled them to perform their work-related functions better. Some of the functions include providing training to the community, sending information about upcoming training, and reporting on fieldwork activities to the stakeholders (community members and SE employees). The use of mobile technology made these tasks easier to provide service to the community. There is a positive intention to use technology because of the benefits that mobile technology features provide in providing services to community members (such as providing training and doing follow-ups with community gardens). One participant expressed some of the benefits as follows:

"We have horizontal learning platforms where we bring organisations together, and we encourage the participants of the year-long program to share learning experiences via WhatsApp group to consolidate and have access. So we found that using Whatsapp and SMS is fairly useful" (ACSE,03,571).

Other technical factors affecting both community members and staff of SE organisations in providing and receiving services are computing network infrastructure and continued occurrences of electricity load-shedding. In South Africa, Load-shedding means the scheduled interruption of electricity supply by the national power utility, Eskom. Power outages occur across different areas as determined by a predefined schedule during load-shedding. This prevents the demand for electricity from exceeding the available supply because of reduced generation capacity. (Walsh et al., 2021). These technical factors affect network coverage. The intention to make use of technology for communication purposes is influenced by poor mobile network coverage. Consequently, there were times when staff members of SE did not have mobile network coverage and could not receive messages, some of which were important information (updates). This hampered the organisation's operations.

Another implication of load-shedding was that some employees of the SE could not be reached through telephones. This happened because cellular phone towers were switched off during load-shedding, which delayed reports (documentation) and reporting about events. The staff would improvise by using their phones' offline features and upload reports or send messages when mobile coverage is restored. An employee explained as follows:

"When there are power outages, the cell phone towers in the leafy suburbs are stronger and last longer than those in the townships where there are many more constraints on the cellphone towers. The power outages are noticeable when I cannot get hold of team members" (WGSE,17,1008).

Some of the non-technical factors influencing behavioural intentions from a community perspective include affordability and accessibility. Affordability, in this case, is a monetary implication. Some farmers and community members linked to SE organisations could not afford smartphones with the latest communication features. The community was categorised as a low-income earner. This could be ascribed to why smartphone was not on top in the order of priority. Many community members who received services from SE were older people who might be dependable on social security grants and, therefore, could not afford a smartphone.

Affordability refers to access to mobile devices and platforms where communication can be shared and received. For instance, many families in the community being served had no laptop (or desktop computer) where they could use email services and internet services to receive or search for important information about gardening. Although the community showed an intention to use the services of SE, not having access to the technology hindered them from benefiting from the available information related to training, gardening, and the resale of garden produce.

The challenges of affordability led some community members to improvise for themselves. Thus, some community members sourced information about gardening and other services from their local library. One participant shared his experience of self-improvisation as follows:

> *"I don't have a problem finding information because we have the library, and I am using it, which helps me a lot. I don't have a problem now because I can continue learning more using the library. There is more information at the library" (COM,11,127).*

The two main tenets of TAM, namely Perceive Usefulness (PU) and Perceive ease of use (PEOU), impact a person's readiness to use a particular technology. These two perceptions influence a person or organisation's readiness or willingness to use technology for activities that could help them in their daily tasks (Almaiah, 2022). The readiness to use or not to use technology is aligned with the intended outcome of a task, and should the perceived PU and PEOU be favourable, a person would develop an intention to use it.

The intention is revealed when a person shows interest in knowing more about the available technology or system. This seems to follow an order. For example, community members would first enquire about the services provided by the organisation (people speaking about the service provided to the community). Secondly, when the community members have attended training sessions, they would give their mobile numbers to receive further communication (information being shared using WhatsApp application). SE's challenge is that some community members do not engage on the platforms they enrol themselves on. When asked about whether people would make use of help offered to them, the response was as follows:

> *"No, they don't do that. I'm not sure if they were doing it before. I later realised that they were doing that. We have a lot of WhatsApp groups. We encourage the farmers to post their challenges, but they don't" (WGSE, 18, 1192).*

There might be a gap between showing intention to actual improvisation by the SE or self-improvisation by community members in using mobile technology to provide or receive services. Both community members and staff of SE have shown positive intentions to use WhatsApp as a communication channel for receiving and distributing information. The participants' responses indicated they perceived the WhatsApp application as useful and easy to use, even though some community members had mobile phones that were incompatible with the application. This means that both community members and employees of the SE were ready to use the platform should they have the appropriate device (smartphone).

Actual Use

In TAM, as explained by Mortano et al. (2020), there is a relationship between intention to use and actual use as behavioural intention influences actual use. Also, PU and PEOU are the base determinants influencing behavioural intention and leading to actual usage behaviour (Iyamu, 2021). This means that people's perception of technology usage leads them to form a behavioural intention, which in turn, leads to them either using or not using the technology.

The staff members of ACSE felt positive about accessing email services on their mobile phones while being away from work premises. They saw that the need for them to stay informed about what is happening in the organisation and keep up to date about their duties is greatly assisted by features provided through mobile applications. Features such as email service and messaging services were perceived as useful which eventually led them to use the service provided by the technology. One of the participants expressed how they make use of email services for work-related activities:

"I receive information that is communicated to me via emails, which I access through my cellphone when I am in the field. This includes work emails and other emails" (ACSE,01,173).

Several technical and non-technical factors influenced behavioural intention and led to actual usage. As stated by Bagozzi (2007), between the intention to act and the action, considerations take place, which include several steps that could impede on or further strengthen the actual use of the technology. In the case of WGSE, workers were expected to use technology for their daily routines in recording data on how farmers and community gardens are doing. The company suggested that they use a mobile application called Kobo, which will allow them to fulfil their tasks of recording data during on-site visits.

" Besides using WhatsApp, there is another tool that we use which is called Kobo Collect which fieldworkers use to collect data from farmers while doing site visits" (WGSE,01,968).

One technical factor in this case is the features provided by the mobile application called Kobo which allows them to record data while being on their site visits. The application has several forms which allow the workers to capture data related to farmers and their progress as well as the state of the actual community garden. The main objective of capturing data and reporting on farmers and their activities (as well as the activities of the fieldworkers themselves) is greatly assisted by the mobile application usage as determined by the company. Another technical factor is the application's ability to record data even while not having an internet connection. One of the employees explained how the technology assists them to perform their tasks, as follows:

"When you are out in the field, you fill in the form and when you're back in the office (where there is data connectivity) you upload it to the hard drive for storage. Kobo then collates the information on the back end" (WGSE,01,982).

Although technology such as Kobo enables employees to perform their tasks, at the same time, it disrupts work-related activities. For example, while on fieldwork, employees hardly get an Internet connection. As a result, the employees travel back to the office premises to complete their various tasks. This is prohibitive from both cost and time perspectives to the WGSE employees and farmers that the services are improvised.

Non-technical features which led to the actual usage of mobile phones, to improvise services relate to the company's decision to use a particular mobile application or software to accomplish work-related tasks. In the case of WGSE, the employees adopted and used WhatsApp application for sharing information and announcements to the stakeholders. Staff are required to use WhatsApp and are also provided with phones to do so. Preference is a non-technical factor which led to actual use and is based on WGSE's perceived usefulness of the WhatsApp application as a messaging service. According to one of the employees who experienced it:

"We use our WhatsApp groups a lot. That is where we would send a WhatsApp flyer. We don't print anything. It will just be a photograph with the date and time and the training that's happening and that we will distribute via the various WhatsApp groups" (WGSE,01,840).

The actual usage of the WhatsApp application as a messaging service had consequences for both the SE who provided the service and the community who received the services. In WGSE improvising services, the organisation sent out information to those in their database. This includes those who attended their workshops and contact details were gathered from them. Some of the community members did not have WhatsApp-enabled phones and the SE, therefore, reverted to sending out bulk SMSes in addition to the WhatsApp messages. The SE has thus adopted another platform, called SMS Portal, for sending out SMSes to communicate important information to the community farmers. One of the participants explained as follows:

"We also engage with farmers through SMS. We also have an SMS database, and we use an SMS portal to distribute bulk SMSs when needed. Last year we had our 40th anniversary and we had a huge pharma festival with over 1200 people attending" (WGSE,01,875).

For the community, the use of multiple platforms means they receive service-related information sent by WGSE regardless of the type of mobile device they have. This translates to the actual usage of technology because the farmers and home garden owners (recipients) could access the service improved, using their mobile devices. Further to this, the recipients participated by either responding to the messages or forwarding them to other stakeholders (friends and family members). Thus, community members benefited from information about community gardening that was sent to as part of services. According to one of the beneficiaries:

> *"We have two big groups. The Khayelitsha farmer's WhatsApp group and then the Nyanga Home Gardens WhatsApp group as well as for Nyanga. People are added to these groups and they are very active, always showing what they are doing, and how they're doing it, with photographs, advice, and all kinds of things" (WGSE,01,784).*

Benefits derived from the engagement with the information using the messaging service include quality garden produce, healthy meals for families and the ability to sell accessible produce to retailers. Community farmers also had employment opportunities through the sale of produce. This adds to income generation for the low-income earners in the communities. These are some of the benefits that have shown how the actual use of technology contributes to social development through improvised services.

DISCUSSION OF FINDINGS

Subjective reasoning is employed in the interpretation of the findings. Primarily, the subject approach was selected for three reasons. First, it is a qualitative study allowing for an interpretive approach. Secondly, it enables the researcher to construct meanings socially (Maines, 2000). Thirdly, with the approach, new insights can emerge and be induced into the phenomenon being studied. Also, subjectivity leans toward interpretivism because people see things differently within their lived experiences (Iyamu, 2020).

Thus, the findings were viewed from different consequential and implicative standpoints, and meanings were constructed. In constructing the meanings, technical and non-technical perspectives were the focus, on how services were improvised to the communities using mobile technologies. This was geared towards two: to gain a deeper understanding of the contribution of SE to communities and for a better comprehension of using mobile devices, to facilitate and enable the ease of access to information and service distribution. Seven impact factors were highlighted in the analysis. The factors were categorised into technical and non-technical factors that influenced how SE and community members use technology to share important information related to service delivery. The technical factors are connectivity, network infrastructure, and capabilities. Non-technical factors include affordability (cost-effectiveness), accessibility, contextualisation, language translation, and knowledgeability. The technical and non-technical factors depend on each other and are inseparable in their use to improvise services to the community.

Connectivity

Connectivity has been used as a metaphor to study interactions enabled by digital technologies for many years (Aljabr, Petrakaki & Chamakiotis, 2024; Kolb, Collins & Lind, 2008). In the context of this study, connectivity refers to the ability to connect entities, humans and services using technology solutions such as mobile devices to share and access information. This means that connectivity can be via mobile data or Wi-Fi. SE improvise service delivery by sharing important information using technology solutions including WhatsApp, short message services (SMS) and electronic mail (email) applications. Connectivity thus means that SE who provide a service to the community can connect via a service provider to distribute information to the community.

Connectivity happens using mobile technology, which plays an important role when it comes to information sharing. According to Sonnad et al. (2022), organisations employ electronic systems to connect and interact with other systems. Most community members have access to a mobile device, which allows them to benefit from the services provided by SE. Those who connect to the services can share the information with others in their community either through word of mouth or by passing on WhatsApp messages. The improvisation of service using mobile technology by SE and community members reaches many in the community, People who would not have known about the services now also have access to information as it is being passed on by those who received first-hand information (through attending training).

Network Infrastructure

Much emphasis is placed on the impact of telecommunication network infrastructure towards digital transformation and quality of services, in developing countries. The cost and quality of services provided to mobile users by internet service providers (ISP) are dependent on proper network infrastructure, which includes fibre optic cables, data centres and mobile phone towers (Inusah et al., 2024; Houngbonon et al., 2023).

Within the context of this study, network infrastructure means the systems and physical components that enable connectivity between computers and mobile devices for communication and information-sharing purposes. Network infrastructure has an impact on the quality of communication and information distribution between SE and community members who rely on mobile connectivity to access the distributed information. Network downtime is often the result of network infrastructure components that are failing or stolen such as mobile phone tower batteries. Network downtime refers to the interruption of access to systems, services, or applications due to hardware failure or power outage (Dzedzy & Ayyub, 2024).

When adequate Network infrastructure is not in place, which is sometimes the case within low-income areas, people experience poor internet connectivity, as empirically revealed in this study. Poor internet or mobile connectivity negatively impacts the services provided by SE to the communities because they use mobile technology. Sometimes the cellular phone towers are affected by electricity interruption and internet, or mobile connectivity is interrupted. This has an impact on the availability of information as well as the inability of fieldworkers to share or store critical information online.

Capabilities

Regarding sharing information and providing learning opportunities through training events, mobile technology is regarded as a crucial tool in providing quality services (KR et al., 2024). The features and capabilities that mobile technology, such as smartphones, provide can potentially increase productivity in rural and urban farming communities (Tulinayo et al., 2022). Features and capabilities within messaging applications such as WhatsApp and text readers allow for quality communication between service providers and community members and between community members. The technical factor of capabilities is important in this study as it relates to what people (service providers and recipients) can do using their mobile devices, which enhances their communication and economic status.

As revealed in the study, SE often would like to improvise their services using different platforms, including face-to-face training sessions, and providing one-on-one assistance to farming communities. An extension to these services includes mobile devices, which the community can access additional resources to help them in their farming practices. It thus becomes crucial that the features and capabilities exist within the suggested mobile applications and platforms to help community members continue their development.

The enabling capabilities and features within mobile technology can result in quality communication between SEs and the communities they are serving. Sharma et al. (2021) discuss the importance of mobile capabilities in providing higher data rates for improved communication. The point of higher data rates for improved communication is also emphasised by Agrawal et al. (2015) when discussing how wireless network technologies have evolved from first-generation (1G) to fifth generation (5G) technologies. Service providers and recipients benefit when information can be accessed seamlessly using enabling capabilities These benefits include greater participation in creating new content and information (Emeana et al., 2020). The community can use social media platforms to share their experience and exchange best agricultural practices (e.g. How and where to grow crops and sell produce).

Accessibility

Research done by Cheng et al., (2021); Myovella et al., (2020), and Solomon & van Klyton (2020) shows that there is a strong relationship between access to the Internet and economic development. This relationship is ascribed to the widespread Information and Communication Technologies, devices, and platforms that have created various services, products, and processes that expose people to economic growth opportunities (Myovella et al., 2020).

Accessibility within the context of this study refers to how information and activities are made available, reachable, and usable for those who need to benefit from the available information and services. Emeana et al. (2020) note the need for accessibility which includes access to mobile devices and network coverage which supports the distribution of agricultural information. This means that the information distributed to farmers and community members needs to be accessible so that they can benefit from it. As noted by Al-Sakran and Alsudairi (2021), this accessibility also refers to the platforms where the information is distributed and the format in which it is shared.

Lack of access to advanced technologies such as smartphones coupled with limited internet access are factors that work against accessibility to important information. Mapiye et al. (2023) note these limitations while stressing the need for device capabilities to support information accessibility. Accessibility is also limited by the lack of digital literacy, which relates to the understanding and knowledge to use information presented in multiple formats on an electronic device (Pangrazio et al., 2020). Accessibility in the context of this study also refers to the ability of the community members to navigate to content using their mobile devices (e.g. smartphones). SE should thus ensure that the information and content they share are accessible by targeting different device users.

Contextualisation

The distribution and accessibility of information often need to be tailored to fit within the context or domain within which the users or recipients find themselves (Kaipia et al., 2017). To enhance the relevance of information, much must be understood about the users and the environment they find themselves in. For SE it thus becomes important to know the community they are servicing so that they can provide contextualised and relevant information.

Context is described as the connection of cultural, spatial, and political influences, amongst other factors (De Bruin et al., 2023). SE thus improvises its services by distributing information within the context of what the community needs. Many of the community members have a farming background. This is coupled with their need to be sustainable and use the available land to their advantage, such as growing crops. Information will make sense to them when contextualised around community members' lived experiences. Contextualised information implies that community members get value from the services that are provided to them. The information the community receives leads to productive farming and sustainable living while also addressing malnutrition. The community members become co-produces of knowledge and information because they, understanding the context, share the information with others in similar settings.

Language Translation

Research shows that many factors hinder communities from benefiting from technological interventions to improve livelihood within developing countries (Alao et al., 2021). Low levels of literacy and language barriers are among the hindering factors impeding the use of technologies like the Internet and mobile devices for information sharing. Language translation is therefore important to gain maximum benefit from information distribution. The language used by people within a specific grouping or culture carries meaning that is particular to the cultural setting. Language translation in the context of this study is making sure that the terminology used aligns with people's conceptualized thoughts, feelings, and behaviour as noted by Young & Lecy (2014). In their improvisation of services, SE should thus ensure that the terminology they use is understood by their target audience. The process of translation according to Corina (2021) ensures an accurate rendering of meaning from one language (the source) to another (the target).

The SE that provides services to the farming community needs to ensure that when distributing information, it is understood and contextualised. If language translation does not take place, it can lead to a breakdown in communication-based on cultural or educational grounds. Language translation is thus important to ensure that content is correctly presented and that it becomes useful to those for whom the information is intended. This leads to greater participation and richer content creation by both service providers and the community.

Knowledgeability

For many people and communities, knowledge and skill come through informal learning over many years. Knowledge in turn is defined as having an awareness or familiarity of something (or skills, descriptions, etc) which have been acquired through experience, discovery, or learning (Fidelugwuowo, 2021). This means that, apart from formal learning, people have some knowledge base developed through their daily activities. This provides them with a basis for being able to search for new knowledge. Knowledgeability within the context of this study refers to people's understanding of things and concepts within their living environment, enabling them to engage with content and processes.

For SE the community members need to have some base knowledge and understanding of their environment and the challenges they face. For example, community members are faced with challenges like food security and unemployment. They do things that supplement their income and provision of nutrition. Knowing the challenges they face leads them to look for ways to improve their livelihood. The improvisation of services by SE thus targets community members wishing to learn more about farming, income generation and food security. When the community is knowledgeable, it makes it easy for SE to provide ongoing service to the community. The community becomes appreciative of what they learn through the training provided because they can put the things learned into practice. Enhanced communication based on knowledgeability between SE and the community leads to new knowledge and understanding.

CONCLUSION

This study contributes to the literature by identifying key factors influencing the integration of mobile technology with services of SE to the community, and by demonstrating an understanding of this complex phenomenon. Practically, our findings suggest that SEs need to focus on training and gaining insights from both technical and non-technical factors, to integrate mobile technology with their services. Future research could explore these issues in other cultural contexts or investigate the long-term impacts of these technologies on SE services including policy development.

REFERENCES

Alambaigi, A., & Ahangari, I. (2016). Technology acceptance model (TAM) as a predictor model for explaining agricultural experts' behaviour in acceptance of ICT. [IJAMAD]. *International Journal of Agricultural Management and Development, 6*(2), 235–247.

Alharbi, S., & Drew, S. (2014). Using the Technology Acceptance Model in Understanding Academics '. *Behavioural Intention to Use Learning Management Systems, 5*(1), 143–155.

Almaiah, M. A., Al-Otaibi, S., Lutfi, A., Almomani, O., Awajan, A., Alsaaidah, A., Alrawad, M., & Awad, A. B. (2022). Employing the TAM model to investigate the readiness of M-learning system usage using SEM technique. *Electronics (Basel), 11*(8), 1–14.

Bagozzi, R. P. (2007). The legacy of the technology acceptance model and a proposal for a paradigm shift. *Journal of the Association for Information Systems, 8*(4), 244–254.

Bansal, S., Garg, I., & Vasa, L. (2023). Can social enterprises aid sustainable development? Evidence from multi-stage investigations. *PLoS One, 18*(2), e0281273.

Bazoobandi, S. (2020). The Middle East North Africa Socio-economic Challenges. *The New Regional Order in the Middle East: Changes and Challenges*, 1-25.

Bilbao-Osorio, B., Dutta, S., & Lanvin, B. (2014). The global information technology report 2014: Rewards and risks of big data. *In World Economic Forum*, 1-369.

Bozhikin, I., Macke, J., & da Costa, L. F. (2019). The role of government and key non-state actors in social entrepreneurship: A systematic literature review. *Journal of Cleaner Production, 226*, 730–747.

Castro-Arce, K., & Vanclay, F. (2020). Transformative social innovation for sustainable rural development: An analytical framework to assist community-based initiatives. *Journal of Rural Studies, 74*, 45–54.

Choi, D., & Park, J. (2024). Local government as a catalyst for promoting social enterprise. In *The Third Sector, Social Enterprise and Public Service Delivery* (pp. 33-54). Routledge.

Chundu, M., Masara, E., & Mucheri, T. (2022). Contribution of Social Entrepreneurship to Sustainable Community Development in Zimbabwe. A Case of Virtuous Women Trust Operating in Harare. *Journal of Human Resource and Sustainability Studies*, *10*(3), 380–402.

Cortis, N. (2017). Access to philanthropic and commercial income among nonprofit community service organisations. *Voluntas*, *28*, 798–821.

Davis, F. D. (1989). Perceived usefulness, perceived ease of use, and user acceptance of information technology. *Management Information Systems Quarterly*, •••, 319–340.

Dzomonda, O. (2021). Demystifying the challenges faced by social entrepreneurs in pursuit of their social mission in South Africa. [AEJ]. *Academy of Entrepreneurship Journal*, *27*(4), 1–17.

Granic, A., & Marangunic, N. (2015). Technology acceptance model : A literature review from 1986 to 2013. *Universal Access in the Information Society*, *14*(1), 81–95.

Guner, H., & Acarturk, C. (2018). The use and acceptance of ICT by senior citizens: A comparison of technology acceptance model (TAM) for elderly and young adults. *Universal Access in the Information Society*, *19*(2), 311–330.

Halsall, J. P., Snowden, M., Clegg, P., Mswaka, W., Alderson, M., Hyams-Ssekasi, D., & Winful, E. C. (2022). Social enterprise as a model for change: Mapping a global cross-disciplinary framework. *Entrepreneurship Education*, *5*(4), 425–446.

Han, K., Shih, P. C., Rosson, M. B., & Carroll, J. M. (2016). Understanding local community attachment, engagement and social support networks mediated by mobile technology. *Interacting with Computers*, *28*(3), 220–237.

Hansson, P., & Wihlborg, E. (2016). Development of quality management in education : A comparative case study in the Swedish multi-level governance system. In *The 10th International Multi-Conference on Society, Cybernetics and Informatics*. Orlando, Florida, USA: IMSCI, 43–48.

Hynes, B. (2009). Growing the social enterprise–issues and challenges. *Social Enterprise Journal*, *5*(2), 114–125.

Iyamu, T. (2020). A case for applying Activity Theory in IS research. [IRMJ]. *Information Resources Management Journal*, *33*(1), 1–15.

Iyamu, T. (2021). *Applying theories for information systems research*. Routledge.

Jayawardhana, K., Fernando, I., & Siyambalapitiya, J. (2022). Sustainability in social enterprise research: A systematic literature review. *SAGE Open*, *12*(3), 21582440221123200.

Kajiita, R. M. (2022). Social Enterprises as Drivers of Community Development in South Africa: The Case of Buffalo City Municipality. *Southern African Journal of Social Work & Social Development*, *34*(3).

Laha, A., Koner, N., & Ghosh, S. K. (2024). Assessing the Role of Social Enterprises in Shaping Eco-Social Agriculture.

Lo, C., Chuang, I., Lai, P., Guo, B. & Kuo, Y. (2015). A Community-Based Data Dissemination Scheme in Opportunistic Networks., 4(5), 305–310.

Maines, D. R. (2000). The social construction of meaning. *Contemporary Sociology*, *29*(4), 577–584.

Maksum, I. R., Rahayu, A. Y. S., & Kusumawardhani, D. (2020). A social enterprise approach to empowering micro, small and medium enterprises (SMEs) in Indonesia. *Journal of Open Innovation*, *6*(3), 50.

Ngubane, M. Z., Mndebele, S., & Kaseeram, I. (2023). Economic growth, unemployment and poverty: Linear and non-linear evidence from South Africa. *Heliyon*, *9*(10).

Nxele, L. (2018). Citizens' knowledge and perspectives on social accountability information access and distribution in Grahamstown. *Journal of Public Administration*, *53*(4), 919–930.

Park, S. H., & Park, J. Y. (2024). Exploring the Model of Social Enterprise in Sport: Focused on Organization Form (Type) and Task. *Journal of Industrial Convergence*, *22*(2), 73–83.

Saka, M. (2024). Bridging the divide: Addressing socioeconomic inequality in post-apartheid South Africa within the framework of millennium development goals (2000-2015). *Journal of International Students*, *20*(1), 201–231.

Sofyani, H., Riyadh, H. A., & Fahlevi, H. (2020). Improving service quality, accountability and transparency of local government: The intervening role of information technology governance. *Cogent Business & Management*, *7*(1), 1–21.

Suriyankietkaew, S., Krittayaruangroj, K., & Iamsawan, N. (2022). Sustainable Leadership practices and competencies of SMEs for sustainability and resilience: A community-based social enterprise study. *Sustainability*, *14*(10), 5762.

Tauringana, V. & Afrifa, G.A. (2013). The relative importance of working capital management and its components to SMEs' profitability, 20(3), 453–469.

Teeroovengadum, V., Heeraman, N. & Jugurnath, B. (2017). Examining the antecedents of ICT adoption in education using an Extended Technology Acceptance Model (TAM) Viraiyan Teeroovengadum, Nabeel Heeraman and Bhavish Jugurnath University of Mauritius. *International Journal of Education and Development using ICT*, 13(3), 4–23.

Ureche, A. (2023). The Salience of Social Enterprise: a 'Fictional', Functional Tale of Three Sectors Cooperation. In *Proceedings of the International Conference on Business Excellence* 17(1), 870–881.

Verver, M., Dahles, H., & Soeterbroek, I. (2024). Scaling for social enterprise development: A mixed embeddedness perspective on two Dutch non-profit organisations. *Journal of Social Entrepreneurship*, *15*(2), 659–685.

Walsh, K., Theron, R., & Reeders, C. (2021). Estimating the economic cost of load shedding in South Africa. In *Paper submission to Biennial Conference of the Economic Society of South Africa (ESSA)*, 22(1), 1-22.

Young, D. R., & Lecy, J. D. (2014). Defining the Universe of Social Enterprise: Competing Metaphors. *International Society for Third Sector Research*, *25*, 1307–1332.

Compilation of References

Aaronson, S. A. (2019). Digital trade agreements: What's on the table? *Journal of International Commerce. Economic Policy*, *10*(2), 1950007.

Aaronson, S. A., & Leblond, P. (2018). Mapping the challenges of digital trade governance. *Journal of International Commerce. Economic Policy*, *9*(2), 1850009.

Aavakare, M., & Nikou, S. (2020a). Challenging the Concept of Digital Nativeness. In M. Cacace, R. Halonen, H. Li, T. P. Orrensalo, C. Li, G. Widén, & R. Suomi (Eds.), *Well-Being in the Information Society. 8th International Conference, WIS 2020* (Vol. 1270). Springer. https://doi.org/DOI: 10.1007/978-3-030-57847-3

Aboud, A., Saleh, A., & Eliwa, Y. (2024). Does mandating ESG reporting reduce ESG decoupling? Evidence from the European Union's Directive 2014/95. *Business Strategy and the Environment*, *33*(2), 1305–1320.

Acquisti, A., Taylor, C., & Wagman, L. (2016). The economics of privacy. *Journal of Economic Literature*, *54*(2), 442–492. DOI: 10.1257/jel.54.2.442

Adeusi, N. K. B., Amajuoyi, N. P., & Lucky, N. (2024). Utilizing machine learning to predict employee turnover in high-stress sectors. *International Journal of Management & Entrepreneurship Research*, *6*(5), 1702–1732. DOI: 10.51594/ijmer.v6i5.1143

Agárdi, I., & Alt, M. A. (2022). Do digital natives use mobile payment differently than digital immigrants? A comparative study between generation X and Z. *Electronic Commerce Research*, *24*, 1463–1490. DOI: 10.1007/s10660-022-09537-9

Agrawal, A., Gans, J., & Goldfarb, A. (2019). The Economics of Artificial Intelligence: An Agenda. University of Chicago Press. Available in: https://press.uchicago.edu/ucp/books/book/chicago/E/bo35780726.html

AI-HLEG. (2019) Ethics guidelines for trustworthy AI. High-Level Expert Group on Artificial Intelligence (AI-HLEG). Publication Office of the European Union. 2019. Brussels. ISBN 978-92-76-11994-4. doi:. Available on https://data.europa.eu/doi/10.2759/346720. (Accessed 10 March 2024)DOI: 10.2759/14078

Ajzen, H., & Fishbein, M. (1980). *Understanding attitudes and predicting social behavior*. Prentice-Hal.

Alambaigi, A., & Ahangari, I. (2016). Technology acceptance model (TAM) as a predictor model for explaining agricultural experts' behaviour in acceptance of ICT. [IJAMAD]. *International Journal of Agricultural Management and Development*, *6*(2), 235–247.

Albareda, L., Lozano, J. M., Tencati, A., Midttun, A., & Perrini, F. (2008). The changing role of governments in corporate social responsibility: drivers and responses. *Business ethics: a European review, 17*(4), 347-363. https://doi.org/DOI: 10.1111/j.1467-8608.2008.00539.x

Albareda, L., Lozano, J. M., & Ysa, T. (2007). Public Policies on Corporate Social Responsibility: The Role of Governments in Europe. *Journal of Business Ethics*, *74*, 391–407. DOI: 10.1007/s10551-007-9514-1

Albrecht, S. L., Bakker, A. B., Gruman, J. A., Macey, W. H., & Saks, A. M. (2015). Employee engagement, human resource management practices and competitive advantage: An integrated approach. *Journal of Organizational Effectiveness: People and Performance*, *2*(1), 7–35. DOI: 10.1108/JOEPP-08-2014-0042

Alharbi, S., & Drew, S. (2014). Using the Technology Acceptance Model in Understanding Academics '. *Behavioural Intention to Use Learning Management Systems*, *5*(1), 143–155.

Allen, N. J., & Meyer, J. P. (1990). The measurement and antecedents of affective, continuance and normative commitment to the organization. *Journal of Occupational and Organizational Psychology*, *63*(1), 1–18.

Almaiah, M. A., Al-Otaibi, S., Lutfi, A., Almomani, O., Awajan, A., Alsaaidah, A., Alrawad, M., & Awad, A. B. (2022). Employing the TAM model to investigate the readiness of M-learning system usage using SEM technique. *Electronics (Basel)*, *11*(8), 1–14.

Alowais, S. A., Alghamdi, S. S., Alsuhebany, N., Alqahtani, T., Alshaya, A., Almohareb, S. N., Aldairem, A., Alrashed, M., Saleh, K. B., Badreldin, H. A., Yami, A., Harbi, S. A., & Albekairy, A. M. (2023). Revolutionizing Healthcare: The Role Of Artificial Intelligence In Clinical Practice. *BMC Medical Education*, *23*(1). Advance online publication. DOI: 10.1186/s12909-023-04698-z PMID: 37740191

Alves, J., Lima, T. M., & Gaspar, P. D. (2023). Is Industry 5.0 a Human-Centred Approach? A Systematic Review. *Processes (Basel, Switzerland)*, *11*(1), 193. DOI: 10.3390/pr11010193

Alwin, D. F. (2012). Integrating Varieties of Life Course Concepts. *The Journals of Gerontology: Series B*, *67B*(2), 206–220. DOI: 10.1093/geronb/gbr146

Ananny, M., & Crawford, K. (2018). Seeing without knowing: Limitations of the transparency ideal and its application to algorithmic accountability. New Media & Society, 20(3), 973–989. Available in: https://journals.sagepub.com/doi/10.1177/1461444816676645

Andrejevic, M. (2020). *Automated media*. Routledge.

Angrave, D., Charlwood, A., Kirkpatrick, I., Lawrence, M., & Stuart, M. (2016). HR and analytics: Why HR is set to fail the big data challenge. *Human Resource Management Journal*, *26*(1), 1–11. DOI: 10.1111/1748-8583.12090

Arikan, R. H., & Jiang, C. (2018). An expectancy model of green product consumption and green brand equity. *Back to the Future: Using Marketing Basics to Provide Customer Value: Proceedings of the 2017 Academy of Marketing Science (AMS) Annual Conference*, 685–696.

Aristotle, The Politics. Book I, part II, 1253a27-29. Book VII, part I, 1323a-1324a.

Arner, D. W., Barberis, J., & Buckley, R. P. (2016). The evolution of FinTech: A new post-crisis paradigm? *Georgetown Journal of International Law*, *47*, 1271–1319.

Arthur, P. L., & Nuenen, T. (2019). Travel in the Digital Age. In Das, N., & Youngs, T. (Eds.), *The Cambridge History of Travel Writing* (pp. 504–518). Cambridge University Press.

Ashcroft, B. (2015). Travel and Utopia. In Kuehn, J., & Smethurst, P. (Eds.), *New Directions in Travel Writing Studies* (pp. 249–262). Palgrave Macmillan.

Ates, A., Garengo, P., Cocca, P., & Bititci, U. (2013). The development of SME managerial practice for effective performance management. *Journal of Small Business and Enterprise Development*, *20*(1), 28–54.

Atzori, L., Iera, A., & Morabito, G. (2010). The Internet of things: A survey. *Computer Networks*, *54*(15), 2787–2805. DOI: 10.1016/j.comnet.2010.05.010

AWS. (2024). *Artificial Intelligence and Machine Learning: Now is the Time to Invest in Skilling Your Workforce | AWS Executive Insights*. Amazon Web Services, Inc. https://aws.amazon.com/executive-insights/content/artificial-intelligence-and-machine-learning-now-is-the-time-to-invest-in-skilling-your-workforce/

Ayres, R. U., & Williams, E. (2004). The digital economy: Where do we stand? *Technological Forecasting and Social Change*, *71*(4), 315–339. DOI: 10.1016/j.techfore.2003.11.001

Bagozzi, R. P. (2007). The legacy of the technology acceptance model and a proposal for a paradigm shift. *Journal of the Association for Information Systems*, *8*(4), 244–254.

Baigorri, A. (2008). ¿De la generación del 98 a la Chiki Chiki? *El País*. https://elpais.com/diario/2008/06/08/sociedad/1212876003_850215.html#?prm=copy_link

Baily, M. N., & Lawrence, R. Z. (2001). Do we have a new e-conomy? *The American Economic Review*, *91*(2), 308–312. DOI: 10.1257/aer.91.2.308

Bakker, A. B., & Demerouti, E. (2007). The Job Demands–Resources model: State of the art. *Journal of Managerial Psychology*, *22*(3), 309–328. DOI: 10.1108/02683940710733115

Ballestero Izquierdo, A. (2011). Notas Para Una Ética Social Del Consumo Individual. *Estudios Filosóficos*, *60*(175), 551–559.

Bamberger, K. A., & Mulligan, D. K. (2015). *Privacy on the ground: Driving corporate behavior in the United States and Europe*. MIT Press.

Bamberger, K. A., & Mulligan, D. K. (2019). Privacy on the books and on the ground. *Stanford Law Review*, *71*(2), 247–313.

Bansal, S., Garg, I., & Vasa, L. (2023). Can social enterprises aid sustainable development? Evidence from multi-stage investigations. *PLoS One*, *18*(2), e0281273.

Barocas, S., Hardt, M., & Narayanan, A. (2019). Fairness and Machine Learning: Limitations and Opportunities. Available in: https://fairmlbook.org

Basnet, S. (2024). The Impact of AI-Driven Predictive Analytics on Employee Retention Strategies. *International Journal of Research and Review*, *11*(9), 50–65. DOI: 10.52403/ijrr.20240906

Bauer, J. M., Bohlin, E., Welfens, P. J. J., & Yoo, C. S. (Eds.). (2016). *The network code economy: Digital platforms and the governance of the new economy*. Springer.

Bazoobandi, S. (2020). The Middle East North Africa Socio-economic Challenges. *The New Regional Order in the Middle East: Changes and Challenges*, 1-25.

Beauchamp, T. L., & Childress, J. F. (1998). *Principios de ética biomédica*. Ed. Masson, 1999. Cap. 3.

Becker, G. S. (1964). *Human capital: A theoretical and empirical analysis, with special reference to education*. University of Chicago Press.

Becker, J., & Englisch, J. (2019). The OECD approach to addressing the tax challenges of the digitalisation of the economy. *Intertax*, *47*(5), 415–430.

Beddaa, M., & Bentalha, B. (2025). Optimizing Local Attractiveness Through Territorial Digital Communication. In Sustainable and Intelligent Territorial Marketing and Entrepreneurship (pp. 159-192). IGI Global.

Bekbolatova, M., Mayer, J., Ong, C. W., & Toma, M. (2024). Transformative Potential of AI in Healthcare: Definitions, Applications, and Navigating the Ethical Landscape and Public Perspectives. *Health Care*, *12*(2), 125–125. DOI: 10.3390/healthcare12020125 PMID: 38255014

Belkhir, L., & Elmeligi, A. (2018). Assessing ICT global emissions footprint: Trends to 2040 & recommendations. *Journal of Cleaner Production*, *177*, 448–463.

Benkler, Y., Faris, R., & Roberts, H. (2018). *Network propaganda: Manipulation, disinformation, and radicalization in American politics*. Oxford University Press.

Bennett, S., & Maton, K. (2011). Intellectual field or faith-based religion: Moving on from the idea of "digital natives." *Deconstructing Digital Natives: Young People, Technology, and the New Literacies, January 2011*, 169–185.

Bennett, C. J., & Raab, C. D. (2020). *The governance of privacy: Policy instruments and the public interest in information states*. MIT Press.

Bennett, S., Maton, K., & Kervin, L. (2008). The "digital natives" debate: A critical review of the evidence. *British Journal of Educational Technology*, *39*(5), 775–786. DOI: 10.1111/j.1467-8535.2007.00793.x

Bentalha, B. (2025). A Prospective Analysis for Robotic Mobile Fulfillment Systems: Assessing the Benefits of Automated Logistics. In Digital Transformation and Innovation in Emerging Markets (pp. 251-278). IGI Global.

Bentalha, B., & Alla, L. (2024). Revealing the subtleties: The art of qualitative studies in science and management. In *Applying qualitative research methods to management science* (pp. 1–21). IGI Global.

Biersteker, T. J., & Hall, R. B. (2002). 10 Private authority as global governance. *The emergence of private authority in global governance*, 85, 203.

Bilbao-Osorio, B., Dutta, S., & Lanvin, B. (2014). The global information technology report 2014: Rewards and risks of big data. *In World Economic Forum*, 1-369.

Binns, R. (2018). Fairness in machine learning: Lessons from political philosophy. Proceedings of the 2018 Conference on Fairness, Accountability, and Transparency. Available in: https://proceedings.mlr.press/v81/binns18a.html

Blau, P. M. (1964). *Exchange and power in social life*. Wiley.

Bonifacio, R. A., Baui, A. F., Uy, M. Y. T., Bandojo, A. J., & Etrata, A. (2024). Generation Z's Purchasing Intention of Cruelty-free Cosmetic Products: The Moderating Role of Environmental and Animal Welfare Concerns. *International Business Education Journal, 17*(1), 118–132. DOI: 10.37134/ibej.Vol17.1.10.2024

Bosnjak, M., Ajzen, I., & Schmidt, P. (2020). The Theory of Planned Behavior: Selected Recent Advances and Applications. *Europe's Journal of Psychology, 16*(3 SE-Special Thematic Section), 352–356. https://doi.org/DOI: 10.5964/ejop.v16i3.3107

Boudri, R., Bentalha, B., & Benjelloun, O. (2024). Phygital marketing and the pain of paying: An Amazon Go netnographic case study. In *AI and data engineering solutions for effective marketing* (pp. 348–363). IGI Global.

Bouhtati, N., Alla, L., & Bentalha, B. (2023). Marketing big data analytics and customer relationship management: A fuzzy approach. In *Integrating intelligence and sustainability in supply chains* (pp. 75–86). IGI Global.

Bounfour, A. (2016). *Digital Futures, Digital Transformation: From Lean Production to Acceluction*. Springer International Publishing.

Boyatzis, R. E. (2018). *The competent manager: A model for effective performance*. John Wiley & Sons.

Bozhikin, I., Macke, J., & da Costa, L. F. (2019). The role of government and key non-state actors in social entrepreneurship: A systematic literature review. *Journal of Cleaner Production, 226*, 730–747.

Brammer, S., Millington, A., & Rayton, B. (2007). The contribution of corporate social responsibility to organizational commitment. *International Journal of Human Resource Management, 18*(10), 1701–1719.

Brécard, D., Lucas, S., Pichot, N., & Salladarré, F. (2012). *Consumer Preferences for Eco, Health and Fair Trade Labels. An Application to Seafood Product in France. 10*(1). https://doi.org/doi:10.1515/1542-0485.1360

Brennen, J. S., & Kreiss, D. (2016). Digitalisation. The International Encyclopedia of Communication Theory and Philosophy, 1-11.

Bresnahan, T. F., & Trajtenberg, M. (1995). General purpose technologies: 'Engines of growth'? *Journal of Econometrics, 65*(1), 83–108. DOI: 10.1016/0304-4076(94)01598-T

Bristow, P. (2010). *The digital divide: Is it an age old question?* https://doi.org/DOI: 10.1109/ITICT.2009.5405933

Broby, D. (2022). The use of predictive analytics in finance. *The Journal of Finance and Data Science, 8*(1), 145–161. ScienceDirect. https://doi.org/DOI: 10.1016/j.jfds.2022.05.003

Brown-Crawford, D. (2022). The Effects of Leadership Organizational Culture on Employee Performance Resulting in High Turnover, Low Morale, and Decreased Productivity. *Doctoral Dissertations and Projects*. https://digitalcommons.liberty.edu/doctoral/3676/

Brundtland, G. H. (1987). Our common future - Call for action. *Environmental Conservation, 14*(4). Advance online publication. DOI: 10.1017/s0376892900016805

Brynjolfsson, E., & McAfee, A. (2017). The Second Machine Age: Work, Progress, and Prosperity in a Time of Brilliant Technologies. W. W. Norton & Company. Available in: https://wwnorton.com/books/the-second-machine-age/

Brynjolfsson, E., & Hitt, L. M. (2003). Computing productivity: Firm-level evidence. *The Review of Economics and Statistics, 85*(4), 793–808.

Brynjolfsson, E., & McAfee, A. (2012). *Race against the machine: How the digital revolution is accelerating innovation, driving productivity, and irreversibly transforming employment and the economy*. Brynjolfsson and McAfee.

Buhalis, D. (2020). Technology in tourism-from information communication technologies to eTourism and smart tourism towards ambient intelligence tourism: A perspective article. *Tourism Review, 75*(1), 267–272. DOI: 10.1108/TR-06-2019-0258

Buhalis, D., & Deimezi, O. (2004). E-tourism developments in Greece: Information communication technologies adoption for the strategic management of the Greek tourism industry. *Tourism and Hospitality Research*, *5*(2), 103–130. DOI: 10.1057/palgrave.thr.6040011

Bukht, R., & Heeks, R. (2017). Defining, Conceptualising and Measuring the Digital Economy. *Research.*manchester.ac.uk. https://research.manchester.ac.uk/en/publications/defining-conceptualising-and-measuring-the-digital-economy

Burrell, J. (2016). How the machine 'thinks': Understanding opacity in machine learning algorithms. Big Data & Society, 3(1). Available in: https://journals.sagepub.com/doi/abs/10.1177/2053951715622512?utm_source=chatgpt.com

Caballero, M., & Baigorri, A. (2019). Glocalising the theory of generations: The case of Spain. *Time & Society*, *28*(1), 333–357. DOI: 10.1177/0961463X18783374

Cabeza-Ramírez, L. J., Fuentes-García, F. J., Cano-Vicente, M. C., & González-Mohino, M. (2022). How Generation X and Millennials Perceive Influencers' Recommendations: Perceived Trustworthiness, Product Involvement, and Perceived Risk. In *Journal of Theoretical and Applied Electronic Commerce Research* (Vol. 17, Issue 4, pp. 1431–1449). https://doi.org/DOI: 10.3390/jtaer17040072

Cadwalladr, C., & Graham-Harrison, E. (2018, March 17). Revealed: 50 million Facebook profiles harvested for Cambridge Analytica in major data breach. *The Guardian*. https://www.theguardian.com

Calo, R. (2013). Consumer subject review boards: A thought experiment. *Stanford Law Review Online*, *66*, 97–102.

Cameron, K. S., Dutton, J. E., & Quinn, R. E. (2003). *Positive organizational scholarship: Foundations of a new discipline*. Berrett-Koehler Publishers.

Campbell, T. (2007). The normative grounding of corporate social responsibility: a human rights approach. In D. McBarnet, A. Voiculescu, & T. Campbell (Eds.), *New Corporate Accountability: Corporate Social Responsibility and the Law* (1 ed., pp. 529-564). [18] Cambridge University Press.

Caragliu, A., Del Bo, C., & Nijkamp, P. (2011). Smart cities in Europe. *Journal of Urban Technology*, *18*(2), 65–82. DOI: 10.1080/10630732.2011.601117

Cardillo, A. (2024, March 4). *How Many Companies Use AI? (New Data)*. Exploding Topics. https://explodingtopics.com/blog/companies-using-ai#companies-using-ai-percentage

Carlock, R. S., & Ward, J. L. (2010). *When family businesses are best: The parallel planning process for family harmony and business success*. Palgrave Macmillan.

Carlsson, B. (2004). The Digital Economy: What is new and what is not? *Structural Change and Economic Dynamics, 15*(3), 245–264. DOI: 10.1016/j.strueco.2004.02.001

Carrington, M. J., Neville, B. A., & Whitwell, G. J. (2014). Lost in translation: Exploring the ethical consumer intention–behavior gap. *Journal of Business Research, 67*(1), 2759–2767. https://doi.org/https://doi.org/10.1016/j.jbusres.2012.09.022

Casalegno, C., Candelo, E., & Santoro, G. (2022). Exploring the antecedents of green and sustainable purchase behaviour: A comparison among different generations. *Psychology and Marketing, 39*(5), 1007–1021. DOI: 10.1002/mar.21637

Casino, F., Dasaklis, T. K., & Patsakis, C. (2019). A systematic literature review of blockchain-based applications: Current status, classification and open issues. *Telematics and Informatics, 36*, 55–81.

Castro-Arce, K., & Vanclay, F. (2020). Transformative social innovation for sustainable rural development: An analytical framework to assist community-based initiatives. *Journal of Rural Studies, 74*, 45–54.

Cerrato, D., & Ferrando, T. (2020). The Financialization of Civil Society Activism: Sustainable Finance, Non-Financial Disclosure and the Shrinking Space for Engagement. *Accounting, Economics, and Law : A Convivium, 10*(2), 1–28. DOI: 10.1515/ael-2019-0006

Cha, J.-m., Shin, J., & Yeom, C.-S. (2015). A Review on Applicability of Big Data Technology in Nuclear Power Plant: Focused on O&M Phases. *Transactions of the Korean Nuclear Society Spring Meeting*. https://www.researchgate.net/publication/278329620_A_Review_on_Applicability_of_Big_Data_Technology_in_Nuclear_Power_Plant_Focused_on_OM_Phases

Chaffey, D. (2022). *Digital business and e-commerce management: Strategy, implementation, and practice* (8th ed.). Pearson.

Chancel, L. (2014). Are younger generations higher carbon emitters than their elders?: Inequalities, generations and CO2 emissions in France and in the USA. *Ecological Economics, 100*, 195–207. https://doi.org/https://doi.org/10.1016/j.ecolecon.2014.02.009

Chander, A., & Sun, U. (2019). The romance of cyberlaw in China. *The American Journal of International Law, 113*(3), 519–563.

Chang, C. W., & Chang, S. H. (2023). The Impact of Digital Disruption: Influences of Digital Media and Social Networks on Forming Digital Natives' Attitude. *SAGE Open, 13*(3), 1–10. DOI: 10.1177/21582440231191741

Chen, L., Mislove, A., & Wilson, C. (2021). Personalization and filter bubbles. *Communications of the ACM, 64*(10), 90–98.

Cheong, C. (2023). How to spot a "zillennial" in the wild, according to TikTok. *Business Insider*. https://www.businessinsider.com/spotting-zillennials-millenial-gen-z-tiktok-2023-7

Chesney, R., & Citron, D. (2019). Deepfakes and the new disinformation war. *Foreign Affairs, 98*(1), 147–155.

China (2017) China's State Council Notice on the Issuance of the Next Generation Artificial Intelligence Development Plan. 20 July 2017. Traslation Aavailable on https://digichina.stanford.edu/work/full-translation-chinas-new-generation-artificial-intelligence-development-plan-2017/ Original available on https://www.gov.cn/zhengce/content/2017-07/20/content_5211996.htm (Accessesd 22 March 2025)

China (2021a) China's 14th Five-Year Plan for National Informatization. The Central Commission for Cybersecurity and Informatization. 28 December 2021. Traslation Aavailable on https://digichina.stanford.edu/work/translation-14th-five-year-plan-for-national-informatization-dec-2021/ Original available on https://www.gov.cn/xinwen/2021-12/28/5664873/files/1760823a103e4d75ac681564fe481af4.pdf (Accessesd 22 March 2025)

China (2021b) Ethical Norms for New Generation Artificial Intelligence Released. Traslation of Ethical Norms for New Generation Artificial Intelligence Released. The National New Generation Artificial Intelligence Governance Specialist Committee. Ministry of Science and Technology. Center for Security and Emerging Technology. 21 Octiber 2021. Traslation Aavailable on https://cset.georgetown.edu/publication/ethical-norms-for-new-generation-artificial-intelligence-released/. Original available on https://www.most.gov.cn/kjbgz/202109/t20210926_177063.html (Accessesd 22 March 2025)

China (2022) China's Provisions on the Management of Algorithmic Recommendations in Internet Information Services. 1 April 2022. The Central Commission for Cybersecurity and Informatization. Traslation Aavailable on https://www.chinalawtranslate.com/en/algorithms/ Original available on https://www.gov.cn/zhengce/zhengceku/2022-01/04/content_5666429.htm (Accessesd 22 March 2025)

Cho, A., Byrne, J., & Zoe, P. (2020). Digital civic engagement by young people. In *UNICEF Office of Global Insight and Policy*. https://www.unicef.org/globalinsight/reports/digital-civic-engagement-young-people

Cho, C. H., Laine, M., Roberts, R. W., & Rodrigue, M. (2018). The frontstage and backstage of corporate sustainability reporting: Evidence from the Arctic National Wildlife Refuge Bill. *Journal of Business Ethics*, *152*, 865–886. DOI: 10.1007/s10551-016-3375-4

Choi, D., & Park, J. (2024). Local government as a catalyst for promoting social enterprise. In *The Third Sector, Social Enterprise and Public Service Delivery* (pp. 33-54). Routledge.

Choi, C. H., Kim, T. T., Lee, G., & Lee, S. K. (2014). Testing the stressor-strain-outcome model of customer-related social stressors in predicting emotional exhaustion, customer orientation and service recovery performance. *International Journal of Hospitality Management*, *36*, 272–285. DOI: 10.1016/j.ijhm.2013.10.009

Chowdhury, S., Dey, P., Joel-Edgar, S., Bhattacharya, S., Rodriguez-Espindola, O., Abadie, A., & Truong, L. (2023). Unlocking the Value of Artificial Intelligence in Human Resource Management through AI Capability Framework. *Human Resource Management Review*, *33*(1), 100899. DOI: 10.1016/j.hrmr.2022.100899

Chrisman, J. J., Chua, J. H., De Massis, A., Minola, T., & Vismara, S. (2021). Management processes and strategy execution in family firms: From "what" to "how". *Small Business Economics*, *56*(3), 1085–1122.

Chundu, M., Masara, E., & Mucheri, T. (2022). Contribution of Social Entrepreneurship to Sustainable Community Development in Zimbabwe. A Case of Virtuous Women Trust Operating in Harare. *Journal of Human Resource and Sustainability Studies*, *10*(3), 380–402.

Cockfield, A. J. (2018). The OECD proposal for taxing the digital economy: A critical evaluation. *Canadian Tax Journal*, *66*(4), 859–906.

Cooke, F. L. (2023). Nikolai Rogovsky, Premilla D'Cruz, Kubo, K., Lee, B.-H., Nho, Y., & Noronha, E. (2023). The Human-Centered Approach to Increasing Workplace Productivity. *Proceedings - Academy of Management*, (1). Advance online publication. DOI: 10.5465/amproc.2023.11052symposium

Cortina, A. (2002). Por una ética del consumo:la ciudadanía del consumidor en un mundo global. In *Pensamiento: Vol. 2ª* (pp. 1–119; 265–349). https://ibdigital.uib.es/greenstone/collect/cd2/index/assoc/consumca.dir/consumcat0001.pdf

Cortis, N. (2017). Access to philanthropic and commercial income among nonprofit community service organisations. *Voluntas*, *28*, 798–821.

Couldry, N., & Mejias, U. A. (2019). *The costs of connection: How data is colonizing human life and appropriating it for capitalism*. Stanford University Press.

Crane, A., Matten, D., Glozer, S., & Spence, L. J. (2019). *Business ethics: Managing corporate citizenship and sustainability in the age of globalization*. Oxford university press.

Crawford, K., & Calo, R. (2016). There is a blind spot in AI research. Nature, 538(7625), 311-313. DOI: . Available in: https://www.nature.com/articles/538311aDOI: 10.1038/538311a

Creswell, J. W., & Clark, V. L. P. (2017). *Designing and conducting mixed methods research*. Sage publications.

Cueto Cedillo, C., & De la Cuesta González, M. M. (2023). *La Administración Pública de la responsabilidad social corporativa y la sostenibilidad. Fundamentos, políticas y herramientas de gestión*. Editorial UNED.

Cutler, A. C. (2001). Critical reflections on the Westphalian assumptions of international law and organization: A crisis of legitimacy. *Review of International Studies*, *27*(2), 133–150. DOI: 10.1017/S0260210500001339

Dahlsrud, A. (2008). How corporate social responsibility is defined: An analysis of 37 definitions. *Corporate Social Responsibility and Environmental Management*, *15*(1), 1–13. DOI: 10.1002/csr.132

Danks, D., & London, A. J. (2017). Algorithmic bias in autonomous systems. In *Proceedings of the 26th International Joint Conference on Artificial Intelligence* (pp. 4691–4697). IJCAI.

Darwish, D. (2024). Human-AI Collaboration in Industry 5. *Advances in Computational Intelligence and Robotics Book Series*, 44–70. https://doi.org/DOI: 10.4018/979-8-3693-6806-0.ch003

Dave, D., & Parikh, A. (2022). Preferences of Gen Z for Investing in Socially Accountable Funds. *Journal of Social Commerce*, *2*(4), 154–166.

Davis, F. D. (1989). Perceived usefulness, perceived ease of use, and user acceptance of information technology. *Management Information Systems Quarterly*, •••, 319–340.

De Massis, A., Frattini, F., Kotlar, J., Petruzzelli, A. M., & Wright, M. (2016). Innovation through tradition: Lessons from innovative family businesses and directions for future research. *The Academy of Management Perspectives*, *30*(1), 93–116.

De Massis, A., Frattini, F., Majocchi, A., & Piscitello, L. (2018). Family firms and the circular economy's entry and extension strategies in biology-based markets. *Journal of Business Research*, *82*, 345–355.

De Pelsmacker, P., & Janssens, W. (2007). A model for fair trade buying behaviour: The role of perceived quantity and quality of information and of product-specific attitudes. *Journal of Business Ethics*, *75*(4), 361–380. DOI: 10.1007/s10551-006-9259-2

De Stefano, V. (2016). The rise of the "just-in-time workforce": On-demand work, crowdwork, and labor protection in the gig economy. *Comparative Labor Law & Policy Journal*, *37*(3), 471–504.

de Vries, A. (2018). Bitcoin's growing energy problem. *Joule*, *2*(5), 801–805.

Deegan, C. (2002). Introduction: The legitimising effect of social and environmental disclosures–a theoretical foundation. *Accounting, Auditing & Accountability Journal*, *15*(3), 282–311. DOI: 10.1108/09513570210435852

Degryse, C. (2016). *Digitalisation of the Economy and its Impact on Labour Markets. European Trade Union Institute*. ETUI.

Delannon, N., & Raufflet, E. (2021). Impeding corporate social responsibility: Revisiting the role of government in shaping business—Marginalized local community relations. *Business Ethics, the Environment & Responsibility*, *30*(4), 470–484. DOI: 10.1111/beer.12378

Deloitte. (2020). The future of social commerce: How digital platforms are shaping retail. *Deloitte Insights*. https://www2.deloitte.com

Dickinson, J. E., Ghali, K., Cherrett, T., Speed, C., Davies, N., & Norgate, S. (2014). Tourism and the smartphone app: Capabilities, emerging practice and scope in the travel domain. *Current Issues in Tourism*, *17*(1), 84–101. DOI: 10.1080/13683500.2012.718323

Diéguez-Soto, J., López-Delgado, P., & Rojo-Ramírez, A. A. (2018). Identifying and classifying family businesses. *Review of Managerial Science*, *12*(4), 983–1023.

Dignum, V. (2019). *Responsible artificial intelligence: How to develop and use AI in a responsible way*. Springer.

Diprose, K., Valentine, G., Vanderbeck, R. M., Liu, C., & McQuaid, K. (2019). Building common cause towards sustainable consumption: A cross-generational perspective. *Environment and Planning E*, *2*(2), 203–228. DOI: 10.1177/2514848619834845

Divasson-J, A., Aguayo-Mendoza, A., Quesada, C., Casado-Mansilla, D., & Borges, C. E. (2025). Climate change from B to Z: A cross-generational perception study in Spain. *Frontiers in Environmental Science*, *13*(February), 1–10. DOI: 10.3389/fenvs.2025.1511398

Djafarova, E., & Foots, S. (2022). Exploring ethical consumption of generation Z: Theory of planned behaviour. *Young Consumers*, *23*(3), 413–431. DOI: 10.1108/YC-10-2021-1405

Domingo, A., & Peñarrubia, J. P. (2024) Faros en la niebla: Herramientas de ética aplicada para sistemas de IA. Conferencia en XXV World Congress of Philosophy: "Philosophy across Boundaries". 1-8 August 2024. Roma. Congress web site https://wcprome2024.com

Domingo, A., & Peñarrubia, J. P. (2025) Proposal of tools for the practical development of ai ethics in business. Ramon Llull Journal of Applied Ethics, 2024, núm. 16, 2025. In press, accepted for publication 3 February 2025. ISSN paper: 2013-8393. ISSN electrònic: 2938-4362. Available on https://raco.cat/index.php/rljae

Doran, C. J. (2009). The Role of Personal Values in Fair Trade Consumption. *Journal of Business Ethics*, *84*(4), 549–563. DOI: 10.1007/s10551-008-9724-1

Drake, W. J., Jørgensen, R. F., & Miège, B. (2019). *Internet governance: Origins, current issues, and future possibilities*. Lynne Rienner Publishers.

Durkheim, E., Lukes, S., & Halls, W. D. (2014). The division of labor in society. In *TA - TT* - (Free Press). Free Press. https://doi.org/LK - https://worldcat.org/title/876277501

Dwesini, N. (2019). Causes and prevention of high employee turnover within the hospitality industry: A literature review. *African Journal of Hospitality, Tourism and Leisure*, *8*(3), 1–15. https://www.ajhtl.com/uploads/7/1/6/3/7163688/article_38_vol_8_3__2019.pdf

Dwivedi, Y. K., Kshetri, N., Hughes, L., Slade, E. L., Jeyaraj, A., Kar, A. K., & Wright, R. (2022). "So you want to talk about the metaverse?": Conceptual underpinnings, synthesis, and research agenda. *Journal of the Association for Information Systems*, *23*(5), 1–61.

Dwork, C., Roth, A., ... (2014). The algorithmic foundations of differential privacy. Foundations and Trends® in Theoretical Computer Science, 9(3–4), 211–407. DOI: . Available in: https://www.nowpublishers.com/article/Details/TCS-042DOI: 10.1561/0400000042

Dyer, W. G. (1986). *Cultural change in family firms: Anticipating and managing business and family transitions*. Jossey-Bass.

Dzomonda, O. (2021). Demystifying the challenges faced by social entrepreneurs in pursuit of their social mission in South Africa. [AEJ]. *Academy of Entrepreneurship Journal*, *27*(4), 1–17.

Edmondson, A. C. (1999). Psychological safety and learning behavior in work teams. *Administrative Science Quarterly*, *44*(2), 350–383. DOI: 10.2307/2666999

Elkington, J. (1998). Partnerships from cannibals with forks: The triple bottom line of 21st-century business. *Environmental Quality Management*. Advance online publication. DOI: 10.1002/tqem.3310080106

Ellerich-Groppe, N., Pfaller, L., & Schweda, M. (2021). Young for old—Old for young? Ethical perspectives on intergenerational solidarity and responsibility in public discourses on COVID-19. *European Journal of Ageing*, *18*(2), 159–171. DOI: 10.1007/s10433-021-00623-9

Ellerich-Groppe, N., Schweda, M., & Pfaller, L. (2020). #StayHomeForGrandma – Towards an analysis of intergenerational solidarity and responsibility in the coronavirus pandemic. *Social Sciences & Humanities Open*, *2*(1), 100085. https://doi.org/https://doi.org/10.1016/j.ssaho.2020.100085

Elmore, T. (2022). *A new kind of diversity: Making the different generations on your team a competitive advantage*. Simon and Schuster.

Engwall, L. (2006). Global enterprises in fields of governance. In Djelic, M., & Sahlin-Andersson, K. (Eds.), *Transnational Governance: Institutional Dynamics of Regulation* (pp. 161–179). Cambridge University Press., DOI: 10.1017/CBO9780511488665.009

Etilé, F., & Teyssier, S. (2016). Signaling Corporate Social Responsibility: Third-Party Certification versus Brands. *The Scandinavian Journal of Economics*, *118*(3), 397–432. DOI: 10.1111/sjoe.12150

Eubanks, V. (2018). Automating Inequality: How High-Tech Tools Profile, Police, and Punish the Poor. St. Martin's Press. Available in: https://us.macmillan.com/books/9781250074317/automatinginequality

Eubanks, V. (2018). *Automating inequality: How high-tech tools profile, police, and punish the poor*. St. Martin's Press.

European Commission. (2021). Proposal for a Regulation laying down harmonised rules on artificial intelligence (Artificial Intelligence Act). Available in: https://digital-strategy.ec.europa.eu/en/library/proposal-regulation-laying-down-harmonised-rules-artificial-intelligence

European Commission. (2023) C(2023)3215 – Standardisation request M/593 commission implementing decision of 22.5.2023 on a standardisation request to the European Committee for Standardisation and the European Committee for Electrotechnical Standardisation in support of Union policy on artificial intelligence. vailable on https://ec.europa.eu/growth/tools-databases/enorm/mandate/593_en (Accessed 2 April 2025)

European Commission. (2024) Regulation (EU) 2024/1689 of the European Parliament and of the Council of 13 June 2024 laying down harmonised rules on artificial intelligence and amending Regulations (EC) No 300/2008, (EU) No 167/2013, (EU) No 168/2013, (EU) 2018/858, (EU) 2018/1139 and (EU) 2019/2144 and Directives 2014/90/EU, (EU) 2016/797 and (EU) 2020/1828 (Artificial Intelligence Act) Official Journal of the European Union, DO L, 2024/1689, 12.7.2024. Available on https://eur-lex.europa.eu/eli/reg/2024/1689/oj (Accessed 2 April 2025)

Evrard, Y., Pras, B., Roux, E., Desmet, P., Dussaix, A.-M., & Gary, L. (2009). *Market - Fondements et méthodes des recherches en marketing*. Dunod.

Fealy, G., McNamara, M., Treacy, M. P., & Lyons, I. (2012). Constructing ageing and age identities: A case study of newspaper discourses. *Ageing and Society*, *32*(1), 85–102. https://doi.org/DOI. DOI: 10.1017/S0144686X11000092

Feldman, M., Friedler, S. A., Moeller, J., Scheidegger, C., & Venkatasubramanian, S. (2015). Certifying and removing disparate impact. Proceedings of the 21st ACM SIGKDD International Conference on Knowledge Discovery and Data Mining. DOI: . Available in: https://dl.acm.org/doi/10.1145/2783258.2783311DOI: 10.1145/2783258.2783311

Ferrell, O. C., Fraedrich, J., & Ferrell, L. (2021). *Business Ethics: Ethical Decision Making and Cases* (13th ed.). Cengage Learning.

Festinger, L. (1957). Social comparison theory. *Selective Exposure Theory*, *16*(401), 3.

Fichman, R. G., Dos Santos, B. L., & Zheng, Z. E. (2014). Digital innovation as a fundamental and powerful concept in the information systems curriculum. *Management Information Systems Quarterly*, *38*(2), 329–353.

Fields, T. D., Lys, T. Z., & Vincent, L. (2001). Empirical research on accounting choice. *Journal of Accounting and Economics, 31*(1-3), 255–307. DOI: 10.1016/S0165-4101(01)00028-3

Fjeld, J., Achten, N., Hilligoss, H., Nagy, A. C., & Srikumar, M. (2020). *Principled artificial intelligence: Mapping consensus in ethical and rights-based approaches to principles for Artificial Intelligence*. Berkman Klein Center Research Publication.

Floridi, Luciano. (2021) The End of an Era: from Self-Regulation to Hard Law for the Digital Industry Philosophy and Technology 34 (4), 619–622 https://doi.org/DOI: 10.1007/s13347-021-00493-0

Floridi, L., & Cowls, J. (2019). A unified framework of five principles for Artificial Intelligence in society. *Harvard Data Science Review, 1*(1). Advance online publication. DOI: 10.1162/99608f92.8cd550d1

Floridi, L., Cowls, J., Beltrametti, M., Chatila, R., Chazerand, P., Dignum, V., & Vayena, E. (2018). AI4People—An ethical framework for a good AI society: Opportunities, risks, principles, and recommendations. *Minds and Machines, 28*(4), 689–707.

Fox, T., Ward, H., & Howard, B. (2002). *Public sector roles in strengthening corporate social responsibility: A baseline study*. World Bank.

Franklin, A., & Crang, C. (2001). The Trouble with Tourism and Travel Theory? *Tourist Studies, 1*(1), 5–22.

Freeman, C., & Louçã, F. (2001). *As time goes by: From the industrial revolutions to the information revolution*. Oxford University Press.

Freitag, C., Berners-Lee, M., Widdicks, K., Knowles, B., Blair, G. S., & Friday, A. (2021). The real climate and transformative impact of ICT: A critique of estimates, trends, and regulations. *Patterns (New York, N.Y.), 2*(9), 100340. PMID: 34553177

Frynas, J., & Stephens, S. (2015). Political Corporate Social Responsibility: Reviewing Theories and Setting New Agendas. *International Journal of Management Reviews: IJMR, 17*(4), 483–509. DOI: 10.1111/ijmr.12049

Fukukawa, K. (2003). A theoretical review of business and consumer ethics research: Normative and descriptive approaches. *The Marketing Review, 3*(4), 381–401.

Fullscreen. (2019). Cuspers: Creative, Stressed, Impulsive - Fullscreen Generational Study Shines Light on the Unique Life Stage Between Millennials and Gen Z. *Business Wire*. https://www.businesswire.com/news/home/20190617005597/en/Cuspers-Creative-Stressed-Impulsive-----Fullscreen-Generational-Study-Shines-Light-on-the-Unique-Life-Stage-Between-Millennials-and-Gen-Z

Furr, N., & Shipilov, A. (2016). Digital doesn't have to be disruptive. *Harvard Business Review*, *94*(7-8), 94–103.

Galea, P. (2012). Grandparenting and Extended-Family Support: The Silent Generation. *Int'l J. Jurisprudence Fam.*, *3*, 283.

García-Allen, J. (2015). *Disonancia cognitiva: la teoría que explica el autoengaño.* Psicología y Mente. https://psicologiaymente.com/psicologia/disonancia-cognitiva-teoria-autoengano

Gardas, R., & Narwane, S. (2024). An analysis of critical factors for adopting machine learning in manufacturing supply chains. *Decision Analytics Journal*, *10*, 100377. DOI: 10.1016/j.dajour.2023.100377

Garg, R., Kiwelekar, A. W., Netak, L. D., & Ghodake, A. (2021). I-Pulse: A NLP-Based Novel Approach for Employee Engagement in Logistics Organization. *International Journal of Information Management Data Insights*, *1*(1), 100011. DOI: 10.1016/j.jjimei.2021.100011

Garg, S., Sinha, S., Kar, A. K., & Mani, M. (2021). A Review of Machine Learning Applications in Human Resource Management. *International Journal of Productivity and Performance Management*, *71*(5), 1590–1610. DOI: 10.1108/ijppm-08-2020-0427

Gee, E. M. T., & Gutman, G. (2000). *The Overselling of Population Ageing: Apocalyptic Demography, Intergenerational Challenges, and Social Policy*. https://api.semanticscholar.org/CorpusID:153842482

Gendron, B. (2004). *Why emotional capital matters in education and in the labour market: Toward an optimal use of human capital and knowledge management. Centre for Educational Research and Innovation (CERI)*. OECD., DOI: 10.1787/870020048750

Gens, F., Levitas, D., & Pone, S. (2016). The Digital Universe in 2020: Big Data, Bigger Digital Shadows, and Biggest Growth in the Far East. IDC iView.

Gentina, E., & Tang, T. L. P. (2024). Youth materialism and consumer ethics: Do Gen Z adolescents' self-concepts (power and self-esteem) vary across cultures (China vs. France)? *Ethics & Behavior*, *34*(2), 120–150. DOI: 10.1080/10508422.2022.2151012

Gerke, S., Minssen, T., & Cohen, G. (2020). Ethical and Legal Challenges of Artificial Intelligence-driven Healthcare. *Artificial Intelligence in Health, 1*(1), 295–336. DOI: 10.1016/B978-0-12-818438-7.00012-5

Ghoshal, S. (2005). Bad management theories are destroying good management practices. *Academy of Management Learning & Education, 4*(1), 75–91. DOI: 10.5465/amle.2005.16132558

Giamporcaro, S., Gond, J.-P., & O'Sullivan, N. (2020). Orchestrating Governmental Corporate Social Responsibility Interventions through Financial Markets: The Case of French Socially Responsible Investment. *Business Ethics Quarterly, 30*(3), 288–334. DOI: 10.1017/beq.2019.40

Gillespie, T. (2018). *Custodians of the internet: Platforms, content moderation, and the hidden decisions that shape social media*. Yale University Press.

Gilpin, L. H., Bau, D., Zoran, D., Pan, Y., Bajwa, A., & Explainable Artificial Intelligence team. (2018). Explaining explanations: An overview of interpretability of machine learning. arXiv preprint arXiv:1806.00069.

Global Reporting Iniciative. (2015). *Sustainability and Reporting Trends in 2025*. Disponible en https://www.globalreporting.org/resourcelibrary/Sustainability-and-Reporting-Trends-in-2025-1.pdf

Goldfarb, A., & Tucker, C. (2012). Privacy and innovation. *Innovation Policy and the Economy, 12*(1), 65–90.

Goldfarb, A., & Tucker, C. (2019). Digital economics. *Journal of Economic Literature, 57*(1), 3–43.

Goleman, D. (1995). *Emotional intelligence: Why it can matter more than IQ*. Bantam Books.

Gond, J. P., Kang, N., & Moon, J. (2011). The government of self-regulation: On the comparative dynamics of corporate social responsibility. *Economy and Society, 40*(4), 640–671. DOI: 10.1080/03085147.2011.607364

Gordon, R. J. (2000). Does the "new economy" measure up to the great inventions of the past? *The Journal of Economic Perspectives, 14*(4), 49–74. DOI: 10.1257/jep.14.4.49

Granic, A., & Marangunic, N. (2015). Technology acceptance model : A literature review from 1986 to 2013. *Universal Access in the Information Society, 14*(1), 81–95.

Grawitch, M. J., Gottschalk, M., & Munz, D. C. (2006). The Path to a Healthy Workplace: A Critical Review Linking Healthy Workplace Practices, Employee Well-Being, and Organizational Improvements. *Consulting Psychology Journal, 58*(3), 129–147. DOI: 10.1037/1065-9293.58.3.129

Gray, R. (2010). Is accounting for sustainability actually accounting for sustainability… and how would we know? An exploration of narratives of organisations and the planet. *Accounting, Organizations and Society*, *35*(1), 47–62. DOI: 10.1016/j.aos.2009.04.006

Greene, J. C., Caracelli, V. J., & Graham, W. F. (1989). Toward a Conceptual Framework for Mixed-Method Evaluation Designs. *Educational Evaluation and Policy Analysis, 11*(3), 255-274. https://doi.org/ (Original work published 1989) DOI: 10.3102/01623737011003255

Greenleaf, G. (2019). Global convergence of data privacy law: The paths are different. *International Data Privacy Law*, *9*(3), 147–172.

Greenleaf, G. (2022). Global data privacy laws 2022: Accelerating coverage but with significant weaknesses. *Privacy Laws & Business International Report*, *176*, 3–16.

Green, P. E., Johnson, R. M., & Neal, W. D. (2004). In Wind, Y., & Green, P. E. (Eds.), *The Journal of Marketing Research: Its Initiation, Growth, and Knowledge Dissemination BT - Marketing Research and Modeling: Progress and Prospects: A Tribute to Paul E. Green* (pp. 245–264). Springer US., DOI: 10.1007/978-0-387-28692-1_12

Gretzel, U., Sigala, M., Xiang, Z., & Koo, C. (2015). Smart tourism: Foundations and developments. *Electronic Markets*, *25*(3), 179–188. DOI: 10.1007/s12525-015-0196-8

Gretzel, U., Zhong, L., & Koo, C. (2016). Application of smart tourism to cities. *International Journal of Tourism Cities*, *2*(2), 216–233. DOI: 10.1108/IJTC-04-2016-0007

Grober, U. (2007). Deep roots: A conceptual history of 'sustainable development' (Nachhaltigkeit). *WZB Discussion Paper P 2007-002, February*, 1–30. http://skylla.wz-berlin.de/pdf/2007/p07-002.pdf

Grossi, D., Royakkers, L., & Dignum, F. (2007). Organizational structure and responsibility. *Artificial Intelligence and Law*, *15*(3), 223–249. DOI: 10.1007/s10506-007-9054-0

Grzesiuk, A., & Wanat, T. (2010). Consumer ethics: Some evidence from young consumers from Poland. *Proceedings on the 9th International Marketing Trends Conference, Venice-Paris, ESCP Europe.*

Guay, T., Doh, J., & Sinclair, G. (2004). Non-Governmental Organizations, Shareholder Activism, and Socially Responsible Investments: Ethical, Strategic, and Governance Implications. *Journal of Business Ethics*, *52*(1), 125–139. DOI: 10.1023/B:BUSI.0000033112.11461.69

Guberman, N., Lavoie, J.-P., Blein, L., & Olazabal, I. (2012). Baby Boom Caregivers: Care in the Age of Individualization. *The Gerontologist*, *52*(2), 210–218. DOI: 10.1093/geront/gnr140

Guerranti, F., & Dimitri, G. M. (2022). A Comparison of Machine Learning Approaches for Predicting Employee Attrition. *Applied Sciences (Basel, Switzerland)*, *13*(1), 267. DOI: 10.3390/app13010267

Guest, D. E. (2017). Human resource management and employee well-being: Towards a new analytic framework. *Human Resource Management Journal*, *27*(1), 22–38. DOI: 10.1111/1748-8583.12139

Guner, H., & Acarturk, C. (2018). The use and acceptance of ICT by senior citizens: A comparison of technology acceptance model (TAM) for elderly and young adults. *Universal Access in the Information Society*, *19*(2), 311–330.

Hagendorff, T. (2020). The Ethics of Artificial Intelligence Ethics: An Evaluation of Guidelines. *Minds and Machines*, *30*(1), 99–120.

Haipeter, T., Manfred Wannöffel, Daus, J.-T., & Schaffarczik, S. (2024). Human-centered AI through employee participation. *Frontiers in Artificial Intelligence*, *7*. Advance online publication. DOI: 10.3389/frai.2024.1272102 PMID: 38496830

Halsall, J. P., Snowden, M., Clegg, P., Mswaka, W., Alderson, M., Hyams-Ssekasi, D., & Winful, E. C. (2022). Social enterprise as a model for change: Mapping a global cross-disciplinary framework. *Entrepreneurship Education*, *5*(4), 425–446.

Hamilton, R. H., & Davison, H. K. (2021). Legal and Ethical Challenges for HR in Machine Learning. *Employee Responsibilities and Rights Journal*, *34*(1). Advance online publication. DOI: 10.1007/s10672-021-09377-z

Han, K., Shih, P. C., Rosson, M. B., & Carroll, J. M. (2016). Understanding local community attachment, engagement and social support networks mediated by mobile technology. *Interacting with Computers*, *28*(3), 220–237.

Hanlon, R. J. (2011). Engineering corporate social responsibility: Elite stakeholders, states and the resilience of neoliberalism. *Contemporary Politics, 17*(1), 71–87. DOI: 10.1080/13569775.2011.552689

Hannam, K. (2009). 'The End of Tourism? Nomadology and the Mobilities Paradigm', Philosophical Issues in Tourism 37: 101–114. Hannam, K., G. Butler and C. M. Paris (2014) 'Developments and Key Issues in Tourism Mobilities'. *Annals of Tourism Research, 44*(1), 171–185.

Hansson, P., & Wihlborg, E. (2016). Development of quality management in education : A comparative case study in the Swedish multi-level governance system. In *The 10th International Multi-Conference on Society, Cybernetics and Informatics*. Orlando, Florida, USA: IMSCI, 43–48.

Harari, T. T., Sela, Y., & Bareket-Bojmel, L. (2022). Gen Z during the COVID-19 crisis: A comparative analysis of the differences between Gen Z and Gen X in resilience, values and attitudes. *Current Psychology (New Brunswick, N.J.)*, •••, 1–10. DOI: 10.1007/s12144-022-03501-4

Hartley, N., Kunz, W., & Tarbit, J. (2024). The corporate digital responsibility (CDR) calculus: How and why organizations reconcile digital and ethical trade-offs for growth. *Organizational Dynamics, 53*(2), 101056. https://doi.org/https://doi.org/10.1016/j.orgdyn.2024.101056

Hassan, R. (2016). The Role of Human Capital Management in Enhancing Engagement and Retention Among Top Talent in Organization: A Critical Literature Revie. *Journal of Emerging Economies and Islamic Research, 4*(4), 54. DOI: 10.24191/jeeir.v4i4.9103

Helbing, D. (2019). *Societal self-engineering*. MIT Press.

Heller, J., Chylinski, M., de Ruyter, K., Mahr, D., & Keeling, D. I. (2019). Embracing digital technology: Clients' perspective on future affordances of makerspaces. *Futures, 109*, 82–97.

Helve, H. M. (2023). Values and Solidarity of Young Finnish Millennials and Generation X. In *Youth* (Vol. 3, Issue 1, pp. 401–413). https://doi.org/DOI: 10.3390/youth3010027

Henderson, J. (2021, September 14). Google commits to carbon-free energy by 2030. *Utility Dive*. https://www.utilitydive.com

Hidayat, C., Asep Hermawan, & Dita Oki Berliyanti. (2024). The influence of organizational culture, transformational leadership on organizational citizenship behaviors, and organizational commitment through employee engagement. *Indonesian Journal of Education and Social Science, 3*(2), 100–120. DOI: 10.56916/ijess.v3i2.635

Higgs, P., & Gilleard, C. (2015). In Torp, C. (Ed.), *Generational Justice, Generational Habitus and the 'Problem' of the Baby Boomers BT - Challenges of Aging: Pensions, Retirement and Generational Justice* (pp. 251–263)., DOI: 10.1057/9781137283177_13

Hobfoll, S. E. (1989). Conservation of resources: A new attempt at conceptualizing stress. *The American Psychologist, 44*(3), 513–524. DOI: 10.1037/0003-066X.44.3.513

Hoffmann, A. L., Katzenbach, M., & Gollatz, K. (2020). Between coordination and regulation: Finding the governance in data governance. *Internet Policy Review, 9*(2), 1–16.

Holzer, H. (2022, January 19). *Understanding the Impact of Automation on workers, jobs, and Wages*. Brookings. https://www.brookings.edu/articles/understanding-the-impact-of-automation-on-workers-jobs-and-wages/

Hontañon Pombo, R. (2023). Los Zillenials y su relación con las marcas. Así es la micro-generación más reciente. *PuroMarketing*. https://www.puromarketing.com/88/212041/zillennials-relacion-marcas-micro-generacion-reciente

Hoofnagle, C. J., van der Sloot, B., & Metzger, A. (2019). The European Union general data protection regulation: What it is and what it means. *Information & Communications Technology Law, 28*(1), 65–98.

Hoyer, W. D., Kroschke, M., Schmitt, B., Krafft, M., & Shankar, V. (2020). Transforming the customer experience through new technologies. *Journal of Interactive Marketing, 51*, 57–71.

Huang, M.-H., & Rust, R. T. (2021). Artificial intelligence in service. *Journal of Service Research, 24*(2), 155–172.

Hubbard, T. N. (2003). Information, decisions, and productivity: On-board computers and capacity utilization in trucking. *The American Economic Review, 93*(4), 1328–1353.

Hunt, S. D., & Laverie, D. A. (2004). Experiential learning and the Hunt-Vitell theory of ethics: Teaching marketing ethics by integrating theory and practice. *Marketing Education Review, 14*(3), 1–14.

Hunt, S. D., & Vitell, S. (1986). A General Theory of Marketing Ethics. *Journal of Macromarketing*, *6*(1), 5–16. DOI: 10.1177/027614678600600103

Huselid, M. A. (1995). The impact of human resource management practices on turnover, productivity, and corporate financial performance. *Academy of Management Journal*, *38*(3), 635–672.

Huws, U., Spencer, N. H., & Coates, M. (2019). *The platformisation of work in Europe: Results from research in 13 European countries*. Foundation for European Progressive Studies.

Huy, Q., & Shipilov, A. (2012). The key to social media success within organizations. MIT Sloan Management Review, 54(1), 73. Melé, D. (2003). Organizational humanizing cultures: Do they generate social capital? *Journal of Business Ethics*, *45*(1), 3–14.

Hwang, J., Park, H.-Y., & Hunter, W. C. (2015). Constructivism in smart tourism research: Seoul destination image. *Asia Pacific Journal of Information Systems*, *25*(1), 163–178. DOI: 10.14329/apjis.2015.25.1.163

Hynes, B. (2009). Growing the social enterprise–issues and challenges. *Social Enterprise Journal*, *5*(2), 114–125.

ICEX (2024) El ecosistema de la Inteligencia Artificial (AI) en China 2024. Oficina Económica y Comercial de España en Pekín. . 20 de diciembre de 2024 . Editado por ICEX España Exportación e Inversiones, E.P.E. NIPO: 224240096

ICEX (2025) Esquema regulatorio e institucional en inteligencia artificial de los EE. UU. Oficina Económica y Comercial de la Embajada de España en Washington. 31 de enero de 2025. Washington. Editado por ICEX España Exportación e Inversiones, E.P.E. NIPO: 224240096

Idemudia, U., & Kwakyewah, C. (2018). Analysis of the Canadian national corporate social responsibility strategy: Insights and implications. *Corporate Social Responsibility and Environmental Management*, *25*(5), 928–938.

Ilieva, J., Baron, S., & Healey, N. M. (2002). Online Surveys in Marketing Research. *International Journal of Market Research*, *44*(3), 1–14. DOI: 10.1177/147078530204400303

InbuiltData. (2024, October 6). *AI-Powered Predictive Analytics for Workforce Planning*. Linkedin.com. https://www.linkedin.com/pulse/ai-powered-predictive-analytics-workforce-planning-inbuiltdata-qld9c

Inglehart, R. (1977). *The silent revolution: Changing values and political styles among Western publics.* Princeton University Press.

Isaak, J., & Hanna, M. J. (2018). User data privacy: Facebook, Cambridge Analytica, and privacy protection. *Computer, 51*(8), 56–59.

Isham, A., Verfuerth, C., Armstrong, A., Elf, P., Gatersleben, B., & Jackson, T. (2022). The Problematic Role of Materialistic Values in the Pursuit of Sustainable Well-Being. *International Journal of Environmental Research and Public Health, 19*(6). Advance online publication. DOI: 10.3390/ijerph19063673

ISO. (2018) Discovering ISO 26000. International Organization for Standardization – ISO. Ginebra. Available on https://www.iso.org/files/live/sites/isoorg/files/store/en/PUB100258.pdf (Accessed 11 April 2024)

ISO. (2022a) ISO/IEC 22989:2022 Information technology — Artificial intelligence — Artificial intelligence concepts and terminology. International Organization for Standardization – ISO. Geneva. Available on https://standards.iso.org/ittf/PubliclyAvailableStandards/ISO_IEC_22989_2022_ed.1_id.74296_Publication_PDF_(en).zip (Accessed: 10 March 2025)

ISO. (2022b) ISO/IEC 38507:2022 Information technology — Governance of IT —Governance implications of the use of artificial intelligence by organizations. International Organization for Standardization – ISO. Ginebra. Disponible en: https://www.iso.org (Accessed 11 April 2024)

ISO. (2022c) ISO/IEC TR 24368:2022 Information technology — Artificial intelligence — Overview of ethical and societal concerns. International Organization for Standardization – ISO. Ginebra. Disponible en: https://www.iso.org (Accessed 10 March 2025)

ISO. (2023a) ISO/IEC 23894:2023 Information technology — Artificial intelligence — Guidance on risk management. International Organization for Standardization – ISO. Geneva. Available in: https://www.iso.org (Accessed 10 March 2025)

ISO. (2023b) ISO/IEC 42001:2023 Information technology — Artificial intelligence — Management system. International Organization for Standardization – ISO. Geneva. Available in: https://www.iso.org (Accessed 10 March 2025)

ISO. (2024a) ISO/IEC 5339:2024 Information technology — Artificial intelligence — Guidance for AI applications. International Organization for Standardization – ISO. Geneva. Available in: https://www.iso.org (Accessed 10 March 2025)

ISO. (2024b) ISO/IEC TR 24030:2024 Information technology — Artificial intelligence (AI) — Use cases. International Organization for Standardization – ISO. Geneva. Available in: https://www.iso.org (Accessed 10 March 2025)

ISO. (2025a) ISO/IEC 42005: 2025 Information technology — Artificial intelligence — AI system impact assessment. International Organization for Standardization – ISO. Geneva. Available in: https://www.iso.org (Accessed 10 March 2025)

ISO. (2025b) ISO/IEC AWI TS 22443 Information technology — Artificial intelligence — Guidance on addressing societal concerns and ethical considerations. International Organization for Standardization – ISO. Ginebra. Disponible en: https://www.iso.org (Accessed 10 March 2025)

ISO. (2025c) ISO/IEC AWI TS 25568 Information technology — Artificial Intelligence — Guidance on addressing risks in generative AI systems. International Organization for Standardization – ISO. Ginebra. Disponible en: https://www.iso.org (Accessed 10 March 2025)

Iunius, R. F., Cismaru, L., & Foris, D. (2015). Raising competitiveness for tourist destinations through information technologies within the newest tourism action framework proposed by the European commission. *Sustainability, 7*(9), 12891–12909. DOI: 10.3390/su70912891

Ivanova, O., Flores-Zamora, J., Khelladi, I., & Ivanaj, S. (2019). The generational cohort effect in the context of responsible consumption. *Management Decision, 57*(5), 1162–1183. DOI: 10.1108/MD-12-2016-0915

Iyamu, T. (2020). A case for applying Activity Theory in IS research. [IRMJ]. *Information Resources Management Journal, 33*(1), 1–15.

Iyamu, T. (2021). *Applying theories for information systems research*. Routledge.

Jain, N., Tomar, A., & Jana, P. K. (2020). A novel scheme for employee churn problem using multi-attribute decision-making approach and machine learning. *Journal of Intelligent Information Systems*. Advance online publication. DOI: 10.1007/s10844-020-00614-9

Januszewska, M., Jaremen, D. E., & Nawrocka, E. (2015). The effects of the use of ICT by tourism enterprises. Zeszyty Naukowe Uniwersytetu Szczecińskiego. Scientific Journal. *Supervisory Management, 16*, 65–73. DOI: 10.18276/smt.2015.16-07

Jan, Z., Ahamed, F., Mayer, W., Patel, N., Grossmann, G., Stumptner, M., & Kuusk, A. (2023). Artificial intelligence for industry 4.0: Systematic review of applications, challenges, and opportunities. *Expert Systems with Applications, 216*(216), 119456. DOI: 10.1016/j.eswa.2022.119456

Jayawardhana, K., Fernando, I., & Siyambalapitiya, J. (2022). Sustainability in social enterprise research: A systematic literature review. *SAGE Open*, *12*(3), 21582440221123200.

Jebarajakirthy, C., Sivapalan, A., Das, M., Maseeh, H. I., Ashaduzzaman, M., Strong, C., & Sangroya, D. (2024). A meta-analytic integration of the theory of planned behavior and the value-belief-norm model to predict green consumption. *European Journal of Marketing*, *58*(4), 1141–1174. DOI: 10.1108/EJM-06-2021-0436

Jecker, N. S. (2021). The time of one's life: Views of aging and age group justice. *History and Philosophy of the Life Sciences*, *43*(1), 24. DOI: 10.1007/s40656-021-00377-8

Jette, S. K., & Moon, J. (2022). Corporate social responsibility and government: The role of discretion for engagement with public policy. *Business Ethics Quarterly*, *32*(2), 243–271. DOI: 10.1017/beq.2021.17

Ji, H., & Miao, Z. (2020). Corporate social responsibility and collaborative innovation: The role of government support. *Journal of Cleaner Production*, *260*, 121028. DOI: 10.1016/j.jclepro.2020.121028

Jobin, A., Ienca, M., & Vayena, E. (2019). The global landscape of Artificial Intelligence ethics guidelines. *Nature Machine Intelligence*, *1*(9), 389–399. DOI: 10.1038/s42256-019-0088-2

Jovanovic, B., & Rousseau, P. L. (2005). General purpose technologies. In Aghion, P., & Durlauf, S. (Eds.), *Handbook of Economic Growth* (Vol. 1, pp. 1181–1224). Elsevier.

Kahn, W. A. (1990). Psychological Conditions of Personal Engagement and Disengagement at Work. *Academy of Management Journal*, *33*(4), 692–724. DOI: 10.5465/256287

Kajiita, R. M. (2022). Social Enterprises as Drivers of Community Development in South Africa: The Case of Buffalo City Municipality. *Southern African Journal of Social Work & Social Development*, *34*(3).

Kallio, H., Pietilä, A. M., Johnson, M., & Kangasniemi, M. (2016). Systematic methodological review: Developing a framework for a qualitative semi-structured interview guide. *Journal of Advanced Nursing*, *72*(12), 2954–2965. PMID: 27221824

Kanfer, R., (2010). Kanfer Motivation Theory in Handbook Indus Orgl Psych.

Kant, I. 1797. *Metaphysics of Morals*. A87.

Kellermanns, F. W., Eddleston, K. A., Sarathy, R., & Murphy, F. (2012). Innovativeness in family firms: A family influence perspective. *Small Business Economics, 38*(1), 85–101.

Kelsey, J. (2018). Trade, security and sovereignty in the digital economy. *Journal of World Trade, 52*(6), 947–970.

Kemp, S. (2021). Digital 2021: Global overview report. *DataReportal.* https://datareportal.com/reports/digital-2021-global-overview-report

Khan, L. (2021). Amazon's antitrust paradox. *The Yale Law Journal, 126*(3), 710–805.

Khanna, P., Kumari, J., & Karim, R. (2024). Human-Centric PHM in the Era of Industry 5.0. *PHM Society European Conference, 8*(1), 7–7. https://doi.org/DOI: 10.36001/phme.2024.v8i1.4121

Kinderman, D. (2016). Time for a reality check: Is business willing to support a smart mix of complementary regulation in private governance? *Policy and Society, 35*(1), 29–42. DOI: 10.1016/j.polsoc.2016.01.001

Knudsen, J. S., & Moon, J. (2017). *Visible hands: Government regulation and international business responsibility.* Cambridge University Press.

Knudsen, J. S., Moon, J., & Slager, R. (2015). Government policies for corporate social responsibility in Europe: A comparative analysis of institutionalisation. *Policy and Politics, 43*(1), 81–99. Retrieved July 15, 2025, from. DOI: 10.1332/030557312X656016

König, A., Kammerlander, N., & Enders, A. (2013). The family innovator's dilemma: How family influence affects the adoption of discontinuous technologies by incumbent firms. *Academy of Management Review, 38*(3), 418–441.

Kontogianni, A., & Alepis, E. (2020). Smart tourism: State of the art and literature review for the last six years. *Array (New York, N.Y.), 6,* 100020. DOI: 10.1016/j.array.2020.100020

Koo, C., Joun, Y., Han, H., & Chung, N. (2016). A structural model for destination travel intention as a media exposure: Belief-desire-intention model perspective. *International Journal of Contemporary Hospitality Management, 28*(7), 1338–1360. *Scopus.* Advance online publication. DOI: 10.1108/IJCHM-07-2014-0354

Kraus, S., Fink, M., & Rössl, D. (2019). From family succession to incubation: A perspective shift in the study of entrepreneurship. *International Journal of Entrepreneurial Behaviour & Research, 25*(6), 1183–1187.

Krupas, M., Kajati, E., Liu, C., & Zolotova, I. (2024). Towards a Human-Centric Digital Twin for Human–Machine Collaboration: A Review on Enabling Technologies and Methods. *Sensors (Basel)*, *24*(7), 2232. DOI: 10.3390/s24072232 PMID: 38610442

Kshetri, N. (2021). The economics of cybersecurity. *IT Professional*, *23*(1), 42–47.

Kumari, P., Anand, A., Praveen, P., Verma, A.R., & Godiyal, A. (2024). Infrastructure Potential and Human-Centric Strategies in the Context of Industry 5.0. *Advances in Web Technologies and Engineering Book Series*, 199–214. https://doi.org/DOI: 10.4018/979-8-3693-0782-3.ch012

Kuner, C. (2020). The CJEU's Schrems II decision: Adequacy undermined, SCCs strengthened? *European Data Protection Law Review*, *6*(4), 481–496.

Kuner, C., Cate, F. H., Millard, C., Lynskey, O., & Svantesson, D. (2021). *Transborder data flows and data privacy law*. Oxford University Press.

Kuron, L. K. J., Lyons, S. T., Schweitzer, L., & Ng, E. S. W. (2015). Millennials' work values: Differences across the school to work transition. *Personnel Review*, *44*(6), 991–1009. DOI: 10.1108/PR-01-2014-0024

Ladner, R. D. (2019). *Accessible technology and the developing world*. Oxford University Press.

Laha, A., Koner, N., & Ghosh, S. K. (2024). Assessing the Role of Social Enterprises in Shaping Eco-Social Agriculture.

Lange, C., Combris, P., Issanchou, S., & Schlich, P. (2015). Impact of information and in-home sensory exposure on liking and willingness to pay: The beginning of Fairtrade labeled coffee in France. *Food Research International*, *76*, 317–324. https://doi.org/https://doi.org/10.1016/j.foodres.2015.06.017

Law, R., Chan, I. C. C., & Wang, L. (2018). A comprehensive review of mobile technology use in hospitality and tourism. *Journal of Hospitality Marketing and Management, 27*(6), 626–648. *Scopus*. Advance online publication. DOI: 10.1080/19368623.2018.1423251

Lazarevic, V. (2012). Encouraging brand loyalty in fickle generation Y consumers. *Young Consumers*, *13*(1), 45–61. DOI: 10.1108/17473611211203939

Lessig, L. (2001). *The future of ideas: The fate of the commons in a connected world*. Random House.

Leung, D., Law, R., Van Hoof, H., & Buhalis, D. (2013). Social media in tourism and hospitality: A literature review. *Journal of Travel & Tourism Marketing*, *30*(1-2), 3–22. DOI: 10.1080/10548408.2013.750919

Lewandowsky, S., Ecker, U. K. H., & Cook, J. (2017). Beyond misinformation: Understanding and coping with the "post-truth" era. *Journal of Applied Research in Memory and Cognition*, *6*(4), 353–369.

Liang, J., & Xu, Y. (2018). Second-hand clothing consumption: A generational cohort analysis of the Chinese market. *International Journal of Consumer Studies*, *42*(1), 120–130. DOI: 10.1111/ijcs.12393

Lin, R., Lin, Y., Hsia, Y., & Kuo, C. (2021). Long working hours and burnout in health care workers: Non-linear dose-response relationship and the effect mediated by sleeping hours—A cross-sectional study. *Journal of Occupational Health*, *63*(1). Advance online publication. DOI: 10.1002/1348-9585.12228 PMID: 33957007

Llanos Anaya, P. M., & Paredes Quenta, F. K. (2023). *Creación de contenido para Instagram utilizando inteligencia artificial (IA) en la marca weCOOL, enfocado en la generación Zillennial* [Universidad Peruana de Ciencias Aplicadas]. http://hdl.handle.net/10757/670777

Lo, C., Chuang, I., Lai, P., Guo, B. & Kuo, Y. (2015). A Community-Based Data Dissemination Scheme in Opportunistic Networks., 4(5), 305–310.

Lobschat, L., Osinga, E. C., Tompkins, L., & Woratschek, H. (2021). Consumer–brand relationships in the subscription economy: A conceptual framework and research directions. *Journal of the Academy of Marketing Science*, *49*(3), 519–536.

Löfgren, O. (1999). *On Holiday: A History of Vacationing*. University of California Press.

Longoria, B. C. (2022). The widowed identity: Identity transformations of the silent generation and the influence of time. *Journal of Women & Aging*, *34*(6), 773–784. DOI: 10.1080/08952841.2021.1948790

Lu, A. C. C., & Gursoy, D. (2015). A conceptual model of consumers' online tourism confusion. *International Journal of Contemporary Hospitality Management, 27*(6), 1320–1342. *Scopus.* Advance online publication. DOI: 10.1108/IJCHM-04-2014-0171

Lu, J., Ren, L., Qiao, J., Yao, S., Strielkowski, W., & Streimikis, J. (2019). Corporate social responsibility and corruption: Implications for the sustainable energy sector. *Sustainability*, *11*(15), 4128. DOI: 10.3390/su11154128

Lu, L.-C., Chang, H.-H., & Chang, A. (2015). Consumer personality and green buying intention: The mediate role of consumer ethical beliefs. *Journal of Business Ethics, 127*, 205–219.

Lumpkin, G. T., Brigham, K. H., & Moss, T. W. (2010). Long-term orientation: Implications for the entrepreneurial orientation and performance of family businesses. *Entrepreneurship and Regional Development, 22*(3-4), 241–264.

Luszcz, M. A., & Fitzgerald, K. M. (1986). Understanding cohort differences in cross-generational, self, and peer perceptions. *Journal of Gerontology, 41*(2), 234–240. DOI: 10.1093/geronj/41.2.234

Luthans, F., Youssef, C. M., & Avolio, B. J. (2007). *Psychological capital: Developing the human competitive edge*. Oxford University Press.

Madzik, P., & Falat, L., Jum'a, L., Vrábliková, M. & Zimon, D. (2024). Human-centricity in Industry 5.0 – revealing of hidden research topics by unsupervised topic modeling using Latent Dirichlet Allocation. *European Journal of Innovation Management*. Advance online publication. DOI: 10.1108/ejim-09-2023-0753

Maines, D. R. (2000). The social construction of meaning. *Contemporary Sociology, 29*(4), 577–584.

Maksum, I. R., Rahayu, A. Y. S., & Kusumawardhani, D. (2020). A social enterprise approach to empowering micro, small and medium enterprises (SMEs) in Indonesia. *Journal of Open Innovation, 6*(3), 50.

Manuti, A., & Giancaspro, M. L. (2019). People make the difference: An explorative study on the relationship between organizational practices, employees' resources, and organizational behavior. *Sustainability, 11*(5), 1499. DOI: 10.3390/su11051499

Manyika, J., Chui, M., Farrell, D., Van Kuiken, S., Groves, P., & Doshi, E. A. (2016). *Digital America: A tale of the haves and have-mores*. McKinsey Global Institute.

Mariscal-Crespo, M. I., Coronado-Vázquez, M. V., & Ramirez-Duran, M. V. (2017). Global analysis of the readability of informed consent documents used in public hospitals in Spain. *Revista de Calidad Asistencial, 32*(4), 200–208. PMID: 28268150

Markowitz, E. M., & Shariff, A. F. (2012). Climate change and moral judgement. *Nature Climate Change, 2*(4), 243–247. DOI: 10.1038/nclimate1378

Marron, D. (2020). *50 Teorías económicas sugerentes y desafiantes*. Blume.

Marsden, C. T. (2018). *Internet co-regulation: European law, regulatory governance and online services*. Cambridge University Press.

Marvin, G., Jackson, M., & Alam, Md. G. R. (2021). A Machine Learning Approach for Employee Retention Prediction. *2021 IEEE Region 10 Symposium (TENSYMP)*. https://doi.org/DOI: 10.1109/tensymp52854.2021.9550921

Mathur, A., Acar, G., Friedman, M. G., Lucherini, E., Mayer, J., Chetty, M., & Narayanan, A. (2019). Dark patterns at scale: Findings from a crawl of 11K shopping websites. *Proceedings of the ACM on Human-Computer Interaction, 3*(CSCW), 1–32.

Matt, C., Hess, T., & Benlian, A. (2015). Digital transformation strategies. *Business & Information Systems Engineering, 57*(5), 339–343.

Mayer, J. D., Salovey, P., & Caruso, D. R. (2000). Emotional intelligence as zeitgeist, as personality, and as a mental ability. In Bar-On, R., & Parker, J. D. A. (Eds.), *The handbook of emotional intelligence* (pp. 92–117). Jossey-Bass.

McAfee, A., & Brynjolfsson, E. (2017). *Machine, platform, crowd: Harnessing our digital future*. W. W. Norton & Company.

McCrindle, M. (2014). *The ABC of XYZ: Understanding the Global Generations* (Issue October). McCrindle Research. https://mccrindle.com.au/resources/The-ABC-of-XYZ_Chapter-1.pdf

McKinsey & Company. (2023, August 1). *The state of AI in 2023: Generative AI's breakout year*. Mckinsey. https://www.mckinsey.com/capabilities/quantumblack/our-insights/the-state-of-ai-in-2023-generative-ais-breakout-year

Meira, J. V. de S., & Hancer, M. (2021). Using the Social Exchange Theory to Explore the Employee-organization Relationship in the Hospitality Industry. *International Journal of Contemporary Hospitality Management, 33*(2), 670–692. DOI: 10.1108/ijchm-06-2020-0538

Meltzer, J. P. (2020). *The impact of the digital economy on developing countries*. Brookings Institution Press.

Mendez, E. N. (2009). *Intergenerational Responsibility and Accountability*. Royal Roads University.

Mennella, C., Maniscalco, U., Pietro, G. D., & Esposito, M. (2024). Ethical and regulatory challenges of AI technologies in healthcare: A narrative review. *Heliyon, 10*(4), e26297–e26297. DOI: 10.1016/j.heliyon.2024.e26297 PMID: 38384518

Mesenbourg, T. L. (2001). *Measuring the digital economy*. U.S. Bureau of the Census.

Meyer, J. P., & Allen, N. J. (1997). *Commitment in the Workplace: Theory, Research, and Application*. Sage Publications.

Meziane, B., Alla, L., & Bentalha, B. (2025). Transformational Trends of Territorial Economic Intelligence Strategies in the Digital Era: A Systematic Theoretical Exploration. In Utilizing Technology to Manage Territories (pp. 455-490). IGI Global.

Mihardjo, L. W. W., Jeremic, J., & Shahriari, S. (2019). The digital transformation of SMEs. In *Proceedings of the 2019 International Conference on Information Technology & Systems* (pp. 277-286). Springer.

Mill, J. S. (2014). On Liberty. Akal Publishing. *Letter to John Elliot Cairnes, XVII*, 1831–1832.

Minghetti, V., & Buhalis, D. (2010). Digital divide in tourism. *Journal of Travel Research, 49*(3), 267–281. DOI: 10.1177/0047287509346843

Miorandi, D., Sicari, S., De Pellegrini, F., & Chlamtac, I. (2012). Internet of things: Vision, applications and research challenges. *Ad Hoc Networks, 10*(7), 1497–1516. DOI: 10.1016/j.adhoc.2012.02.016

Mishra, A. (2025). The Impact of Predictive Analytics on Employee Engagement and Turnover in Knowledge-based Teams: A Systematic Literature Review. SSRN *Electronic Journal*. https://doi.org/DOI: 10.2139/ssrn.5038568

Mitchell, J. V. (Ed.). (1998). Companies in a World of Conflict: NGOs, Sanctions and Corporate Responsibility; *Papers from a Workshop Organized in Oslo by the Royal Institute of International Affairs, April 1997*. Earthscan.

Mladjan, M. M., & Marković, D. Z. (2021). Generational responsibility in consumption as a response to global economic crises. *Sustainability, 13*(6), 3329.

Moon, J., & Vogel, D. (2008). Corporate social responsibility, government, and civil society. In Crane, A. (Eds.), *The Oxford Handbook of Corporate Social Responsibility.*, DOI: 10.1093/oxfordhb/9780199211593.003.0013

Morley, J., Floridi, L., Kinsey, L., & Elhalal, A. (2021). From what to how: An initial review of publicly available Artificial Intelligence ethics tools, methods and research to translate principles into practices. *Science and Engineering Ethics, 27*(4). Advance online publication. DOI: 10.1007/s11948-019-00165-5 PMID: 31828533

Munawar, M., & Suriyanti, S. (2024). The Effect of Organizational Culture, Work-Life Balance, and Job Satisfaction on Non-Commercial Employee Work Engagement. *Golden Ratio of Human Resource Management, 4*(1), 53–66. DOI: 10.52970/grhrm.v4i1.452

Muncy, J. A., & Vitell, S. J. (1992). Consumer ethics: An investigation of the ethical beliefs of the final consumer. *Journal of Business Research, 24*(4), 297–311. DOI: 10.1016/0148-2963(92)90036-B

Munsch, A. (2021). Millennial and generation Z digital marketing communication and advertising effectiveness: A qualitative exploration. *Journal of Global Scholars of Marketing Science, 31*(1), 10–29. DOI: 10.1080/21639159.2020.1808812

Murillo, S., & Mena, L. (2006). *Detectives y camaleones: el grupo de discusión: una propuesta par la investigación cualitativa*. Talasa.

Murire, O. T. (2024). Artificial Intelligence and Its Role in Shaping Organizational Work Practices and Culture. *Administrative Sciences, 14*(12), 316. DOI: 10.3390/admsci14120316

Naci Çoklar, A., & Tatli, A. (2021). Examining the Digital Nativity Levels of Digital Generations: From Generation X to Generation Z. *Shanlax International Journal of Education, 9*(4), 433–434. DOI: 10.34293/education.v9i4.4224

Nagata, J. M., Chu, J., Ganson, K. T., Murray, S. B., Iyer, P., Gabriel, K. P., Garber, A. K., Bibbins-Domingo, K., & Baker, F. C. (2023). Contemporary screen time modalities and disruptive behavior disorders in children: A prospective cohort study. *Journal of Child Psychology and Psychiatry, and Allied Disciplines, 64*(1), 125–135. https://doi.org/https://doi.org/10.1111/jcpp.13673

Nagy, L., Abonyi, J. & Ruppert, T. (2024). Knowledge Graph-Based Framework to Support Human-Centered Collaborative Manufacturing in Industry 5.0. *Applied Sciences (Basel, Switzerland), 14*(8), 3398–3398. DOI: 10.3390/app14083398

Nahapiet, J., & Ghoshal, S. (1998). Social capital, intellectual capital, and the organizational advantage. *Academy of Management Review, 23*(2), 242–266. DOI: 10.5465/amr.1998.533225

Nakova, R. (2024). Generational differences in grocery shopping behaviour. *Industrial Growth Conference 2024*, 376–385. https://doi.org/DOI: 10.53656/igc-2024.32

Nambiar, R., & Parmar, N. (2024). A Study on Impact of Culture on Creating an Engaged Workforce. *International Journal of Research Publication and Reviews, 5*(4), 2161–2165. DOI: 10.55248/gengpi.5.0424.0956

Nankya, M., Mugisa, A., Usman, Y., Upadhyay, A., & Chataut, R. (2024). Security and Privacy in E-Health Systems: A Review of AI and Machine Learning Techniques. *IEEE Access : Practical Innovations, Open Solutions, 12*, 148796–148816. DOI: 10.1109/access.2024.3469215

Napoli, C. (2020). Zennials: The In-Between Generation. *WGSN*. https://www.wgsn.com/insight/p/article/88103?lang=en

Napoli, P. M. (2019). *Social media and the public interest: Media regulation in the disinformation age*. Columbia University Press.

Narayana, A. (2023). Futuristic HRM and the Implications of Integration with Industry 5.0 for Sustainable Business. *Management Insight*, *19*(01), 71–78. DOI: 10.21844/mijia.19.1.7

Narayanan, S. (2022). Does Generation Z value and reward corporate social responsibility practices? *Journal of Marketing Management*, *38*(9–10), 903–937.

Negroponte, N. (1995). *Being digital*. Knopf.

Ng, E., Schweitzer, L., & Lyons, S. (2010). New Generation, Great Expectations: A Field Study of the Millennial Generation. *Journal of Business and Psychology*, *25*, 281–292. DOI: 10.1007/s10869-010-9159-4

Ngubane, M. Z., Mndebele, S., & Kaseeram, I. (2023). Economic growth, unemployment and poverty: Linear and non-linear evidence from South Africa. *Heliyon*, *9*(10).

Nikou, S., Cavalheiro, S., & Widén, G. (2020). In Sundqvist, A., Berget, G., Nolin, J., & Skjerdingstad, K. I. (Eds.), *Digital Natives and Digital Immigrants in the Creative Economy BT - Sustainable Digital Communities* (pp. 343–362). Springer International Publishing.

Nimri, R., Dharmesti, M., Arcodia, C., & Mahshi, R. (2021). UK consumers' ethical beliefs towards dining at green restaurants: A qualitative evaluation. *Journal of Hospitality and Tourism Management*, *48*, 572–581.

NIST. (2023) National Institute of Standards and Technology (NIST) Artificial Intelligence Risk Management Framework (AI RMF 1.0) Available on https://nvlpubs.nist.gov/nistpubs/ai/nist.ai.100-1.pdf (Accessed 20 March 2025)

Norman, D. A. (2013). *The design of everyday things: Revised and expanded edition*. Basic Books.

Norman, D. A., & Verganti, R. (2014). Incremental and Radical Innovation: Design Research vs. Technology and Meaning Change. *Design Issues*, *30*(1), 78–96. DOI: 10.1162/DESI_a_00250

Nunnally, J. C., & Bernstein, I. H. (1994). *Psychometric theory* (3rd ed.). McGraw-Hill.

Nxele, L. (2018). Citizens' knowledge and perspectives on social accountability information access and distribution in Grahamstown. *Journal of Public Administration, 53*(4), 919–930.

O'Neil, C. (2016). *Weapons of math destruction: How big data increases inequality and threatens democracy*. Crown Publishing.

Observatorio de Responsabilidad Social Corporativa. (2021), *La responsabilidad social corporativa en las memorias anuales de las empresas del IBEX 35, análisis del ejercicio 2019*. Disponible en: https://observatoriorsc.org/inicio/que-hacemos/estudios/)

OECD. (2018). *Tax challenges arising from digitalisation: Economic analysis and evaluation of the impact of the proposals*. OECD Publishing.

OECD. (2020). *The digital economy outlook 2020*. OECD Publishing.

OECD. (2021). *OECD privacy framework*. OECD Publishing.

OECD. (2024) Futures of Global AI Governance: Co-Creating an Approach for Transforming Economies and Societies. 2024 OECD Global Strategy Group. Organisation for Economic Co-operation and Development OECD October 2024. Paris. JT03551355. Available on https://www.oecd.org/content/dam/oecd/en/about/programmes/strategic-foresight/GSG%20Background%20Note_GSG(2024)1en.pdf/_jcr_content/renditions/original./GSG%20Background%20Note_GSG(2024)1en.pdf (Accessed 20 March 2025)

Okoye, A. (2009). Theorising corporate social responsibility as an essentially contested concept: Is a definition necessary? *Journal of Business Ethics*, *89*, 613–627. DOI: 10.1007/s10551-008-0021-9

Oliner, S. D., & Sichel, D. E. (2000). The resurgence of growth in the late 1990s: Is information technology the story? *The Journal of Economic Perspectives*, *14*(4), 3–22.

Onyemelukwe, I. C., Ferreira, J. A. V., & Ramos, A. L. (2023, July). Exploring human centricity in industry 5.0: a systematic review. In *Proceedings of the International Conference on Industrial Engineering and Operations Management*.

Otegui Carles, A., Brea, J. A., & Araújo, N. (2023). The Ethical Attitudes of Generation Z in Spain Toward Animal-Based Tourism Attractions. *Tourism (Zagreb)*, *71*, 285–300. DOI: 10.37741/t.71.2.4

Pandey, J. (2018). Managing emotional labor for service employees: An HRM-based approach. *Human Resource Management International Digest*, *26*(4), 1–4. DOI: 10.1108/HRMID-03-2018-0044

Papadopoulos, T., Baltas, K. N., & Balta, M. E. (2020). The use of digital technologies by small and medium enterprises during COVID-19: Implications for theory and practice. *International Journal of Information Management*, *55*, 102192. PMID: 32836646

Papathanassiou, C., & Nieto, M. J. (2025). Different shades of green: EU corporate disclosure rules and their effectiveness in limiting "greenwashing". *ECB Occasional Paper*, (2025/370).

Pappas, I. O., Mikalef, P., Giannakos, M. N., Krogstie, J., & Lekakos, G. (2021). Big data and business analytics ecosystems: Paving the way towards digital transformation and sustainable societies. *Information Systems and e-Business Management*, *19*(4), 885–902. 10.1007-s10257-018-0377-z

Pardee, R. L. (1990, February). *Motivation Theories of Maslow, Herzberg, McGregor & McClelland. A Literature Review of Selected Theories Dealing with Job Satisfaction and Motivation.* Ed.gov; ERIC. https://eric.ed.gov/?id=ED316767

Parker, G. G., Van Alstyne, M. W., & Choudary, S. P. (2016). *Platform revolution: How networked markets are transforming the economy and how to make them work for you.* W. W. Norton & Company.

Park, J., Yoo, J. W., Cho, Y., & Park, H. (2024). Understanding switching intentions between traditional banks and Internet-only banks among Generation X and Generation Z. *International Journal of Bank Marketing*, *42*(5), 1114–1141. DOI: 10.1108/IJBM-06-2023-0338

Park, S. H., & Park, J. Y. (2024). Exploring the Model of Social Enterprise in Sport: Focused on Organization Form (Type) and Task. *Journal of Industrial Convergence*, *22*(2), 73–83.

Pasipamire, N., & Muroyiwa, A. (2024). Navigating algorithm bias in AI: Ensuring fairness and trust in Africa. *Frontiers in Research Metrics and Analytics*, *9*. Advance online publication. DOI: 10.3389/frma.2024.1486600 PMID: 39512269

Pasquale, F. (2015). *The black box society: The secret algorithms that control money and information.* Harvard University Press.

Patil, K. P., & Kulkarni, M. S. (2024). Harmonising human and robotic workforces in Industry 5.0: Creating a resilient, human-centric, and sustainable organisational ecosystem. In *Modern Technologies and Tools Supporting the Development of Industry 5.0* (pp. 179–208). CRC Press.

Patten, D. M. (2002). The relation between environmental performance and environmental disclosure: A research note. *Accounting, Organizations and Society*, *27*(8), 763–773. DOI: 10.1016/S0361-3682(02)00028-4

Pekerti, A. A., & Arli, D. (2017). Do Cultural and Generational Cohorts Matter to Ideologies and Consumer Ethics? A Comparative Study of Australians, Indonesians, and Indonesian Migrants in Australia. *Journal of Business Ethics*, *143*(2), 387–404. DOI: 10.1007/s10551-015-2777-z

Peñarrubia, J. P (2024) ¿Quién cuida el jardín?: Cuidado humanizador de los cimientos individuales y sociales ante el impacto de las tecnologías digitales. SCIO Revista de Filosofía, n.º 26, Julio de 2024, 123-149, ISSN: 1887-9853 DOI: https://doi.org/DOI: 10.46583/scio_2024.26.1155

Peñarrubia, J. P. (2022a) Etica profesional TIC para una sociedad digital sostenible. Conference on XXIX Congress European Business Ethics Network - EBEN España. 25-27 May 2022. ESIC University. Pozuelo de Alarcón.

Peñarrubia, J. P. (2022b) El papel de la ética profesional de la ingeniería informática como elemento necesario para la construcción y la sostenibilidad de la sociedad digital. Communication on VI International Congress on Bioethics / Congreso Internacional de Bioética: Bioética y Democracia ante el reto de la Inteligencia Artificial. 24-28 October 2022. University of Costa Rica. San José. In press, accepted for publication 25 August 2022.

Peralta, A. (2024). ¿Millenials, Generación Z o Zillennials? Te decimos a cuál perteneces según éstas características. *Milenio*. https://www.milenio.com/cultura/entre-la-generacion-z-y-los-millenias-se-encuentran-los-zillenials?utm_source=chatgpt.com

Peruzzini, M., & Prati, E., & Pelicciari, M. (2023). A framework to design smart manufacturing systems for Industry 5.0 based on the human-automation symbiosis. *International Journal of Computer Integrated Manufacturing*, •••, 1–18. DOI: 10.1080/0951192x.2023.2257634

Philippon, T. (2016). The FinTech opportunity. *NBER Working Paper No. 22476*. https://doi.org/DOI: 10.3386/w22476

Pilkington, M. (2016). Blockchain technology: Principles and applications. In Olleros, X., & Zhegu, M. (Eds.), *Research handbook on digital transformations* (pp. 225–253). Edward Elgar.

Pluta, A., & Rudawska, A. (2016). Holistic approach to human resources and organizational acceleration. *Journal of Organizational Change Management, 29*(2), 293–309. DOI: 10.1108/JOCM-04-2015-0060

Porter, M. E., & Kramer, M. R. (2019). Creating shared value. *Harvard Business Review, 97*(1), 62–77.

Prasad, H. C. S., Suar, D., & Taraban, R. (2014). Antecedents and moderators of software professionals' performance. *SAGE Open, 4*(1), 1–11. DOI: 10.1177/2158244014522633

Prensky, M. (2001). Nativos e Inmigrantes Digitales. *Cuadrenos SEK 2.O*, 21.

Preston, S. H. (1984). Children and the elderly in the US. *Scientific American, 251*(6), 44–49.

Pullen, A., & Vachhani, S. J. (2021). Feminist Ethics and Women Leaders: From Difference to Intercorporeality. *Journal of Business Ethics, 173*(2), 233–243. DOI: 10.1007/s10551-020-04526-0

PYMNTS. (2023). *The ConnectedEconomy Monthly Report: Meet the Zillenials.* https://www.pymnts.com/study/the-connectedeconomy-monthly-report-zillennials-generation-trends/

Rachinger, M., Rauter, R., Müller, C., Vorraber, W., & Schirgi, E. (2018). Digitalization and the labour market: Theoretical knowledge and empirical project findings. *International Journal of Environmental and Science Education, 13*(7), 537–556.

Radu, R. (2020). *Digital sovereignty: The search for power in a data-driven world.* Oxford University Press.

Ragnedda, M., & Muschert, G. W. (Eds.). (2018). *Theorizing digital divides.* Routledge.

Rahman, M. A. (2023, December 20). *HR Analytics: Association with Big Data and Machine Learning Algorithms. An Empirical Study.* https://doi.org/DOI: 10.13140/RG.2.2.35545.49768

Rahman, S., & Thelen, K. (2019). The gig economy and the future of work: A comparative analysis of labor platforms across sectors and countries. *Comparative Political Studies, 52*(11), 1652–1680.

Raji, I. D., Gebru, T., Mitchell, M., Buolamwini, J., Lee, J., & Denton, E. (2020). Saving face: Investigating the ethical concerns of facial recognition auditing. *Proceedings of the AAAI/ACM Conference on Artificial Intelligence, Ethics, and Society.* DOI: DOI: 10.1145/3375627.3375820

Rajuroy, A. (2024, December 22). *AI-Driven Solutions for Monitoring and Addressing Employee Engagement in High-Stress IT Roles*. https://www.researchgate.net/publication/387312543_AI-Driven_Solutions_for_Monitoring_and_Addressing_Employee_Engagement_in_High-Stress_IT_Roles

Ramos-Hidalgo, E., Diaz-Carrion, R., & Rodríguez-Rad, C. (2022). Does sustainable consumption make consumers happy? *International Journal of Market Research*, *64*(2), 227–248. DOI: 10.1177/14707853211030482

Rane, N. L., Desai, P., Rane, J., & Mallick, S. K. (2024). *Using artificial intelligence, machine learning, and deep learning for sentiment analysis in customer relationship management to improve customer experience, loyalty, and satisfaction*. Using Artificial Intelligence, Machine Learning, and Deep Learning for Sentiment Analysis in Customer Relationship Management to Improve Customer Experience, Loyalty, and Satisfaction., DOI: 10.70593/978-81-981367-4-9_7

Rashid, A. B., & Kausik, A. K. (2024). AI Revolutionizing Industries Worldwide: A Comprehensive Overview of Its Diverse Applications. *Hybrid Advances*, *7*(100277), 100277–100277. DOI: 10.1016/j.hybadv.2024.100277

Rathore, R., & Rathore, S. P. S. (2024). Machine Learning Applications in Human Resource Management: Predicting Employee Turnover and Performance. *International Journal for Global Academic & Scientific Research*, *3*(2), 48–59. DOI: 10.55938/ijgasr.v3i2.77

Rawlins, B. (2008). Measuring the Relationship Between Organizational Transparency and Employee Trust. *The Public Relations Journal*, *2*(2), 1–21.

Reinhardt, F. (1998). Environmental product differentiation: Implications for corporate strategy. *California Management Review*, *40*(4), 43. DOI: 10.2307/41165964

Ribeiro, M. T., Singh, S., & Guestrin, C. (2016). Why should I trust you? Explaining the predictions of any classifier. *Proceedings of the 22nd ACM SIGKDD International Conference on Knowledge Discovery and Data Mining*. DOI: DOI: 10.1145/2939672.2939778

Ritu, R. (2024). A Comprehensive Study On Employee Engagement Strategies. *Educational Administration: Theory and Practice*, 5894–5899. https://doi.org/DOI: 10.53555/kuey.v30i4.2309

Rochet, J.-C., & Tirole, J. (2003). Platform competition in two-sided markets. *Journal of the European Economic Association*, *1*(4), 990–1029.

Rodgers, W., Murray, J. M., Stefanidis, A., Degbey, W. Y., & Tarba, S. Y. (2022). An artificial intelligence algorithmic approach to ethical decision-making in human resource management processes. *Human Resource Management Review*, *33*(1), 100925. DOI: 10.1016/j.hrmr.2022.100925

Rodrigues, M. A. B., & Morais, A. I. (2021). How to Challenge University Students to Work on Integrated Reporting and Integrated Reporting Assurance. *Sustainability*, *13*(19), 10761. DOI: 10.3390/su131910761

Rodriguez-Rad, C. J., & Ramos-Hidalgo, E. (2018). Spirituality, consumer ethics, and sustainability: The mediating role of moral identity. *Journal of Consumer Marketing*, *35*(1), 51–63. DOI: 10.1108/JCM-12-2016-2035

Rolnick, D., Donti, P. L., Kaack, L. H., ... (2019). Tackling Climate Change with Machine Learning. arXiv preprint arXiv:1906.05433. Available in: https://arxiv.org/abs/1906.05433

Ruggerio, C. A. (2021). Sustainability and sustainable development: A review of principles and definitions. *The Science of the Total Environment*, *786*, 147481. DOI: 10.1016/j.scitotenv.2021.147481

Ruggie, J. G. American Exceptionalism, Exemptionalism and Global Governance (February 6, 2004). Available at *SSRN*: https://ssrn.com/abstract=517642 or http://dx.doi.org/DOI: 10.2139/ssrn.517642

Saadat, S., Rahmati, D., & Lahooti, V. (2020). The underlying paradigms of industry 4.0-based societies. *IEEE Access : Practical Innovations, Open Solutions*, *8*, 173825–173836.

Sachse, U. (2022). Digital transformation in family firms: An exploratory analysis. *Journal of Business Research*, *144*, 143–162.

Saka, M. (2024). Bridging the divide: Addressing socioeconomic inequality in post-apartheid South Africa within the framework of millennium development goals (2000-2015). *Journal of International Students*, *20*(1), 201–231.

Saks, A. M. (2006). Antecedents and Consequences of Employee Engagement. *Journal of Managerial Psychology*, *21*(7), 600–619. DOI: 10.1108/02683940610690169

Salazar, N. B. (2010). *Envisioning Eden: Mobilizing Imaginaries in Tourism and Beyond.* Berghahn Books., Available at https://books.google.nl/books?id=Vx85TX9T3h0C

Salovey, P., & Mayer, J. D. (1990). Emotional intelligence. *Imagination, Cognition and Personality*, *9*(3), 185–211. DOI: 10.2190/DUGG-P24E-52WK-6CDG

Sammu, J., & Joy, J. (2024, November 22). *Predictive Analytics in Employee Retention and Engagement Strategies*. ResearchGate; unknown. https://www.researchgate.net/publication/386050620_Predictive_Analytics_in_Employee_Retention_and_Engagement_Strategies

Samson, B., None Olukunle Oladipupo Amoo, None Akoh Atadoga, Abrahams, O., None Femi Osasona, & None Oluwatoyin Ajoke Farayola. (2024). Ethical AI in practice: Balancing technological advancements with human values. *International Journal of Science and Research Archive, 11*(1), 1311–1326. DOI: 10.30574/ijsra.2024.11.1.0218

Saputra, W. (2024). Pengaruh Gaya Kepemimpinan dan Budaya Organisasi Terhadap Keterlibatan Karyawan. *Indo-Fintech Intellectuals: Journal of Economics and Business, 4*(4), 1559–1567. DOI: 10.54373/ifijeb.v4i4.1662

Saraiva, A. (2023). Ethics and Responsibility in Artificial Intelligence: A Global Perspective and Portugal's AI Governance. 186. Call for AI – GEE Papers. GOV. Available in: https://www.gee.gov.pt/pt/estudos-eseminarios/gee-papers-category/33900-ethics-and-responsibility-in-artificial-intelligence-a-global-perspectiveand-portugal-s-ai-governance

Saraiva, A., & Silva, M. (2024). Governance and Transparency: Ethical Leadership in the information age. In Machado, A., Sousa, M., Pequeira, A., Brambila, A., & Alavaro, A. (Eds.), *Environmental, Social And Governance And Digital Transformation In Organizations*. Springer.

Sari, R. E., Min, S., Purwoko, H., Furinto, A., & Tamara, D. (2020). Artificial Intelligence for a Better Employee Engagement. *International Research Journal of Business Studies, 13*(2), 173–188. DOI: 10.21632/irjbs.13.2.173-188

Sartor, G., & Luciano, F. (2020). Legal reasoning with machine learning: A critical survey. *Artificial Intelligence and Law, 28*(3), 333–381.

Scherer, A., & Palazzo, G. (2007). Toward a Political Conception of Corporate Responsibility: Business and Society Seen from a Habermasian Perspective. *Academy of Management Review, 32*(4), 1096–1120. DOI: 10.5465/amr.2007.26585837

Schewe, C. D., & Meredith, G. (2004). Segmenting global markets by generational cohorts: Determining motivations by age. *Journal of Consumer Behaviour: An International Research Review, 4*(1), 51–63.

Schneier, B. (2015). *Data and Goliath: The hidden battles to collect your data and control your world*. W. W. Norton & Company.

Schwab, K. (2016). The Fourth Industrial Revolution. World Economic Forum.

Schwab, K., & Davis, N. (2020). *Shaping the Future of the Fourth Industrial Revolution*. Currency. DOI.

Schwartz, R., Dodge, J., Smith, N. A., & Etzioni, O. (2020). Green Artificial Intelligence. *Communications of the ACM*, *63*(12), 54–63. DOI: 10.1145/3381831

Seethamraju, R., & Krishna Sundar, D. (2013). Influence of ERP systems on business process agility. *IIMB Management Review*, *25*(3), 137–149.

Shafiee, S., Ghatari, A. R., Hasanzadeh, A., & Jahanyan, S. (2019). Developing a model for sustainable smart tourism destinations: A systematic review. *Tourism Management Perspectives*, *31*, 287–300. DOI: 10.1016/j.tmp.2019.06.002

Shah, S., & Suhaimi Mhd. Sarif. (2023). Building a Culture-Conscious Workforce. *International Journal of Culture and Education*, *1*(3). Advance online publication. DOI: 10.59600/ijcae.v1i3.15

Sharma, S. (2022). How ethical are my millennials? A qualitative study. *Journal of Information. Communication and Ethics in Society*, *20*(4), 531–545.

Shaw, W. H. (2009). Marxism, business ethics, and corporate social responsibility. *Journal of Business Ethics*, *84*, 565–576. DOI: 10.1007/s10551-008-9725-0

Shchepkina, N., Ramnarayan, Dhaliwal, N., Ravikiran K, & Nangia, R. (2024). Human-Centric AI Adoption and Its Influence on Worker Productivity: An Empirical Investigation. *BIO Web of Conferences, 86*, 01060–01060. https://doi.org/DOI: 10.1051/bioconf/20248601060

Sheehan, M. (2023) China's AI Regulations and How They Get Made Carnegie Endowment for International Peace. Available on https://carnegieendowment.org/research/2023/07/chinas-ai-regulations-and-how-they-get-made (Accessed 22 March 2025)

Sheller, M., & Urry, J. (2004). *Tourism Mobilities: Places to Play, Places in Play*. Routledge.

Shiel, C., do Paço, A., & Alves, H. (2020). Generativity, sustainable development and green consumer behaviour. *Journal of Cleaner Production*, *245*, 118865. https://doi.org/https://doi.org/10.1016/j.jclepro.2019.118865

Shiller, R. J. (2000). *Irrational exuberance*. Princeton University Press.

Shneiderman, B. (2020). Bridging the Gap between Ethics and Practice. *ACM Transactions on Interactive Intelligent Systems*, *10*(4), 1–31. DOI: 10.1145/3419764

Siau, K., & Wang, W. (2018). Building trust in artificial intelligence, machine learning, and robotics. Cutter Business Technology Journal, 31(2), 47–53. Available in: https://www.cutter.com/article/building-trust-artificial-intelligence-machine-learning-and-robotics-498981

Singh, S., Rai, M., Pandey, J. K., & Saxena, A. K. (2024). Emotional Intelligence and Collaborative Dynamics in Industry 5.0 for Human-Machine Interactions. *Advances in Computational Intelligence and Robotics Book Series*, 190–204. https://doi.org/DOI: 10.4018/979-8-3693-6806-0.ch010

Singh, D., & Cohen, V. (2024). Socio-economic dimensions and human centricity in Industry 5.0: A study on manufacturing sectors in central and Eastern European economies. *Journal of Economic Studies (Glasgow, Scotland)*. Advance online publication. DOI: 10.1108/jes-02-2024-0067

Singh, S., & Prakash, N. (2020). Are Values A Differentiation Criterion for Generational Cohorts? International Journal of Current Advanced Research. *International Journal of Current Advanced Research*, *9*(12), 23505–23510. DOI: 10.24327/ijcar.2020.23510.4655

Sirmon, D. G., Arregle, J. L., Hitt, M. A., & Webb, J. W. (2011). Resource orchestration to create competitive advantage: Breadth, depth, and life cycle effects. In Corbett, A. C., & Katz, J. A. (Eds.), *Insights to a Changing World* (Vol. 2, pp. 63–88). Emerald Group Publishing Limited.

Siu, A. (2023). What marketers need to know about 'Generation Zennial,' from social media to buying habits. *Digiday*. https://digiday.com/marketing/what-marketers-need-to-know-about-generation-zennial-from-social-media-to-buying-habits/

Sivarajah, U., Kamal, M. M., Irani, Z., & Weerakkody, V. (2021). Critical analysis of big data challenges and analytical methods. *Journal of Business Research*, *70*(1), 263–286. https://www.sciencedirect.com/science/article/pii/S014829631630488X

Sofyani, H., Riyadh, H. A., & Fahlevi, H. (2020). Improving service quality, accountability and transparency of local government: The intervening role of information technology governance. *Cogent Business & Management*, *7*(1), 1–21.

Solove, D. J. (2013). Privacy self-management and the consent dilemma. *Harvard Law Review*, *126*(7), 1880–1903.

Solove, D. J. (2020). *Understanding privacy*. Harvard University Press.

Solove, D. J., & Schwartz, P. M. (2020). *Privacy law fundamentals* (6th ed.). IAPP.

Soluk, J. (2018). How digitalization is changing today's business. *European Scientific Journal, 14*(13), 59–66.

Soluk, J., & Kammerlander, N. (2021). Digital transformation in family-owned Mittelstand firms: A dynamic capabilities perspective. *European Journal of Information Systems, 30*(6), 636–671.

Steurer, R. (2010). The role of governments in corporate social responsibility: Characterising public policies on CSR in Europe. *Policy Sciences, 43*, 49–72. DOI: 10.1007/s11077-009-9084-4

Steurer, R., Martinuzzi, A., & Margula, S. (2012). Public policies on CSR in Europe: Themes, instruments and regional differences. *Corporate Social Responsibility and Environmental Management, 19*, 206–227. DOI: 10.1002/csr.264

Strauss, W., & Howe, N. (1991). *Consumer Behaviour.* The Dryden Press.

Stromberg, S. (2019, September 17). Why baby boomers' grandchildren will hate them. *The Washington Post.* https://www.washingtonpost.com/opinions/2019/09/17/why-baby-boomers-grandchildren-will-hate-them/

Strubell, E., Ganesh, A., & McCallum, A. (2019). Energy and policy considerations for deep learning in NLP. *Proceedings of the 57th Annual Meeting of the Association for Computational Linguistics.* DOI: DOI: 10.18653/v1/P19-1355

Subramaniam, M., & Youndt, M. A. (2005). The influence of intellectual capital on the types of innovative capabilities. *Academy of Management Journal, 48*(3), 450–463. DOI: 10.5465/amj.2005.17407911

Sun, Y., & Jung, H. (2024). Machine Learning (ML) Modeling, IoT, and Optimizing Organizational Operations through Integrated Strategies: The Role of Technology and Human Resource Management. *Sustainability, 16*(16), 6751–6751. DOI: 10.3390/su16166751

Sun, Y., Ma, H., & Chan, E. H. W. (2018). A model to measure tourist preference toward scenic spots based on social media data: A case of Dapeng in China. *Sustainability (Switzerland), 10*(1). *Scopus.* Advance online publication. DOI: 10.3390/su10010043

Supanti, D., Butcher, K., & Fredline, L. (2015). Enhancing the employer-employee relationship through corporate social responsibility (CSR) engagement. *International Journal of Contemporary Hospitality Management, 27*(7), 1479–1498. DOI: 10.1108/IJCHM-06-2014-0286

Suriati, S., Ibrahim, M. B. H., Irawan, A., Akbar, M. A., & Yendra, Y. (2024). Effective Strategies for Retaining and Nurturing Employees in Organizations. *Advances: Jurnal Ekonomi & Bisnis*, *2*(3), 151–162. DOI: 10.60079/ajeb.v2i3.191

Suriyankietkaew, S., Krittayaruangroj, K., & Iamsawan, N. (2022). Sustainable Leadership practices and competencies of SMEs for sustainability and resilience: A community-based social enterprise study. *Sustainability*, *14*(10), 5762.

Swiss Life. (2016). *Study intergenerational solidarity*. https://www.swisslife.com/en/home/blog/intergenerational-solidarity.html

Tabouli, E. M. A., Habtoor, N. A., & Nashief, S. M. (2016). The impact of human resources management on employee performance: Organizational commitment mediator variable. *Asian Social Science*, *12*(9), 176–192. DOI: 10.5539/ass.v12n9p176

Tauringana, V. & Afrifa, G.A. (2013). The relative importance of working capital management and its components to SMEs' profitability, 20(3), 453–469.

Teeroovengadum, V., Heeraman, N. & Jugurnath, B. (2017). Examining the antecedents of ICT adoption in education using an Extended Technology Acceptance Model (TAM) Viraiyan Teeroovengadum, Nabeel Heeraman and Bhavish Jugurnath University of Mauritius. *International Journal of Education and Development using ICT*, 13(3), 4–23.

Teo, S. T. T., Nguyen, D., Meurer, M., & Bentley, T. (2021). High commitment HRM and burnout of frontline food service employees: A moderated mediation model. *Employee Relations*, *43*(6), 1342–1361. DOI: 10.1108/ER-10-2020-0484

Tetlock, P. E. (1985). Accountability: A social check on the fundamental attribution error. *Social Psychology Quarterly*, *48*(3), 227–236. DOI: 10.2307/3033683

Tetlock, P., Skitka, L., & Boettger, R. (1989). Social and Cognitive Strategies for Coping With Accountability: Conformity, Complexity, and Bolstering. *Journal of Personality and Social Psychology*, *57*, 632–640. DOI: 10.1037//0022-3514.57.4.632

Thakkar, D. (2021). Leveraging AI to Transform Talent Acquisition. *ResearchGate*. https://doi.org/DOI: 10.13140/RG.2.2.27746.54722

Thomas, A., Chawla, Y., Varma, A., & Szleter, P. (2024). The Role of Business Leaders in Industry 5.0. *Springer Proceedings in Complexity*, 629–640. https://doi.org/DOI: 10.1007/978-3-031-44721-1_47

Tiainen, L. (2024). *Unmasking Greenwashing : An Examination of Generation Z 's Perception of Sustainable Business* [LAB University of Applied Sciences]. https://www.theseus.fi/handle/10024/852630

Tikkinen-Piri, C., Rohunen, A., & Markkula, J. (2018). EU general data protection regulation: Changes and implications for personal data collecting companies. *Computer Law & Security Review*, *34*(1), 134–153.

Timsina, S. (2024). Employee Turnover and Engagement Programs for Retention. *Theseus.fi, 1*(1). https://www.theseus.fi/handle/10024/851623

Toleikienė, R., Balciunas, S., & Juknevičienė, V. (2020). Youth Attitudes Towards Intolerance to Corruption in Lithuania. *Scientific Papers of the University of Pardubice, Series D. Faculty of Economics and Administration*, *28*, 1–13. DOI: 10.46585/sp28020109

Treviño, L. K., & Nelson, K. A. (2021). *Managing Business Ethics: Straight Talk About How to Do It Right* (8th ed.). Wiley.

Treviño, L. K., Weaver, G. R., & Reynolds, S. J. (2006). Behavioral ethics in organizations: A review. *Journal of Management*, *32*(6), 951–990. DOI: 10.1177/0149206306294258

Tu, Q., & Liu, A. (2014). Framework of smart tourism research and related progress in China. In A. Kong (Ed.), International conference on management and engineering (CME 2014) (pp. 140-146). Shanghai, China.

Twenge, J. M., Cooper, A. B., Joiner, T. E., Duffy, M. E., & Binau, S. G. (2019). Age, period, and cohort trends in mood disorder indicators and suicide-related outcomes in a Nationally Representative Dataset, 2005 – 2017. *Journal of Abnormal Psychology*, *128*(3), 185–199. https://doi.org/https://dx.doi.org/10.1037/abn0000410

Uche, S. C. (2018). *Generation Z and corporate social responsibility*. Syracuse University.

UNESCO. (2021). Recommendation on the Ethics of Artificial Intelligence. Available in: https://unesdoc.unesco.org/ark:/48223/pf0000380455

United Nations (UN). (2015). Transforming our world: The 2030 Agenda for Sustainable Development. Available in: https://sdgs.un.org/2030agenda

Ureche, A. (2023). The Salience of Social Enterprise: a 'Fictional', Functional Tale of Three Sectors Cooperation. In *Proceedings of the International Conference on Business Excellence* 17(1), 870–881.

Utting, P. (2008). The struggle for corporate accountability. *Development and Change*, *39*(6), 959–975.

Vajravelu, A., Thanikachalam, Y., Abd Wahab, M. H. B., Jamil, M. M. B. A., & Sivaranjani, S. (2024). Human-Machine Collaboration and Emotional Intelligence in Industry 5.0. In Human-Machine Collaboration and Emotional Intelligence in Industry 5.0 (pp. 220-232). IGI Global.

Valentine, S., Godkin, L., & Lucero, M. (2002). Ethical Context, Organizational Commitment, and Person–Organization Fit. *Journal of Business Ethics*, *41*(4), 349–360. DOI: 10.1023/A:1021243117958

Van Kenhove, P., Vermeir, I., & Verniers, S. (2001). An Empirical Investigation of the Relationships between Ethical Beliefs, Ethical Ideology, Political Preference and Need for Closure e of Dutch-Speaking Consumers in Belgium. *Journal of Business Ethics*, *32*, 347–361. DOI: 10.1023/A:1010720908680

Vanka, S., Rao, M. B., Singh, S., & Pulaparthi, M. R. (2023). *Sustainable Human Resource Management: Transforming Organizations, Societies and Environment.* Routledge., DOI: 10.4324/9781003258220

Vannini, P. (2010). Mobile Cultures: From the Sociology of Transportation to the Study of Mobilities. *Sociology Compass*, *4*(2), 111–121.

Varian, H. R. (2019). Artificial intelligence, economics, and industrial organization. In Agrawal, A., Gans, J., & Goldfarb, A. (Eds.), *The economics of artificial intelligence: An agenda* (pp. 399–419). University of Chicago Press.

Veale, M., & Binns, R. (2017). Fairer machine learning in the real world: Mitigating discrimination without collecting sensitive data. *Big Data & Society*, *4*(2). Advance online publication. DOI: 10.1177/2053951717743530

Venugopal, M., Madhavan, V., Prasad, R., & Raman, R. (2024). Transformative AI in human resource management: Enhancing workforce planning with topic modeling. *Cogent Business & Management*, *11*(1). Advance online publication. DOI: 10.1080/23311975.2024.2432550

Verver, M., Dahles, H., & Soeterbroek, I. (2024). Scaling for social enterprise development: A mixed embeddedness perspective on two Dutch non-profit organisations. *Journal of Social Entrepreneurship*, *15*(2), 659–685.

Visconti, P., Rausa, G., Del-Valle-Soto, C., & Velázquez, R., Donato Cafagna, & Fazio, R. D. (2024). Machine Learning and IoT-Based Solutions in Industrial Applications for Smart Manufacturing: A Critical Review. *Future Internet*, *16*(11), 394–394. DOI: 10.3390/fi16110394

Vitell, S. J., & Muncy, J. (2005). The Muncy-Vitell consumer ethics scale: A modification and application. *Journal of Business Ethics*, *62*(3), 267–275. DOI: 10.1007/s10551-005-7058-9

Vitell, S. J., Singhapakdi, A., & Thomas, J. (2001). Consumer ethics: An application and empirical testing of the Hunt-Vitell theory of ethics. *Journal of Consumer Marketing*, *18*(2), 153–178.

Vitell, S., Ramos-Hidalgo, E., & Rodríguez-Rad, C. (2018). A Spanish perspective on the impact on religiosity and spirituality on consumer ethics. *International Journal of Consumer Studies*, *42*(6), 675–686. https://doi.org/https://doi.org/10.1111/ijcs.12438

Voelsen, D. (2021). Democracy and Digital Technology. German Institute for International and Security Affairs. Available in: https://www.swp-berlin.org/10.18449/2021RP03/

Voigt, P., & Von dem Bussche, A. (2017). *The EU General Data Protection Regulation (GDPR): A Practical Guide*. Springer., DOI: 10.1007/978-3-319-57959-7

Walker, A. (2012). The New Ageism. *The Political Quarterly*, *83*(4), 812–819. https://doi.org/https://doi.org/10.1111/j.1467-923X.2012.02360.x

Walker, B., Gunderson, L. H., Kinzig, A., Folke, C., Carpenter, S., & Schultz, L. (2006). A Handful of Heuristics and Some Propositions for Understanding Resilience. *Ecology and Society*, *11*(1), 13.

Wallimann-Helmer, I., Terán, L., Portmann, E., Schübel, H., & Pincay, J. (2021). An Integrated Framework for Ethical and Sustainable Digitalization. *2021 Eighth International Conference on EDemocracy & EGovernment (ICEDEG)*, 156–162. https://doi.org/DOI: 10.1109/ICEDEG52154.2021.9530972

Walsh, K., Theron, R., & Reeders, C. (2021). Estimating the economic cost of load shedding in South Africa. In *Paper submission to Biennial Conference of the Economic Society of South Africa (ESSA)*, 22(1), 1-22.

Wang, D., Li, X. R., & Li, Y. (2013). China's "smart tourism destination" initiative: A taste of the service-dominant logic. *Journal of Destination Marketing & Management*, *2*(2), 59–61. DOI: 10.1016/j.jdmm.2013.05.004

Wang, D., Park, S., & Fesenmaier, D. R. (2012). The role of smartphones in mediating the touristic experience. *Journal of Travel Research*, *51*(4), 371–387. DOI: 10.1177/0047287511426341

Wang, D., Xiang, Z., & Fesenmaier, D. R. (2016). Smartphone use in everyday life and travel. *Journal of Travel Research*, *55*(1), 52–63. DOI: 10.1177/0047287514535847

Wang, Q., Myers, M. D., & Sundaram, D. (2013). Digital natives and digital immigrants: Towards a model of digital fluency. *Business & Information Systems Engineering*, *5*(6), 409–419. DOI: 10.1007/s12599-013-0296-y

Ward, J. L. (2004). *Perpetuating the family business: 50 lessons learned from long-lasting, successful families in business*. Palgrave Macmillan.

Wayne, S. J., Shore, L. M., & Liden, R. C. (1997). Perceived organizational support and leader-member exchange: A social exchange perspective. *Academy of Management Journal*, *40*(1), 82–111.

White House. (2022) Blueprint for an AI Bill of Rights. White House Office of Science and Technology Policy (OSTP). October 2022. Available on https://www.whitehouse.gov/wp-content/uploads/2022/10/Blueprint-for-an-AI-Bill-of-Rights.pdf (Accessed 25 March 2025)

White House. (2023) National artificial intelligence research and development strategic plan: 2023 update. The White House Office of Management and Budget. Available on https://www.whitehouse.gov/wp-content/uploads/2023/05/National-Artificial-Intelligence-Research-and-Development-Strategic-Plan-2023-Update.pdf (Accessed 20 March 2025)

White House. (2024) Advancing Governance, Innovation, and Risk Management for Agency Use of Artificial Intelligence. The White House Office of Management and Budget. Available on https://www.whitehouse.gov/wp-content/uploads/2024/03/M-24-10-Advancing-Governance-Innovation-and-Risk-Management-for-Agency-Use-of-Artificial-Intelligence.pdf (Accessed 20 March 2025)

Whitehouse, L. (2003). Corporate Social Responsibility, Corporate Citizenship and the Global Compact. *Global Social Policy*, *3*(3), 299–318. DOI: 10.1177/146801810300330

Winterton, J., & Cafferkey, K. (2019). Revisiting human capital theory: progress and prospects. *Elgar Introduction to Human Resources and Employment Relations Theories*, 218–234. https://doi.org/DOI: 10.4337/9781786439017.00023

Wood, J., & Winston, B. (2007). Development of three scales to measure leader accountability. *Leadership and Organization Development Journal*, *28*, 167–185. DOI: 10.1108/01437730710726859

World Travel & Tourism Council. (2019). Economic impact. https://wttc.org/Research/Insights

Wright, P. M., & McMahan, G. C. (2011). Exploring human capital: Putting 'human' back into strategic human resource management. *Human Resource Management Journal, 21*(2), 93–104. DOI: 10.1111/j.1748-8583.2010.00165.x

Wright, P. M., & Ulrich, M. D. (2017). A Road Well Travelled: The Past, Present, and Future Journey of Strategic Human Resource Management. *Annual Review of Organizational Psychology and Organizational Behavior, 4*(1), 45–65.

Xiang, Z., & Fesenmaier, D. R. (2017). Big data analytics, tourism design and smart tourism. In Xiang, Z., & Fesenmaier, D. R. (Eds.), *Analytics in smart tourism design* (pp. 299–307). Springer., DOI: 10.1007/978-3-319-44263-1_17

Xiang, Z., & Gretzel, U. (2010). Role of social media in online travel information search. *Tourism Management, 31*(2), 179–188. DOI: 0.1016/j.tourman.2009.02.016

Xiang, Z., Wang, D., O'Leary, J. T., & Fesenmaier, D. R. (2015). Adapting to the Internet: Trends in travelers' use of the web for trip planning. *Journal of Travel Research, 54*(4), 511–527. DOI: 10.1177/0047287514522883

Youndt, M. A., Subramaniam, M., & Snell, S. A. (2004). Intellectual capital profiles: An examination of investments and returns. *Journal of Management Studies, 41*(2), 335–361. DOI: 10.1111/j.1467-6486.2004.00435.x

Young, D. R., & Lecy, J. D. (2014). Defining the Universe of Social Enterprise: Competing Metaphors. *International Society for Third Sector Research, 25*, 1307–1332.

Yusuf, F. A., & Widodo, W. (2023). The secret of reducing turnover intention: Evidence from Indonesia. *Cogent Business & Management, 10*(2), 2202026. DOI: 10.1080/23311975.2023.2202026

Zaikauskaitė, L., Butler, G., Helmi, N. F. S., Robinson, C. L., Treglown, L., Tsivrikos, D., & Devlin, J. T. (2022). Hunt–Vitell's General Theory of Marketing Ethics Predicts "Attitude-Behaviour" Gap in Pro-environmental Domain. *Frontiers in Psychology, 13*(March), 1–19. DOI: 10.3389/fpsyg.2022.732661

Zeng, B., & Gerritsen, R. (2014). What do we know about social media in tourism? A review. *Tourism Management Perspectives, 10*, 27–36. DOI: 10.1016/j.tmp.2014.01.001

Zhang, L.-y., Li, N., & Liu, M. (2012). On the basic concept of smarter tourism and its theoretical system. *Luyou Xuekan, 27*(5), 66–73.

Zhu, W., Zhang, L., & Li, N. (2014). Challenges, function changing of government and enterprises in Chinese smart tourism. In Z. Xiang, & I. Tussyadiah (Eds.), Short paper proceedings of the ENTER 2014 conference on information and communication technologies in tourism. https://ertr.tamu.edu/enter-2014-volume-4-research-notes/

Zimand-Sheiner, D., & Lissitsa, S. (2024). Generation Z - factors predicting decline in purchase intentions after receiving negative environmental information: Fast fashion brand SHEIN as a case study. *Journal of Retailing and Consumer Services, 81*, 103999. https://doi.org/https://doi.org/10.1016/j.jretconser.2024.103999

Zuboff, S. (2019). *The Age of Surveillance Capitalism: The Fight for a Human Future at the New Frontier of Power*. PublicAffairs.

Zueva, A., & Fairbrass, J. (2021). Politicising Government Engagement with Corporate Social Responsibility: "CSR" as an Empty Signifier. *Journal of Business Ethics, 170*, 635–655. DOI: 10.1007/s10551-019-04330-5

About the Contributors

Sandra Castro-González is Associate Professor in the Department of Business Organization and Marketing at the Universidade de Santiago de Compostela. She completed her BA in Business Administration in 2013 and a Master's Degree in Business Management in 2014, both from the Universidade de Santiago de Compostela. In 2017, she completed her PhD in Economics and Business at the same institution. Her research primarily focuses on consumer behavior, corporate social responsibility and sales management. Her publications include contributions to prominent journals such as the Corporate Social Responsibility and Environmental Management, Sustainable Production and Consumption, Current Psychology, Journal of Cleaner Production, or Social Responsibility Journal; she has also attended a number of national and international conferences.

Lucía Rey-Ares is Associate Professor in the Department of Financial Economics and Accounting at the Universidade de Santiago de Compostela. She completed her BA in Economics in 2012 and a Master's Degree in Business Management in 2013, both from the Universidade de Santiago de Compostela. In 2018, she completed her PhD in Economics and Business at the same institution. She belongs to the Interuniversity Research Center Economics and Business Administration for Society (ECOBAS). Her research primarily focuses on household finance, with particular emphasis on household saving and investment decisions, financial literacy, and financial vulnerability. Her publications include contributions to leading journals such as the International Journal of Bank Marketing, Journal of Cleaner Production, and Journal of Economic Surveys, among others. In addition, she has presented papers at various national and international conferences and has actively contributed to a range of research projects and contracts.

***

Ayyoob A is a Senior Research Scholar at the School of Business Studies, University of Calicut, specializing in sustainability, corporate governance, and strategic corporate social responsibility (CSR). A seasoned academic, Ayyoob has served as a resource person for numerous workshops on research methodology and data analysis. His scholarly contributions include publishing book chapters and articles in reputed platforms and presenting research papers at prestigious national and international conferences, both in India and abroad, organized by renowned universities. Additionally, Ayyoob actively reviews manuscripts for esteemed journals, showcasing his expertise and commitment to advancing research in his fields of interest.

Al Anoud Saad Al-Naemi is a PhD student in the Department of Business Organization at the Universitat Politècnica de València, conducting research on the application of predictive analytics and machine learning in talent management to improve organizational productivity and support evidence-based decision-making. She holds a Master's degree in Strategic Business Unit Management from HEC Paris and brings over 18 years of experience in senior leadership roles in human capital management within the Qatari public sector. She currently serves as Director of Government's Manpower Planning at the Civil Service and Governmental Development Bureau (CGB-Qatar), where she leads national workforce planning strategies, talent optimization initiatives, and human capital development programs aimed at building a resilient and future-ready public sector. Her work emphasizes aligning workforce capabilities with Qatar's national development goals through data-driven and forward-looking approaches. Her research interests focus on talent management, strategic workforce planning, leadership development, organizational transformation, and the integration of artificial intelligence and predictive modeling in talent management practices. She has authored multiple academic articles and continues to contribute to bridging the gap between academic research and public policy through her scholarly and professional endeavors.

Paula Antón-Maraña has Master's Degree in Business Intelligence and Big Data in Cyber-Secure Environments, Master's Degree in Teaching and Bachelor's Degree in Business Administration. Currently, she is a PhD student in Economics at the University of Burgos (Spain). Her research expertise lies in the application of quantitative methods to tourism, business analytics, and impact assessment, with a strong focus on sustainability, operational optimization, and AI-driven decision-making. Additionally, she has actively contributed to research projects and conferences in the fields of big data, business intelligence, metaheuristic optimization applied to healthcare, tourism, sustainability and business ethics. She also contributes as a reviewer for international scientific journals and collaborates on interdisciplinary projects aimed at enhancing data-driven decision-making through AI in both public and private sectors.

Jesus Barrena Martinez is an Associate Professor in the Department of Business Management at the University of Cadiz, Spain. His teaching and research interests include Human Resource Management, Corporate Social Responsibility, Sustainability and Intellectual Capital. He works in the University of Cadiz since 2009, participating in international and national research projects, transference agreements with companies as well as publishing several articles and chapters.

Badr Bentalha teaches Supply Chain and Operations Management at National School Of Business and Management – Fez, Sidi Mohamed Ben Abdellah University – Morocco. Dr. Bentalha investigates the structural dynamics and control of complex networks, applying his findings to supply chain management, Industry 4.0, risk analysis, and digital supply chains. His work emphasizes the intersection of supply chain management, operations research, industrial engineering, and digital technology. As a professor, he teaches undergraduate, graduate, and, doctoral courses in operations management, supply chain management, logistics, management information systems, and strategic management. Through guest lectures, webinars, and scholarly presentations, he engages students and fosters an active learning environment.Professor Bentalha specializes in supply chain and operations management, operations research, and service management. He is passionate about integrating knowledge across disciplines to solve real-world problems. He has delivered numerous invited plenary talks, keynotes, and panel discussions at conferences and global webinars.

Dolores Botella is an Associate Professor in the Department of Business Organization at the Universitat Politècnica de València. She has nearly 20 years of teaching experience in undergraduate and master's programs, and has held various university management positions. Her research interests focus on Talent Management, as well as Entrepreneurial and Digital Skills. She has published over 35 articles in journals indexed in the Journal Citation Reports (JCR), as well as several books and book chapters with publishers such as IGI Global, Thomson Reuters, and Springer. She currently serves as guest editor for special issues of the journals ESIC Market (Q2) and Journal of Enterprising Communities: People and Places in the Global Economy (Q3), and is a member of the editorial board of leading journals including the Journal of Innovation & Knowledge (Q1). She has participated as a researcher in more than 10 research projects and is currently the principal investigator (PI) of a project focused on analyzing junior talent turnover in the technology sector.

Neelatphal Chanda is an assistant professor at the Department of Media Studies, CHRIST (Deemed to be University) BGR Campus. His study area revolves around Media Literacy, Media Pedagogical research, and technology-aided Communication. He pursued doctoral research at the Department of Mass Communication, Assam University (A Central University). Before joining media research and academia, he was a NEWS PRODUCER at News 18 Group (Etv News), Hyderabad.

Julieta Díez-Hernández holds a Master's degree in Circular Economy and Bachelor's Degree in Business Management. Currently, she is pursuing a PhD in Social Sciences the University of Burgos (Spain), where she works as a researcher on different European projects and as assistant professor in the Business and Economics Department. Her research focuses on sustainability, business ethics, circular economy, and impact assessment, analysing the social and ethical impact of novel materials and developing methodologies for life cycle sustainability assessment. She has worked on different European Horizon Europe projects in the field of materials development and innovation, fraud prevention and local revalorisation of waste.

María-José Foncubierta-Rodríguez is a PhD in Economics and Business Sciences (UNED). Associate Professor of Business Organization at the University of Cádiz (UCA). She has published articles in specialized journals within her field of expertise, all indexed in leading academic databases and catalogs (WoS, Scopus, Latindex, Scielo, etc.). She is a co-founder and researcher of the International University Network for Multidisciplinary Studies on Happiness and Creativity, part of INDESS, in which UCA is a pioneering institution in Spain. She actively contributes to the training of early-career researchers and serves as co-supervisor of several doctoral theses. She previously served as Director of the Faculty of Economics and Business Sciences at the Bahía de Algeciras Campus. Currently, she is the Principal Investigator (PI) of the research group SEJ-058: "Chair of Legal and Economic Studies of the Campo de Gibraltar", part of the PAIDI program of the Andalusian Regional Government.

Ishayu Gupta is a Student pursuing Media Studies from Christ University, Bengaluru and holds a special interest in covering and reporting politics and sports. He is looking forward to pave a career in the field of Broadcast Media. He has worked with News Organisations like the Statesman, the Telegraph and has more than 50+ by-lines for the same. He is currently working as an Accredited Reporter for the Indian Super League.

Dara Hernandez Roque began research activity began with the development of their doctoral thesis, during which they started exploring the concept of resilience. This line of inquiry led them to delve deeper into the theory of psychological capital and its relationship with entrepreneurship—specifically, academic entrepreneurs and academic spin-offs. Over the years, they have completed various courses related to research in the social sciences and have participated in both national and international conferences and academic meetings. They have also authored research articles published in peer-reviewed journals. In the field of teaching, they have delivered numerous courses across various degree programs within the Department of Business Organization. Among the most notable subjects they have taught are those related to human resources, logistics, and operations management. They have also taken part in teaching innovation projects. In terms of academic administration, They was appointed Head of Section of their department at the Algeciras Campus in the 2013/2014 academic year, a position they continue to hold.

Tiko Iyamu holds a PhD in information systems from the University of Cape Town, South Africa. Currently, Iyamu is Research Professor at the Faculty of Informatics and Design, Cape Peninsula University of Technology (CPUT), Cape Town, South Africa. Previously, he was with the Tshwane University of Technology, South Africa, and Namibia University of Science and Technology, Namibia. Iyamu served as a Professor Extraordinaire at the Department of Computer Science, University of the Western Cape, from 2006 to 2015. In 2014, he was a visiting Professor at the Flensburg University of Applied Sciences, Germany. Professor Iyamu's areas of focus include enterprise architecture, health informatics, big data analytics, and mobile computing. In addition, he has keen interest in the application of sociotechnical theories, such as actor-network theory, structuration theory, and diffusion of innovation in information systems research. He has authored 6 books, and over 150 peer-reviewed research articles in journals, conference proceedings and book chapters.

William Olivier is a lecturer in Information and Communication Technology Research Areas: - Information Systems and Mobile Technology - Information Systems in Healthcare

María del Carmen Peces-Prieto is an Assistant Professor (Profesora Ayudante Doctora) in the Department of Spanish and International Economics, Econometrics, Economic History and Institutions at the Faculty of Law and Social Sciences, UCLM, Ciudad Real Campus. Academic Background: Ph.D. in Economics and Business Sciences from the University of Córdoba (2014–2020). Research Interests: Intellectual Capital Applied Economics Energy Economics, with a focus on renewable energies and energy efficiency Sustainable Development Innovation and Technological Change in Productive Structures Research Group: Member of the Sustainable Economy Seminar (Seminario de Economía Sostenible) at

UCLM, which concentrates on creating value and distributing goods and services to enhance well-being while minimizing externalities. The group's research aligns with Castilla-La Mancha's RIS3 strategy, particularly in the environment and energy sector. Teaching Roles: Coordinator for the second year of the Bachelor's Degree in Business Administration and Management at UCLM. Instructor in various subjects within the Department of Spanish and International Economics, including International Economics and European Union Economics. Publications: Dr. Peces Prieto has authored several research articles published in peer-reviewed journals indexed in major academic databases such as Web of Science (WoS) and Scopus.

Maria Albertina Barreiro Rodrigues completed her PhD in Management in 2022 by the Europeia University of Lisbon and Member of CETRAD. Professor of ISCAL, is the President of the scientific counsil of Portuguese Association of Business Ethics.

Aparna Sajeev is an Assistant Professor at the Department of Commerce and Management Studies, School of Business Studies, University of Calicut. She pursued her doctoral degree in macro-policy management at the Faculty of Management Studies, University of Delhi. Her key research areas include sustainable Development and Climate Change, Sustainable Finance, Psychometric Analysis, and Impact Assessment. She has three years of Education industry experience as a Senior Research Manager - Impact Assessment and continues her work in education sector engagements as a consultant. She collaborated with the Berkeley Evaluation and Assessment Research Center. With over a decade of research experience, she is presently a research supervisor at the Department of Commerce, University of Calicut. She received a 2 million Won - Selected Research Paper award from Kyunghee University, Seoul (2020).

Ana Saraiva completed her PhD in Management in 2022 by the Lusíada University of Lisbon and Master in Hotel Management in 2016 by ESHTE. She has published relevant papers in specialized journals, in conferences, and participated as a Researcher in various projects. Her research interests focus on Management, Education, E-Commerce and Philosophy.

Orencio Jesús Vázquez Oteo is a Professor of Economics at UNED. Graduate in Law. PhD in Economics, cum laude. Extraordinary Award. Coordinator of the Corporate Social Responsibility Observatory. Member of the International Commission of Experts on Social Responsibility of the Ministry of Labor. Member of the Advisory Council of the National Contact Point. Member of the Spanish Council for Corporate Social Responsibility (CERSE).

Index

F

G

H

I

L

M

O

P

R

S

T

U

W

www.ingramcontent.com/pod-product-compliance
Lightning Source LLC
LaVergne TN
LVHW080911300926
849162LV00003B/645